Ogma

Ogma

Essays in Celtic Studies
in honour of Próinséas Ní Chatháin

EDITED BY
Michael Richter & Jean-Michel Picard

FOUR COURTS PRESS

Set in 10 pt on 12.5 pt Garamond by
Carrigboy Typesetting Services, County Cork for
FOUR COURTS PRESS LTD
Fumbally Court, Fumbally Lane, Dublin 8, Ireland
e-mail: info@four-courts-press.ie
http://www.four-courts-press.ie
and in North America for
FOUR COURTS PRESS
c/o ISBS, 5824 N.E. Hassalo Street, Portland, OR 97213.

ISBN 1–85182–6/1–8

ACKNOWLEDGMENT

The publisher and editors gratefully acknowledge the generous grants given by
University College Dublin and Universität Konstanz.

Printed in England
by MPG Books, Bodmin, Cornwall

Contents

CONTENTS vii

Abbreviations

AASS	*Acta Sanctorum … a Sociis Bollandianis*
AB	*Analecta Bollandiana*
AClon.	*Annals of Clonmacnois*, ed. D. Murphy (Dublin 1896, repr. Felinfach 1993)
AConn.	*Annals of Connacht*, ed. A.M. Freeman (Dublin 1944)
AESC	*Annales, Economies Sociétés Civilisations*
AFM	*Annals of the kingdom of Ireland by the Four Masters*, ed. J. O'Donovan, 7 vols (Dublin 1848–51), repr. New York 1966; Dublin 1990
AH	G.M. Dreves and C. Blume (eds), *Analecta Hymnica Medii Aevi*, 55 vols (Leipzig 1886–1922)
AI	*The Annals of Inisfallen*, ed. S. Mac Airt (Dublin 1951)
AL	*Annales Laubienses*
ALC	*Annals of Loch Ce*, ed. W.M. Hennessy, 2 vols, RS 54 (London 1871), reflex facsimile (Dublin 1939)
ABoyle	A.M. Freeman, 'The annals in Cotton MS Titus A. xxv' in *RC* 41 (1924) pp 301–30; 42 (1925) pp 283–305; 43 (1926) pp 358–84; 44 (1927) pp 336–61
AR	*The Annals of Roscrea*, ed. D. Gleeson and S. Mac Airt, in *PRIA* 59 (1958) pp 137–80
ATig.	*Annals of Tigernach*, ed. W. Stokes in *RC* 16 (1895) pp 374–419; 17 (1896) pp 6–33, 119–263, 337–420; 18 (1897) pp 9–59, 150–97, 267–303, repr. in 2 vols (Felinfach 1993)
AU	S. Mac Airt and G. Mac Niocaill (eds), *The Annals of Ulster (to 1131)*, Part i: text and translation (Dublin 1983)
BAR	*British Archaeological Reports*
BB	*The Book of Ballymote*
BBCS	*Bulletin of the Board of Celtic Studies*
BFer.	*The Book of Fermoy*
BHL	*Bibliotheca Hagiographica Latina*, ed. Bollandists, 2 vols, Brussels 1898–1901, and supplement (1911)
CCCM	*Corpus Christianorum, Continuatio Mediaevalis*
CCSL	*Corpus Christianorum, Series Latina*
GDG	Thomas Parry, *Gwaith Dafydd ap Gwilym* (Caerdydd 1952)
CGH	M.A. O'Brien, *Corpus Genealogiarum Hiberniae* (Dublin 1962)
CIH	*Corpus Iuris Hibernici*, ed. D.A. Binchy, 6 vols (Dublin 1978)
CLA	E.A. Lowe, *Codices Latini Antiquiores*, 12 vols (Oxford 1934–72)
Clm	*Codices latini monacenses*
CMCS	*Cambridge/Cambrian Medieval Celtic Studies*
CS	*Chronicum Scotorum: a chronicle of Irish affairs from the earliest times to a.d. 1135, with a supplement 1141–50*, ed. William Hennessy (London 1866, repr. Wiesbaden 1964)

DA	*Deutsches Archiv für die Erforschung des Mittelalters*
DIL	*Royal Irish Academy, Dictionary of the Irish language based mainly on Old and Middle Irish materials* (Dublin 1913–75)
EHR	*English Historical Review*
ÉtC	*Études Celtiques*
FA	Joan Radner (ed.), *Fragmentary annals of Ireland* (Dublin 1978); same text as that edited by J. O'Donovan, *Three fragments (Annals of Ireland: three fragments copied from ancient sources by Dubhaltach Mac Firbhisigh* (Dublin 1860)
GL	H. Keil and H. Hagen, *Grammatici Latini*, 7 vols (Leipzig 1857–80, repr. Hildesheim 1961)
HBS	Henry Bradshaw Society
HE	Bede, *Historia Ecclesiastica*
HGC	Henry Lewis, *Hen Gerddi Crefyddol* (Caerdydd 1931)
IER	*The Irish Ecclesiastical Record*
IF	*Indogermanische Forschungen*
IHS	*Irish Historical Studies*
IT	E. Windisch and W. Stokes (eds), *Irische Texte*, 4 vols (Leipzig 1880–1909)
ITS	*Irish Texts Society*
JRSAI	*Journal of the Royal Society of Antiquaries of Ireland*
LEIA	*Lexique Étymologique de l'Irlandais Ancien*, ed. J. Vendryes, E. Bachellery, P.-Y. Lambert (Paris/Dublin 1959–)
LL	*The Book of Leinster*, i–vi ed R.I. Best, O. Bergin, M.A. O'Brien, A. O'Sullivan (Dublin 1954–83)
LU	*Lebor na hUidre*, ed R.I. Best and O. Bergin (Dublin 1929)
MGH	*Monumenta Germaniae Historica*
MGH NG	*— Necrologia Germaniae*
MGH, AA	*— Auctores Antiquissimi*
MGH, PL	*— Poetae Latini Medii Aevi*
MGH, SRG	*— Scriptores Rerum Germanicarum*
MGH, SRM	*— Scriptores Rerum Merovingicarum*
MGH, SS	*— Scriptores*
PBA	*Proceedings of the British Academy*
PL	J.-P. Migne, *Patrologia Latina*, 221 vols (Paris 1844–64)
PMLA	*Publications of the Modern Language Association*
PRIA	*Proceedings of the Royal Irish Academy*
RB	*Revue Bénédictine*
RC	*Revue Celtique*
RIA	Royal Irish Academy
RS	Rolls Series
SC	Sources Chrétiennes (Paris 1941–)
Settimane	*Settimane di studio del Centro Italiano di Studi sull' Alto Medioevo* (Spoleto 1954–)
SBB	*Sitzungsberichte der königlich Preussischen Akademie der Wissenschaften*
SHR	*Scottish Historical Review*
SLH	*Scriptores Latini Hiberniae* (Dublin 1955–)
TAPhA	*Transactions and Proceedings of the American Philological Association*

TOS	*Transactions of the Ossianic Society*
TPS	*Transactions of the Philological Society*
UJA	*Ulster Journal of Archaeology*
VSH	C. Plummer (ed.), *Vitae Sanctorum Hiberniae*, 2 vols (Oxford 1910, repr. 1968)
YBL	*The Yellow Book of Lecan*
ZCP	*Zeitschrift für celtische Philologie*
ZKG	*Zeitschrift für Kirchengeschichte*
ZRPh	*Zeitschrift für Romanische Philologie*

The abbreviations for biblical sources are those of R. Weber (ed.), *Biblia Sacra iuxta Vulgatam Versionem* (Stuttgart 1975)

List of plates, maps and figures

Foreword

GEORGE HUXLEY
Trinity College Dublin

Professor Próinséas Ní Chatháin is a person of quality, and, as the present volume shows, her scholarship is praised far beyond the shores of Ireland. It is an honour to write, by invitation, this foreword; I am not one of the *lucht eolais*, but she is a dear friend, with whom I have enjoyed over the years many a philological conversation. Her delight in dialogue helps to explain the generosity and effectiveness of her teaching.

Professor Ní Chatháin came early to Irish language and literature. Her father, from his youth onwards, strove to revive the tongue, and her mother, of the Ó Conaill line at Baile Bhúirne in West Cork, was a native speaker. More Irish than English was spoken at home in New Ross. After schooling at the Convent of Mercy there, she went, with a Scholarship, to University College Galway, where she graduated B.A. in 1956. Her knowledge of Celtic Studies was widened and deepened by a visit to Bonn during tenure of a Travelling Studentship awarded by the National University of Ireland. She received her Doctorate from the University of Edinburgh in 1966. By then she had grasped two principles upon which much of her scholarship has been founded: the historical continuity of the Irish language and the enduring heritage of Christianity in Irish society.

She learnt more about linguistic theory – though she is a most empirical scholar – and about Indo-European philology in 1965 and 1966, when she was a Visiting Lecturer at the University of Pennsylvania. Thereafter she came to work on the Old Irish Dictionary in the Royal Irish Academy as an arranger, under the meticulous direction of Professor E.G. Quin, on what Quin called 'the lengthy letter C'. She thus joined a long tradition of lady-lexicographers, among whom shine in memory such luminaries as Maud Joynt and Eleanor Knott. For her accuracy and linguistic insight she won high commendation, but no bibliographical acclaim. Her power of analysis had already been recognised in the Dublin Institute for Advanced Studies, where she was a Scholar from 1962 to 1965. Her perceptions of historical continuity in Irish, almost certainly, owe something to the doctrines of the venerable Osborn Bergin.

In 1967 she took up an Assistant Lectureship in Early Irish at University College Dublin, where she has remained, except for temporary appointments oversea – a sojourn in Austria was especially rewarding to her hosts and to herself.

Administrative capability was shown in the running of a M. Phil. programme in Mediaeval Studies, which included seminars in history and literature; not rarely, the gatherings were enlivened by her judicious choice of speakers from other institutions as well as from UCD itself. The College acknowledged her intellect and practicality by appointing her to the Chair of Early and Medieval Irish in 1986. In the following decade and a half she and her colleagues have progressed steadily in teaching and research. The merit of lectures contributed to the inter-departmental courses in 'Celtic Civilisation' has been outstanding. She herself designed the inclusive and coherent syllabus.

Two aspects of her life must be emphasized. The first is her devotion to her family. Her pride in the literary and professional attainments of her brothers is a joy to behold, and her kindly monitoring of their offspring reflects the disciplined gentleness of her own conduct. She is a paradigm of the universal aunt, such as every family needs, but alas, nowadays, few possess. The second aspect is her power of self-criticism. It is a virtue enhancing her pithy and droll – but never malign – comments upon social pretensions and professional posturings, and it has enabled her usually to remain detached from the personal fissions intermittently disfiguring Old Irish studies. Her manner reminds me of the just ruler in *Audacht Morainn* (§12) who keeps plagues and great lightnings from the people.

Self-criticism also explains her reluctance to publish. She is by inclination a writer of articles, not of books, though she has been a conscientious co-editor of large books. Her style is spare, neat, apt. Some may deem the pages few, but in the life of the mind quality, not quantity, counts. The quality is consistently high, and to a Hellenist onlooker there is to be seen in her prose a poetical elegance, almost Callimachean, of 'fewlinèdness' (ὀλιγοστιχία).

Three of her writings are, I believe, particularly markworthy. In the first, understanding of the Derrynavlan chalice is increased by deft use of liturgical arguments[1] – how wise were the fellows of the Royal Society of Antiquaries of Ireland to choose her to be their President. The second study, 'Swineherds, seers, and druids', not only assembles accurate botanical evidence for 'earth-nuts', but also offers an arboreal explanation of the name Deirdriu, together with an illuminating discussion of the role of swineherds in the tradition about the supremacy of Cashel.[2] The third examines the cult of the horse in early Irish sources.[3] The cult is shown to be connected with chariots, kings, and charioteers, and, Professor Ní Chatháin argues, its ethos is to be found, euhemerized, in the actions of Medb, Fergus, and Sualdaim mac Róich in *Táin Bó Cúailnge*, as also in Cú Chulainn's ancestry. A significant gain here is the explanation of the name *Róch* as a petrified feminine o-stem in Old Irish; the name means 'the great mare', and in *Róch* we have the Irish equivalent of *Epona*. The sharpness of the reasoning is typical of its author (*ex ungue leonem*): here is the claw-mark of the lioness, not afraid to correct even the great Thurneysen.

Próinséas, with gratitude and affection we honour you, and since your mind is keener, and your memory better-stocked, than ever, we pray that the Muses, daughters of Mnemosyne, will continue to smile upon you, while you in your turn enlighten us, in the years to come. Long may you say, with the scholar in the Carinthian text:

do thabairt doraid do glé
for mo mud céin am messe.

1 'The liturgical background of the Derrynavlan altar service', *JRSAI* 110 (1980) pp 127–48.   2 'Swineherds, seers, and druids', *Studia Celtica* 14–15 (1979–8) pp 200–11.   3 'Traces of the cult of the horse in Early Irish sources', *Journal of Indo-European Studies* 19 (1991) pp 123–32.

Early Irish queens and royal power:
a first reconnaissance

DORIS EDEL

Women have an important place in Old and Middle Irish literature. Not only are the female characters in the narrative texts more numerous than in the contemporary European literatures, they are also more varied. In real life their role was undoubtedly much more restricted. Epic tradition has a tendency to exaggerate, and this not only with regard to female characters; however, one can only exaggerate what already exists in one way or another.

The problem, to quote Professor Mac Cana, is whether a society which in its literature attributes such independence to its women characters as does much of early Irish literature would on the other hand deny it or rigidly curtail it in real life. In his view the solution for the problem lies in the domain of mythology: the female characters in the literary texts have to be seen as adaptations of the archetypal sovereignty goddess.[1]

My intention is to approach the problem from the historical angle. Limiting myself to the figure of the queen, I hope to get a glimpse of the socio-political reality underneath the myth by sifting the available evidence in the light gained from other parts of early medieval Europe.

In the first part of the article I shall discuss the functions of the queen in her role of royal consort, in the second part, the relation between the literary image of the female independent ruler and historical reality. But before I begin I wish to make some general remarks. First, when we speak of independent rulers, we have to bear in mind that the early medieval king did not have absolute authority; he could only act with the support of at least some strategically placed nobles.[2] Secondly, when using the terms king and queen, I do not have the title as such in mind, but the whole complex of duties, rights, privileges, expectations, etc. that was attached to early kingship. In Ireland and elsewhere in the Barbarian West there were higher and lower kings, and some of the Continental equivalents of Irish kings had the lower title *dux*.[3] Thirdly, there are great differences in the source materials of the various parts of early medieval Europe.[4] As the king's duties are described both in Irish literary and non-literary texts in a very schematic and summary manner,[5] it would be extremely unrealistic to expect from these sources a more detailed account of the queen's tasks and functions. Add to this the relative rarity of descriptive passages in the

1 P. Mac Cana, 'Women in Irish mythology', in M.P. Hederman et al. (eds), *The Crane Bag book of Irish studies 1977 1981* (Dublin 1982) pp 521–4. Also the approach of M J. Enright, *Lady with a mead cup. Ritual, prophecy and lordship in the European warband from La Tène to the Viking Age* (Dublin 1996) is essentially mythological, particularly in the fifth chapter, which deals with the Celtic world.   2 J.M. Wallace-Hadrill, *Early Germanic kingship in England and on the continent* (Oxford 1971) p. 3.   3 Ibid. pp 2–8, referring to Tacitus, *Germania*, ch. 7. *Reges* were chosen *ex nobilitate, duces ex virtute* 'for prowess in the field'. The Germanic equivalent of *dux* was *herizogo*.   4 As pointed out by P. Wormald, 'Celtic and Anglo-Saxon kingship: some further thoughts', in P.E. Szarmach (ed.), *Sources of Anglo-Saxon culture* (Kalamazoo 1986) with regard to Anglo-Saxon England and Ireland.   5 I refer to the well-known passage in the *Táin*, at the beginning of the Boyhood Deeds, and in *Críth Gablach*, ch. 41. See C. O'Rahilly (ed.), *Táin Bó Cúailnge: Recension I* (Dublin 1976; hereafter referred to as *TBC I*) ll. 402–4, and D.A. Binchy (ed.), *Críth Gablach* (Dublin 1941, repr. 1979) p. 21.

narrative texts coupled to their tendency to focus on the action rather than on the actor,[6] and on inanimate objects rather than on human figures,[7] and it need not come as a surprise that quite often the available evidence consists of no more than a few disjointed remarks.

Professor Kelly states that the Irish annals do not provide any instances of female political or military leaders.[8] He only knows of one reference to a female ruler or military leader in a non-literary source, which he regards as dubious. It is found in the Old Irish law-text on sick-maintenance, *Bretha Crólige*, in the list of the twelve classes of women in whose case the actual sick-maintenance (*othrus*) is replaced by a fixed fee. Among these twelve classes are the *ben sues srutha coctha for cula* 'the woman who turns back the streams of war' and the *rechtaid géill* 'the ruler entitled to hostages'. The glosses on the passage mention the abbess of Kildare (*bancomarba cille dara*) as an example of the first,[9] and queen Medb of Connacht (*meadb cruacan*) as an example of the second type. Like their male equivalents in the list of the male exceptions these classes of women were excluded from *othrus* to save the defendant from the unreasonable burden of providing sick-maintenance to persons of such elevated rank.[10] To Professor Kelly's suggestion that the male imagery surrounding the office of kingship precluded even the possibility of a female ruler[11] I shall come back towards the end of the article. Here I only call attention to the fact that although the Irish annals make no mention of independent female rulers, Irish scribes have preserved a collection of genealogical lore about women which is unparalleled elsewhere, the *Banshenchas*.

I. The queen as royal consort

I shall begin with the queen's functions in the royal hall (*aula regis*), then sketch her roles as the king's adviser and as battle-leader, and conclude this part with her position *vis-à-vis* the succession of the king.

The queen of the aula regis

The queen's prime area of activity was domestic and, rather than a drawback, this placed her in a position of strength. As Lois L. Huneycutt points out, 'at least until the middle of the twelfth century, the medieval world drew little distinction between 'public' and 'private' spheres of life and authority, or between public and private rights.'[12] On the elevated level of the royal hall, the

---

6 As evinced, for instance, by the frequent use of impersonal verbal forms.   **7** See, for instance, the description of the royal hall of king Conchobar in *Tochmarc Emire*, ch. 2–4, in A.G. van Hamel (ed.), *Compert Con Culainn and other stories* (Dublin 1933, repr. 1978) pp 20–1, where it is said that the famous beer vat *Iarngúala* could satisfy all the men of Ulster in one turn. No ladies are mentioned, not even Conchobar's queen, as opposed to the description of the royal hall of Ailill and Medb in *Fled Bricrend*, ch. 55; see G. Henderson (ed.), *Fled Bricrend. The feast of Bricriu*, ITS 2 (London 1899, repr. 1993) pp 68–71.   **8** F. Kelly, *A Guide to early Irish law* (Dublin 1988) p. 69. As we shall see, this statement has to be mitigated.   **9** The position of abbess was the most authoritative one available to women. Abbesses, like abbots, had an important politial role, not only in Ireland, but also on the continent: see Janet L. Nelson, 'Early medieval rites of queen-making and the shaping of medieval queenship', in Anne Duggan (ed.), *Queens and queenship in medieval Europe* (Woodbridge, Suffolk 1997) pp 301–15, at p. 310.   **10** D.A. Binchy, 'Sick-maintenance in Irish law', *Ériu* 12 (1938) pp 78–136, at p. 121; idem (ed.), 'Bretha Crólige', *Ériu* 12 (1938) pp 1–77, ch. 32 (female exceptions) ch. 12 (male exceptions).   **11** Similarly, with respect to Cartimandua, T.M. Charles-Edwards, 'Native political organization in Roman Britain and the origin of MW brenhin', in M. Mayrhofer et al. (eds), *Antiquitates Indogermanicae. Gedenkschrift für Hermann Güntert* (Innsbruck 1974) pp 35–45, at p. 45.   **12** 'Female succession and the language of power in the writings of twelfth-century churchmen', in J.C. Parsons (ed.), *Medieval queenship* (Stroud 1994) pp 189–201, at p. 190. In Ireland the separation between the two

organisation of the household – the distribution of food, drink, clothing and other gifts; the nurturing of the young men; the maintenance of friendly relations between the adult warriors; the reception of embassies from other kingdoms – was a political function.[13]

Enright begins his recent book *Lady with a mead cup* with a discussion of the important passage in *Beowulf* in which the wife of king Hrothgar enters the royal hall and greets the warriors. She first offers the ceremonial cup to her husband and then to his retinue, to begin with to the veterans, then to the younger men, and finally to the guest, Beowulf, who is seated among the latter category.[14] How essential the queen's role in the mead-hall was also in the Irish setting, is illustrated in the scene towards the end of *Tochmarc Étaine* (The Wooing of Étain) when king Eochaid has to identify his wife Étain among the troop of fifty identical women led by an old crone which his opponent Midir has sent to him: he attempts to distinguish her from the other women by examining their way of serving drink:[15]

'Mo bensa as deach oc dáil a nEre. Atagensa ocon dail.' Tochorastair a coic .xx. it a leth thighi innonn, 7 a .u.xx.it a leth a tighi illé, 7 tucad lestar co lind for lár an tighe. Dothiced iarom ben disiu 7 ben anall […].

'My wife is the best at serving drink in Ireland. I shall recognise her by her serving.' Twenty-five were placed at that side of the house and twenty-five at this, and a vessel filled with liquor was placed in the midst of the house. Then a woman would come from this side and from that […].

A fundamental function of the mead-hall, where the networks of friendship and clientship were maintained, where the hierarchy was made public in the sitting order,[16] was the prevention of feud. The queen played a central role in this, not only as provider of hospitality, but also as maintainer of the warband and peace-weaver. In *Fled Bricrend* (Bricriu's Feast), one half of Bricriu's house is set apart for king Conchobar of Ulster and his warriors, the other for queen Mugain and her ladies.[17] Conchobar's queen is usually a secondary figure, but she receives full attention in her

spheres came later. **13** Janet L. Nelson, 'Queens as Jezebels: the careers of Brunhild and Balthild in Merovingian history', in D. Baker (ed.), *medieval women, dedicated and presented to Professor Rosalind M.T. Hill* (Oxford 1978) pp 31–77, at pp 74–5, referring to J.M. Wallace-Hadrill, *The long-haired kings* (London 1962) pp 237–8; Pauline Stafford, *Queens, concubines, and dowagers. The king's wife in the early middle ages* (Athens, GA, 1983) pp 99ff (for the queen as peace-maker, see pp 44–5 and 117; as vengeance-taker, p. 110). Not surprisingly, the *De ordine palatii* by Adalhard of Corbie (d. 826) revised by Hincmar of Reims *c.*882, pays considerable attention to the queen's duties in this domain, which enabled 'the king to fix his hope on God the Allmighty and to give his mind to the rule and conservation of the entire realm' (*omnis rex omnipotenti Deo spem suam indesinenter committens ad totius regni statum ordinandum vel conservandum animum semper suum promptum haberet*): see T. Gross and R. Schieffer (eds), *Hincmarus De ordine palatii*, MGH Fontes iuris N.S. 3 (Hannover 1980) ll. 360–72; English translation by me. Some queens had the control of the royal treasure: for examples, see Stafford, op. cit., pp 104ff and eadem, 'Emma: the powers of the queen in the eleventh century', in Duggan, *Queens and queenship*, pp 3–26, at p. 6; Nelson, art. cit., p. 40; Joan Nicholson, '*Feminae gloriosae:* women in the age of Bede', in Baker, *Medieval women*, pp 15–29, at p. 24; Edith Ennen, *Frauen im Mittelalter* (Munich 1984) p. 56. For the possibility that Irish kings also had tresors, see Wormald, 'Celtic and Anglo-Saxon kingship', p. 167. As Nelson points out, the realisation and effective exploitation of the possibilities which the position of the queen provided go far to explain the achievements by the Merowingian queen-regents Brunhild and Balthild (see section on the queen-regent below). **14** For this description of Wealhtheow in ll. 607–41, quoted by Enright, *Lady with a mead cup*, pp 3–4, see Fr. Klaeber (ed.), *Beowulf and the fight at Finnsburg* (Boston 1922, repr. 1950) pp 23–4. **15** O. Bergin and R.I. Best (eds), 'Tochmarc Étaine', *Ériu* 12 (1938) pp 137–96, at pp 186–7 (ch. 18). **16** For example, see *Críth Gablach*, ch. 46 (p. 23 in Binchy's edition) and the English translation by F.J. Byrne, *Irish kings and high-kings* (London 1973, repr. Dublin 2001) p. 33. The sitting arrangements are also accorded great importance in the Welsh *Pedeir Keinc y Mabinogi*. **17** *Fled Bricrend*, ch. 12 (pp 12–13 in Henderson's edition). In the only description of Cráebrúad,

role of nurse to the *iuvenes* and stabilising factor *vis-à-vis* the warband in the scene towards the end of Cú Chulainn's Boyhood Deeds when the boy returns from his first ride in a war-chariot in a heroic frenzy. She and her ladies confront him with bared breasts to bring him back to his senses, that is, to make him realise his place in society; and when he has cooled down, she clothes him before he is accorded his permanent seat at the king's knee:[18]

Tothéit iarom bantrocht nEmna ara chend im Mugain mnaí Conchobair meic Nessa, 7 donnochtat a mbruinni friss. 'It é óic inso condricfat frit indiu', or Mugain. Foilgis-[s]eom a gnúis. La sodain atnethat láith gaile Emna 7 focherdat i ndabaig n-úarusci. [...] Dotháet ass íarom 7 dobeir in rígan íar sudiu .i. Mugain, bratt ngorm n-imbi 7 delg n-argit n-and 7 léne chulpatach. Ocus suidid fo glún Conchobair íarom, 7 ba sí sin a lepaid do grés íar sudiu.	The women of Emain Macha went forth to meet him, with Mugain, the wife of Conchobar mac Nessa at their head, and they bared their breasts to him. 'These are the warriors who will encounter you today', Mugain said. He hid his face. Then the warriors of Emain seized him and plunged him in a vat of cold water. [...] Then he came out and the queen, Mugain, put on him a blue mantle with a silver brooch therein, and a hooded tunic, and he sat at Conchobar's knee, and that was his seat ever after.

The queen in her role as the king's adviser
Besides being provider of hospitality, maintainer of the *comitatus* and peace-weaver, the queen acted as her husband's adviser. Sedulius Scottus, in his 'Book on Christian Governors' in the chapter dedicated to the queen, exhorts her to have the prudence of a good counsellor; notwithstanding feminine frailty, the husband of a prudent queen should be grateful for her advice.[19]

Mugain only appears in the role of Conchobar's adviser in the tale known under the titles *Tochmarc Ferbe* (The Wooing of Ferb) and *Fís Conchobuir* (Conchobar's Vision), where she is called *miadmas co morchéil* 'rich in honour and wisdom'.[20] A good example is the wife of the Leinster king Mac Dathó in *Scéla Mucce Meic Dathó* 'The Tale of Mac Dathó's Pig', who advises her husband how to act in the difficult situation into which he has been manoeuvred when both Ulster and Connacht request from him his famous warhound:[21]

in *Tochmarc Emire*, Mugain is not mentioned: see above, note 7.   **18** *TBC I*, ll. 811–21; my translation based on those by C. O'Rahilly and T. Kinsella, *The Táin* (Oxford 1970) p. 92. As I understand the scene, it is not the aim of the women to awaken sexual shame in the boy, as surmised by R. Thurneysen, *Die irische Helden- und Königsage* (Halle 1921) p. 139, and later by G. Dumézil, *Horace et les Curiaces* (Paris 1942) pp 44–50, but rather to remind him that he is returning to the bosom of his people. (I postulated this earlier in the *Stellingen* presented by me as part of the defence of my doctoral dissertation at the University of Utrecht on 20 June 1980.) The episode may be compared with the scene in Caesar's *De Bello Gallico* VII, 47, when the *matres familiae* of Gergovia bare their breasts to the Roman attackers, not to seduce them, but to appeal to their clemency towards women and children, that is, the non-combatant part of their people.   **19** See Nelson, 'Early medieval rites of queen-making', pp 304–5. For Sedulius's *Liber de rectoribus christianis*, written in 869 for Charles the Bald, see S. Hellmann (ed.), 'Sedulius Scottus', *Quellen und Untersuchungen zur lateinischen Philologie des Mittelalters* i/1 (Munich 1906) pp 1–91, ch. 5 at pp 34–7. Significantly, Sedulius calls the queen *rectrix*: she governs and rules alongside the king (p. 37, l. 21). **20** E. Windisch (ed.), 'Tochmarc Ferbe', in W.H. Stokes and E. Windisch, *Irische Texte* iii/2 (Leipzig 1897) pp 445–556, at p. 523 ('ehrenreich mit grossem Verstand'); similarly pp 473 and 550. Cf. Thurneysen, *Heldensage*, pp 351–9.   **21** R. Thurneysen (ed.), *Scéla Mucce Meic Dathó* (Dublin 1935, repr. 1986) p. 4, ll. 20–1; translation by me. The passage reminded Thurneysen, *Heldensage*, p. 495 n. 3 of 1 Kgs 21: 4 (Jezebel's advice to her husband Ahab). Similarly K. McCone, *Pagan past and Christian present in early Irish literature* (Maynooth 1990) p. 77: 'One does not, of course, need to go beyond chapter three of Genesis to appreciate the disastrous consequences of following female councel [...].' However, the advice of Mac Dathó's wife is not deceitful like Jezebel's, but merely shrewd:

Táthut airle lim-sa fris	I have advice for you in this,
ní olc fri íarmairt n-indi,	its outcome will not be bad:
tabair dóib-sium dib línaib,	give the dog to both sides,
cumma cía thóetsat imbi.	even if they get killed about it.

There is historical evidence for the queen's role as her husband's adviser. The Irish examples all belong to the Early Modern period, which may have to do with the extreme scantiness of the information from the preceding centuries.[22] One of the examples is the famous Finnghuala (Finola), who will be discussed in her function as battle-leader. Early medieval evidence is provided by Anglo-Saxon England, among others by Bede,[23] and the Continent. I limit myself to the German Ottonian Empire, where from the inauguration of king Otto I (d. 973) as German emperor in 962 onwards, the queen was officially acknowledged as *consors regni, particeps imperii*.[24] Otto's son, the later emperor Otto II, married in 972 the Byzantine princess Theophanu,[25] and she too was solemnly accepted into the *consortium imperii*[26] and acknowledged as *coimperatrix augusta necnon imperii regnorumque consors*. The title of *consors regni*, apparently of Late Classical origin, appeared first in Italy. In Germany it existed until the twelfth century.[26a] The reason that it disappeared then may be sought in the institutionalisation of the power of the royal administration; however, queens continued to represent their absent husbands.

To return to the Insular world, albeit not the Celtic-speaking part, and the domain of art and fiction, the queen in her role as adviser is depicted in the so-called Lewis Chessmen, which had probably been made in a twelfth-century Scandinavian artistic milieu.[27] Significantly, the figure of the queen holds a drinking horn in her left hand and supports her head with her right hand in

by following it her husband manages to extricate himself from a highly threatening situation. Moreover, the Old Testament also contains positive female role-models such as Judith and Esther (cf. below, note 61) besides negative ones like Jezebel and Eve. And last but not least, the mysoginist passage in section 16 of *Tecosca Cormaic*, to which Mc Cone refers, is much less characteristic for the early Irish (gnomic) literature than is sometimes suggested.   **22** The Irish annals list a number of queens, but, as observed by D. Ó Corráin, 'Women in early Irish society', in Margaret Mac Curtain and D. Ó Corráin (eds), *Women in Irish society: the historical dimension* (Dublin 1978) pp 1–13, at p. 10, they are usually called the wife of a king or the queen of a king. Limiting ourselves to the Annals of Ulster and to Irish examples, this does not apply to Cellach, daughter of the king of Uí Liatháin and wife of Cathal mac Finguine (AD 732), Gormlaith, daughter of Donnchadh, *regina Scotorum* (AD 861), Der bhFáil, daughter of Mael Finnia, *regina Temrach* (AD 931), Flann daughter of Donnchadh, *righan Ailigh* (AD 940). The question is, however, what positions these queens held.   **23** See Nicholson, '*Feminae gloriosae*', pp 24–6. This role of the queen is reflected in the secular literature.   **24** The wife of Otto I was Adelheid, daughter of king Rudolf II of Burgundy and queen Bertha. She was first married to king Lothar of Italy. After his death on 22 November 950, according to law she had the right to designate a successor. However, the following month she was taken prisoner by margrave Berengar of Ivrea, who arranged that he himself was chosen and installed as king, together with his son. Adelheid managed to escape and after an adventurous flight married in 951 the widowed German king Otto I, who thus acquired a claim to the Italian kingship. At Otto's inauguration as emperor in Rome on 3 March 962, she was inaugurated as empress, and subsequently took an active part in the governance of the empire, as her interventions in the royal charters show. On her and on her daughter-in-law Theophanu, see Ennen, *Frauen im Mittelalter*, pp 63–7, 75; K.-U. Jäschke, 'From famous empresses to unspectacular queens', in Duggan, *Queens and queenship*, pp 75–108, at pp 75–6.   **25** Theophanu (*c.*955–991) was not a Byzantine princess by birth, but the daughter of the Armenian general and usurper John Tzimiskes.   **26** *In copulam legitimi matrimonii consortiumque imperii*: see Ennen, *Frauen im Mittelalter*, p. 63.   **26a** A. Fössel, *Die Königin im mittelalterlichen Reich* (Stuttgart 2000) p. 55 signals that the *consors regni*-title occurs first in the Vulgate version of the Old Testament with regard to Esther. According to Fössel, the title was in use in Germany until the transition to the venecular in the first half of the fourteenth century.   **27** For these chess figures, which were found in 1831 on the Hebridean island Lewis, see M. Taylor, *The Lewis chessmen* (London 1978). In his view 'the queens seem aghast' (p. 7); however, the expression on the kings' faces is not much different. Karen Pratt, 'The image of the queen in Old French literature', in Duggan, *Queens and queenship*, pp 235–59, at 259 n. 108 suggests that the replacement of the figure of the vizir as second-in-command in the chess game by the queen 'is indicative of the important political role played by queens in the Middle Ages'.

a pensive pose which resembles that of the Middle High German poet Walther von der Vogelweide in the *Manesse Codex*.[28]

An Irish literary example of the queen as representative of her absent husband is found in the middle section of *Tochmarc Étaine* when king Eochaid departs on a circuit of his country and leaves his wife behind to pay the last rites to his brother after the latter's imminent death.[29]

The king's wife in her role as battle-leader

Until now I have alluded to queen Medb of Connacht only briefly, for as a queen in her own right she has a special position. In addition to the roles just reviewed[30] she also appears in the one function which is generally regarded by modern scholars as distinguishing masculine from feminine roles, that of battle-leader. The glosses on the Old Irish law tract *Bretha Crólige*, referred to at the beginning, adduce her as an example for this. The scenes in *Táin Bó Cúailnge* in which she inspects the camp of the armies and calms the warriors when they are assailed by panic portray her as an experienced war-leader.[31] A comparable character is Macha Mongrúad, the protagonist of the origin legend of Emain Macha, who defeats her male rivals for the kingship in a series of battles. As both she and Medb are presented as *banchomarbai*, I shall discuss them in the second part, in the section on the concept of the female successor to the kingship.

As mentioned earlier, according to Professor Kelly these literary characters have no historical parallels. He is right insofar as no *independently* operating female political or military leader is found in the Irish annals. However, the annals occasionally mention wives of rulers as commanders of troops. In the web of conflicting tribal and family interests which surrounded the kingship the queen sometimes had followers of her own, whose loyalty belonged to her personally. The conflict between Ailill and Medb about the Galióin troops in the Táin thus may have its roots in the clash of loyalties between their respective followers, Ailill being of Galióin provenance.[32]

As I have pointed out, the Irish historical evidence belongs to the Early Modern period.[33] My first example comes from the second half of the sixteenth century. The afore-mentioned Finnghuala, styled as *Inghean Dubh*, the mother of Aodh Rúad Ó Domhnaill (Red Hugh O'Donnell), the lieutenant of the Great O'Neill in the latter's war against the English, brought to her husband at their marriage some thousands of Scots mercenaries; and likewise did her mother at her marriage to the

---

28 The early 14th-century Manessische Liederhandschrift from Zurich is kept in the University Library, Heidelberg. The miniature on fol. 126r depicts the poet as he describes himself in his political poem 'Der Reichton', composed *c*.1298: 'Ich saz uf eime steine / und dahte bein mit beine. / dar uf satzt ich den ellenbogen, / ich hete in mine hand gesmogen / daz kinne und ein min wange. […]' (I sat on a stone and placed one leg over the other. I put my elbow on it, supporting with my hand my chin and one of my cheeks). See F. Maurer (ed.), *Die Lieder Walthers von der Vogelweide. I. Die religiösen und die politischen Lieder* (2nd ed., Tübingen 1960) pp 19–20; English translation by me. **29** Bergin and Best, 'Tochmarc Étaine', pp 166–7 (ch. 4). **30** As a provider of hospitality she is presented in a negative light in *Táin Bó Fraích*, ch. 8–12, ed. W. Meid (Dublin 1967, repr. 1994) pp 3–4. **31** *TBC I*, ll. 136ff and 210–3. This positive picture is not contradicted by her final defeat; indeed, not victory, but death and defeat on the battle-field are the epic themes *par excellence*. **32** J. Carney, 'Early Irish literature: the state of research', in G. Mac Eoin et al. (eds), *Proceedings of the sixth international congress of Celtic studies held in University College, Galway, 6–13 July 1979* (Dublin 1983) pp 113–30, at pp 120–1. For the Galióin episode, see *TBC I*, ll. 147–83. The underlying conflict, which appears to be deliberately concealed in the Táin, is that between the Laigin and the Uí Néill of Tara. It plays a prominent role in *Orgain Dind Ríg* and *Esnada Tige Buchet* (see below, note 54). The passage in Caesar's *De Bello Gallico* VI, 19, on the fate which expected a wife whose husband died in suspect circumstances, refers in my view to the aristocracy, and within it to those cases in which the wife's first loyalty did not belong to her husband, but to the faction that supported her personally. **33** For both examples I am indebted to K. Simms, 'Women in Norman Ireland', in Mac Curtain and Ó Corráin, *Women in Irish society*, pp 14–25. Significantly, as soon as the Annals become more informative, they provide examples of powerful women. A thorough investigation

Great O'Neill's immediate predecessor Toirdhealbhach Luineach Ó Néill (Turlough Luineach O'Neill), which took place in the same year 1569.[34] These Scots, of whom it was said that each of them had the worth of two Irishmen, formed an important element in the build-up towards that last great uprising which ended so tragically with the defeat at Kinsale in 1601. But the presence of these highly professional troops, whose loyalty belonged to Finnghuala, was also a great boost to her own position. The Annals of the Four Masters report how she used them to rid her son of a serious rival in his claim to the chieftaincy, while he was held captive in Dublin by the English:[35]

Ro eccaoín a himneadh, 7 a héttualang fris an amhsaidh Albanaigh baoí for a ttuillmhe 7 for a ttuarustal do grés, 7 ina comaitecht in gach maighin go ro tingheallsat sidhe fria gomdis ellma for a for congraissi daithe a neccraittis for a mbíodhbaibh cecib tan do tochrad chuca. […] Iar ttocht dósomh don bhaile ro aiccill si a sainmmuntir .i. na hAlbanaigh, 7 ro ráidh friú 7 ro aslaigh iad im chomhalladh in ro geallsat. Do rónadh fúirresi sin […].

She complained of her troubles and injuries to the Scottish mercenaries, who were constantly in her service and pay, and who were in attendance on her in every place; and they promised that they would be ready at her command, to wreak vengeance upon their enemies, whenever they should meet with them. […] When he (= the rival) had come to the place (where she was), she addressed her faithful followers, i.e. the Scots; and she told them, and requested of them to perform what they had promised. This was accordingly done for her […].

There was not only rivalry between her children and her husband's adult kinsmen, but also between her own 'Scottish' children and the 'Irish' children her husband had from earlier unions. According to her son's biography, *Beatha Aodha Rhuaidh Uí Dhomhnaill* (Life of Red Hugh O'Donnell), the children born by her were the only illustrious offspring her husband had.[36] Her portrayal in this work reminded the editor, Paul Walsh, of the queen Medb of the Pillow Talk. Indeed, *Beatha Aodha* suggests that her husband would have passed into obscurity if she had not been his wife. The following scene in the Life describes her presence at the council of nobles at Kilmacrenan, the traditional inauguration seat of the Ó Domhnaills, at which her son Aodh Ruadh was elected to succeed to his father's authority:[37]

---

of the material is needed.   **34** Finola's father was James O'Donnell, Lord of the Isles and of the Glynnes of Antrim, who was killed at Glenshesk in 1565 according to the Annals of Loch Cé. Her mother was Agnes Campbell, daughter of the 4th earl of Argyle, who after the death of her first husband married Turlough Luineach O'Neill, who was later ousted by Hugh (the Great) O'Neill from the chieftaincy of Tír Eóghain.   **35** J. O'Donovan (ed.), *Annala Rioghachta Eireann. Annals of the kingdom of Ireland by the Four Masters*, 7 vols (Dublin 1848–51, repr. 1998) *s.a.* 1588. The rival was Hugh son of Galvach O'Donnell, the son of her husband's elder brother, whom her husband had succeeded to the chieftaincy. See P. Walsh (ed.), *Beatha Aodha Ruaidh Uí Dhomhnaill. The Life of Aodh Ruadh O Domhnaill*, 2 vols, *ITS* 42, 45 (London 1948–57) II, p. 88 n. 12. E. Curtis, *A history of Ireland* (London 1936, repr. 1961) p. 208, characterized her as a 'mother of the Macchabees'.   **36** See Walsh, *Beatha Aodha*, II, pp 24–5 and 212; as to her children's relative fame, see ibid., I, pp 2–3. Rivalry between a ruler's offspring from various unions was common, and so was the tendency of wives to secure the position of their own children.   **37** See Walsh, ibid., I, pp 38–9; cf. II, p. 24.

Ba feirrde dana a tuidhechtsidhe isin dail ar así ba cend airle 7 athchomhairc do Chenél Conuill 7 gerbhó fosaidh ionmálla 7 gerbo hadhmolta i nairrdhibh mná ro bhaoi croidhe curaidh 7 inntinn fhiannusa aice illeith fria forngaire ittir forsan ccách conetestair 7 fora cele sainred occ aithe a huilc 7 a héccorafor gach naon donairilledh 7 no bhiodh buidhne iomdha a hAlbain 7 araill dÉirendchoibh fora cor 7 fora commus 7 fora tuillmhe 7 fora tuarustal badhdein dogres 7 go sainredhach in airett baoi a mac (an Ruadh) hi ccimbidhecht 7 hi cuimreach og Gallaibh.

It was an advantage that she came to the gathering, for she was the head of advice and counsel of the Cenél Conaill, and though she was calm and very deliberate and much praised for her womanly qualities, she had the heart of a hero and the mind of a soldier, inasmuch as she exhorted in every way each one that she was acquainted with, and her husband especially to avenge his injuries and wrongs on each according to his deserts. She had many troops from Scotland, and some of the Irish at her disposal and under her control, and in her own hire and pay constantly, and especially during the time that her son (the Ruadh) was in prison and confined by the English.

Finnghuala's role was not exceptional. Also her mother Agnes Campbell was reported to be a good counsellor to her (second) husband, Turlough Luineach O'Neill.[38] Queens held a recognized position comparable to that of the *tánaiste*, being likewise endowed with certain lands and revenue from taxation.[39]

An even more striking example of a female military leader occurred some 300 years earlier, when Edward Bruce, the brother of the victor of Bannockburn, invaded Ireland. It is Dearbfhorgaill, daughter of Maghnus Ó Conchobhair (Magnus O'Connor) and wife of Aedh Ó Domhnaill (Hugh O'Donnell) of Tír Conaill. The Connacht dynasty of the Ó Conchobhair was already badly weakened by a long succession war at the beginning of the Bruce invasion. When Gaelic Connacht started to revolt upon the defeat of one of the leading Anglo-Normans in the North[40] by Bruce, the Ó Domhnaills took advantage of the situation and extended their power southwards. Dearbfhorgaill not only assisted her husband in attacking the territory of her own kinsmen, the Ó Conchobhair, but even conspired in the killing of one of them. The Annals of Connacht have the following entries on her.[41]

AD 1315:

Aed h. Domnaill ri Thiri Conaill do techt hi Carpre 7 crich Cairpri uili do milled leis tria comarli a mna .i. ingine Magnusa h. Conchobair, 7 dol di fein mar oen re a bfuair do gallocclaechaib 7 do Clainn Murcertaig fo templaib Droma Cliab 7 moran do clerchib Droma Cliab do arcain le. Caislen Slicig do lecad la hOed h. Domnaill don toisc-sin 7 eddala mora d'fagbail doib and.

Aed O Domnaill, king of Tir Conaill, came into Carbury and ravaged the whole district, being advised thereto by his wife, the daughter of Magnus O Conchobair. She herself, with all the gallowglasses and men of the Clan Murtagh that she could obtain, marched against the churches of Drumcliff and plundered many of its clergy. Sligo castle was ravaged by Aed O Domnaill on this occasion, and they got much booty in it.

38 In a letter by the Lord Deputy Sir Henry Sidney to Sir Francis Walsingham, Secretary to Queen Elizabeth I. See Walsh, ibid., II, p. 206.   **39** See K. Simms, 'The legal position of Irishwomen in the later middle ages', *Irish Jurist* 10 (1975) pp 96–111, at pp 108–9 (the earliest example mentioned is 11th-century) and eadem, *From kings to warlords. The changing political structure of Gaelic Ireland in the later middle ages* (Woodbridge 1987) p. 72.   **40** The Red Earl of Ulster, Richard de Burgh, who had earlier acquired the Sligo lordship from the Geraldines.   **41** A.M. Freeman (ed., trans.),

AD 1316:

Aed h. Domnaill 7 Cenel Conaill uili do tinol sluaig moir 7 techta a Carpri aridisi do 7 a dul co Caislen Meic Conchobair don toisc-sin, 7 Ruaidri mac Domnaill h. Conchobair do scarthain rena braithrib fein 7 sid do denam do re h. nDomnaill 7 tigernus Cairpri do thabairt do; 7 Derbforgaill ingen Magnusa h. Conchobair do fastod ceitherni galloclaech 7 luach do tabairt doib do chind marbtha Ruaidri meic Domnaill h. Conchobair, 7 a marbad leo iarom dar sarugad minn Tiri Conaill tucad do reme, 7 creca mora do denam do Chenel Conaill iar sin ar orecht Cairpre.	Aed O Domnaill and all the Cenel Conaill assembled a great army and came into Carbury again, reaching Castleconor this time. And Ruaidri son of Domnall O Conchobair parted with his kinsmen and made a peace by himself with O Domnaill, yielding to him the lordship of Carbury. But Derbforgaill daughter of Magnus O Conchobair hired a band of gallowglasses and gave them a reward for killing Ruaidri son of Domnall O Conchobair; so by them he was killed, in violation of oaths sworn to him previously on the relics of Tirconnell. After this the chief families of Carbury were extensively plundered by the Cenel Conaill.

Also Dearbfhorgaill seems to have had an army of gallowglasses at her command.[42]

I end this section with an example from the neighbouring island of Britain: the Welsh princess Gwenllian (c.1098–1136). The two famous battling queens of Celtic Britain, Cartimandua and Boudicca, and the Anglo-Saxon Aethelflaed of Mercia belong to the category of (virtually) independent female rulers and will be discussed under that heading. Gwenllian was the daughter of Gruffudd ap Cynan of Gwynedd and the daughter-in-law of Rhys ap Tewdwr of Deheubarth, the two princes who established themselves in 1081 as the leaders of their respective kingdoms and thus inaugurated a Welsh renaissance.[43] The death of king Henry I of England in 1135 brought new manifestations of independence in Wales: Gwenllian's brothers became active in the northern half and invaded Ceredigion; and her husband, with their help, began to reconquer the lost parts of Deheubarth. In 1136, while he was seeking the support of her brothers, Gwenllian marched against the stronghold of Kidwelly, some ten kilometres to the south of Carmarthen, which had come into Norman hands in 1102, but she was routed at a spot later known as Maes Gwenllian (Gwenllian's Field).[44] Gerald of Wales describes her heroic death in his *Welsh Itinerary* in the following words:[45]

Annála Connacht. The annals of Connacht (Dublin 1944; repr. 1996), pp 240–3. Dearbfhorgaill died in 1316: see ibid., pp 248–9. Her father Magnus belonged to the cadet branch Clan Murcertach or Murtagh, the line of Murchertach, a younger brother of Rory (d. 1198) and Cathal (d. 1224).   **42** The first mention of gallowglasses, by that name, occurs in the Annals of Connacht *s.a.* 1290.7, in connection with the temporary deposition of Aedh Ó Domhnaill by his (half-)brother; however, the first actual reference to these troops, and to the custom of the bride bringing a company of them with her at her marriage, is found *s.a.* 1259.6.   **43** At the battle of Mynydd Carn, fought at the return of Gruffudd ap Cynan (c.1055–1137) from his Irish exile, he and Rhys ap Tewdwr of Deheubarth defeated three rivaling Welsh princes, who had Anglo-Norman connections. In 1116 Gwenllian married Rhys ap Tewdwr's son Gruffudd ap Rhys (1090–1137); one of her sons was the powerful Lord Rhys (1132–97). A. Breeze, *Medieval Welsh literature* (Dublin 1997) pp 74–8, 108 suggests that she is the author of the *Pedeir Keinc y Mabinogi*, dated by him c.1128.   **44** For the name Maes Gwenllian, see Sir Richard Colt Hoare (trans.), *The itinerary of Archbishop Baldwin through Wales*, first published in 1806 and edited in revised form in T. Wright, *The historical works of Giraldus Cambrensis* (London 1913) pp 325–476, at p. 393 n. 3. Hoare knew the work of antiquarians such as Henry Wharton.   **45** Giraldus Cambrensis, *Itinerarium Cambriae*, I.9. For the text, see J.F. Dimock (ed.), *Giraldi*

[...] Anglorum rege Henrico primo rebus humanis exempto, dum Griphinus Resi filius, Sudwalliae tunc princeps, in Norwallium auxilium corrogaturus ivisset, uxor ejus Guendoloena, tanquam Amazonum regina et Pentesilea secunda, in partes illas exercitium ducens, a Mauricio Londoniensi, loci illius tunc domino, et viro egregio Gaufrido, praesulis constabulario, bellico in certamine confecta, interempto ibidem filio ejusdem Morgano, et altero capto, silicet Mailgone, quos pueros secum in expeditionem arroganter adduxerat, cum aliis multis ipsa demum ferro confossa caput amisit.

It was in this region (near Kidwelly Castle), after the death of Henry I, king of the English, and at a moment when her husband, Gruffydd ap Rhys, Prince of South Wales, had gone to North Wales for reinforcements, that the Princess Gwenllian rode forward at the head of an army, like some second Penthesilea, queen of the Amazons. She was beaten in battle by Maurice of London, who ruled over the district at that time, and by Geoffrey, the Bishop's constable. She was so sure of victory that she had brought her two sons with her. One of them, called Morgan, was killed, and the other, called Maelgwn, was captured. Gwenllian herself had her head cut off, and so did many of her followers.

The Welsh historian John Edward Lloyd wrote about her in his pioneer work on the early history of Wales that she had chosen to play a part which was deemed unfitting for her sex in a Christian society.[46] His verdict on this female battle-leader is characteristic for the greater part of the nineteenth and twentieth centuries. But as Pauline Stafford pointed out some seventy years later, the wife or mother of the early medieval king was often the most loyal and trustworthy defender of his interests in the insecurity and rivalry in which he had to operate.[47] The fact that some queens had their own supporters does not contradict this.

A Continental example of a woman actively engaged in warfare is Mathilda, margrave of Tuscany, who was an important supporter of pope Gregory VII in his power struggle with the German emperor Henry IV. Although a distant cousin of the latter, she intervened with her own troops on behalf of the pope.[48]

The queen's position with regard to the king's succession
Enright argues convincingly that the queen did not only have a stabilising influence on her husband's followers during his lifetime, but also after his death.[49] In the early Middle Ages the

Cambrensis Opera, RS 21, vol. 6 (London 1868) p. 79; for the translation, L. Thorpe, *Gerald of Wales. The Journey through Wales and The Description of Wales* (London 1978) p. 137. Gwenllian's defeat was merely a casual triumph for the Normans.   **46** J.E. Lloyd, *A History of Wales*, 2 vols (London 1911) p. 470: 'She had chosen to play a part which, in Wales, as in other Christian lands, was deemed unfitting to her sex, but patriotism has lovingly preserved her memory in the name, still borne by the battle-field, of Maes Gwenllian.'   **47** Stafford, *Queens and Concubines*, p. 119.   **48** See Ennen, *Frauen im Mittelalter*, p. 71 and the illustration facing p. 49 (the Canossa scene with Henry IV kneeling before Mathilde, from Donizo of Canossa, *Vita Mathildis celeberrimae principis Italiae* [1114], Biblioteca Vaticana, Codex Vaticanus latinus 4922, fol. 49r); P. Golinelli, *Mathilde und der Gang nach Canossa*, German translation by A. Avella (Düsseldorf/Zürich 1998). Mathilda lived 1046–1115. Canossa, where Henry IV did penance to the pope in 1077, belonged to her. Other historical examples of female commanders of troops are the mother of Charles the Bald, Judith, who supported her son with an army in the decisive battle for his share in the inheritance (cf. below, p. MM) and Ageltrudis, the widow of margrave Wido I of Spoleto, who defended Rome and the imperial dignity for herself and her son, albeit without success (for both, see Ennen, ibid., pp 58–9.). A literary example is Guibourc, the exemplary wife of Guillaume d'Orange, who defends the city of Orange in her husband's absence in the Old French *Chanson de Guillaume* (Gyburg in Wolfram von Eschenbach's early 13th-century reworking *Willehalm*).   **49** For this and the

succession of the king was often a matter of fierce competition. The rules of succession were fluid; kings frequently had children from several unions; there was much rivalry between the various segments of the ruling lineages; last but not least, the larger kingdoms often had a federate character. In this situation, a claimant to the throne who succeeded in marrying the king's widow achieved two things: he legitimised his claim, and he gained the support of her followers and allies. The desirability of widows as wives for kings and nobles, already high in the sixth and seventh centuries, gained a peak in the turbulences of the tenth century.[50]

Marriages between wives of kings or nobles and their husbands' successors, including their husbands' conquerors, were part of the Irish historical reality, as, indeed, were abductions. The latter quite often took place with the consent of the lady in question.[51] Unions of this kind also have a prominent place in Irish literature, particularly in narrative texts with a political bias – not surprisingly, for a society so strongly dominated by family interests as that of medieval Ireland tends to couch its political arguments in the language of lineage and genealogy.[52] The contradictory genealogical 'explanations' provided by different texts are merely a reflection of the ever-shifting political relations. As I hope to have shown elsewhere, the thirteenth-century text *Ferchuitred Medba* (Medb's Share of Husbands), in which Medb of Crúachain marries a number of successive candidates for the Connacht throne, is not a tale of marital chaos, but provides a justification – a model – for the political aspirations of various population groups and dynasties *vis-à-vis* the kingship of Connacht, as well as for the Uí Néill interests in the Fifth.[53] Similarly the fifteenth-century (?) text about the multiple marriages of her namesake Medb Lethderg gives literary expression to the age-old conflict between the Uí Néill and the Laigin dynasty, which lies at the basis of a number of tales: Medb Lethderg is first married to Cú Corb, an ancestor of the Leinster king Catháer Mór, and then to his killer Fedlimid, the father of Conn Cétchathach and so the ancestor of (the Connachta and) the Uí Néill.[54] Medb of Crúachain and Medb Lethderg are still commonly interpreted as manifestations of the goddess of sovereignty with whom the claimant to the throne must mate in order to become king. However, as we shall see in the second part, two earlier texts, the Pillow Talk and *Esnada Tige Buchet*, significantly present them as wielders of royal power and claimants to the throne in their own right, not as mythical spouses of the rightful king.

following, see Enright, *Lady with a mead cup*, pp 22–37. At p. 34: 'As *mediatrix* and covenant bearer of the *comitatus* the queen is the appropriate emissary to the new lord and that is why her capture and marriage, voluntary or involuntary, are so important to usurpers, rebels, royal claimants and warband alike.' Similarly Nelson, 'Queens as Jezebels', p. 37.   **50** Stafford, *Queens and concubines*, pp 49ff. In some instances, the bride had at least twice the age of her husband, as in the case of Adelaide and Louis V (ibid., p. 50).   **51** A famous example of an abduction with the woman's consent is that of the Meath princess Derbfhorgaill, wife of Tighearnán O'Rourke, king of Bréifne, the principal ally of Rory O'Connor (d. 1198) who was abducted by Rory's rival Dermot MacMurragh in 1151.   **52** How strongly Irish thinking was governed by the concept of kinship is evinced by the Old Irish law text on the rules for conducting water across neighbours' land to power a water-mill, in which the claims of the partners are regulated in accordance with the claims of the various kin-groups to the estate of a deceased member of the kin: see D.A. Binchy (ed., trans.) 'Irish law-tracts re-edited. I. *Coibnes Uisci Thairidne*', *Ériu* 17 (1955) pp 52–85.   **53** It is also known under the title *Cath Boinne*. For the text, see J. O'Neill (ed., trans.), '*Cath Boinne*', *Ériu* 2 (1905) pp 173–85, and K. Meyer (ed.), '*Ferchuitred Medba inso*', in O.J. Bergin et al. (eds), *Anecdota from Irish manuscripts*, vol. 5 (Halle 1913) pp 17–22. See also Thurneysen, *Heldensage*, pp 531–4, and for my interpretation of the tale, D. Edel, 'Caught between history and myth? The figures of Fergus and Medb in the "Táin Bó Cúailnge" and related matter', *ZCP* 49/50 (1997) pp 143–69, at pp 162–4. On the relation between the Uí Néill and the Connachta, and the ability of the former to take their share as kings among the Connachta, see T.M. Charles-Edwards, *Early Irish and Welsh kingship* (Oxford 1993) pp 159–64.   **54** For this text, which is found in the facsimile of the Book of Leinster, p. 380a53, and thus belongs to a 15th-century addition to the manuscript, see T. Ó Máille, 'Medb Chruachna', *ZCP* 17 (1928) pp 129–46, at pp 137–8. The conflict between the Laigin and the Uí Néill is also

I add two literary examples from the southern kingdom of Munster. In the traditions around the Battle of Mag Mucrama, Sadb, a daughter of Conn Cétchathach, is first married to Lugaid Loígde, ancestor of the Corcu Loígde, a population group in Munster, and then to his successor, king Ailill Ólomm of the Éoganacht. In the first part of the tale the two opponents are Lugaid Mac Con, according to some traditions Sadb's son by her first husband, and Éogan, her eldest son by her second husband, the former disputing the latter's claim to the kingship.[55] The second example has been discussed by Professor Mac Cana in his article 'Aspects of the theme of king and goddess in Irish literature'. As I understand the tale about the Munster queen Mór Muman, who is first married to an Éoganacht king of the Cashel branch and subsequently to one of the Glenamain branch, it provides a justification for the alternation of the kingship between the two dynastic branches from the beginning of the seventh century to the middle of the eighth.[56]

The concept of the *hieros gamos* between mortal ruler and sovereignty figure, which became increasingly important as a literary topos in the Early Modern and Modern period, should not render us blind for the historical reality behind it. The widowed queen was not merely a passive instrument of legitimization. Provided she had enough political acuity and the necessary means to stay near the centre of power, why would she have accepted to fade into the periphery?

The Irish examples have historical parallels in the early Germanic kingdoms. Paul the Deacon reports in his *Historia Langobardorum* that after the death of the Langobard king Authari in 590 the nobles of the kingdom and the members of his retinue 'allowed [his widow Theudelinda] to remain in her royal dignity, advising her to choose for herself [as her husband] whomsoever she might wish from all the Lombards; such a one, namely, as could profitably manage the kingdom.'[57] Which the queen did, *consilium cum prudentibus habens* 'taking council with the prudent'.

Anglo-Saxon England provides several examples of marriages between the widowed queen and her husband's son and successor. Bede reports that when king Aethelberht died in 616 in recently Christianized Kent, the latter's son and successor Eadbald, then still a pagan, married *uxorem patris* 'his father's wife' – a union which the Benedictine monk condemned in harsh terms.[58]

---

reflected in *Orgain Dind Ríg* and in *Esnada Tige Buchet*, and, implicitly, in the Galióin episode in the *Táin* (see above, note 32). For the relation between the Uí Néill and the Connachta, see note 53.   **55** In *Scéla Moshauluim*, ch. 1, in Máirín O Daly (ed.), *Cath Maige Mucrama. The battle of Mag Mucrama* (London 1975) pp 74–5, according to one variant Lugaid Mac Con is Sadb's son by her first husband, according to the other variant, and according to *Cath Maige Mucrama*, ch. 1–2 (ibid., pp 38–9) Lugaid Mac Con of the Corcu Loígde is a fosterson of her and Ailill. From the three sons born by her to Ailill Ólomm, Éogan, Cían and Cormac Cas, are descended the Éoganacht, Cíannacht, and Dál Cáis. O Daly suggests that the story in its original form was a purely Munster tale and that it was later altered and added to by the partisans of the Connachta in order to lend support to the claim of the race of Conn to the kingship of Tara (ibid., p. 3).   **56** P. Mac Cana, 'Aspects of the theme of king and goddess in Irish literature', *ÉtC* 7 (1955/56) pp 76–114, 356–413, *ÉtC* 8 (1958/59) pp 59–65; see *ÉtC* 7, pp 81–4. The tale has been edited by T.P. O'Nolan under the title 'Mór Muman ocus Aided Cuanach meic Ailchine', *PRIA* 30 (1912) pp 261–82. The death of this Mugain Mór, who apparently had West Munster associations, is recorded in the Annals of Ulster *s.a.* 632 in an addition to the work of the first scribe; cf. M. O'Brien, *Corpus Genealogiarum Hiberniae*, vol. 1 (Dublin 1962; repr. 1976) p. 221 (151a17).   **57** '[…] *permiserunt eam in regia consistere dignitatem, suadentes ei, ut sibi quem ipsa voluisset ex omnibus Langobardis virum eligeret, talem scilicet qui regnum regere utiliter possit.*' For the text, see G. Waitz (ed.), *Pauli Historia Langobardorum* (Hannover 1878: MHG SS rer. Germ.) p. 140, for the translation, W.D. Foulke, *Paul the Deacon. History of the Lombards* (Philadelphia 1974) p. 149. Theudelinda chose a relative of her husband, Agilulf of Turin. According to Lombard law the widowed queen had the right to designate a successor: cf. note 24 above. The view that the queen was a vehicle on which claims to the royal succession could be carried to a second husband was apparently also held in Visigothic Spain, but not in Merowingian Gaul: see Nelson, 'Queens as Jezebels', pp 37–8 and n. 28.   **58** HE II.5, using the term *fornicatio*. Assuming that Eadbald was the son of Bertha, the widow in question would have been a second or secondary wife of Aethelberht. Secondary wives were certainly not uncommon. In fact, Bertha's own father, Charibert, one of the

However, Eadbald's behaviour was less exceptional than is often assumed.[59] Nearly 250 years later, in 858, upon the death of the powerful king Aethelwulf of Wessex, Aethelbald, his oldest living son by his first wife, also married his father's widow, the youthful Judith, daughter of Charles the Bald, and the union was acknowledged both by her father and the Church.[60] Aethelbald must have seen in her a highly prestigious mother for his future children, for she had been anointed queen on the occasion of her marriage to the aging Aethelwulf by her father's bishop, Hincmar of Reims – the first queenly consecration which is not only relatively well documented in the contemporary sources, but whose *ordo* has been preserved.[61]

There is Continental evidence of widowed queens who extended their influence through their sons by successfully defending the latter's claims both against the brothers of their husbands and the half-brothers of their sons.[62] The mother of the afore-mentioned Charles the Bald, whom Louis the Pious, the son of Charlemagne had married when the sons of his deceased first wife were already approaching adulthood, defended her son's interests so successfully against his half-brothers that after his father's death he obtained the western third of the empire as his share in the inheritance. When Charles the Bald forced his son Louis the Stammerer to divorce his first wife and marry Adelaide, the latter, after Louis's death, managed to keep her posthumously born son, the future Charles the Simple, safe from her husband's first wife until circumstances were favourable to his ascension to the West Frankish throne.

In Ireland, the genre of 'kingly literature' which provides this kind of information elsewhere comes late. As we have seen, conflicts of this sort are alluded to in *Beatha Aodha Rhuaidh Uí Dhomhnaill* and in the Annals of the Four Masters, both from the first decades of the seventeenth century.[63] In the literary texts these struggles are reflected, among others, by the theme that the ancestor of a new dynasty is the son of a secondary wife, as in the case of the Uí Néill.[64]

four sons of Clothar I of Neustria, who was king of Paris 661–7, provides us with a well documented example of polygamy: see D.P. Kirby, *The earliest English kings* (London 1991) p. 33; Stafford, *Queens and concubines*, pp 72ff. Oswiu of Northumbria had an Irish wife (the mother of Alhfrith) besides the Deiran princess Eanfled (the mother of Aldfrith and Ecgfrith); moreover, according to the early 9th-century *Historia Brittonum*, ch. 57 he had a British wife. For secondary wives on the Continent, see Ennen, *Frauen im Mittelalter*, p. 59. Charlemagne had (at least) four full wives and six secondary wives. **59** Cf. J.M. Wallace-Hadrill, *Bede's Ecclesiastical history of the English people. A historical commentary* (Oxford 1988) p. 61: 'To marry one's father's widow was sound Germanic practice.' **60** Ennen, *Frauen im Mittelalter*, pp 60–1; Pauline Stafford, 'Charles the Bald, Judith and England', in Margaret Gibson and Janet Nelson (eds), *Charles the Bald: court and kingdom* (Oxford 1981) pp 137–51; Kirby, *The earliest English kings*, pp 200–1. Judith was only about thirteen at her marriage to Aethelwulf in 856, who was then about fifty. At that time, Aethelbald was already representing his absent father as regent. Aethelwulf had been married to Judith for two years when he died in 858, and Aethelbald for two and a half when he died in 860. For Judith's later history, see Ennen, *Frauen im Mittelalter*, pp 61–3. After her return to France, Judith managed to escape in 862 with a man of her own choice, Baudouin, count of Flandres, and thus became the ancestress of the Flemish dynasty. **61** Nelson, 'Early medieval rites of queen-making', pp 306–8; for the text of the *ordo*, in which Hincmar, adapting a king's *ordo*, referred to the Old Testament examples of Judith and Esther, see pp 313–14. The prayer has nothing about fertility. However, cf. Stafford, 'Charles the Bald', p. 141 and *Queens and concubines*, p. 131, who regards the ceremony partly as a fertility rite. As Nelson, art. cit., p. 302 states, the evidence for the blessing of queens does not go further back than the advent of the Carolingian dynasty in 751. The custom may have had been introduced because in the case of these upstarts, as they are characterized by Nelson in 'Women at the court of Charlemagne: a case of monstruous regiment', in Parsons, *Medieval queenship*, pp 43–61, at pp 50–1, the royal family was a nuclear, small family, which asked for a highlighting of the royal couple as couple. **62** For the following examples, see Ennen, *Frauen im Mittelalter*, pp 58–9 and Stafford, *Queens and concubines*, pp 69, 112, 130, 164. The name of Charles the Bald's mother was also Judith. **63** See above and notes 35 and 36. For comparable information contained in the genealogies, see Charles-Edwards, *Early Irish and Welsh kinship*, pp 114–15. **64** In *Echtra mac n-Echach Muigmedóin*: see M. Dillon, *The cycles of the kings* (London etc. 1946) pp 38–41. This theme also occurs

II. The literary image of the female ruler and historical reality

In this second part, I shall subsequently discuss the queen as virtually independent ruler, the queen-regent, and the concept of the female successor to the kingship.

The queen as virtually independent ruler

The word 'queen' originally designates the wife of the king,[65] and in general the queen is envisaged in the secondary role of royal consort, but there is the possibility of a more or less primary, independent role. However, the female ruler is an anomaly, and the few historical examples are the product of extraordinary circumstances, such as the turmoils of the Roman conquest of Britain or those of the Viking age. Boudicca turned against the Romans when, after her husband's death, they looted his kingdom. The Icenian king Prasutagus, a *foederatus* of Rome, had named the emperor his heir together with his two daughters – as Tacitus suggests, to place his kingdom and household beyond the risk of injury –, but when he died, his people and his family were treated as prizes of war. In this crisis his widow rose to power and proclaimed the revolt.[66] Cartimandua, on the other hand, may have owed her dominant position at least in part to her pro-Roman policy. Professor Charles-Edwards has suggested that she was the last survivor of the ruling family of her people, with no surviving male kinsmen. In these circumstances, marrying the foremost war-leader among the Briganti would have been the expected thing for her to do. (The marriage has a parallel in the origin legend of Emain Macha, as we shall see.) However, while she was supported by the pro-Roman element in the Brigantian confederation, her husband followed an increasingly anti-Roman policy. It was probably for this reason that she divorced him, captured his kinsmen and followers, and married his shield-bearer (*armiger*). In the ensuing war the Romans took her side, thus pursuing their own aims.[67]

The Anglo-Saxon Aethelflaed may be regarded as a successful parallel of Cartimandua. The marriage of this first-born child of Alfred the Great of Wessex and his Mercian wife with the Mercian *ealdorman* Aethelred served as a confirmation of the West Saxon overlordship over Mercia. Aethelflaed was the prominent partner in this marriage. She first ruled Mercia jointly with her husband, who was seriously ill for many years before his death in 911; from then until her own death in 918 she ruled it virtually independently. As a result of her important successes against the Vikings and the Welsh she became the leader of a great North-English alliance. She was known in Ireland, as is evinced by the Annals of Ulster, which recorded the death of Eithilfleith, *famosissima regina Saxonum*.[68]

The queen-regent

A special type of virtually independent female rulership is found among the widows who assumed the regency for their underage sons and grandsons. While the queen-regent made her appearance

---

in other traditions. For an African example, see J. Vansina, *Oral tradition. A study in historical methodology*, English trans. H.M. Wright (London 1965) p. 83.   **65** It is the Indo-European word for woman, cognate with Irish *ben*. **66** According to Tacitus, *Annals*, XIV.35, she stated that it was customary for the Britons to fight under female leadership; she was seeking revenge, not as a queen of glorious ancestry, but as a woman of the people.   **67** Cf. Charles-Edwards, 'Native political organization in Roman Britain', p. 45; Tacitus, *Annals*, XII.40, *Histories*, III.45. Tacitus describes Venantius as *post captum Caratacum praecipuus scientia rei militaris*. Compare Tacitus's harsh words on female rule in Cartimandua's case (Annals, XII.40) with his favourable verdict of Agrippina, the wife of Claudius, who claimed a partnership in the empire that her ancestors had created (*Annals*, XII.37).   **68** AU *s.a.* 918. For Aethelflaed, see

in Merovingian Gaul as early as the latter part of the sixth century, in Ireland she is unknown, and this despite the many resemblances between the two countries. Whence this contrast? In this case I do not seek the cause in the paucity of the Irish source material, for Anglo-Saxon England, whose historical sources contain an impressive amount of influential female figures, seems to have managed without the queen-regent too. It seems to me that at least part of the explanation lies in the superabundance of dynastic families in Ireland and England and the fierce competition that was the result of this. Merovingian Gaul, on the other hand, was already well on the road towards dynastic strengthening, although its succession system was still to a certain extent fluid.

Ireland may not have had queen-regents of its own, but it became acquainted with at least two through its *peregrini*: Brunhild (d. 613), through the contacts of St Columbanus with her, and Balthild (d. *c.*680), through the support the Irish-Frankish monastic movement received from her. The Visigothic princess Brunhild, who had actively supported her husband Sigibert I of Austrasia during his lifetime, assumed the regency for their son Childebert after her husband was murdered at his brother's instigation. Against all odds, she managed to secure Childebert the thrones of Austrasia and Burgundy. After his untimely death she ruled as regent for his underage sons and secured the two kingdoms for them. Her last attempt to keep the two kingdoms together, after their early deaths, led to her tragic downfall.[69] Janet Nelson has suggested that Brunhild was not motivated by the ambition to strengthen the Merovingian *regnum*, but had only her own position in mind.[70] However, the two may well have gone together. Her ideas of a strong kingship, ideas for which she was in all probability indebted to her homeland, must have been shared by the faction whose support she had, *viz.* those same circles which had favoured Sigibert's marriage to the Visigothic princess half a century earlier.

While the hagiographic sources blackened Brunhild's picture – the result of her clash with St Columbanus[71] –, Balthild was idealised in a near-contemporary *vita* of her own.[72] An Anglo-Saxon ex-slave, she was the wife of Clovis II. Already very influential during her husband's lifetime, upon his death in 657 she became regent for their eldest son Clothar III. Her motivation was comparable to that of Brunhild:[73] to strengthen the Merovingian *regnum* by safeguarding her own royal line. Both she and Brunhild are depicted as royal figures, with the same traits as their male equivalents.[74]

Stafford, *Queens and concubines*, pp 118–19; Ann Williams et al., *A biographical dictionary of Dark Age Britain, England, Scotland and Wales, c.500–c.1050* (London 1991) pp 21–2. Alfred the Great of Wessex was the youngest son of Aethelwulf of Wessex (see above, p. 13). Under him Mercia came under the overlordship of Wessex. **69** Her younger grandson Theuderic of Burgundy, who always remained close to her, defeated in 612 his brother Theudebert and thus gained control over Austrasia. While he was marching against Clothar II of Neustria, he suddenly died, possibly through murder. The failure of Brunhild's last attempt to maintain the union between the two kingdoms, by having Theuderic's eldest son, Sigibert, succeed his father, led to her judicial murder at the orders of Clothar II in 613. **70** Nelson, 'Queens as Jezebels', p. 45 and n. 79. **71** Jonas's *Vita Columbani*, ch. 19. The life is edited by B. Krusch in *MGH SRM* 4 (Hannover/Leipzig 1902) pp 1–152. Her clash with the saint was caused by his refusal to bless Theuderic's two sons, born to him by a concubine. If Theuderic indeed did not take a full wife because Brunhild was opposed to this, her attitude may be compared to that of ruling kings, who considered the marriage of their sons as an act of rebellion. **72** The *Vita Balthildis*, written at Balthild's nunnery at Celles-sur-Cher, whereto she was forced to retire on Clothar's coming of age, was also edited by B. Krusch, *MGH SRM* 2 (Hannover 1887) pp 475–508). Another important foundation of hers was the Luxeuil daughter Corbie. Also Jumièges and St-Wandrille received large donations from her. **73** In her case too, Nelson, 'Queens as Jezebels', p. 48 is critical about the suggestion that as queen-regent she pursued a policy of reunifying the Merovingian *regnum*. **74** See Nelson, ibid., p. 76. Gregory of Tours said of Brunhild that she was *prudens consilio et blanda colloquio* (*Liber Historiae Francorum* IV.27) and Balthilt is described in her Life, ch. 2 as *prudens et astuta virgo* (see Nelson, ibid., pp 40, 46).

I end this section with the afore-mentioned Theophanu. Upon her husband's death in 983 she assumed the regency for their only son, Otto III, who was then only three years old. The power wielded by her until her death in 991 was matched only by a handful of contemporary kings and surpassed by none. One of the two charters she signed independently bears the male form of her name, *Theophanius gratia divina imperator augustus*, and is dated *anno vero imperii domni Theophanii imperatoris xviii.*[75]

The concept of the female successor to the kingship

While Ireland provides no historical examples of female rulers, whether as rulers in their own right or as queen-regents, there are several literary examples of female successors to the kingship.

As I have signalled earlier, Medb of Crúachain and Medb Lethderg, whose role in two Early Modern texts has led scholars to interpret them as manifestations of the divine spouse of the rightful king, appear in two earlier texts as successful claimants to the throne, the one as the king's widow, the other as the king's daughter. In the tenth-century *Esnada Tige Buchet* (The Melodies [or Cries] of Buchet's House), Medb Lethderg, upon the death of her husband Art, the son of Conn Cétchathach, assumes the kingship, not allowing Cormac, his son by another woman, into Tara.[76] In the twelfth-century Pillow Talk, Medb of Crúachain, the daughter of the Irish high-king Eochu Feidlech, presents herself as *banchomarbae* 'female heir' and calls her husband Ailill *fer ar bantinchur* 'a man upon woman-input' because she has received Connacht from her father. Her husband Ailill, on the other hand, regards himself as a claimant to the kingship of Connacht through his mother.[77]

Alan Bruford, at the Belfast conference on the Ulster cycle, called attention to a contemporary historical parallel: the Empress Matilda.[78] Henry I of England, who was since 1120 without a male heir, wished to be succeeded by his daughter Matilda. To secure her accession, he even took the unusual step of demanding a public oath in support of her at a court gathering in 1127. However, when he died in 1135, the throne was claimed by his sister's son, Stephen of Blois, and the ensuing civil war ended only with the accession of Matilda's son Henry II to the throne in 1154. Henry I was probably not the only nor the first king who preferred a female successor of his own line to a

---

75 That is, to the year 900, the eighteenth year since her marriage to Otto II. See Theophanu 2, in T. von Sickel (ed.), *Ottonis III Diplomata*, MGH DRG ii/2 (Hannover 1893) pp 876–7. **76** W. Stokes (ed. and trans.) 'The songs of Buchet's house', *RC* 25 (1904) pp 18–39, 225–7, at pp 24–5 (ch. 7). The passage is found in what D. Greene (ed.), *Fingal Rónáin and other stories* (Dublin 1955, repr. 1993) p. 27 regarded as an interpolation into the tale and therefore presented on p. 31 as an appendix (dinnshenchas of Odra). In the main narrative (ch. 12 in Stokes's edition) Cormac abducts Eithne, the daughter of Cathaer Mór, who has many brothers, because her foster-father Buchet does not give her to him, as the right to give her belongs to her father. After she gives birth to his (Cormac's) son Cairpre Lifechar, he takes her as his queen. Both the so-called interpolation and the main narrative refer to the conflict between the Laigin dynasty and the line of Conn: cf. above note 54. **77** C. O'Rahilly (ed.), *Táin Bó Cúalnge from the Book of Leinster* (Dublin 1970) ll. 1– 50. Máta Muirisc, Ailill's mother, is of the Fir Ól nÉcmacht (the old name for the Connachta): cf. O'Brien, *Corpus Genealogiarum Hiberniae*, pp 22–3 (118 b 7–12). **78** A. Bruford, 'Why an Ulster Cycle', in J.P. Mallory and G. Stockman (eds), *Ulidia. Proceedings of the first international conference on the Ulster cycle of tales, Belfast and Emain Macha, 8–12 April 1994* (Belfast 1994) pp 23–30, at p. 23 and n. 2. He was apparently unaware of the more recent studies about Matilda by Marjorie Chibnall and others. For a more modern view on this female claimant to the throne, see, for instance, Huneycutt, 'Female succession' (as above, note 12) p. 198, who comes to the conclusion that contemporaries of Matilda like Orderic Vitalis and John of Salisbury 'realized and accepted that the political and social realities of their day inevitably meant that women, acting to secure familial claims, would sometimes exercise public authority'. However, while Matilda and that other well-known example of a medieval female claimant, Melisende of Jerusalem (also mid-12th century) 'saw themselves as true heirs and rulers in their own right' (ibid., p. 192) their commentators, with few exceptions, portrayed them as representatives of their

male one of a collateral branch. As Ireland came increasingly into contact with England at that time, we may safely assume that the problems around Henry I's succession were followed on the island with interest.

An earlier parallel of Medb in Irish literature is the afore-mentioned Macha Mongrúad, the protagonist of the origin tale of Emain Macha. In the oldest version of the tale, which may be as early as the first half of the eighth century,[79] Macha is the only child of a certain Rúad who rules Ireland in turn with two other kings, Cimbaeth and Dithorbae. When Cimbaeth dies, he is succeeded by his five sons, who complete his turn, but when subsequently Rúad dies, his daughter is not accepted as joint ruler. However, Macha does not acquiesce in this refusal and seizes the kingship by force, taking Cimbaeth as her husband and leader of her troops.[80]

How do we interpret these literary figures? I suggest that although they do not mirror Irish historical reality, they may mirror historical polemics.[81] Is there not a striking resemblance between the claims presented by Medb and Ailill to the kingship of Connacht in the Pillow Talk and the claims of Matilda and Stephen of Blois to the English throne?

An interesting historical example comes from the Low Countries. In the discussion about Ada of Holland (c.1188–1223), the only child of duke Dirk VII of Holland, two phases may be distinguished, the former early-thirteenth-, the latter late-fifteenth-century. When Ada's father died in 1203, her mother married her off without delay to a neighbouring duke in order to ensure Ada's succession. However, the father's brother, with the support of one of the noble factions, seized the duchy and had Ada imprisoned and brought to England. (The affair was part of an international conflict, in which besides a number of local powers also two popes and the English king were involved.) While the contemporary sources are rather indifferent to Ada's fate, she is rehabilitated as *comitissa Hollandiae* in some late-fifteenth-century texts. The explanation for this late interest in her is that at that time the Low Countries were confronted with a similar problem in the person of Jacoba of Bavaria. By retrospectively acknowledging Ada's reign, a precedent was created for acknowledging the reign of Jacoba.[82]

To return to the daughter of Henry I, although she did not succeed in gaining the throne, her son Henry II did. My question is: how can we be certain that among the substantial percentage of Irish kings of unknown lineage – plus great-great-grandsons and further removes[83] – there were not some who had successfully claimed the kingship through their maternal line?

Fergus Kelly has suggested that the male imagery surrounding the office of kingship precluded even the possibility of a female ruler. As the material evidence for the rituals surrounding the inauguration of kings in the Barbarian West is extremely scarce, the only way to test his suggestion is by comparison with other periods and cultures. As Egypt has abundant archaeological and

families, agents for their fathers, husbands, and sons (ibid., p. 196). **79** Thurneysen, *Heldensage*, p. 17 assumed that it was contained in the Cín Dromma Snechta. **80** See K. Meyer (ed.), 'The dindshenchas of Emain Macha', in W. Stokes and K. Meyer (eds), *Archiv für celtische Lexicographie*, vol. 3 (Halle 1907) pp 325–6. (As far as I know, there is no published translation of this earliest version.) The tale ends as follows: Dithorbae's sons, who have retreated into the wilderness of Connacht – in order to reconquer the kingship from there? – are captured by Macha and brought to Emain, where they have to build an earthen rampart around her. **81** Participants in the polemic around Matilda, besides the afore-mentioned Orderic Vitalis and John of Salisbury, were William of Malmesbury and the anonymous author of the *Gesta Stephani*. See Huneycutt, 'Female succession' and Pauline Stafford, 'The portrayal of royal women in England, mid-tenth to mid-twelfth centuries', in Parsons, *Medieval Queenship*, pp 143–67, at pp 158–60. **82** F.W.N. Hugenholtz, 'Ada van Holland', in R.E.V. Stuip *et al.* (eds), *Middeleeuwers over vrouwen* [Medieval authors on women], vol. 1 (Utrecht 1985) pp 12–26, 177–9. **83** D. Ó Corráin, 'Irish regnal succession, a reappraisal', *Studia Hibernica* 11 (1971) pp 7–39, found 7% of unknown lineage

textual information from early times onwards, I have chosen two examples from there. The first one is Hatscheput. She reigned from 1490 until her death in 1468 BC, the first two years as regent for her stepson and subsequently as the official ruler, while her stepson was reduced to a purely formal co-rulership. At her solemn installation in 1488 she entered into the male role of the pharaoh, including all its martial traits. Yet, although she was forced by the royal ideology to have herself depicted as a man or as a male sphinx, she managed within this fixed scheme to express something of her femininity, for instance, by showing her female forms under the robes of office, or by assuming the names Female Horus or Daughter of Re. However, her case contains a harsh lesson: some time after her death the attempt was made to destroy all material traces of her – statues, reliefs, inscriptions – and in later royal genealogies her reign is ignored as being illegitimate.[84] The second example is Tausret, who ruled independently from c.1188–1186 BC. She followed Hatscheput's example in assuming the official title of ruling king and in having her grave built in the sacred area reserved for ruling kings. On the cover of her sarcophagus she is depicted holding the pharaoh's insignia, lash and crook.[85]

An example closer to the Barbarian West is the Empress Irene of Byzance. When her son Constantine VI, for whom she had acted as regent from AD 780 to 790, proved to be unsuited as emperor, she took over the government in 797 and ruled alone until 802, using the male title *basileus* and issuing coins which show her wearing the imperial *loros* and holding the cross-scepter and orb.[86]

With this very tentative reconnaissance of the Irish material against the background of the Anglo-Saxon and Continental evidence I hope to have shown that the renewed attention for the Irish kingship must be accompanied by an investigation of Irish queenship. Possibly royal women had less scope in Ireland than elsewhere. In the early phase the reason for this may have been the strong competition between the numerous ruling lineages and branches of lineages. From the

and 20% great-great-grandsons and further removes among the Uí Chennselaig kings (p. 28). **84** See E. Hornung, *Grundzüge der ägyptischen Geschichte* (2nd rev. ed. Darmstadt 1978) pp 78–84. Hatscheput was the half sister and wife of Thutmosis II (1493–90) from her mother Ahmes's side descending from the founder of the New Realm. She and Thutmosis II only had one daughter, Nofrurê, who was under-age at his death in 1490. However, he left behind an under-age son by Isis, his secondary wife (the later Thutmosis III, 1490/1468–36). Hatscheput reigned first for two years as regent for her stepson, but in 1488 she got herself proclaimed and solemnly crowned as ruling king, thereby entering the purely male role of pharaoh. From then until her death in 1468, her stepson was only formally her co-ruler, the power lying entirely with her and the ministers appointed by her. The first grave she had prepared for her was situated outside the Valley of Kings, the sacred area reserved for the burial of ruling kings; however, after her accession to the throne she had a new grave built for herself within the Valley, although in a simple, undecorated style: see E. Hornung, *Tal der Könige* (Zurich/Munich 1982) pp 51–2; cf. pp 38, 217. Her wish to be succeeded by her daughter was not fulfilled due to Nofrurê's early death. After her death, her stepson assumed the kingship. Whereas her reign had been prosperous and peaceful, he became the lasting terrifying symbol of Egypt's greatness both for his subjects and the neighbouring peoples. An earlier example of a female ruler is Sobeknofru (1789–85 BC) who after the death of her brother Amenemhât IV (1798–89 BC) assumed the title of a ruling king. Her short reign left many traces from the Nile delta until the second cataract, contrary to the historically non-documented "Nitokris" at the end of the 6th dynasty. See Hornung, *Grundzüge*, pp 63–4. **85** Tausret ruled first together with her husband Sethos II (1204–1194), the real power being then apparently with her, and subsequently for the under-age Siptah (c.1194–88), probably a son of Sethos II from another union. After Siptah's early death she ruled independently from 1188 to 1186, assuming the official title of ruling king like Hatscheput before her. She also followed Hatscheput's example in having her grave prepared in the Valley of Kings. Hers is the only decorated queen's grave in this holy area. See Hornung, *Grundzüge*, p. 109; idem, *Tal der Könige*, pp 54, 217–19 and the illustrations and photos on pp 64, 87, 109, 196 (cover of her sarcophagus). **86** Irene lived c.753–803, Constantine VI was born in 870. See Sir Steven Runciman, 'The Empress Irene the Athenian', in Baker, *Medieval women*, pp 101–18; Nelson, 'Women at the court of Charlemagne', pp 47–9 (with illustration showing a

tenth century onwards, when Ireland came increasingly into line with the rest of Europe, the queen-consort seems to have gained in importance, but this development came apparently again to an end in the Anglo-Norman period. While elsewhere lineages narrowed into dynasties and royal administrations gained in strength, Ireland seems to have reverted to more horizontal structures, at least in part. The ruling families, in order to hold on to their bases of power, safeguarded their material resources in the tail male system, which was unfavourable to female descendants. However, as Pauline Stafford has recently pointed out, power can be both competitive (usually associated with male authority) and relational (usually associated with female authority),[87] and so the investigation of Irish queenship should perhaps begin with an enquiry into the working of power itself.

coin with her image). Referring to contemporary annals, Nelson points out that Irene's *femineum imperium* has an important part in explaining why Charlemagne became emperor in 800. **87** Cf. Stafford, 'Emma' (see above, note 13) p. 11.

Further reflections on royal ordinations in the *Vita Columbae*

MICHAEL J. ENRIGHT

In two studies published in the mid 1980s, I argued that certain passages in Adomnán's *Vita Columbae* and in the *Collectio Canonum Hibernensis*, among other texts, suggest that some contemporary churchmen wished to reform the traditional royal inauguration ritual by introducing the Old Testament rite of anointing kings.[1] While this thesis has attracted considerable attention, it has also evoked criticism on several counts. It may thus be helpful to examine briefly a few additional aspects in order to develop more fully their implications for the overall argument and to provide further material for an assessment of Adomnán's sources, methodology and politics.

From the rather lengthy discussion in *Iona, Tara and Soissons*, two episodes may be considered anew: one is Adomnán's description of the sacring of Áedán mac Gabráin as king of Dál Riata, and the second in his reference to the ordination of Diarmait mac Cerbaill as king of all Ireland. As both passages are frequently cited and have also been covered more fully in the work mentioned, I shall deal here only with those elements that are immediately relevant to the present purpose and otherwise seek to avoid repetition as far as possible. I shall then not be dealing with all of the evidence but primarily with additional evidence in two cases. Because the Áedán chapter is crucial to any interpretation, it must be cited in full:

De angelo domini qui ad sanctum Columbam in Hinba commorantem insula per visum apparuit, misus ut Aidanum in regem ordinaret

Alio in tempore, cum vir praedicabilis in Hinba commoraretur insula, quadam nocte in extasi mentis angelum domini ad se misum vidit, qui in manu vitreum ordinationis regum habebat librum. Quem cum vir venerandus de manu angeli accipisset ab eo jusus legere coepit. Qui cum secundum quod ei in libro erat commendatum Aidanum in regem ordinare recussaret, quia magis Iogenanum fratrem ejus dilegeret, subito angelus extendens manum sanctum percussit flagillo, cujus livorosum in ejus latere vestigium omnibus suae diebus permansit vitae. Hocque intulit verbum: 'Pro certo scias' inquiens, 'quia ad té a deo misus sum cum vitreo libro, ut juxta verba

Of the angel of the Lord who was sent to St Columba to bid him to ordain Áedán as king, and who appeared to him in a vision while he was living in the island of Hinba

Once, when the praiseworthy man was living in the island of Hinba, he saw one night in a mental trance an angel of the Lord sent to him. He had in his hand a glass book of the ordination of kings, which St Columba received from him, and which at the angel's bidding he began to read. In the book the command was given him that he should ordain Áedán as king, which St Columba refused to do because he held Áedán's brother Éoganán in higher regard. Whereupon the angel reached out and struck the saint with a whip, the scar from which remained with him for the rest of his life. Then the angel addressed him sternly: 'Know then as

1 M.J. Enright, *Iona, Tara, and Soissons: the origin of the royal anointing ritual* (Berlin and New York 1985); 'Royal succession and abbatial prerogative in Adomnán's *Vita Columbae*,' *Peritia* 4 (1985) pp 83–103.

quae in eo legisti Aidanum in regnum ordines. Quod si obsecundare huic nolueris jusioni, percutiam te iterato'.

Hic itaque angelus domini cum per tris contenuas noctes eundem in manu vitreum habens codicem apparuisset, eademque domini jusa de regis ejusdem ordinatione commendasset, sanctus verbo obsequtus domini ad Iovam transnavigavit insulam, ibidemque Aidanum hisdem adventantem diebus in regem sicut erat jusus ordinavit. Et inter ordinationis verba de filiis et nepotibus pronepotibusque ejus futura profetizavit, inponensque manum super caput ejus ordinans benedixt.[2]

a certain truth, I am sent to you by God with the glass book in order that you should ordain Áedán to kingship according to the words you have read in it. But if you refuse to obey this command, I shall strike you again.'

In this way the angel of the Lord appeared to St Columba on three successive nights, each time having the same glass book, and each time making the same demand that he should ordain Áedán as king. The holy man obeyed the word of the Lord and sailed from Hinba to Iona, where Áedán had arrived at this time, and he ordained him king in accordance with the Lord's command. As he was performing the ordination, St Columba also prophesied the future of Áedán's sons and grandsons and great-grandsons, then he laid his hand on Áedán's head in ordination and blessed him.[3]

In my opinion, this passage from the *vita* is inspired by the story of Samuel's unction of Saul as told in *I Reges*. It indicates, among other things, that Adomnán wished to identify closely Columba with that famous prophet and judge of the Old Testament. In the context of his time (but not that of Columba) there were sound political and ideological reasons for such identification. This interpretation has been challenged by T.M. Charles-Edwards, however, who argues that the 'principal Old Testament background' to the consecration passage is not Samuel's dealings with Saul and David but rather 'owes a great deal to the account in Genesis of Isaac's dealings with his twin sons, Esau and Jacob, where blessing is mixed with dynastic prophecy and confers, by means of a kiss and the imposition of hands, supreme authority on the one blessed.' He considers these passages and others like them as being 'far more appropriate for Irish purposes because the Irish were not concerned to make a family royal which had not been so previously [as in the Frankish case of Pippin III in 751], but rather to choose the next king from within a kindred whose royal claims no one denied.'[4] This latter remark is based on the erroneous impression that I advocated such an undifferentiated interpretation.[5]

Charles-Edwards's approach would seem to seek to relate Adomnán's concerns to inheritance law and to the associated quarrels among sons about property and precedence. Certainly these

2 A.O. and M.O. Anderson (eds), *Adomnán's Life of Columba* (London 1961) pp 472–4. Essential background studies are M. Herbert, *Iona, Kells, and Derry: the history and hagiography of the monastic familia of Columba* (Oxford 1988, repr. Dublin 1996); J.-M. Picard, 'The purpose of Adomnán's *Vita Columbae*', *Peritia* 1 (1982) pp 160–77; id. 'Bede, Adomnán and the writing of history', *Peritia* 3 (1984) pp 50–70; F.J. Byrne, 'The Ireland of St. Columba', *Historical Studies* 5 (1965) pp 37–58; *Irish kings and high-kings* (London 1973, repr. Dublin 2001); T.O. Clancy and G. Màrkus (eds), *Iona: the earliest poetry of a Celtic monastery* (Edinburgh 1995). 3 The translation is that of Richard Sharpe, *Adomnán of Iona. Life of St Columba* (London 1995) p. 208f. 4 T.M. Charles-Edwards, 'A contract between King and people in early medieval Ireland? *Críth Gablach* on kingship', *Peritia* 8 (1994) pp 107–19 at p. 109 n. 9, p. 118. 5 In *Iona, Tara, and Soissons*, I maintain that Pippin III and his advisors were influenced by passages in the *Hibernensis* and not by any other work. I do argue, however, that Adomnán's views had an effect on the compilers of the *Hibernensis*. The two theses should not be confused. Similarly, it is not correct

were profoundly important in Irish society where they often affected claims and attitudes about royal succession. As Charles-Edwards rightly notes, however, Adomnán's writings about kingship express a greater interest in the relations between a ruler and God than between a ruler and people.[6] Perhaps equally significant for Adomnán, I would suggest, is the relationship between abbot and king, ordainer and ordained, Columba and Áedán. Adomnán is less interested in 'Irish purposes' and far more so with the specific purposes of the *familia* of Columba, namely its status with regard to the kings of Dál Riata and with the kings of Ireland, particularly the Uí Néill then being courted by followers of Patrick and Armagh. Iona's high level of interest in royal politics is well reflected in the extract from abbot Cumméne Find's book (cited in the Schaffhausen manuscript) on the miraculous powers of St Columba. The saint is there made to warn Áedán about their political alliance:

Cummeneus albus in libro quem de virtutibus sancti Columbae scripsit sic dixit, quod sanctus Columba de Aidano et de posteris ejus et de regno suo profetare coepit, dicens: 'Indubitanter crede, O Aidane, quoniam nullus adversariorum tuorum tibi poterit resistere, donec prius fraudulentiam agas in me et in posteros meos. Proptera ergo tu filiis commenda, ut et ipsi filiis et nepotibus et posteris suís commendent, ne per consilia mala eorum sceptrum regni hujus de manibus suis perdant. In quocumque enim tempore malum adversum me aut adversus cognatos meos qui sunt in Hibernia fecerint, flagillum quod causa tui ab angelo sustenui per manum dei super eos in magnum flagitium vertetur; et cor virorum auferetur ab eis, et inimici eorum vehimenter super eos confortabuntur'.

Cumméne the White in the book which he wrote on the miraculous powers of St Columba gives this account of St Columba's prophecy about Áedán and his descendants and his kingdom: 'Make no mistake, Áedán, but believe that, until you commit some act of treachery against me or my successors, none of your enemies will have the power to oppose you. For this reason you must give warning to your sons, as they must pass it on to their sons and grandsons and descendants, so that they do not follow evil counsels and so lose the sceptre of this kingdom from their hands. For whenever it may happen that they do wrong to me or to my kindred in Ireland, the scourge that I have suffered for your sake from the angel will be turned by the hand of God to deliver a heavy punishment on them. Men's hearts will be taken from them, and their enemies will draw strength mightily against them.'

Hoc autem vaticinium temporibus nostris conpletum est in bello Roth, Domnallo Brecco nepot[e] Aidani sine causa vastante provinciam Domnail nepotis Ainmuireg. Et a die illa usque hodie adhuc in proclivo sunt ab extraneis: qoud suspiria doloris pectori incutit.[7]

This prophecy was fulfilled in our own time, at the battle of Mag Roth, when Áedán's grandson Domnall Brecc laid waste the territory of the saint's kinsman Domnall Ua Ainmirech. From that day to this the family of Áedán is held in subjection by strangers, a fact which brings sighs of sorrow to the breast.[8]

to hold that the only reason for anointing is to make a previously non-royal family royal. If that were the case then unctions after the first generation would be superfluous and unnecessary – an interpretation contradicted by Carolingian practice and that of other later dynasties. Nor does a similarity of ritual at any time necessarily mean a similarity in political situation. There is a large literature on the political significance of various Carolingian anointings and I cite a good deal of it in my work. For the *Hibernensis* and Pippin, see *Iona, Tara and Soissons*, pp 79–106.   **6** T.M. Charles-Edwards, 'Contract between king and people', p. 118.   **7** Anderson, *Life of Columba*, p. 474. Translation by Sharpe, *Life of St Columba*, p. 209.   **8** On Cumméne's book and the prophecy, see Sharpe's lengthy notes

This passage is of great significance because it was inserted (perhaps by Dorbbéne although that is uncertain) immediately after Adomnán's reference to Columba's prophecy about the future of Áedán's sons made during the ordination itself. It is thus probable that the writer wished to ensure that Columba's exact words were remembered. They seemed to have constituted a kind of contract.[9] A close and permanent political alliance is clearly presumed in the excerpt, so much so that from one perspective the ordination might be seen as that ritual which expresses it. Thus, Columba guarantees the security of Áedán's kingship and that of his sons and descendants as long as they do not oppose the saint or his succeeding abbots. Royal dominion hinges on maintaining faith with Iona since otherwise Dál Riata's kings will 'lose the sceptre of this kingdom.' Aside from God's support, what Columba has offered is dynastic protection in return for loyalty. It is, therefore, largely the political interest of the Iona abbot that is expressed by the ordination and any 'Irish interests'(whatever those may be) are at best ancillary.

As the excerpt shows (and other examples could be cited) the Iona abbots were principally interested in close reciprocal relations with kings in which they defined the conditions of reciprocity. What ideological sustenance then could the Isaac/Jacob material lend to a community committed to such policies? That is the question that must be answered. At first glance these texts look promising as vehicles for inspiration since they do provide examples of prophecy, a choosing between brothers, an imposition of hands and a conferral of authority. If one interprets Columba's ordination in a minimalist fashion, then some level of comparison seems reasonable. But analysis reveals that such sources would present more problems for Iona than solutions. The difficulties are fourfold. First, although the Isaac/Jacob passages may be attired in the garb of lordship they are not easily suited to fit kings. None of the figures mentioned are royal and the authority conferred is not royal either. Jacob does not become a king after his father's blessing. Nor will it do to argue that kings are simply lords writ large. To do so would not only skirt the issue, it would ignore the heavy ideological and religious freight that accompanies Irish kingship (and which we shall soon see Adomnán himself employing). Consider also that any propagandist who wished to persuade a royal candidate of the correctness of such Genesis precedents must now get the candidate to agree to a double novelty: he must not only convince him to accept a new model of inauguration, he must also persuade him that his status is not diminished by following the example of those who are not kingly. That would be no easy task in a society where status was crucial.

Second, the Isaac/Jacob material is fraught with danger to a clerical user because it omits the clergy. The familial power that is being conferred is passed on by the patriarch himself. There is no need for an outside ordainer and hence no leverage, no political advantage for the outsider. What then would tempt Adomnán to draw on it? If control over an extended family and its dependants may be transferred by a simple blessing of father to son, then the establishment of that ritual as a political model by an extra – familial institution is not only foolhardy, it is positively suicidal. Adomnán was too capable a thinker to base his arguments on precedents that eliminated any need for himself or his descendants. The Áedán episode conclusively demonstrates that the actions and speech of an ordaining Columban abbot are indispensable.[10]

in *Life of St Columba*, pp 357–60. **9** This may be Charles-Edwards's view as well since he refers to an 'agreement', an 'alliance', and 'explicit instructions': 'Contract between king and people', 118. The contract that he analyzes is a different one however. **10** That is why this passage cannot easily be compared, for example, to *Timna Chathaír Máir*, the 'Testament of Chathair Már', in which a ruler alone bequeaths kingship to one of his sons. This text, as Myles Dillon pointed out, does seem to draw upon the Jacob blessing of Genesis so that it is clear that a concept of the passage of kingship could be adapted to that form. But that is the opposite of what Adomnán wants because it eliminates the outside holy man. The *Testament* is a bequest, moreover, and thus lends itself to the Genesis

Third, a real problem of credibility exists in supposing that Adomnán would wish to draw on texts lacking reference to both kings and outside consecrators. After all, a great many of both figures can be found elsewhere in the Old Testament. Not only are they present, they are frequently depicted in close and contingent relationships that privilege the holy man while also providing illustrations of practically every lesson that a thoughtful or beleaguered abbot might wish to inflict on an unworthy king. That aspect of contingency is also especially prominent in the Cumméne find extract. Hence, turning to Genesis when the Books of Kings are available is like throwing a pebble when a cannon is at hand. At best, it provides only a weak basis for the warnings and precepts that Adomnán wishes to emphasise so as to protect Columba's authority.

Fourth, and very significantly, both structure and content of the Isaac/Jacob verses are deficient as evidence for inspiration in that they demonstrate a complete absence of any relationship with the pattern of thought and event in the Áedán chapter. The Samuel/Saul material does just the opposite: it confirms one.

This final item requires lengthier exposition. In *Iona, Tara, and Soissons*, aside from the consecration itself, I placed much emphasis on the comparable coincidences of timing, secrecy, and unusual site in I *Reges* and the Áedán chapter.[11] These motifs seemed to correspond rather well and thus to suggest borrowing. In fact, however, the texts immediately preceding these events in the bible also offered persuasive evidence and it would have better served the thesis to have examined them more closely. I shall now attempt to remedy that neglect.

Adomnán's description of the Iona kingship ritual contains several additional aspects worthy of comment. These include the chagrin of the saint at God's command, the triple appearance of the angel, the choice between candidates, and the strangely persistent focus on the book carried by the angel. The inspiration for these details continues to be I *Reges* but chapter 8 now becomes as relevant as 9 and 10. When God's angel appeared to Columba with the order to hallow Áedán, the saint reacted with obstinacy because he preferred Áedán's brother Éoganán. Indeed, the saint had to be repeatedly scourged until he was driven to agree. There is simply no parallel to these motifs in the cited Genesis material. Something quite reminiscent of the saint's reaction does appear in I *Reges* 8:6, however, where the elders of Israel approach Samuel. They demand that he appoint a king over them. We are told that Samuel was 'displeased' by this: *displicuitque sermo in oculis Samuhelis*.[12] Here, then, we actually find two comparable items – one, a demand from an outside source to create a king, and two, the holy man's displeasure when he hears it. Neither is fully comparable to the *vita* in that the elders of Israel are obviously not God's angel and neither is Samuel's annoyance so extreme as to require a whipping. Nonetheless, the partial parallels of outside demand to make a king combined with the ordainer's displeasure are impressive enough. Both serve the same functional requirement of setting the stage for a kingmaking which then follows in *each* source. Nor can the pattern simply reflect a common story line since dismay at the prospect of a royal inauguration is hardly a predictable response on the part of him who is to perform the ordaining.

precedent. It is not a kingmaking ritual at all. In that sense, the *Testament* is better compared to the choosing of Eochaid Buide in *Vita Columbae* I, 9 which, however, is carried out by Columba, as in the Áedán episode, and is also based on Samuel's actions in I *Reges*. *Oirdnidir, ordinatio*, are fluid terms in Irish as well as Latin and here we see two usages in play. That of the Testament fits well with Charles-Edwards's interpretation whereas that in the *Vita Columbae* is a separate one with a different meaning. See Myles Dillon (ed.), *Lebor na Cert. The Book of Rights* (Dublin 1962) pp 148–53. Further commentary on such material in F.J. Byrne, 'Seanchas: The nature of Gaelic historical tradition', *Irish Historical Studies* 9 (1974) pp 137–59 at p. 155 f.; D. Ó Corráin, 'Irish origin legends and genealogy: recurrent aetiologies', in T. Nyberg et al., *History and heroic tale* (Odense 1985) pp 51–96 at p. 53 f.; 'Creating the past: The early Irish genealogical tradition', *Peritia* 12 (1998) pp 177–208 at p. 204 f. **11** The dominant position of the holy men with regard to the king is also important. See *Iona, Tara and Soissons*, p. 18 f. *et passim*. **12** R. Weber et al., *Biblia Sacra Iuxta Vulgatam Versionem* (Stuttgart 1994) p. 276.

The possibility that these comparisons may strain the evidence is rendered improbable by what immediately follows in that God's command to Samuel to make a king is expressed three times (I *Reges* 8:7,9,22), on each occasion in essentially the same words: *audi vocem populi*.[13] This is paralleled in the *vita* by the angel's three successive appearances bearing God's command. A recognition of the correspondence here is also significant in that it provides an additional perspective which helps us to understand Columba's recalcitrance. His repeated refusal to obey divine commands is surprising, not to say shocking. Part of this at least is to be explained by the nature of Irish culture and religiosity since we do find other saints that display a similar kind of stubbornness.[14] But another part lies in God's own ambivalence expressed after his first and second commands to Samuel to make a king. God is Himself displeased at the people since they are rejecting His kingship over them in favour of another's. He complains bitterly of this to Samuel. There is then a choice of kings in both texts – between God and Saul, Áedán and Éoganán – and it is because of the nature of the choice in both cases that the ordainers (Samuel and Columba) are displeased. Each prefers another. Later on (I *Reges* 15: 35), the Lord will state that he regrets having made Saul king over Israel. It is thus possible to gain some insight into the subtlety of Adomnán's thought by these comparisons: an important part of his aim is to make Columba more like Samuel, an effort repeated on other occasions. The vita motifs of displeasure, choice and recalcitrance are thereby all illuminated once we accept the Samuel/Saul paradigm even though Adomnán radicalises it in his version. Admittedly, however, differences stand out as well since Columba was not averse to earthly kingmaking but only to the choice of Áedán. Adomnán was willing to accept a lesser disparity for the sake of the larger parallel that he wished to establish.

The book carried by the angel is highly significant. I believe that I explained it broadly correctly in *Iona, Tara,* and *Soissons* although I would now change a few remarks. Nonetheless, it is clear to me that more needs to be said about its background and the reason for its presence. This book is certainly the dominant motif in the entire passage. It is described as a 'glass book of the ordination of kings'. Columba must read from it. He must then ordain Áedán 'according to the words you have read in it.' Since Adomnán chooses to mention this book four times in such a brief space, it must have had a pivotal, indeed overwhelming, meaning for him. It is surprising then that it is absent from the Genesis passage from which it is alleged that he drew his inspiration. On the other hand, it does appear in I *Reges* 10:25 where, after an election of Saul by lot that Samuel supervises, he writes down the *legem regni* in a book and places it before the Lord. Both book and context have a background. Both seem to be related to a prophetic command by God in Deuteronomy 17: 15–19 where a book is mentioned among a listing of the laws by which the people of Israel must live. Verse 15 proclaims that once the people come into the promised land, they must set over themselves a king chosen by God. (Now we can see why God's angel appears to Columba in the first place. He is the bearer of God's will about His chosen king and God's choice is the one to be followed, not Columba's. The angel is the vehicle by which Adomnán wishes to express this will.) The two verses that follow contain

13 Charles-Edwards writes of *Críth Gablach*'s contract between a king and his people as being 'an extraordinarily precocious venture in political thought': 'Contract between king and people', p. 116. He places the idea within the context of other early Irish law texts which, he suggests, makes it seem less improbable. This is a stimulating interpretation. Before accepting it, however, I would wish to see an analysis of Old Testament references like *audi vocem populi*. There is reason to think that such references might well have played a role in this aspect of Irish thinking.   **14** For this cultural pattern, see M. Enright, '*Iromanie – Irophobie* revisited: a suggested frame of reference for considering continental reactions to Irish *peregrini* in the seventh and eighth centuries,' in Jörg Jarnut et al. (eds), *Karl Martell in seiner Zeit* (Sigmaringen 1994) pp 367–80. For comparisons of saints with regard to the Old Testament, see my 'Royal succession', pp 83–103.

a set of injunctions about royal behaviour. Since these are partially recalled in I *Reges* 8: 11–18, a connection between the texts is confirmed. Verse 18 then states God's order that when the king is enthroned he shall make a copy of the law from the book in the custody of the Levitical priests. He shall then read it every day in order to observe carefully all the words of the law.[15]

We now apprehend why Adomnán laid such dramatic stress on the angel's book; a legitimate kingmaking that follows Old Testament law has to have one. A book is not only important because Samuel writes one after anointing Saul and then places it before the Lord – the probable implication is that it is the same copy carried by the angel – it is also important because divine prophecy, book and God's choice of king are all related by passages in both Deuteronomy and Kings. Samuel's actions thus look like the necessary fulfilment of an earlier prophecy from which God did not veer, and his book must be an implied part of it. In such a significant case – in which the *creation* of a king is linked to a book in two *related* biblical texts, Columba could not veer from precedent either; he too had to have a book, and Áedán had to be ordained in the manner prescribed in it because that was the law that Samuel administered and wrote down.

A critic has several openings here. He might well reply that God's command that his chosen king have a book is not the same thing as Samuel's book, and neither are necessarily the same as the angel's book. All of that would be correct but still overlooks the scriptural requirement that a book appear. From Adomnán's point of view, the heavenly book is necessary because of what Samuel did and what God said. That was enough; it was more than enough, it created an obligatory condition for correct ritual action in making kings.

Adomnán's approach has its own understandable justification. As propaganda, it can also carry conviction and encourage assent as long as the various parallel movements from biblical model to Iona copy that are taken to achieve assent are easily recognisable. But that is where, in modern terms, Adomnán goes wrong. His subtlety becomes too subtle and his variations too unexpected. That is surely part of the rationale for the sceptical air with which the Áedán episode is sometimes greeted by scholars. As I see it, Adomnán is deeply committed to imitating Samuel but his very familiarity with the relevant texts interferes with his good judgement and propagandistic flair. He expects too much knowledge from his readers and thus he compresses the material to the point that he nearly obscures the lesson. That would seem to be one reason why, in the case of the ordination contract, a sympathetic observer who recognises the problem adds the clarifying Cumméne Find extract. Adomnán's desire for brevity has made his message cryptic so that it requires explication. At the same time, Adomnán gives his material an Irish cultural twist that tends to divert attention from the legitimating Samuel/Saul elements present in its makeup. Samuel is satisfied with God's voice; Adomnán wants a scourging messenger angel. Samuel has a book; Adomnán wants a 'glass' book – its fits well with the Irish view that associates glass objects with the Otherworld. The difficulty is that these additions stray from his well-chosen model that is already supernaturally based. That aspect then becomes saturated and the result is a sense of excessive unreality – not so much for Adomnán's milieu in which the additions probably augmented verisimilitude – but rather for our own in which they act to diminish it.

While the evidence for Adomnán's borrowing from the I *Reges* paradigm is convincing, it is curious that the hagiographer does not draw attention to the future result of the ordination

15 It may be that I placed too much emphasis on the probable existence of an 'angelic' book in reality in *Iona, Tara and Soissons*. Nonetheless, given Adomnán's close following of Old Testament precedents, together with God's command that the king actually possess such a book in Deuteronomy, a somewhat better context for the book's

contract, namely the faithlessness of Áedán's descendants; that would have fortified the message by offering an instructive parallel with the behaviour of Saul. In fact, however, it is done by the writer of the Cummène Find extract who makes Adomnán's reference to Columba's prophecy more explicit by referring to possible loss of the sceptre, treachery and rightful heavy punishment by the hand of God. Following such a warning, one would normally expect a strongly moralistic message about loyalty and duplicity. What one actually gets is a doleful and even sympathetic tone: 'from that day to this the family of Áedán is held in subjection by strangers, a fact which brings sighs of sorrow to the breast.' Significantly, this is much like what one finds in I *Reges* where Saul is repeatedly scolded and warned by Samuel who, nonetheless, 'mourns' for Saul for some considerable time after God has rejected him. Indeed God upbraids Samuel for its duration (I *Reges* 16:1). The extract thus seems to serve two purposes: one is to expand on Adomnán's overly terse recital of Columba's prophecy. The other completes the Samuel/Saul pattern by alluding to warnings, failure and subsequent mourning. The fact that it does both is arresting in itself. Adomnán's strategy is thereby maintained and elucidated.

Let us now examine Adomnán's presentation of the death of Diarmait mac Cerbaill. Here too I have explained the various politico-religious aspects more fully in previous work and so I offer only a limited supplementary analysis that aims primarily to develop additional evidence. In this chapter, Adomnán tells us first about the advent of Áed Dub mac Suibni in Britain. Áed was a Dál nAraidi king or overking of Ulster who had taken the habit of a priest and wished to remain a pilgrim. Adomnán regards him as an utterly depraved sinner because he had killed Diarmait who had been 'ordained by God's will as king of all Ireland': *qui scilicet Aidus Niger valde sanguinarius homo et multorum fuerat trucidator. Qui et Diormitium filium Cerbulis totius Scotiae regnatorem deo auctore ordinatum interfecerat.*[16] Diarmait had been a Uí Néill king and was a famous ancestor of the contemporary dynasty of Tara rulers. Adomnán goes on to explain Áed Dub's background and the reason why Columba curses him:

Hic itaque idem Aidus post aliquantum in perigrinatione transactum tempus accito episcopo quamvis non recte apud supradictum Findchanum prespiter ordinatus est. Episcopus tamen non est ausus super caput ejus manum inponere, nisi prius idem Findchanus Aidum carnaliter amans suam capiti ejus pro confirmatione inponeret dexteram.

This same Áed, having spent some time in pilgrimage, was ordained priest in Finchán's monastery, but the ordination was invalid even though a bishop had been brought. This was because the bishop had not dared to place his hand on Áed's head until Findchán (who had a carnal love for Áed) had first laid his right hand on his head in confirmation.

Quae talis ordinatio cum postea sancto intimaretur viro egre tulit. Tum proinde hanc de illo Findchano et de Aido ordinato formidabilem profatur sententiam, inquiens:

When this ordination was later made known to the saint, he took it ill, pronouncing thereupon this fearful judgement on Findchán and Áed, now ordained saying:

'Illa manus dextera, quam Findchanus contra fas et jus eclesiasticum super caput filii perditionis inpossuit, mox conputrescet et post magnos dolorum cruciatus ipsum in terram sepelienda praecedet. Et ipse post suam humatam manum

'That right hand which Findchán, against the law of God and of the Church, laid on the head of a son of perdition will soon grow rotten. It will give him great pain, and be dead and buried before him though he will live

historicity now exists. **16** Andersons, *Life of Columba*, p. 280.

per multos superstes victurus est annos. Ordinatus vero indebete Aidus sicuti canis ad vomitum revertetur suum. Et ipse rursum sanguilentus trucidator existet, et ad ultimum lancea jugul[a]tus de ligno in aquam cadens submersus morietur. Talem multo prius terminum promeruit vitae, qui totius regem trucidavit Scotiae'.

Quae beati viri profetia de utroque adimpleta est. Nam prespiteri Findchani dexter prae pugnus putrefactus in terram eum praecessit, in illa sepultus insula quae Ommon nuncupatur. Ipse vero juxta verbum sancti Columbae per multos post vixit annos. Aidus vero Niger, solummodo nomine prespiter, ad sua priora reversus scelera dolo lancea transfixus de prora ratis in aquam lapsus stagneam disperiit.[17]

many year after his hand is buried. Áed, however, who was ordained unfittingly, will return as a dog to his vomit; he will again be a bloody murderer and in the end, killed by a spear, he will fall from the wood into water and die drowning. He deserved such an end to life long ago for having killed the king of all Ireland.' The blessed man's prophecy concerning both of them was fulfilled. First, the right fist of the priest Findchán became rotten and preceded him into the earth, being buried on the island called Ommon. The man himself, inaccordance with St. Columba's words, lived on for many years. Áed Dub, priest in name only, returned to his old wickedness and, being pierced by a treacherous spear, he fell from the prow of a ship into waters of a lake an perished.[18]

Adomnán had clear political reasons for cursing Áed Dub; he hoped thereby to attract greater support for the *paruchia Columbae* from his Uí Néill relatives. By establishing Columba's special power to protect and avenge kings (both before and after the saint's death), he would advance an especially tempting incentive and persuasive argument. While Columba is angry at Findchán as well because of this wrongful ordination, his chief ire, marked by the fact that he curses him to death and not just to suffering ('he deserved such an end to life long ago'), is reserved for Áed Dub. But on what rationale does Adomnán base this extreme condemnation? And how could it be so strongly legitimised that he could not be accused of simply supporting his relatives as other saints did? Here is where his thinking about the nature and meaning of royal ordination becomes most sharply definable. Adomnán's approach to the killing of Diarmait demonstrates beyond any doubt that he is strongly influenced by the biblical concept of royal anointing. It is this concept – and this one only – that holds that the killing of an anointed king (whom God has thereby chosen for a sacral office) is on act of such evil that it brands the killer as an irredeemable outlaw, and those who aid him, like Findchán, as dangerously corrupt. Consequently, Adomnán must have been drawing on this aspect of Old Testament law. He could not otherwise have reasonably described Columba as reacting in the way in which he did. The killing of Irish kings around 700 is hardly uncommon and would not normally have been viewed by anyone as uniquely sinful, certainly not by Adomnán who does not object in other cases and who sees no impediment to cursing the royal Áed Dub mac Suibni to death. Adomnán's approach, therefore, is certainly that of one who expects a reader to make a close connection between royal ordination and anointing. The fact that *ordinatio* is a fluid term that can also have other meanings, as in the case of Áed Dub, has no significance in Adomnán's usage (or in that of the *Hibernensis*) because he clearly distinguishes between kings who have been specially graced and those who have not. Irish thinkers of the period held that a number of different kinds of ordinations existed and that these could be classed for various reasons as appropriate or righteous or otherwise.[19] It is this kind of model that

17 Ibid.   **18** Sharpe, *Life of St Columba*, pp 138–9.   **19** See for example the chapters in the *Hibernensis: De*

Adomnán is thinking of and thus here we see two examples of ordination in which one is tied to unction but the other is not. The differences are easily understandable and there is no conflict between them.

Adomnán's approach can also be explicated in another way that casts new light on the Diarmait chapter as a whole. This passage, regardless of where it falls in the manuscript, would appear to be a companion piece to the Áedán chapter. That seems probable because each centers on a royal ordination, and that sets them off from other materials. They are also joined by a singular pattern of repetition. In the Áedán passage, Adomnán marks his special interest in a book through this device of repetition; he simply hammers away at it until it is driven into the reader's consciousness. One or two mentions are not enough. He does the same in the Diarmait chapter where he constantly focuses on hands – on the bishop's hand, on Finchán's hand, on his right hand, on his diseased hand, on his hand that is buried before him. By implication of course, Áed Dub's hand, that which had killed an ordained king, is also cursed but it is not worth specifically mentioning because he is to die in any case.

As with the Áedán material, one must again turn to I *Reges* (and not Genesis) for an understanding of why Adomnán desires this kind of focus. Chapter 24 describes a situation in which Saul is following David in order to kill him. But God turns the tables in David's favour and gives him an opportunity to do what he will to the king. David refuses to kill Saul. He cuts off a piece of Saul's robe and explains to his men that God's law forbids him to stretch out his hand against the Lord's anointed. David then calls out to Saul and tells him that he has not turned his hand against him for that reason. As soon as one reads this chapter, it becomes clear, excruciatingly clear in fact, that the scribe wishes to establish an unbreakable connection between a royal opponent's hand, his ill intent and a prohibition against killing the Lord's anointed. He refers to it twice formally and explicitly, but in total refers to a link between hand and killing no less than five times in a chapter of only 23 verses. Chapter 25 makes some more general references to this theme of life, hand and righteousness but the whole matter comes to a head in chapter 26. Once again, Saul is insufficiently guarded and David and his companion Abishai secretly enter the king's camp. Saul is sleeping with a spear and jug of water by his head. Abishai urges David to kill him and David refuses: 'for who can stretch forth his hand against the Lord's anointed and be guiltless.' Instead, David takes the spear and the jug of water as proofs of his erstwhile presence. He then calls out to Abner, Saul's man, and reproaches him. He has not guarded his lord the king but has wrongfully left a means for someone to enter the camp and destroy him. Abner's like is not to be found in Israel. He and his people deserve death:

> Non est bonum hoc quod fecisti vivit Dominus quoniam filii mortis estis vos qui non custodistis dominum vestrum christum Domini nunc ergo vide ubi sit hasta regis et ubi scyphus aquae qui erat ad caput eius.[20]

It is these chapters, and especially I *Reges* 26:7–12, 16 that are the sources for Adomnán's Áed Dub/Diarmait material. Chapter 24 provides the inspiration for the 'hand' repetition. Chapter 26 then provides the parallel items that appear in Columba's curse. A spear and water are mentioned

---

ordinatione regis; De ordinatione regis cum sorte; De IIII generibus ordinationum; De eo, quod Dominus solus successorum ordinat; De consensu populi cum principe in ordinando successore; De eo, quod non degradandi sunt principes a Domino uncti; etiam maligni; Hermann Wasserschleben (ed.), *Die irische Kanonensammlung* (Leipzig 1885) pp 76, 131, 136, 139. **20** Weber, *Biblia Sacra*, pp 409–10.

in both texts and each are directly related to the theme of *nolite tangere christos meos*. Such conjunction cannot be coincidence. Admittedly, there are significant contrasts as well. Most notably, a jug of water is not a body of water and there is no reference to falling from wood and drowning. These features are interesting for other reasons as we shall see below, but they are insufficient to shake the correspondences that indicate a relationship between passages. In case of doubt, one has the additional testimony of David's rebuke (curse?) of Abner – his deserving of death – because he has allowed the Lord's anointed to be endangered.

It now seems difficult to suppose that Genesis has anything to do with Adomnán's concept of kingship. In all cases, Adomnán is drawing on consecutive chapters from a later and different book so that Columba can be more vigorously identified with Samuel, the chooser and anointer of kings. In addition, all of the sources that Adomnán draws on refer to an anointing ritual and the concept that he applies to Diarmait is directly dependent upon it. It hardly makes sense to suppose that he would repeatedly exploit these precedents only to exclude in his ritual the central element which gives them their greatest meaning. I can think of no reason why he could wish to do so and several why he would not.

Adomnán was a reformer who wished to introduce royal anointing because that was the pattern that God favoured for kings. It would also benefit the *paruchia Columbae* because anointing would accord increased political leverage to its chief abbot to be applied in times of transition. If the Columban ritual became necessary, then the Columban abbot could not be excluded from succession decisions – in choosing between brothers or sons for example. In order to achieve that reform, however, Adomnán needed the support of kings. He angled for it by presenting Columba as the saint who would protect and avenge kings while also (as in the case of the ordained Oswald of Northumbria) granting them victory. The basis for the promised protection, of course, comes from the very anointing rite that inspires his examples. Ideally at least, it would provide greater security for the royal person, a potential that should not be underrated. It should also have an effect on bolstering the king's status with regard to others and hence be pertinent to his dealings in general. A clerical ritual that excludes an anointing, on the other hand, also reduces its value. The protective element that is promised no longer has the same warrant because it lacks biblical legitimization and God cannot be appealed to on that basis. A rival *paruchia* seeking advantage could mount a serious challenge to Columban claims on the issue of deviation alone. It is worth noting, for example, that David avenges Saul's death in II *Reges* 1:13–16 precisely because of Saul's anointed character. Like Áed Dub, the sinful Amalekite is executed because he has stretched forth his hand against the Lord's anointed. In both cases it is unction that makes the difference and not a blessing or simple hand-laying. Anointing cannot therefore be omitted from Adomnán's thinking about kingship. His fulfilling of biblical precedents makes good political and religious sense while deviation from them not only has nothing to recommend it, it would immediately undermine the very rationale for his arguments.

A further examination of the Diarmait chapter has thus established two related points: first, Adomnán applies the concept of royal unction in order to justify avenging an ordained king; second, he applies it knowingly and deliberately in relation to its origin so that David's rebuke of Abner becomes the source of Columba's curse of Áed Dub. There can be no question then of his arbitrarily appealing to an idea alone in relation to a clerical ordination without an unction as, for example, might be claimed for the Áedán episode. That cannot be the case since it has now been demonstrated that the *vita* concept is targeted and directly tied to its source in biblical text and ritual. This has the further consequence of bolstering the view that *ordinatio* in the Áedán episode must be understood as including an anointing since the only conceivable reason that it would not would be if Adomnán were to contradict his own usage and practice. That he would not wish to do so has been shown in the preceding paragraph. Moreover, Adomnán himself calls attention to the importance that he assigns to relating the Áedán and Diarmait stories by the fact that he employs the unusual device of repetition for each one. Of course, an historical royal unction ritual is not demonstrable even if it is now clear that Adomnán wanted to make it so. If his intentions have been elucidated, the question of their realisation is an entirely different matter. Adomnán knew that his proposals could only be successful if they were taken up by the Uí Néill kings. His association of unction with the equally novel concept of *imperium*, therefore, is suggestive in several regards.

While a biblical royal anointing component is pivotal in Adomnán's thinking, other aspects are of secondary value and might be manipulated to create a stronger or more desirable impression. The hagiographer does exactly this in his story of Áed Dub. David's remarks to Abner, for example, could be considered as more like an insulting reproach than a curse but Adomnán seizes on the latter possibility in order to demonstrate Columba's power to achieve results. A similar change occurs with the spear and water jug. In the biblical passage they appear as tokens only, but Adomnán see the opportunity to make them fit into Irish kingship tradition. Hence, he relates them to the 'threefold death' motif.[21] An interesting point here, again indicative of Adomnán's methodology, is the fact that it is the biblical text that provides the initial inspiration (note too the biblical emphasis from Proverbs 26:11 in Áed's returning like a dog to his vomit).[22] The threefold death motif is thereby linked to unction as well. But it is turned to the protection of rulers, rather than against them as in some other cases, because Columba's curse is directed at the king's slayer and not the king. The matter is more complicated because Áed Dub was also a king and would die as such in 588 (according to *AU*) when the curse took effect. Adomnán probably knew this and thus it appears significant that he artfully obscures the question by stating that Áed Dub is of Cruithnian race and royal lineage, implying royal lineage alone but not necessarily kingship. It looks as if he does so for the sake of his message, namely that it is the Columban intention that king-killers suffer severely but not kings themselves.[23] In both the Áedán and Diarmait episodes, then, Adomnán feels free to embellish his source for the sake of an association with Irish tradition, but he does so in a way that avoids any conflict with the unction component. That approach is chosen, and his additions designed, in order to make an innovative ritual more attractive. It's existence affirms the view that the unction ritual is his lever for influencing kings and achieving a reform that will favour his community.

In the investigation so far I have presented additional evidence in two ordination cases – now to be seen as closely and artfully related – in order to demonstrate more fully Adomnán's reliance on the I *Reges* model. It seems unsatisfactory to leave it at that, however, since one also needs to appreciate how these examples fit into his larger plan and conceptual pattern. Despite reference to a number of rulers, the *Vita Columbae* contains only a few ordained kings, Áedán, Diarmait and Oswald of Northumbria. Adomnán must have had a special reason for this selection for he involves Columba significantly with all three and signals a special connection through ritual terminology. If we now understand more about the latter, the former issue is still unclear. What

---

21 On this topic in the vita, see J.-M. Picard, 'The strange death of Guaire mac Áedáin', in D. Ó Corráin et al. (eds), *Sages, saints, and storytellers: Celtic studies in honour of Professor James Carney* (Maynooth 1989) pp 367–75 at p. 372 f.   **22** As is noted by Picard, ibid. and note 47.   **23** This is in keeping with Adomnán's theme that Columba will provide victories for kings.

exactly is it that Adomnán is doing when he describes Columba's dealings with this trio? What is his rationale for mentioning the things that he does?

A plausible answer is suggested by the way in which the Cummene Find extract depicts the political meaning of the ordination ritual. A balance is described in which the maintenance of the sceptre for sons and grandsons and the powerlessness of enemies is contrasted with the suffering to follow if wrong is done to Columba or to his kindred. The writer clearly views the ordination ritual as creating a binding contract which provides permanent dynastic security for Áedán and his descendants as long as they remain faithful to the Columban community. This reciprocal binding then includes a political alliance based on promises of mutual support. The extract author focuses on it in graphic and threatening terms. Adomnán is more subtle; he tends to emphasise the positive side of the agreement. Thus, in VC I 8, he depicts Columba as praying for victory for Áedán, which the king is then granted by a God who listens to the saint. In the following chapter, Columba raises the matter of royal succession, and this also turns out well for Áedán since the saint promises that his son, Eochaid Buide, will become king.

The manner of Eochaid Buide's choosing is significant for it is performed by Columba and associates the concepts of contract and unction. Acting through Columba, the Lord will choose Eochaid Buide when he is called in by his father but runs directly to the saint's arms. When the boy enters, he leans on the saint's bosom:

> 'The saint kissed and blessed him and said to his father: 'This one will survive to be king after you and his sons will be kings after him.'[24]

God thus extends the benefits of the contract to Eochaid Buide because, out of the sons who were called and present, he is the one who demonstrates the next generation's love for Columba. That is the basis for the contract's continuation. The choosing is also notable because it is patterned on I Reges 16:6–13, where Samuel conducts a similar parade of sons in order to choose Saul's successor. Like Columba, the holy man then chooses the youngest, David, whom he anoints. Because Columba's act is also a matter of choosing the next king, and because he follows so complicated a procedure, there can be no doubt as to the Old Testament source of the method employed. So too with the succession promise for Eochaid's sons which, because it follows the choosing of David precedent, is probably based on God's promise to David to set up his seed as kings after him (II Reges 7:12 and elsewhere). We can now understand a good part of what dynastic protection means to Adomnán. In the process, we have also seen several consecutive and related biblical acts followed by consecutive and related vita acts, which draw on them. There are two significant differences, however. Unlike Eochaid Buide, David is not the king's son, and unlike Samuel, Columba does not anoint the successor. These differences are linked and actually follow because of Adomnán's close study of the reasoning behind his precedents. In I Reges Samuel is only permitted to anoint David because God has rejected Saul who has sinned. That is not the case in Dál Riata. God has not only not rejected Áedán, He has, on the contrary, confirmed his righteousness in the selection of his son to succeed him. Hence, Adomnán can only follow the precedent up to the point of anointing but not beyond it. He envisages a situation in which Saul has not been rejected and acts accordingly by designating Áedán's son as king, the most that he can do under the circumstances. We may thus also perceive a piece of negative evidence in that Adomnán's precedent refers to an unction but he

---

24 Sharpe, Life of St Columba, p. 120.

refers only to a kiss and a blessing and does not call it an ordination. A kiss and a blessing, therefore, are not sufficient to constitute an ordination and the only thing that remains is a laying on of hands which can clearly include an oiling.

In these examples, we see Adomnán's view of the Columban side of the ordination contract. It is fulfilled by Columba's prayers, which bring victory to his favoured king, by a son following in his father's rule (although Columba must have a say in it), and by a guarantee of security for the dynasty. These must be the key components for they appear again with regard to Diarmait and, less fully, for Oswald. In Diarmait's case, it now becomes clear that the promise of dynastic protection also includes personal protection. Columba will seek to protect him and, if that fails, will avenge him by cursing his killer to death. Like Áedán, Diarmait is an ordained king and protection is due to him because of it. We note that it too is part of the contract and hence its basis in unction must apply to Áedán as well as Diarmait. This confirms the argument presented earlier based on concept and terminology but without reference to any alliance agreement. Moreover, as in the Eochaid Buide episode, Columba also guarantees kingship for Diarmait's son, Áed Sláine. The 'kingship of all Ireland' is predestined for him although he loses it through the sin of kin-killing. As Columba warns him before the fact, the result is not the saint's fault. In fact, it would seem to be the case that the warning he issues is part of the theme of dynastic protection. In the case of Oswald, Columba does not deliver this dynastic promise but he does assure victory. In case anyone might think of this result as affecting only one king, Adomnán is careful to state that Columba can always bestow victory. God has granted this 'special privilege' to him as to a powerful champion, even after his death. Oswald thus gets his great victory, returns home to 'reign happily' and is 'ordained by God as emperor of all Britain'.[25] Aside from the ordination reference, there is nothing in the Oswald passage that suggests that Adomnán is thinking in Old Testament terms; his description is general and leaves too many possibilities open. But then he states that Columba spoke to Oswald in the same words that the Lord spoke to Joshua when he too was troubled (Joshua 1:9): 'Be strong and act manfully. Behold, I will be with thee.' It looks as if Adomnán is frequently thinking of Old Testament precedent, even when one would not expect it.

While Adomnán's motives for appealing to powerful rulers are fairly clear, the reason for his joining them to Áedán through ordination is a different matter. One must, I think, speak of them as being joined to Áedán, despite the political power differential, because the Áedán episode contains the only relatively full description of ordination whereas the others are brief references whose meaning is best interpreted in relation to it. All associations can be explained, however, if one assumes that Adomnán wishes Diarmait and Oswald to be bound in the same kind of contract that is described by the extract writer. As we have seen, ordination is the ritual that settles the contract. Columba's ordination of Áedán is thus the model, and the saint's miracles for the other kings are attuned to it so that the model stands out and its general efficacy is displayed. Adomnán cannot duplicate the ordination model precisely for Diarmait and Oswald because he is conscious of the historical anomalies. Hence, he has God ordain them but depicts the associated miracles as occurring through Columba's influence in order to demonstrate that it is the saint's involvement that is crucial and his contract that is at issue. Whether a king is dead, as in the case

---

25 On Oswald, see Sharpe, *Life of St Columba*, pp 250–3; Clare Standcliffe, 'Oswald, 'Most Holy and Most Victorious king of the Northumbrians' in C. Stancliffe and E. Cambridge (eds), *Oswald: Northumbrian king and European saint* (Stamford 1995) pp 33–83; Barbara Yorke, *Kings and kingdoms of early Anglo-Saxon England* (London 1992) p. 81 f.

of Diarmait, or whether the saint is dead, as in the case of Oswald, makes no difference; Columba will still enforce the victory/protection contract and ensure it for the royal sons and their sons who follow.

It is Adomnán's hope that the contemporary descendants and successors of these kings will recognise the message and favourably weigh the potential benefits. In the case of *imperium* the benefits are especially great. Columba can guarantee overlordship over all other kings in the islands. In return, he expects the same degree of support for the overlordship of the *paruchia Columbae* in ecclesiastical affairs, something that Armagh and Patrick's community are now wrongfully claiming.[26] A contract created through the most solemn kind of hierarchical ritual known to the bible should put an end to that. If the contract can create overlords in the secular world, it can also create them in the ecclesiastical sphere. The saint who creates *imperium* by choosing, ordaining and protecting kings must himself be imperial; he must be like Samuel, the high priest of Israel and preeminent kingmaker.

We now have a coherent theoretical approach that can explain the ordained kings and the related Columban miracles on their behalf. They fit unto a contractual context of mutual obligations. As Adomnán presents it, the Columban side of the contract is detailed in the archetypical acts of the saint. Now some such acts, like prophecy, blessing or victory for example, might be occasionally granted to other rulers. But what Adomnán offers to ordained kings is decidedly different: it is a package containing *continuous* favour in the form of personal safety, dynastic continuity through sons (not brothers), victory in battle and warning when in danger of loss. All of these promises, some directly and some indirectly, are related to the anointing precedents discussed above. That is also true of victory in battle and warning to kings which God delivers on a number of occasions through Samuel to Saul and David in I and II *Reges*. I have not dealt with these two issues separately because they are routine in miraculous terms; saints frequently warn kings and grant victory without any special ritual being involved. In this case, however, these miracles too must be linked to ordination because the extract writer views them as terms of the ordination contract, and so does Adomnán who provides the relevant wonders for those ordained. They thus belong in the contract package. Looked at from this perspective, all of the major acts that Columba performs for the three kings are causally related to the fact of their ordination. In other words, it is not just royal safety and succession (as with Diarmait and Eochaid Buide) that are linked to Samuel's royal anointing, it is also victory and warnings of danger. Adomnán regards them all as terms within a divinely sanctioned agreement that should apply to rulers in Ireland as well as Israel. He views Samuel and Columba as the carriers, administrators and judges of God's contract with kings.

Important consequences follow from this finding. First, although contractual alliances between powers based upon detailed pledges of mutual support are frequent in medieval society, the contract discussed here is conspicuously odd because it is created in a unique manner – through the royal ordination of a candidate by a holy man prompted by God. The only other place where that occurs in context is I *Reges*. The inspiration for this contract, therefore, also derives from I

---

26 Thus see a link between the ecclesiastical overlordship claimed by Armagh and Adomnán's concept of *imperium* applied to kings and by implication I think to Iona abbots. On Armagh's claims, see Liam de Paor, 'The aggrandisement of Armagh', *Historical Studies* 8 (1971) pp 95–110; Richard Sharpe, 'St Patrick and the See of Armagh', *CMCS* 4 (1982) pp 35–59; Edel Bhreathnach, 'Temoria: Caput Scotorum', *Ériu* 47 (1996) pp 67–88. For the literary analysis of Patrician and Columban texts, see Joseph Falaky Nagy, *Conversing with angels and ancients: literary myths of medieval Ireland* (Dublin 1997) pp 40–198.

Reges where it appears as God's covenant with the house of David. We recall that Columba's prophecy for Eochaid Buide and his sons is based upon God's promise to David. Second, since ordination, contract and the several contract specifics are a coherent cluster in the *vita*, and since we have now found that they reflect the same clustering of events and ideas in I *Reges*, the discovery of these additional conjunctions changes the character of the associations between the two texts. The relationships can no longer be classified as partial or incidental; they are pervasive. The constellation of common features that have been established is now too large and internally complex to be regarded as having developed independently. The conclusion is, therefore, inevitable: Adomnán's chapters on ordained kings and their sons are consciously shaped to imitate the fabric of I *Reges*. It is that book that provides the source for Adomnán's opinions about politics; it is also the source for his programme of ritual renovation.

What Adomnán does is brilliantly original. He assesses, aligns and reconstructs a series of key elements in I *Reges* and then fits them to the background of three royal houses in Ireland and Britain whose support is needed by the *familia Iae*. God's Samuel-created covenant with the house of David becomes the inspiration for God's Columba-created covenant with the house of Áedán, and it is also meant to be extended to the houses of Diarmait and Oswald. We can now see why God had to play a role in Áedán's ordination. His presence through a scourging angel has always been interpreted as a grandiose piece of exaggeration or, if one accepts the fabulous as routine Irish hagiography, as a typically spectacular magnification that confers an air of visionary fantasy. It must now, however, be seen as essential to the pattern, in fact if not in mode, since it is God who chooses the candidate, directs the ordination and sanctions the unction based contract in I *Reges*. As soon as that covenant/contract condition is recognized, the other kinds of miracles for ordained kings fall easily into line. Indeed, they become very nearly predictable, a sure sign that they have finally been interpreted according to Adomnán's wishers. Not that his views in this area have ever been easy to decipher. Even around 700 that would seem to have been the case because it would be difficult to establish the contractual significance of ordination without reference to the Cumméne Find extract. Because it fits so well with what he wrote about kingship and ritual, the evidence now suggests that this earlier work by Cumméne Find influenced Adomnán's approach, just as his views on anointed kings would go on to influence those of the compilers of the *Collectio Canonum Hibernensis*. That is why the small world of Irish monastic scholarship could produce two works referring to and recommending royal unctions in a brief space, and at a time when the rest of Europe was unaware of the enormous potential for ideological and political change that resided therein.

A renewed investigation of royal ordinations has thus produced additional evidence to support (and in some ways to modify) the conclusions reached in my earlier work. Its also enables one to be more emphatic about the formulations there presented. Adomnán not only employs *ordinatio* to mean anointing, he actually presents a new theory of clerically mediated kingship based upon the unction created covenant of the Old Testament. It is a theory in which the new sacrality and *imperium* of some rulers would be balanced by the ecclesiastical *imperium* of Iona and her abbots in the Irish church. Outside of Visigothic Spain, this is the first theory of royal anointing to be developed in the West even though actual royal anointings may not have occurred in Ireland during the period.

A Frankish aristocrat at the battle of Mag Roth

HERMANN MOISL AND STEFANIE HAMANN

A main achievement in the study of early Ireland over the past several decades has been the integration of Irish history and culture with that of contemporary Europe. Próinséas has been a prime mover in this [Ní Chatháin and Richter 1984, 1987, 1996], and it therefore seems appropriate to offer her something that advances the integration, even if only in a small way.

Irish ecclesiastical interaction with Britain and the continent in the early Middle Ages has been extensively researched and described. Much less has been done on such interaction at the level of secular politics. The reason for this is quite simple: the relevant evidence is sparse and difficult to interpret satisfactorily. The evidence that does exist is, however, worthy of careful scrutiny, for at least two reasons. Firstly, the main goal of the historiography of early medieval Europe to date has been as complete and accurate a reconstruction of the period as possible; if one subscribes to this goal, then any increase in historical knowledge of the period is intrinsically worthwhile. And, secondly, understanding of Irish ecclesiastical interaction with the rest of Europe is deepened by awareness of its secular political context: endowments to Irish missionaries were made and maintained by secular lords whose prime motivation was usually political advantage, and the interests of churchmen typically became closely identified with those of their patrons. This discussion aims to develop our knowledge of secular political interaction between Ireland and the rest of Europe in the early medieval period, and more particularly between Ireland and Francia in the seventh century.

There was at least one secular political link between Ireland and continental Europe in the mid-seventh century: the Merovingian prince Dagobert II lived in Ireland for two decades between *c.*656 and 675. The reason for his presence and its implications have been much discussed, and have now been – in our view satisfyingly – elucidated by J.-M. Picard [Picard 1991b; see also Wooding 1996 and Richter 1999, 154–6], who argued that Dagobert's Irish sojourn was a consequence of high-level Frankish politics in which the monastic community established in Francia by the Irish monk Fursey and his bothers Foillán and Ultán was deeply involved. We will argue that, a generation before Dagobert II, a Frankish aristocrat named Madelgarius was sent to Ireland by the Merovingian king Dagobert I, and that Madelgarius fought at the battle of Mag Roth in 637.

The discussion is in three main parts. The first part presents and evaluates the Irish evidence for the Madelgarius' presence at Mag Roth, the second does the same for the Frankish evidence, and the third combines the two. The conclusion then evaluates the results of the discussion, and suggests avenues of further research.

The Irish evidence

Two medieval Irish vernacular texts, *The Battle of Dún na nGéd* (BDG) [O'Donovan 1842; Lehman 1964] and *The Battle of Mag Roth* (BMR) [O'Donovan 1842; Marstrander 1911], give narrative accounts of the battle of Mag Roth and of the circumstances which led to it. In both

Congal Cáech, king of Ulster, fights Domnall mac Áeda, king of the Cenél Conaill branch of the northern Uí Néill, at Mag Roth in northern Ireland, and is defeated and killed. In Congal's army are various allies. These are referred to at various places in both texts, and include the Irish of Dál Riata in western Scotland as well as Britons, Saxons, and Franks. The allies' leaders are named, but only Domnall Brecc, king of Dál Riata (ob. 642) is demonstrably historical [Mac Niocaill 1972, 87–9, 96]. The British leader is Conan Rod, which seems a plausible enough British name of the early medieval period, but to our knowledge there was no such person in the historical record at or around the time of the battle. The leader of the Franks was Dairbhre mac Dornmhar, which means 'Oak son of Great Fist' in Irish, and the Saxon leader is called Garbh mac Rogairbh, which means 'Rough son of Very Rough'; both names are clearly invented. We are interested in the Saxons and the Franks, and apart from the mere fact of their presence and the spurious names of their leaders, the two texts say nothing about them that is of any use to the historian.

The battle of Mag Roth is an historical event that took place in 637. Relative to that date, our two texts are very late. The published consensus at the moment is that the extant copy of BMR was written in the tenth century [Dillon 1946], and BDG in the late eleventh – mid-twelfth [Herbert 1989]. As such, they suffer from the usual problem with regard to the use of noncontemporary texts as historical sources: such texts can, and often do, incorporate historically accurate information, but there is no general way of determining which aspects are historically reliable, and which are not. The question for present purposes is, therefore, whether or not the claim that there were Franks and Saxons at Mag Roth can be believed.

The rest of this section presents arguments in support of that claim. These arguments are preceded by a sketch of the context in which the battle occurred, since some knowledge of this context is required to understand the supporting arguments.

Historical sketch

The battle of Mag Roth is one of the more securely historical events of early Irish history [Herbert 1989]. It is mentioned in two contemporary or near-contemporary sources. One of these sources is a chronicle begun and maintained at the monastery of Iona in either the later sixth or the mid-seventh century, and based on contemporary local information [Smyth 1972; Anderson 1973; Moisl 1983; Herbert 1988, ch. 1]. This chronicle is now attested in the pre-740 entries in several sets of extant Irish annals, which name Congal Cáech and Domnall mac Áeda as the chief protagonists of the battle, record Congal's defeat and death, and date the event to 637. The other source is a short extract from a *Life* of St Columba written by Cumméne, abbot of Iona from 657 to 669 [Anderson and Anderson 1991; Herbert 1988, 24–6; Richter 1999, 75–84], now included in the late seventh-century *Life of St Columba* written by Abbot Adomnán [Anderson and Anderson 1991; Herbert 1988, ch.1; Richter 1999, 80–83]. Cumméne writes that Columba had warned the Dál Riatan king Áedán mac Gabráin that if he or his descendants should ever show any hostility to his own, that is, Columba's kindred, 'sceptrum regni huius de manibus suis perdant', and further notes that this had come to pass as a result of the battle of Mag Roth: 'Et a die illa usque hodie, adhuc in proclivo sunt ab extraneis'.

These sources moreover have a particularly close association with the protagonists in the battle, which gives them a special authority. By *c.*500, the small kingdom of Dál Riata in north-east Ireland had colonised the closely adjacent parts of western Scotland, and its royal family ruled from the Scottish side [for what follows see Bannerman 1966, 1968; Mac Niocaill 1972, ch. 4;

Byrne 1973, chs. 4–7; Anderson 1973, 134 ff; Nieke and Duncan 1988; Ó Cróinín 1995, 48–52]. As far as the kings of the province of Ulster were concerned, however, the Dál Riatan kings remained subject to them, and it appears that at least one, Báetán mac Cairill (ruled 572–81) managed to realise that claim. In 575 an alliance was made at Druim Cett on the Irish mainland between Áedán mac Gabráin, king of Dál Riata, and Áed mac Ainmerech, king of the northern Uí Néill. From the Dál Riatan point of view this alliance was almost certainly intended to counter the claims of Báetán mac Cairill. The Uí Néill, who were only beginning the rise to political pre-eminence which they enjoyed in later centuries, for their part gained a useful ally against an Ulster still capable of asserting itself. The agreement eventually outlived both its originators and was terminated in 637 at Mag Roth, where Congal Cáech, king of Ulster, in alliance with Domnall Brecc, king of Dál Riata, attacked the northern Uí Néill king Domnall mac Áeda, and was defeated. In siding with Congal Cáech, Domnall Brecc broke the long-standing alliance with the Uí Néill; the consequence, it seems, was that the Dál Riatan kings lost control over their Irish territories.

The Uí Néill / Dál Riata connection also had an ecclesiastical dimension, and it is from this that the authority of the two Iona sources on Mag Roth derives. The monastery of Iona was established in 563 in Dál Riata by St Columba, a member of the Cenél Conaill branch of the northern Uí Néill, and all but one of the saint's eight successors in the abbacy of Iona up to the end of the seventh century were demonstrably of the same stock [Herbert 1988, chs. 2, 3]. In other words, Iona began as an Uí Néill *Eigenkirche* within the kingdom of Dál Riata, and remained so at and long beyond the date of the battle of Mag Roth. It is also clear that there was a close association between Iona and the Dál Riatan kingship from the start. Columba was present at Druim Cett: given his family ties on the one hand and the location of his monastery on the other, it can hardly be doubted that he was instrumental in arranging the alliance between his cousin Áed mac Ainmerech and Áedán mac Gabráin [Richter 1999, 59–61]. Adomnán's *Life of Columba* also describes the saint otherwise involving himself in Áedán's political affairs – for example, his attempt to influence the Dál Riatan royal succession [Richter 1999, 58–61] – and the very fact of Iona's continued existence shows that Dál Riatan royal patronage was maintained after the founder's death. Iona for its part kept a detailed record of the Dál Riatan royal house and its affairs, and, as the writings of abbots Cumméne and Adomnán show, there were hagiographical traditions which stressed the benefits of reverence for Columba and his heirs to the Dál Riatan kingship. The early Iona references to the battle of Mag Roth are, therefore, pretty much guaranteed to be accurate about the facts of the battle.

Arguments

Two main arguments are offered in support of the claim that BMR and BDG are reliable with respect to the Frankish presence at Mag Roth despite their late date. The first (i) is that the two texts preserve demonstrably accurate information about the historical battle, and that there is consequently a priori reason to believe that other aspects of the narrative, such as the Frankish presence, are accurate as well. The second (ii) is that if the presence of other foreign allies of Congal Cáech can be substantiated, then the case for the Frankish presence becomes stronger. In combination, the two arguments are held to constitute a good but not conclusive case for the Frankish presence.

i. We have noted that BMR and BDG are of indeterminate historical reliability on account of their lateness relative to the event they describe. They both also contain elements that are clearly intended for literary effect, such as direct speech and accounts of the doings of individual fighters, which one can safely discount as invention. Both texts are, moreover, completely unaware of the historical context of the battle, and instead attribute it to a trivial cause. Nevertheless, they do get the protagonists and the outcome of the battle right, and, as such, are not entirely unhistorical. There is consequently some basis for thinking that other aspects of the narrative, such as the Frankish presence, might be historically accurate as well.

ii. There is a good case for the reliability of the claim that Anglo-Saxons were involved at Mag Roth:

- Because kingship [Yorke 1990, ch. 8] did not necessarily or even usually pass from father to son among the Anglo-Saxons, and because there was no generally agreed mechanism for a king to designate his successor, the *æðeling* who was able to realise his claim to kingship over other – often quite numerous – candidates did so by force. This led to dynastic infighting as successful claimants tried to eliminate as many actual and potential rivals as possible. If they were wise, dynasts belonging to disenfranchised lines fled into exile and canvassed support at foreign courts for an eventual return to power [Kirby 1974]. The presence of Anglo-Saxon noblemen among the Irish is, therefore, not surprising in principle.

- We know that Bernician dynasts and their supporters did in fact take refuge among the Irish, and more specifically in Dál Riata, on at least two occasions. The first time was in the late sixth century when, on the accession of Ethelfrith to the Bernician kingship, his predecessor Hussa's son Hering fled to the court of Áedán mac Gabráin, king of Dál Riata [Moisl 1983]. The second time was after the death of the Bernician king Ethelfrith (616) and subsequent accession of the Deiran Edwin to the throne of Northumbria. As Bede tells us, 'siquidem tempore toto quo regnavit Eduini, filii praefati regis Aedilfridi, qui ante illum regnaverat, cum magna nobilium iuventute apud Scottos sive Pictos exulabant' [Colgrave and Mynors 1969, III.1]; at least two of these sons of Ethelfrith, Oswald [Colgrave and Mynors 1969, III.3] and Oswiu [Colgrave and Mynors 1969, III. 25], fled to Dál Riata with their retinues. Corroboration, if such is needed, comes from Adomnán's *Life of Columba*, which says that Oswald was baptised 'cum xii viris … cum eo Scotos inter exsolante' [Anderson and Anderson 1991, I.1]. The presence of Anglo-Saxon dynasts among the Irish is, therefore, not only plausible in principle, but was the case in practice in the late sixth and early seventh centuries.

- We know that Anglo-Saxon dynasts not only took refuge but also fought alongside Irish kings at least twice [Moisl 1983]. In 603, the above-mentioned Hering and Áedán mac Gabráin attacked Ethelfrith at Degsastan somewhere in Anglo-Saxon territory; from Hering's point of view this was presumably a bid to capture the Bernician kingship, but he and Áedán were defeated. And, in 628, an Anglo-Saxon *æðeling* whom the Irish annals name as Oisiricc mac Albruit fought on the side of Connad Cerr, king of Dál Riata, at Fid Eóin on the Irish mainland, where they were defeated at the hands of Máel Caích mac Scandail, king of Ulster. Not only is the presence of Anglo-Saxon dynasts among the Irish both inherently plausible and historically attested, then, but such dynasts are known to have fought alongside Irish kings on at least two occasions.

- In terms of the political context in which the battle of Mag Roth was embedded, there is good reason to expect Anglo-Saxons to have been involved. Very soon after his return from Dál

Riata and his accession to the throne of Northumbria in 634, Oswald extended his patronage to Iona, a monastery wholly controlled by the Cenél Conaill branch of the northern Uí Néill [Colgrave and Mynors 1969, III.3]. A few years later, at Mag Roth, Domnall mac Áeda of the Cenél Conaill fought and defeated an Ulster / Dál Riata alliance. As a consequence of the victory Oswald became overlord of Dál Riata [Moisl 1983; on Northumbrian overlordship in the North see Kirby 1991, ch. 5] and maintained his patronage of Iona, as Bede's accounts of Lindisfarne and its various English daughter houses attests. The natural inference is that Oswald was on the Cenél Conaill side in the battle, supporting the family that controlled the mother house of his newly-established Northumbrian Church.

But BMR and BDG claim that the Anglo-Saxons were on the Ulster / Dál Riata side: it looks like either we or the two texts are wrong about the nature of the Anglo-Saxon involvement at Mag Roth. Not necessarily so, however. The early Iona chronicle referred to above records that, on the same day as Mag Roth, the forces of Cenél Conaill fought those of Dál Riata and of the other main northern Uí Néill branch, the Cenél nEógain, in a naval battle off Kintyre [Mac Airt and Mac Niocaill 1983, 119; Stokes 1896, s.a. 636]; it appears that the Cenél nEógain were part of the alliance against Cenél Conaill, which is not surprising given the history of rivalry between the two dynastic branches [Mac Niocaill 1973, chapters 1, 2, 4; Byrne 1973, 113]. Why is this significant with respect to the Anglo-Saxon presence at Mag Roth? Because another Bernician exile in Ireland, Oswald's brother Oswiu, had married a Cenél nEógain princess [Moisl 1983; Ireland 1991]. This indicates that the outcome at Mag Roth was not only significant for the Ulster – Dál Riata alliance, but also for Uí Néill and Bernician dynastic rivalries. Given the cut-throat nature of dynastic politics at this time, there is no reason to think that Oswiu would have been loyal to Oswald just because they were brothers – they might in fact only have been half-brothers [Plummer 1896, vol. 2, 161] – and every reason to think that he was plotting his own accession to the Northumbrian kingship. Indeed, such tension is manifest in the relationship between Oswald's son Ethelwald and Oswiu: after Oswald's death, Ethelwald allied himself with Penda in an attack on his uncle [Colgrave and Mynors 1969, III.14 and III.24]. On this view, Oswiu aligned himself with the anti-Cenél Conaill alliance at Mag Roth in the hope of supplanting Oswald, though in the event he failed and had to wait until Oswald's death in 642.

A final argument is offered in support of the proposal just made. The references to Congal Cáech's foreign allies in BMR and BDG are but two examples of a tradition of Anglo-Saxons and other foreigners fighting in Ireland which is attested in a variety of early Irish vernacular prose texts [Moisl 1983]. In one of them, *Togail Bruidne Da Derga* (TBDD), three of the Anglo-Saxon leaders are actually named. Listed among the warriors in the retinue of Conaire, a mythical king of Tara, are [Best and Bergin 1929, 233]:

> Osalt and his two brothers in fosterage, Osbrit Lamfota and his two brothers in fosterage, Lindas and his two brothers in fosterage. These were three princes (rigdomna) of the Saxons with the king.

All three names are genuine Anglo-Saxon/Germanic [Moisl 1983]. *Osalt* corresponds to Old English *Oswald*, and *Osbrit* to Old English *Osfrith* or *Osberht*. *Lindas* is a little problemmatical, but its components *lind* and *æsc* are certainly Germanic name elements. We make the following observations about this passage:

- The tradition of Anglo-Saxons fighting in Ireland for Irish kings, or at least the version that TBDD represents, was not derived from the above-quoted Fid Eóin annal entry: the entry does not mention Osalt, Osbrit, or Lindas, and TBDD does not mention the annals' Oisiricc.

- The TBDD tradition contains genuine Anglo-Saxon names.

- The TBDD tradition refers to the Anglo-Saxon leaders not as kings, but as *rigdomnai*, which corresponds directly to Old English *æðeling*, 'heir-apparent'. [Ó Corráin 1971; Dumville 1979].

- One of TBDD's *rigdomnai* is called Osalt / Oswald; we know from Bede that stories about the Northumbrian king Oswald were current in seventh-century Ireland [Colgrave and Mynors 1969, III.13], and that during his time in exile among the Irish he was a *rigdomna*.

There is, then, a secure historical basis for Anglo-Saxon dynasts fighting in Ireland very near the time of the battle of Mag Roth, and a good case for thinking that Oswald, the Bernician king of Northumbria, and his brother and successor Oswiu, fought at Mag Roth. This lends strong support to the historicity of our two texts' claim that Anglo-Saxons were present at Mag Roth, and by transitivity to the Frankish presence. Despite all that, of course, one can always argue that the Franks were just a bit of literary decoration extrapolated from the presence of the Anglo-Saxons, so none of this is conclusive.

The Frankish evidence

The *Vita S. Madelgarii I* [Poncelet 1893] recounts the career of a Frankish aristocrat named Madelgarius who was born in Strepy, near present-day Binche in the Hennegau region of Flanders/ Artois, of minor noble stock. According to the *Vita*, Madelgarius was sent to be fostered at the court of Dagobert I, the Merovingian king of Austrasia from 623 and of Francia from 629. While there he married Waldetrude, daughter of a certain 'nobilissimus vir' Waldebert. As a wedding present, Dagobert gave him lordship of the whole of Ireland. Madelgarius travelled to Ireland with a band of companions, where he was received with great honour; his wife soon joined him there, and they remained for some considerable time. On their return to Francia they had four children, after which Madelgarius founded a monastery in Haumont where he became a monk, taking the name Vincentius, and in about 652 he founded another monastery at Soignies [Pertz 1841, 11]. The passage which recounts Madelgarius' Irish stay reads as follows [Poncelet 1893, chs. 8–10]:

> Audiens interea gloriosus rex Francorum Dagobertus de iam dicto viro Madelgario, quia oboedisset parentibus et copulatus esset matrimonio, valde hilaris effectus est. Honoravit ergo eum censu dignissimo, deditque ei omnes confines Hiberniae in possessionem. Qui accipiens viros industrios atque nobiles, profectus est in possessionem sibi collatam. Susceperuntque eum pagenses terrae illius pacifice cum honore maximo, nullo modo audentes resistere dominationi eius, audientes a compluribus quod honorem maximum apud regem Dagobertum haberet. Demoratus autem ibi multis diebus, non ferens eius coniunx adhuc rudis eius amorem senioris, accipiens fidelissimos viros atque consanguineos suos, profecta est post eum in Hiberniam. At ille cernens eam, valde admiratus est fidem eius, suscepitque eam cum mago triumpho et dixit: 'Quae te ratio fecit tam magnum iter arripere?'. At illa dixit: 'Amor tuus, quia desiderabam perspicere decorem vultus tui'. Et

osculantes se invicem atque tripudiantes sumpserunt cibum ex omnibus divitiis terrae illius, egeruntque magnum gaudium tam ipsi quam comites illorum de adventu coniugis. Devoluto ibi itaque multo tempore, reversi sunt in fines Francorum cum opibus magnis.

Dagobert I reigned from 623 to 639. The preface to the *Vita S. Vincentii Madelgarii II* [1867], a twelfth-century work [van der Essen 1907, 288], suggests that Madelgarius was born *c*.615, and proposes 635 as the year of Madelgarius' entry into Dagobert's service, but these dates are not reliable. The most one can say is that the above passage relates to the period 623 to 639, the years of Dagobert's rule. Van der Essen [1907, 284–8] took the view that our text, the *Vita S. Madelgarii I*, dates from the beginning of the eleventh century. Work on the *Vita* since then has not greatly advanced knowledge of its provenance [Nazet 1967; Helvetius 1994]: it is possibly based on a lost tenth-century *Vita*, to which the *Vita Gisleni V* [de Smedt 1887], itself a tenth-century work [van der Essen 1907, 257–58], refers. This leaves us in much the same position as the Irish texts did, that is, the passage of interest is of unknown historical reliability because the text from which it is taken is very late relative to the time with which it deals. As before, an attempt will be made to substantiate the passage by arguing that some aspects of the *Vita* are historically reliable, and that this supports the reliability of the passage in question.

For van der Essen [1907, 286–7] the *Vita Madelgarii* is an epitome of hagiographical plagiarism, which view he substantiates by citing borrowed passages from Gregory of Tours' *Vitae Patrum*, from Sulpicius Severus, and from a range of other *Vitae*. When one discounts textual borrowings, however, our text contains much information about Madelgarius that appears also in other sources:

- Madelgarius' origins in the Hennegau, together with both his own monastic foundations and those of other members of his family, appear in the *Lives* of several contemporary local saints: the eleventh-century *Vita S. Autberti* [de Ghesquière 1785], the early tenth-century *Vita S. Gisleni V* [de Smedt 1887], the *Vita S. Gisleni III* [de Smedt 1886] of *c*.1000, and the eleventh-century *Vita S. Foillani IV* [1883].

- Waldebert, with whose family Madelgarius is alleged to have been connected via marriage to Waldetrude (first mentioned in the *Vita Aldegundis*, which dates from the first half of the ninth century [Krusch and Levison 1913, chs. 2, 4]), is referred to also by Fredegar [Krusch 1888a, IV, 54] as *domesticus* to Chlothar II, as are her uncles Landrich and Gundeland, successively *maior domus* in Neustria 584–616/7 [Krusch 1888a, IV.25,26,45; see also *Liber Historiae Francorum* [Krusch 1888b, chs. 35, 36, 40, 42] and *Vita Gaugerici* [Krusch 1896, ch. 9].

- Madelgarius appears as a nobleman in the service of Dagobert I in the *Vita Aldegundis* [Krusch and Levison 1913, ch. 4], in a trio of texts which depend on the *Vita Aldegundis* (*Vita Waldetrudis*, *Vita Aldetrudis*, and *Vita Madelbertae*, for which see [van der Essen 1907, 219–44]), and in the *Vita Gisleni II* [1866, ch. 10] and V [de Smedt 1887, ch. 7].

- Madelgarius' involvement in Irish affairs appears also in the *Vita S. Foillani III* [1883, ch. 14], the *Vita S. Foillani IV* [1883, ch. 31], and – in somewhat different terms – the *Vita Ettonis* [1867, chs. 5–7, 12]. No clear interrelationship of these texts has been established [van de Essen 1907, 160, 161, 282–4, 288].

- Madelgarius is also mentioned in the *Gesta Episcoporum Cameracensium* [Pertz 1846, 409] and the *Annales Laubienses* for the year 652 [Pertz 1841, 11].

The corroborative value of a set of texts relative to information of interest – here Madelgarius' career – depends crucially on them being independent in the sense that the texts' authors did not use one anothers' work or a common source. But such independence is impossible in principle to demonstrate. One can show that author *x* **did** use author *y's* work, or that the two used a common source, by citing textual borrowing or influence, or by arguing on good grounds that he is likely to have done so. It cannot, however, be shown that author *x* **did not** use author *y's* work, or that the two did not use a common source: absence of formal textual criteria or of strong plausibility arguments for borrowing of information does not logically imply that there was no borrowing. In the present instance, a few of the above texts have been argued to be interdependent and thus lack corroborative value, and a few have been asserted to be independent, but, as far as we are aware, their textual interdependence is for the most part unknown because it has not been properly studied. All one can hope for in this situation is probabilistic corroboration: the greater the number of texts, the less likely it is that they are all interrelated. That is the argument here. Given the relatively large number of texts that refer to Madelgarius, and also that these texts bring him into contact with persons whose historicity is beyond doubt, such as Dagobert I and the family of Waldebert, it is pretty much certain that Madelgarius is an historical figure and that the main facts of his life as they appear in the textual record are true. His connection with Ireland depends on a small number of texts whose interdependence is unknown, and which thus lack corroborative value; since the *Vita S. Madelgarii I* is reliable in other respects of Madelgarius' historical context, however, there is reason to believe it in this respect as well.

Irish and Frankish evidence combined

We have two sources of evidence in support of our claim that a Frankish aristocrat named Madelgarius was sent to Ireland by the Merovingian king Dagobert I and fought at the Irish battle of Mag Roth in 637. The Irish one says that Franks were present at the battle, and the Frankish one that Madelgarius was sent to Ireland by Dagobert sometime between 623 and 639. Both sources are very late in relation to the events they describe, and there is a good but by no means conclusive case for both that the information of interest which they offer is historically reliable. One step remains.

It is possible, in principle, to establish historical truth – the assertion that there was a specific state of the world at some point in the past – with near certainty. This depends on the availability of two or more textual sources of historical evidence which (i) describe the same state of affairs, and (ii) are independent of one another in the sense that the authors of the respective texts and those of their sources were unaware of or did not use one another's work. In such a case, the features on which their accounts agree can be regarded as historically true for practical purposes because of the low probability of authors independently inventing identical states of the world: the features in which their accounts agree must be based ultimately on observation of reality [Moisl 1999]. The texts are thereby said to corroborate one another. For corroboration to be effective, however, the source texts must be truly independent, and it is not generally possible to establish independence conclusively, as noted earlier. Where independence cannot be conclusively demonstrated, the effectiveness of corroboration is proportional to the conviction which the case made for independence carries.

In the present case, the question is therefore whether Irish vernacular texts of the tenth and twelfth centuries on the one hand, and an early eleventh-century Frankish saint's life on the other, are independent. Our intuition is that they are very likely to be so, and hence that their corroborative value is very high – in other words, that Dagobert I really did send Madelgarius to Ireland, and that Franks really did fight in the Irish battle of Mag Roth in 637. All that then remains is to extrapolate from this to the claim that Madelgarius led the Franks at Mag Roth. We stress that our assumption of independence is purely intuitive, however, and there may well be good grounds for questioning it.

Conclusion

We have made what we take to be a strong case that the Frankish aristocrat Madelgarius was sent to Ireland by the Merovingian king Dagobert I and fought at the Irish battle of Mag Roth in 637. If accepted, this raises an interesting question whose elucidation might well shed further light on secular political links between Ireland and the rest of Europe in the seventh century. The question is: what might have motivated Dagobert to send Madelgarius to Ireland?

No serious attempt at an answer is made here. We do, however, suggest three avenues of investigation which we feel might lead to one.

a) Dagobert might have sent Madelgarius to Ireland in an attempt to influence succession to the kingship of Northumbria. To see this, consider the following:

i. Dagobert had reason to be interested in Northumbrian royal succession. There was a family relationship between him and the Deiran king Edwin of Northumbria: Edwin was married to Ethelburh, daughter of Ethelbert king of Kent and his wife Bertha, herself the daughter of the Merovingian king Charibert of Neustria [Colgrave and Mynors 1969, I.25; Wood 1994, 176]. When Edwin was killed in 633 [on Edwin's dates see Higham 1995, 103 note 19], Ethelburh took refuge with her brother King Eadbald of Kent, and subsequently sent her son Uscfrea and her grandson Yffi to her second cousin Dagobert in Francia, 'qui', says Bede, 'erat amicus illius' [Plummer 1896, vol. 2, 117; Colgrave and Mynors 1969, II.20; Wood 1994, 177–8; Lohaus 1974, 25–6]. It is therefore conceivable that Dagobert would have supported a bid by the Deiran branch of the Northumbrian royal dynasty to reclaim the kingship from the Bernician Oswald, who had taken the throne in 634 after a brief period of turmoil. Support for this comes from a contemporary example of Merovingian kings interfering on behalf of a relative married to a foreign dynast: in 623/4 and again in 631/2 Chlothar II and Chlodwig II respectively threatened to intervene in Lombardy when the distantly-related Gundeperga appeared to be in danger [Krusch 1888a, IV.51, 71; Wood 1994, 167].

ii. Edwin's potential successors from his immediate family died or were eliminated soon after his death. One of Edwin's sons, Osfrith, was killed in the same battle as his father; another son, Eadfrith, sided against his father with Penda of Mercia, who subsequently had him murdered; both his youngest son Uscfrea and his grandson Yffi died in Francia 'in infantia' [Colgrave and Mynors 1969, II.20].

iii. When Oswiu succeeded Oswald he married Eanfled [Colgrave and Mynors 1969, III.15], Edwin's daughter, whom Ethelburh had taken to the Kentish court [Colgrave and Mynors 1969, II.20].

iv. Oswald may have been on the Cenél Conaill side of the conflict, and Oswiu on the Ulster / Dál Riata side.

One possible interpretation of (i)–(iv) is as follows. Dagobert initially intended to promote the claims of the Deiran Uscfrea or Yffi against the Bernician Oswald, and to that end sent Madelgarius to fight Oswald in Ireland. After the death of the two princes Dagobert supported the only direct descendant of Edwin's still remaining: Eanfled. Once in Ireland – the *Vita I* says that he stayed *multo tempore* – Madelgarius found himself unexpectedly involved not only in Northumbrian but also in Uí Néill dynastic rivalries, culminating in the battle of Mag Roth. Since Oswald was linked to the Cenél Conaill, Madelgarius and his Franks found themselves in alliance with the Cenél nEógain / Ulster / Dál Riata party, and thus backing Oswiu. Later, having acceded to the throne, Oswiu reciprocated by marrying Eanfled. This is all very impressionistic, of course, but a careful development of the argument seems worthwhile to us.

b) There may be a connection between Madelgarius and the later coming of the brothers Fursey [Richter 1999, 126–33], Foillán, and Ultán to Francia, their Merovingian patronage, their involvement in Merovingian politics, and Dagobert II's despatch to Ireland. Madelgarius turns up in the *Vita S. Foillani III* [1883 ch. 14], which says:

> Scottia vero et Hibernia quam abundaverint sanctis viris, ex hoc satis apparet, quod eorum peregrinatio adhuc Gallias sanctificat: huius peregrinationis maxima causa fuisse dicitur dux Madelgarius qui et Vincentius, qui potens in Francia, et ut dicunt, potens etiam in Hibernia, multos ad peregrinandum pro Christo animavit et auxilio fovit.

c) There may be a connection with the *Franci Patricii* mentioned in the Patrician texts in the *Book of Armagh* [Bieler 1979, 128] – early founders of churches in Ireland that Armagh was, in the seventh century, claiming as its own. Such an Armagh connection would tie up nicely with (b) above, since Fursey and his brothers had clear Patrician links: the *Virtutes S. Fursei* says Fursey himself had brought relics of Patrick with him [Krusch 1902, ch. 19], and the brothers had a strong association with Louth, a church that was in the Armagh orbit in the seventh century [Doherty 1991; Picard 1991b, 34].

Finally, a straw in the wind. The *Vita Ettonis* [1867] claims that Madelgarius was born in Ireland, and that he brought seven Irish saints with him to Francia, including Fursey, Foillán, and Ultán. This flatly contradicts all the other sources on Madelgarius, and of course the argument that has been made here, but if that argument is ever to gain full acceptance, the *Vita's* claim will have to be dealt with.

References

M.O. Anderson, 1973, *Kings and kingship in early Scotland*, Edinburgh
A.O. and M.O. Anderson, 1991 (eds), *Adomnán's Life of Columba*, revised edition, Edinburgh
J. Bannerman, 1966, 'The convention of Druim Cett', *Scottish Gaelic Studies* 11
J. Bannerman, 1968, 'The Dál Riata and northern Ireland in the sixth and seventh centuries', *Celtic Studies*, ed. J. Carney and D. Greene, Glasgow
R. Best and O. Bergin (eds), 1929, *Lebor na Huidre*, Dublin
L. Bieler, 1979 (ed.), *The Patrician texts in the Book of Armagh*, Dublin

F. Byrne, 1973, *Irish kings and high-kings*, London; repr. Dublin 2001

B. Colgrave and R. Mynors (eds), 1969, *Bede's Ecclesiastical history of the English people*, Oxford

M. Dillon, 1946, *The cycles of the kings*, Oxford

C. Doherty, 1991, 'The cult of St Patrick and the politics of Armagh in the seventh century', in *Ireland and Northern France, AD 600–850*, ed. J.-M. Picard, Dublin

D. Dumville, 1979, 'The *ætheling*: a study in Anglo-Saxon constitutional history', *Anglo-Saxon England* 8, 1–33

A. Duncan, 1981, 'Bede, Iona, and the Picts', *The writing of history in the early middle ages*, ed. R. Davis and J. Wallace-Hadrill, Oxford

L. van der Essen, 1907, 'Etude critique et litteraire sur les vitae des saints merovingiens', Louvain

J. de Ghesquière (ed.), 1785, *Vita S. Autberti*, in *Acta Sanctorum Belgii Selecta 3*, Brussels, 539–64

A.–M. Helvetius, 1994, *Abbayes, évêques et laïques une politique du pouvoir en Hainaut au Moyen Age (VIIe–XIe siècle)*, Brussels

M. Herbert, 1988, *Iona, Kells, and Derry*, Oxford

M. Herbert, 1989, '*Fled Dúin na nGéd*: a reappraisal', *CMCS* 18, 75–87

H. Higham, 1995, *An English empire. Bede and the early Anglo-Saxon kings*, Manchester

C. Ireland, 1991, 'Aldfrith of Northumbria and the Irish Genealogies', *Celtica* 22, 64–78.

D.P. Kirby, 1974, 'Northumbria in the time of Wilfred', *Saint Wilfrid at Hexham*, ed. D.P. Kirby, Newcastle

D.P. Kirby, 1991, *The earliest English kings*, London

B. Krusch (ed.), 1888a, *Fredegarii et aliorum Chronica*, MGH, SS rer. Merov. 2, 20–168

B. Krusch (ed.), 1888b, *Liber Historiae Francorum*, in *Fredegarii et aliorum Chronica*, MGH SS rer. Merov 2, 241–328

B. Krusch (ed.), 1896, *Vita Gaugerici*, in *Passiones vitaeque sanctorum aevi Merovingici et antiquiorum aliquot I*, MGH SS rer. Merov. 3, 652–8

B. Krusch (ed.), 1902, *Virtutes S. Fursei*, in *Passiones vitaeque sanctorum aevi Merovingici II*, MGH SS er. Merov. 4, 440–49

B. Krusch and W. Levison (eds), 1913, *Vita S. Adelgundis*, in *Passiones vitaeque sanctorum aevi Merovingici IV MGH SS rer. Merov. 6, 85–90

R. Lehmann (ed.), 1964, *Fled Dúin na nGéd*, Medieval and Modern Irish Series 21, Dublin

A. Lohaus, 1974, 'Die Merowinger und England', *Münchner Beiträge zur Mediävistik und Renaissance–Forschung* 9

S. Mac Airt and G. MacNiocaill, (ed.), 1983, *Annals of Ulster (to AD 1131)*, Dublin

G. Mac Niocaill, 1972, *Ireland before the Vikings*, Dublin

C. Marstrander, 1911, 'A new version of *The Battle of Mag Roth*', *Ériu* 5, 226–47

H. Moisl, 1983, 'The Bernician royal dynasty and the Irish in the seventh century', *Peritia* 2, 103–26

H. Moisl, 1999, *Lordship and tradition in Barbarian Europe*, Lampeter

A. Molinier, 1901, *Les Sources de l'Histoire de France I*, Paris

J. Nazet, 1967, 'La transformation des abbayes en chapitres ... le cas de Saint-Vincent de Soignies', *Revue du Nord* 49, 267–80

P. Ní Chatháin and M. Richter (eds), 1984, *Ireland and Europe. The early Church*, Stuttgart

P. Ní Chatháin and M. Richter (eds), 1987, *Ireland and Christendom. The Bible and the missions*, Stuttgart

P. Ní Chatháin and M. Richter (eds), 1996, *Ireland and Europe in the early middle ages. Learning and literature*, Stuttgart

M. Nieke and H. Duncan, 1988, 'Dalriada: the establishment and maintenance of an early historic kingdom in northern Britain, in *Power and politics in early medieval Britain and Ireland*, ed. S. Driscoll and M. Nieke, Edinburgh

D. Ó Corráin, 1971, 'Irish regnal succession: a reappraisal', *Studia Hibernica* 11, 7–39

D. Ó Cróinín, 1995, *Early medieval Ireland, 400–1200*, London.

J. O'Donovan (ed.), 1842, *The Banquet of Dun na n-Gedh and the Battle of Magh Rath*, Dublin

G. Pertz (ed.), 1841, *Annales Laubienses*, in *Annales, chronica et historiae aevi Carolini et Saxonici*, MGH SS 4, 9–28

G. Pertz (ed.), 1846, *Gesta Episcoporum Cameracensium, Lib I*, in *Chronica et gesta aevi Salici*, MGH SS 7, 402–54

J-M Picard (ed.), 1991a, *Ireland and Northern France, AD 600–850*, Dublin

J.-M. Picard, 1991b, 'Church and politics in the seventh century: the Irish exile of king Dagobert II', in *Ireland and Northern France, AD 600–850*, ed. J.-M. Picard, Dublin

C. Plummer, (ed.), 1896, *Venerabilis Baedae Opera Historica*, Oxford

P. Poncelet (ed.), 1893, *Vita I Sancti Vincentii Madelgarii*, Analecta Bollandiana 12, 426–440

M. Richter, 1991, 'The English link in the Hiberno-Frankish relations in the seventh century', in *Ireland and Northern France, AD 600–850*, ed. J.-M. Picard, Dublin

M. Richter, 1999, *Ireland and her neighbours in the seventh century*, Dublin

C. de Smedt et al. (eds), 1886, *Vita S. Gisleni III*, AB 5, 216–39

C. de Smedt et al. (eds), 1887, *Vita S. Gisleni V*, AB 6, 257–70

A. Smyth, 1972, 'The earliest Irish annals: their first contemporary entries and the earliest centres of recording',
   PRIA 72

W. Stokes, 1896, 'The Annals of Tigernach', *RC* 17, 119–263

Vita Ettonis, 1867, *AA SS*, Jul. III, 57–60

Vita S. Foillani III, 1883, *AA SS*, Oct. XIII, 391–5

Vita S. Foillani IV, 1883, *AA SS*, Oct. XIII, 395–408

Vita S. Gisleni II, 1866, *AA SS*, Oct. IV, 1030–35

Vita S. Vincentii Madelgarii II, 1867, *AA SS*, Jul. III, 640–53

I. Wood, 1994, *The Merovingian kingdoms, 450–751*, London

J. Wooding, 1996, *Communication and commerce along the western sealanes AD 400–800*, *BAR*, International Series
   654, Oxford

B. Yorke, 1990, *Kings and kingdoms of early Anglo-Saxon England*, Seaby

Cuthbert, Boisil of Melrose and the Northumbrian priest Ecgberht: some historical and hagiographical connections

D.P. KIRBY

The contributions of members of the monastic community of Melrose to the eighth-century hagiography of Cuthbert of Melrose and Lindisfarne enables some analysis to be made of the process by which hagiographical tradition concerning Cuthbert evolved. Moreover, though nothing is said directly in Bede's *Historia Ecclesiastica Gentis Anglorum* about the monastic community of Melrose being at the centre of a discussion in the early eighth century concerning the correct attitude for the Northumbrian Church to adopt towards non-Catholic observances in the Columban churches and among the Picts, the indications are that Melrose was in the vanguard of this debate.

The efflorescence of the cult of Cuthbert[1] on Farne and Lindisfarne after his death as bishop of Lindisfarne in 687 and controversy surrounding Cuthbert and the future of Lindisfarne as an episcopal see within the Northumbrian Church[2] led directly to the successive *Lives* of Cuthbert and to Bede's inclusion of so much material concerning the saint in his *Ecclesiastical History*. In this hagiographical and historical literature the focus was naturally on Cuthbert at Lindisfarne and on Farne. But Cuthbert probably lived more of his life at Melrose than he did at Lindisfarne. The monastery of Melrose emerges most clearly in Bede's *Vita sancti Cuthberti prosaica*, written before the death in 721 of Eadfrith, bishop of Lindisfarne, to whom it is dedicated[3] and in his *Historia Ecclesiatica Gentis Anglorum*, which reached an important stage in its production in 731,[4] as the community Cuthbert first entered in order to pursue the monastic life – but it features only incidentally in this respect in the *Vita sancto Cuthberti auctore anonymo*, written between 699 and 704[5] or even in Bede's first *Life* of Cuthbert, based on the anonymous *Life*, the *Vita sancti Cuthberti metrica*, produced between 704 and 716 but probably nearer 704 and possibly revised at a later stage.[6]

The writer of the anonymous *Life* of Cuthbert knew that Cuthbert had been prior of Melrose (*VCA* iii, 1) and that on one occasion in the middle of winter he journeyed from Melrose by sea to the land of the Picts (*VCA* ii, 4) but says nothing else about Cuthbert's time at Melrose. When he came to write his prose *Life* Bede was in a position to draw on two sources of information which did provide him with relevant detail. One source was Sigfrith, a priest of Jarrow at the time Bede knew him but before that of Melrose, who told him how favourably Cuthbert was received by Prior Boisil when he first joined the community there (*VCP* 6). The other was Herefrith, a

1 G. Bonner, D. Rollason, C. Stancliffe (eds), *St Cuthbert, his cult and his community to AD 1200* (Woodbridge 1989).
2 D.P. Kirby, 'The genesis of a cult: Cuthbert of Farne and ecclesiastical politics in Northumbria in the late seventh and early eighth centuries', *Journal of Ecclesiastical History* 46 (1995) pp 383–97.   3 B. Colgrave (ed.), *Two Lives of Saint Cuthbert* (Cambridge 1940) pp 141–307 (henceforth abbreviated in the text as *VCP*).   4 C. Plummer (ed.), *Baedae Historia ecclesiastica gentis Anglorum: Venerabilis Baedae opera historica*, 2 vols (Oxford 1896); B. Colgrave and R.A.B. Mynors (eds), *Bede's Ecclesiastical History of the English people* (Oxford 1969) (henceforth abbreviated in the text as *HE*).   5 Colgrave, *Two Lives of Saint Cuthbert*, pp 59–139 (henceforth abbreviated in the text as *VCA*).
6 W. Jaeger (ed.), *Vita sancti Cuthberti metrica auctore Beda*, in *Bedas metrische Vita sancti Cuthberti* (Leipzig 1935) (henceforth abbreviated in the text as VCM). On the date of this work see M. Lapidge, 'Bede's metrical *Vita S.*

priest of Melrose originally, who was with Cuthbert when he died and who was subsequently abbot of Lindisfarne (*VCP* 8, 37).[7] Herefrith was able to provide Bede with what purports to be Cuthbert's own account of how he survived the plague at Melrose in which Boisil died (*VCP* 8), an account which very much highlights Boisil's formative influence on the young Cuthbert. Bede, therefore, tapped a rich vein of testimony about Cuthbert at Melrose when he talked with Sigfrith and Herefrith, and not just about Cuthbert at Melrose. Herefrith told Bede how a piece of linen which Cuthbert, when prior of Lindisfarne, sent as a gift to Aelfflaed, abbess of Whitby, cured her (and another Whitby nun) of pain (*VCP* 23) and presented Bede with a detailed account of Cuthbert's last days and death on Farne (*VCP* 37–40) which in a somewhat revised form[8] became central to Bede's account of the *passio* of the saint. Herefrith was also among those who read and commented on the draft materials for Bede's prose *Life* (*VCP* Preface). It is clear that his testimony was greatly valued by Bede and his standing high among the circle of those who had known Cuthbert and were in a position to talk about him.

So it is particularly surprising that the writer of the anonymous *Life* should not have drawn at all on what Herefrith had to say. For the writer not to be aware of Sigfrith some reasonable explanation is perhaps possible. Sigfrith was living at Jarrow when Bede wrote his prose *Life* and may have been away from Melrose or Lindisfarne for many years, so that he and the anonymous author never met. Or, given the localised nature of oral tradition in this period, it is conceivable, if unlikely, that the anonymous was simply indifferent to stories about Cuthbert at Melrose. But for the writer never to have encountered Herefrith or anyone who was familiar with his testimony not just about Cuthbert at Melrose but about his last days and final hours is extremely odd. If Herefrith returned from Lindisfarne to Melrose after the death of Cuthbert, some contact with so important a witness could surely still have been made when the two houses clearly experienced a close association. Even if Herefrith were dispatched still further afield, it is difficult to imagine no attempt being made to enquire what he remembered. Could Herefrith have been too insignificant a figure at the time the anonymous wrote for any attention to be paid to his recollections? Hardly, because many humble priests contributed their testimony to Cuthbert's sanctity. Nor can there have been a degree of reservation in writing about Cuthbert's last days to make Herefrith's account too sensitive to use. A certain brother, Walhstod, is said by the anonymous author frequently to have told how he was made well by ministering to Cuthbert in his cell during his final illness (*VCA* iv, 12), testimony which Bede subsequently subsumed into his version in the prose *Life* of Herefrith's account of Cuthbert's last days (*VCP* 38).

One possible explanation of these features of the Cuthbert material is that Herefrith's testimony about Cuthbert at Melrose and his account of Cuthbert's death had not been formulated when the anonymous author wrote. It may not then have existed in any coherent narrative form for the anonymous author to avail himself of it. The dynamic behind the growth of the cult of Cuthbert was the need on the part of the community on Lindisfarne to establish for itself a former bishop as a saintly figure on a heroic scale to guarantee its own survival as a bishopric. The mainsprings of Melrose hagiography would be quite different. Consequently at first there may have been no formed tradition at Melrose about Cuthbert's life there which was relevant to Lindisfarne.

Cuthberti', in *St Cuthbert, his cult and his community*, as above note 1, pp 77–93.   **7** Herefrith was probably abbot some time after the death of Cuthbert but he seems to have resigned by the time Bede wrote his prose *Life*, see Kirby, 'The genesis of a cult', as above note 2, p. 386, note 15.   **8** W. Berschin, '*Opus deliberatum ac perfectum*: why did the Venerable Bede write a second prose Life of St Cuthbert?', in *St Cuthbert, his cult and his community*, as

Herefrith's testimony is certainly not without its difficulties. According to Herefrith, Boisil prophesied that Cuthbert would one day be made a bishop (*VCP* 8). Bede attempted to resolve the enigma thereby created, for the anonymous *Life* gives no hint of any such prophecy or that Cuthbert's elevation to a bishopric was anticipated years before, by paraphrasing Cuthbert's alleged words in the anonymous *Life* to Abbess Aelfflaed on being offered a bishopric, humbly accepting that neither on sea or land could he hide from such an honour (*VCA* iii, 6), to read that he would never be free from the entrapments of this world were he to become a bishop even if he were to hide himself away on a rock in the sea, which statement he is said to have made several times to the brethren who visited him on Farne (*VCP* 8). The prophecy, attributed by Herefrith to Boisil, does not seem to have been part of the tradition about Cuthbert before Bede wrote his prose *Life*. For Herefrith, Boisil emerges as an absolutely pivotal figure in the life of Cuthbert, as his teacher and mentor. Herefrith's meditation on Cuthbert had clearly led him to stress the importance of Cuthbert's time with Boisil at Melrose for his spiritual development. The testimony of Sigfrith implies an identical process. As Bede reports it, it was Sigfrith himself who testified that Boisil's greeting of Cuthbert on his arrival at Melrose was Christ's response to Nathanael in the Gospel of John (Jn 1:47) – 'Behold an Israelite in whom there is no guile' (words also used by Sulpicius Severus of Martin of Tours) – and had thereby supported his narrative with appropriate scriptural and hagiographical cross-references. The suspicion must be that both Sigfrith's and Herefrith's stories about Cuthbert and Boisil at Melrose were conceived at about the same time and in the same milieu. Given the apparent ignorance of the author of the anonymous *Life of Cuthbert* about the role of Boisil in the early *Life* of Cuthbert, the indications are that the time these stories took shape was between the writing of the anonymous *Life* and the writing of Bede's prose *Life*, that is to say across the first two decades of the eighth century, and, with the emphasis as it is on the person of Boisil, that the setting was the monastery of Melrose.

That Herefrith's material was being adapted to changing circumstances is clear from one detail in particular in the account of Cuthbert's dying injunctions, namely Cuthbert's alleged command to his community not to enter into any communion with those who departed from the unity of the Catholic peace, either in not celebrating Easter at the proper time or in evil living (*VCP* 39). Bede's account of the vision and ascetic practices of Dryhthelm, who became a monk at Melrose (*HE* v, 12), reveals explicitly what has been described as the continuing 'pervasive Irish background' of the cultural world at Melrose at the close of the seventh century.[9] Such a cultural identity was established at Melrose, which Cuthbert entered in 651 or soon after, in the time of Aidan.[10] In the early 660s Cuthbert went with Eata, abbot of Melrose, to Eata's new foundation at Ripon (*VCP* 7) but when the monastery was given to another company of monks under the young Wilfrid (later bishop of York) Eata and Cuthbert returned to Melrose (*VCP* 8), preferring, according to Bede, to renounce the site at Ripon rather than abandon their Columban Irish customs (*HE* iii, 25). Eata was a disciple of Aidan (*HE* iii, 26) whose soul Cuthbert was said to have seen ascending to Heaven (*VCA* i, 5; *VCM* 4; *VCP* 4). In the aftermath of the synod of Whitby the outgoing bishop of Lindisfarne, Colmán, requested that Eata be placed over those who preferred to remain on the island when the Irish leaders departed (*HE* iii, 26). And in

above note 1, pp 95–102, at p. 98, 102. **9** C. Ireland, 'Penance and prayer in water; an Irish practice in Northumbrian hagiography', *CMCS* 34 (1997) pp 51–66, at p. 65. **10** C. Stancliffe, 'Oswald "most holy and most victorious king of the Northumbrians"', in C. Stancliffe and E. Cambridge (eds), *Oswald: Northumbrian king to European saint* (Stamford 1995) pp 33–83, considers the possibility that Melrose was originally a British foundation,

retreating to Farne Cuthbert was imitating the practices of Aidan (*HE* iii, 6). Moreover, Cuthbert's recorded visit (according to Bede as prior, in which case after the synod of Whitby) on behalf of the Melrose community to the Picts for the mid-winter feast of Epiphany (*VCA* ii, 4; *VCM* 9; *VCP* 11) suggests an established and sustained relationship between Melrose and the Columban communities among the Picts and Cuthbert's evident familiarity with the Pictish situation in the mid-680s, when he advised the Northumbrian king not to invade (*HE* iv, 26), correctly as it transpired, makes it likely that his contacts with the Picts continued until the end of his life. Whatever compromises Cuthbert was obliged to make in the years following the synod of Whitby, and adapt to new practices he must have done even within a more diverse Northumbrian regime than that epitomised by the Wilfridian communities, the ascription to him of such sentiments as those to which Herefrith attests in Bede's prose *Life* is incongruous.[11] The report of Herefrith's testimony on this matter represents attitudes and prejudices of the period when the account was constructed in the first two decades of the eighth century, not the thoughts and pronouncements of Cuthbert himself or necessarily either contemporary attitudes at Melrose.

Even by the time Bede was writing the *Vita sancti Cuthberti prosaica*, the situation was changing. Biographical and hagiographical anecdotes about a new generation of leading figures were pointing in a direction away from non-communion with Columban religious communities and towards a programme of integration. In 716, according to Bede, a Northumbrian priest, Ecgberht, arrived on Iona, head of the Columban foundations in Pictland, from Ireland to seek to persuade the community there to accept the Roman Easter and a change in the shape of the tonsure (*HE* v, 22). It is important to stress that Bede does not say that Ecgbert effected an alteration in the shape of the tonsure and the date on which Easter was celebrated on Iona in 716 except in so far as he comments that the monks on Iona accepted Catholic practices while Dúnchad was abbot (*HE* v, 22), and Dúnchad, whose actual status is ambiguous,[12] died in 717; otherwise Bede's meaning is clearly that Ecgberht arrived in 716 and Iona adopted the Catholic Easter and the Petrine tonsure thereafter. And for these changes to have occurred after 716 would make better sense of the expulsion by Nechton, king of the Picts, of the Columban communities from Pictland in 717 for non-compliance with the changes he was introducing to the dating of Easter (than the assumption that these communities were simply recalcitrant even in the face of change at home) and help to explain why it is only in 718 that the Annals of Tigernach record the imposition of the (Petrine) tonsure on the *familia* of Iona.[13] The probability is that Bede's allusion to the acceptance of Catholic ways of life on Iona while Dúnchad was abbot is an elaboration of the simple fact that Ecgberht arrived in Dúnchad's time, that is to say this was the start of the process. It will have been between Ecgberht's arrival and the completion of a programme of change on Iona that King Nechton approached Bede's monastery for guidance on the true date of Easter (*HE* v, 21).

These developments indicate that the issue of the date of Easter was a serious one among the Picts in the second half of the second decade of the eighth century but not necessarily earlier. There is no evidence that Northumbrian pressure to change had been brought to bear to any significant extent on Iona and its dependent Pictish communities before this. The only exception is Bede's monastery of Wearmouth and Jarrow, though the evidence here is ambiguous. According

---

p. 79.   **11** Cf. Kirby, 'The genesis of a cult', as above note 2, pp 387–9.   **12** M. Herbert, *Iona, Kells, and Derry: the history and hagiography of the monastic familia of Columba* (Oxford 1988, repr. Dublin 1996) pp 57–9.   **13** Ed. W. Stokes, *RC* 17 (1896) p. 226. The matter of the tonsure may have been regarded as an issue separate from the date of Easter (Herbert, *Iona, Kells and Derry*, p. 60) but Bede places the resolution of the tonsure difficulty in

to Bede, Adomnán, abbot of Iona, had come to recognise the Roman Easter and correct canonical rites of the Catholic Church during a visit to Northumbria in the 680s, afterwards attempting unsuccessfully to convert Iona, from whence he then departed to go to Ireland where he met with success among non-Columban houses before returning to Iona and encountering defeat there a second time (*HE* v, 5 and cf. v, 21). Adomnán certainly visited Wearmouth and Jarrow and is said to have discussed the shape of the tonsure with Abbot Ceolfrith (*HE* v, 21). But rather than championing the Roman Easter to the extent of estranging himself from his own community, Adomnán appears to have remained on good terms with the brethren on Iona, for whom he wrote the *Vita sancti Columbae c.*700, and supporting evidence that he campaigned in Ireland for the acceptance of the Roman Easter is non-existent.[14] What had probably been, after Adomnán's visit to Northumbria, at most a general discussion of issues involved was magnified in the *Ecclesiastical History* into a personal crusade on Adomnán's part.

According to an 'aged and venerable' and 'most truthful' priest who was Bede's source of information at this point, the Northumbrian nobleman and priest, Ecgberht, had taken a vow at the time of the plague of 664 while studying at Rath Melsigi (Clonmelsh)[15] in Ireland as a young man, never to return to his home and Ecgberht's companion, Aethelhun, received visionary confirmation that Ecgberht would keep his vow (*HE* iii, 27). He remained, however, in close contact with Northumbrian ecclesiastical centres. Rath Melsigi was among the principal monastic sites in Ireland to which Anglo-Saxons from Northumbria flocked. Ecgberht had been a fellow-student in Ireland with Chad (*HE* iv, 3), one of Aidan's pupils, and Aethelhun was the brother of Aethelwine, who became bishop of Lindsey after 679 (*HE* iii, 11, 27; iv, 12). Higebald, abbot of a monastery in the diocese of Lindsey, is known to have visited Ecgberht in Ireland (*HE* iv, 3). Between 704 and 716 Eanmund, who intended to found a monastery in Northumbria, was put in touch, probably by Eadfrith, bishop of Lindisfarne, with Ecgberht in Ireland, who not only sent Eanmund an altar dedicated to St Peter for his new church but told him exactly where to build it.[16]

The indications are that another house Ecgberht remained in touch with either directly or indirectly was Melrose. According to Bede, he had begun to think in terms of missionary activity among the continental Germans when a one-time member of the community at Melrose, then also living in Ireland, told him how his former master and tutor Boisil had appeared in a vision to him, instructing him to tell Ecgberht not to go to the Germanic tribes on the continent but to Iona and the monasteries of Columba among the Picts. Though Ecgberht is not otherwise known to have had any connection with the monastery of Melrose, some close association there must have been for it to have been supposed in Bede's story that the name of Boisil would be enough to influence Ecgberht to redirect his life. The implication has to be that at one time Boisil had also been Ecgberht's master and tutor. Ecgberht is said to have asked his companion to say nothing of the vision to anyone else and to have been unwilling to alter his plans. Much concerned, Boisil's former pupil informed Ecgberht that the same vision had occurred again with greater urgency. Even so, only when his ship was wrecked in a storm in the harbour did Ecgberht abandon his original intention (*HE* v, 9). Bede dates this confrontation between Ecgberht and the monk from Melrose some two years before the commencement (in 690) of the mission of

---

716 in exactly the same way as he does the change in the dating of Easter.   **14** J.-M. Picard, 'Bede, Adomnán, and the writing of history', *Peritia* 3 (1984) pp 50–70, at pp 60ff.   **15** D. Ó Cróinín, 'Rath Melsigi, Willibrord, and the earliest Echternach manuscripts', *Peritia* 3 (1984) pp 17–49 at p. 23.   **16** A. Campbell (ed.), *Aethelwulf De Abbatibus* (Oxford 1967) pp 10ff.

Willibrord to the Frisians. But Ecgberht did not arrive on Iona until 716, twenty-eight years later. Although he did not go to the Germanic tribes himself, he continued, according to Bede, to be involved in launching the mission of Willibrord (*HE* v, 10), but this would not have prevented him for twenty-eight years from obeying the visionary command. It would be far more understandable if Ecgberht were to have been inspired by the report of the visionary injunction to act sooner rather than later in response to it.

Moreover, other indicators suggest that there are no grounds for ascribing to Northumbrian communities a clearly expressed resolve to instruct the monastery of Iona and the Picts in correct Catholic observances before the second decade of the eighth century. The words which Herefrith attributed to Cuthbert suggest rather a pronounced antagonism to any such association. That such antagonism was already becoming a thing of the past by *c*.720 is clear from Ecgberht's arrival on Iona in 716. It is not so clear that it was already out of date by the late 680s. The prominence of Boisil in Bede's account of the vision said to have been vouchsafed to Ecgberht's companion may be the key which enables us to locate Ecgberht's Melrose-inspired commission in a more appropriate time-frame. The material relating to Cuthbert suggests that the community at Melrose was developing its traditions about Boisil in the first two decades of the eighth century. Bede's story of the monk of Melrose's claim to have experienced a vision of Boisil is almost certainly part of the same phenomenon. The desire of the community of Melrose (evidently expressed in terms of a vision of Boisil) that Ecgberht should proceed to Iona to argue for a change there in the date of Easter was probably communicated to Ecgberht, therefore, not all that long before 716 and reflected real concern at Melrose, with its long-established Pictish connections, that new approaches needed to be made to Columban communities across northern Britain.

There were certainly still monks from Melrose in Ireland in the early eighth century. Haemgils, an aged Melrose monk and 'eminent' priest who provided Bede with his account of the vision and ascetic practice of Dryhthelm of Cunningham, was living in Ireland as Bede wrote (*HE* v, 12). There must be a possibility that Haemgils was the 'aged and venerable' priest who was the source of Bede's story of Ecgberht's original vow never to return to his homeland, in which a visionary element is also present, and even perhaps the source, directly or indirectly, of the story of the monk of Melrose's vision of Boisil and the command to Ecgberht to preach to the Columban foundations. In Bede's hagiographical legend this vision of Boisil and his special commission for Ecgberht was placed in association with Ecgberht's failure to go to the Germanic tribes as he had been intending, thereby providing a dramatic explanation of that failure and a miraculous revelation of divine purpose.

It seems clear that Ecgberht's personal inspiration for his activities on Iona and among the Picts derived ultimately from Melrose and that Boisil had come to be conceived of in that community as an important validating figure. In the same way as in the stories of Sigfrith and Herefrith about Boisil he is represented as proclaiming the sanctity of Cuthbert, so in the story of the vision of the brother from Melrose Boisil is seen as authorising and endorsing Ecgberht's work among the Columban communities in the north. It seems reasonable to suggest that the correct approach to be adopted by the Northumbrian Church to the non-Catholic practices of the Columban communities was a burning issue at Melrose in the early eighth century and that its resolution in favour of inclusion through conversion to Catholic norms led directly to the landing of Ecgberht on Iona in 716.

Chiasmus and hyperbaton in the Annals of Ulster

FRANCIS JOHN BYRNE

When some fifteen years ago Próinséas Ní Chatháin, Jean-Michel Picard, Charles Doherty and myself were studying the *Collectio Canonum Hibernensis* with the late Professor Maurice Sheehy we had occasion to discuss the colophon to this text found in the Paris manuscript BN lat. 12021: 'Hucusque nuben & cucuiminiae. & du rinis', i.e. 'Hucusque Ruben et Cú Cuimni Iae et Durinis', explained by Thurneysen as a chiasmic construction 'Ruben of Dairinis and Cú Chuimne of Iona'.[1] Thurneysen says that we must emend to *Cu Cuimne Iæ* and *Daurinis* and treat both place-names as Latin genitives. That *Iæ* or *Iae* is indeed Latin seems confirmed by the evidence of the annals,[2] but I am not convinced that *Durinis* (for the normal Old Irish *Dairinse*) can be so explained: furthermore the first syllable could be understood as *dar-* due to the misreading of an open *a* just as *nuben* shows a mistaken reading of initial short-tailed *r*. As examples of the chiasmus A B b a Thurneysen cites Wb. 30d 19: *tonica … lacerna .i. sái … fúan* and *Fís Adamnáin* §4: *Naim thuascirt in domain … ocus a descirt ina ndib nairechtaib dermáraib tess ocus tuaid* and also *Serglige Con Culaind* §3: '*Ní fírfidir*', ol *Cu-Chulainn, 'co tí Conall ocus Fergus*'; *fo bith ba haiti dó Fergus ocus ba comalta Conall Cernach.* Then he cites the listing of 5 types of speech in *Revue celtique*, xiii, p. 269, where the examples are given in reverse order to their listing (i.e. ABCDE are illustrated by examples edcba), and a similar arrangement in *Irische Verslehren*, §§ 99–102 of the tasks allotted to the tenth year of study. None of these parallels are quite as striking as some examples from the Annals of Ulster.[3]

In the case of the following entry (i.e. the obits of Do Dímmóc anchorite abbot of Clonard and of Do Chumma the Wise of Kildare) the chiasmus in AU apparently misled the compiler of ATig. and certainly the Four Masters, who do not mention Do Chumma. I fell into the same error when compiling the lists of abbots of Clonard and Kildare in Moody, Martin and Byrne, *A New History of Ireland*, ix (Dublin 1984) pp 243 and 260.

1 Thurneysen, *ZCP*, vi (1908), pp 1–5; see Kenney, *Sources*, p. 248, note 273. According to Wasserschleben, *Die irische Kanonensammlung* (Leipzig 1874; 2nd revised ed. 1885) this manuscript (his Cod.3 'Sangermanensis') has the ascription to Ruben and Cu Cuiminiæ after the *Hibernensis*, and also at the end a long colophon of Arbedoc *clericus* who wrote for the abbot Haelhucar. It was used by Wasserschleben as his basis for the first two Books missing in Sangallensis. It was formerly at St Germain, and previously at Corbie, but originally written in Brittany. L. Bieler, *The Irish Penitentials* (Dublin 1963) denotes it as MS P (*Sangermanensis 121*), and dates it to the beginning of the tenth century, and as from Corbie, adding that it is earlier (but not much earlier) than Paris 3182, another early tenth-century Breton manuscript of canon law texts. Léon Fleuriot, *Dictionnaire des gloses en vieux Breton* (Paris 1964) p. 5, no. 11 says it was written in continental script with frequent use of insular g, and that is has twelve Breton glosses (edited by Stokes, *RC* 4 (1878) pp 327–8) as well as three short phrases in OIr. (ibid. p. 325, n. 3), for which see Stokes and Strachan, *Thesaurus Palaeohibernicus* (Cambridge 1903) vol. ii, pp xi, 38. Fleuriot does not give a date. Lapidge and Sharpe *A bibliography of Celtic-Latin literature 400–1200* (Dublin 1985) p. 157, date it to the tenth century. 2 See for instance the entry at AU 717 cited below on p. 63. 3 The annalistic texts in this paper

AU 748: Dormitatio Do Dimóc anchoritæ abbatis Cluana Irairdd 7 Cille Daro Do Cumai sapientis [THE FALLING ASLEEP of Do Dímmóc THE ANCHORITE ABBOT of Clonard and of Do Chumma THE WISE of Kildare].

ATig. [748]: Dormitatío Do Dimoc ancorite abbad Cluana hIraird 7 Cille Dara. Do Chummai sapientis quies [THE FALLING ASLEEP of Do Dímmoc THE ANCHORITE abbot of Clonard and of Kildare. REPOSE of Do Chumma THE WISE].

AI [748]: Quies Mo Dimmóc Cluana Iraird [REPOSE of Mo Dímmóc of Clonard].

AFM 743: Do Dimmóc ancoiri abb Cluana hIraird & Cille Dara d'écc [Do Dímmóc the anchorite abbot of Clonard and of Kildare dies].

With this we might compare the following entries from the seventh century

1. AU 658: Mors Gureit regis Alo Cluathe Fergaileque filii Domnaill [DEATH of Guriat, KING of Ail Cluaid (= Dumbarton) AND of Fergal SON of Domnall].

This entry unique to AU could possibly be read as containing the obit of Domnall mac Fergaile rather than of Fergal mac Domnaill. But as no person of the name Fergal is attested in the annals before this date the reference is most probably to an otherwise unknown Fergal son of Domnall mac Áedo or possibly son of Domnall Brecc.

2. AU 687: Mors Osseni episcopi Monosterii Finntin filii Finnguine [DEATH of Osséne SON of Finguine BISHOP OF THE MONASTERY of Fintan (= Taghmon)].

ATig. [687]: Mors Osení espuic Monasteri Finntan .i. Mundu mc. Tulcháin [DEATH of Osséne bishop OF THE MONASTERY of Fintan, i.e., Munnu mac Tulcháin].

CS [683]: Mors Ossene episcopi Monosterii Fintani .i. Munnu mic Tulcani [DEATH of Osséne BISHOP OF THE MONASTERY OF FINTAN, i.e., Munnu son of TULCHANUS].

AR §148: Mors Osseni episcopus Monosterii Fiontain mc. Thaulchain .i. Mundu [DEATH of Osséne BISHOP OF THE MONASTERY of Fintan mac Tulcháin i.e. Mundu].

AFM 685: Osseni epscop Mainistreach Fiontain mac Tulchain d'écc [Osséne bishop of the Monastery of Fintan mac Tulcháin dies].

The mention of Finguine is peculiar to AU and probably puzzled the redactors of the other annals. However Adomnán says that Osséne was son of Ernán:

Haec mihi quodam narrante relegioso sene praespitero Christi milite Oisseneo nomine Ernani filio gente mocu Neth Corb indubitanter didici; qui sé eadem omnia supra memorata uerba eiusdem ab ore sancti Finteni filii Tailchani audisse testatus est ipsius monacus.[4]

Note that Adomnán does not call him a bishop, but a priest and a monk. Note also that the following chapter-heading deals with an Ernán or Ernéne whose obit occurs together with that of Fintan in the annals at 635.

represent the manuscript readings of the originals: emendations (correct or otherwise) incorporated in the current published editions are ignored. The English translation is my own and is as literal as possible: words which are in Latin in the originals are printed in small caps.   4 Adomnán, *Vita Columbae*, I. 2 (13b) [Anderson, pp 212–14]. I have omitted commas and restored *i* and *u* for the editors' *j* and *v*.

De Erneneo filio Craseni sancti Columbae profetia

[...] Hic erat Erneneus filius Craseni postea per omnes Scotiae eclesias famosus et ualde notissimus; qui haec omnia supra scripta uerba Segeneo abbati de sé profetata enarrauerat meo decessore Failbeo intentius audiente qui et ipse cum Segeneo praesens inerat. Cuius reuelatione et ego ipse cognoui haec eadem quae enarraui.[5]

AU 635: Quies Fintain m. Telchain 7 Erneni m. Creseni [REPOSE of Fintan mac Tulcháin and of Ernéne mac Creséne].

ATig.[634]: Quies Finntain .i. Mundu mc. Tulcháin húi .xii. Kl. Nouembris et Ernáine mc. Cresene [REPOSE of Fintan i.e. Munnu mac Tulcháin on the twelfth of the Kalends of November (= 21 October) AND of Ernáine mac Creséne].

CS [634]: Quies Fintani (Munnu) filíí Telchan in .xíí. Kl. Nouembris et Ernaine mic Cresine [REPOSE of FINTANUS (Munnu) SON OF Tulchán ON THE TWELFTH OF THE KALENDS OF NOVEMBER and of Ernáine mac Creséne].

AI [637]: Quies Munnu m. Thilchain [REPOSE of Munnu mac Tulcháin].

AR §114: Quies Fiontain (.i. Mundu) filii Tealcain 12. Kal. Nouembris 7 Ernaine m. Creasaini [REPOSE of Fintan (i.e. Munnu) SON of Tulchán ON THE TWELFTH OF THE KALENDS OF NOVEMBER AND OF ERNÁIC MAC CRESÉNE.

AClon.634: Fintann of Tymonna & Ernany m[c]Cressine Died the 12th of the calends of Nouember and of Ernáine mac Creséne].

AFM 634: S. Fionntain mac Telchain d'écc an 21 d'October [St Fintan mac Tulcháin dies on the 21 October].

Another Osséne is recorded as founder of the Columban church of Clonmore in Ferrard (Cluain Mór Fer nArda).[6] The Middle Irish Life of Colum Cille, §41, states that Columba placed Osséne mac Cellaig there:

Facbais Ossine mac Cellaig i Cluain Mor Fher nArda.[7]

The only Osséne or Ossíne mentioned in Ó Riain, *Corpus gen. SS. Hib.* (Dublin 1985), §705.235, p.138 is in the list *De sacerdotibus* without any further information, but whose name is juxtaposed with that of Munnu of Taghmon:

S Oísine
[S] Munnu

Ernéne mac Crasséni is commemorated in the *Félire Óengusso* at 18 August.[8]

Mac Cresséni m'Ernóc*
mórais Fiadat fairinn

---

5 Adomnán, *Vita Columbae*, I. 3 (14a and 15b) [Anderson, pp 214 and 218].   6 See M. Herbert, *Iona, Kells, and Derry* (Oxford 1988, repr. Dublin 1996) pp 189, 281, who refers to *Mart. Tall.*, 1 January, commemorating *Ossine Clúana Mór*, and to W. Reeves, *The Life of Columba* (Dublin 1857) pp 280–1.   7 Herbert, *Iona, Kells, and Derry*, pp 233, 258.   8 W. Stokes (ed.), *Félire Óenguso Céli Dé. The Martyrology of Oengus the Culdee* (London 1905, repr. Dublin 1984) pp 177, 186.

M'Ernoc .i. mac Creisine ó Raith Nui inhUib Garrchon i Fortuathaib Laigen 7 o Chill draignech inhUib Drona.

and in Ó Riain, *Corpus gen. SS. Hib.* §707.766, p. 151:

Moernoc m. Cruissin.

Peculiar word order (hyperbaton) occurs at:

1. AU 718: Fiannamail nepos Boghaine m. Finn Insolæ princeps Maige Samh 7 Dub Duin nepos Faelain episcopus abbas Cluana Irairdd [Fiannamail mac Find DESCENDANT of Bóguine PRINCEPS OF THE ISLAND of Mag Sam (= Inishmacsaint); and Dub Dúin DESCENDANT of Fáelán THE BISHOP ABBOT of Clonard].
    ATig. [718]: Hí sunt uiri sapientis qui mortuí sunt: Fianamail hua Bogaine mc. Find Insola princeps Muige Sam 7 Dub Duin hua Faelain espoc ab Cluana Iraird [THESE ARE THE WISE MEN WHO DIED: Fiannamail mac Find ua Bógaine PRINCEPS OF THE ISLAND of Mag Sam and Dub Dúin ua Fáeláin the bishop abbot of Clonard].
    AR §171: Hi sunt viri sapientes qui mortui sunt: Dub Duin hua Faolain episcopus ab Cluana Iraird Fiannamail o Bogaine [THESE ARE THE WISE MEN WHO DIED: Dub Dúin ua Fáeláin THE BISHOP abbot of Clonard; Fiannamail ua Bógaine].
    AFM 716: Dubh Dúin Ua Faoláin epscop & abb Cluana hEraird d'écc. [...] Fionamhail Ua Boghaine mac Finn [Dub Dúin ua Fáeláin bishop and abbot of Clonard dies. ... Fiannamail ua Bógaine mac Finn].

2. AU 732: Bellum inter Genus Conaill 7 Eugain in quo filius Fergaile Aid <.i. Aedh> de Flaithbertacho filio Loingsich <mc. Aengusa mc Domnaill mc. Aedha mc Ainmireach> triumphauit hiis ducibus cessis a dicione eius: Flann Gohan filius Conghaile m. Fergussa Flaithgus m. Duib Dibergg [A BATTLE BETWEEN THE RACE of Conall (= Cenél Conaill) and of Eógan (= Cenél nEógain) IN WHICH Áed SON of Fergal <i.e. Áed> TRIUMPHED OVER FLAITHBERTHACHUS (= Flaithbertach) SON of Loingsech <son of Óengus son of Domnall son of Áed mac Ainmerech> THESE LEADERS FROM (= those under) HIS AUTHORITY BEING SLAUGHTERED: Flann Goan SON of Congal mac Fergusa (and) Flaithgius mac Duib Díbergg].

This entry is unique to AU. The chiasmus is more obvious if we omit the interpolations and additional information:

> Bellum inter Genus Conaill 7 Eugain in quo filius Fergaile Aid de Flaithbertacho filio Loingsich triumphauit.

Here there is a double chiasmus in that Áed mac Fergaile belonged to the Cenél nEógain and Flaithbertach mac Loingsig to the Cenél Conaill. Note also the Latinisation of Flaithbertach. This is unusual in secular names, but is found in the references to Selbach of Cenél Loairn *s.aa.* 712, 714, 719 and 727 and to Nechtan king of the Picts *s.a.* 717, as well as to the Picts Bruide and Talorc *s.a.* 731 (see next section). The entry should be read in connection with the following:

AU 733: Congressio iterum inter Aedh m. Fergaile 7 Genus Conaill in Campo Itho ubi ceciderunt Conaing m. Conghaile m. Fergusso 7 ceteri multi [AN ENCOUNTER ONCE MORE BETWEEN Áed mac Fergaile AND THE RACE of Conall (= Cenél Conaill) IN THE PLAIN of Íth (= Mag nÍtha) WHERE Conaing son of Congal mac Fergusa AND MANY OTHERS FELL].

ATig.[733]: Congressio iterum inter Aedh mac Fergaili et Genus Conaill in Campo Itha ubí cecidit Conaing mac Congaile mc. Fergusa Fanat et ceteri multi. Flaithbertach clasem Dal Riada in Iberniam duxit et ceades magna facta est de is in Insola hOíne uibí hí trucidantur uiri: Concobar mac Locheni et Branchu mac Brain et multí in flumine demersí sunt[9] dicitur in Banna [AN ENCOUNTER ONCE MORE BETWEEN Áed mac Fergaile AND THE RACE of Conall IN THE PLAIN of Íth WHERE Conaing son of Congal mac Fergusa Fánat AND MANY OTHERS FELL. Flaithbertach LED THE FLEET of Dál Riata TO IRELAND AND A GREAT SLAUGHTER WAS MADE OF THEM IN THE ISLAND of Oíne (= Inis Óine : Island Heaghey near Coleraine?) WHERE THE FOLLOWING MEN WERE MASSACRED: Conchobar mac Lóchéne AND Branchú mac Brain AND MANY WERE DROWNED IN THE RIVER [WHICH] IS CALLED the Bann].

AU 734: Congressio in Campo Itho inter <Flaithbertach> filium Loingsich 7 <Aed Allan mc.> Fergaile natum ubi Nepotes Echdach <do Cinel Eogain> ceciderunt 7 ceteri [AN ENCOUNTER IN THE PLAIN of Íth BETWEEN <Flaithbertach> THE SON of Loingsech AND <Áed Allán son of> THE [MAN] BORN of Fergal WHERE THE DESCENDANTS of Eochaid <of the Cenél nEógain> AND OTHERS FELL].

Again here the chiasmus is clearer without the interpolations:

Congressio in Campo Itho inter filium Loingsich 7 Fergaile natum …

ATig.[734]: Cath i Muig Itha iter mac Loingsig 7 mac Fergaile .i. Sil Eachach 7 Cenel Eogain 7 tucadh a n-ar leath ar leath and [A battle in Mag nÍtha between the son of Loingsech and the son of Fergal i.e., the Síl nEchdach <and> the Cenél nEógain and they were slaughtered on both sides].

Here ATig. are mistaken in their interpretation of Síl nEchdach's role.

AClon.730: Fergus brought an army out of Dalriada into Inis Owen in Ulster upon whom there was a great slaughter made amongst whom Connor son of Locheny and Branchowe the son of Bran were slaine and many others Drowned in the river of Banne.

AFM 727: Iomairecc etir Aodh mac Feargaile & Cenel cConaill i Maigh Iotha bail in ro marbhadh Conaing mac Congaile mic Feargusa & sochaidhe ele do Cenel Eoghain [An encounter between Áed mac Fergaile and the Cenél Conaill in Mag nÍtha where Conaing son of Congal mac Fergusa and many others of the Cenél nEógain were killed].

AFM 728: Iomairecc hi Maigh Iotha etir cloinn Loingsich mic Aongusa & cloind Fearghaili mic Maoile Dúin du inro marbhadh sochaidhe do Cenel Eoghain. Flaithbhertach do thochuiredh mur-chobhlagh do Dail Riata dochum nEreann & iarna ttorachtain níro airiseatar co rangatar Inis hOinae & ro fearadh cath eitir Flaithbheartach cona amhsaibh & Ciannachta & araill d'Ultoibh & do Chenel Eoghain & ro múdhaigheadh drong di-rimhe

9 [quod] *add.* Stokes.

d'Ultoibh do Chenel Eoghain & do Chiannachtaibh ann im Conchubhar mac Loichene & im Branchoin mac Brain & ro baidheadh líon dí-rímhe dibh isin mBanda iar sraoineadh forra [An encounter in Mag nÍtha between the progeny of Loingsech mac Óengusa and the progeny of Fergal mac Maíle Dúin where many of the Cenél nEógain were killed. Flaithbertach invited a fleet of Dál Riata to Ireland and after their arrival they did not stop until they reached Inis Oíne and a battle was fought between Flaithbertach with his mercenaries and the Cianachta and some of the Ulstermen and of the Cenél nEógain and an innumerable multitude of the Ulstermen, of the Cenél nEógain and of the Cianachta were destroyed there around Conchobar mac Lóchéne and Branchú mac Brain and an innumerable number of them were drowned in the Bann after they had been routed].

Note here that the Four Masters have misinterpreted both *filium* and *natum* as *clann* 'the progeny of'. The use of *natum* is unusual but has a parallel in an early entry in AI which has a peculiar semi-Latinisation of the name Findlug:

AI [486]: Natiuitas Brændini Albilogi <.i. Findloga> gnati <.i. filii> [BIRTH OF BRENDINUS (= Brendan) OFFSPRING <I.E. SON> OF ALBILOGUS <i.e. of Findlug>].

This may explain the curious reference to Brendan as 'bishop of Armagh' in the Annals of Roscrea and the Annals of Clonmacnois:

AR §101: Quies Brendainn episcopi Aird Macha eodem anno quo repertum est corpus B. Barnabae apostoli per reuelationem et euangelium Matthei.
AClon. 454: Brandon Bushopp of Ardmagh dyed.

I suggest that these derive from a notice of the birth (not the death) of Brendan, who may have been styled *maccu Alti* (i.e. 'of the Altraige') and that this was misread as *Mache Alti* and understood as Armagh.

3.   AU 736: Uir sapiens 7 anchorita Insole Uaccæ Albæ Dublittir 7 Samson nepos Corcrain dormierunt [Dublitter WISE MAN AND ANCHORITE OF THE ISLAND OF THE WHITE COW (= Inis Bó Finne = Inishbofin) AND SAMSON DESCENDANT of Corcrán FELL ASLEEP].
      ATig.[736]: Uir sapiens et ancorita Insola Uaccae Ailbe Indsi Bó Finde <do Cianachtaib Bregh dó> [A WISE MAN AND ANCHORITE OF THE ISLAND OF THE WHITE COW Inis Bó Finne <he was of the Cianachta Breg>].

Here Dublitter's name occurs in an unusual position. Stokes added *Dublittir et Samson nepos Corcrain dormierunt* to his translation of ATig., but these words do not occur in the text. The obit of Samson is unique to AU while ATig. has missed the name of Dublitter and AFM 731 omit the whole entry. It might not be inconceivable to read the entry as the obits of the *Uir sapiens Samson* and of the *anchorita … Dublittir*. The interlined gloss in ATig. is misplaced and should refer to Conmál ua Lóchéni abbot of Clonmacnois, who died in 737.

AU 737: Conmal nepos Locheni abbas Clona maccu Nois pausat [Conmál DESCENDANT of Lóchéne ABBOT of Clonmacnois DECEASES].

ATig.[737]: Conmael hua Loichene ab Cluana mc. Noiss pausat [Conmáel ua Lóchéne abbot of Clonmacnois DECEASES].

AI [737]: Quies huí Lóchíne abb Cluana m. Nóis [REPOSE of ua Lóchéne abbot of Clonmacnois].

AClon.734: Convall or Conmoyle O'Locheny abbot of Clonvicnois Died.

AFM 732: Conamhail Ua Loichene abb Cluana muc Nóis do Ciannachtaibh Breagh … [Conamail ua Lóchéne abbot of Clonmacnois of the Cianachta Breg …].

4.   AU 737: Fælbe filius Guaire Mæl Rubi .i. heres Crosan in profundo pilagi dimersus est cum suis nautis numero .xx.ii [Faílbe SON of Guaire i.e. HEIR (Latin = coarb) of Máel Rubai of <Apor> Crossan (= Applecross) WAS DROWNED IN THE DEPTH OF THE SEA WITH HIS SAILORS TO THE NUMBER OF 22].

ATig.[737]: Failbe mac Guaire .i. haeres Mael eíre bai eiris .i. Apuircrosan in profundo filaighi demersus est cum suis nautis nuno .xxii [Faílbe mac Guaire i.e. HEIR of Máel Rubai i.e. of Apor Crossan WAS DROWNED IN THE DEPTH OF THE SEA WITH HIS SAILORS TO THE NUMBER OF 22].

AClon.734: The work done in Upercroossann was sunk in the Debth of the sea & certaine sea-fareing men to the number of 22.

AFM 732: Failbhe mac Guaire comharba Maoile Rubha do bháthadh go bfoirinn a luinge amaille fris. Dias ar fichit a llíon [Faílbe mac Guaire coarb of Máel Rubai drowned with the crew of his ship along with him, 22 their number].

Here, the hyperbaton *Máel Rubi heres Crossan* gave the scribes of the annals some difficulty. The scribe of AU seems to have been somewhat puzzled by the word-order and has inserted an *.i.* at the wrong point. ATig. have garbled the entry and AClon. have apparently misinterpreted *Apor* as Irish *opair* (suggesting that the word, which is not in AU, occurred twice in the exemplar) and missed the personal names altogether, whereas AFM have undertsood the sense but omitted the reference to Applecross. For *in profundo pilagi* compare Muirchú's Preface: *in hoc periculossum et profundum narrationis sanctae pylagus.*[10]

Two examples from the ninth century are:

AU 817: Mors Dathail episcopi scribae 7 ancoritæ hui Duibleni [DEATH of Dathal BISHOP SCRIBE AND ANCHORITE descendant of Duibléne].

In this entry unique to AU there is ambiguity as to whether it represents one obit or two – i.e. that of Dathal the bishop and scribe and that of Ua Duibléni the anchorite. If one obit is intended there is hyperbaton; if two, a chiasmus of the type AabB.

AU 869: Martan abbas Cluana maccu Nois 7 Daiminnsi scriba Niallán episcopus Slane dormierunt [Martan ABBOT of Clonmacnois and SCRIBE of Devenish [and] Niallán BISHOP of Slane FELL ASLEEP].

10 L. Bieler (ed.), *The Patrician texts in the Book of Armagh* (Dublin 1979) p. 62.

CS [869]: Martan do Dartraigib Daiminnsi ab Cluana muc Nois ocus Daiminnse quieuit [Martan of the Dartraige of Devenish abbot of Clonmacnois and of Devenish RESTED].

AR §258: Martan ab Cluana Mc. Nois 7 Daiminsi scriba Niallan episcopus Slaine dormierunt [Martan abbot of Clonmacnois and SCRIBE of Devenish [and] Niallán BISHOP of Slane FELL ASLEEP].

FA §367: Niallan epscop Slaine obiit [Niallán bishop of Slane MET HIS DEATH].

AFM 867: Niallán epscop Sláine d'écc. … Martan abb Cluana mic Nóis & Daimhinsi scribhnidh eisidhe do Dhartraighibh Dhaimhnisi a chenél [Niallán bishop of Slane dies. … Martan abbot of Clonmacnois and of Devenish: he was a scribe of the Dartraige of Devenish his race].

Again there could be ambiguity as to whether this represents two obits or three – i.e. that of Martan abbot of Clonmacnois and that of Niallán scribe of Devenish together with that of an unnamed bishop of Slane. But most likely the first obit is that of Martan, abbot of Clonmacnois and scribe of Devenish, with chiasmus of the type AabB in his titles.

These are the latest examples that I have so far found in the Annals of Ulster. Otherwise the devices of chiasmus and hyperbaton seem peculiar to the eighth century, with two possible occurrences in the seventh (at 658 and 687).

For hyperbaton elsewhere in the eighth century see Muirchú (though I suspect the paragraph is not his work), where Bieler reads (following a transposition made by Gwynn): *Orientales et nepotes Neill contra Ultu acriter ad certamen ruunt.*[11] This is an unnecessary emendation of the manuscript reading: *Orientales et contra Ultu Nepotes Neill acriter ad certamen ruunt.* On p. 19 Bieler remarks: '… in his use of rhetorical devices, for example of the hyperbaton, Muirchú is far more restrained than is Adamnán', adding in a footnote: 'I note that *hyperbaton* … … is rather frequent (23 instances) from I 29 (BII 1) onwards, but almost non-existent in the earlier part. This could have some significance. Had Muirchú's style at one time come under the influence of Adamnán's?' But the evidence of Probus' *Vita Patricii* and of the Novara epitome of Muirchú together with that of the *Vita Tertia* makes it almost certain that Muirchú (or whoever was responsible for Book II of his Life of Patrick) made no mention of the Uí Néill in his account of the contest for the saint's body. Stylistic grounds alone would make us suspect that they have been dragged into the narrative by the hair of their heads.[12]

An example in eighth-century Old Irish verse occurs in Fíacc's Hymn (*Thesaurus Palaeohibernicus*, ii, p.309):

macc Calpuirn, maicc Fhotide
haue[13] deochain Odissi

where we should read *haui* and translate 'son of Calpurn mac Fotide, of the deacon grandson of Odissus', not with Stokes and Strachan 'a descendant of the deacon Odisse'. Whereas Calpuirn and Fotide have been naturalised into Irish (from *Calpurnius* and *Potitus*) Odissi is a Latin genitive and is accented on the penultimate, thus alliterating with *deochain*. Hyperbaton later in the same

11 Ibid. p.120.   12 On word order in seventh-century hagiography and on the different styles of Muirchú and Adamnán, see J.-M. Picard, 'Sur l'ordre des mots dans la prose latine des hagiographes irlandais du VIIe siècle' in D. Conso, N. Fick and B. Poulle, *Mélanges François Kerlouégan* (Paris 1994) pp 483–500.   13 MSS hóa.

text also misled the editors (p. 317) into translating *tuatha adortais síde* as 'the peoples used to worship *síde*' instead of 'they used to worship the peoples of the *síd*'.

Instances of Latin forms of Irish secular personal names

The name of Selbach of Cenél Loairn occurs with Latin declensional endings in several entries.

> AU 712: Obsesio Aberte apud Selbachum [THE SIEGE of Abert BY SELBACHUS (= Selbach)].

This entry is unique to AU.

> AU 714: Dun Ollaigh construitur apud Selbachum.
> ATig.[714]: Dun Ollaig construitur apud Selbacum [Dún Ollaig (Dunolly) IS BUILT BY SELBACHUS].

> AU 719: Bellum maritimum Ardæ Nesbi inter Dunchad mBecc cum Genere Gabrain 7 Selbachum cum Genere Loairn 7 uersum est super Selbachum prid Non. Septimbris <–l– Octimbris> die .ui. feriæ in quo quidam comites conruerunt [THE SEA BATTLE of Ard Nesbi BETWEEN Dúnchad Bec WITH THE RACE of Gabrán (= Cenél nGabráin) AND SELBACHUS WITH THE RACE of Loarn (= Cenél Loairn) AND SELBACHUS WAS OVERTHROWN ON THE DAY BEFORE THE NONES OF SEPTEMBER (= 4 September) <OR OCTOBER (= 6 October)> ON THE 6TH FERIA (= Friday) IN WHICH SOME <of his> COMPANIONS SUCCUMBED].
> ATig.[719]: Cath maritimum Ardde Anesbí eter Dunchadh mBecc cum Genire Gabraín 7 Selbaccum # Genere Loairn et uersum est super Selbacom .ii. Nonas Octimbris die septime feriae in quo quidam comites corruerunt [THE SEA battle of Arda Anesbi […] between Dúnchad Bec WITH THE RACE of Gabrán and SELBACHUS <with> THE RACE of Loarn AND SELBACHUS WAS OVERTHROWN ON THE 2ND OF THE NONES OF OCTOBER (= 6 October) ON THE 7TH FERIA (= Saturday) IN WHICH SOME <of his> COMPANIONS SUCCUMBED].

> AU 727: Congressio Irrois Foichnæ ubi quidam ceciderunt dendibh Airgiallaib inter Selbacham 7 familiam Echdach nepotis Domnaill [THE ENCOUNTER of Irros Foichne BETWEEN SELBACHUS AND THE HOUSEHOLD of Eochaid THE DESCENDANT of Domnall WHERE SOME of the Airgialla FELL].

This entry is unique to AU.

But his name is given in the Irish genitive at 723, 733 and 736 (where note that Bruide is Latinised as *Brudeum* and *Brudeus*) and in the nominative at his obit in 730:

> AU 723: Clericatus Selbaich [RELIGIOUS RETIREMENT of Selbach].
> ATig.[723]: Clericatus Selbaigh reghes Dal Ríada [RELIGIOUS RETIREMENT of Selbach KING of Dál Riata].
> AFM 719: Sealbhach tighearna Dal Riada do dhol i cclercecht [Selbach lord of Dál Riata goes into religious retirement].

AU 733: Dungal m. Selbaich dehonorauit Toraich cum traxit Brudeum ex ea 7 eadem uice Insola Cuilenrigi inuassit. <cuiren rigi> [Dúngal mac Selbaig DISHONOURED TORY WHEN HE DRAGGED BRUDEUS (= Bruide) FROM IT AND ON THE SAME OCCASION HE INVADED THE ISLAND of Cuilenrige <Cuirenrigi> (Malin Head?)].

ATig.[733]: Dungal mac Selbaig do-ríndi toisc a Toraigh 7 toisc aile a nInis Cuirennrighe cor airg [Dúngal mac Selbaig made an expedition to Tory and another expedition to Inis Cuirenrige and plundered it].

This entry does not occur in AFM.

AU 736: Oengus m. Fergusso rex Pictorum uastauit regiones Dail Riatai 7 obtenuit Dun At 7 combussit Creic 7 duos filios Selbaich catenis alligauit .i. Donngal 7 Feradach 7 paulo post Brudeus m. Oengusa filii Fergusso obit [Óengus mac Fergusa KING OF THE PICTS RAVAGED THE TERRITORIES of Dál Riata AND OCCUPIED Dunadd AND BURNED Creic AND BOUND THE TWO SONS of Selbach WITH CHAINS i.e. Donngal and Feradach AND SHORTLY AFTERWARDS BRUDEUS (= Bruide) son of Óengus SON of Fergus MET HIS DEATH].

ATig.[736]: Aengus mac Fergusa rex Picctorum uastauit regionis Dail Riata et obtenuit Dun Ad et compuisit Creic et duos filios Selbaiche cathensiss aligauit .i. Dondgal et Feradach et pauló prae Brudeus mac Aengusa mc. Fergusa obit.

AClon.733: Enos mcffergos K. of Picts wasted the Region of Dalriada or Redshankes tooke Dunatt and burnt Cregg & bound the 2 sonnes of Sealuy with coardes Dungall and fferaagh. A little while after Brudeus the son of Enos who was son of †Cron Moyle mcColgann abbot of Lusk Died.† ffergus died.

AClon. have wrongly inserted the obit of Crundmáel mac Colgen abbot of Lusk into the middle of this entry.

AU 730: Bran filius Eugain Selbach m. Fercair mortui sunt [Bran son of Eógan [and] Selbach mac Ferchair died].

This entry is unique to AU.

Compare the entries on Nechtan, king of the Picts:

AU 717: Expulsio familiæ Iæ trans Dorsum Brittaniæ a Nectano rege [EXPULSION OF THE HOUSEHOLD (= community) OF IONA ACROSS THE RIDGE OF BRITAIN (Latin = Druim nAlban) BY NECTANUS (= Nechtan) THE KING].

ATig.[717]: Expulsio Familiæ Íe tras dorms Britonie a Nectono rege.

CS [713]: Expulsio familiae Iae trans Dorsum Britaniae a Nectonio rege.

AR §170: Expulsio familiae Iae trans dorsum Britanniae a Nechtano rege.

The names of the Pictish Bruide and Talorc are also Latinised at:

AU 731: Bellum inter filium Oengussa 7 filium Congussa sed Brudeus uicit Talorcum fugientem [A BATTLE BEWEEN THE SON of Óengus AND THE SON of Congus BUT BRUDEUS (= Bruide) CONQUERED THE FLEEING TALORCUS (= Talorc)].

ATig.[731]: Cath eter mac Aengusa 7 mac Congusa sunt. Bruidhens uicit Talorcum fugentem [A battle beween the son of Óengus and the son of Congus. BRUIDEUS CONQUERED THE FLEEING TALORCUS].

AClon.728: There was a battle between the sonn of Enos and the son of Congus where Brudeus vanquished Tolorg flying.

Also note in a purely Irish context:

AU 737: Congressio inuicem inter Nepotes Aedho Slane ubi Conaing m. Amalghaidh Cernachum uicit 7 Cathal m. Aedho cecidit. Iuxta Lapidem Ailbe ab orientali parte gesta est [AN ENCOUNTER BETWEEN THE DESCENDANTS of Áed Sláine (= Síl nÁeda Sláine) THEMSELVES WHERE Conaing mac Amalgada CONQUERED CERNACHUS (= Cernach) and Cathal mac Áeda FELL. IT WAS WAGED BESIDE THE STONE of Ailbe (= Lia Ailbe) TO THE EAST].

ATig.[737]: Congresió inuitcem inter Nepotes Aeda Slaine ubi Conaing mac Amalgaidh Cearnacum uicit et Catal mac Aedha cecidit iuxta Lapitem Ailbe ab orientaili pairtí gesta est [AN ENCOUNTER WAS WAGED BESIDE THE STONE of Ailbe to the EAST BETWEEN THE DESCENDANTS of Áed Sláine THEMSELVES WHERE Conaing mac Amalgada CONQUERED CERNACHUS and Cathal mac Áeda FELL].

AFM 732: Scainnear etir Shiol Aodha Sláine in ro marbhadh Cathal mac Aodha don taobh thoir do Lícc Ailbhe la Conaing mac Amhalgadha [A skirmish between the Síl nÁeda Sláine in which Cathal mac Áeda was killed on the eastern side of Lia Ailbe by Conaing mac Amalgada].

The Four Masters have omitted all mention of Cernach.

All of these entries (with the possible exception of the last) derive from the Iona annals, the Latinity of which merits further examination. As Cú Chuimme of Iona died in 747 (his collaborator Ruben died in 725) he may have been responsible for some of the instances of chiasmus and hyperbaton in the annals.

St Gallen and the Irish in the early Middle Ages

MICHAEL RICHTER

The activity of Irishmen outside Ireland in the time between the late sixth and the twelfth centuries is well researched[1] even though not always sufficiently appreciated, especially outside Ireland. In any case, the Irish were the most influential foreign ethnic group linked to the Christian religion in early medieval continental Europe, and they have contributed in manyfold ways to the shaping of this dynamic part of the world. But the benefit was not one-sided. For we still have, from the continent, a considerable corpus of scholarly work written in the Old Irish language. Anyone who begins to study Old Irish systematically is exposed to glosses marked variously as Wb (for Würzburg), Ml (for Milan, material mainly from Bobbio), Ag (*Augiensis*, one of the early names for Reichenau), Sg (for St Gallen). This and other, less extensive, material has been gathered in two substantial volumes in the *Thesaurus Palaeohibernicus* which appeared almost exactly a century ago.[2]

It is obvious that this work of glossing Latin texts in Irish was done by scholars educated in Irish and Latin, and it is equally obvious that the glossing was done for the benefit of other scholars, more precisely scholars who also had a knowledge of Old Irish since the Irish material was intended to throw light on the Latin text that was glossed. Unfortunately the work of glossing was normally done anonymously. Of the four places mentioned above, only one, Bobbio, has an impeccable Irish pedigree, originating in the last phase of the work of Columbanus who died as abbot of Bobbio in 615. By contrast, the monastery of Reichenau, little as we know for certain of its early history,[3] was apparently a foundation by a local Alamannic person; its first abbot, Pirmin (724–727), was not an Irish *peregrinus*.[4] The early history of the bishopric of Würzburg (where we do not know for certain of any early monastery to be associated with Kilian and his companions who were martyred in 687) is Anglo-Saxon/Frankish rather than Irish. Würzburg emerges in 742 as the seat of a bishopric, and its first bishop was Burghard.[5] How writings in Old Irish came to be in these places has not been fully elucidated.

The following contribution will concentrate on one of these major places, St Gallen It is rightly famous, and the high degree of institutional continuity has had the effect that much St Gallen material has been there for many centuries. St Gallen has been a favourite object of international research, so much so that one might hold that with all the work done on the Irish there over the

---

1 The most comprehensive review is Heinz Löwe (ed.), *Die Iren und Europa im früheren Mittelalter* (Stuttgart 1982). For a cartographical representation see T.W. Moody, F.X. Martin, F.J. Byrne (eds), *A new history of Ireland, vol. IX, maps, genealogies, lists* (Oxford 1984) map 17; for a recent discussion of the important Carolingian period see M. Garrison, 'The English and the Irish at the court of Charlemagne', in P.L. Butzer et al. (eds), *Karl der Große und sein Nachwirken. 1200 Jahre Kultur und Wissenschaft in Europa* (Turnhout 1997) pp 97–123. **2** *Thesaurus Palaeohibernicus*, ed. W. Stokes and J. Strachan, originally 1902, repr. Dublin 1975. **3** M. Richter, 'Neues zu den Anfängen des Klosters Reichenau', *Zeitschrift für die Geschichte des Oberrheins* 146 (1996) pp 1–18. **4** See the discussion by A. Angenendt, *Monachi peregrini. Studien zu Pirmin und den monastischen Vorstellungen des frühen Mittelalters* (Munich 1972) who remains ultimately ambivalent about Pirmin's origins. **5** A. Wendehorst, *Das Bistum Würzburg. Teil 1. Die Bischofsreihe bis 1254* (Berlin 1962).

past century, by Heinrich Zimmer,[6] J.M. Clark[7] or Johannes Duft,[8] to name only the most prominent scholars who have published in this field, everything that can be stated has been written. However, this is not the case; while I do not have any new sources to analyse, a review of the available studies shows that new insights are possible. Scholarly work[9] is prone to fashion, and the imaginative dimension in the historian's craft which is indispensable differs from scholar to scholar, as does their academic background and indeed purpose. In the following pages I shall concentrate only on those issues that appear to yield new insights.

Gallus

The patron of the monastery of St Gallen, Gallus, belonged to the group of monks under the guidance of Columbanus who had been expelled from Burgundy around 610 and who eventually turned towards northern Italy. En route, south of Lake Constance, there arose a quarrel between Columbanus and Gallus. Significantly, this incident is not mentioned in the *Vita Columbani* by Jonas[10] presumably because it would have reflected poorly on Columbanus as well as on Gallus. It is found instead, and is indeed indispensable here, in the early hagiographical work on Gallus. It can be reconstructed from three works, the fragmentary anonymous *Vita vetustissima*, and the completely transmitted ninth-century writings from the Reichenau authors Wetti (died 824) and Walahfrid Strabo (died 849).[11] Gallus overstepped one of the central tenets of early Irish monastic principles, unconditional and unresentful obedience to the abbot.[12] He refused to remain part of the group heading south across the Alps, due to ill health, according to Wetti and Walahfrid. In response, Columbanus forbade Gallus to say mass as long as he, Columbanus, was alive. Wetti writes that Columbanus excommunicated Gallus, uncharacteristically, *cum hilaritate* (ch. 9).[13] According to the *Vita vetustissima*, Gallus showed obedience at least in this sanction. The surviving text opens with the account that he had a dream informing him that Columbanus had died. After waking he sent messengers to Italy who came back with the message that this was indeed the case. Gallus was free to resume the celebration of mass.

There are many things about Gallus which we do not know. His Irish descent has been questioned,[14] and indeed his name is not Irish. However, both Wetti and Walahfrid present him as an Irishman of noble descent and a follower of Columbanus. One ninth-century manuscript

---

6 See esp. Heinrich Zimmer, 'Über die Bedeutung des irischen Elements für die mittelalterliche Kultur', *Preußische Jahrbücher* 59 (1887) pp 27–59.   **7** J.M. Clark, *The abbey of St Gall as a centre of literature and art* (Cambridge 1926). **8** His most detailed discussion, inconsiderably modified in later publications, is in Johannes Duft, P. Meyer, *Die irischen Miniaturen der Stiftsbibliothek St Gallen* (Olten 1953) introduction. The publications of Johannes Duft down to 1979 are listed in O.P. Clavadetscher et al. (eds), *Florilegium Sangallense. Festschrift für Johannes Duft zum 65. Geburtstag* (Sigmaringen 1980) pp 289–301.   **9** The bibliographical references in what follows are highly selective but can be taken as guides to earlier works.   **10** B. Krusch (ed.), *Ionae Vitae Sanctorum Columbani, Vedastis, Iohannis*, MGH SRG us, 1905. Gallus is mentioned in that Vita only once, as an informant of Jonas, ch. 11, pp 171–72.   **11** *MGH SRM* 4, pp 251–56 (*vetustissima*, for which see also below, note 62), 257–89 (Wetti), 280–357 (Walahfrid). On the three texts see W. Berschin, 'Gallus abbas vindicatus', *Historisches Jahrbuch* 95 (1975) pp 257–77 as well as W. Berschin, *Biographie und Epochenstil* III, (Stuttgart 1991) esp. pp 282–303. **12** Characteristically, Columbanus's *Regula monachorum* opens with a chapter *De oboedientia*, ed. G.S.M. Walker (Dublin 1958) p. 122. **13** Berschin does not know of any other instance of the excommunication of a future saint, *Epochenstil* III, p. 27; however, this is what happened to Colum Cille, see *Adomnán's Life of Columba*, ed. A.O. Anderson and M.O. Anderson (Edinburgh 1961) III, 3, pp 468ff.   **14** See B. and H. Helbling, 'Der Heilige Gallus in der Geschichte', *Schweizerische Zeitschrift für Geschichte* 12 (1962) pp 1–62.

from St Gallen, Cod. 553, gives a brief account of his Irish background, allegedly provided by Irishmen in the monastery: *Ista sunt ergo nomina venerabilium virorum, quos aliqui venerabiles Scotti nobis legendo conprobaverunt ... < rex Kethérnach> genuit filium nimia bonitate pollentem, qui Callehc nuncupatus fuerat in eorum lingua, et apud Latinos Gallus vocitatus.*[15] This entry was viewed by its nineteenth-century editor as *fabulosa*, which it may well be. On the other hand, it attests the existence, temporary or more permanent, of Irishmen in St Gallen who were mindful of their compatriot. On a different basis and more reliably, a Romano-Frankish origin of Gallus is highly unlikely. Columbanus's earliest biographer, Jonas, reports that when Columbanus was expelled from Burgundy he was not allowed to take the Frankish members of his community with him but only those he had brought: *nequaquam hinc se sequi alios permissuros, nisi eos quos sui ortus terra dederat, vel qui e Britannica arva ipsum secuti fuerant; ceteros, qui Gallico orti solo, preceptis esse regiis inibi remansuros.*[16] This passage, hardly ever referred to in the literature, receives some kind of further credibility from the letter which Columbanus wrote to the brethren he had left behind on his expulsion from Burgundy.[17] Thus here we have circumstantial evidence for considering Gallus as not Romano-Frankish. Later Irish visitors of St Gallen were said to go there to visit their compatriot.[18]

We know next to nothing about Gallus after the excommunication had lapsed, nor the date or circumstances of his death. The official commemoration has settled for 16 October 651. The monastery that was to bear his name was established about two generations later, c.720.[19] Its first abbot, Otmar, was of Raetish descent, from Chur. One would hardly call him a local man, but he was certainly not a product of the milieu in which Gallus had been active. The circumstances of how Gallus came to be the patron of the monastery remain unknown. Clark posits the continuous existence of a small community living under Gallus and after him according to the rule of Columbanus and obtaining Irish manuscripts if not actually producing them.[20] There is no evidence to support these constructs.

Manuscripts

To this day the Stiftsbibliothek of St Gallen houses some of the most valuable Irish manuscripts, Irish in writing and/or in language. These manuscripts and manuscript fragments have been described more than once, and the most recent and thorough discussion comes from Johannes Duft from 1953. There is nothing I can add to this discussion as far as the palaeographical evidence is concerned. But the more general historical approach allows for some additional insights.

Isidore

By far the oldest of these manuscripts written in Irish script are small fragments of Isidore of Seville's Etymologies (Cod. Sangall. 1399a).[21] These fragments are believed to date from the mid-

15 *MGH SS* 2, 34. **16** *Vita Columbani*, ch. 20, p. 196. **17** *Sancti Columbani Opera*, ed. G.S.M. Walker, (Dublin 1957) ep. IV. This would have been the most likely constellation for Columbanus to write his *regula*, namely for the brethren left behind. For the others it was his personal authority that ruled. **18** Ekkehard, *Casus sancti Galli*, ch. 2 p. 18. **19** Clark, pp 23f. Against this Duft 1953, pp 26 ff who writes: 'Von einem klösterlichen Konvent unter Leitung eines Abtes und von einer irischen Gemeinschaft kann keine Rede sein', ibid. 26b. **20** Clark writes: 'We may safely assume that all the thirty-two *libri scottice scripti* of the old catalogue were either brought to St Gall, or were written there before the introduction of the Benedictine Rule, i.e. before the middle of the eighth century', p. 25. **21** Three fragments were

seventh century; they are the earliest preserved specimens of this text by far. If the suggested mid-seventh-century date is correct, we can say with confidence that this manuscript could not have originated from the scriptorium of the monastery of St Gallen since this monastery did not exist at the time; the same holds for the monastery of Reichenau. This strengthens the probability of the origin of that manuscript in Ireland[22] from where we have comparably accomplished manuscripts from that time,[23] and where there is independent evidence that Isidore's writings were known then.

Libri Scottice Scripti

Cod. Sangallensis 728 contains on pp 4–22 what is the oldest list of books of the monastic library, dating from the mid-ninth century.[24] All of page 4 is filled with material headed *libri scottice scripti*, containing 31 item in all:[25]

Metrum Juvenci in volumine I.
Epistolae Pauli in volumine I.
Actus Apostolorum in volumine I.
Epistolae canonicae VII in volumine I.
Tractatus Bedae in proverbia Salomonis in volumine I.
Ezechiel propheta in volumine I.
Evangelium secundum Iohannem in volumine I.
Enchiridion Augustini in volumine I.
Item Juvenci metrum in volumine I.
Apocalypsis in volumine I.
Item apocalypsis in volumine I.
Metrum Sedulii in volumine I.
De gradibus eclesiasticis in volumine I.
Arithmetica Boetii, volumen I.
Missalis in volumine I.
Vita sancti Hilarii in codicillo I.
Passio sanctorum martyrum Marcellini et Petri.
Metrum Virgilii in volumine I.
Eius glosa in altero.
Quaternio I de inventione corporis sancti Stephani.
Quaternio I de relatione translationis sancti Galli in novam eclesiam.
Bedae de arte metrica in quaternionibus.

found in 1936, the fourth in 1955, see J. Duft, 'Ein vor anderthalb Jahrhunderten entdecktes, aber damals nicht bestimmbares, dann verschollenes, jetzt wiedergefundenes irisches Isidor-Bruchstück des 7. Jhs', *Texte und Arbeiten Beuron* 31 (1955) , Anhang, pp 7–12.   **22** This is the view of B. Bischoff, *Mittelalterliche Studien* I (Stuttgart 1966) p. 180 whereas Duft, Löwe, *Iren*, p. 931 opts for Bobbio.   **23** Cf. especially the Eusebius-Rufinus fragment discovered in 1984, for which see B. Bischoff and V. Brown, 'Addenda to the *Codices Latini Antiquiores*', *Mediaeval Studies* 47 (1985) *CLA* A 1864, p. 348f.   **24** The following list is taken from Paul Lehmann, *Mittelalterliche Bibliothekskataloge Deutschlands und der Schweiz. Erster Band, Die Bistümer Konstanz und Chur* (München 1918, repr. 1969), pp 66–82, here p. 72, which expands the abbreviations throughout. It is also found in Duft 1953, p. 41 and Duft 1982, p. 923. Duft consistently discusses the later fate of these items but not the issues brought up here below.   **25** This page is reproduced in Löwe, *Iren*, vol. 2, plate 20.

> Instructio eclesiastici ordinis in codicillo I.
> Liber I genesis in quaternionibus.
> Actus apostolorum et apocalypsis in volumine I veteri.
> Quaternio I in natali innocentium legenda.
> Orationes et sententiae variae in volumine I.
> Orationes in quaternionibus.
> Expositio in cantica canticorum in quaternionibus II.
> Item in regum quaternio I.

We notice the spelling *eclesia-* which occurs twice in our list. It is a kind of spelling not uncommon with Irish authors.

It is obvious from the list that the term *scottice* in the heading refers to the script, not the language of the manuscripts. Naturally, this list has caught scholars' attention for a long time, and various suggestions have been made concerning these items in Irish script. With one exception to be treated shortly, the titles are very general,[26] and the manuscripts listed could have been written by scribes trained in Irish script anywhere, though preferably in an Irish centre. There is, however, one item that is specifically associated with St Gallen: *Quaternio I de relatione translationis sancti Galli in novam eclesiam.* There were two 'new' churches in St Gallen after Gallus's death: the stone building erected under Otmar after 719 and the rebuilding of the church of St Gallen under abbot Gozbert between 830 and 837.[27] The second rebuilding is associated with the famous drawing of the layout of a monastery which was carried out in Reichenau *c.*816, for St Gallen, where the original is still preserved.[28] The account of the translation of Gallus is most likely to be associated with this second rebuilding[29] and a medium-term effect of the hagiography from Wetti's pen.[30] Here we have evidence, admittedly of an indirect kind, that writing in Irish script was practiced in St Gallen in the second quarter of the ninth century, and it is reasonable to assume that the scribe came to St Gallen after he had acquired this skill. In this case it is highly plausible that more of the *libri scottice scripti* may have been written in the scriptorium of St Gallen.[31] This of course would be of greatest interest to historians as well as palaeographers.

We may add that according to Notker Balbulus (d. 916), another famous scholar of St Gallen, Walahfrid had written his Life of Gallus on the initiative of the same abbot Gozbert who initiated the rebuilding of the monastic church.[32] It would thus appear that Walahfrid's Life of Gallus and the *Relatio translationis sancti Galli in novam eclesiam* were written very close to each other. Obviously the contacts between Reichenau and St Gallen were particularly close then. It is worth mentioning here that there was apparently also close contact between Reichenau and the Irish world, as attested by Walahfrid's poem on the martyrdom of Blathmac on Iona whose death the Annals of Ulster record under the year 825.[33]

---

26 It may be pointed out that the seven Catholic Epistles were the object of Irish exegetes in the seventh century, see M. Richter, *Ireland and her neighbours in the seventh century* (Dublin and New York 1999) pp 192f.   **27** Duft 1953 suggests the year 835 but fails to draw the obvious conclusions from the item.   **28** J. Duft (ed.), *Studien und Forschungen zum St Galler Klosterplan* (St Gallen 1962).   **29** On the Gallus crypt of this church see J. Gantner, A. Reinle, *Kunstgeschichte der Schweiz*, vol. I (Frauenfeld 1968) pp 145f. For more detail see H.R. Sennhauser, *Das Münster des Abtes Gozbert (816–37) und seine Ausmalung unter Hartmut* (St Gallen 1988).   **30** The explicit information concerning the script of this work virtually excludes it having been written under abbot Otmar whose community would appear to have been exclusively Alemannic.   **31** On the subsequent fate of these *libri scottice scripti* see Duft 1953, pp 42f, and with no further suggestions Duft 1982.   **32** '*Causa autem carminis huius scribendi haec quidem erat: Gozpertus abbas noster Walafrido Augiae abbati vitam sancti Galli a Scotis semilatinis corruptius scriptam …*', *Versus Sangallenses, MGH, PL* 4, p. 1096, 6–9. Notker's text is quoted and discussed more fully below.   **33** *Versus Strabi de*

Priscian

For scholars of Old Irish the richest manuscript from St Gallen is undoubtedly Cod. Sangallensis 904, containing a substantial part of Priscian's grammar and glossed in Old Irish.[34] It is one of the handful of manuscripts containing the bulk of Old Irish material. In marginal entries the names of several Irish scribes are given: *Calvus Patricii* (p. 157), *Coibbre* (p. 194), *Finguine* (p. 182), *Donngus* (p. 194, 207), *Cobthach* (p. 219).[35] An unnamed scribe declares: *do inis maddoc dún .i. meisse 7 coibbre.*[36] The manuscript as well as the Irish glosses are believed to have been produced in Ireland, possibly at Nendrum or Bangor.[37] Ludwig Traube associated its later history with the circle of Sedulius at Liège.[38] When it came to St Gallen is not clear; Duft suggests that this may have happened as late as the tenth century.[39]

Both Johannes Duft[40] and Bernhard Bischoff[41] argued strongly against the idea that Irish script was ever written at St Gallen, or any items in the Irish language. We have shown that there was at least one item produced in St Gallen in Irish script in the second quarter of the ninth century, and this in turn increases the plausibility that others of the *libri Scottice scripti* had been produced there as well.

We may add here another observation. The scriptorium of St Gallen was one of the earliest continental scriptoria where *scriptura continua* began to be replaced by leaving space between words. This scribal practice is now held to have been developed first in Irish scriptoria in the seventh century, most likely inspired by the layout of Syriac Gospel books.[42] The earliest St Gallen manuscript to show this feature is Cod. Sangallensis 913, the *Vocabularius Sancti Galli* of c.780–90.[43] It should be emphasized that the same feature is also visible in the list of the *libri scottice scripti* which was written in Caroline script.

These ideas might appear in a somewhat different light when we turn to the Irish monks who must be associated with this monastery in the ninth century.

Irish monks in St Gallen in the ninth century

The personnel of the monastery of St Gallen in the early Middle Ages is unusually fully attested. There have survived the *libri confraternitatum,* of St Gallen as well as of other neighbouring monasteries, the St Gallen *Necrologia,* the book of monastic professions as well as a great number of charters providing altogether many thousands of names. Some of these names are unmistakably Irish, and in most cases we get a bare mention of the name in one or another of the sources mentioned. Other names, not Irish, are known from other sources to be those of Irish monks; one

beati Blaithmaic vita et fine, MGH, PL II (Berlin 1885) pp 297–301. Walahfrid's Latinity here is particularly inappropriate to the subject but his language deserves closer analysis.   **34** *Thes.* II, 49–224. See most recently R. Hofman, *The Sankt Gall Priscian commentary,* 2 vols (Münster 1996) and for the description of the manuscript vol. I, p. 12ff.   **35** Lastly Duft 1953, p. 73. He lists another Irish name, *Fogella,* but see *Thes.* II, xxi, noted 6: 'it seems rather a verb'.   **36** See *Thes.* II, p. xxi.   **37** Hofman, pp 22f.   **38** Ludwig Traube, 'O Roma nobilis. Philologische Untersuchungen aus dem Mittelalter', *Abhandlungen der Akademie der Wissenschaften München* 19 II (1891) pp 299–395, esp. 338 ff.   **39** Duft 1953, 73b.   **40** Duft 1953 surprisingly does not comment on the work on the translation of Gallus. He writes on the other Irish manuscripts now in St Gallen: 'Für die früher oft geäußerte Vermutung, sie seien teilweise in St Gallen selbst von Iren geschrieben und gemalt worden, läßt sich weder in den Handschriften noch in der lokalen Geschichte irgendein Hinweis finden'. p. 67b.   **41** *Mittelalterliche Studien* III, p. 47: 'von keiner Handschrift, von keiner Glosse oder Korrektur in irischer Schrift läßt sich beweisen, daß sie in St Gallen selbst geschrieben wäre'.   **42** For a thorough account of this phenomenon see P. Saenger, *Space between words. The origins of silent reading* (Stanford 1997) p. 83 and see Index s. v. Ireland.   **43** Saenger p. 103.

would think that there may have been yet more Irishmen in the community. The vast majority of the names are Germanic, showing that the local monks, unlike most Irish monks,[44] did not assume specific Christian monastic names. Generally speaking, the Irish element was small, but this does not imply that it was for that reason insignificant.

The Book of Confraternities of St Gallen lists under the heading ITEM CLERICORUM a Maeltuili (I, 43/19).[45] In the same manuscript, among the monks who professed obedience to Abbot Werdo (784–812), there occurs a Maelchomber (I 391/9);[46] he is likewise listed (Mealchomber) in the Book of Confraternities of Reichenau under the heading NOMINA FRATRUM DE MONASTERIO SANCTI GALLI CONFESSORIS (II, 49/26).[47] This name is also listed in the St Gallen necrology under Jan. 28.[48] In the Book of Confraternities of Reichenau, in the column adjacent to Mealchomber, we find a Marcellus alias Moengal (II, 49/23);[49] Marcellus m appears likewise as a monk of St Gallen in the Book of Confraternities of Pfäfers. (III, 31/20).[50] Marcellus/Moengal does not occur in the St Gallen Book of Confraternities; on the other hand, his death is listed under 30 September in the necrology of St Gallen: (*Ob. Moengal*) *cognomento Marcelli, viri doctissimi et optimi.*[51] The entries in these documents do not give any indication of the precise years during which these Irish monks were part of the St Gallen community. We will come back to Marcellus/Moengal anon. From the entries listed here it appears that the Book of Confraternities of St Gallen is incomplete as far as their own community is concerned.

It should be mentioned at least in passing that the St Gallen necrology commemorates a number of Irish clerics who had not been part of the community. These are, in chronological order:

> Jan. 6 Macharius abb. et Scotus pie memorie. Dominus Abb. et Scotus.
>   Adamnanus diac. et Scotus
> June 3 Ob. Faillani Scotti doctissimi et benignissimi magistri
> July 2 Ob. Clementis Scotti
> Sept. 12 Et est ob. Dubsalani Scoti m atque pb
> Oct. 17 Et ob. dominus abb. et Scottus Gallus
> Nov. 16 Gregorius pie memorie abb. et Scotus
> Nov. 19 Brendanus m. et Scottus
> Nov. 27 David m. et Scotus ob.

While it cannot be stated in each case when these names were entered precisely, the commemoration of Irish ecclesiastics from outside the community would have been facilitated both by the Irish patron of the monastery and by Irish members of the community.

---

44 An exceptional case is Gallus. 45 P. Piper (ed.), *Libri confraternitatum Sancti Galli, Augiensis, Fabariensis, MGH NG* (Berlin 1884) p. 25. A man of that name is listed in the *Annals of Ulster*, s.a. 871.7. 46 Ibid., p. 127. This part of the St Gallen manuscript has been edited in facsimile: P.M. Krieg, *Das Professbuch der Abtei St. Gallen* (Augsburg 1931). Our entry is on plate XVII. It would appear to be in the same hand as the previous and the following entries and thus not an autograph. 47 Ed. Piper, p. 169. 48 *MGH NG, I. Dioceses Augustensis, Constantiensis, Curiensis*, ed. F.L. Baumann (Berlin 1888, repr. Munich 1983) p. 466. 49 Ed. Piper p. 169. This Reichenau list has been re-edited in facsimile: J. Autenrieth, D. Geuenich und K. Schmid (eds), *Das Verbrüderungsbuch der Abtei Reichenau, MGH Libri Memoriales et Necrologia Nova Series* I (Hannover 1979) here p. 11 B3. 50 Ed. Piper, p. 364. 51 Ed. Baumann, p. 481. For an Irish flavour of the term *optimus* in connection with learning see M. Richter, *The formation of the medieval West Studies in the oral culture of the barbarians* (Dublin and

Moengal

Whereas the Irish monks Maeltuile and Maelchomber remain mere names to us, Marcellus/
Moengal is much better known and deserves closer scrutiny. We know of only one St Gallen
monk of that name from the Books of Confraternities as well as the necrology. Thus it is plausible
to suggest, as indeed it has been done in the past, that the scribe of four St Gallen charters named
Marcellus is Marcellus/Moengal. These charters date from 853 (W 424), 854 (W 429), 855 (W 441)
and 860 (W 470).[52] To be the scribe of a charter was obviously a prestigious affair, as attested by
the phrase in W 429: *Ego itaque Marcellus indignus monachus vize Gozberti prepositi scripsi et
subscripsi.* These St Gallen charters are preserved in the original. The charters written by Marcellus
do not show Irish script but Caroline minuscule. Had Marcellus not been trained in Irish script
or was he an expert in two hands?

We have seen already that at his death (the year of which is unknown) Marcellus was commemorated for his considerable learning.[53] In this respect it is not surprising that his learning was
referred to by a later learned member of the St Gallen community, Notker Balbulus ('the
stammerer') who died in 916. Here we must refer to an account from his pen on Gallus, written
*c.*885.[54] In his introduction Notker states his reason for writing yet another account on Gallus:
*Causa autem carminis huius scribendi haec quidem erat: Gozpertus abbas noster Walafrido Augiae
abbati vitam sancti Galli a Scotis semilatinis corruptius scriptam, ut facundia sua, qua ipse prae aliis
tunc temporis diffamatus est, luculentioris leporis stilo describeret, iniunxit.*[55] We have seen above that
the line of dependence in the various lives of Gallus was different: first the fragmentary anonymous *Vita vetustissima*, then the prose account by Wetti, thereafter the account by Walahfrid,
drawing on Wetti as well as the *Vita vetustissima*. Notker now presents what could be taken as the
result of the developing collective memory of the community of St Gallen: Walahfrid was asked
to improve on a version written by Irishmen in poor Latin. In the eyes of Notker, Latin stylishness
was a relative term: as his fellow-scholar Tuotila[56] pointed out to him in conversation, Walahfrid's
text contained several passages in which the verb forms of the vernacular (here apparently
German[57]) showed that Walahfrid as a Latin scholar was overated.

Obviously, the education of the school of St Gallen had improved in the second half of the
ninth century, and this was due, to no small extent, to the learning brought there by Marcellus.
For in a passage right at the beginning of his account Notker tells: *At vero quinque hos post illum
Marcellus Scotus, Moengal Ibernice vocatus, (cum) Marco quidem episcopo avunculo apud nos
commanens septem liberalibus instruxerat artibus. Quorum tandem singuli singulares columpnae facti
sunt monasterii sancti Galli, ut in cantilenis ipsorum dulcisonis, quibus singulus eorum apud nos
adscriptus est, sciolis apparet.*[58]

New York 1994) pp 203 f.   **52** W refers to H. Wartmann (ed.), *Urkundenbuch der Abteil Sankt Gallen*, vol. II (Zürich
1866). Bernhard Bischoff points out that a bilingual psalter, in Greek and Latin, now preserved in Basel, contains a
marginal entry next to Ps 30: *hucusque scripsi. Hic incipit ad Marcellum nunc.* 'Irische Schreiber im Karolingerreich',
in id., *Mittelalterliche Studien* III (Stuttgart 1981) p. 46.   **53** However, he should not be credited with the introduction
of word separation into the scriptorium of St Gallen as does Saenger, p. 111.   **54** See Berschin, *Biographie und
Epochenstil* II (Stuttgart 1988) p. 99.   **55** *MGH PL* IV, 1096 l. 6–9. A new edition of this text has been provided by
W. Berschin, 'Notkers *Metrum de vita sancti Galli*. Einleitung und Edition', in: *Florilegium Sangallense* (FS Johannes
Duft) pp 71–121. Since this work is less accessible than the *MGH*, I quote according to the older edition.
56 E. Schlumpff, *Tuotila, Mönch und Künstler* (St Gallen 1953).   **57** Ibid., l. 22f.: *cum id quidem nec teutonicum sit nec
latinum. Cf.* also earlier l. 17f: *dissertissimum illum passim barbarico modo et more latina dixisse ut illud 'quam habuit
desponsatam', quod quidem latinius esset, si 'quam desponsaverat' posuisset?*   **58** Ibid., p. 1095.

In this account the learning of Marcellus, referred to in the necrology in general terms, is specified: he was educated in the *septem artes liberales*, and his teaching had obviously been so successful that Notker and his circle could look down on Walahfrid with condescension.

We should note that Notker is the first to inform us that Marcellus had come to the monastic community together with his uncle Marcus who was a bishop. The reliability of this information is not evident although it may be stated that Notker was active in the generation after Marcellus and was one of those who benefited, on his own admission, greatly from the latter's expertise. We have seen that Marcellus is not listed in the Book of Confraternities of St Gallen even though he was part of the community as evidenced from the other sources. On the other hand, there is a Marcus listed as a monk of St Gallen in the Book of Confraternities of Reichenau. (II, 49/15). The St Gallen necrology lists under 1 March *Marcus episcopus* which would indicate that the uncle of Marcellus whom Notker mentions did in fact end his life in St Gallen.

More than a century after Notker, we get yet more detailed information concerning bishop Marcus and his nephew Marcellus. In his *Casus Sancti Galli* Ekkehard IV reports as early as chapter 2 the arrival in the monastery of the Irish bishop Marcus and his nephew Marcellus, a great scholar. They both decided eventually to stay. In the course of time Marcellus was made teacher of the monastic school. To this point the information which Ekkehard provides is virtually identical with that of Notker. What is not in Notker is the following: Marcus and Marcellus came to St Gallen from Rome with an entourage of notable even though unspecified size, carrying a rich supply of books and valuables. Marcus and Marcellus eventually decided to remain in St Gallen, keeping the books, gold and cloth. Their companions carried on (it is not said, but presumably back to Ireland).[59]

The stark entry in the St Gallen necrology concerning the learned Marcellus and Ekkehard's florid account are separated by a gap of a century and a half. It is not necessary that Ekkehard should be charged with the invention of the additional information, but neither is it advisable to treat this additional information in Ekkehard as factual, as is often done.[60] We are dealing with some stages in the growth of a full-bodied story in the community of St Gallen where the bare bones are fleshed out with accretions over time.

Heinrich Zinmer, for one, took Ekkehard's account at face value in his attempt to explain the existence of a Pelagian manuscript on Paul in St Gallen. For good measure he also equated the books which Marcus and Marcellus brought with them to St Gallen with the *libri Scottice scripti*. Finally, he identified Marcellus as the pilgrim abbot Moengal of Bangor whose death the Annals of Ulster list in 871 in old age (*vitam senilem*) report.[61]

We have shown that the traces of Irishmen in St Gallen and their contributions are more fragmented and fragmentary. They appear as a trickle rather than a stream but cover most of the ninth century between Maelcomber and Marcellus.

---

59 *Casus Sancti Galli*, ed. K.F. Haefele (Darmstadt 1980) pp 18–20 (also *MGH* SS II): *Marcus quidam Scotigena episcopus Gallum tamquam compatriotam suum Roma rediens visitat. Comitatur eum sororis filius Moengal, postea a nostris Marcellus diminutive a Marco avunculo sic nominatus. Hic erat in divinis et humanis eruditissimus. Rogatur episcopus loco nostro aliquandiu stare allecto nepote . Diu secum deliberantes vix tamen consenserant ... Libros vero, aurum et pallia sibi et sancto Gallo retinuit. ... Remanserat episcopus cum nepote et paucis sue lingue apparitoribus. Traduntur post tempus Marcello scole claustri cum Notkero, postea cognomine Balbulo, et ceteris monachici habitus pueris ... ;* in ch. 33 of the same work Marcellus's learning is once more referred to in vitually identical terms: *Qui in divinis eque potens et humanis, septem liberales eos duxit ad artes, maxime autem ad musicam,* p. 76.   **60** Even Duft 1953, who initially expressed some reservations about Ekkehard's account, subsequently treated it as factual, pp 35f.
61 Heinrich Zimmer, *Pelagius in Irland* (Berlin 1901) pp 219–25.

Irish symptoms in the Vita Vetustissima

We have seen that the view was current in St Gallen in the later ninth century that the earliest Life of St Gallus had been written by an Irishman in Latin of poor quality. We have also mentioned that the anonymous and fragmentarily preserved *Vita vetustissima* lies behind later accounts on Gallus. The latest editor of this work, Iso Müller, has shown that the author would have been familiar with Jonas's Life of Columbanus as well as the *Regula Benedicti*.[62] We may point out that this fragment contains more possible Hibernicisms than have been recognised so far. The fragments have been dated to the second half of the ninth century by Bernhard Bischoff, earlier than anybody else.[63] They are at best a copy of the original, and this copy was most likely made at St Gallen where at that time the Irish element was particularly strong.

In chapter 1 there is the orthography *gresus* for *gressus*. Iso Müller noted throughout the text the frequent use of hypochoristic forms[64] which is likewise a frequent feature in Hiberno-Latin.[65] In chapter 3 the term *abbas* is used synonymously with princeps, and Iso Müller considered here, with reference to the *Collectio Canonum Hibernensis*, a possible Hibernicism. The term occurs of course in many more Irish texts.[66] Finally there is the use of the preposition apud (Old Irish *le*) for *cum: invenit omnia, sicut revelatum fuit magistro suo per visionem et permansit apud fratres noctem unam.*[67]

While none of these features taken on its own would point to an Irish author of the *Vita vetustissima*, the cumulative evidence strengthens the likelihood, particularly when taken together with Notker's remark about the authorship, disparaging as it may be. It should be added that the place where the *Vita vetustissima* was written remains a mystery.[68] If the dating of the early chapters is correct, then it would have been written before the foundation of either St Gallen or Reichenau. In view of our ignorance, why not fly a kite and suggest Bobbio?

Results

The glamour of Latin learning of the school of St Gallen derived, on the admission of some of their best representatives, from the scholarship conveyed to them, directly or indirectly, by Marcellus. Athough it would appear that he could not be linked either with the *libri scottice scripti* or to the execution of Irish script in the monastery of St Gallen, it could be shown that the collective memory of the community, over two centuries, not only preserved the degree of his learning but cast it in growing elaboration. The latest version, that of Ekkehard, cannot, certainly, be taken as the carrier of factual information, but there can be little doubt that one Irishman, Marcellus, made a decisive contribution to the Latin learning in one of the most important cis-Alpine monasteries of the late Carolingian era. His is a good case for not counting heads but weighing talent and its repercussions.

62 Iso Müller, 'Die älteste Gallus-Vita', *Zeitschrift für Schweizerische Kirchengeschichte* 66 (1972) pp 209–49. **63** Müller, p. 212. **64** Müller, pp 222f. **65** See Richter, *Ireland and her neighbours*, esp. pp 86f. **66** Müller, p. 229 and notes 3 and 5. For the latest treatment of this issue see J.-M. Picard, '*Princeps and principatus* in the early Irish Church: a reassessment', in *Seanchas. Studies in early and medieval Irish archaeology, history and literature in honour of Francis J. Byrne* (Dublin 2000) pp 146–60. **67** Müller, p. 213; Krusch p. 251, l. 32 f. **68** Berschin, 'Gallus abbas vindicatus', 270 f. posits the composition of the earliest chapters of the *Vita vetustissima c.* 689 but does not say anything about where this writing should have been located. He does not modify this position in his

There are also faint traces of the presence and activity of other Irish or Irish-trained members of the St Gallen community and scriptorium since the late eighth century.

In casting the net somewhat wider than both Duft and Bischoff had done, looking beyond palaeography, we can suggest that the Irish dimension in St Gallen in the early Middle Ages was somewhat stronger than these two experts had suggested as the last in a long and distinguished series of scholars. Naturally, the maximalist position of a Heinrich Zimmer is no longer tenable. But it is desirable to come to a conclusion that does full justice to all the elements available between either Iromania or Irophobia.[69]

later publications. **69** J. Duft, 'Iromanie – Irophobie. Fragen um die frühmittlelalterliche Irenmission exemplifiziert an St Gallen und Alemannien', *Zeitschrift für schweizerische Kirchengeschichte* 50 (1956) pp 241–62.

The Life of Martin of Tours:
a view from twelfth-century Ireland

MÁIRE HERBERT

The writings of Sulpicius Severus about Martin of Tours, compiled in the final decade of the fourth century, were known in Irish monastic circles at least by the close of the seventh century, when they served as an important model for Adomnán's *Vita Columbae*.[1] Indeed, the Martinian writings were also used in the composition of the Lives of two other Iona saints, Baithéne and Adomnán, author of the *Vita Columbae*.[2] Liturgical commemoration of Martin, attested in the *Vita Columbae*, reinforces the sense that the Columban monastic community particularly venerated Martin as an exemplar of asceticism who had privileged access to the supernatural world.[3] Yet Martin's veneration in early Christian Ireland was not solely a Columban prerogative, as the evidence of surviving hymns, Mass invocations, and calendar commemorations reveals.[4] Moreover, the beginnings of Martin's cult among the Irish may be earlier than indicated by the surviving records, if Columbanus's reported pilgrimage to Tours be deemed to reflect a devotion dating back to his monastic formation in sixth-century Ireland.[5]

What emerges significantly from all of the foregoing testimony is that in early Christian Ireland Martin was appropriated in his monastic rather than in his episcopal persona. We note, for instance, that the names of Antony and of Martin are linked together in the epilogue to *Félire Oengusso*, composed around the beginning of the ninth century.[6] While the works of Sulpicius Severus may have been known to Muirchú when he was compiling his Life of Patrick in the late seventh century, it is not Martin's *Vita* but apocryphal *acta* of New Testament apostles which provided the most significant literary template for the depiction of Ireland's premier bishop-apostle.[7]

---

1 Reference is made to the *Vita Martini* edition by J. Fontaine, *Sulpice Sévère, Vie de Saint Martin*, 3 vols (Paris 1967–9). For the *Dialogi*, see edition by C. Halm, *CSEL* 1 (Vienna 1866). English translations in A. Roberts, *Nicene and Post-Nicene Fathers* vol. XI (repr. Edinburgh 1991) pp 1–54. On the use of Sulpicius's works, see G. Brüning, 'Adamnans Vita Columbae und ihre Ableitungen', *ZCP* 11 (1917) pp 213–304 (especially pp 247–9); J.M. Picard, 'Structural patterns in early Hiberno-Latin hagiography', *Peritia* 4 (1985) pp 67–82; id. 'Tailoring the sources: the Irish hagiographer at work', in P. Ní Chatháin and M. Richter (eds), *Irland und Europa im früheren Mittelalter: Bildung und Literatur* (Stuttgart 1996) pp 261–74. **2** *Vita S. Baithini*, ed. W.W. Heist, *Vitae Sanctorum Hiberniae ex codice olim Salmanticensi nunc Bruxellensi* (Brussels 1965) pp 379–82; *Life of Adomnán*, ed. M. Herbert and P. Ó Riain, *Betha Adamnáin: The Irish life of Adamnán* (London 1988). See also M. Herbert, *Iona, Kells, and Derry: the history and hagiography of the monastic familia of Columba* (Oxford 1988, repr. Dublin 1996) pp 148–50, 170–74. **3** *Adomnán's Life of Columba*, ed. A.O. and M.O. Anderson (revised ed. Oxford 1991) Book III. 12. See R. Sharpe, *Adomnán of Iona: Life of St Columba* (London 1995) note 379, p. 366. **4** On Martinian commemoration in Ireland, see, in particular, P. Grosjean, 'Gloria postuma S. Martini Turonensis apud Scottos at Britannos', *AB* 55 (1937) pp 300–48; A. Gwynn, 'The cult of St Martin in Ireland', *IER* 5 ser. 105 (1966) pp 353–64; M. Richter, *Ireland and her neighbours in the seventh century* (Dublin and New York 1999) pp 225–31; M. Lapidge, 'A new Hiberno-Latin hymn on St Martin', *Celtica* 21 (1990) pp 240–51. **5** Jonas, *Vita Columbani abbatis*, I. 22 (ed. B. Krusch, *MGH, SRM* 4 (Hannover 1902) pp 61–152. **6** *Félire Óengusso Céli Dé: The Martyrology of Oengus the Culdee*, ed. W. Stokes (London 1905) p. 276, n° 273. **7** For Muirchú's use of Sulpicius, see Picard, 'Structural patterns', pp 71–2. On alternative influences, see A. O'Leary, 'An Irish apocryphal apostle: Muirchú's portrayal of Saint Patrick', *Harvard Theological Review* 89 (1996) pp 287–301.

Evident promotion of Martin among Patrick's devotees in Armagh seems to be attested securely only from about the beginning of the ninth century. The most significant indication is, of course, the copy of Sulpicius Severus's *Vita* of Martin, together with two of his *Dialogues*, entered into the Book of Armagh, alongside the New Testament and the dossier of texts relating to St Patrick, around the year 807.[8] It would seem that the ninth century was also the time when contact with Martin was first depicted in Patrician hagiography.[9] The vernacular *Vita Tripartita* provides the most elaborated version of this contact. It represents Patrick, in the course of his studies in Gaul, visiting Tours and receiving the monastic tonsure from Martin. Moreover, the two saints are linked by kinship as well as by ecclesiastical association, since Patrick's mother is identified as a sister of Martin.[10]

Set in historical context, the Armagh evidence suggests that Martin receives new prominence there in a period of institutional repositioning, when *abbas* is attested as a designation of the successor of Patrick, the representative of his community in ecclesiastical and secular assemblies.[11] Learned activity in Armagh, documenting a special relationship with Martin, seems to reflect contemporary propaganda regarding Armagh's status within the Irish church. Martin, favoured saint of Ireland's leading monastic churches, is shown as having superior personal links with Patrick. The Book of Armagh, copied for the abbot Torbach at the beginning of the ninth century, may be seen as a collection of core documents sustaining the current ecclesiastical status of the successor of Patrick. Thus, the New Testament represented his general Christian allegiance, the Patrician dossier, his particular allegiance, while the Martinian writings linked Patrick's church and community with the well-spring of Western monasticism.[12]

There is little indication, however, that the actual text of Sulpicius Severus's writings had any more than symbolic significance in Armagh in the period after it was copied at abbot Torbach's behest. Surviving evidence indicates that Martin's veneration owed little to detailed knowledge about his life and deeds. Only a few broad brush-strokes delineated Martin's portrait, highlighting his intercessory powers and his links with Patrick.[13] As the ninth century progressed Viking attacks disrupted ordered ecclesiastical life, and secular power encroached. From the tenth century onward, successive holders of Armagh's highest ecclesiastical office were lay members of a prominent local family, who held the temporalities of Armagh as a hereditary possession.[14] The vernacular supplanted Latin as the main medium of ecclesiastical writing, and scholarship itself must have been constantly hindered. The Latin works of Sulpicius Severus evidently lay dormant during this time.

Yet some continuity seems to have been maintained in Armagh scholarly circles, and by the eleventh century signs of resurgence are in evidence. Many factors played a part – a renewal of pilgrimage to Rome, contact with Irish monastic houses established on the continent in the tenth

---

8 Diplomatic edition by J. Gwynn, *Liber Ardmachanus* (Dublin 1913). For the texts on Martin (*LA* fol. 192r-222r), see Gwynn, pp 377–438. On the status of the Armagh copy in the text tradition of Sulpicius's works, see Fontaine, *Vie de Saint Martin* I, p. 219; Richter, *Ireland and her neighbours*, p. 228. **9** The date is suggested on the grounds that reference to Martin does not form part of the common source shared by the *Vita Secunda, Vita Quarta* and *Vita Tripartita* of Patrick. See L. Bieler (ed.), *Four Latin Lives of St Patrick* (Dublin 1971) pp 1–13. **10** *Bethu Phátraic: The Tripartite Life of Patrick*, ed. K. Mulchrone (Dublin 1939) lines 83–84, pp 249–51. I hold that this text has a stratum of ninth-century material, but was reworked in the tenth century, and subsequently edited in its present tripartite homily form in the eleventh century. **11** See, for instance, *AU* at the years 804, 811. **12** A different view has been expressed by R. Sharpe, 'Palaeographical considerations in the study of the Patrician Documents in the Book of Armagh', *Scriptorium* 36 (1982) pp 3–28. **13** See anecdotes published by Grosjean, 'Gloria postuma', pp 321–2, 344–5. **14** T. Ó Fiaich, 'The Church of Armagh under lay control', *Seanchas Ardmhacha* 5 (1969) pp 75–127 (particularly 75–90).

and eleventh centuries, contact with English monastic reform, and, by the latter part of the eleventh century, contact with the nascent movement for Irish ecclesiastical reform, primarily centred on Munster.[15] While hereditary succession of laymen was still in evidence in the governance of Armagh, ecclesiastical scholars like Máel Ísa Ua Brolcháin, who died in the year 1086, produced new devotional writings which witness to a revival in Latin as well as in vernacular scholarship.[16] The view that renewal of intellectual and spiritual life should be accompanied by institutional reform evidently began to take root. By the beginning of the twelfth century, it had gained momentum.

Cellach, a member of the Ua Sinaich family who held hereditary rights to the headship of Armagh, took ecclesiastical orders on his accession, and subsequently received episcopal ordination in the year 1106.[17] In his person, therefore, Cellach was a transitional figure between hereditary and reformed structures in the governance of Armagh. Fusion between tradition and innovation, moreover, was a feature of Armagh artistic and scholarly output in the eleventh and twelfth centuries. Manuscript decoration reveals continuity with the decoration of the Book of Armagh as well as newer influences.[18] Textually, a collection of homilies, apparently begun around this time, gives fresh currency to Latin exegesis and sermon material of previous centuries by setting these in new vernacular contexts.[19] The library of Armagh thus provided resources from the past to be reworked in the interests of present and future.

The transition into a new era proved most difficult at the level of ecclesiastical structures of authority. After Cellach's death in the year 1129, his chosen successor, was Malachy (Máel Máedóc Ua Morgair), a monk who had received sacerdotal and episcopal orders. The latter's assumption of Armagh authority was vigorously opposed by the holders of hereditary privilege. It took about three years for Malachy's succession to be established. Then, in accordance with his wishes, once the principle that clerical orders were the *sine qua non* of Armagh headship had been established Malachy resigned from Armagh office in the year 1137.[20] His designated successor, Gilla Mac Liag, (Gelasius) had also begun his ecclesiastical career as a monk, and had been head of the Columban community in Derry prior to his episcopacy and accession to Armagh.[21] During the latter's long term of office which extended until his death in 1174, Armagh participation in ecclesiastical reform was effectively consolidated.

In retrospect, then, the first half of the twelfth century was a pivotal era in the establishment of ecclesiastical reform in the north of Ireland. Intellectual and artistic endeavours both reflected and promoted the ideals of the reformers, as they sought a new synthesis between the best of the

15 See, for instance, A. Gwynn, *The twelfth-century reform* (Dublin 1968); idem, *The Irish Church in the 11th and 12th centuries*, ed. G. O'Brien (Dublin 1992); D. Bethell, 'English monks and Irish reform in the eleventh and twelfth centuries', *Historical Studies* 8 (1971) pp 111–35. 16 M. Ní Bhrolcháin, *Maol Íosa Ó Brolcháin* (Maigh Nuad 1986). 17 AU 1105, 1106; Ó Fiaich, 'Lay control', 94–5. 18 F. Henry, *Irish Art in the Romanesque Period 1020–1170 AD* (London 1973) pp 63–73. 19 F. Mac Donncha, 'Medieval Irish homilies', *Biblical Studies: the medieval Irish contribution*, ed. M. McNamara (Dublin 1976) pp 59–71; J. Rittmueller, 'The Hiberno-Latin background of the Leabhar Breac homily *In Cena Domini*', *Proceedings of the Harvard Celtic Colloquium* 2 (1982) pp 1–10; eadem, *The Leabhar Breac Latin and Middle-Irish homily 'In Cena Domini': An edition and source analysis*, Harvard Ph.D. Thesis 1984. 20 Bernard of Clairvaux, *Vita Sancti Malachiae*, ed. J. Leclercq and H.M. Rochais, *Sancti Bernardi Opera* III (Rome 1963) pp 197–378; Irish annal entries relating to Malachy include ATig. 1134, 1140, 1148; AFM 1132, 1134, 1135, 1136, 1147, 1148. See also A. Gwynn, 'Saint Malachy and the see of Armagh, 1121–37' *The Irish Church in the 11th and 12th Centuries*, pp 193–217. On his surname and genealogical background, see H.J. Lawlor's notes to his translation, *St Bernard of Clairvaux's life of St Malachy of Armagh* (London 1920) note 5; Gwynn, *Sancti Bernardi Opera*, p. 310. 21 *Annála Uladh: The Annals of Ulster* ed. W.M. Hennessy and B. MacCarthy, 4 vols (Dublin 1887–1901) vol. II, s.a. 1174.

past and the innovation of the present. Among the written works revived and recreated in this era were the writings of Sulpicius Severus on Martin. The Latin *Vita Martini* and the *Dialogi* on the saint were reintroduced into Irish public consciousness in the form of a vernacular homily.

The text of the homily now survives in three manuscript copies. The earliest, Royal Irish Academy 23 P 16, An Leabhar Breac, (hereafter B), fol. 59a16–61b21, is dated to the beginning of the fifteenth century. The other two copies are found in sixteenth-century manuscripts, British Library Egerton 91, fol. 42–44b (E) and King's Inns MS 10, ff 48d1–51a22 (K).[22] While all three copies derive ultimately from a common exemplar, the version in B is distinct from that in E and K. The latter two, however, are not directly related to each other. In fact, the relationship between the textual witnesses parallels that of the B, E, and K copies of another hagiographical homily, the Middle-Irish version of the Life of Colum Cille (hereafter CC).[23] The joint evidence of language and content has been used to date the latter work around the mid-twelfth century.[24] Though Stokes suggested a thirteenth-century date for the homily on Martin (hereafter *Mart*),[25] its linguistic profile reveals evident correspondences with the language of CC. Certainly the combined manuscript testimony regarding *Mart* reveals no features characteristic of a date later than that of CC.[26] For instance, the proportion of infixed to independent pronouns in *Mart* is 3:2, while that in CC is 6:6.[27] The verbal system shows similar features in both texts, and one must be very tentative in seeking to differentiate between them. There are, however, a few instances in which the earlier verbal form occurs in *Mart*, such as *co ndessid* (§ 34) and *forémdid* (§ 17), where CC correspondingly has *ro suid* (481) and *ro fhemid* (191).[28] Overall, the sum of linguistic evidence indicates that *Mart* belongs generally to the same era as CC, but probably comes before CC in order of compilation. Therefore, the date of *Mart* may be placed within the first half of the twelfth century.

What was the provenance of *Mart*? The availability in the Book of Armagh of the full range of Martinian writings used in the homily is an important consideration.[29] Moreover, the case has long been made for Armagh as a centre of homiletic activity within the period 1050–1150.[30] The main source of the homiletic *exordium* of *Mart* has been identified as Bede's commentary *In Lucae Evangelium*, a text available in Armagh, and cited in exegetical commentary in an Armagh gospel-

---

22 The B text has been edited by W. Stokes, 'A Middle-Irish homily on S. Martin of Tours', *RC* 2 (1873–5) pp 381–402. Textual references throughout are denoted by the chapter-numbers of Stokes's edition. **23** See the edition of this homily in Herbert, *Iona*, pp 211–88. For an account of the manuscripts and text tradition, see in particular pp 211–17. **24** The arguments are set out in Herbert, *Iona*, pp 180–99. **25** 'Middle-Irish homily', p. 383. **26** Dating criteria are set out in Herbert, *Iona*, pp 185–88. See also K.H. Jackson (ed.), *Aislinge Meic Conglinne* (Dublin 1990) Appendix, pp 73–140. **27** I have examined and compared all three manuscript versions of *Mart*, using microfilm and photostat copies. I base my statistics on forms common to all manuscripts. **28** Herbert, *Iona*, pp 186–8. I have compared the evidence from *Mart* with the full evidence of my study of the language of CC and have also taken account of Rittmueller's examination of the linguistic profile of the comparable *Leabhar Breac* homily *In cena Domini* (Ph.D. thesis, pp 134–74). **29** Published by Gwynn, *Liber Ardmachanus* (note 8 above). The Irish text of *Mart* is printed in parallel with the corresponding Latin text of Sulpicius from the Book of Armagh in E. Hogan, *The Latin Lives of the Saints as aids towards the translation of Irish texts and the production of an Irish dictionary* (Dublin 1894) pp 87–100. Quotations from Sulpicius in *Mart* show occasional variations from the wording of the Armagh text. However, such variation might well have arisen through scribal misunderstanding. We must be mindful that there are two centuries between the date of compilation of Mart and the date of its earliest surviving copy. **30** Mac Donncha, 'Medieval Irish homilies', sets out the arguments, and also links the compilation of a homily-collection with a particular scholar, Máel Ísu Ua Brolcháin, head of the school of Armagh, who died in 1086. While this identification cannot be substantiated, the independent work of Rittmueller on a specific homily confirms Armagh provenance, and supports a dating 1050–1150 for a corpus of homiletic materials. However, the largest collection of homilies in the *Leabhar Breac* includes some compositions from 1200 or later, indicating that homily writing continued beyond the upper dating limit suggested by Mac Donncha; see K. Jackson, 'The historical grammar of Irish: Some actualities and some desiderata', *Proceedings of the Sixth*

book, now British Library MS Harley 1802, dated to the year 1138.[31] Indeed, the foregoing
commentary contains one short passage paralleled in the *exordium* of *Mart*.[32] The evidence is
cumulative, therefore, that the scholarly resources used by the compiler of *Mart* were all available
in the library of twelfth-century Armagh.

The homily's opening gospel text, *Nemo potest duobus dominis seruire* (Mt 6:24), sets the
narrative tone for a sermon which stresses that worldly concerns and enslavement to wealth are
incompatible with the service of God. While certain Irish hagiographical homilies reveal a lack of
integration between the account of the saint's career and the sermon material which encloses it,
Mart reveals purposeful unity between the two. Thus, the account of Martin's career may be seen
to exemplify the counsel of the *exordium*, while the homiletic *peroratio* sums up the saint's virtues
in phrases derived from the *Vita Martini* (*VM*) itself. The works of Sulpicius Severus provide the
narrative substance of *Mart*. Following the homiletic *exordium* (§ 1–8), the narrative of § 9–34
in broad outline follows *VM* II – XXIV. There is a switch of source to the *Dialogi* at this point, so
that § 35–37 of *Mart* are based successively on § 2, 4, and 9 of Sulpicius's second book of
Dialogues, while *Mart* § 38–41 represent the content of § 2, 14, 8, and 15 of Sulpicius's third book
of Dialogues. The closing *peroratio* reverts for its material to *VM* § 25–27.[33]

At first sight, then, *Mart* appears as a skilful condensation of the works of Sulpicius, renewing
access to a hagiographical classic through the vernacular. There is a concern to follow Sulpicius's
lead in the ordering of events, and an avoidance of additional commentary and interpolation. Yet
there is more in question than simply recreation in a new medium. There is a process of omission
as well as of retention, a process of decision rather than of default. The writer of *Mart* does not
take a neutral attitude to his source. He actively shapes it in accordance with his own priorities.

Shifts in emphasis are discernible throughout, when the Irish account of Martin's career is set
alongside that of Sulpicius. We see, for instance, that the Martin of Sulpicius's narrative was often
a controversial figure, who was vilified, and even physically attacked on occasions. The author
of *Mart*, however, views his subject at greater distance, presenting him as a heroic exemplar rather
than as a contemporary recalled in personal detail. The author of *Mart* generally omits any
material which reveals the saint on the defensive, or subject to human fear or doubts. There is no
mention of Arian opposition to Martin, for instance, nor is there a sense of the enforced nature
of his withdrawal to Gallinaria.[34] The opposition to his episcopal consecration by bishop Defensor
is not mentioned, nor are two attempts on Martin's life.[35] Even incidents showing the saint
turning the tables on his attackers are, for the most part, avoided.[36] A very abbreviated account of
Bricio's denunciation of Martin is used by the Irish homilist to point the lesson of the saint's
scripturally-guided forbearance.[37]

While secular nobles are among Martin's opponents in Sulpicius's narrative, they also figure
among those impressed by the saint's holiness and by the divine power channelled through him.

International Congress of Celtic Studies, ed. G. Mac Eoin (Dublin 1983) pp 1–18.   **31** *Beda: In Lucae evangelium
expositio*, ed. D. Hurst, *CCSL* 120 (Turnhout 1960) pp 299–300 (= Lk 16:13). See Mac Donncha, p. 66, and
Rittmueller, (Ph.D. thesis, p. 312). The homily material consists of a series of extracts from Bede's work rather than
a direct transcript. On the Armagh gospel commentary, see J. Rittmueller, 'The Gospel commentary of Máelbrigte
ua Máeluanaig and its Hiberno-Latin background', *Peritia* 2 (1983) pp 185–214; eadem, *Peritia* 3 (1984) pp 215–18.
32 I have examined the microfilm copy of Harl. 1802. Its commentary on Mt 6:24 is very brief, but the content
parallels matter in *Mart* § 6, on the definition of Mammon, and on the distinction between possession of riches
and enslavement to them.   **33** The Book of Armagh contains only the Dialogues on Martin's life (Dialogues II and
III). On the layout of the Martinian texts in the Book of Armagh, see Gwynn, 'The cult of St Martin', p. 355.
34 *VM* VI.4–5.   **35** *VM* IX.4–7; XV.1–3.   **36** For example, *Dial.* II.3, 5; III.4.   **37** *Dial.* III.15, *Mart* §41.

The Irish author of *Mart*, however, is wary of depicting his subject in any relation with societal magnates. He evidently seeks to sustain the uncompromising counsel of his scriptural lesson *Nemo potest duobus dominis seruire* Martin's youthful declaration to the Caesar Julian that he was renouncing earthly for heavenly service thus takes on a heightened significance in *Mart* as does the saint's certainty that Christ would not manifest himself on earth in royal apparel.[38] The homilist conveys the view that Martin prevails through his own trust in God rather than through association with earthly potentates.

Martin is portrayed in the homily as a person committed to divine service, whether as soldier, monk, or bishop. The text discloses a strong partiality for the monastic life. It is that which Martin contemplates in his youth; in his military days 'he was not deemed a soldier but a monk', and when compelled from his monastery to take the bishopric of Tours, 'he relinquished not his monk's way of life'.[39] *Mart* does not differ from Sulpicius in any of the foregoing, but the statements are thrown into higher relief in the shorter Irish text. Martin is shown as the epitome of true monastic values in his denial of worldliness, in his humility and in his asceticism. Yet the author of *Mart* is concerned to show a pastoral aspect also. He chooses from Sulpicius incidents in which Martin's demeanour and miraculous deeds bring about conversions.[40] Accounts of the raising from the dead of an unbaptised catechumen and of a suicide are concerned with spiritual as well as bodily regeneration.[41] Martin's powers to discern truth from falsehood are shown to be deployed on behalf of the whole community. He unmasks the bogus martyr who was being publicly commemorated, and exposes the demonically-inspired misinformation about an attack on the city.[42] Martin's empathy with those in need brings about individual healings as well as the communal freeing of the Senones from yearly hailstorms.[43] Thus, while monastic virtues accorded the saint access to supernatural power, his use of power is clearly shown to have extended beyond monastic confines, to benefit church and community.

Indeed, in recounting miraculous deeds and signs of divine affirmation, the author of *Mart* clearly is not concerned with accumulating as many instances as possible. There are omissions in the case of all of the main categories of Martinian *uirtutes* recounted by Sulpicius, nature miracles, healings, exorcisms, supernatural encounters and revelations.[44] Certainly the homily format required some abbreviation of Sulpicius's narratives, and the Irish writer evidently seeks to avoid excessive repetition of similar types of story. Beyond that, however, the homilist seems to favour incidents which have didactic or directly beneficial import over those which primarily evoke wonder. Thus, we may note that *Mart* omits nature miracles like the immobilisation of hounds to save a hare, as well as supernatural signs such as the appearance of a fiery globe above the saint's head during Mass.[45] The Irish hagiographer evidently wishes to portray a saint whose wonderworking was primarily concerned with human welfare, both spiritual and temporal.

The sum of evidence has indicated a date of compilation for *Mart* within the first half of the twelfth century. Its scholarly context fits that of contemporary Armagh, where texts from early Irish Christianity were being revived and recreated. The historical context of *Mart* coincides with the era of ecclesiastical reform in Armagh. The homily presents Martin as a saintly exemplar for this era, as a man who lived out the biblical exhortation to serve God with single-minded purpose,

---

38 *Mart* §13, 34.   **39** *Mart* §9, 11, 21. The quotations are from Stokes's translation.   **40** *VM* V.4–6=*Mart* §15; *VM* XIII=*Mart* §25.   **41** *VM* VII=*Mart* §19; *VM* VIII=*Mart* §20.   **42** *VM* XI=*Mart* §23; *VM* XVIII.1–2 = *Mart* §31. **43** For example, *VM* XVI.2–8=*Mart* §28; *VM* XVII.1–4 = *Mart* §29; *Dial.* II.2 = *Mart* §35; *Dial.* III.7 = *Mart* §38. **44** For a valuable listing by category of Sulpician narratives, see C. Stancliffe, *St Martin and his hagiographer: history and miracle in Sulpicius Severus* (Oxford 1983) pp 363–71.   **45** *Dial.* II.9; II.2.

renouncing earthly attachments. Indeed, the Martin of the homily is even more austerely removed than is Sulpicius's Martin from any circumstance that might conceivably be read as earthly distraction, such as contact with secular rulers or, indeed, with females.[46] Martin's way of life is shown to be vindicated by supernatural signs. Angels support him, and he triumphs over demons.[47] The ecclesiastical context of Martin's spiritual triumph is also important. Leaving military service for monasticism, he yielded to the entreaties of the faithful and received episcopal consecration. The ideal presented thereby in *Mart* is of a bishop whose ministry eschewed the trappings of authority and worldly privilege in favour of monastic humility and asceticism. He exemplified responsiveness to community needs, both pastoral and material, combining monastic self-effacement with episcopal commitment to preaching the Word. The homilist seeks to demonstrate that the role of bishop did not supplant the monastic role, but rather complemented it, and derived strength and benefit from it.

At a fundamental level, the Irish homily conveys the blend of tradition and innovation which characterised the intellectual and artistic world of contemporary Armagh. Implicitly it expresses the view that church reform was to be considered as renewal rather than as rejection of the past. Martin, a revered saint linked with Patrick himself, provided a prototype of transition and fusion between the monastic and the episcopal states. Thus, he served as a model for ecclesiastical authority in Armagh, a model that responded to the need for diocesan government while remaining sensitive to the importance of monastic ideals within the Irish church.[48] In addition, as reformers sought to end contemporary abuses such as secularisation and politicisation of clerical office, the subject of *Mart* set a standard of ecclesiastical conduct which rejected earthly attachments in favour of commitment to the spiritual.

Overall, the homily on Martin seeks to shape, and is shaped by, its contemporary context. It promotes renewal of ecclesiastical life while validating change with the sanction of antiquity. It revives the memory of a saint who was venerated from the early days of Irish Christianity, conveying the view that Martin's era resonated with the twelfth-century present. Indeed, the successive roles of Martin's life could be seen to harmonise with the career trajectories of successive reforming churchmen in contemporary Armagh. The saint's early involvement in secular society before becoming an ecclesiastic could find a parallel in the career of Cellach, originally a lay 'heir of Patrick' who took holy orders. Martin's reluctant elevation to the episcopacy and his continuing adherence to his monastic ideals set a paradigm which finds correspondences in Malachy's ecclesiastical career. Moreover, the pattern of monk becoming bishop also provided a precedent for the succession of Gelasius, who was a monk of Derry before he followed Malachy in the episcopacy of Armagh in the year 1137.[49]

That Martin's Life did, indeed, offer an apposite model in northern Irish reform circles in the twelfth century seems to be affirmed by an apparently unlikely hagiographical source, Bernard of Clairvaux's *Vita Sancti Malachiae* (*VMal*).[50] This Life of the reformer, Malachy, was compiled soon

---

46 Note the omission from *Mart* of *VM* XIX.1–3; XX; *Dial.* II.5–6, 11–12; III.3–4, 8, 11–13.   **47** Examples of angelic assistance, *Mart* §27, 32; contests with demonic presences, *Mart* §16, 30, 34.   **48** Monastic reform was, of course, many-faceted, involving change within existing structures as well as introduction of new orders. See, for instance, Gwynn, *The twelfth-century reform*; A. Gwynn and R.N. Hadcock, *Medieval religious houses: Ireland* (Dublin 1970). **49** See above, notes 17, 20, 21.   **50** The edition used is that cited in note 20. The text is abbreviated as *VMal*, with chapters numbered in accordance with the edition. For English translations and notes to the text see also H.J. Lawlor, *St Bernard of Clairvaux's Life of St Malachy of Armagh* (London 1920); R.T. Meyer, *Bernard of Clairvaux: the life and death of Saint Malachy the Irishman* (Kalamazoo 1978); A.B. Scott, *Malachy* (Dublin 1976).

after the death of the Irish churchman in Clairvaux in the year 1148. Bernard had first-hand acquaintance with his subject through Malachy's visits to Clairvaux in 1140 and 1148.[51] Yet this information would have been insufficient for a full Life, and, as his text reveals, Bernard drew on additional materials supplied by Irish informants. The correct transmission of a significant amount of historical and onomastic detail indicates, moreover, that at least some of Bernard's Irish accounts of Malachy were received in written form.[52] Much of what historians today know of Malachy's career derives from Bernard's work, and this affirms the importance of the Irish evidence in *VMal*. However, while its contribution to the historical record of twelfth-century Ireland is rightly acknowledged, the hagiographical aspect of *VMal* has not received its due attention.

Yet like all hagiographical works, *VMal* is fundamentally concerned with demonstrating its subject's sanctity. Narratives of Irish provenance catalogue a variety of supernatural signs of the saint's favour with God. What is striking is that the mould of sanctity in which these testimonies of Malachy have been shaped seems clearly Martinian. Exorcisms and demonic encounters credited to Malachy are only attested elsewhere in Irish hagiography in works influenced by Martin's Life.[53] Healing miracles attributed to Malachy and reminiscent of those of Martin include cures of dumbness and of paralysis.[54] The Lives of both Martin and Malachy refer to the miraculous efficacy of the saint's bedding, and of other objects touched by him.[55] Moreover, both Lives credit their subjects with resuscitation of the dead. The narrative in *VMal* particularly recalls Martin's revival of a catechumen, for in both cases the miracle is linked with a sacramental need. Thus, the resuscitation reverses unexpected death before baptism in Martin's case, and, in the case of Malachy, it reverses the unexpected death of a woman whose anointing had been deferred.[56]

Bernard's commentary on the latter narrative supports the view that he is the amanuensis rather than the contributor. Immediately after the resuscitation account in *VMal* he relates how Malachy converted a woman's anger to gentleness, and expresses the view that the latter miracle, which brought the inner person back to life, should take precedence over a miracle of reviving the body. Indeed, before proceeding to recount any of Malachy's miracles, Bernard puts on record that 'the first and greatest miracle that he presented was the man himself'.[57] Other writings by Bernard confirm his unease with a concept of sanctity primarily based on wonderworking. His sermon on the life of Martin distinguishes between the admirable and the imitable. Bernard places his main emphasis on the latter, on Martin's exemplification of virtues, especially of obedience, rather than on extraordinary signs.[58]

Certainly *VMal* reflects Bernard's literary skill and rhetoric. His was a task of compilation as well as of composition, however, so that a body of Irish-derived materials fitted within his text. The content of these materials suggests that veneration of Malachy as a saint had already begun among his Irish contemporaries, who stylised their reminiscences in accordance with a prevailing model of sanctity, a model derived from Martin's Life. We must also consider the possibility that this model of sanctity had influenced Malachy himself. Biographical data such as Malachy's reluctant acceptance of the episcopacy of Armagh, his desire to return to monastic contemplation,

51 *VMal* XVI, 37; XXXI, 70.   52 Note, for instance, *VMal* Preface and chapters VI, 12; X, 19–20; XX, 46.
53 *VMal* XX, 45, 46. See C. Stancliffe, ' The miracle stories in seventh-century Irish Saints' Lives', *The seventh century: change and continuity*, ed. J. Fontaine and J.N. Hillgarth (London 1992) pp 87–115 (especially 101–10).
54 *VMal* XX, 46, 47; XVII, 41.   55 *Dial.* II.8; *VMal* XXI, 46, 47.   56 *VM* VII; *VMal* XXIV, 53.   57 *VMal* XXV, 54; XIX, 43.   58 *PL* 183, 489–500. Note also Bernard's comments in *VMal* XIX, 43, 44; XXIX, 66. See J. Leclercq, 'S. Martin dans l'hagiographie monastique du moyen age', *Studia Anselmiana* 46 (1961) pp 175–87; S.L. Reames, 'Saint Martin of Tours in the *Legenda Aurea* and before', *Viator* 12 (1981) pp 131–64.

his humility and his rejection of hierarchical privilege,[59] all may witness to a complex interaction between the exemplary Life of Martin, the lived experience of a churchman familiar with Martin's Life, and the manner in which this lived experience was, in turn, recalled in hagiographical form within a shared cultural milieu.

Occasionally, indeed, we glimpse an intervention by Bernard that seeks to resolve what, in his terms, seemed anomalous. For example, Malachy's continued residence in a monastic community after his episcopal consecration is represented by Bernard as a practical convenience, being 'near the city'.[60] Yet in actual fact diocesan centre and monastery were not at all closely situated.[61] Viewed within a Martinian framework, however, Malachy's remaining within a monastic community was perfectly in accord with Martin's practice, as reported by Sulpicius and by the Irish homilist. It is possible that Malachy's decision, and its subsequent retelling in *VMal* were both informed by the hagiographical precedent.

Twelfth-century evidence, therefore, reinforces the view that hagiographical accounts of Martin provided a 'lexicon of images' which could be reconstructed and adapted in accordance with changing circumstances.[62] Martin had been a model and patron of monks in early Christian Ireland. In the era of Irish ecclesiastical reform, as the transition to a diocesan structure of ecclesiastical government was in train, Martin came to be perceived as a mediator *par excellence*, an embodiment of synthesis between monastic and episcopal roles. The recreation of the Latin writings of Sulpicius Severus in vernacular form helped to bridge past and present. Martin came to embody reform ideals, as a bishop who respected true monastic values, and as a churchman whose service of God was unmingled with earthly considerations. At the level of ideology as well as of literary representation, the narrative of Martin's Life offered a compelling medium through which change could be perceived as renewal of the custom of Christianity's foundational era.[63]

59 *VMal*X, 20, 21; XIX, 43, 44. 60 *Mal*VII, 15. 61 See Lawlor, *The Life of St Malachy*, p. 35, notes 1, 2. 62 R. Van Dam, 'Images of Saint Martin in late Roman and early Merovingian Gaul', *Viator*, 19 (1988) pp 1–27 (2). For evidence regarding Martin's veneration in twelfth-century Derry, in a period when Derry was closely associated with Armagh, see Herbert, *Iona*, pp 190–3. 63 In this regard, see G. Constable, *The Reformation of the Twelfth Century* (Cambridge 1996, repr. 2000), pp. 160–1.

Early contacts between Ireland and Normandy: the cult of Irish saints in Normandy before the conquest

JEAN-MICHEL PICARD

The arrival of King Henry II in the bay of Waterford in 1171 can be seen as the beginning of new and stronger links between Ireland and Normandy in the larger context of the vast Plantagenêt empire. It is also true that contacts between these two countries are far older and are attested for the Merovingian and Carolingian period, for the Viking period, and for the time of the early dukes of Normandy. The main difficulty in assessing the extent of these contacts is the lack of original sources, mostly due to the Scandinavian raids which took place both in Ireland and in Normandy in the ninth-century. Fighting between local lords and plundering of monasteries, even at a later period, must also be taken into account. With the exception of rare and expensive Gospel books, which finally found their way back to the monasteries of Europe after a series of market transactions, few manuscripts survived the burning of monastic buildings which ended most plundering, foreign or local. The remarks made by Lucien Musset – the great historian of medieval Normandy – about the lack of Norman sources for the seventh, eighth, ninth and tenth centuries also apply to Ireland.[1] In recent years, historians have realised that a great deal can be learned from the study of saints' cults and hagiography. The testimony of saints' Lives copied in later manuscripts and the dedication of churches and parishes often provide the missing links needed by the historian. But even in that branch of research, the Norman evidence is quite scant. In contrast with the neighbouring regions of Northern France and Brittany, where the cult of Irish saints is well attested and has been the subject of a number of studies,[2] few traces remain in Normandy and, in general, little is known about the Irish influences there. However, I believe there is enough evidence to warrant a reassessment of the situation. The review of the cult of Irish saints in Normandy which I propose below may also help us to gain a better understanding of some aspects of early Norman settlement in Ireland.

Saint Columbanus

The cult of Columbanus was introduced in Normandy shortly after the saint's death in 615. I have shown elsewhere how Columbanus himself had travelled through Normandy in 610 and how one of his disciples, Potentinus, had founded a monastery at Orval near Coutances.[3] The founding of Jumièges and St-Wandrille along the Seine valley in 637 and 649 is also linked to the presence of

---

1 L. Musset, 'Discours de Clôture' in H. Atsma, *La Neustrie. Les pays au nord de la Loire de 650 à 850*, 2 vols (Sigmaringen 1989) vol. 2, pp 471–8, p. 472.   2 On Irish saints in these regions, see L. Gougaud, *Les saints irlandais hors d'Irlande* (Louvain 1936); B. Bischoff, 'Il monachesimo irlandese nei suoi rapporti col continente', *Settimane di Studio* 4 (Spoleto 1957) pp 121–38; T. Ó Fiaich, 'Irish peregrini on the continent', *IER* 103 (1965) pp 233–400; J.-M. Picard (ed.), *Ireland and Northern France, AD 600–850* (Dublin 1991).   3 J.-M. Picard, 'L'Irlande et la Normandie avant les Normands (VIIe-IXe siècles)', *Annales de Normandie* 47 (1997) pp 3–24, at pp 4–8.

Columbanus on the continent. The founders of both monasteries, Filibertus and Wandregisel, were great admirers of Columbanus and considered Luxeuil and Bobbio as ideal monastic houses: as a result, the *Rule of Columbanus* was in use in both monasteries. Likewise, Évroul (†706), who founded the monastery of St-Évroult in the second half of the seventh century, was also influenced by Columbanus's way of life and spirituality.[4] In the eighth-century *Life of Évroul*, it is said that the saint knew not only the Roman, Gallican and Benedictine cursus, but also that of the Irish, namely that of saint Columbanus.[5] At St-Wandrille, Abbot Wando had his own copy of the *Rule of Columbanus:* this was considered valuable enough to be mentioned separately in his will among the items he left to the monastery at his death in 754.[6]

Writing around 750, the author of the *Life of Saint Filibertus* indicates how important the cult of Columbanus was at Jumièges. While the altars of continental saints like Martin, Denis and Germanus were housed in small oratories outside the church, the altar dedicated to Columbanus was in the main church together with that of Saint John the Evangelist, both on either side of the tomb of the founder of the monastery.[7] Due to the destruction of Jumièges by the Vikings in 851, no manuscript or artefacts from the early period have survived which could tell us more about the extent of the Columbanian tradition there. But from the eleventh century onwards we have tangible evidence of the interest in Columbanus among the monastic communities in Normandy. We know that the *Life of Columbanus* written by Jonas of Bobbio in the 640s was known in Normandy before the Viking invasions since the author of the seventh-century *Life of saint Wandregisel* uses it.[8] When the monasteries were restored, in the tenth and eleventh centuries, the librarians requested copies from other parts of Europe. By the twelfth century, Jumièges, Fécamp, St-Ouen and St-Évroult had copies of the *Life of Columbanus.*[9] They all belong to the same textual family in the manuscript tradition of the *Vita Columbani* and their model originated in Northern France.[10]

Apart from the manuscript evidence, Orderic Vital's *Ecclesiastical History* provides further proof of Norman awareness concerning Columbanus. Writing at St-Évroult between 1114 and 1141, Orderic shows great admiration for saint Columbanus. For example, in book VIII, chapter 27, which deals with the founders of the new monastic orders, Bernard of Tiron and Vital of Savigny, he specifies that he only mentions these reformers for the benefit of posterity, but that, personally, he does not think that they are any better than the old monastic founders, especially saint Columbanus.[11] He then reminds the reader that Columbanus was Irish, that he was the founder of Luxeuil and Bobbio, that he was the first to introduce in Gaul a monastic rule inspired by the Holy Spirit and that his reputation is justified by many signs and miracles. He was the teacher of many seventh century abbots and these disciples composed a mixed rule, mostly inspired by that of Benedict, but devised so that they would not have to reject the precepts of their good master

---

4 See M. Chibnall, 'The Merovingian monastery of St Évroul in the light of conflicting tradition', in Derek Baker (ed.), *Popular belief and practice*, Studies in Church History VIII (Cambridge 1972) pp 31–40.   **5** *Vita primitiva Ebrulfi* (ed. M. Chibnall, *The Ecclesiastical History of Orderic Vitalis*, 6 vols, Oxford, 1969–80, vol. 1, pp 204–11) pp 208–9: '*Et ut omnes cursus compleret, scilicet Romanum, Gallicanum, Sancti Benedicti, Scotticum seu Sancti Columbani, per diuersa horarum spacia psallebat*'.   **6** Gesta *Abbatum Fontanellensium* (ed. F. Lohier and J. Laporte, Rouen-Paris 1936) c.13.   **7** *Vita Filiberti*, c.8, ed. W. Levison, *MGH, SRM* 5, pp 583–604.   **8** *Vita Wandregiseli, c.*1 and 2, ed. B. Krusch, *MGH, SRM* 5, pp 13–24.   **9** The *Vita Columbani* is found in the following manuscripts: Rouen 1333 (s. XI) and Rouen 1399 (s. XII) both from Jumièges; Rouen 1404 (s. XII) from Fécamp; Rouen 1410 (s. XIII) from St-Ouen in Rouen. It is also mentionned in the twelfth-century library catalogue of St-Évroult (Paris, Lat. 10062, fol. 80v).   **10** This is the group A2b in the stemma proposed by B. Krusch, *Ionae vitae sanctorum Columbani, Vedastis, Johannis* (Hannover 1905).   **11** Chibnall, *The Ecclesiastical History of Orderic Vitalis*, vol. 4,

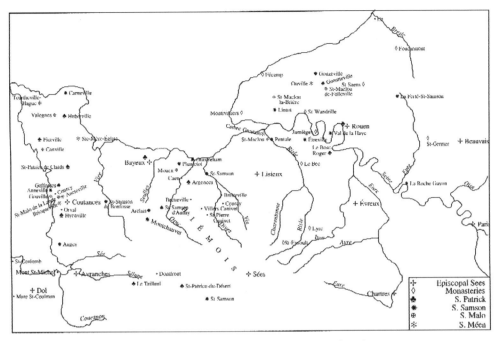

1 Map of medieval Normandy: sites mentioned in the text

Columbanus.[12] And to conclude the chapter, Orderic gives a list of his sources,[13] showing that in the first half of the first century St-Évroult had succeeded in gathering a significant dossier of Carolingian texts relating to Columbanus.

Saint Columcille

Compared to Columbanus, Columcille is less well known on the continent. Adomnán's *Life of Columcille* was a major factor in the spread of the his cult, but it circulated mostly in Irish circles. Only five manuscripts were written in French monasteries: three in the Metz region and two in western France.[14] Thus it is quite interesting to note that in the twelfth century, the library of St-Évroult had a copy of the *Life of Columcille*.[15] Orderic Vital, confirms that interest in Columcille and in Iona was kept up to date in Normandy during his lifetime. Writing about the good deeds of Queen Margaret of Scotland (†1093), wife of King Malcolm III, Orderic tells us that 'she reconstructed the monastery of Iona which the servant of Christ Columba had built at the time of Bruide son of Maelchon, king of the Picts, but which had fallen into ruins on account of the

pp 326–36. **12** *Historia Ecclesiastica*, VIII, 27 (vol. 4, p. 334): '*Ipsi reor beatum Maurum eiusque socios et discipulos nouerunt utpote uicini, et ab ipsis sicut ab aliis scripta doctorum aedificationis causa sancti normam suscepere Benedicti, ita tamen ut non abhorrent sui statua magistri almi uidelicet Columbani*'. **13** *HE*, VIII, 27 (vol. 4, p. 334): '*Qualis predictus doctor ante Deum et homines quantusque fuerit, liber uitae eius signis plenus et uirtutibus ostendit. In gestis etiam sepe memoratur Audoeni Rotomagensis archiepiscopi et Nouiomagensis Eligii aliorumque uirorum qui ab illo educati sunt ac ad apicem uirtutum per eius documenta prouecti sunt*'. **14** See J.-M. Picard, 'Adomnán's *Vita Columbae* and the cult of Colum Cille in continental Europe', *PRIA* 98 (1998) pp 1–23. **15** Paris, Bibliothèque Nationale de France, Latin 10062 (s. xii) < St-Évroult, fol. 80v, line 6: '*Vita S[an]cti Columbae*'.

havoc of wars and of being so ancient. So the pious queen gave to the monks enough finance for its upkeep and restored it for divine worship'.[16]

Saint Brigit

The main agents of the spread of the cult of Brigit on the continent were the Irish communities of Péronne and Fosses in Northern France and their Frankish contacts of Nivelles and St-Amand.[17] Even today, saint Brigit is venerated as a powerful protector of cattle in the region of Namur with no less than 120 churches and oratories dedicated to her.[18] The *Life of Saint Brigit* written at Kildare by Cogitosus *c*.650 has survived in more than one hundred manuscripts of continental origin. This text was known in Normandy from at least the eleventh century as attested by the existence of several manuscripts.[19] The Norman abbeys went to some trouble to source surviving manuscripts of the *Life of Saint Brigit*. No less than three independent versions of the Life circulated in Normandy in the twelfth century: two from two different areas of Northern France and one from Western France.[20]

Saint Fursa

The cult of Fursa was widespread in the neighbouring regions of Picardy and Île de France. The oldest *Life of Fursa* was written around 670 by an Irish monk living in the monastery of Nivelles and has been handed down to us in more than 150 Latin manuscripts and several translations in Medieval French, Italian and German. The Latin Life was known in Normandy in the eleventh century in a version belonging to type B2 in the edition by Bruno Krusch (*BHL* 3210).[21] Apparently, it came to Normandy through the same channels as the *Life of Brigit*: it is found in the same manuscripts (Paris, Bibliothèque Mazarine, 1711 (s. XI) from St-Ouen in Rouen; Rouen 1384 (s. XI) from Jumièges) and, as in the case of the *Vita Brigitae*, the text in the Jumièges manuscript is very close to that of Cambrai 864. The abbey of Fécamp also had a copy of the same version.[22] St-Évroult does not seem to have owned a copy of the seventh-century Vita Fursei, but had a 'Story of Saint Fursa' (*Narratio de sancto Furseo*) based on Bede's account of the life and visions of Saint Fursa (BHL 3212).[23] In the twelfth century, the abbey of Foucarmont had yet another version of the *Vita Fursei* (BHL 3209) which was the standard version circulating among the Cistercians.[24]

16 *HE*, VIII, 22 (vol. 4, p. 272): '*Inter caetera bona quae nobilis hera fecerat, Huense cenobium quod seruus Christi Columba tempore Brudei regis Pictorum filii Meilocon construxerat, sed tempestate preliorum cum longa uetustate dirutum fuerat, fidelis regina reedificauit datisque sumptibus idoneis ad opus Domini monachis reparauit*'. **17** On the contacts between these monasteries, see Picard, *Ireland and Northern France*, pp 27–52. **18** C. Hoex, *Enquête sur le culte et l'iconographie de sainte Brigide d'Irlande en Wallonie* (Bruxelles 1973). **19** Paris, Bibliothèque Mazarine, 1711 (s. XI) < St-Ouen in Rouen; Rouen 1384 (s. XI) < Jumièges; Rouen 1401 (s. XIII) < Jumièges; Paris, Bibliothèque Nationale de France, Latin 5352 (s. XIII) < Bonport. **20** Paris, Bibliothèque Mazarine, 1711 (s. XI) < St-Ouen de Rouen: Type a, linked to MSS from St-Amand, Marchiennes, St-Ghislain; Rouen 1384 (s. XI) < Jumièges: (Type b) linked to Cambrai 865 (s. X) < St-Sépulchre, Cambrai and Paris, Lat. 10862 (s. X) < Echternach; Paris, Bibliothèque Nationale, Latin 5352 (s. XIII) < Bonport: Type γ, linked to Paris, Latin 3788 (s. XII) < Maine/Anjou; Paris, Latin 5318 (s. XII) < Maine/Anjou; Angers 807 (s. XII) < St- Serge d'Angers. **21** B. Krusch (ed.), *Vita uirtutesque Fursei, MGH, SRM* 4, pp 434–40, pp 429–30. **22** Rouen 1400 (s. XI) < Fécamp, fol. 42–44v. **23** Rouen 1467 (s. XII) < St-Évroult; cf Bede, *HE*, III, 19. **24** Paris, Latin 5291 (s. XIII) < Foucarmont, fol. 79v-83.

Saint Kilian (= Cilléne)

Out of the sixteen Kilians mentioned by John Colgan in the *Acta Sanctorum Hiberniae*,[25] two were known in Normandy. The first was Saint Kilian of Aubigny, who was a member of the group of Irish monks surrounding Bishop Faro of Meaux and was active in the Artois region until his death in 672.[26] This Kilian was celebrated at St-Wandrille and his name is included in the *Martyrology of Fontenelle* both on 21 and 24 January. His cult may have been brought to the Seine valley by Bainus, abbot of St-Wandrille from 699 to 706 and bishop of Thérouanne in the Artois region. The other Kilian was the Irish martyr killed at Würzburg in 689. He is also commemorated in the Martyrology of St-Wandrille on 8 July. In the twelfth century, the monastic library of St-Évroult had a copy of the *Passio sancti Kiliani*, which is an account of the life and martyrdom of Kilian of Würzburg.[27] The manuscript must have disappeared from the library quite early since the title was crossed out in the twelfth-century catalogue. Two Lives or *Passiones* of Kilian were written in the ninth century and have survived in a number of manuscripts.[28] It is probably one of those which was known at St-Évroult. It is possible that the cult of Kilian of Würzburg was introduced at St-Évroult by Ainard, a German monk who, between 1046 and 1078, was abbot of St-Pierre-sur-Dives, a monastery closely associated with St-Évroult. In his *Historia Ecclesiastica*, Orderic Vital tells us that Ainard was a man of exceptional talents, both literary and musical, and that the proof of his achievement could be seen in the works he composed for the feasts of saint Kilian of Würzburg and saint Catherine.[29] According to Geneviève Nortier, who studied the library catalogue of St-Évroult, the entry concerning Saint Kilian belongs to the set of entries added during the life time of Orderic Vitalis.[30] The interest in Kilian may not have been older than the eleventh century and did not last beyond the twelfth century. Apart from the mention in the St-Évroult catalogue, Kilian is not commemorated in any of the collection of saints Lives compiled in Normandy.

Saint Saëns = Sidonius = Setna

The monastery of St-Saëns, 25 miles north of Rouen, was founded in the 680s by an Irishman called Sidonius. The Irish origin of Sidonius has been questioned, mostly on the grounds that his name does not sound Irish. In fact the Latin forms *Sidonius* and *Sedonius* are used in Hiberno-Latin sources to render the Irish *Setna*. Several Carolingian sources mention the presence of Sidonius in Normandy between 670 and 690 and clearly state that he was of Irish origin. The *Second Life of Saint Audoen*, written in the ninth century, mentions Sidonius among the companions of Audoen as they prepare to leave for Rome: 'among them was Sidonius, an Irishman and the founder of a monastery which is now called by metonymy Saint Sidonius'.[31] The *Life of Filibert*, written around 750 and modified in the ninth century, tells us that when Filibert

---

25 *Acta sanctorum Hiberniae*, t. 1, p. 331.   **26** B. Krusch, *MGH, SRM* 5, pp 173–4.   **27** Paris, Latin 10062, fol. 80v, n° 121.   **28** W. Levison, *MGH, SRM* 5, pp 711–28.   **29** *HE*, IV, 18 (vol. 2, pp 352–54): '*Hic fuit natione Teutonicus, geminaque scientia pleniter imbutus uersificandi et modulandi cantusque suaues edendi peritissimus. Hoc euidenter probari potest in historiis Kiliani Guirciburgensis episcopi et Katerinae uirginis …*'; see also the eulogy of Ainard at the beginning of Book IV (vol. 2, pp 296–8).   **30** G. Nortier, *Les Bibliothèques médiévales des abbayes bénédictines de Normandie* (Caen 1966) pp 106–8.   **31** *Vita secunda Audoini*, 32: '*… multi etiam uenerabiles uiri et Deo deuoti una cum illo ire gaudebant; inter quos erat sanctus Sidonius, genere scottus, aedificator monasterii quod nunc per metonymiam Sanctum Sidonium dicunt*'; see also the note by W. Levison, *MGH, SRM* 5, p. 560, n. 1.

had to leave Jumièges to live in exile at Noirmoutier, his cellarer was Sidonius and, while he was in charge, the clothes and shoes for the monks were bought from Irish traders.[32] The *Life of Leutfred*, written in the ninth century, tells at length of Sidonius and of his good influence on Leutfred: 'Having heard of the reputation of holy Sidonius, the man of God Leutfred speedily arrived to the town of Rouen, where our man of God Sidonius, a native of Ireland, an island in Britain, was held in the highest respect for his splendid virtues'.[33] In spite of the critiques concerning the historical value of these individual saints Lives, they nevertheless confirm that at least from the ninth century, the hagiographic tradition about Sidonius the Irishman was alive and strong in the diocese of Rouen. Two Lives of Saint Saëns were written at the end of the tenth century and again in the twelfth century: both mention the Irish origin of the saint.[34] Orderic Vitalis knew of Sidonius and had read one of the Lives: 'Sidonius, Ribert, Germer, Leutfred and many other monks were active in the diocese of Rouen and all their good deeds were fostered by the zeal and help of the venerable archbishop Audoen, as the eager readers can clearly see in their Lives'.[35]

Saint Brendan

By the twelfth century, Saint Brendan of Clonfert had become one of the best known Irish saints on the continent. His legendary life and travels circulated in a variety of texts: (1) The *Vita Brendani*, probably written in the seventh century, by rewritten subsequently: it has survived in a number of fourteenth-century manuscripts and it is the source of the Irish version;[36] (2) The *Nauigatio Brendani*, written in Ireland in the second half of the eighth century and promoted on the continent in the tenth century by the Irish milieus in Lotharingia;[37] (3) A text also called *Vita Brendani*, which combine elements of the original *Vita* with episodes from the *Nauigatio*.[38] The most widespread text was that of the *Nauigatio Brendani*, which survives in more than 120 Latin manuscripts and was translated in most vernacular European languages from the twelfth century onwards.[39] Sometime between the end of the eighth century and the tenth century the *Nauigatio Brendani* must have travelled through Wales or Brittany as the close links between the hagiography of Saint Brendan and Saint Malo clearly show.[40] The manuscript tradition of the *Nauigatio Brendani* in Normandy illustrates the diversity of contacts and influences in eleventh- and twelfth-century Normandy. The text is found in four manuscripts: Alençon 14 (s. XI) from St-Évroult; Rouen 661 (s. XII) from St-Évroult; Rouen 1393 (s. XIII) from Jumièges, and Paris, Latin 5284 (s. XIII) from Foucarmont.

---

32 *Vita Filiberti*, 37 and 42 (ed. W. Levison, *MGH, SRM* 5, pp 583–604). **33** *Vita Leutfredi*, 8 (ed. W. Levison, *MGH, SRM* 7, pp 1–18): '*Audita fama beati Sydonii, uir Dei Leutfredus Rotomagensem urbem protinus aduenit, ubi prædictus homo Dei Sydonius, Hibernia Brittaniae insula ortus, uirtutum splendore uenerabilis habebatur*'. **34** A. Legris, 'Vie de saint Saëns, abbé au diocèse de Rouen, VIIe siècle', *AB* 10 (1891) pp 406–40. **35** *HE*, V, 9 (vol. 3, p. 62): '*Sidonius quoque et Ribertus, Geremarus, Leudfredus aliique plures monachi florebant in Rotomagensi diocesi, quibus omnibus ad omne bonum fauebat studium et auxilium Audoeni uenerabilis archiepiscopi, sicut feruidi lectores in eorum gestis possunt lucide contemplari*'. **36** BHL 1442; see J.F. Kenney, *The Sources for the early History of Ireland. Ecclesiastical* (New York 1929; repr. Dublin 1993) pp 412–14; G. Orlandi, *Navigatio sancti Brendani. I– Introduzione* (Milan 1968) pp 9–41; *Betha Brénainn*, ed. Ch. Plummer, *Bethada Náem nÉrenn. Lives of Irish Saints*, 2 vols (Oxford 1922) vol. 1, pp xvi–xxiii and 44–95. **37** BHL 1436–1439; C. Selmer (ed.), *Navigatio Sancti Brendani Abbatis from early Latin manuscripts* (Notre Dame, Indiana 1959) pp xxviii–xxix; D.N. Dumville, 'Two approaches to the dating of *Nauigatio Sancti Brendani*', *Studi Medievali* 29 (1988) pp 87–102. **38** BHL 1440–1441, 1446. **39** C. Selmer, 'The vernacular translations of the *Navigatio Sancti Brendani*: A bibliographical study', *Mediaeval Studies* 18 (1956) pp 145–57. **40** See S. Mac Mathúna, 'Contributions to a study of the voyages of St Brendan and St Malo', in C. Laurent and H. Davis (eds), *Irlande et*

Alençon 14 is one of the oldest manuscripts of the *Nauigatio* and, as Carl Selmer has shown, it is closely connected to Paris, Latin 15076 (s. XII) which belonged to the abbey of St-Victor in Paris. The original text came from Northern or Belgium: it is related to that in Gent 401 (s. XI) and Brussels 9920–31 (s. XI), which comes from St Laurent in Liège.[41]

Paris, Latin 5284 from Foucarmont also shows continental links and is related to manuscripts produced in Southern Germany.[42]

The other two manuscripts (Rouen 661 et Rouen 1393) present a more interesting case: they both belong to the series of nine manuscripts attesting a Breton connection in the textual transmission of the *Nauigatio*.[43] All these manuscripts include an interpolation in chapter two, which specifies that Malo was one of the fourteen disciples of Brendan and asks the public to read the *Life of Saint Malo* if they want to know more about this outstanding saint.[44] The author of this interpolation obviously knew the *Vita Machutis* and attempts to reconcile the hagiographic traditions concerning the two saints. The redactor of the Jumièges manuscript goes further in that direction by crediting Malo with the authorship of the *Vita Brendani*.[45] Linked with that of Saint Malo, the cult of Brendan may owe its continuous presence in Normandy throughout the Middle Ages to the vitality of Breton communities in that region.

Saint Patrick

The case of Saint Patrick is ambiguous, because although he is celebrated as the Apostle of Ireland, he was of British origin and, as in the case of Brendan, the Bretons played an important part in the spread of his cult in Normandy. The cult of Saint Patrick has left very little trace in France: there are only three town lands called *Saint-Patrice* in France, but out of the three, two are located in Normandy: Saint-Patrice-de-Claids and Saint-Patrice-du-Désert (see map); the third is Saint-Patrice in the district of Indre-et-Loire. But there are many dedications to Saint Patrick in Norman parishes: churches and altars are dedicated to Patrick in western Normandy at Huberville, Fierville-les-Mines, Hyenville and Le Teilleul, near Caen at Argences and near Rouen at Bosc-Roger.[46] The parish churches of St-Patrice at Bayeux and Rouen are also well known. It is difficult to ascertain when these dedications were made. In Rouen, the parish of St-Patrice was already well established in 1228 when the fire destroyed most of the town in that year. It was located outside the city walls in the quarter which housed the leather industry.[47] The location and the name of the saint are strongly evocative of the commercial contacts which existed between Ireland and Normandy in the tenth and eleventh centuries and which were reinforced from 1145 by a charter of Henry Plantagenêt, duke of Normandy, granting the town of Rouen a monopoly on commercial exchanges with Ireland.[48] Throughout the

Bretagne – Vingt siècles d'Histoire (Rennes 1994) pp 41–55.   **41** Selmer, *Navigatio Sancti Brendani*, pp xxxiii–xlix. **42** Munich Clm 29061 (s. X–XI) <Tegernsee; Munich, Clm 17740 (s. X) < St-Mang, Stadtamhof; Munich, Clm 22248 (s. XII) < Windberg.   **43** Rouen 661 (s. XII) < St-Évroult; Chartres 1036 (s. XIV); Paris, Lat. 5348 (s. XIII); Paris, Lat 2333A (s. XIII); Rouen 1393 (s. XIII) < Jumièges; Bruxelles 4241 (s. XVII) < Anchin; London, BL, Cotton. Vesp. B. X (s. XIII–XIV) < Durham; London, BL, Cotton. Vesp. A. XIV (s. XII–XIII) < Monmouth; Dublin, TCD, 580 (E 3.8) (s. XVII).   **44** *Navigatio S. Brendani*, § 2: '*Igitur sanctus Brendanus, de omni congregacione sua electis bis septem fratribus, [inter quos fuit preclarus ac Deo dignus adolescens Macutus qui ab infancia sua est electus quique usque ad finem uite sue permansit in Dei laudibus. Quod si quis noscere uoluerit perlegens eius uenerabila gesta inueniet eius opera prima et nouissima que preclara habentur] conclusit se in uno oratorio cum illis …*'   **45** Rouen 1393, fol. 178: '*Vita sancti Brendani abbatis et confessoris edita a uenerando discipulo eius Machuto*'.   **46** See G.H. Doble, 'Dedications to Celtic saints in Normandy', *Old Cornwall* 3 (1940) pp 275–82.   **47** A. Reneault, *La paroisse Saint-Patrice de Rouen* (Fécamp 1942) pp 1–3.   **48** J.H. Round, *Feudal England*, p. 467.

Middle Ages the main export products associated with Ireland were precisely leather and fur.[49] Again, it may not be fortuitous that a number of dedications to Saint Patrick are found in the area of Cotentin where a number of Hiberno-Norse families had settled in the tenth century (Muiredac > La Meurdraquière; Dicuil > Digulleville; Néill > Néhou).[50] But this is not necessarily so as the dedications to saint Patrick do not occur in isolation but appear in the context of dedication to Breton saints, especially Samson, Malo and Méen (see map). Léon Fleuriot has shown that these dedications, associated with place-names containing the words Brette, Bretteville and Canivet, coincide with the areas of Breton settlement in Normandy.[51] Uurdisten, abbot of Landévennec, wrote c.880 a *Life of Saint Guénolé*, in which he mentions the strength of the cult of Saint Patrick among the Bretons in the ninth century.[52] But, we know that the cult of Patrick, which is well attested in Breton liturgical texts, has left few traces in the geography of Brittany. On the other hand, Uurdisten's paragraph on the influence of Patrick on 'the churches of the whole world'[53] is better understood if one supposes that the abbot of Landévennec refers to the Breton churches outside Brittany.

Breton influence may also be responsible for the confusion between Patrick and Brendan in the Fleury manuscript of the *Martyrology of Fontenelle*.[54] The text shows that Patrick was celebrated in Avranches before the tenth century, but the date of the feast day, 16 May, and the use of the word Abbot instead of Bishop, suggests a confusion with Brendan. In the Corbie version of the same martyrology, the feast of Patrick is correctly entered under 17 March and the saint is given his proper titles of Bishop and Confessor.[55] In the twelfth century Patrick was commemorated at Bayeux and Fécamp.[56]

The text of St Patrick's *Confession* has survived in only eight manuscripts and one of them comes from Normandy. This is Rouen 1391, which dates from the eleventh century. The *Confession of Patrick* seems to have travelled through the same network as the *Life of Brigit* and the *Life of Fursa*, from Louth to Péronne and then to other continental monasteries with a strong Irish presence. The monks of Péronne had promoted the cult of St Patrick on the continent from the seventh century onwards,[57] and the early manuscripts of the *Confession* come from that area of Northern France.[58] The circulation of manuscripts was part of the general climate of close contacts between the regions of Picardy/Flanders and Normandy in the eleventh century.

De Courcy and the Order of Savigny

When members of the Anglo-Norman aristocracy finally settled in Ireland in the late twelfth century, they could not have been unaware of the earlier religious contacts nor of the importance

---

49 See A.F. O'Brien, 'Commercial relations between Aquitaine and Ireland c.1000 to c.1550' in J.-M. Picard, *Aquitaine and Ireland in the middle ages* (Dublin 1995) pp 31–80, at pp 31–43.   **50** L. Musset, 'Participation des Vikings venus des pays celtes à la colonisation scandinave de la Normandie', *Cahiers du centre de recherches sur les pays du nord et du nord-ouest* 1 (1978) pp 107–17; G. Fellows-Jensen, 'Les noms de lieux d'origine scandinave et la colonisation viking en Normandie', *Proxima Thulé* 1 (1994) pp 63–103.   **51** L. Fleuriot, *Les origines de la Bretagne* (Paris 1980) pp 102–3; pp 150–57 and map 7.   **52** *Vita Winwaloei*, c.19, ed. A. de la Borderie, *Cartulaire de l'abbaye de Landevenec* (Rennes 1888) pp 1–135.   **53** Ibid. c.19, p. 46: '… cunctas Hyberniae insulae illuminaret aecclesias, et non solum illas, sed etiam totius mundi omnes ad quas fama eius meritumque deferri potuisset …'   **54** Paris, Nouv. Acqu. Lat. 1604 (s. X) < Fleury-sur-Loire (cf. *Martyrologium Hieronymianum*, in *AASS*, Nov. 2/1): 'XVII Kl Iun. in Abrincatino Patricii Abbatis'.   **55** Paris, Lat. 12410 (s. XII) and 17767 (s. XII): 'XVI Kl Apr. Depositio Patricii episcopi et confessoris'.   **56** Bayeux Missal = Paris, Bibliothèque Mazarine 404 (s. XII) fol. 186v; Fécamp Missal = Rouen 290 (s. XII) fol. 169.   **57** See C. Doherty, 'The cult of St Patrick and the politics of Armagh in the seventh century', in Picard, *Ireland and Northern France*, pp 53–94.   **58** Paris, Latin 17626 (s. X) < Compiègne; Arras 450 (s. XII) < St-VaaSt

of the cult of specific saints in Irish society. For example, when John de Courcy undertook to issue his own money in Ulster, he had his own name minted on one side of the coins, but the other side bore the name of St Patrick. He was also responsible for the translation of the relics of Patrick, Brigit and Columcille at Downpatrick in 1185 and he commissioned a new Life of St Patrick, not from a local hagiographer, but from a monk of the Norman foundation of Furness.[59] In Normandy, the Courcy came from the areas of Breton settlement where the cult of St Patrick was prominent (Coutances and Hiémois; see map). Even though the continental branch and the insular branch of the family were quite distinct in the twelve century,[60] contacts were still alive. In the 1130s and 1140s Robert de Courcy frequently travelled between Normandy, where he was active as a Lord of the Exchequer and England, where he functioned as a royal judge.[61] William de Courcy, a close relative of John de Courcy, was Seneschal of Normandy in the 1170s.[62] The interest of John de Courcy in the cult of St Patrick must be viewed not only in the context of local politics in Down and Antrim, but in the wider context of the expansion of Norman ecclesiastical orders, especially the order of Savigny.

The order of Savigny had been founded in Normandy at the beginning of the twelfth century by Vital, monk of St-Évroult and chaplain of Count Robert de Mortain, a close relative of William the Conqueror. With the support of the Norman aristocracy, the monks of Savigny founded fourteen houses in Normandy, eleven in England, one in the Isle of Man and two in Ireland. The English foundations included Basinwerk and Furness in Lancashire, and the two Irish houses were Erenagh (i.e. Carrig, south of Downpatrick) founded in 1127 and St Mary's Abbey in Dublin, founded in 1139.[63] All the Savigniac foundations were amalgamated to the Cistercian order in 1147 but remained under the jurisdiction of the abbot of Savigny.[64] Six papal bulls were issued between 1148 and 1162 in order to protect the status – and the assets – of the order of Savigny. A bull of Pope Anastasius IV, dated 20 April 1154, is addressed to Richard de Courcy, fourth abbot of Savigny, and confirms his authority over the monasteries of Basingwerk and Furness in England and St Mary's in Dublin.[65] It may not be fortuitous that the new texts written in the 1180s in support of a renewed and stronger cult of St Patrick originate from this group of monasteries. The story of knight Owein's visit to Lough Derg which forms the core of the *Treatise on St Patrick's Purgatory* is presented as the authoritative account of Gilbert, abbot of Basingwerk,[66] and the new *Life of St Patrick*, written at John de Courcy's behest, is the work of Jocelyn, a monk at Furness. One of the manuscripts of the *Treatise on St Patrick's Purgatory* comes from Savigny.[67] In that context, it seems unlikely that John de Courcy discovered the importance of the cult of Patrick only after his arrival in the north of Ireland in 1177. I would suggest that, given his family background, he was well aware of the existence of Patrick as a major Irish saint and that this awareness played a significant role in his initial success in the Downpatrick area.

---

59 Ed. Bollandists, *AASS*, Mart. II, pp 540–80; J. Szövérffy, 'The Anglo-Norman conquest of Ireland and St Patrick: Dublin and Armagh in Jocelin's *Life of St Patrick*', *Repertorium Novum* 2 (1957–60) pp 6–16. **60** S. Duffy, 'The first Ulster plantation: John de Courcy and the men of Cumbria', in T. Barry, R. Frame and K. Simms (eds), *Colony and frontier in medieval Ireland* (London 1995) pp 1–27. **61** J. Le Patourel, *Normandy and England, 1066–1144* (Reading 1971) pp 33–4; M. Chibnall, *The Ecclesiastical History of Orderic Vitalis*, vol. 6, p. 517 and n. 3. **62** M. T. Flanagan, *Irish society, Anglo-Norman settlers, Angevin kingship. Interactions in Ireland in the late twelfth century* (Oxford 1989) pp 296–302. **63** A. Gwynn and R.N. Hadcock, *Medieval religious houses, Ireland* (Dublin 1970) pp 114–15. **64** A. Gwynn, 'The origins of St Mary's Abbey, Dublin', *JRSAI* 79 (1949) pp 110–25. **65** Ed. M. Sheehy, *Pontifica Hibernica*, 2 vols (Dublin 1962) vol. I, pp 11–12. **66** J.-M. Picard (tr.) and Y. de Pontfarcy, *Saint Patrick's Purgatory* (Dublin 1985) pp 14–15. **67** Paris Nouv. Acq. Lat. 217 (s. XIII).

Irish church reform in the twelfth century and Áed Ua Cáellaide, bishop of Louth: an Italian dimension

MARIE THERESE FLANAGAN

In 1982, in an article exploring the possible influence of Cluniac monasticism on the reform movement within the Irish church of the eleventh and twelfth centuries, Neithard Bulst drew attention to a marginal entry in the necrology of the Benedictine monastery of San Savino in Piacenza under 24 August which recorded *obiit Edanus lugdunensis episcopus 7 prior canonicorum mona 7 sanctimonialium per hiberniam*.[1] Bulst's main concern was to highlight the occurrence of an Irish bishop in the San Savino necrology, a house which had close connections with Cluny, and the Cluniac-influenced monastery of St Bénigne in Dijon, and to suggest that at least informal channels of influence between the Irish Church and Cluniac houses could have existed, which might serve to modify Aubrey Gwynn's contention that Cluniac monasticism had exerted virtually no influence on the church reform movement in Ireland.[2] Bulst was at a loss to identify the Irish bishop thus commemorated at San Savino, but suggested emending *Lugdunensis to Enagdunensis* and proposing an identification with a bishop of the Connacht diocese of Annaghdown, though he was unable to name a specific individual. The bishop, however, may be identified as Áed Ua Cáellaide, bishop of Louth (1138-resigned ante 1179, died 1182), who is attested in Latin sources of Irish provenance as *Edanus, episcopus Lugdunensis*.[3] The identification is confirmed more certainly by his description as 'prior of the monk canons and nuns of Ireland' which bears close analogy with his death notices in the Irish annals. Áed was described in the Annals of Loch Cé, 1182, as *espac Airgialla acus cend canánach* and in the Annals of the Four Masters as *espoc Airghiall 7 cend canánach Ereann*.[4] In 1138 Áed had been chosen by the leading reformer, Máel Máedóc Ua

---

1 Neithard Bulst, 'Irisches Mönchtum und cluniazenische Klosterreform' in *Die Iren und Europa im früheren Mittelalter*, ed. Heinz Löwe, 2 vols (Stuttgart 1982) pp 958–69 at p. 968, n. 61. The necrology was edited by Franz Neiske, *Das ältere Nekrolog des Klosters S. Savino in Piacenza: Edition und Untersuchung der Anlage*, Münstersche Mittelalter-Schriften, 36 (Munich 1979). The marginalia were not included, but I am very grateful to Dr Neiske, Institut für Frühmittelalterforschung, Westfälische Wilhelms-Universität, Münster, for kindly supplying me with a xerox reproduction of Piacenza, Bibl. com. MS 16, fol. 51v which contains the marginal entry. *Mona* occurs without abbreviational sign, but almost certainly should be expanded as *monachorum*, signifying regular or monastic canons as distinct from secular canons. Although the latter might live a common life in refectory and dormitory, they could retain personal property, whereas regular canons, like monks, held their worldly goods in common. It is particularly appropriate that the present study originated with a footnote in the published proceedings of the first international colloquium on Ireland and Europe held under the auspices of the Europa Zentrum with which Professor Ní Chatháin has had such a close association. **2** A. Gwynn, 'Irish monks and Cluniac reform', *Studies*, 29 (1940) pp 409–30 reprinted in A. Gwynn, *The Irish church in the 11th and 12th centuries*, ed. Gerard O'Brien (Dublin 1992) pp 1–16. **3** *Registrum Prioratus Omnium Sanctorum*, ed. R. Butler (Dublin 1845) pp 11, 50. Cf. *Gesta Henrici secundi Benedicti abbatis*, ed. W. Stubbs, 2 vols, *RS* (London 1867) i, p. 26; *Chronica Rogeri de Houedone*, ed. W. Stubbs, 4 vols, *RS* (London 1868–71) ii, p. 30, where he is described as *Edanus Lugdunensis episcopus* on Henry II's arrival in Ireland in 1171. **4** Cf. the entry in the catalogue of early Irish bishops in MS Rawl. B 480 fol. 63r, 'Aodh Ó Caolluidhe, epscop Airgiall is ceann canonach Ereann, quievit 1182' and the entry in the Mac Fhirbisigh-Ware catalogue of Irish bishops, 1665, in BL Add. MS 4799, fol. 19r, 'Aedh Úa Caellaidhe, .i. Aedh Ó Caellay, bishop of Oirgiall, superior of the *canonicorum Hiberniae quieuit*'. I am very grateful to Dr

94

Morgair, otherwise known as St Malachy of Armagh, from among 'three of his disciples' to be bishop of the diocese of Airgialla in succession to Malachy's own brother, Gilla Críst (Cristianus) Ua Morgair, who had held the office between 1135 and 1138.[5] From the very outset of his career, therefore, Áed, was identified closely with the reformist party, and he was installed, furthermore, in a diocese where Malachy's brother had already laid the groundwork, and where, with the support and patronage of Donnchad Ua Cerbaill, king of Airgialla (ante 1133–1168), Malachy was to achieve notable success in establishing reform structures. Donnchad Ua Cerbaill had been instrumental in installing Malachy as archbishop of Armagh in 1134 in the face of strenuous opposition from the hereditarily entrenched Clann Sínaich who had exerted a monopoly over the headship of the church of Armagh from AD 965. Although Malachy was first bishop of Connor (1124–6), then archbishop of Armagh (1132–6), and subsequently bishop of Down (1136–48), it was in the diocese of Airgialla and with the patronage of the Airgiallan king, Donnchad Ua Cerbaill, that the first Irish Cistercian house was established at Mellifont in 1142. Also in or about 1142 the first community of Augustinian canons of the Arroasian observance was established at the early Irish monastic site of St Mochta of Louth.[6] Like the Cistercian rule, the Arroasian customs were introduced by St Malachy following his journey to the Continent in 1139–40, when he had visited Arrouaise and inspected and approved its *consuetudines*, and had its *libri* and *usus*

Nollaig Ó Muraile, Dept of Celtic, the Queen's University of Belfast, for affording me access to his forthcoming edition of both these lists. In *A new history of Ireland: maps, genealogies, lists*, ix; ed. T.W. Moody, F.X. Martin, F.J. Byrne (Oxford 1984) p. 273, Áed's date of death is given as 29 March 1182. I can find no authority for that date other than a tentative suggestion that *Edanus episcopus* listed under that day in a fifteenth-century breviary from St Mary's Abbey, Trim, which was an Arroasian house, might perhaps commemorate Bishop Áed Ua Cáellaide: M.T. Flanagan, 'St Mary's Abbey, Louth and the introduction of the Arrouaisian observance into Ireland', *Clogher Record* 10 (1980) pp 223–34 at pp 232–3. As also pointed out there, however, the feast of Áedán of Doire Bruchais (Derrybrughas, par. Drumcree, bar. Oneilland West, County Armagh as identified in Pádraig Ó Riain, *Corpus genealogiarum sanctorum Hiberniae* (Dublin 1985) p. 320; Edmund Hogan, *Onomasticon Goedelicum* (Dublin 1910; repr. Dublin 2000) p. 326) is recorded under 29 March in the martyrologies of Tallaght, Uí Gormáin, and Donegal. Unfortunately, the Trim breviary lacks the months of July and August. It cannot therefore be ascertained whether it might have contained an entry for the day of death of Bishop Áed on 24 August as given in the San Savino necrology. Twelfth-century charters relating to the church of Louth indicate an association with a cult of a St Edanus. Thus, the church of Clonkeen, County Louth, granted by Cristinus, bishop of Louth, and Thomas, prior of Louth, to Peter Pipard and subsequently granted by Richard de Stormi to St Mary's Abbey, Dublin, was dedicated to St Edanus: *Chartularies of St Mary's Abbey, Dublin*; ed. J.T. Gilbert, 2 vols, RS (London 1884–6) i, p. 153; H.J. Lawlor, 'A charter of Cristin, bishop of Louth', *PRIA* 32 (1913–15) pp 28–40. He may be identified as Áed of Cluain Cháin in *Comainmigud noem hErenn* (as in *Corpus genealogiarum sanctorum Hiberniae*, p. 140, 707.24), but, unfortunately, his feast day is not included in the extant martyrologies. **5** *Sancti Bernardi opera*; ed. Jean Leclercq, C.H. Talbot and H.M. Rochais, 8 vols in 9 (Rome 1957–77) iii (1963) p. 341; H.J. Lawlor, *St Bernard of Clairvaux's life of St Malachy of Armagh* (London 1980) p. 67; Bernard of Clairvaux, *The life and death of Saint Malachy the Irishman*, trans. Robert T. Meyer (Kalamazoo 1978) pp 49–50. Gilla Críst's date of accession is determined by the death of his predecessor, Cináeth Ua Baígill, as 'bishop of Clogher' in 1135: *ATig.*, *AFM* 1135, *CS* 1131=1135. Gilla Críst's own death is recorded in 1138 when, according to *AFM*, he was buried in the church of St Peter and Paul, Armagh. His obit is recorded as 12 June in *Félire Húi Gormáin: the martyrology of Gorman*; ed. Whitley Stokes, *HBS* ix (London 1895) pp 114–15. His standing as a reformer is confirmed by his appearance in heaven in the *Visio Tundali* alongside St Patrick, Cellach of Armagh, St Malachy of Armagh, and Nehemias, bishop of Cloyne: *The vision of Tnugdal*; ed. J.M. Picard and Yolande de Pontfarcy (Dublin 1989) p. 155. Although titled 'bishop of Clogher' in *AFM*, Gilla Críst is styled 'bishop of Louth' in the *Visio Tnugdali* as well as in *Chartul. St Mary's Abbey, Dublin*, ii, p. 258. This suggests that the see of the diocese of Airgialla, that had been named as Clogher at the Synod of Ráith Bressail, 1111, which first drew up an island-wide framework of dioceses for the Irish church, moved from Clogher to Louth during the episcopate of Gilla Críst Ua Morgair. At the same time, a portion of the diocese of Armagh was transferred to the diocese of Airgialla, broadly coinciding with the territorial expansion of the kingdom of Airgialla that took place under the dynamic rulership of Donnchad Ua Cerbaill: Katherine Simms, 'The origins of the diocese of Clogher', *Clogher Record* 10 (1980) pp 180–98. **6** Flanagan, 'St Mary's Abbey, Louth', pp 223–34.

ecclesiae transcribed, and introduced its *ordo* and *officium* to Irish episcopal sees, because, as recorded at Arrouaise itself, he judged them to be particularly suited for that purpose.[7] Indeed the Arroasian canons established at Louth served also as the cathedral chapter of Áed's diocese. As such, they had the right to elect the bishop of the diocese. A desire to secure canonically valid episcopal elections that would be free from secular pressures and hereditarily entrenched family ties, such as Malachy himself had encountered in his roles as abbot of Bangor, bishop of Connor, archbishop of Armagh, and bishop of Down,[8] may have been one reason why Malachy deemed the introduction of the Arroasian observances as particularly appropriate for Irish *sedes episcopales*, though equal weight probably should also be accorded to the fact that, in imitation of the *vita apostolica* of the early church,[9] the property of the see would be held in common between the bishop and the community of canons, for the appropriation and privatisation of church property can be identified as another signal abuse in the twelfth-century Irish church that impeded the progress of reform, as Malachy knew from all too painful personal experience. Malachy undoubtedly also would have been aware that the recent Second Lateran council, 1139, had decreed that the 'goods of deceased bishops are not to be seized by anyone at all, but are to remain freely at the disposal of the treasurer and the clergy for the needs of the church and the succeeding incumbent'.[10] The introduction of Arroasian canons into Irish cathedral chapters might afford one means of enabling that decree to be better observed. Additionally, Louth Abbey, as the first Arroasian house established in Ireland, served not only as a cathedral chapter, but also as the mother-church of a filiation of houses of the Arroasian observance.[11] That is what the title 'head of the canons' accorded Áed in his annalistic death notices signified and which is echoed also in the San Savino necrology.

The entry in the San Savino necrology is interesting on a number of counts. First, it describes Áed as *prior*. The title of prior rather than abbot is precisely what was used at Louth Abbey, as attested, for example, in an original extant charter issued *c.*1187–8 in the joint names of Cristinus

7 *Fundatio monasterii Arroasiensis auctore Gualtero abbate*; ed. O. Holder-Egger, *MGH, SS*, XV, pp 1121–2; P.J. Dunning, 'The Arroasian order in medieval Ireland', *IHS* 4 (1945) pp 97–301 at p. 300, n. 1; Ludo Milis, *L'ordre des chanoines réguliers d'Arrouaise*, 2 vols (Brugge 1969) i, pp 345–8. Milis argues that *usus ecclesiae* is synonymous with *consuetudines* while the *libri* referred to liturgical books such as missals, graduals, and antiphonaries and that Malachy attached special importance to the recitation of the office. As pointed out by Milis, pp 324–6, 600–1, Malachy first encountered the Arrouaisian observance in a cathedral location at Carlisle on his way to the continent, where it had just recently been introduced by Bishop Aethelulf, *c.*1138–9. 8 M.T. Flanagan, 'John de Courcy, the first Ulster plantation and Irish church men' in *Britain and Ireland, c.900–1300: insular responses to medieval European change*; ed. B. Smith (Cambridge 1999) pp 154–78 at p. 165. 9 See Colin Morris, *The papal monarchy: the western church from 1050 to 1250* (Oxford 1989) pp 74–8; David Ganz, 'The ideology of sharing: apostolic community and ecclesiastical property in the early middle ages' in *Property and power in the early middle ages*; ed. W. Davies and P. Fouracre (Cambridge 1995) pp 17–31. The apostolic ideal of common property was highlighted as the attribute of coenobitic monks in the *Collectio Canonum Hibernensis*: H. Wasserschleben, *Die irische Kanonensammlung*, 2nd edn (Leipzig 1885) pp 147, 151. Milis places greater emphasis on Malachy's interest in the liturgical *ordo* and *officium* of Arrouaise than its institutional practices, a view based primarily on the fact that the attendance of Irish abbots at the general chapter of Arrouaise appears to have been unsatisfactory: Milis, *L'ordre des chanoines réguliers d'Arrouaise*, pp 345–6; Irish abbots were prescribed a penance *c.*1180–93 for non-attendance at the annual general chapter: Ludo Milis, *Constitutiones canonicorum regularium ordinis Arroasiensis*, CCCM 20 (Turnhout 1970) p. xlv, 196. 10 *Decrees of the ecumenical councils*; ed. N.P. Tanner (London 1990) p. 197. About 1102 Anselm, archbishop of Canterbury, wrote to Samuel Ua hAingliu, bishop of Dublin, complaining that various objects given by Anselm's predecessor, Archbishop Lanfranc, to Samuel's predecessor, his uncle, Donngus (Donatus), had not been intended as a personal gift but for the use of the church of Dublin: J.F. Kenney, *Sources for the early history of Ireland* (New York 1929, repr. Dublin 1993) no. 643; *Sancti Anselmi Cantuariensis archiepiscopi opera omnia*; ed. F.M. Schmitt, 6 vols (Rome 1938–61) iv, p. 192, no. 278; *The letters of St Anselm of Canterbury*; ed. Walter Fröhlich, 3 vols (Kalamazoo 1990–4) ii, p. 281, no. 278. 11 Flanagan, 'St Mary's Abbey, Louth', pp 228–33.

(Gilla Críst Ua Máel Chiaráin), bishop of Louth, and Thomas (Gilla Tigernaig), prior of Louth.[12] Secondly, the San Savino necrology described Áed not only as prior of the canons, but also of the *sanctimoniales* of Ireland. The latter titulature is not included in his annalistic death notices. Female religious foundations as an aspect of the twelfth-century reform movement in the Irish church have tended to be overlooked. It is noteworthy, however, that the *Visio Tnugdali* written *c*.1149 described Malachy as the 'builder of fifty-four congregations of monks, canons and nuns to whom he provided all the necessities of life and kept nothing at all for himself'.[13] There was a concentration of Malachy's monastic innovations in the diocese of Airgialla during the episcopate of Áed Ua Cáellaide, and at least one important female community following the Arroasian observance can be shown to have been established at Termonfeckin near Louth Abbey, during the reign of Donnchad Ua Cerbaill, king of Airgialla. An entry copied into the fifteenth-century so-called Antiphonary of Armagh from an earlier source, runs:

> A prayer for Donnchad Ua Cerbaill, over-king of Airgialla, by whom were made the book of Cnoc na n-Apstal [Knock] at Louth and the chief books of the order of the year, and the chief books of the mass. It is this great king who founded the entire monastery both stone and wood, and gave territory and land to it for the prosperity of his soul in honour of Paul and Peter. By him the church throughout the land of Airgialla was reformed, and a regular bishopric was established, and the church was placed under the jurisdiction of the bishop. In his time tithes were received and marriage was assented to, and churches were founded and *teampaill* and bell-houses were made, and monasteries of monks and canons and nuns were re-edified, and *neimheda* were made. These are especially the works which he performed for the prosperity [of his soul] and reign in the land of Airgialla, namely the monastery of monks on the banks of the Boyne [the Cistercian abbey of Mellifont], both stone and wooden furniture and books, and territory and land, in which there are one hundred monks and three hundred conventuals, and the monastery of canons of Termann Feichin, and the monastery of nuns, and the great church of Termann Feichin, and the church of Lepadh Feichin, and the church of ... [14]

Termonfeckin, then, had a community both of canons and of female religious at the same location, a pattern attested also at other early Arroasian houses, and since there is evidence that Termonfeckin was affiliated to St Mary's Abbey, Louth,[15] of which Áed Ua Cáellaide was head, he could indeed be regarded as head not only of canons but also of nuns, as described in the San Savino necrology. It is noteworthy that Giraldus Cambrensis in a chapter on Ireland in his *Speculum ecclesiae*, an attack on contemporary monastic orders, cited the scandal of the close vicinity of houses of canons and nuns of the Arroasian observance in Ireland, that were separated neither by wall nor bank but only thin and all too penetrable fences, and that he located those houses specifically *in Ardmacensi provincia et Urielensis diocesis parochia*, that is in the diocese of

12 H.J. Lawlor, 'A charter of Cristin, bishop of Louth', *PRIA* 32 (1913–15) pp 28–40; cf H.J. Lawlor, 'A charter of Donatus, prior of Louth', idem, pp 313–33.   13 *Vision of Tnudgal*, p. 155. The emphasis on his lack of personal property is in conformity with the conception of the *vita apostolica*. For female religious within the Arrouaisian *ordo* see Milis, *L'ordre des chanoines réguliers d'Arrouaise*, i, pp 248–9, 502–17.   14 Obituary notice as cited in George Petrie, *The ecclesiastical architecture of Ireland: an essay on the origins and uses of the round towers of Ireland* (Dublin 1845, repr. Shannon 1970) p. 394, which gives both the Irish text and a translation; also in translation in *Félire Húi Gormáin*, p. xx; H.J. Lawlor, *St Bernard of Clairvaux's life of St Malachy of Armagh*, as above note 5, p. 170; Brendan Smith (ed.), *Colonisation and conquest in medieval Ireland: the English in Louth, 1170–1330* (Cambridge 1999) p. 16; cf Kenney, *Sources*, no. 658.   15 Flanagan, 'St Mary's Abbey, Louth', pp 229–30.

Airgialla or Louth.[16] The San Savino entry reveals, then, an accurate knowledge of Bishop Áed's role in the Irish church. Furthermore, its insertion in the necrology may also almost certainly be dated before 1196 by which date the female community of St Mary's, Termonfeckin, had come under the authority of Agnes, abbess of the Arroasian convent of St Mary's Clonard, Co. Meath, as evidenced by a confirmation of Pope Celestine III which listed thirteen other conventual churches as subject to the abbess of Clonard.[17] The papal confirmation reveals that Agnes was by then acknowledged as grand abbess of a filiation of female Arroasian communities. In the early stages of the introduction of the Arroasian observance Áed, as head of the first such house established in Ireland, may be expected to have played a key role in relation not only to the male but also the female communities, but there is evidence for restructuring and rearrangement of filiations following his death. In the case of the Arroasian house of All Hallows, Dublin, for example, the circumstance whereby Áed had jurisdiction over a religious community in the diocese of Dublin struck the Anglo-Norman incomer, John Cumin, who was elected archbishop of Dublin in 1181, as anomalous, and he took steps to amend it. Áed Ua Cáellaide's successor as bishop of Louth, Máel Ísu (Malachias) Ua Cerbaill (*ante* 1179–1186/7), was obliged to renounce to John Cumin any claims by his successors to All Hallows, retaining his rights there only for the duration of his lifetime.[18]

It is interesting to speculate on how Áed Ua Cáellaide's death came to be recorded at San Savino in Piacenza. A *hospitium* for Irish pilgrims had been established at Piacenza in AD 850. The Irishman Donatus, bishop of Fiesole (829–876), on 20 August 850, had bestowed on St Columbanus's foundation of Bobbio a church dedicated to St Brigit located just outside the

16 *Giraldi Cambrensis opera*; ed. J.S. Brewer and J.F. Dimock, 8 vols, *RS* 21 (London 1861–91) iv, p. 183. **17** M.P. Sheehy, *Pontificia Hibernica: medieval papal chancery documents concerning Ireland, 640–1261*, 2 vols (Dublin 1962–5) i, no. 29. The confirmation to Agnes probably was occasioned by the death in the same year of *In banab mor ingen hUi Maeilsechlainn: A.L.C.* She occurs as 'Caillech Mór, daughter of Ua Máel Sechlainn, *ceand caillech Erend*' in the *Banshenchas*: Margaret Dobbs, 'The Ban-Shenchus', *RC* 48 (1931) pp 163–234 at p. 234. Her mother was Sadb, daughter of Ua Nualláin, king of Fotharta, and she herself was the mother of Máel Ruanaid and Dunlaing and Cremthainn, sons of Mac Dalbaig Ua Domnaill, king of Uí Felmeda. She probably therefore entered the convent as a widow. The distinction between *sanctimoniales* or choir canonesses and lay *conversae* has to be borne in mind, but there can be little doubt that Clonard contained *sororibus … regularem vitam professis*: Sheehy, *Pontificia Hibernica*, i, no. 29. Cf Avicia de la Corner, *vidua*, who founded and became the first prioress of the convent of Lismullin: *Pontificia Hibernica*, ii, no. 493.   **18** The text of the quit-claim is printed as an appendix in *Registrum Prioratus Omnium Sanctorum*, p. 100, where the bishop's initial is given as E representing Edanus, that is Áed Ua Cáellaide. The text is taken, however, from Archbishop Alen's register and the initial has been emended silently from R. to E: *Calendar of Archbishop Alen's register, c.1172–1534*; ed. Charles McNeill (Dublin: Royal Society of Antiquaries of Ireland, 1950) p. 35. Another version of the text in the *Crede mihi* gives M as the bishop's initial: J.T. Gilbert, *Crede mihi: the most ancient register book of the archbishops of Dublin before the Reformation* (Dublin 1897) p. 70, no. lxxx. This would equate with Áed's immediate successor, Máel Ísu Ua Cerbaill (Malachias), and on chronological grounds must be judged more likely. Although John Cumin was elected archbishop of Dublin at Evesham in September 1181, and was consecrated by Pope Lucius III at Velletri on 21 March 1182, he did not visit his diocese until 1184 when he was dispatched by Henry II in advance of the expedition of his son, John, to Ireland in 1185: *Gesta Henrici*, i, pp 280, 287, 320; *Chronica Rogeri de Houedone*, ii, p. 263, 267; Giraldus Cambrensis, *Expugnatio Hibernica*; ed. A.B. Scott and F.X. Martin (Dublin 1978) pp 198–9, and p. 342, n. 385. Cumin is unlikely to have been in a position to negotiate severance of the link between All Hallows and the bishop of Louth before his arrival in Dublin in 1184. It may be noted, however, that Cumin secured from Pope Lucius III (1181–5) a comprehensive papal privilege, *tuis iustis postulationibus*, dated 13 April 1182 at Velletri, pertaining to the rights of his new see which exhibits detailed knowledge of local conditions and exhorts him to treat his clergy with pastoral affection 'so that even those opposed to your rule may by good will be joined to you': Sheehy, *Pontificia Hibernica*, i, no. 11. This probably refers to the clergy of his cathedral church of Holy Trinity, Dublin. The register compiled by Archbishop John Alen, the first Henrician archbishop of Dublin (1529–34) and an assiduous investigator of the archives of his diocese, makes reference to a no longer extant bull of Pope Lucius III in favour of the canons of Holy Trinity, Dublin: *Alen's register*, p. 8.

south-west angle of the city wall in Piacenza on the condition 'that if any *peregrinus* of my people comes, I want and require that two or three shall stay and be taken care of there under the protection of a provost employed for this work'.[19] Piacenza was located along the well-trodden trans-Appenine route through Francia to Rome.[20] The foundation of the *hospitium* at Piacenza may be linked to what Kathleen Hughes discerned as a change in the motivation of Irish travellers to the continent during the ninth century,[21] when they went either on Roman-style pilgrimages *ad limina* or settled for longer periods under local patronage in hospices. Carolingian legislation had attempted to regulate for the maintenance of such hospices so that pilgrims would not constitute a drain on normal diocesan funds. Donatus's association with the Carolingian court is well documented. As bishop of Fiesole he was the direct vassal of the Carolingian king and an important representative of Carolingian interests in northern Italy. Most of the historical notices that mention Donatus record his presence at church councils or royal meetings acting in the interests of Carolingian kings, and in the memorial poem which he himself wrote shortly before his death he recalls 'how loyally I served the kings of Italy, Lotharius the great and Ludovicus the good'.[22] One of the strategies that the Carolingian kings used to implant themselves in the kingdom of Lombardy, following its conquest by Charlemagne in AD 774, was to accord much greater power to bishops than had their predecessors, the Lombard kings. For that very reason the Carolingians preferred non Italo-Lombard ecclesiastics who might be subject to constraints and pressures emanating from their local connections. The Irish *peregrinus*, Dungal, who was installed as head of the cathedral school of Pavia in 825 by royal decree of the Carolingian king, Lothar, and who wrote a treatise rebutting Claudius, bishop of Turin, at the height of the Iconoclastic controversy, affords a pertinent example of such Carolingian *Kirchenpolitik*.[23] Whether or not Bishop Donatus was a Carolingian appointee at Fiesole, positioned to manage a strategically sensitive region, what is certain is that during his forty-seven year episcopate he acted in close association with the Carolingian kings. It need therefore occasion no surprise that, in compliance with Carolingian legislation relating to the management of *hospitia*, he endowed a hospice for Irish *peregrini* at Piacenza under the auspices of the Irish foundation of Bobbio. The earliest

---

19 *Si de gente mea aliquis peregrinus advenerit, volo et instituo ut duos aut tres ibi sub tutela praepositi praefati degant et alantur.* Carlo Cipolla and E.G. Buzzi, *Codice diplomatico de monastero di San Colombano di Bobbio fino all'anno MCCVIII*, 3 vols, Fonti per la Storia d'Italia, vols 52, 53, 54 (Rome 1918) i, no. 44, pp 165–9 and cf ii, pp 230–1; Simon Young, 'Donatus and the cult of St Brigit in Italy', *CMCS* 35 (1998) pp 13–26, from which the English translation given here is derived. For details of the metrical life of Brigit attributed to Donatus see Michael Lapidge and Richard Sharpe, *A bibliography of Celtic-Latin literature, 400–1200* (Dublin 1985) no. 693; Kenney, *Sources*, no. 151 (i). For an epitaph poem attributed to Donatus see *MGH, PL* III (Berlin 1896) pp 691–2; cf Kenney, *Sources*, no. 421; Lapidge and Sharpe, no 694. A later life of Bishop Donatus is included in *ASS*, Oct. 22 (Paris 1869) pp 648–62; cf Kenney, *Sources*, no. 421.   **20** It is significant that Piacenza is shown on the map included in the manuscript of Giraldus Cambrensis's Irish works, National Library of Ireland, MS 700, fol. 48, which depicts the British Isles in relation to Rome and is based on contemporary routes used by travellers to Rome from the British Isles: Thomas O'Loughlin, 'Giraldus Cambrensis's map of Europe', *History Ireland*, 8, no. 2 (2000) pp 16–21.   **21** Kathleen Hughes, 'The changing theory and practice of Irish pilgrimage', *Journal of Ecclesiastical History* 11 (1960) pp 143–51, reprinted in Kathleen Hughes, *Church and society in Ireland, AD 400–1200* (London 1987) chapter 14.   **22** *MGH PL* III, pp 691–2; Young, 'Donatus', pp 13–15.   **23** Claudio Leonardi, 'Gli irlandesi in Italia: Dungal e la controversia iconoclastica' in Löwe, *Iren*, as above note 1, pp 746–57; Lapidge and Sharpe, nos 657–9; Kenney, *Sources*, pp 516, 535, 538–42, 550, 563. More recent scholarship, as detailed by Leonardi, has reduced Kenney's suggested three individuals by the name of Dungal – one associated with St Denis in Paris, another with Pavia, and a third with the monastery of Bobbio – to a single individual; see also Mary Garrison, 'The English and the Irish at the court of Charlemagne' in *Karl der Grosse und sein Nachwirken: 1200 Jahre Kultur und Wissenschaft in Europa/Charlemagne and his heritage: 1200 years of civilization and science in Europe*, ed. P. Butzer, M. Kerner and W. Oberschelp (Turnhout 1997) pp 97–123.

reference in Carolingian legislation to specifically *hospitalia Scottorum* occurs in canon 40 of the acts of the Council of Meaux, 845, which legislated for the restoration to their original use of such houses, indicating that they had been in existence for some time, and which sought the intervention of the west Frankish king, Charles the Bald (847–77), to effect such restitution. This was approved by Charles at a *conventus* at Épernay in 846. In 858 the bishops of the dioceses of Reims and Rouen wrote to the east Frankish king, Louis II, the German (843–76), urging him to ensure that the *hospitalia Scottorum* were properly administered.[24] That is the ninth-century context in which Bishop Donatus's endowment of a *hospitium* for Irish *peregrini* in Piacenza should be set.

The entry relating to Edanus, bishop of Louth, inserted into the San Savino necrology attests to an Irish presence at Piacenza in the late twelfth century where the *hospitium* for Irish travellers may still have been in operation. By some means, the date of death of Bishop Edanus was made known to San Savino. How did this come about? Had Áed himself once passed through Piacenza while travelling en route to Rome? His patron, St Malachy, had travelled to Rome in 1139 and it was Malachy's intention to do so again in 1148, had he not been prevented by his untimely death at Clairvaux. St Malachy is reputed to have petitioned confirmation from Pope Innocent II (1130–43) that the *quartam episcopalem per totam Ergalliam dari episcopis Clogherensibus*, suggesting early contact between Áed's diocese and the papal court.[25] It is not inconceivable that during Áed's long episcopate, 1138–79, he might have journeyed to Italy, especially as his diocese of Airgialla was perhaps the most important trial ground for reformist structures within the Irish church during that period.[26] Normally, inclusion in a necrology was no chance occurrence. It had to be earned in some way. The person was either a member of the religious house in which the necrology was kept, or a member of a house under the same rule, or of another religious community filiated via a formal confraternity of prayer. Edanus was not a follower of the Cluniac observance, nor even a Benedictine monk. Alternatively, though less usually, insertion in a necrology might result from some form of personal contact either directly with the individual or a close associate. Names were almost always included in necrologies in the case of recently dead, and indeed the hand-writing of the San Savino entry accords with a late twelfth-century or early thirteenth-century date. The fact that it is a marginal insertion at the foot of the page suggests also that it was not copied from another necrology, as might sometimes be the case, but recorded at San Savino itself.

Although the evidence is almost invariably chance and incidental, a substantial amount of Irish traffic to and from Rome may be assumed by the late twelfth century. Aubrey Gwynn first drew attention to a series of annalistic entries recording Irish royal pilgrims travelling to Rome in the first half of the eleventh century, presumably because they were more noteworthy than clerical

---

24 Kenney, *Sources*, pp 600–2.   25 K.W. Nicholls, 'The Register of Clogher', *Clogher Record* 7 (1971–2) pp 361–431 at p. 371n., 384. The context in which the papal privilege was sought may have been the transfer of a portion of the diocese of Armagh to the diocese of Airgialla: below n. 26.   26 In return for the support of Donnchad Ua Cerbaill, king of Airgialla, Malachy had enlarged the diocese of Airgialla at the expense of the diocese of Armagh. There is evidence to suggest that following Malachy's death in 1148, his successor at Armagh, Gilla meic Liac, with the support of Muirchertach Mac Lochlainn, king of Cenél nEógain, sought to recover the ceded territory. It is significant that Áed Ua Cáellaide is not listed as present at the Synod of Kells, 1152: Geoffrey Keating, *Foras feasa ar Éirinn*, ed. P.S. Dinneen, iii, *ITS*, ix (1908) pp 316–17. His absence may be linked to an annalistic entry recording that 'Gilla meic Liac, successor of Patrick, was mortally wounded by Ua Cerbaill, king of Airgialla, when outraging him, and because of that Ua Cerbaill was plundered and deposed by the son of Mac Lochlainn': *ATig.*, cf *AFM*. It is conceivable that a dispute over diocesan boundaries between Gilla meic Liac and Áed Ua Cáellaide could have occasioned the latter's recourse to the papal court. The use of the title 'bishop of Louth' was politically charged, for Louth was situated in that part of the diocese of Airgialla which had been acquired at the expense of the diocese of Armagh.

travellers or lesser lay pilgrims, while an entry in the Annals of Inisfallen in 1095 recording the death of *Eogan cend manach na Gaedel hi Roim* affords the sole Irish evidence for the existence of an Irish community of monks there, though valuable corroborative testimony comes from a Vatican manuscript containing two lists of latinized Irish names, the second list being written in a distinctively Irish hand.[27] Gilla Espaic or Gilbertus, bishop of Limerick, who on the testimony of Bernard of Clairvaux was the first native papal legate in Ireland,[28] may be presumed to have been appointed to that office as a result of an otherwise unknown continental visit in the early twelfth century. Imar Ua hÁedacáin, St Malachy's teacher according to St Bernard of Clairvaux, and builder of the stone church of Saints Peter and Paul at Armagh which was consecrated on 21 October 1126 according to the Annals of Ulster, died in Rome in 1134.[29] In 1140, on the testimony of St Bernard, Malachy spent a month in the city of Rome visiting holy places and was intending a return visit when he died at Clairvaux in November 1148. Malachy had hoped to request *pallia* for the Irish archbishoprics from Pope Eugenius III, and, in the wake of Malachy's death, the pope sent Cardinal John Paparo as papal legate to Ireland in 1152. Paparo, as reported by the English chronicler, John of Hexham, travelled to Ireland in the company of an Irish bishop, who is named in the annals of St Mary's Abbey, Dublin, as Gilla Críst Ua Conairche, bishop of Lismore, native papal legate, and former first abbot of Mellifont.[30] Gilla meic Liac, archbishop of Armagh, received his pall at the hands of Cardinal Paparo in 1152, but when he died on 27 March 1174, his successor, Conchobar mac Meic Con Caille (Concors), formerly abbot of the monastery of St Peter and Paul, Armagh, and probably therefore an Arroasian canon, travelled in person to Rome to receive his *pallium*, dying on the continent in 1175 on his return journey.[31] Two archbishops and four Irish bishops attended the third Lateran council which met between 5–19 March 1179, Lorcán Ua Tuathail, archbishop of Dublin, who had introduced the customs of Arrouaise to his cathedral church of Holy Trinity, Dublin, *c.*1162, Cadla (Catholicus) Ua Dubthaig, archbishop of Tuam, Brictius, bishop of Limerick, Constantín Ua Briain, bishop of Killaloe, Augustinus Ua Selbaig, bishop of Waterford, and Felix, bishop of Lismore.[32] On 2 July 1186 Pope Urban III issued a confirmation to All Hallows, Dublin, *vestris iustis postulationibus*, confirming it in its use of the Augustinian rule and Arroasian *institutio*, and in its possessions, privileges, rights and immunities, and, on the same date, two confirmations in similar form were also issued to the prior of the Arroasian house of Holy Trinity, Dublin.[33] A dispatch to Rome to obtain those confirmations may be assumed. In his confirmation to Holy Trinity, Dublin, Pope Urban III refers to exemplars of his predecessors, Alexander III (1159–81) and Lucius III (1181–5), indicating yet earlier Arroasian traffic from Ireland to the papal court, and allowing for the possibility of a journey in 1182.[34] It is noteworthy that the priory of All Hallows, Dublin, owed its

27 *AI*, 1095.13; André Wilmart, 'La Trinité des Scots à Rome et les notes du Vat. Lat. 378', *RB* 41 (1929) pp 218–30; 'Finian parmi les moines romains de la Trinité des Scots', *RB* 44 (1932) pp 359–61; Aubrey Gwynn, 'Ireland and the continent in the eleventh century', *IHS* 7 (1953) pp 193–216, reprinted in Gwynn, *Irish Church in the 11th and 12th centuries*, pp 34–49.   **28** He was most likely appointed by Pope Paschal II (1099–1118). I accept the arguments against Máel Muire Ua Dunáin, bishop of Meath, having been native papal legate prior to Bishop Gilla Espaic: Donnchadh Ó Corráin, 'Máel Muire Ua Dúnáin 1040–1117, reformer' in P. de Brún et al. (eds), *Folia Gadelica* (Cork 1983) pp 47–53.   **29** *Sancti Bernardi opera*, iii, p. 313, 317, 323; *AU*2, 1126.11; *AFM* 1134. His day of death is recorded as 13 August in *Félire Húi Gormáin*, pp 156–7.   **30** *Symeonis monachi opera omnia*; ed. T. Arnold, *RS* (London 1885) ii, p. 36; *Chartul. St Mary's, Dublin*, ii, p. 263.   **31** *AU, AFM, A. Boyle*. The day of death of Gilla meic Liac was recorded in *Félire Húi Gormáin*, pp 62–3.   **32** J.D. Mansi, *Sacrorum conciliorum nova et amplissima collectio*, 31 vols (Florence-Venice, 1759–98; reprinted and continued 53 vols in 60 Paris-Arnhem) xx, col. 217.   **33** Sheehy, *Pontificia Hibernica*, i, nos. 13, 14, 15.   **34** See above, n. 18. According to the early thirteenth-century

origins to a land-grant made *c*.1162 to Bishop Áed Ua Cáellaide as head of the Arroasian canons in Ireland by Diarmait Mac Murchada, king of Leinster, and overlord of the city of Dublin.[35] An Irish traveller, or supplicant on a mission to the papal court, with Arroasian connections halting at Piacenza in or around the time of death of Áed Ua Cáellaide in 1182, may have been responsible for securing the insertion of the entry in the San Savino necrology.

Although Áed Ua Cáellaide died in 1182, he can be shown to have resigned his bishopric no later than 1179 for his successor, Máel Ísu (Malachias) Ua Cerbaill, is attested as bishop of Airgialla in that year when he was present at the synod of Clonfert, convened by Lorcán Ua Tuathail, archbishop of Dublin, as native papal legate on his return from the third Lateran council.[36] How and where did Áed spend his last days? Although the year of his death is recorded in the Irish annals under 1182 it is not stated where he died. Could he have died in Italy? Probably he was too old by then to have undertaken a journey to the continent in person, and it might be better to assume that another Irish traveller, almost certainly an Augustinian *confrater*, in view of the title accorded Áed as head of the canons and nuns of Ireland, conveyed the news of his recent death to the San Savino community. If so, however, it tells us less about possible Cluniac influence on the Irish Church, as suggested by Bulst, than it does about Irish, and probably Arroasian, travellers in Italy, and specifically at Piacenza which may be assumed to have been a traditional halting point for Irish travellers not only because of the tradition of an *hospitium Scottorum* there, but also because of its proximity to St Columbanus's foundation at Bobbio which Irish pilgrims are also likely to have wished to visit. It is worth noting that in an Irish context Arroasian canons were especially active in recording death days, as the compilation of no less than four martyrologies in the late twelfth century indicates. First there is the *Félire Uí Gormáin* compiled *c*.1170–4 which takes its name from Máel Muire Ua Gormáin, abbot of the Arroasian house of Knock, located near Louth, comprising a vernacular metrical martyrology combining the feast days of Irish and foreign saints, and which drew on continental sources, in itself telling evidence for the continental

life of St Lorcán Ua Tuathail, on his translation from the abbacy of Glendalough to the see of Dublin, he introduced the Arrouaisian *usus et consuetudines* to Holy Trinity, Dublin, *c*.1162 and sent two of his canons to Rome to seek papal confirmation: Charles Plummer, 'Vie et miracles de St Laurent, archevêque de Dublin', *AB* 33 (1914) pp 121–86 at p. 138; cf *Chartul. St Mary's, Dublin*, ii, p. 268. **35** *Registrum Prioratus Omnium Sanctorum*, p. 50; Flanagan, 'St Mary's Abbey, Louth', pp 228–33. **36** *AClon.* 1170 recte 1179 pp 213–14. The date of Áed's resignation is given as *ante* May 1178 in *A new history of Ireland*, ix, p. 273. This is unreliably based on the fact that Áed Ua Cáellaide heads the list of witnesses in a charter-text of Lórcán Ua Tuathail, archbishop of Dublin, in favour of Holy Trinity, Dublin, in which Áed is styled simply *Edano episcopo* while the second witness is given as Malachias, bishop of Louth: M. P. Sheehy, 'The registrum novum, a manuscript of Holy Trinity Cathedral: the medieval charters', *Reportorium novum* 3 (1963–4) pp 249–81 at p. 280; cf 'Calendar to Christ Church deeds' in *Report of the Deputy Keeper of the Public Records in Ireland*, xx, (Dublin, 1888) pp 36–122 at pp 102–4, no. 364 (a); *Chartae privilegia et immunitates, being transcripts of charters and privileges to cities, towns, abbeys, and other bodies corporat, … 1171–1395* (printed for the Irish Record Commission, Dublin 1829–30; published 1889) p. 2 *ex antiq. rotulo in archiv. eccles. S. Trin. Dublin*. The date, 14 May, given for the charter in the Registrum Novum and in the Christ Church calendar almost certainly should be interpreted as referring to the date of an inspeximus of 3 Edward IV, 1463, which, in turn, was exemplified on 10 May 11 Henry VII, 1496, and not to Archbishop Lorcán's original charter, since it would have been highly unusual for a twelfth-century charter to be so dated, and it does not accord with the diplomatic of other charters issued by Lorcán. Cf also Gwynn, *Irish church in the 11th and 12th century*, p. 137, where the same dating assumption as in *A new history of Ireland*, ix, p. 273, is made. It appears to have originated with H.J. Lawlor, 'The genesis of the diocese of Clogher', *Journal of the Co. Louth Archaeological Society* 4 (1916–20) pp 129–53 at p. 135. Another exemplification of Archbishop Lorcán's charter made on 5 May 1364 by Thomas White, notary public, at the behest of Stephen de Derby, prior of Holy Trinity, Dublin, and transcribed into the *Liber Albus* significantly did not include any dating clause for Archbishop Lorcán's charter: H.J. Lawlor, 'A calendar of the Liber Niger and Liber Albus of Christ Church, Dublin', *PRIA* 27 (1908) pp 1–93 at pp 24–5.

contacts of the Arroasian canons.[37] Áed Ua Cáellaide is mentioned in the preface as bishop of Airgialla at the time of its compilation, while the death of his predecessor, Bishop Gilla Críst Ua Morgair, is entered under 12 June.[38] The annals of the Four Masters recorded under 1148 that 'the church of Cnoc na Sengán [Knock, County Louth] was finished by Bishop Ua Cáellaide and Donnchad Ua Cerbaill, and was consecrated by Ua Morgair, a successor of Patrick, and a *nemed* was assigned to it in Louth', clear evidence of the affiliation between Louth and Knock. Secondly, there is a prose Latin martyrology known as the Drummond missal which Professor Pádraig Ó Riain attributes to a Glendalough redactor, where there was also an Arroasian community, and which likewise combines Irish and foreign saints.[39] Thirdly, there is evidence that by the late twelfth century the Arroasian community at Holy Trinity, Dublin, had a martyrology, no longer extant in its twelfth-century form, but which was incorporated into a later version.[40] More directly comparable typologically with the San Savino necrology is the book of obits of Holy Trinity, Dublin, which in its current form was compiled in the course of the fifteenth and sixteenth centuries, but it too drew on a twelfth-century record as evidenced by the inclusion of the day of death of eleventh and twelfth-century bishops of Dublin,[41] of Malachias, bishop of Kildare, who died in 1175,[42] of Earl Richard fitz Gilbert, otherwise known as Strongbow, who died on 20 April 1176,[43] of Prior Gervasius, who died c.1177,[44] of Macrobius, bishop of Glendalough who died before 1192, and of Cristinus, *sacerdos et canonicus noster*, who may be identified with the sacristan of the same name attested in two original extant charters issued by the community of Holy Trinity and by Lorcán Ua Tuathail, archbishop of Dublin, c.1176–7.[45] Fourthly, a fifteenth-century martyrology as well as the sanctorale portion of a breviary of the Arroasian house of St Peter and Paul, Trim, also shows evidence of drawing on a twelfth-century source.[46] According to the consuetudines of Arrouaise at the daily chapter the commemorative list of the dead who were to be remembered on that day, was read out,[47] which accounts at least in part for the compilation of necrologies in Arroasian circles. The mother-house of Arrouaise apparently actually prayed for the deceased *fratres Hibernenses* though no names of individual Irish men appear to have been recorded in extant continental Arroasian necrologies.[48]

37 See above n. 4 and Jacques Dubois, 'Les sources continentales du martyrologe irlandais de Gorman', *AB* 100 (1982) pp 607–17; Cf the death notice on 20 March 1174 of 'Flann Ua Gormáin, chief lector of Armagh and of all Ireland, a learned observant man in sacred and secular learning after having twenty-one years learning in France and England': *ALC, AFM*. He almost certainly was related to Abbot Máel Muire Ua Gormáin of Knock. **38** *Félire Húi Gormáin*, pp 4–5; cf above n. 4. **39** See *Beatha Bharra: Saint Finbarr of Cork, the complete life*: ed. Pádraig Ó Riain, *ITS* 57 (1993) p. 24; cf Kenney, *Sources*, no. 566. **40** *The book of obits and martyrology of the cathedral church of the Holy Trinity, commonly called Christ Church, Dublin*; ed. J.C. Crosthwaite (Dublin: Irish Archaeological Society, 1844). **41** *Book of obits*, pp 21, 23, 31, 42, 45, 51 and cf pp xxvi, xxxii. **42** *ATig., AFM*. **43** *Book of obits*, pp 21, 57; according to Ralph of Diss, Strongbow died on 5 April, according to Giraldus Cambrensis on 1 June, but his commemoration was kept on 20 April by Holy Trinity, Dublin, where he was buried, the funeral rite being performed by Archbishop Lorcán, and that date is supported by his obituary notice preserved at Tintern Abbey, Monmouthshire: *Radulphi de Diceto opera historica*; ed. William Stubbs, 2 vols, *RS* (London 1876) i, p. 407; Giraldus Cambrensis, *Expugnatio Hibernica*, pp 164–5; William Worcestre, *Itineraries*; ed. J.H. Harvey, Oxford Medieval Texts (Oxford 1969) pp 54–5. **44** For Gervasius, prior of Holy Trinity, see *Register of the Abbey of St Thomas, Dublin*; ed. J.T. Gilbert, *RS* (London 1889) pp 161, 285; Sheehy, 'Registrum novum:', p. 258; Calendar to Christ Church deeds' in *Report of the Deputy Keeper of the Public Records in Ireland*, xxiii (Dublin 1890) pp 75–152 at p. 75, no. 468 (a) and (f); and cf *Book of obits*, p. xxvi. **45** M.P. Sheehy, 'Diplomatica: unpublished medieval charters and letters relating to Ireland', *Archivium Hibernicum*, 25 (1962) pp 123–35 at p. 127, 128; cf Sheehy, 'Registrum novum', p. 258; Calendar to Christ Church deeds', pp 75–152 at p. 75, no. 468 (a) and (f). **46** See Aubrey Gwynn, 'A breviary from St Mary's Abbey, Trim', *Ríocht na Midhe* 3 (1963–6) pp 290–8 and cf above n. 4. Trim's observance of the custom of Arrouaise was confirmed by Pope Celestine III (1191–8) almost certainly in 1196, that is around the same time as his confirmation to the Arrouaisian house of St Mary's Abbey, Clonard: above n. 17. **47** Milis, *Constitutiones*, p. 38 and cf. pp 154–5, 165, 185, 198. **48** Milis, *Constitutiones*, p. 144. They

Augustinians of the Arroasian filiation in twelfth-century Ireland can be shown therefore to have been actively engaged in the compilation of martyrologies, calendars, and necrologies, and it is not inappropriate to suggest that one of their number passing through Piacenza may have been responsible for securing the insertion of Áed's death notice into the San Savino necrology. It is certainly possible to suggest a plausible reason why Arroasian canons from Ireland may have been travelling through Italy specifically in 1182: the circumstances of the Anglo-Norman John Cumin's election in September 1181 to the see of Dublin, which most exceptionally took place at Evesham rather than in Dublin, and his consecration at the papal court at Velletri in March 1182, thereby avoiding any possibility of his having to make a profession of obedience to the archbishop of Armagh as primate, may well have generated such traffic to Rome. The manner of Cumin's election and consecration undoubtedly would have raised serious concerns for the Arroasian canons of Holy Trinity, Dublin, who had been introduced c.1162 into his cathedral church by Archbishop Lorcán Ua Tuathail, since their right to act as electoral chapter had been by-passed. It is not inconceivable that, in the wake of Cumin's irregular election and consecration at the papal court, canons of Holy Trinity may have been dispatched as emissaries to the papal court to argue the case against the diminution of their rights; these may have passed through Piacenza and imparted the details of the recent death of Bishop Áed and his role as head of the Arroasian filiation in Ireland.[49]

A chance entry in an Italian manuscript serves to emphasise yet again how heavily reliant historians of the twelfth-century Irish Church reform movement are on externally generated sources. How little would be known of the origins of the church reform movement without the correspondence of the Canterbury archbishops, Lanfranc and Anselm, with Irish kings and bishops, while it would be well nigh impossible to reconstruct the career of St Malachy of Armagh without Bernard of Clairvaux's Life of Malachy. And not surprisingly perhaps, it does not convey the full story. From an English source we learn incidentally that Malachy met the English monastic reformer, St Gilbert of Sempringham, at Clairvaux[50] while in a similar way it is only from an account of Abbot Gualterus of Arrouaise, that we ascertain that Malachy had visited that house and had introduced its customs to the Irish church. The San Savino entry affords one more tiny, albeit, given the dearth of information, valuable piece of evidence, and invites us to keep an open mind about an Italian dimension to the Irish Church reform movement and continental contacts of Irish Augustinian canons of the Arroasian observance.[51]

were to be remembered, along with deceased brethren of the Premonstratensian order, on the feast of Saint Grisogonus on 24 November. Cf the reference to *confraternitates cum Hibernensibus* in Douai, Bibliothèque Municipale, MS 822, fol. 271v as cited by Milis, *Constitutiones*, p. 144. The manuscript contains a *historia monastica* compiled by François de Bar *ante* 1600 which drew on a now lost compilation of Marc Théry compiled in 1596 which, in turn, was based on original sources relating to Arrouaise no longer extant: see Milis, *L'ordre des chanoines réguliers d'Arrouaise*, p. 67, 64, 74 n. 4, also p. 484, 493, 545. **49** See above n. 18. Other Irish traffic to the papal court around this time is indicated by the confirmation issued by Pope Lucius III on 15 February 1183 at Velletri to Killenny Abbey (De Vallis Dei), County Kilkenny: Sheehy, *Pontificia Hibernica*, i, no. 12. **50** Raymonde Foreville and Gillian Keir (eds), *The book of St Gilbert* (Oxford 1987) pp 44–5. **51** It is worth noting that in 1177 a special cemetery 'for Scots, Irish and other pilgrims' was added to the Arroasian house at Wissant, the port of disembarkation for travellers crossing from England to Flanders: Milis, *L'ordre des chanoines réguliers d'Arrouaise*, p. 212.

Two contributors to the Book of Leinster: Bishop Finn of Kildare and Gilla na Náem Úa Duinn

EDEL BHREATHNACH

In recent decades, scholars have sought to unravel the complexities of the great Irish manuscripts of the late medieval era from the twelfth-century onwards and of the scholarship of their compilers. This note considers the origins and affiliations of two such compilers whose work is found in the twelfth-century codex known either as *Lebar na Núachongbála* or more popularly as the Book of Leinster: Bishop Finn of Kildare and Gilla na Náem Úa Duinn.[1]

The bishops Finn of Kildare

The earliest personal letter in Irish sources[2] is the letter preserved on folio 206 of the Book of Leinster. Finn, bishop of Kildare, sends greetings to his correspondent Áed mac Crimthainn, *comarba* of Colum of the church of Terryglass, County Tipperary and requests that the *dúanaire* of Mac Lonáin be brought to him *co faiccmis a cialla na nduan filet ann* 'that we may discover the meaning of the poems that are in it'.[3] Finns additions to Cináed úa hArtacáin's poem *Fíanna bátar i nEmain* are noted as such in the same codex in the margin of folio 32a: *Find episcopus Cilli Dara hoc addidit.*[4] Most commentators to date have identified this bishop of Kildare with a certain Finn mac Gormáin whose death is recorded in 1160 in the Annals of Ulster (*AU*), the Annals of the Four Masters (*AFM*) and the Annals of Tigernach (*ATig.*). The three annals record his death as follows:

> *AU*: Finn hUa Gorma[i]n, epscop Cille-dara, abb manach Ibhair-Cinntrachta fri ré, ad Christum migrauit.
> *ATig.*: Mac Gorman, espoc Cilli dara, quieuit.
> *AFM*: Fiond mac Gormáin, epscop Cille dara 7 abb manach Iubhair Chind trachta frí ré, dég.

He is usually identified as the bishop of Kildare who attended at the Synod of Kells in 1152. However, the source of this information, Geoffrey Keating, in his treatise *Foras Feasa ar Éirinn*,[5] lists the bishop in question as *Fionn mac Cianáin easpog Chille Dara*. Byrne in his list of bishops of Kildare records correctly that Finn mac Máel Muire mac Cianáin probably acceded to the

---

1 Note on use of *úa* / *Úa* : Since the twelfth century is a period of transition between *úa* / *Úa* / *Ó*, I use *úa* where the name is relating to an earlier period (e.g. Cináed úa hArtacáin) or where the person is a genuine grandson (e.g. Finn úa Cianáin). Otherwise, I use *Úa* to indicate a surname (e.g. Gilla na Náem Úa Duinn). 2 For consideration of the letter's context as *ars dictaminis*, see S.L. Forste-Grupp, 'The earliest Irish personal letter', *Proceedings of the Harvard Celtic Colloquium* 15 (1995) pp 1–11. 3 For the full text of the letter see R.I. Best, O. Bergin and M.A. O'Brien, *The Book of Leinster formerly Lebar na Núachongbala*, vol. I (Dublin 1954) p. xvi. 4 Ibid. p. 132. 5 P.S. Dinneen (ed.), *Foras Feasa ar Éirinn le Seathrún Céitinn, D.D. The History of Ireland by Geoffrey Keating, D.D.*, vol. III, *ITS* 9 (London

bishopric before March 1152 and was followed by Finn mac Gussáin Úa Gormáin.[6] *AFM* and Sir James Ware[7] appear to have duplicated the obit of Finn mac Gussáin Úa Gormáin at 1085 and to have conflated the two twelfth-century bishops of Kildare at 1160. Colgan noted the confusion in his *Trias Thaumaturga*:

> Finnius filius Gormani, secundum Ketinum filius Kianani Episcopus Killdarien. & aliquandiu Abbas Monachorum de Iubhar-Cinntrachta obiit [in 1160].

Colgan also records Finn mac Gussáin Úa Gormáin's death at 1085 and states that he was buried at Cell Achaid (Killeigh, County Offaly).[8] While Byrne accepts that Finn mac Gussáin Úa Gormáin was abbot of the Cistercian monastery at Newry who died in 1160 and was buried at Cell Achaid, it is significant that he is not included among the witnesses to that monastery's foundation charter, dated to *c.*1156/7.[9] No record of an abbot of Newry before 1404 survives.[10]

Both bishops Finn of Kildare were inextricably linked with prominent families in Leinster and both could have contributed to the compilation of the Book of Leinster. Finn mac Gussáin Úa Gormáin belonged to the royal lineage of Uí Bairrche. His grandfather, Muiredach, died in 1124, and although his father Gussán's obit is unrecorded, he is included in the regnal list of the Uí Bairrche in the secular genealogies.[11] The family's ecclesiastical affiliations were probably primarily to the church of Killeshin, County Laois, the source from which certain material included in the other twelfth-century codex, Rawlinson B502, originated.

The existence of a bishop Finn úa Cianáin of Kildare is confirmed by an entry in the twelfth-century compilation on the mothers and wives of Irish kings known as the *Banshenchas*.[12]

> (Lecan) Mael Febail ingen Fhaeillechain m. Goriatha m. Duithir m. Idchon do Breatnaib i nAidni Conain, mathair Con Aifni hUi Chonchobair rig hUa Failgi: 7 Fhind m. Mail Muiri m. Cianain.

> (RIA Ms D.2.1) Mael Feabuil ingen Faelachain m. Goriath m. Tuithir m. Fidchuind, mathair Con Aifne hUi Concobair rig hUa Failge: 7 Find m. Mail Muire m. Finain espog Cille Dara.

Finn úa Cianáin had illustrious relatives who were closely associated with Kildare. His stepbrother was Cú Aifne Ua Conchobair Failgi, king of Uí Fhailge.[13] He was distantly related to Mór daughter of Domnall Ua Conchobair Failgi (d. 1115) who was imposed as the abbess of Kildare by the Uí Fhailge in 1127 and who was deposed by the Uí Chennselaig in 1132.[14] She died in 1167. Finn úa Cianáin's attendance at the Synod of Kells in 1152 would fit chronologically with the date

1908) p. 316. **6** T.W. Moody, F.X. Martin and F.J. Byrne, *A new history of Ireland IX: Maps, genealogies, lists. A companion to Irish history*, Part II (Oxford 1984) p. 313. **7** J. Ware and W. Harris, *The works of Sir James Ware concerning Ireland revised and improved in three volumes* (Dublin 1739) vol. 1, pp 382, 384. Ware's entry at 1160 records the death of Finan (Mac-Tiarcain) O-Gormain. **8** J. Colgan, *Trias Thaumaturga*, with an introduction by Pádraig Ó Riain (reprint Dublin 1997) p. 630. **9** W. Dugdale, *Monasticon Anglicanum*, ed. J. Caley, H. Ellis and B. Bandinel, 6 vols (London 1817–30; repr. 1846) vol. 6, part 2, pp 1133–4. **10** G. Mac Niocaill, *Na manaigh liatha in Éirinn 1142-c.1600* (Dublin 1959) pp 9–10, 175. **11** M.A. O'Brien, *Corpus genealogiarum Hiberniae*, vol. I (Dublin repr. 1976) p. 10 (117a32). **12** M.E. Dobbs, 'The Ban-shenchus', *RC* 48 (1931) pp l99, 231. **13** Best et al., *Book of Leinster*, p. 188 (LL40d, l.5640). Cú Aifne is described in his obit in 1130 as *rí H. Failgi* (*AU*). **14** *ALC* 1132, *AClon* 1135.

of the stanzas added to *Fíanna bátar i nEmain* which include a reference to the battle of Móin Mór fought in 1151.[15] His collaboration with Áed mac Crimthainn in compiling the Book of Leinster might account for the inclusion of poems which probably emanated from Kildare, including three poems ascribed to Orthanach úa Cáelláma Cuirrig and two poems concerning Brigit's people, the Fothairt.[16] Undoubtedly, these poems could also have been included at the instigation of Finn mac Gussáin Ua Gormáin. However, the poem celebrating the superiority of Uí Fhailge over other Leinster dynasties, *Clanna Falge Ruis in ríg,* bears all the hallmarks of Uí Fhailge propaganda which Finn úa Cianáin might have passed onto Áed mac Crimthainn. It would seem that the poem was included by Áed in the Book of Leinster in 1161, since he notes the death of Domnall mac Congalaig, *tánaise* of Uí Fhailge, in that year in the margin (fol. 49b).[17]

Gilla na Náem Úa Duinn, fer léigind *of Inis Clothrann*

The Annals of Tigernach record the death of Gilla na Náem Úa Duinn in 1160 according him the accolades:

> fer léighind Indsi Clothrann 7 ughdar Erenn re senchus 7 re dan 7 aenollam na nGaedhel [*fer léigind* of Inis Clothrann and (chief) author of Ireland in *senchas* and in poetry and *ollam* without equal of the Irish].

The Annals of the Four Masters use their usual hyperbole:

> Giolla na Naemh Ua Duinn ferléighinn Insi Clothrann, saoi seanchusa 7 dána 7 deaghfhear labhra, ro fhaidhsein a spirat co a athardha etir coraidh aingel an 17 do December iars an ochtmhadh bliadhain ar chaogad a aoise [Gilla na Náem Úa Duind, lector of Inis Clothrann, sage of *senchas* and poetry and skilled in speech, released his spirit to his maker (patrimony) among choirs of angels on the 17th of December [1160] in his fifty-eighth year].

Why this particularly detailed and praiseworthy obit for a scholar in a seemingly insignificant church? The answer probably has to do with Gilla na Náem Úa Duinn's renown as a poet and scholar and also with his ecclesiastical and familial connections. His literary work, as far as we can identify it, reflects the typical activity of twelfth-century men of learning, involving the compilation of manuscripts and redaction of texts, and in his case, particularly of regnal and topographical material. Six poems are attributed to Gilla na Náem Úa Duinn:

1. *Cúiced Lagen na lecht ríg:* a regnal poem on the Christian kings of Leinster which ends with Diarmait mac Murchada (†1171) who is still alive at the time of writing. Copies are preserved in many manuscripts, the earliest being in the Book of Leinster (folios 32a–33b) and the Book of Ballymote (folios 55d–57a).

---

15 *Best et al. Book of Leinster,* p. 133 (LL32a4163).   **16** *A chóicid chóem Chairpri chrúaid* (43a1ff); *Slán seiss, a Brigit co mbúaid* (49b9ff); *Masu de chlaind Echdach aird* (5lb29ff); *Fothart for trebaib Con Corbb* (35a11ff); *Feidlimid athair Echach* (35b1ff).   **17** Best et al., *Book of Leinster,* p. 242.

2. *Cruachu Condacht raith co rath:* a regnal poem on the Christian kings of Connacht which ends with Toirdelbach Úa Conchobair (†1156) who is alive at the time of writing. The earliest copy is in the Book of Ballymote (folio 58a).

3. *Oirgialla a Eamain Macha:* a genealogical poem on the Airgíalla preserved in the Book of Uí Maine (folio 42vb) and the Book of Lecan (folio 81d).

4. *Eri íarthar talman tortigh:* a précis in four parts of *Dinnshenchas Érenn* preserved in the Book of Uí Maine (folio 172ra).[18]

5. *Finnaid úaim, co ségda suairc:* the *dinnshenchas* of Sliab Fúait. A version found in the Book of Lecan (folio 257va) and in a series of other manuscripts.[19]

6. *Aibhind sin a Eriu ard* : A *dinnshenchas* poem found in National Library of Ireland MSS G2 (folio 30*ra*) and G131 (97 *i*).

The final stanza of *Cúiced Lagen na lecht ríg* seems to verify that the poem was composed by Gilla na Náem Úa Duinn:

Hua Duind fer na n-érgna n-óc	Hua Duind, the man of agile understanding,
ro chren a berla cach mbrúit	his language (poetic craft) redeemed every brute (?),
ro shil don Banba can bét	he enumerated for Banba, without injury,
trét na ríg calma fo chóic	the host of the brave kings by five

This final line implies that he composed five regnal poems, although only the two poems on the Christian kings of Leinster and Connacht have been identified. *Cruachu Condacht raith co rath* lacks any internal reference to the poet similar to the final stanza of *Cúiced Lagen na lecht ríg*. The Book of Ballymote (BB) copy simply notes *Hua Duind cc* as an introduction. Nonetheless, there are indications that this is a genuine ascription. The Uí Briúin Bréifne genealogies, as preserved in BB and in the Mac Fhirbisigh Book of Genealogies (Fir), quotes the stanza on Domnall mac Tigernáin, king of Connacht (†1102) from *Cruachu Condacht raith co rath* prefacing it with the phrases (BB) *amail asbert .H. Duind* and (Fir) *amhail aspert Giolla na Naomh Ua Duinn* 'as Gilla na Náem Úa Duinn said'.[20] While not conclusive evidence, it points to a belief by later scholars that Gilla na Náem was the author of *Cruachu Condacht raith co rath*. There is also a strong similarity of style between the Leinster and Connacht regnal poems. They are not especially complicated compositions, but are versified regnal lists, mostly based on annalistic material, in which many of the verses follow a similar pattern: the length of each king's reign followed by his name and his *aided*, the manner or place of his death. The attribution of *Oirgialla a Eamain Macha* to Gilla na Náem is based on an ascription in the Book of Uí Maine. The Book of Lecan does not include the ascription in its copy. Byrne, in his edition of the regnal poem *Clann ollaman uaisle Emna* on the Christian kings of the Ulaid, written during the reign of Eochaid mac Duinnshléibe (1158–66), considered Gilla na Náem as a possible author on the basis of numerous similarities of diction with the Connacht and Leinster poems.[21] Most significantly all three regnal poems are a series of summarised *aideda*, possibly used in schools as mnemonic verses.

---

18 E.J. Gwynn, 'The Dindshenchas in the Book of Uí Maine', *Ériu* 10 (1926–8) pp 76–89.   19 E. Gwynn, *The metrical Dindshenchas*, Part IV (Dublin 1924; reprint 1991) pp 166–9.   20 M.V. Duignan, 'The Uí Briúin Bréifni genealogies', *JRSAI* 64 (1934) pp 216–18 (XXXVI). I wish to thank Eoghan Ó Mórdha for bringing this reference to my attention.   21 F.J. Byrne, 'Clann Ollaman Uaisle Emna', *Studia Hibernica* 4 (1964) pp 60–1.

The two topographical *dinnshenchas* poems ascribed to Gilla na Náem Úa Duinn, *Eri íarthar talman tortigh* and the *dinnshenchas* poem on Slíab Fúait, though not necessarily from his pen, include an insight into either his own view of himself or that of a near contemporary. The Slíab Fúait poem includes the sentiments:[22]

Doárim úa Duinn duibe	Úa Duinn of the dark speech told the tale
fót Cinn builid Berraide	of the sod of blooming Cenn Berraide
do sheol co becht dar'fuaig lib	when he accurately wove for you for your instruction
cert sléibe Fúait, is finnaid.	the exact [story] of Slíab Fúait – and learn it.

The lengthy précis of *dinnshenchas* in *Eri íarthar talman tortigh* ends with the even more informative lengthy stanza:[23]

Gilla na Naemh na ndhuan níamhdha	Gilla na Náem of the illustrious poems,
O Duind fer sgailti na sgel	Úa Duind, the man who let the tales be known,
Darighni duain fhir-glaein amra	he composed true, pure, famous poems
do righraidh Banbha na fhér	for the kings of Banba ?of the pastures.
a n-Inis Clochrand na cuiri	In Inis Clothrand of the hosts
tar nach loch-mall tuili tren	over any sluggish, slow current . . . (?)
ni lag gan tathaeir dia tapadh	not weak without blame for its/his bravery,
cathaeir na n-abhadh is na n-eir.	the city of the abbots and of the nobles.

Following the theme in the final stanza of *Cúiced Lagen na lecht ríg*, this stanza again notes that Gilla na Náem's fame was due to his enumeration in verse of the kings of Banba.

Despite his importance Gilla na Náem Úa Duinn does not appear in genealogical records. His Leinster affiliation, which presumably caused him to compose a poem on the Christian kings of Leinster, were through his family, the Uí Duinn, also known by the name Uí Riacáin, who were part of the greater group known as Uí Fhailge.[24] By the twelfth century the Uí Duinn were not in a particularly strong position in north-west Leinster and an entry in the Book of Leinster prose list of the kings of Uí Fhailge suggests that they were embroiled in internecine warfare involving the two main dynasties of the Uí Fhailge, Uí Chonchobair Failgi and Uí Diummasaig.[25] The Uí Duinn appear to have supported Uí Diummasaig claims to the kingship of Uí Fhailge. Given that Uí Chonchobair Failgi kings were not Diarmait mac Murchada's most loyal subjects, as evidenced by their decision to submit to Diarmait Úa Máelsechlainn, king of Mide, rather than to Diarmait in 1166, perhaps Gilla na Náem's mildly favourable comments towards Diarmait were influenced by the Uí Duinn's role in Uí Fhailge struggles:

Sínid ria Lagnib na lán	He rules beyond Leinster of the multitudes,
i tírib nad sadbir slóg	into lands whose hosts are not wealthy,
arcgid na benna 'ma mbúar	he destroys the horns around their cattle (?)
Mar is dúal d'ú Mella mór.	as is fitting for the descendant of mighty Mella.

22 Gwynn, *Metrical Dindshenchas*, pp 168–9. **23** Gwynn, 'Book of Uí Maine', p. 89 verse 121. **24** For a survey of the Irish lordship of Ó Duinn (territory of Iregan) in the late medieval period, see K.W. Nicholls (ed.), *The O Doyne (Ó Duinn) manuscript. Documents relating to the family of O Doyne (Ó Duinn) from Archbishop Marsh's Library, Dublin MS Z.4.2.19* (Dublin 1983). **25** Best et al., *Book of Leinster*, p. 188 (LL 40d5650–1): *Murchertach (i. in t-athclerech) mac Murchertaich .iii. coro marbad la Áed Hua nDuind i mmebail i Feraib Cell* 'Muirchertach son

It is also possible that Diarmait's latimer, Morice O'Regan mentioned by Giraldus Cambrensis and in *The Song of Dermot and the Earl*[26] hailed from the same area or family as Gilla na Náem Úa Duinn.

The church to which Gilla na Náem was affiliated, Inis Clothrann (Inchcleraun, County Longford) was a crossing point on Lough Ree between the midlands and Connacht. The island is said to have taken its name from Clothru daughter of Eochaid Feidlech, Medb of Connacht's sister. The tale *Aided Medba* 'Medb's deathtale' tells how Medb's nephew Furbaide, Clothru's son, killed Medb on Inis Clothrann. In the text, the comment is made *Is and didiu do-meled Clothru dligeda Connacht i n-Inis Clothrand for Loch Rí*[27] 'Thus it was on Inis Clothrand in Lough Ree that Clothru used to exercise authority in Connacht', suggesting an association between the island and the kingship of Connacht. Inis Clothrann was reputedly founded by Diarmait mac Lugnai of Uí Fhiachrach of Connacht. That the island functioned as a stopping-point between Leinster and Connacht is implied in a passage in the notes to *Féilire Óengusso* at the feast-day of Óenu moccu Laigsi, abbot of Clonmacnois (†570/577). Óenu set out from the territory of Laiges Laigen to go into military service (*amsaine*) with the king of Connacht. Crossing Loch Rí on his journey westward he came to Inis Clothrann (*co ndeachaid co port Innsi Clothrann og trial tar Loch Rib síar*). There he met Ciarán of Clonmacnois who succeeded in recruiting him into the service of God (and to be his own successor), rather than into the service of the king of Connacht.[28]

The names of ecclesiastics of Inis Clothrann are recorded in the annals from 720 onwards. Inis Clothrann had a dependent church, Fochlaid (Faughalstown on Lough Derravaragh, County Westmeath) and also had links with Clonmacnois. Cináed Úa Cethernaigh, priest of Inis Clothrann (†1167), was probably a member of a prominent family associated with Clonmacnois.[29] In 1170 Diarmaid Úa Braoin, who also belonged to an important Clonmacnois family, and who was *comarba* of Commán (Roscommon) died at Inis Clothrann. The church seems to have functioned, like Cong,[30] as a place of retirement. For example, Dubchoblaig daughter of Úa Cuinn and wife of Mac Carrgamna died and was buried there in 1168, notably the same year in which her son was killed by the Úa Máelsechlainn of Mide. Donnchad, bishop of Elphin and descendant of Toirdelbach Úa Conchobair, king of Connacht (†1156), died at Inis Clothrann in 1244 (*AConn.*) and was buried at Boyle. Gilla na Náem Úa Duinn was not the only learned man to die at the monastery. As early as 871 there is an obit for Cú Roí mac Aldniad of Inis Clothrann and Fochla, described as *peritissimus historiarum Scotticarum* (*AU*). This tradition continued to the late fourteenth century as the Miscellaneous Irish Annals record the death in 1393 of Domhnall mac Sairbhreathaigh Mhic Aedhagáin an *ollam fénechais* (of Irish law) to Muintir Anghaile or Uí Fhergaile. The latter family, who belonged to Conmaicne of Connacht, were closely associated with Inis Clothrann. In 1150 (*AFM*), for example, Murchad mac Gilla na Náem Úa Fergaile, a venerable member of the family, died there.

Inis Clothrann was constantly implicated in the complicated politics of the midlands and of Uí Conchobair kings of Connacht. Ruaidrí Úa Cerbaill, king of Éile, a territory close to Uí Duinn lands, was killed by his own brother at Inis Clothrann in 1174 (*ATig.*). During the dispute between Ruaidrí Úa Conchobair and his son Conchobar Máenmaige, it would seem that the

of Muirchertach (namely, the former cleric) was treacherously killed by Áed Úa Duind in Fir Cell'. **26** G.H. Orpen (ed.), *The Song of Dermot and the Earl* (Oxford 1892) lines 420–40, 1656–73. **27** V. Hull (ed.), 'Aided Meidbe: the violent death of Medb', *Speculum* 13 (1938) pp 55, 59. **28** W. Stokes (ed.), *Félire Óengusso Céli Dé. The martyrology of Oengus the Culdee* (London 1905, repr. 1984) pp 48–51. **29** A. Kehnel, *Clonmacnois – the church and lands of St. Ciarán. Change and continuity in an Irish monastic foundation (6th to 16th century)* (Münster 1997) p. 289. **30** I wish to thank Dr Colmán Etchingham for drawing this analogy to my attention.

latter's hostages were kept at Inis Clothrann. On Conchobar's death in 1189, Ruaidrí took possession of these hostages. Given the church's political affiliations, Gilla na Náem was probably well aware of the need to praise kings of Connacht when he wrote *Cruachu Condacht raith co rath*.

The inclusion of the poem *Cúiced Lagen na lecht ríg* in the Book of Leinster lessens to a certain extent the perception that twelfth-century codices such as Rawlinson B502 and the Book of Leinster were 'antiquarian' compilations, containing, as they do, the texts of an earlier age. The compilers of both manuscripts were far from ignorant of contemporary compositions. The remarkable final folios of Rawlinson B502 (163a-166b) contain regnal poems which refer to kings of the most important provinces at the time of compilation. Among them (folio 165a) is the poem on the kings of Connacht *A fhir théit i mMaig Medba, do scéla bat scothmebra* which was also composed during the reign of Toirdelbach Úa Conchobair.[31] Similarly *Cúiced Lagen na lecht ríg* is a contemporary poem, as are Bishop Finn of Kildare's additional verses to *Fíanna bátar i nEmain* which allude to the battle of Móin Mór fought in 1151. This suggests that Áed mac Crimthann, Gilla na Náem Úa Duinn and Bishop Finn's work should be viewed not simply as antiquarian collections. They were indeed continuing a long-established tradition of copying and preserving earlier texts. However, they were involved in the revision and re-invention of old texts[32] and they ensured that contemporary compositions and translations were included in their codices. Such was their keen interest in contemporary events that they up-dated genealogies and regnal lists, and, in doing so, occasionally remarked on such events.[33] The compilers' *modus operandi* is best summarised by Glenisson when considering the nature of the medieval manuscript:[34]

> Le manuscrit médieval n'est généralement pas l'œuvre d'un seul individu (à moins qu'il n'écrive pour son propre usage), mais d'une équipe de personnes qui se relaient ou qui collaborent selon un scénario organisé.

Áed mac Crimthann, Bishop Finn of Kildare and Gilla na Náem Úa Duinn were the *équipe* that compiled the Book of Leinster in mid twelfth-century Ireland.

31 M. F. Liddell, 'A poem on the kings of Connaught', *ZCP* 9 (1913) pp 461–9.   **32** T. Ó Concheanainn, 'The manuscript tradition of two Middle Irish Leinster tales', *Celtica* 18 (1986) pp 13–33.   **33** The most quoted of these comments is Áed Mac Crimthainn's observation at the end of the prose regnal list of Leinster (Best et al., *Book of Leinster*, p. 184: LL39d5504) *Saxain. iar sain* [the death of Diarmait mac Murchada] *miserabiliter regnant. Amen a. amen.*   **34** J. Glénisson, *Le livre au moyen age* (CNRS 1988) p. 67.

The Cross triumphant: high crosses in Ireland

HILARY RICHARDSON

The crosses set up by Irish sculptors over a thousand years ago are still a living force in the land-scape of Ireland today. They are among the most remarkable works of art of the early medieval world. Along with their counterparts in Britain they have a unique place in west Christian art. Dating in the main to the ninth and early tenth centuries, they are a series of impressive free-standing monuments which were erected at a time when there was little opportunity in Western Europe to commission sculpture on any large scale or carry out major architectural schemes. For their period the Irish high crosses stand unrivalled in stone in the grandeur of their conception and execution.

Now at long last they are beginning to receive the attention they deserve. Possibly their location in a visual backwater has been against them. Their importance is apparent, yet they have been sadly ignored over the years despite the efforts of a handful of exceptional scholars. It is no accident that two of their finest exponents in the twentieth century have been foreigners, Kingsley Porter and Françoise Henry, one a Harvard professor and the other initially from the Musée des Antiquités Nationales, St Germain-en-Laye. Both individually came upon the crosses from a wide international knowledge of art and architecture. They saw the extraordinary character of the Irish carvings and were attracted to investigate them further, devoting many years to their study.[1]

The visual aspects are certainly the most striking feature of the crosses but are not their only source of interest. They are the meeting point for diverse disciplines, including theology, archae-ology, local history, the study of monasticism, of liturgy and of early Irish society. Many crosses are still in their original situation and are still potent, charged with meaning, even if it may have been modified by time. On a Sunday in September, I was visiting some sites in Co Kilkenny with an antiquarian society from a town nearby, and as it happened the Feast of the Exaltation of the Cross was the very next day. When we arrived at Killamery, a secluded spot, already in the graveyard a small crowd was assembled, gathered around the splendid cross which is unique for its shape and beautiful ornament. A local priest was leading prayers and the people had come together to celebrate the Triumph of the Cross. Although the Killamery Cross dates to the ninth century, it still has a living function after eleven hundred years.

Ireland has preserved relatively intact a sequence of Christian monuments from the seventh to the twelfth centuries. They are extremely valuable documents for a rather obscure period of history when destruction and reconstruction marked neighbouring European countries. The Irish carvings had a long evolution of five centuries and although foreign elements were introduced, these were absorbed and often transformed into something fresh and original. The cross-based monuments of Britain share certain aspects in common with the Irish crosses, but it is only a group in western Scotland, in the area evangelised by the monastery at Iona, that belongs to the

---

1 A.K. Porter (1883–1933) studied early Irish carvings following his research in origins of Romanesque sculpture, v. *The crosses and culture of Ireland* (New Haven 1931); F. Henry (1902–82) began her life's work on early Irish art with her doctoral thesis, *La Sculpture Irlandaise pendant les douze premiers siècles de l'ère chrétienne* (Paris 1933).

1 The High Cross at Killamery, Co. Kilkenny

Irish high cross tradition. There are even a few of these ringed in the typical Irish style. Iona, founded by St Colmcille in 563, occupied a key position in the seventh and eighth centuries as an active centre for the Irish Church, radiating outwards to Northumbria, Pictland and further afield, while keeping in touch with Ireland. Some scholars have persuaded themselves that the idea of the high cross infiltrated through this corner of southwest Scotland into Ireland, but the preponderance of evidence in Ireland itself does not tally with this theory. The extent of resources, apart from archaeology, is often not appreciated; for example, the immense heritage of early Irish texts is only partially tapped at present.

The Killamery cross illustrates the general structure of a high cross (see plate). There are several schools of sculptors and local groupings, but the broad plan is much the same. A stone shaft, like a pillar carved on four sides, is set into a separate base. The upper part of the shaft terminates in a cross, and an open ring, connecting the cross-arms to the upright, creates the familiar outline of the ringed or Celtic cross.

Imagery found in an Old-Irish gloss in the Würzburg manuscript, m.p.th.f.12, gives a spiritual dimension to the shape of the cross. The scribe comments on Ephesians 3, verses 18 and 19. The text runs: 'With deep roots and firm foundations, may you be strong to comprehend with all God's people, what is the breadth and length and height and depth of the love of Christ, and to know it, though it is beyond knowledge'. The scribe notes that the four measurements are said to be in the secrets of the Godhead, and also in the Cross of Christ, i.e. the four limbs of the cross. 'Knowledge' he says, refers to the divine nature of Christ. 'With His right hand He saved the left of the world, i.e., the North; with His left hand He saved the right part of the world, i.e., the South; His head redeemed the East, and His feet the West.'[2]

A capstone on top of the cross completes the monument. It is usually made in the shape of a small oratory or church and is normally carved from a separate block. The Killamery capstone however is rather damaged, and apparently it was removed from time to time since it was believed to have healing properties. The remains of an inscription survives on a panel at the base of the shaft, where a plain surface is often reserved for lettering. It has been rendered as – OR DO MAELSECHNAILL or 'A prayer for Máelsechnaill', which if correct is an important link with the cross at Kinnitty, Co Offaly. Here one of the inscriptions, recently deciphered, reads: A prayer for King Máelsechnaill son of Máelruanaid, A prayer for the king of Ireland.[3] Máelsechnaill reigned from 846–862, and it was his son, Flann Sinna, whose name is recorded on the Cross of the Scriptures at Clonmacnois, along with that of Colman, the abbot who put up the cross. Perhaps Colman was the actual sculptor. F. Henry notes that the entry for his death in the *Annals of the Four Masters* (924) calls him *Colman Cluana gair gach tuir* 'Colman of Cluain, the joy of every tower'.[4] At all events the magnificence of the crosses reflects a patronage of wealth and vision. The crosses were commissioned by people of substance, kings and abbots, just as the luxury Gospel books bear witness to the prosperity of the monasteries in whose scriptoria they were illuminated.

The continuity of a pre-Christian, prehistoric tradition adapted to spread the Christian message, makes Irish art very special. The conditions for artistic work were also special because it was concentrated in the monasteries which had sprung up with great rapidity. Monastic life, so

2 T. Olden (trans.) *The holy scriptures in Ireland one thousand years ago; selections from the Würzburg glosses* (Dublin 1888) p. 90.   3 D. Ó Murchadha and G. Ó Murchú, 'Fragmentary Inscriptions from the West Cross at Durrow, the South Cross at Clonmacnois, and the Cross of Kinnitty', *JRSAI* 118 (1988) pp 53–66.   4 F. Henry, 'Around an inscription: the cross of the Scriptures at Clonmacnois', *JRSAI* 110 (1980) p. 45.

congenial in Ireland, took its model from the Egyptian desert. Hence St Paul and St Antony, the pioneers of monasticism, were figures of consequence and can be seen on many crosses. Sometimes they are receiving the bread from the raven, and sometimes they are in the act of breaking it between them, adding a Eucharistic meaning. St Jerome relates how they hesitated out of politeness, neither wishing to be first, and finally broke the bread in unison. Ireland kept alive in western Europe certain features of Christian art that had been widespread throughout Christendom at one time but had been lost or obliterated in the convolutions of the Dark Ages. It had a vital link not only with its own Celtic past, but also with initial stages of Christian belief and custom. A number of the ideas behind the setting up of the high crosses go back ultimately to the time of Constantine the Great in the fourth century.

The Sign of Constantine

There were major changes for Christians following the Peace of the Church. From Constantine onwards for several centuries the cross was used principally as a sign of triumph, of the victory of Christ and of the Christian faith. For the Irish crosses the shape of the cross stands not merely as the instrument of Christ's punishment, but is actually the embodiment and symbol of Christ. The idea of a crucifix is found only on the latest group of crosses, dating to the eleventh and twelfth centuries, which have a representation of the Crucifixion carved in bold relief. But the theme of earlier crosses is the Triumph of the Cross, with the cross a powerful symbol of victory, of faith triumphant, linked to the Sign of Constantine the Great and the Finding of the True Cross in Jerusalem.

The word 'sign' dominates two images connected with the cross in medieval thought. *In hoc signo vinces* 'by this sign shalt thou conquer' was the message inscribed on the cross of light seen by Constantine in his vision before the Battle of the Milvian Bridge in 312. The victory he achieved through the sign of the cross had repercussions throughout Christendom, starting with his own conversion. From the time that Constantine came to power, attention tended to concentrate on Jerusalem and interest in the holy places grew steadily with pilgrims flocking to visit the shrines. Already Eusebius speaks of people coming from the ends of the earth soon after 314. The churches built by Constantine, especially the Church of the Holy Sepulchre over Christ's tomb, were of prime importance. Then the story of the Finding of the True Cross by St Helena, his mother, further focussed public awareness on Jerusalem, the Holy City.

A sketch plan of the Church of the Holy Sepulchre at Jerusalem and its surroundings illustrates an early ninth century copy of Adomnán's *On the Holy Places, (De Locis Sanctis)*, Vienna Cod. 458, fol.4v. Adomnán, ninth abbot of Iona (679–704), acquired his information from Bishop Arculf who had lived in Jerusalem for nine months.[5] Arculf drew diagrams on wax tablets for Adomnán and the community at Iona c.683, to explain geographical details. Several buildings are represented on the plan:

1. The Round Church (*Anastasis*) over the Holy Sepulchre.
2. The Sepulchre with twelve lamps always burning, enclosed in a domed rock-cut structure, with entrance at the east.

5 D. Meehan (ed.), *Adamnán's De Locis Sanctis* (Dublin 1958) pp 43–7.

3. The Church of St Mary.

4. The Church of Golgotha, of which Adomnán says: 'From the roof hangs a large bronze wheel for lamps, and below it stands a great silver cross, fixed in the same socket as the wooden cross on which the Saviour of mankind once suffered'.

5. The basilica built by Constantine, showing where the cross was found, buried under debris along with the crosses of the two thieves, according to the story of the Finding of the True Cross by Helena, Constantine's mother.

In the eastern churches the feast of the Exaltation of the Cross celebrates the dedication of the churches built by Constantine on the sites of the Holy Sepulchre and Golgotha, and also commemorates the rediscovery of the true cross in Jerusalem. Egeria, the pilgrim, writing about 384, outlines the ceremonies that she saw during the feast at Jerusalem, and mentions that the date of the dedication of churches coincides with the anniversary of the dedication of Solomon's temple. She describes how the churches were adorned as at Easter and Epiphany, and how the festival similarly lasted for eight days. Crowds were attracted from everywhere, including bishops, monks and pilgrims.[6]

The Feast of the Exaltation was introduced from the east to the western church by Pope Sergius 1 (687–701), who had been born in Sicily of a family which came originally from Antioch. However in the west the Exaltation commemorates the exposition of the relic of the True Cross at Jerusalem around 630, after its recovery by the Emperor Heraclius from the Persians, who had devastated the city earlier in the seventh century. These incidents aroused great interest throughout Christendom and again put the cross before the public eye, adding to the store of images surrounding it.

The stepped base of the high cross, the capstone and the idea of the jewelled cross all relate back to Jerusalem. The steps at the base of the cross refer to the steps up the hill of Golgotha, while the capstone on the top is modelled on the small shrine or house built by Constantine to mark the place of Christ's Resurrection.[7] The motif of the relic of the True Cross appears most clearly in the Ahenny group of crosses, in their creation in stone of precious metal casings that imitate the protective coverings made to enshrine a wooden cross.[8]

The Sign of the Son of Man

The second manifestation of the word 'sign' also has immediate implications for the crosses. The Last Judgement usually occupies the east face of the crosshead, balanced by the Crucifixion on the west. Judgement Day and the Second Coming of Christ loomed large in medieval thought. A key text for the Second Coming is St Matthew's Gospel, chapter 24. 'For as the lightning cometh out of the east, and shineth even unto the west; so shall also the coming of the Son of man be.' Verse 30 begins: 'And then shall appear the sign of the Son of man in heaven', which is the only passage on this subject where the word 'sign' occurs. It must have had a special significance as it is actually one of the readings in the Stowe Missal in an Office for the Visitation

6 L. Duchesne, *Christian worship. Its origin and evolution* (London 1927) pp 570–1.   **7** H. Richardson and J. Scarry, *An introduction to Irish High Crosses* (Cork 1990) pp 24–6.   **8** H. Richardson, 'The jewelled Cross and its canopy', in C. Bourke (ed.), *From the Isles of the North* (Belfast 1995) pp 177–86.

of the Sick. The Stowe Missal, now in the Royal Irish Academy, dates to near 800 and is the earliest missal to survive in Ireland. The famous Gospel Book (London BL Harley 1802), written in Armagh by Máel Brigte in 1138, has an important gloss on *signum* at the same passage. The commentary itself dates to the tenth century or second half of the ninth, according to the most recent scholarship.[9] It refers to the fiery cross that will shine in the east at the end of the world, although the Jews concealed the cross. The Constantine legend seems to fit here. At *signum* the commentator says: 'It must be considered how great is the power of this sign, that is, of the cross. The sun will be darkened but the cross will shine forth, and when the lights of heaven grow dim and the stars fall down, the sun will radiate so that you may know that the cross is brighter than the sun in all God's creation'.

The Last Judgement is the climax of the scenes on the crosses. The fullest composition is on the Cross of Muiredach at Monasterboice where the blessed and the damned are on either side of the figure of Christ in Glory, with the weighing of the souls and St Michael below. The intention of the biblical scenes becomes clear in the light of the Last Judgement, and also in the prayers for salvation, the 'Help of God', which have a Jewish origin but which were adapted and enlarged later on to prefigure the life of Christ, and which are still used to commend the soul of a sick person *in extremis* in the *commendatio animae* prayers. The small selection of subjects in the carved scenes depends on this setting, making a readable scheme of redemption, from the Fall of Man to the Last Judgement. 'Looked at in this way, the high crosses of the ninth and tenth centuries are prayers in enduring stone, rising within the circuit of the monastery wall, visible at all times far and near, a perpetual silent liturgy, a dedication and a hope.'[10]

Conclusion

All these various indications show that the Irish crosses belong to an extremely early tradition in Christian art, and are outstanding in upholding and continuing that tradition long after it had been lost elsewhere in the West. The relative peace prevailing in Ireland allowed for continuity in contrast to the turmoil in Europe and the devastation brought about by repeated incursions of barbarian peoples. A fundamental break with the past occurred in many countries where Christianity had gained some footing in more stable times.

The symbol of Constantine's cross of victory, 'By this conquer', was an important element in the erection and design of free-standing cross monuments and is well represented in the remains of east Christian stonework, e.g. of Armenia and Georgia, where continuity also was maintained.[11] Ireland, Christian from the fifth century, belonged to a large, loosely interconnecting association of Christian communities and shared the same trends and ideas that were already prevalent in Christian art over a wide spectrum. The originality of Irish art is apparent from the beginning and is not in question, but the point here emphasised by the evidence from the high crosses is a remarkable continuation, extending in Ireland right through early medieval times, of concepts that date back to the aftermath of Constantine the Great and the triumph of the faith over paganism.

9 B. Bischoff in M. McNamara (ed.), *Biblical Studies. The medieval Irish contribution* (Dublin 1976) p. 148.   **10** R. Flower, 'Irish High Crosses', *Journal of the Warburg and Courtauld Institutes* 17 (1954) pp 87–97.   **11** H. Richardson, 'Observations on Christian art in early Ireland, Georgia and Armenia' in M. Ryan (ed.), *Ireland and Insular Art, A D 500–1200*, (Dublin 1985) pp 129–37.

Dungiven Priory and the Ó Catháin family

ANN HAMLIN

Introduction

I recall with pleasure several occasions over the years when I have spoken on sites with Próinséas Ní Chatháin, and one of these double acts was at Dungiven.[1] Dudley Waterman described Dungiven Priory in about 1969 as 'not only one of the most impressive of the smaller ecclesiastical buildings to survive in west Ulster but also one of the most difficult to evaluate in terms of its structural development'.[2] Since the ruined church is still imperfectly understood but its connections with the Ó Catháin family are well established, I thought there could be no more appropriate tribute to a dear and respected friend than to consider the Ó Catháin links with the site from an architectural and archaeological viewpoint.[3]

Since Dudley Waterman wrote the words quoted above there have been several advances in our knowledge of the site and of comparative material. Excavations at the Priory in 1968–70, 1974–5 and 1982–3 have told us much about the site's long development but, unfortunately, did not solve all the structural problems. Irish Romanesque architecture has been the subject of systematic study in recent years, both through the British Academy's inventory project and in research papers.[4] Understanding of the Augustinian Canons Regular has increased, including the importance of St Malachy's contacts with Arrouaise in Flanders in 1139–40.[5]

Early History: before the Ó Catháins

There are strong local traditions about St Patrick and the account of the parish in Shaw Mason's collections (1814) records that St Patrick was the only saint particularly respected in the area.[6] Rounds or patterns were recorded by the Ordnance Survey and other workers in the early nineteenth century, involving visits to Tubber Patrick and Clough Patrick as well as the graveyard.[7] It does, however, seem likely that 'noble Nechtán, from Alba', listed in the Martyrology of Oengus

1 County Londonderry, grid reference C 692083.   2 My late predecessor, Dudley Waterman, was very much in my thoughts as I wrote this paper. He was intending to write an article about Dungiven similar to his detailed study of nearby Banagher church. It is likely that he hesitated because of the real difficulties in interpretation and when he died, in 1979, he left only fragments of text. His notes and papers have been valuable in my work and he did publish some views in the Banagher article: D.M. Waterman, 'Banagher Church, County Derry', *UJA* 39 (1976) p. 34.   3 I am not qualified to discuss the family's history, but see J. Scott Porter, 'Some account of the sept of the O'Cathains of Ciannachta Glinne-Geimhin', *UJA* 3 (1855) pp 1–8 and 265–72. The form of the name used locally is O'Cahan or O'Kane, and some writers have used the name Cahan Abbey for the Priory, including Champneys, Leask and Hunt.   4 For the inventory project see Roger Stalley, 'In search of Romanesque sculpture', *Archaeology Ireland* 30 (1994) pp 7–9. Tadhg O'Keefe has published many papers: see his *Medieval Ireland: an archaeology* (Stroud 2000) for a full bibliography.   5 A. Gwynn and R.N. Hadcock, *Medieval religious houses: Ireland* (London 1970) pp 146–52, and M.T. Flanagan, 'St. Mary's Abbey, Louth, and the introduction of the Arrouaisian Observance into Ireland', *Clogher Record* 10, no. 2 (1980) pp 223–34.   6 W. Shaw Mason, *A statistical account or parochial survey of Ireland*, I (Dublin 1814) p. 328.   7 A. Day and P. McWilliams (eds), *Ordnance Survey memoirs*

on 8 January, was associated with the site. The gloss in this source adds 'from the east, from Scotland his kindred, i.e., of Dun Geimin in Ciannachta of Glenn Geimin. Or in Scotland is Nechtain.'[8] Nechtán also appears in the Martyrology of Tallaght, and in the later Martyrologies of Gorman (as a 'holy virgin') and Donegal. If this Nechtán can be identified with Nechtan Ner, whose death is recorded in the Annals of Ulster in 679, the use of the site could be taken back at least to the seventh century. Nothing else is known with certainty about the early church here, although the fourteenth-century Book of Lecan used a Book of Dungiven (*Lebor Dúine Gemin*), now lost, as a source.[9] This would suggest a scholarly tradition here at some time.

The place-name with *dún* is itself interesting as it often denotes an important, perhaps royal, fort and it cannot be ruled out that the strong promontory was the site of an early secular fortification before its ecclesiastical use.[10] The excavations of recent years have produced some tantalising glimpses of activity before the stone church, including a deep trench under the chancel and to its south, a group of stakeholes at the west end of the nave, and some early finds (pottery, crucibles, quernstones), but it was only possible to examine small areas.[11] It is not clear from historical sources or from archaeology whether or not there was a substantial functioning church on the site in the eleventh and early twelfth centuries for the Ó Catháins to 'take over' or 'refound'.

The Ó Catháin connection

Before the twelfth century the Roe Valley area was under the control of the O'Connors, but during that century the Ó Catháins displaced the O'Connors and became lords of *Glenn Geimin*.[12] The date of this take-over is important for the history of the church at Dungiven. The long-accepted tradition was that the Priory was founded by the Ó Catháins as a house of Augustinian Canons Regular in 1100, and this claim has often been repeated and used as 'evidence' in attempts to date the church. It does, however, seem that this 'date' goes back only as far as Ware and Alemand in the seventeenth century,[13] and many writers have pointed out that there can have been no Ó Catháin connection at that early date.[14]

The earliest reference to Ó Catháin control in the area seems to be in 1138, when 'Raghnall, son of Imhar Ua Catháin, lord of Craebh, Cianachta and Fir Li, fell' (Annals of the Four Masters). There are frequent mentions of the family in the area from the 1150s onwards, but there is no date for the founding of the Priory. The earliest reference to a prior is in 1207 (Annals of Ulster), and the Augustinian community could have been established at any time from about 1140 onwards.

of Ireland, vol. 15 (Belfast 1992) 42. O. Davies, 'Dungiven Priory', *UJA* 2 (1939) 285–6, quotes the *Memoir* and reproduces a drawing of Clough Patrick from it, although Shaw Mason, *Statistical account*, p. 303 reports that this name was used by local people for the standing stone on a mound near the graveyard. He describes the rounds on p. 328. **8** W. Stokes (ed.), *Félire Óengusso Céli Dé : the Martyrology of Oengus the Culdee* (London 1905) pp 34 and 42–3. **9** K. Mulchrone (ed.), *The Book of Lecan* (Dublin 1937) pp xiii and xxiv and folio 129vb. Other lost sources were Books of Derry, Down and Saul, and others were unnamed. **10** Deirdre Flanagan, 'Settlement terms in Irish place-names', *Onoma* XVII (1972–3) pp 159–62. **11** The many burials restricted the areas of intact archaeological deposits available for excavation. There are preliminary notes on the excavations in *Excavations 1970* (Association of Young Irish Archaeologists, 1971) p. 7 (the 1968–70 work) and T.G. Delaney (ed.), *Excavations 1975–76* (1977), p. 10 (the 1975 work), but it should be noted that the interpretations offered there were tentative. **12** William Reeves, *Acts of Archbishop Colton in his metropolitan visitation of the diocese of Derry AD MCCCXCVII* (Dublin 1850) pp 36–7. **13** J. Ware, *De Hibernia et Antiquitatibus eius* (1654), in W. Harris, *Ware's Antiquities of Ireland* (1745) p. 265; L.A. Alemand, *Histoire monastique d'Irlande* (Paris 1690) p. 98. The date has been repeated by many writers, including Sampson, Petrie, Lewis and Munn. **14** Scott Porter, 'The sept of the O'Cathains', p. 4; 'Proceedings: Dungiven, St Mary's Priory', *JRSAI* 45 (1915) pp 240–41.

Gwynn and Hadcock suggest that 'it was possibly one of the Arrouaisian establishments in the province of Armagh' at the time of St Malachy, between 1140 and 1148.[15] While this can only remain a suggestion, it is nevertheless interesting to note that in the foundation charter of the Cistercian Abbey at Newry in 1156–7, 'Eachmacach O Cathan rex Fearnacrim et Kennachta' comes first in the list of lay witnesses, following the clergy.[16] His appearance here, in the company of reforming bishops, suggests a sympathy with the cause of reform and this could support the case for an Augustinian foundation in his homeland, at Dungiven, in the middle years of the twelfth century. The Ó Catháins therefore emerge as founders of the Priory, and it will become clear from the study of the fabric that they were generous benefactors and also developed a substantial, and unusual, interest in the site.

The site and the buildings

Dungiven Priory stands on a promontory, high above the River Roe, a situation which greatly appealed to nineteenth-century romantic writers. The Ordnance Survey *Memoir* described the Roe: 'it makes several crooked turns and being shut in by precipices at each side, foams loudly'.[17] Petrie though the Priory was 'remarkable for the romantic beauty and fitness of its situation. It is, indeed, hardly possible to imagine anything more singularly wild and striking'.[18] The ruined church stands in an ancient graveyard and is approached from the east by a long lane which, in earlier days, continued down the steep slope to the river (followed now by a footpath). The buildings consist of a nave and chancel and low excavated foundations to west and south.

Earlier published studies of the church introduced much confusion over its dating. Petrie saw the chancel arch as 'Saxon' and believed that the south-west stair-tower was an early round tower.[19] Champneys in 1910 laid too much emphasis on the claimed 1100 'foundation' and favoured a date of about 1100 for Dungiven's nave.[20] In 1925 Munn claimed that the whole church was a seventeenth-century rebuilding for Protestant worship,[21] while Oliver Davies in the most detailed study to date (1939) attributed much of the fabric to the fourteenth century and significantly underestimated the Romanesque work.[22] Leask increased confusion by suggesting a twelfth-century date for the chancel and the fourteenth century for the nave.[23] The most recent, brief, accounts are by McNeill in 1980 and in the 1983 guide to state care monuments.[24]

Twelfth century

The earliest standing masonry is the nave, built of well-cut, coursed sandstone blocks on a neat cutstone offset. Where this work is well preserved, especially where recently exposed and not too

15 Gwynn and Hadcock, *Medieval religious houses*, p. 174.   **16** I am indebted to Dr Marie Therese Flanagan for this reference: Dugdale, *Monasticon Anglicanum*, vi.2.1133; J.F. Kenney, *The sources for the early history of Ireland: ecclesiastical* (New York 1929, repr. 1993) p. 769.   **17** Day and McWilliams, *Ordnance Survey memoirs*, p. 38.   **18** P. [George Petrie], 'Abbey of Dungiven, County of Londonderry', *Dublin Penny Journal* I.51 (June 1833) pp 404–5. Shaw Mason, *Statistical account*, p. 302 is similarly enthusiastic about the location.   **19** Petrie, 'Abbey of Dungiven', pp 404–5.   **20** A.C. Champneys, *Irish ecclesiastical architecture* (London 1910) pp 60, 102, 136.   **21** A.M. Munn, *Notes on the place names of the parishes and townlands of the county of Londonderry* (1925, reprinted Ballinascreen Historical Society, 1985) p. 155.   **22** Davies, 'Dungiven Priory', fig. 1 and passim.   **23** H.G. Leask, *Irish churches and monastic buildings*, 3 vols (Dundalk 1955–66) vol. 2, p. 148.   **24** T.E. McNeill, *Anglo-Norman Ulster: the history*

heavily weathered, it can be seen to be finely jointed and beautifully dressed. In the south wall is a semicircular-headed window with an external projecting frame with an expanded sill (see pl. I). Internally it has an arch of finely-jointed voussoirs, carefully dressed and finely-jointed jambs and a steeply-sloping sill. It is very closely paralleled in the nave of Banagher church, only 1 ½ miles south-west of Dungiven Priory, including a detail common to both associated with fixing a shutter.[25] Not found at Banagher, however, is the distinctive treatment of the external angles of the nave. This is most clearly seen at the north-east corner where there is a flat pilaster clasping the angle, 26–27cm. wide and projecting only 5–7cm. (see pl. 2). From the pilaster run three flat horizontal bands along the east wall, visible for only a short distance before they are covered by the added chancel wall. They decrease in width from bottom (32cm.) through the central one (27cm.) to the top (about 20cm.). Dudley Waterman, who was in close contact during the conservation work and had access to scaffolding when the chancel was roofed in about 1969–70, left records to show that another shallow pilaster extended to match the angle pilaster, now within the chancel wall,[26] so it seems that the horizontal stripwork may have linked these two vertical projections rather than having run along the whole east wall as observers might imagine. What is suggested is substantial *antae* to the east with clasping pilasters at their angles and decorative stripwork on the space between. *Antae* are found in Romanesque Irish contexts well into the twelfth century, but this kind of decorative stripwork is difficult to parallel in Ireland. Closest, perhaps, is the decoration of the north porch at Cormac's Chapel, Cashel (consecrated in 1134), and stripwork is found in other contexts in Anglo-Saxon England,[27] but it is tempting to suggest a timber model for the strange Dungiven feature. At the south-east corner of the nave (see pl. 3) the angle pilaster survives for a height of about 93cm. (two courses above the offset), and at the south-west angle early fabric is exposed to a height of about 90cm., and on two stones the pilaster is visible on the west face but has decayed on the south.

Great uncertainty surrounds the original west end of the nave. The present west wall comes late in the sequence except for the small area at the south-west angle, exposed only in the late 1980s, with carefully cut and jointed sandstone and the remains of the pilaster, already described. Excavation in 1975 did, however, show that a substantial stone foundation runs north-south at a low level, some 1.20m within (east of) the standing west wall and apparently bonded into the standing north and south walls. If this is to be interpreted as the original west wall of the nave, the 'early' masonry and fragmentary pilaster at the south-west angle have to be explained in some way. One circumstance I can envisage is that there was a small, original projection to the west at the south-west corner (where the later stair-tower was), but it is difficult to suggest any function for it. Another possibility is the very early ruin of the west wall and its rebuilding a little further west at an early date, in the same style as the eastern angles. A third possibility is that the excavated west wall belonged to a church of before the twelfth century, and that the present nave was built on the earlier low foundations, following them except at the west end where the building was made longer.

and archaeology of an Irish barony, 1177–1400 (Edinburgh 1980) pp 45–6 and 50; *Historic monuments of Northern Ireland* (Belfast 1983) pp 50–3 and 127–8.   **25** Waterman, 'Banagher Church' pp 29–30, 34 and fig. 5. Champneys, *Irish ecclesiastical architecture*, p. 102 points out the evidence for the same method of closing a shutter at both sites, at Dungiven a socket cut into the interior face of the sill and traces of another (now filled with mortar) in the window head.   **26** Waterman's records, including measured sketches, done at the time of the roofing when the church was scaffolded, are in the Northern Ireland Monuments and Buildings Record.   **27** McNeill, *Anglo-Norman Ulster*, pp 45–6, and pl. 5A; Liam de Paor, 'Cormac's Chapel, Cashel: the beginnings of Irish Romanesque', *North Munster studies: essays in honour of Monsignor Michael Moloney*, ed. Etienne Rynne (Limerick 1967) pp 133–45; H.M. Taylor, *Anglo-Saxon architecture*, vol. III (Cambridge 1978), chaps 10–11, though there are no very close

An issue which may never be satisfactorily solved is the position and form of the original door of the church. The most likely location for a church of this period is at the west end, but the excavated foundation was very deep and the standing west wall is certainly late medieval so there are no clues to an early door here.[28] Davies suggested that the blocked door in the south wall of the nave could have been the original access, but a western door is more likely.[29] For the possible form it is tempting to look to the west door at nearby Banagher church and the rather more distant west door at Maghera, 12 miles away to the south-east across the mountains. These doors are conservative in form, with massive lintels, but accomplished in execution, with a turned semicircular arch to the interior, fine roll mouldings on the Banagher door and at Maghera magnificent Romanesque Irish carving on the lintel and exterior frame.[30]

On the interior of the surviving east wall, where not cut away by the later chancel arches, are the remains of two arches of what must have been a blind arcade. In each corner is a three-quarter round attached shaft. On the north side there are remains of a capital and a base, both with scalloped decoration but both cut away towards the nave in later remodelling. In the south angle the base is missing and the capital is weathered beyond recognition, but three decayed yellow sandstone voussoirs survive from the semicircular arched head of the arcade (see pl. 4–5).[31] Excavation in 1975 showed that the foundations of the east wall continue across the area of the chancel arch at a low level confirming that the nave was originally a single-cell church, without a chancel. What we cannot know, unless loose fragments are ever found, is what form the original east window took. The blind arcade could have framed a single window, or perhaps two, as at Aghowle (Wicklow).[32] Blind arcades are not very common in Irish Romanesque churches, but a few general parallels can be cited, usually in external contexts. Cormac's Chapel, Cashel, has interior and exterior arcades. There are arcades on the west front of Ardmore cathedral (Waterford) containing sculptured panels, and blind arcades flank the Romanesque portal at Roscrea (Tipperary), while at Ardfert (Kerry) there are remains of blind arcades on the exterior west wall.[33]

There are at least two possible models for dating the single-cell church which now survives as the nave, both involving the Ó Catháins, but in different ways. The first is to regard the main construction, with the south window, angle pilasters and stripwork-decorated *antae*, as of the early to mid twelfth century, before the Ó Catháin take-over and the Augustinian foundation. The east wall arcade, with its clearly Romanesque decoration, would then be the first Ó Catháin imprint

parallels.   **28** Day and McWilliams, *Ordnance Survey memoirs*, reproduce a drawing on p. 38 from the O.S. papers with the caption 'View of O'Cathan's priory'. This drawing must be of Banagher Church, 1½ miles away, with its distinctive west door and two windows in the south wall. I have looked at the original drawing in the Royal Irish Academy and it is certainly labelled as above, and it is on the back of a sheet of Dungiven drawings, but the nearness of Banagher allows the possibility of a mistake in captioning having been made.   **29** Davies, 'Dungiven Priory', fig. 1 and p. 280. Internally the blocking is plastered over and only one dressed stone is visible, a long stone with a shallow curve on the upper left, and there seems to be a long lintel above.   **30** Waterman, 'Banagher Church', fig. 5 and p. 29; for Maghera, F. Henry, *Irish art in the Romanesque period* (*1020–1170 AD*) (London 1970) pp 184–5 and pl. V, and for a suggested mid twelfth-century date, A. Hamlin and R.G. Haworth, 'A crucifixion plaque reprovenanced', *JRSAI* 112 (1982) p. 115.   **31** This feature is visible in the photograph (by Mrs Shackleton) accompanying the account of a visit in July 1902, in the 'Proceedings', *JRSAI* 32 (1902), facing p. 313. During conservation work in the late 1960s the blocking of the two arches was partly removed to show the features and expose the back wall.   **32** Where it is interesting to find the Banagher/Maghera door type: Leask, *Irish churches*, vol. 1, p. 84. I have not been able to trace the possible window fragment mentioned by Waterman in 'Banagher Church' p. 34: 'a carved fragment found in the thirteenth-century blocking of the northern opening incorporated small bosses in its ornamentation'.   **33** Romanesque blind arcades are discussed by de Paor, 'Cormac's Chapel' pp 134–6. Leask, *Irish churches*, vol. 1 illustrates the examples cited: pls VIb, VIIIb, XIX and fig. 68.

of the mid to later twelfth century on an 'inherited' church. Waterman seems initially to have inclined towards this model. He referred to 'some evidence that the east wall is a reconstruction',[34] and I wonder if this was the state of the south-east corner of the nave where, as already noted, the angle pilaster only survives to a height of about 93cm (see pl. 3). The angle above has clearly been rebuilt, as well as some of the adjoining south wall. This work could have proved necessary in the context of remodelling the east wall (interior), but it is perhaps more likely to have happened when the chancel was added.[35]

The second model, which Waterman also considered, would see the nave, with all its features, as a unitary work of the mid twelfth century or a little later, and the first church of the Augustinian Canons introduced by the Ó Catháins. This would require acceptance of a combination of architectural conservatism, seen especially in the south window, and a more up to date element in the blind arcade with its restrained Romanesque decoration. It seems quite likely that, in Waterman's words, the north 'evolved outside the mainstream of the Irish Romanesque',[36] and it may well have embraced the mixture of older and newer features suggested here and still visible at Maghera. The fine quality of the masonry, seen in the south window and the freshly uncovered angles, would certainly suggest a date later than the earliest Romanesque and I would tend to favour the simpler model, of the nave as we now have it being a unitary design, of the third quarter of the twelfth century and so the first contribution of Ó Catháin patronage at Dungiven.

Thirteenth century

The annals record the deaths of three priors of Dungiven in the thirteenth century and indicate the importance of the O'Murray family in the post (continuing to the fifteenth century). Flaithbertach O'Laverty died in 1207, Mael-Poil O'Murray in 1216 and Mael-Pedair O'Murray in 1253. The thirteenth century also saw the addition of the very fine chancel to the earlier nave, without doubt the result of Ó Catháin patronage. Liturgically this would have been the canons' preserve, with an altar under the east windows, choir stalls and some kind of screen separating the chancel from the lay people in the nave.

Architecturally what survives is a space of two formerly vaulted bays, with two narrow east windows and a narrow south window, which shows signs of a defaced roll moulding around its inner jambs and head. There is a trefoil-headed cupboard on each side of the east windows, and in the eastern angles remains of the vault (see pl. 6). Defaced bases on sub-bases would have supported detached (now missing) shafts, with shaft-rings and capitals, and there are remains of the springing of the vault above. Much of the detail is unfortunately weathered and unclear, but the north-east capital has distinctive decoration of stiff stems rising 'through' an intermediate ring to clustered 'flowers' above, with an overhanging ring (the abacus) above (see pl. 7). The south-east capital appears to be plain, but earlier observers have detected traces of decoration and the

34 Waterman, 'Banagher Church' 34. The 1966 edition of *Ancient monuments of Northern Ireland* (Belfast) p. 115 states that the east wall was reconstructed. This probably reflects Waterman's views in the early to mid-1960s, but by the time of the Banagher paper in 1976 he left the issue more open. 35 The north-east corner of the nave was not similarly affected. There was no attempt to reproduce the distinctive early treatment of antae with angle pilasters and stripwork; rather there are small, neat, largely dressed sandstone quoins. 36 Waterman, 'Banagher Church' 34. In the de Paor dating scheme, arising from Cormac's Chapel, the distinct capitals and bases and simple treatment would point to an early date, but the decoration at Maghera is clearly quite advanced in terms of Romanesque decorative development.

profile is similar to the other capital, with a concave outline below a ring embellished with a fillet and an overhanging abacus roll. All these features are articulated by a projecting string-course roll, which steps up north and south of the cupboards to link with the shaft-rings of the angle shafts. The roll can be traced along the north wall, where it steps down again and continues either as a projection or as a narrow course of stone where the roll has been cut back (see pl. 6). The feature turns the corner along the south wall but stops short of the tomb.

There are substantial traces of the vault in the walls. Clusters of vaulting ribs rise in the south-east and north-east angles and a wall rib runs over the east windows, partly reconstructed in the nineteenth century. Short lengths of wall ribs surviving at the mid point of the north and south walls will be argued later to belong to the fifteenth century, but above them a shadow of a lost capital can be seen in the plaster, of the same concave profile as those surviving in the eastern angles (see pl. 10). Nothing is left in the western angles of the chancel, but in the north and south walls are traces of the vaulting arches (taken by some early observers to be blocked windows). The vault ribs in the eastern angles have a distinctive profile, of two rolls separated by an angle fillet. The addition of the chancel involved piercing the original east wall and creating a chancel arch. This was wide, cutting the Romanesque arcade, and probably originally pointed, but it was partly filled in and replaced by the present, narrower seventeenth-century chancel arch. There is no trace of it on the north side, but on the south its line can be seen on both sides, to west and east. Towards the nave there was a roll flanked by a deep hollow and short chamfer, and although the detail is now invisible, Dudley Waterman identified the roll as filleted. The roll ends 48cm. above the present ground level of the nave. On the east side only the flanking hollow is visible. The external treatment of the chancel is also careful, with walls of cut, coursed sandstone, seen well in the lower east wall and much of the north wall. It has a sloping basal plinth of dressed stone defined by a projecting roll along its top, only partly surviving and very decayed but possibly of keeled form.[37]

Nineteenth-century paintings and drawings, from about 1800 to the 1860s, show the gradual decay and collapse of the east gable and also contribute some valuable architectural detail (see Appendix). In the 1830s the gable is shown intact, with (in some drawings) a clear horizontal string-course above the windows and a squarish window in the apex of the gable. The inner heads (rear-arches) of the east windows were more acutely pointed than they now appear,[38] and on the exterior were label mouldings, lacking terminals but linked at the springing between the two heads. The narrow south window of the chancel was blocked up and some of its exterior east jambstones were missing. The east gable was clearly insecure, and by the mid nineteenth century the wall was ruined to the top of the east windows, while by 1868 the window heads had fallen and the ground inside had risen to the level of the window sills, with fallen masonry. Unfortunately the subsequent restoration work is not documented or exactly dated, but it is clear that at some point in the later nineteenth century the gable was rebuilt to its now rather rounded outline. This involved restoring the window heads (probably newly-cut), without the external labels, and restoring the lost area of the wall-rib above the windows, which is in distinctively different red stone from the intact work. The tomb was probably restored at the same time (see below).[39]

---

37 McNeill, *Anglo-Norman Ulster*, p. 50 sees the mouldings on both internal and external string-courses as keeled (pointed). While I agree this may be true of the external roll, the internal one at different points seems to show a fillet and scroll form. See Richard K. Morris, 'An English glossary of medieval mouldings: with an introduction to mouldings c.1040–1240', *Architectural History* 35 (1992) fig. 2 for illustrations of these terms.   **38** Several early illustrations of the east windows show the rear-arches as almost triangular: G. Vaughan Sampson, *Statistical survey of the county of Londonderry* (Dublin 1802) facing p. 492, and Shaw Mason, *Statistical account*, facing p. 300.   **39** At present the

Ribbed vaults are not common in thirteenth-century Ireland, especially in smaller churches, and their presence at Dungiven underlines the unusual quality of the work in the chancel. The question obviously arises of the inspiration for the enterprise and the source of the craftsmen who carried it out. We have already noted that an Ó Catháin was prominent in the witness list of the foundation charter for Cistercian Newry Abbey in 1156–7, and the Cistercians were pioneering ribbed vaults in the thirteenth century, so this is one possible source of influence. The chapter house of St Mary's Abbey, Dublin, had a ribbed vault in about 1200, Mellifont in about 1210, and Corcomroe (Clare) in about 1210–20. Anglo-Norman foundations in the east were using ribbed vaults in the second quarter of the century.[40]

Another possible source of influence and craft skills is the major ecclesiastical settlement at Derry. Annals testify to the second half of the twelfth century having been a period of active building in Derry,[41] and the Annals of Ulster record that in 1192 'the door of the refectory of the Penitentiary (*Dubreiclés*) [of Derry] was made by Ua Cathain of the Craib and by the daughter of Ua Inneirghi'. This indicates contact with, and patronage of, Derry by the family in the late twelfth century. Sadly, nothing is left above ground of these buildings, but there must have been craftsmen, masons, joiners, and hewers of stone in Derry at that time, and their descendants could have worked at Dungiven in the thirteenth century.

The weathered, indistinct profiles of the roll mouldings and other features makes it difficult to draw close parallels, but some suggestions can be made. Keeled rolls are found at Augustinian Ballintober (Mayo), which also has ribbed vaulting and similar string-courses in the chancel in about 1220.[42] Rolls with fillets and scroll mouldings, both apparently present at Dungiven, can have a later date-range in the thirteenth century. The distinctive vaulting rib, with two rolls separated by an angle fillet, can be paralleled in late twelfth-century western Britain, as at Buildwas chapter house (Shropshire) and Glastonbury Abbey (Somerset),[43] and it is commonly found in early Gothic work in northern France. The closest parallel I have traced in Ireland is in the vault ribs of the chapter house at St Mary's Abbey, Dublin where there is the same combination in a slightly more complex overall rib form.[44] The distinctive capital in the north-east angle, with the stiff stems, and flowers appearing above a ring, also finds parallels in western Britain, for example at Slimbridge (Gloucestershire), and Llantwit Major (Glamorgan) on loose capitals. There are similar examples in Irish contexts, especially in Christ Church Cathedral (nave triforium) and St Patrick's Cathedral (north choir aisle and elsewhere), both in Dublin, and other possible parallels at Cashel Cathedral (high in the choir) and in the castle chapel at Ferns (Wexford).[45]

Before hazarding a date for the chancel it may be instructive to consider other Ulster churches which can be dated to the early thirteenth century. At nearby Banagher the chancel has windows and *sedilia* embellished with continuous, plain, filleted and pointed bowtell mouldings, characteristic of the 'western' school of Transitional architecture and datable to about 1210–25. A

restoration cannot be dated more closely than to between 1868 and 1896, but I suspect it was before the ruin passed to the state in 1880, and further research may allow the date to be defined more precisely. **40** Roger Stalley, *The Cistercian monasteries of Ireland* (Yale 1987) pp 130–35. **41** K.A. Steer and J.M.W. Bannerman, *Late medieval monumental sculpture in the West Highlands* (Edinburgh 1977) pp 106–7; M. Herbert, *Iona, Kells and Derry: the history and hagiography of the monastic familia of Columba* (Oxford 1988, repr. 1996) pp 119–21. The Ó Brolchán family was prominent in the fifteenth century: see p. 129 below. **42** Leask, *Irish churches*, vol. II 62–3. **43** [John Henry Porter], *A glossary of architecture* (Oxford 1840), pl. 77 (Glastonbury); John Bilson, 'The architecture of the Cistercians', *Archaeological Journal* 66 (1909) 264–5, fig. 13 VIII T. **44** Stalley, *Cistercian monasteries*, pl. 115 and fig. 74. **45** I am very grateful to Roger Stalley for help in identifying parallels from his extensive knowledge and collection of photographs. The Ferns capital appears in his *Architecture and sculpture in Ireland 1150–1350* (Dublin 1971) p. 27, pl. 11.

similar window is found in the Lower Church on Devenish (Fermanagh) for which the same date-range is likely.[46] Dungiven chancel lacks roll mouldings on its windows (except perhaps the south window) and cupboards; indeed they are surprisingly plain in view of the other features, especially the vault. The chancel appears to be fully Gothic, even if the vault rib moulding is conservative, and a date around the middle of the thirteenth century seems likely.[47]

Fourteenth century

Nothing in the visible fabric can be dated to the fourteenth century, but towards the end of the century the Priory did feature in a dramatic event. Archbishop John Colton of Armagh visited Derry diocese in 1397 and an account of his travels and an accompanying rental of the see estates survives. It was edited and published by William Reeves with his usual exemplary notes in 1850.[48] The Archbishop heard a complicated matrimonial case involving Magnus Ó Catháin in Derry, then proceeded to Banagher where he lodged. On 16 October he went from Banagher to the Priory at Dungiven, 'and there, at the request of the Prior and convent, solemnly reconciled the church and cemetery of that place which had been polluted by the spilling of blood'.[49] William Ó Catháin features in the text as Archdeacon of Derry, Maurice Ó Catháin as a canon of Derry, and Magnus Ó Catháin was included in the long list of those excommunicated for usurping the rights of the church at Derry.[50] Some writers have regarded this date of 1397 as the key to the next main building period, assuming that the incident recorded involved damage to the church, but this need not have been the case. The shedding of blood could have arisen from an incident like violation of sanctuary, which may have caused little, if any, damage to the fabric. The dating of the next phase must be considered independently of this documented event, interesting as it is.

The fifteenth and sixteenth centuries

With the increase in the available ecclesiastical sources for this late medieval period we learn quite a lot about Dungiven and its clergy. Earlier indications of the O'Murray family having a hereditary interest in the office of prior are confirmed by their continuing prominence in the fifteenth century. Papal records refer in 1417 to the succession of Philip O'Murray as prior, following John O'Murray.[50] Philip must have been the unnamed prior who was sent a mandate by the pope in 1423 to act in a disputed case of the union of parishes in Armagh diocese.[51] He also appears in the Register of Primate Swayne in 1427 when he seeks protection against several members of the Ó Catháin family.[52] Philip died in 1435 and in that year we read the following description: 'St Mary's priory of *Dungheuhin*, a house of regular canons of St. Austin ... which does not depend on any other house, is reserved to the pope'. It was now vacant by the death of Philip and the pope wished to favour John Omarieadaid (O'Murray).[53]

---

46 Waterman, 'Banagher Church' 34–5; C.A. Ralegh Radford, 'Devenish', *UJA* 33 (1970) p. 59. **47** Perhaps before the death of Maghnus Ó Catháin in the Battle of Down in 1260 when 'fifteen men of the nobles of Clann–Cathain were killed on that spot' (*AU*). **48** Reeves, *Acts of Archbishop Colton*, pp 40–42. **49** Ibid. pp 44–6 and 50–51. **50** M.A. Costello, *De Annatis Hiberniae* (Dublin 1912) p. 215. **51** Ibid. 218–19. **52** D.A. Chart (ed.), *The Register of John Swayne, archbishop of Armagh and primate of Ireland, 1418–1439* (Belfast 1935) p. 59. **53** Costello, *De Annatis*, p. 221.

In 1454 the pope 'issued mandates for Nelanus O'Cahan, a clerk of illegitimate birth, to be received into the monastery for appointment as prior if his accusations against Prior John O'Murray ... were proved'.[54] On the eve of the beginnings of the major changes brought about by the dissolution, in 1535 Archbishop Cromer refers in a letter to an unnamed prior of *Dungewin* as one of three judges delegated from the Holy See to deal with a dispute over the succession to three parishes in Armagh diocese,[55] so there is every indication that community life was continuing at Dungiven into the sixteenth century. It is not known when the house was dissolved, but it is referred to in 1603 as 'a suppressed monastery or house of canons' and its possessions of townlands are listed, but there is no record of buildings.[56]

Against this historical background we can look at the next major changes to the fabric of the Priory which must date from the fifteenth century, perhaps its later years. A tall, two-light window was inserted into the north wall of the nave, towards its east end. Its head is fairly acutely pointed and there are remains of cusped tracery, but not enough to suggest a reconstruction with any confidence.[57] The external label has polygonal stops in the form of small corbels which run into the decoration of interlaced stems and conventional leaves, with the extra elaboration of three small rosettes above the leaves on the left (east) side (see pl. 8).[58] The jambs have a fine roll on the outer face, then are chamfered with a groove for glass, broken-out bar holes in the eastern jamb and holes for vertical bars in the sill. The rear-arch has a simple chamfer and dies into the unadorned jambs.[59]

In the chancel a low door was inserted in the north wall, cut through the external plinth and causing the lower part of the thirteenth-century window above to be built up. The doorway is now blocked on its outer face but is exposed on the interior, showing characteristically late medieval use of only two stones to form the arch, and hollow-chamfered with small triangular stops on the jambs (see pl. 9).[60] These stops are at the present floor level in the chancel, but it seems likely that there was a step up in the eastern bay, suggested by the distance below the sub-bases of the eastern angle shafts.

It also appears that the vault was reworked in the fifteenth century. This would have been a major undertaking, perhaps done in connection with the insertion of the tomb (see below), and perhaps also seeking a fashionably lower pitch and flatter roof profile. The south wall of the chancel is markedly rougher than the other walls in its external stonework and it is possible that it was partly rebuilt, on the original, thirteenth-century plinth, when the vault was reworked.[61] The traces of the fifteenth-century vault are sparse and difficult to interpret, and no loose vault stones have been found.[62] The clearest evidence is in the north wall at the mid point, where there is a wall-rib, the defaced capital already mentioned, and a damaged decorated panel below (see pl. 10). The wall-rib profile is similar to the earlier one, but not identical (with stilted rolls and a very slight projection between instead of the thirteenth-century angle fillet). It is also made of a harder stone and shows clear pecked marks from its dressing. Below is a gap, which could have held a corbel, and below again the panel with stylised leaves, characteristic of the fifteenth century and

54 Gwynn and Hadcock, *Medieval religious houses*, p. 174. Is this a sign of increasing Ó Catháin family power in priory affairs? 55 Aubrey Gwynn, *The medieval province of Armagh* (Dundalk 1946) pp 100–1. 56 'Proceedings: Dungiven', p. 241; Reeves, *Archbishop Colton*, pp 41–2. 57 S. Lewis, *A topographical dictionary of Ireland* (London 1837) p. 581 refers to 'a window ornamented with tracery, in good preservation'. 58 Rosettes do not necessarily indicate a Tudor date. They occur on the west door of Clontuskert Priory, dated by an inscription to 1471: Leask, *Irish churches*, vol. III, pl. X and p. 74. 59 Davies, 'Dungiven Priory', p. 278, fig. 4. 60 Ibid., pl. XV, b3. 61 The Waterman papers include thoughts on this issue, including the possibility that the rebuilding was done in the late thirteenth century, but I am suggesting that the fifteenth century is also possible. 62 There are many records of the clearance of loose stones and soil from the interior of the church since 1883, the first recorded work

similar to the decoration on the exterior of the north window in the nave. The pitch of this reworked vault may be indicated by the wall-rib arching over the east windows. Although this is reconstructed, early illustrations show a rib in this position, at a clearly lower pitch than the thirteenth-century ribs are describing in the north-east and south-east angles.[63]

The glory of the chancel is obviously the grand tomb in the south wall, much illustrated by nineteenth-century artists (see Appendix). Traditionally and popularly attributed to Cooey-na-Gall O'Cahan (Cú-maige), who died in 1385, it has been dated by John Hunt to the last quarter of the fifteenth century,[64] and this seems reasonable. It is, therefore, either a mausoleum for Cooey-na-Gall or the tomb of a member of the family who died in the late fifteenth century. The annals supply several possible candidates, including Godfrey (died 1472), Diarmait (died 1489), and Godfrey and John (both died 1492), but we will probably never know certainly for whom the tomb was made.

The tomb as we see it now has been substantially restored, perhaps more than once. Early and mid nineteenth-century illustrations show the tracery broken, the tomb chest in disarray, with the front panels and figures partly detached and loose, and the main figure without his head.[65] Study of a wide range of illustrations suggests that the openwork canopy was restored on the basis of the stumps of tracery and the effigy was given a new head (with an unlikely cap) between 1868 and the late nineteenth century. One account attributes the restoration to Mr Ogilby of the Pelipar estate a few years before 1903, while another claims that the Revd Ross got a rich relation to restore the tomb, but Canon Ross was rector from 1850 to 1886.[66] One of the albums of Du Noyer drawings shows a fascinating juxtaposition of a brown aquatint of the tomb as it was and another showing an imaginative restoration, with the disclaimer 'The crucifixion on the apex of the dripstone, and the cherubims at the head and foot of the effigy are mere juvenile fancies (- in 1840) so are the nondescript pilasters supporting the theoretical angelics …'[67] His reconstruction of the tracery is exactly as it was reconstructed some decades later, and it is interesting to wonder whether his drawing was available to influence the work. Photographs of the restored tomb in the late nineteenth and early twentieth centuries show the line of 'weepers' intact, with clear facial features, so it seems likely that the whole tomb was reconstructed and restored, including probably some whole figures on the front.[68] An undated photograph by R.J. Welch (active from about 1883 to 1936) presents a problem which has puzzled me. In his view the figures are very much more decayed than in the c.1900 group of photographs, and I can only reconcile this by suggesting that the Welch photo was a late one in his career, and that the restored figures were by then actively weathering, as they have continued to do throughout the twentieth century.[69] Opinions have varied on the quality of the restoration. The account of the Antiquaries' visit in 1915 commented

I have come across, but it is possible that the vault did not survive to the early seventeenth-century reuse of the church and the stones may have been reused and dispersed long ago.   63 'Proceedings: Dungiven', p. 241 suggests that this rib may date from the early seventeenth-century refitting of the church, but I would incline towards the fifteenth century.   64 J. Hunt, *Irish medieval figure sculpture 1200–1600* (Dublin 1974) vol. I, pp 130–12.   65 'Proceedings: Dungiven', p. 242 gives an illustration based on a Du Noyer 'sketch' (1840) showing the tomb in this state. See also Appendix.   66 *Northern Whig* and *Belfast News Letter* 27 October 1903, for Ogilivy connection. Letter in Ministry of Finance file, Rev. I.T. Trelawny–Ross to Dr D.A. Chart, July 1926 for the Ross tradition. J.B. Leslie, *Derry clergy and parishes* (Enniskillen 1937) p. 74 for Canon William Ross's career.   67 Du Noyer Album VII p. 46 (centre) for the tomb in 1840, and p. 47 for the restoration drawing, in the library of the Royal Society of Antiquaries of Ireland.   68 'Proceedings: Dungiven', p. 243 shows the headless main figure and only three clear smaller figures, with perhaps the shadow of a fourth. In his reconstruction drawing (note 67) Du Noyer shows 'weepers' only in arches 2, 3, 5 and 6 (numbering from left to right).   69 Ulster Museum reference numbers W07/26/3 (Welch) and

2 North-east exterior angle of nave at junction with chancel, showing angle pilaster and stripwork.

1 Exterior of window in south wall of nave.

3 Detail of south-east angle of nave to show quality of stonework and rebuilding above.

4 North-east corner of nave, interior, showing remains of arcade.

5 South-east corner of nave, interior, showing remains of arcade.

6 Wide-angle view of chancel, looking east.

8 Detail of label stop and decorated finial, fifteenth-century window in north wall of nave, exterior, left side.

7 Detail of capital in north-east corner of chancel; shaft-ring and string-course also visible.

9 Blocked fifteenth-century door in south wall of chancel, with earlier window above (lower part of window blocked). Signs of vault also visible.

12 Detail of end of tomb, facing west.

10 Fifteenth-century vault-rib and decorated stone below, midpoint, north wall of chancel, with shadow of capital visible above.

11 The tomb and south-east angle of chancel.

13 General view looking east, with tower-house foundation in foreground. Blocking off of chancel also seen.

on the 'careful' work, while John Hunt regarded the restoration as 'drastic and ill-judged'.[70] It is impossible at this distance in time from the restoration in the later nineteenth century to judge the quality of the work, now so weathered, but we must be grateful that the deterioration of the early nineteenth century was halted and reversed.

Despite all its vicissitudes, including recorded vandalism over many years and long weathering of the soft sandstone,[71] it remains the grandest late medieval tomb in the north and a worthy memorial to one of the many military members of the Ó Catháin family (see pl. 11). The main figure lies under a cusped semicircular arch and a magnificent openwork canopy of cusped flamboyant tracery. He wears a long quilted and padded garment (aketon) to the knee and a collar of mail (pisane) over the shoulders, and his helmet was probably originally pointed (a bascinet). He has a belt and his sword lies across his body. On the flat top of the tomb chest is a weathered coat of arms (left of his head), the Ó Catháin arms,[72] and on the right is a small figure, perhaps an angel. The edge of the slab is decorated with nail-head ornament, as is also the label moulding of the arch above. Across the front of the tomb chest are six arched trefoil-headed niches, and in each is a galloglas (gallowglass) warrior weeper, standing on guard for their lord, with hands on swords and one with a spear. They are dressed in the same way as the main figure. On the right corner of the front is a banded shaft, and on the small area of tomb exposed on the west-facing side is a heavily weathered animal, probably the motif from the Ó Catháin crest of an otter catching a fish (see pl. 12).[73]

Although the nail-head decoration and banded shaft look back to the thirteenth century, the arch mouldings, the tracery and the figures all point to the late fifteenth century, and the 'early' elements must be conscious archaising, perhaps to respect the thirteenth-century features in the chancel.[74] The ancestry of the tomb seems to be partly western Scottish and partly western Irish. The gallowglass figures closely resemble figures on the tombs of the Iona School of West Highland stonecarving, and it is quite possible that a mason trained on Iona carried out the work. There were close links between Derry diocese and western Scotland throughout the middle ages, and it is interesting to note a marriage link between the Ó Catháin family and the same area. In the late thirteenth century Aine, daughter of Cú-maige na nGall Ó Cathán of the Ciannachta, married Angus Óg of the Clan Donald.[75] Two Irish families were prominent in the Iona stonecarving community, the Ó Brolcháns and the Ó Cuinns, and Donald Ó Brolchán recorded his work in Iona cathedral in an inscription in about 1450. There are windows in the cathedral with flamboyant tracery which resembles the Dungiven canopy, and this is another pointer to a likely Iona source of influence on the craftsman who made the Dungiven tomb.[76] It is reasonable to imagine an ancient route from Iona by sea to Lough Foyle, and from Derry along the western branch of the great early main road, the Slige Midluachra, which ran close to the Priory on its way east and south to the ford at Toome.[77]

H07/26/3 (Hogg).   **70** 'Proceedings: Dungiven', p. 242; Hunt, *Irish medieval figure sculpture*, vol. I, p. 131.   **71** The O.S. *Memoir* reports damage to the tomb: Day and McWilliams, p. 39. There are local newspaper accounts of damage and moves to fence off the tomb in 1903. In the late 1960s the (then) Ministry of Finance decided it was necessary to roof the chancel and fit a partition into the chancel arch with a lockable door to protect the chancel and tomb from weathering and vandalism.   **72** Scott Porter, 'The sept of the O'Cathains' p. 266 describes the devices on the shield and in the Du Noyer papers in the Royal Irish Academy there are many heraldic drawings, including the Ó Catháin arms. See also J. Barry, 'Guide to records in the Genealogical Office, Dublin, with a commentary on heraldry in Ireland', *Analecta Hibernica* 26 (1970) pp 17–18 (though he follows the late fourteenth-century dating scheme for the tomb).   **73** Clearly seen in a Du Noyer drawing dated 1835 in the National Library of Ireland, ref. 1975 TX 33.   **74** Hunt, *Irish medieval figure sculpture*, vol. I, pp 131–2.   **75** Steer and Bannerman, *Late medieval monumental sculpture*, pp 202–3.   **76** Ibid. pp 106–9.   **77** C. Ó Lochlainn, 'Roadways in ancient Ireland', in *Féil–Sgríbhinn Eóin Mhic Néill* (Dublin 1940, repr. 1995) p. 472 and map.

The West Highland tradition does not, however, account for the openwork tracery canopy and the row of weepers which are such attractive features of the Dungiven tomb. For these elements we have to look west, for example to the Joyce tomb in St Nicholas', Galway, Strade (Mayo), Kilconnell Friary (two examples: Galway), and Sligo Abbey. At Roscommon 'Abbey' there are gallowglass weepers but they wear armour rather than quilted aketons.[78] There is no exact parallel for the Dungiven tracery and figures but it must be to this general background of tomb-carving in the fifteenth century that we must look. It is, however, also worth recalling that there were once fine late medieval tombs in east Ulster, now destroyed or defaced, as in Armagh Franciscan Friary and Newtownards Dominican Friary,[79] and that there may well have been an eastern tradition of tomb-carving.

The insertion of the fifteenth-century door in the south wall of the chancel may have been linked with major changes at the west end of the nave at the same time.[80] It is possible that the (hypothetical) original west door was blocked a this time as part of the structural changes and other arrangements for access had to be made. The blocked door in the south wall of the nave is undatable but could be from this period. A door was cut through the north wall of the nave, very close to the present north-west corner, but this is now blocked and the area around it is very difficult to understand.[81]

The west wall must have been rebuilt in connection with the creation of a rectangular extension to the nave (see pl. 13). Its walls survive incompletely as low excavated foundations and the only clear access is at the south-east corner, where a door leads to a small square stair-tower in the south-east corner of the original nave, from which doors also lead east into the church, with a hollow chamfer to the church, and south to the exterior, with plain chamfers and triangular stops on the outside face. By the plantation period this complex was known as Ó Catháin's 'castle', and by that time it was clearly a defended tower-house. It is, however, just possible that the extension was first made to serve as a house for the prior of the Augustinian community. We are here purely in the realm of speculation, partly because little is known about the conventual buildings which extended south of the church,[82] and partly because excavation threw no light on the early use of the tower. It is unclear even if there was a complete cloister in stone; at Bonamargy Franciscan Friary in north Antrim only the east range appears to have been stone-built.

In the later middle ages there was a growing desire for privacy and comfort in accommodation, and this did sometimes lead to the head of a community seeking his own, private 'house'. There is an early (mid thirteenth-century) Augustinian example at Kilmacduagh (Galway) where a two-storey hall is known as the abbot's house.[83] A late abbot of Cistercian Baltinglass (Wicklow) built a tower-house, and at Holycross (Tipperary) a building south-east of the cloister is traditionally the abbot's house, a two-storey dwelling with comfortable domestic features.[84] The trend towards 'domestication' is also seen in non monastic ecclesiastical contexts. At nearby Banagher, for

---

78 Illustrations in Leask, *Irish churches*, vol. III, pls XXIV–VI and Hunt, *Irish medieval figure sculpture*, vol. II, pls 248–60.   79 *An archaeological survey of County Down* (Belfast 1966) pp 285–6 and pl. 100 for Newtownards, and C.J. Lynn, 'Excavation in the Franciscan Friary church, Armagh', *UJA* 38 (1975) p. 63 and fig. 2.   80 There is no archaeological dating evidence to show that the work at the west end was contemporary with the changes in the chancel, but the insertion of the new window in the nave north wall does, perhaps, lend some support to the suggestion that the tower-house was built in the later fifteenth century, when the other work was done elsewhere in the church.   81 Davies, 'Dungiven Priory', fig. 4.   82 Walls were found during the 1968–70 excavation running south from the south-east corner of the chancel, the junction of chancel and nave, and near the west end of the south wall. These could all belong to the plantation period remodelling, except perhaps for a lower wall at the chancel/nave junction which could relate to conventual buildings. Most of the area of the likely cloister and later bawn is mounded high with dense burials.   83 Waterman, 'Banagher Church', p. 37.   84 Stalley, *Cistercian monasteries*, pp 173–5.   85 Waterman, 'Banagher Church', pp 35–7 and pl. XI.   86 Leask, *Irish churches*, vol. III,

example, there are low foundations of a tower near the church, best explained as a priest's house,[85] and there are residential west towers at Layd (Antrim), Newcastle (Dublin) and Taughmon, Kilpatrick and Templecross (Westmeath).[86] It is just possible that the Dungiven Ó Catháin 'castle' originated in this way.

It seems reasonable to explore this possibility because it is most unusual for a secular defended structure to be added to a church, and it slightly more believeable for an ecclesiastical domestic structure to be 'taken over' and militarised. Excavation produced some late medieval everted-rim pottery which could derive from Augustinian or Ó Catháin activity (or both). Whether the tower originated as the prior's house, or whether it was, from the start, probably in the fifteenth century, a secular defended structure, it is certain that an Ó Catháin tower-house existed at the west end of the nave by the late middle ages.

Seventeenth century

The Ó Catháin link with Dungiven Priory was broken in the early seventeenth century. In 1602 Donnell Ó Catháin submitted and Dowcra placed a garrison at Dungiven, presumably in the tower-house. When the area was granted to the Skinners' Company of London, Captain (later Sir) Edward Doddington transformed the complex. The Priory church was remodelled, with a new chancel arch and a north door with a porch, and was used for Protestant worship until 1711–16, when a new church was built in the village.[87] The tower-house was repaired and probably remodelled, the cloister area was reworked as a bawn, and a manor-house was built where the west range would have been.[88] Manus Ó Catháin was briefly in control of the castle in 1641–2, but it returned to English hands and was occupied by Doddington's wife until her death in 1679, after which it was destroyed by fire and abandoned.[89]

Written and pictorial sources survive from the plantation period through which we can look back to the Ó Catháin church and castle. A drawing in Carew's 1611 survey shows a rectangular tower with large windows, a gabled slated roof behind a crenellation, and a feature which could indicate the top of a stair turret. The chancel is roofed but the nave seems to be roofless. The text beside the drawing reads 'The House and Castle of Dungevan Reeddified and Bult by Captn Dodington'.[90] Pynner's 1618–19 survey records the castle built by Doddington 'of 22 foot broad, four stories high, whereof some part of the walls were standing before … by him well finished and slated'. Adjoining the castle he had built a house 'the walls whereof some parts were standing', and he had 'repaired' a bawn of lime and stone abut the castle and the house.'[91] This suggests considerable reuse of the Ó Catháin and Augustinian fabric by Doddington, including the tower-

pp 18–21 and 87–8. For Layd, see F.J. Bigger and W.J. Fennell, 'Layde, Cushendall, Co. Antrim', *UJA* 5 (1899) pp 35–6.   **87** Munn, *Notes on the place names*, p. 155, gives 'about 1711–1716', while J.B. Leslie, *Derry clergy and parishes* (Enniskillen 1937) p. 216, has 'about 1718'.   **88** N.F. Brannon and B.S. Blades, 'Dungiven Bawn re-edified', *UJA* 43 (1980) pp 93–6.   **89** The 1982–3 excavation produced much evidence for burning and the indications were that the house had been abandoned before the fire: A. Hamlin and C. Lynn (eds), *Pieces of the past: archaeological excavations by the Department of the Environment for Northern Ireland 1970–1986* (Belfast 1988) pp 82–3. Doddington's widow, Dame Anne Cooke, made her will in July 1679 and it was proved on 5 January 1680, so I suggest she died late in 1679. I owe this reference to Nick Brannon.   **90** E.M. Jope, 'Moyry, Charlemont, Castleraw and Richhill: fortification to architecture in the north of Ireland', *UJA* 23 (1960) p. 99, fig. 1.   **91** G. Hill, *An historical account of the Plantation of Ulster at the commencement of the seventeenth century 1608–1620* (Belfast 1877) pp 572–3.

house, the east range of the cloister, and some kind of precinct enclosure, apparently a stone wall.[92] A more elaborate drawing in 1622 by Thomas Raven to accompany Sir Thomas Phillips' survey differs from the 1611 depiction in several ways, not least in how the tower is shown.[93] It has many small slit and cross-shaped windows, a varied outline with crow-stepped crenellations, drop-holes, a chimney, and a clearly projecting and taller circular tower at the south-east angle, with its own crenellations above a string-course. The church is shown fully slated and the new porch is clear, projecting from the north wall of the nave. Unfortunately nothing is known about whether the buildings at Dungiven suffered in the warfare of the late sixteenth and early seventeenth centuries, and it is uncertain what survived, in what condition, for 're-edifying' and reuse. These areas in the western part of the site were ruined at an early date and recent excavation has not yet been able to clarify this issue.

The square foundation in the south-west corner of the nave was the base of the tall tower shown in the drawings, probably containing a spiral stair. It was square below but became circular above the roof-line. Excavation showed the foundations of the stair-tower lapping over the church's south wall and of one build with the west wall, so it can reasonably be dated to the fifteenth century when the tower-house was built. The stair-tower was still standing in the late eighteenth century and was apparently brought down by treasure seekers digging at its base in 1784.[94] It is likely that the fall of this tower did further damage to whatever was still standing at the west end of the church and the tower-house.[95] The stair tower was said to have been about 50 feet high and two early nineteenth-century illustrations show it, though whether drawn from life or from memory is not certain. The drawing published in 1802 is a very distant view, but Shaw Mason's illustration, published in 1814, is more helpful.[96] It shows the church from the north-west, including the remains of the stair-tower with traces of corbelling and a string-course and indications of crenellations, somewhat reminiscent of the 1622 drawing. Petrie was very excited about this tower in 1833, believing it to have been an early round tower, unique in having been attached to the west end of a church.[97] It has appeared in several lists of round towers, but there can be no doubt that it was the last remaining standing element of the Ó Catháin tower-house, as remodelled by Edward Doddington.

It is surprising that the existence of the Ó Catháin castle at the west end of the Priory church was lost sight of, at least in scholarly circles. The existence of a fortification in Dungiven village attracted attention away from the Priory site, and the seventeenth-century descriptions and drawings were taken to refer to the remains in the village. In fact, the west wall of the Priory was known locally as the 'Castle Gable', and in 1833 Petrie wrote of 'the former existence of a fortress adjacent to the ecclesiastical buildings,'[98] while Munn in 1925 reported that the old castle, one of

---

92 During the 1982–3 excavation a short stretch of a medieval ditch was found north-west of the church, a possible enclosure at some period.   **93** J.S. Curl, *The Londonderry Plantation 1609–1914* (Chichester 1986) p. 290, pl. 208 and back of dust jacket in colour; Brannon and Blades, 'Dungiven Bawn', p. 92, pl. 1.   **94** The date of 1784 is not absolutely certain. Shaw Mason, *Statistical account*, p. 302 writes 'fallen within these few years' (from 1814) and Reeves, *Archbishop Colton*, p. 41, suggests 'fell about the year 1784'. Most later sources, like Munn, *Notes on the place names*, p. 155 express no reserve: 'fell in the winter of 1784'.   **95** A plan, probably by Stokes, in the O.S. materials in the Royal Irish Academy, has a note 'ruin of the "Castle Gable"' (Box 39 II 3, No. 72). See also Appendix, Royal Irish Academy 9.   **96** G.V. Sampson, *Statistical survey of the county of Londonderry* (Dublin 1802) facing p. 498 (distant view), also in *JRSAI* 1915, p. 238, and Shaw Mason, *A statistical account*, facing p. 302, also reproduced in Brannon and Blades, 'Dungiven Bawn', p. 95, pl. 2.   **97** Petrie, 'Abbey of Dungiven', p. 404, but in his later book he was more cautious: George Petrie, *The ecclesiastical architecture of Ireland* (Dublin 1845) p. 395 ('of a date but little anterior to the thirteenth century').   **98** Petrie, 'Abbey of Dungiven', p. 405.

the Ó Catháin residences, 'was situated on a cliff to the west of the old Church'.[99] It was not until 1980, however, that Brannon and Blades firmly restored the link between the Priory, the Ó Catháin tower-house and Doddington's manor-house and bawn.[100]

After the disuse of the church in the early eighteenth century the site continued to be used for burial and it was a focus for pilgrimage.[101] Following all the antiquarian interest in the nineteenth century, the Priory ruins were passed by the Church Temporalities Commission to the Commissioners of Public Works in 1880 to be preserved and maintained as a national monument. The site is now in the care of the Department of the Environment for Northern Ireland, and following Nick Brannon's excavations in 1982–3 the tower-house and manor-house are once again exposed and displayed. The site is visited and enjoyed by local people, local schools and visitors from far and near.[102]

Conclusion

The Ó Catháin connection with Dungiven began with the introduction of the Augustinian Canons Regular around the middle of the twelfth century, when the family endowed the building of a single-cell church (or possibly remodelled an earlier church) on a site occupied by an early foundation associated with Nechtán, a saint from Scotland who died in 679. The fine thirteenth-century chancel was added under Ó Catháin patronage, and in the fifteenth century the family's hand is seen again in major structural changes. These included the commissioning of the magnificent tomb and changes in the chancel, and perhaps the building of a secure tower-house at the west end of the nave, although the possibility of an ecclesiastical origin has also been discussed. With the warfare of Elizabeth's reign and the early seventeenth century the site passed to the Skinners' Company of London and the tower-house became part of the plantation manor-house complex. The church was remodelled and was used for Protestant worship until the second decade of the eighteenth century. In the nineteenth century the ruins attracted the attention of scholars like Petrie and Reeves and artists like Du Noyer. The site continued to be valued by local people and those who cared for it in the twentieth century, but there was much confusion and misunderstanding of the ruins. As we enter a new century we must hope that this complex, multiperiod site, so powerfully evocative of Ulster's many-layered history[103] and so closely associated with the Ó Catháin family, will become better understood and more widely appreciated.

Acknowledgments

I am grateful to many people and institutions for help with this paper. I thank my former colleagues in Environment and Heritage Service (EHS) for helpful discussion and access to the

---

99 Munn, *Notes on the place names*, p. 156. **100** Brannon and Blades, 'Dungiven Bawn', passim. **101** Du Noyer recorded many of the heraldic gravestones in and around the church, including Ó Catháin tombs. Sampson, *Statistical survey*, p. 490 points out that Dungiven was 'the burying-place of the sept of Ó Cathan'. The many small crosses incised on the chancel masonry, concentrated on the exterior east and north walls, may be connected with pilgrimage activity, and the bullaun in the graveyard ('wart well') is still frequented. See also note 7. **102** F. Smith, 'Historical evidence in the classroom: a Dungiven example', *Ulster Local Studies* 19 (1984) pp 65–71. I was pleased to coincide with a group from a local school at the Priory in September 2000. **103** C.J. Donnelly, *Living places: archaeology, continuity and change at historic monuments in Northern Ireland* (Belfast 1997) pp 111–14.

Monuments and Buildings Record, especially Nick Brannon, Terence Reeves-Smyth and Gail Pollock, and Caroline Dowling and other members of the EHS Specialised Skills Unit for typing the text. I am also very grateful to Dr Marie Therese Flanagan, Professor Roger Stalley and Rachel Moss for their help. My warm thanks go to the following institutions and individuals for access to their collections: Ulster Museum (Martin Anglesea and Pauline Dickson), National Library of Ireland (Joanne Finegan), Royal Irish Academy (especially Patricia McCarthy) and Royal Society of Antiquaries of Ireland (Nicole Arnould). Finally I thank the staff of the Roe Valley Country Park (EHS) for facilitating my access to the chancel at Dungiven.

Appendix: Pictorial sources

Pictorial sources are important for the information they can give, especially for the period before photography was widely available. These sources do, however, present their own problems of interpretation because we are dependent on the eye and accuracy of the artist, yet we cannot check his depiction if the subject no longer exists. Because of the keen interest in Dungiven Priory in the nineteenth century many drawings and other illustrations survive. Drawings were copied, fair copies were made, engravings from drawings were 'improved', so it is not really surprising that there are variations in how the same subject is shown. It is nevertheless puzzling that many illustrations show a square window in the east gable while others do not, and there are similar inconsistencies in whether a horizontal string-course appears over the wall-rib over the east windows or not. It is often necessary to trace the 'ancestry' of a drawing to see how it has evolved, like the engraving in the *Dublin Penny Journal* for 1833 which is based on a drawing by Andrew Nicholl. The sources listed below are those I have traced and used, but there are probably more (perhaps many more) to be found and this can only be a tentative list.

National Library of Ireland

1. 290 TA Etching of chancel, as in Sampson 1802, facing p. 492.

2. 291 TA Aquatint of distant view of church and tower from mound and standing stone north-east of church, as in Sampson 1802, facing p. 498. Reprinted in *JRSAI* 1915, p. 239.

3. Another drawing in Sampson 1802, facing p. 490, of the tomb, is not in the NLI collection.

4–10. 1975(6) TX Du Noyer album of drawings (fair drawings from O.S. sketches)

4. 1975 TX 28 View of chancel looking east, tomb in disarray, square window in gable, gap in gable's north slope.

5. 1975 TX 29 East windows and cupboards, interior, windows intact but soil spilling over sills from exterior. Dated 1838.

6. 1975 TX 30 East windows, exterior, showing label moulding. Masonry looks loose. With scale in feet.

7. 1975 TX 31(A) Captioned 'Capital of Pillar, Dungiven Old Church', but not like anything surviving (interlaced decoration with leaves and flowers above fluting).

8. 1975 TX 31 South window of nave, exterior and interior, with detail of plan of external frame.

9. 1975 TX 32 Window in south wall of chancel, exterior, some missing jambs on right filled with rubble.

10. 1975 TX 33 Detail of west-facing end of tomb, showing otter eating fish, dated 1835.

Ulster Museum
1–3. Irish Antiquities by Andrew Nicholl 1835–7, vol. 1.

1. N147 (36) Dungiven Old Church, ink drawing, chancel through chancel arch, with east gable intact, wall-rib over windows and horizontal string-course over the rib. Square window in gable.

2. N183(7) Similar to above, ink drawing, less accomplished and no extra information.

3. N183(8) Tomb, drawing, showing weepers leaning but no clear tomb chest. Indications of seven rather than six weepers. Main figure has head and feet.

4. J.H. Burgess, watercolour, probably mid nineteenth-century, showing chancel through chancel arch, east wall ruined to (insecure) window-heads, tomb in disarray, main figure seems dislodged, without head or legs, banded shaft at right angle of tomb loose, leaning against wall. Published in *Portraits and Prospects* (Ulster Museum, Belfast, 1989), p. 90 and pl. 44 as 'Cahan Abbey'.

5. 3199 Dr James Moore (1819–83), watercolour dated 1868, chancel through chancel arch, looking to south-east corner, showing east gable with window heads gone and ground level up to window sills. Tomb appears less ruined than in earlier pictures.

6. Pencil sketch, unsigned and undated, showing tomb, similar to Du Noyer sketches.

7. WO7/26/2 Photograph by R.J. Welch (1859–1936), undated, view from west across ruined west wall, looking east. Although this view might suggest much subsequent rebuilding of the west wall, in fact the ground level has been greatly lowered in excavations since the late 1960s.

WO7/26/3 Photograph by R.J. Welch, undated, of the tomb showing weepers much weathered, especially their faces, and wall behind main figure stone below and plaster above. Reproduced by E. Estyn Evans and Brian S. Turner, *Ireland's Eye: the photographs of Robert John Welch* (Belfast 1977), p. 152 and often elsewhere.

H07/26/2 Photograph by Alexander Hogg (1870–1939), from nave to chancel arch, showing restored east windows and cupboards through the arch, taken in 1907.

H07/26/3 Photograph by Alexander Hogg of the tomb, showing weepers in good condition with facial detail clear and back wall plastered, taken in 1907.

Royal Society of Antiquaries of Ireland Library
G.V. Du Noyer Albums
1. VII, p. 45 v pencil drawing of capital, as NMI 7 above.

2. VII, p. 45 v pencil sketch of Cooey figure with some dimensions.

3. VII, p. 46 left, pencil sketch from nave (very full of tombs) to choir, 'Interior, Dungiven Old Church'.

4. VII, p. 46 centre, brown aquatint, fair drawing of tomb, clearly basis for drawing in *JRSAI* 1915, p. 242. Only three weepers visible, figure lacks head and left arm.

5. VII, p. 47, brown aquatint, 'Restoration of the Tomb of Cooey-na-Gall, Dungiven Old Church, Co. Derry'. Caption (quoted above, see note 67) suggests date of 1840.

Shaw Mason, *Parochial Survey* (1814), text indicates drawings by Mr A. Ogilby of Beaufort Lodge (unknown if originals survive).
1. Facing p. 300, engraving, chancel gable, showing rear-arches of windows as markedly triangular and squarish window in gable, and some damage to gable's north slope.

2. Facing p. 302, engraving, 'Church of Dunalbinn', view from north-west, showing windows and door in north wall and tower at south-west angle, but shading leaves west 'wall' uncertain.

Royal Irish Academy
O.S. Memoirs Box 39 II 3. Sketches and drawings, probably by John Stokes. Not individually recorded but include a drawing of the 'Saxon door' (chancel arch), drawing of main figure, ground plan with notes of features, and drawing of blocked door at west end of nave north wall. Some of these drawings reproduced in Davies, 'Dungiven Priory', figs 2, 5 and 6.

O.S. Sketches by George V. Du Noyer (1817–69)
1. 12.T.7 (77) Pencil sketch of chancel, square window in gable, incomplete wall-rib above east windows and gap on north slope of gable. This or similar basis for NLI 4. Artist included.

2. 12.T.7 (78) Ink drawing with printed caption, dated December 1838, interior east windows and cupboards. Compare NLI 5.

3. 12.T.7 (79) Ink drawing with scale, exterior east windows showing label moulding. Compare NLI 6.

4. 12.T.7 (80a) Ink drawing, interior south window of nave. Compare NLI 8.

5. 12.T.7 (80b) Ink drawing, outside south window of nave, with plan of exterior frame. Compare NLI 8.

6. 12.T.7 (81b) Ink drawing, exterior south window of chancel, 'at present built up'. Compare NLI 9.

7. 12.T.7 (83b) Pencil sketch of detail of west-facing end of tomb, showing otter eating fish and loose weeper, dated December 1835. Compare NLI 10.

8. 12.T.13(13) Pencil sketch of exterior of east windows, showing label mouldings, perhaps preparatory to No. 3 above.

Other Du Noyer drawings are of gravestones in the church and graveyard, also in the 12.T.7 sequence.

9. 12.T.15(25) Pencil sketch of church from south-west, probably by John Stokes. Shows levels inside nave as very high and especially leaning masonry at south-west angle, looks fallen.

Ulster Journal of Archaeology 2 (1895), p. 129, a figure signed F H (?) Lockwood 1895 shows a plan and details, not very accurately but it is clear that the east gable is reconstructed and the tomb is restored. See UM 5 for the latest illustration traced before the restoration.

Note on the Photographs
Most of the photographs were taken during the conservation programme, between 1968 and 1970, often when the joints between stones had been cut out before repointing. Plates 1, 3, and 6–13 are by A.E.P. Collins and are Crown Copyright, reproduced with the permission of the Controller of Her Majesty's Stationery Office. Plates 2 (1967) and 4–5 (1971) are by the author and are her copyright.

Notes on the legend of Louernios

PROINSIAS MAC CANA

One of the passages most often cited in connection with the social and professional role of the Gaulish poets is that in which Athenaeus (fl. *c.*AD 200) recounts the story of king Louernios's generosity as recorded by the philosopher, historian and anthropologist, Posidonios (*c.*135–*c.*51 BC). The Arverni, to whom Louernios belonged, occupied the north of the Massif Central and particularly the modern Auvergne, to which they gave their name. Prior to the period of Caesar's campaign in Gaul they were one of the richest and most powerful of the Gaulish tribes and their influence extended from the Pyrenees to the Rhine.[1] They carried on a long and tenacious policy of opposition to the Roman process of colonization. One notable reflex of their material and political importance is the fact that they introduced their own coinage during the third century BC. A comment by Sidonius Apollinaris (*c.*430–489) that the nobility of the Auvergne had recently rid themselves of the coarseness of their Celtic language (*sermonis celtici squama*m) is sometimes cited as evidence that they had continued to speak Gaulish until his own time, but his words seem open to other interpretations.[2] Louernios, however, was their ruler about the middle of the second century BC, when the Arverni were still a strong and independent people:

> Posidonius, again, when telling of the wealth of Louernius, father of Bituis who was dethroned by the Romans, says that in an attempt to win popular favour he rode in a chariot over the plains distributing gold and silver to the tens of thousands of Celts who followed him; moreover, he made a square enclosure one and a half miles each way, within which he filled vats with expensive liquor and prepared so great a quantity of food that for many days all who wished could enter and enjoy the feast prepared, being served without a break by the attendants. And when at length he fixed a day for the ending of the feast, a Celtic [τῶν βαρβάρων] poet who arrived too late met Louernius and composed a song magnifying his greatness and lamenting his own late arrival. Louernius was very pleased and asked for a bag of gold and threw it to the poet who ran beside his chariot. The poet picked it up and sang another song saying that the very tracks made by his chariot on the earth gave gold and largesse to mankind.[3]

Professor Joseph F. Nagy has recently commented on this anecdote in his extended discussion of the evolution of medieval Irish written literature and its relation to the preceding and underlying oral culture.[4] Drawing a semiotic comparison between Louernios's encounter with the poet and the Celtic/Irish charioteer's skill in reading directional signs and in interpreting the tracks and

---

1 H. Birkhan, Kelten: *Versuch einer Gesamtdarstellung ihrer Kultur* (Wien 1997) pp 174–5.   2 Sidonius Ap., *Epist.* III,3,2 (to Ecdicius): '... *tuae que personae quondam debitum quod sermonis celtici squamam depositura nobilitas, nunc oratorio stylo, nunc etiam camenalibus modis imbuebatur*'. See G. Dottin, *La langue Gauloise* (Paris 1920) p. 70; L. Fleuriot, *Les origines de la Bretagne* (Paris 1980) pp 55–6.   3 Athenæus IV 37 p. 152D-F as translated by J.J. Tierney, 'The Celtic ethnography of Posidonius', *PRIA* 60 (1960) pp 189–275: 248 (text 225–6).

traces of those who have gone before, he suggests that 'the chariot rider and charioteer look ahead for the signs that lead them to their destination while they leave behind tracks for a poet to render into a lasting performative tribute'; he further, though much more tentatively, raises the possibility that the Louernios tale has implications for the semantic progression of the Irish words *slicht* and *lorg* from their primary meaning 'track' to their secondary and literary meaning 'version' or 'recension' of a text. My own purpose in the present note is rather different, if not wholly unconnected: it is merely to juxtapose the Louernios passage with several much later literary citations and to consider – and invite others to consider – whether they reflect essentially the same ideological concept.

As Professor Nagy has recognized, the Louernios legend is an instance of the close coupling of prestation and counterprestation which bound patron and praise-poet through an enduring bond of mutual dependence that underpinned the whole complex institution of poetic learning among the Celtic peoples as among various other peoples of the ancient world. It is significant because it is such an early attestation of a topic that was to become, not surprisingly, a commonplace of medieval panegyric and traditional literature in general among the insular Celts. It is also of particular interest for the form and the circumstance in which it represents the exchange of gifts between king and poet as taking place: the brief but appropriately extravagant account of the king's boundless liberality exemplified by the great communal feast, the hasty arrival of the poet, delayed but not too discomposed to respond to the occasion, and finally the closely compacted sequence of the poet's song of praise, the king's golden recompense, and, in prompt return, the song of acknowledgement in which the poet reacts to the immediate situation with the image of the tracks left by the king's chariot casting forth a bounty of gold.

Another, much condensed version of this episode is recorded in Strabo's Geography (4.2.3):

> But the Arverni had extended their rule as far as the Pyrenees and to the ocean and the Rhine. Luerius, the father of Bituitus, who fought the war against Maximus and Domitius, is said to have been so rich and given to luxury that once in making a display of his wealth to his friends he rode on a carriage over the plain scattering gold and silver coins hither and thither which those who followed him gathered up.[5]

Here the event is stripped of its nuance and presented as little more than a display of personal wealth. Mention of the poet and his poems is omitted and with them the symbolism of the poet's response to the ruler's bounty. Yet in one detail Strabo might seem to repair a minor inconsistency in the narrative of Athenaeus-Posidonios. Where the latter has the ruler throw a bag of gold to the poet running beside his chariot, the former has him scatter gold (and silver) coins to be gathered up by those following behind, a variant that is more in accord with the poet's figure of Louernios's chariot tracks yielding up 'gold and largesse'. While it is not perhaps a matter of primary significance, it is possible that in this detail Strabo is closer to Posidonios's text; it may be noted that σπείρω, the simplex of Strabo's διασπείρω, meant 'to sow (seed, a field, etc.), scatter like seed, strew'.

I am not immediately aware of other close parallels to the Gaulish poet's expressive imagery as reported by Athenaeus, but it is very much in character with the rich mythico-heroic symbolism centred on the chariot in the several cultures of antiquity. It has for example been noted by various

4 J.F. Nagy, *Conversing with angels and ancients: literary myths of medieval Ireland* (Ithaca and Dublin 1997) pp 290–2.   **5** Tierney, 'The Celtic ethnography', p. 264.

commentators on Indic tradition that there is a frequent association between chariot driving and liberality. J.C. Heesterman draws attention to this in discussing the provision and distribution of *dákṣiṇā*, the form of offering given to the brahmins or sacrificers within the framework of ritual sacrifice: the offering, originally of cows, may vary in kind, but according to the *Rigveda* the gift of gold confers eternal life on the donor.[6] In the context of certain rituals 'the king performs a chariot drive (or race), thus symbolically encompassing and regenerating the universe; during this drive he conquers the thousand cows which afterwards are distributed as daksinās,' while gods like Agni, Pūsan and Indra are sometimes pictured in the *Rigveda* as charioteers commanding and bestowing wealth and precious goods.[7]

By the late Middle Ages the chariot was a literary memory, but that the kind of symbolic imagery recorded by Posidonios was still not extinct is evident from an event mentioned by the chronicler from the Limousin, Geoffroi de Vigeois. One of the more extravagant occasions he describes was the court held at Beaucaire in 1174 by king Henri Plantagenet to celebrate the reconciliation of the duke of Narbonne with the king of Aragon. It is cited by Henri-Irénée Marrou in his study of the troubadours to illustrate a social change which came about in the second half of the eleventh century, one which helped to create the artistic refinement and delicacy of conventional courtoisie but by the same token brought a heightened emphasis on the enjoyment and display of luxury among the nobility that was sometimes pushed to the extremes of excess. Marrou can only compare such prodigality to the phenomenon of potlatch among the Canadian Indians of the Pacific coast:

> Non sans étonnement, l'historien découvre, à l'intérieur de cette notion complexe de 'courtousie', un équivalent de ce que nos sociologues, après l'avoir observé chez les Indiens de la côte canadienne du Pacifique, ont défini sous le nom de *potlatch*: l'étalage, la distribution, le gaspillage même, de la richesse apparaissent non comme un scandale (ainsi qu'en aurait jugé un siècle bourgeois; même de nos jours les gens sérieux parlent du Midi futile et frivole), mais comme un titre d'honneur, de gloire, une source de prestige.[8]

At Beaucaire, where members of the nobility sought to outdo one another in their vaunting of wasteful expenditure, one visiting lord who came accompanied by three hundred knights required that his dinner be cooked by the heat of wax candles, another made a bonfire of thirty valuable horses, and – much closer to the topic of the present discussion – still another arranged to have a field ploughed by twelve pairs of oxen and then to have thirty thousand écus (presumably of gold) sown in it. One cannot be sure that these events actually happened as described, but, as Marrou remarks, the fact that they were recounted by the chronicler and accepted as conceivable is in itself significant. Clearly Marrou himself views them solely in terms of contemporary social attitudes without regard to any possibility of ethnico-cultural continuity, and in the first instance that is undoubtedly the counsel of prudence. On the other hand, it may be worth noting, if only to fill out the dossier, that Geoffroi de Vigeois's Limousin was the ancient territory of the Gaulish Lemovices, neighbours to the Arverni on their western border (Limoges < *Lemóvices*, Limousin < *Lemovicínum*), while keeping firmly in mind that there is a temporal gap of well over a millennium between Geoffroi and Posidonios and the events they describe.

---

6 *RV* X.107.2.   **7** J.C. Heesterman, 'Reflections on the significance of the dákṣiṇā ', *Indo-Iranian Journal* 3 (1959) pp 241–58: 248–9. On the association of chariot driving with largesse see also J. Gonda, *Vedic ritual: the non-solemn rites* (Leiden/Köln 1980) p. 161.   **8** H.-I. Marrou, *Les troubadours* (Paris 1971) pp 60–1.

The other obvious disparity between the two anecdotes, the plough for the chariot, is perhaps less significant than might appear at first glance. In both instances the gold is thought of as being sown in the soil by the donor; in the later text this is enacted mimetically, in the earlier it is represented figuratively in the wording of the poet's eulogy. In both the donor is portrayed not only as the direct dispenser of largesse but also as the lord and ruler who renders prosperous and bountiful the land in which he moves and over which he exercises his influence. In the medieval text the immediate instrumentality, the imagery, is that of husbandry and agriculture, whereas in the classical text it is still regal-heroic. Yet the essential symbolism remains the same: the earth is fructified by the precious coinage deposited in it by the noble donor and in return renders its bounty to the beneficiaries of his generosity. In one case the earth is opened up by the conscious operation of the plough, in the other it is opened by the passage of the ruler's chariot (here one may usefully recall not only the poet's imagery as recorded by Athenaeus but also Strabo's variant reference to the scattering of the gold coins). While there were indeed roadways in pre-Roman times to facilitate travel between major centres, elsewhere, one may reasonably suppose, the rims that shod the chariot wheels often cut and churned the terrain they passed over. When Cú Chulainn mocks the clumsy progress of Conall Cernach's chariot in the medieval Irish tale of *Fled Bricrenn* with the phrase: 'how ponderously your chariot moves, with each of its two great wheels raising up a dyke so that every road your chariot travels remains for a year's length a clear track for the young warrors of Ulster', his hyperbole merely overlays a perceived reality.

It is of the nature of traditional eulogy that much of its linguistic and figurative paraphernalia is essentially retrospective, invoking ideal models of heroic or kingly behaviour; yet, whatever its degree of idealization, its system of social allusion cannot be entirely remote from contemporary reality. This was a truth recognized by the Welsh author Ffransis G. Payne, who wrote wisely and well on certain constituent elements of the history of Welsh material culture, and nowhere more so than when dealing with matters relating to agriculture, especially to the tilling and cultivation of the soil. In his scholarly and at the same time semi-popular essay 'Cwysau o foliant cyson' he reviews some of the testimony on this topic gathered from the praise poetry of the period from the fourteenth to the sixteenth century, in other words from the 'poetry of the nobility', *barddoniaeth yr uchelwyr*.[9] Deliberately disregarding consciously factual descriptions of farming and its equipment, he chooses instead phrases and passages where the poets' object was to eulogize men and women in life and elegize them in death, or 'to deal figuratively with objects that had nothing to do directly with ploughing and sowing and reaping' (*neu ddyfalu gwrthrychau nad oedd a wnelynt ag aredig a hau a medi*). Simply by arranging some of these tropes one can, he claims, bring together something of the poets' unconscious testimony to their own everyday background and that of their audience.

The cultivation of crops and getting them ready for the miller comprised a more extended series of discrete agricultural activities than would be the case today, and collectively they furnished the poets with a ready-made system of metaphorical reference for their poems of eulogy and elegy. This metaphorical system, like the farmer's serial labours, was centred on the ox, and 'when a poet was looking for a word which would neatly describe a man who maintained his

---

9 G. Payne, 'Cwysau o foliant cyson', in *Cwysau: casgliad o erthyglau ac ysgrifau* (Llandysul 1980) pp 7–29, to which I am much indebted in the following pages. I had re-read his *Aradr Gymreig* in search of the relevant material and I am grateful to Professor D.J. Bowen for reminding me of this essay in *Cwysau* and also for reading the present paper and allowing me to benefit from his own profound familiarity with the poetry of the *cywyddwyr*.

territory (as well as the poet for the duration of the festal time), *ych* ("ox") is the word that would occur to him more often than not'. Ffransis Payne illustrates the quite elaborate terminology used primarily to define the different roles and the relative locations of the several oxen within the plough-team and secondarily – in its figurative application – to laud those whom he identifies as their human correlatives. The technical vocabulary encompassed also the several articles of gear that joined oxen and plough in a working unit. The wooden yoke (the *iau* or *gwedd*) that linked the oxen had an important function and, as Payne remarks, it might be said that it possessed a small 'figurative literature' of its own: to describe someone as a *ieuawr/ieuor* ('one who bears the yoke') was in itself an expression of respect and admiration. Similarly the chains (*tidau*) which connected the yokes to one another and to the plough are familiar items in this semantically charged vocabulary.

After the oxen and the plough come the allusions to the works they perform. As the ploughshare turns the sod it creates the furrow, one of the most visible signs of the control and cultivation of the earth and of its increased fertility, which is doubtless the reason why in ancient Indian tradition the furrow, *sītā*, was deified as the goddess Sītā, who was wife to Indra and had a special sacrifice in her honour.[10] Given the general predilection of the Welsh poets of the period for agricultural imagery, it is hardly surprising that the word *cwys* 'furrow' should have enjoyed a high frequency in their compositions. Ffransis Payne borrows the title of his essay, *Cwysau o foliant cyson* 'furrows of harmonious praise', from a poem rich in such agricultural reference addressed by the fifteenth-century poet Ieuan Gyfannedd to Ffylib ap Rhys of Cenarth in Sir Faesyfed (Radnorshire) and his wife Gwenllïan daughter of Owain Glyndwr.[11] In similar vein Dafydd ap Maredudd ap Tudur offered his encouragement to Watcyn Fychan of Hergest in the west of Sir Henffordd (Herefordshire) in the exercise of his authority:

Cwysaist megis Siŵl Casar	You have furrowed like Julius Caesar
Trwy'r gwledydd – ni bydd heb âr –	Throughout the kingdoms – he will not be without
Tyn, er cadernid y tir,	ploughed land –
Cwys beunydd, cosba enwir.	Draw, for the strength of the land,
	A daily furrow, punish the unrighteous.

where the denominative verb *cwyso* assumes more or less the meaning 'to take control of, to rule, to govern'.

The normal term for land that is ploughed or tilled in preparation for sowing is *âr*, and, predictably, it is widely used by the praise poets together with its derivative *cyfar* 'co-tillage'. Similarly the act of sowing the seed, *hau*, in order to produce the crop of golden wheat, is symbolically linked to the reciprocal dispensing of benefits between patrons and poets, largesse by the former and fame and honour by the later – as would appear to be already implicit in Strabo's version of the Louernios legend. When Gutun Owain speaks of *llaw yn hau yn Llwyn Hywel* 'a hand sowing in Llwyn Hywel' (in Carmarthenshire) the reference is to the patron dealing out his bounty to the poet.[12] Tudur Aled (*c.*1465–*c.*1525) uses the same figure in a poem to Robert ap Rhys of Dolgynwal in Sir Ddinbych (Denbighshire):

---

10 Gonda, *Vedic ritual,* pp 297, 306, 428. **11** Illegitimate daughter, it would appear (Dafydd Johnston (ed.), *Gwaith Lewys Glyn Cothi* (Cardiff 1995) p. 613). **12** Payne, 'Cwysau o foliant', p. 23.

Hau'r wyd aur, hawdd yw d'eiriol,	You sow gold, easy it is to entreat you,
A'th air a dyf fyth ar d'ôl;	And your fame will forever increase after you;
Heuent dy glod, hwyntau, glêr,	They, the poets, would sow your praise,
Hap i'r undyn, heb brinder.[13]	Prosperity to the person, without scarcity.

Lewys Glyn Cothi (*c*.1420–89) moves the symbolism a stage further in his eulogy of Bedo Chwith ap Dafydd of Elfael in Sir Faesyfed by representing himself in the role of the earth being tilled and fructified by Bedo, and this in a passage where the word *aur* 'gold' is echoed repeatedly:

Bedo'n llafurio fy llaw	Bedo is tilling my hand,
y sydd, bid einioes iddaw;	long may he live;
arnai y rhoes o'r un rhan	on it he placed together
dri o erydr o arian,	three ploughs of silver,
ac ar eu hôl y gŵyr hau	and after them he knows to sow
arnai had aur yn heidiau.[14]	upon it golden seed in great profusion.

Dafydd ap Gwilym (*fl.* 1320–70), in one of his poems to his friend and patron Ifor Hael ('Ifor the Generous') of Gwernyclepa in Masaleg in the south-east of the old region of Morgannwg, draws eloquently on our motif:

O'm pen fy hun, pen-cun cyrdd,	Through the words of my own mouth, chief lord of hosts,
Y'th genmyl wyth ugeinmyrdd.	eight score myriads shall praise you.
Hyd yr ymdaith dyn eithaf,	As far as man travels farthest,
Hyd y try hwyl hy haul haf,	as far as the bold summer sun rises on its course,
Hyd yr hëir y gwenith,	as far as wheat is sown,
A hyd y gwlych hoywdeg wlith,	and as far as fair dew-fall moistens,
Hyd y gwŷl golwg digust,	as far as the unclouded eye can see –
Hydr yw, a hyd y clyw clust,	it is a confident assertion – and far as ear can hear,
Hyd y mae iaith Gymräeg,	as far as the Welsh tongue is known,
A hyd y tyf hadau teg,	and as far as fair seeds grow,
Hardd Ifor, hoywryw ddefod,	splendid Ifor, of noble custom
Hir dy gledd, hëir dy glod.[15]	– long your sword – your praise will be sown.

In keeping with the genre for which he is perhaps best known, Dafydd also applies the motif of sowing praise to the theme of romantic love. In this instance he recalls to Morfudd that he has spread her fame far and wide:

13 T. Gwynn Jones (ed.), *Gwaith Tudur Aled* I (Caerdydd 1926) p. 202.27–30. Cf. Gruffudd Hiraethog in his eulogy of Tegeingl in Flintshire: *Edwin sir, daioni sôn / Am bawb o'i dir, am bob dyn, / A chlywed hau ei chlod hir / I bawb, o wir, i bob un* 'The shire of Edwin, it is right and proper to mention / everyone from his territory, every person, / and to hear its extended praise being sown / to everyone, indeed, to every single one' (the text is cited by D.J. Bowen, 'Canu Gruffudd Hiraethog i Degeingl', *BBCS* 26 (1974–6) pp 281–304: 285.38–41. **14** D. Johnston (ed.), *Gwaith Lewys Glyn Cothi* (Caerdydd 1995) p. 337.21–6. **15** T. Parry, *Gwaith Dafydd ap Gwilym* (Caerdydd 1952) pp 19–20. 25–36; Rachel Bromwich, *Dafydd ap Gwilym: a selection of poems* (Llandysul 1982) 166–7.

Heais mal orohïan	Like a mad lover I have sown
Ei chlod yng Ngwynedd achlân.	her praise through all of Gwynedd.
Hydwf y mae'n ehedeg,	Abundantly it germinates,
Had tew, llyna head teg.	the prolific seed, it was a fine sowing.
Pellwawd yw'r ddyn nid pwyllwael	The girl is praised afar, and not ill-thought of,
Pawb a ŵyr, pob dyn hwyr hael.[16]	Everyone knows this, every unhurried generous one.[17]

The whole complex of panegyric imagery based on the cycle of the sowing and harvesting of crops is neatly epitomized by the poet and genealogist Simwnt Fychan (*c.*1530–1606):

Testun da i foli gwr yw honni ei fod ef yn hwsmon da. A'r hwsmonaeth yw aredig. A'r aredig yw croesawu pawb i'w lys … A gwedi hynny hau. A'r hau hwnnw yw rhoi aur ac arian i feirdd ac i gerddorion ac i bob dyn. Ac o'r rhain y tyf cnwd teg ffrwythlawn, nid amgen clod a moliant …	A good topic for praising someone is to affirm that he is a good husbandman. And the husbandry in question is ploughing. And the ploughing is welcoming everyone to his court … And after that the sowing. And that sowing is giving gold and silver to poets and musicians and all the rest. And it is from these there grows a fine and fruitful crop, namely praise and renown.[18]

Why exactly the combination of panegyric with ploughing and sowing should be so relatively frequent in the period highlighted by Ffransis Payne, namely the fourteenth to sixteenth centuries, I leave to others more skilled in these matters to explain; doubtless it is one of the various features of metrics, ideology and social reference that mark the shift from the Poetry of the Princes (or the poetry of the Gogynfeirdd) to the Poetry of the Nobility during the fourteenth and fifteenth centuries. What I am concerned with here is the semiotic analogy which seems to me to exist between the story of Louernios, the Beaucaire 'potlatch', and this recurrent symbolism in Welsh verse. While some of the externals have changed – notably from chariot to plough – the essentials seem to remain constant: the reciprocity of benefits between poet and patron represented figuratively in the correspondence between, on the one hand, the earth giving forth its fruitful bounty in response to the benign governance of a just and lawful ruler and, on the other, the unstinting generosity of the ruler evoking and responding to the sustaining eulogy of his poet.

---

16 Parry, *Gwaith Dafydd ap Gwilym*, p. 95.13–18; see also Bromwich, *Dafydd ap Gwilym*, pp 30–1.   **17** Occasionally in similar romantic contexts it is the seeds of love rather than of praise or fame that are sown. Perhaps the outstanding example is another poem of Dafydd ap Gwilym's, that titled by its editor Thomas Parry *Hwsmonaeth Cariad* 'Love's husbandry'. Its theme is neatly summarized by Rachel Bromwich (ibid. 22–3, text and translation 12–15; text in Thomas Parry, ibid. pp 238–40): 'Presenting himself as a disappointed lover, the poet here compares his plight to that of a farmer who watches his seed grow and prosper, until at the moment when it is ripe for harvest it is destroyed by a sudden storm.' She notes that the Dutch scholar Th. M. Chotzen pointed out in his *Recherches sur la Poésie de Dafydd ap Gwilym* (Amsterdam 1927) pp 331–2 that the extended husbandry imagery in this poem has a striking parallel in the thirteenth-century *Roman de la Rose* (ed. F. Lecoy (Paris 1965) ll 3932–42), a text which had a wide literary influence in France and England and has been identified as the probable source of several other features in Dafydd ap Gwilym's verse. Chotzen's suggestion is in itself persuasive, though, in the light of the textual references reviewed in the present essay as well as other evidence, his supporting comment is less than telling: 'Il semble peu probable que ces images se soient présentées spontanément à l'esprit d'un de ces montagnards gallois qui, exception faite pour les habitants de Mon, la mère féconde du Pays de Galles, n'ont été pas plus agriculteurs que navigateurs, et dont le mot pour laboureur, *hwsmon*, semble même emprunté au flamand.' Furthermore, whatever the precise relationship involved between the French and Welsh poems in this instance, the burden of the textual evidence would suggest that the topos of sowing the seeds of love is distinct from that of sowing praise, despite their sharing the same material frame of reference. **18** Payne, 'Cwysau o foliant', p. 27.

The sovereignty of Paeonia

YOLANDE DE PONTFARCY

Around the time of Darius I the Great (550–486 BC), king of Persia, Paeonia was a country which lay in the southern part of the Balkan peninsula, between Illyria to the west and Thracia to the east, and between Celtic tribes to the north and Macedonia to the south-west. In other words it occupied part of what is now northern Greece, southern Macedonia and western Bulgaria.[1] Very little is known about this ancient country, the people of which were probably of Thraco-Illyrian origin. However, Herodotus (*Hist.* v, 12–14) relates the circumstances which prompted Darius in 490 BC to order Megabazus, the commander of his army, to remove the Paeonians from their land in Europe and transport them to Asia. While Darius was at Sardis, having left Megabazus conquering Thracia, he decided to give the reward of their asking to two of his generals: Histiaeus, king of Miletus, and Coës the general of the Mytileneans. The first one got Myrcinus, a district in the Edonian land, and the second (who was an ordinary citizen) became ruler of Mytilene in Lesbos (*Hist.* v, 11). It seems that Darius's gift prompted the greed of Pigres and Mantyes, two Paeonian brothers, 'whose ambition it was to obtain the sovereignty over their countrymen' (*Hist.*, v, 12).[2]

> So when Darius crossed into Asia, these men came to Sardis, and brought with them their sister, who was a tall and beautiful woman. Then waiting till Darius sat in state in the capital city of the Lydians they had their sister dressed in the richest gear they could and sent her to draw water, bearing a jar on her head, and leading a horse by the bridle on her arm, while all the way as she went she span flax. Now as she passed by Darius, he took notice of her; for what she did was not in the manner of Persians or the Lydians or any of the peoples in Asia. Darius accordingly noted her, and ordered some of his guard to follow her and watch to see what she would do with the horse. So they followed her; and the woman, when she came to the river, first watered the horse, then filled her vessel and came back the same way, with the jar of water on her head, leading the horse on her arm, while she still kept twirling the spindle. (*Hist.* v, 12)

Darius, full of wonder, commanded that she should be brought to him and asked the young men of what nation the woman was, what part of the world they lived in and what business brought them to Sardis. They replied that they were Paeonians and that she was their sister, that they had come to be his men and that Paeonia was a country upon the Strymon, a river which was not far from the Hellespont. Then Darius asked if all the women of their country worked so hard. The brothers eagerly answered in the affirmative; and that it was 'for this very purpose that they had

1 Irwin L. Merker, 'The ancient kingdom of Paionia', *Balkan Studies* 6 (1965) pp 35–54; for the history of the territorial evolution of Paeonia see also N.G.L. Hammond, *A history of Macedonia*, vol. 1 'Historical geography and prehistory' (Oxford 1972) pp 193–194, 418 f. and 428 f; and A. Fol and N.G.L. Hammond, 'Persia in Europe, apart from Greece', *The Cambridge Ancient History* 4 (1988) pp 234–53. **2** George Rawlinson's translation, Everyman's Library (London 1952); see also A.D. Godley (ed.), *The Loeb Classical Library* (London 1922).

come' (*Hist.* v, 13). So Darius sent orders to Megabazus to 'remove the Paeonians from their own land, and bring them into his presence, men, women and children' (*Hist.*, v, 14).[3]

The gesture of the Paeonian brothers has been judged 'a most charming story [...] since it shows the versatility of Paionian women'.[4] However the full meaning of this staged performance, like that of rituals or myths, is based on a codified language in which thoughts are expressed through symbols. Indeed one cannot help recognising in this woman another example of the personification of Sovereignty equated with the land goddess – the subject of many a myth not only in Ireland but all over the Indo-European world. She has her attributes the vessel, the spindle and the horse, not to mention the idea of totality that she represents and which is expressed by the *coincidentia oppositorum* which surrounds her action: richly dressed and adorned, she fulfils the function of a servant (bringing water) and of a groom (watering the horse) while spinning flax, performing in motion an activity usually practised in a still position.

In India, Sovereignty is Srî, originally a pre-aryan goddess of fertility who in the Vedic ritual, *Dâksayana*, became the king's spouse (*SB.* ii, 4, 4, 6). In the *Mahâbhârata*, she is reincarnated as princess Draupadî who, on the day of the contest for her hand, offered the royal cup to the winner, married him and his brothers, restoring to them half of the kingdom that their cousins had taken.[5] When the gods shared Srî's attributes between them, Varuna, the ancient Vedic sovereign god, took from her Universal Sovereignty (*SB.* xi, 4, 3, 3).[6] Compared to the womb (*SB.* iv, 1, 4, 10), he is represented by a golden jar or a jar with a golden coin.[7] The motif of the offering or the filling of the cup as an accession to kingship is also very rich in the Celtic world. The foundation of Marseilles by the Greeks is explained by the gesture of the daughter of the Gallo-Ligure chief, who, the day of her wedding, offered a cup and marriage to the chief of a Greek expedition who had arrived the day before and whom her father had invited to the banquet.[8] In Ireland many stories[9] represent the birth of kings from the offering either of a cup of red ale by the goddess Sovereignty as related in a tale attached to Conn of the Hundred Battles, the mythical ancestor of the Connachta and the Uí Néill,[10] or by giving to the candidate for kingship access to the water she is guarding like the loathsome hag whom the five sons of king Eochaid Mugmedón met near the fountain while looking for some water to fill the royal cup and quench their thirst. She gave access to the last son, Níall of the Nine Hostages (the historical founder of the Uí Néill dynasty), because he was the only one to accept her dare: to kiss her; and in his arms she became a most beautiful woman who declared herself to be the Sovereignty of Ireland.[11] However

3 Although Megabazus deported a number of tribes who dwelt east of lake Prasias, in the Strymonian plain, to Phrygia (*Hist.* v, 15), he never really managed to subdue Paeonia (*Hist.*, v, 16); and later during the Ionian revolt the deported Paeonians helped by Greek islanders escaped and came back to their own land (*Hist.*, v, 98). See N.G.L. Hammond and G.T. Griffith, *A history of Macedonia*, vol. 2 (Oxford 1979) p. 55 ff.; and N.G.L. Hammond 'The Expedition of Dotis and Artaphernes', *The Cambridge Ancient History* 4 (1988) pp 491–517, who writes p. 495 'In the interior the limit of Megabazus's advance westwards was set by his failure to conquer the Agrianes, a Paeonian tribe of the upper Strymon valley; the Doberes of the Strumitsa valley; the Odomante north-west of Mt Pangeum and the Paeonians of lake Prasias which guarded the approach to the Rupel pass on the Strymon'.   4 L. Merker, op, cit., pp 41–42.   5 A.B. van Buitenen (trans.), *The Mahâbhârata*, vol. 1 (Chicago and London 1968) pp 344–75. 6 *Satapatha Brâhamana*, J. Eggeling (trans.) in Sacred Books of the East, ed. F. Max Müller (Oxford 1882–1900) vols 12, 26, 41, 43, 44.   7 B.J. Kuiper, Varuna and Vidûsaka. On the origin of the Sanskritdrama (Amsterdam 1979) pp 144–7 and 162–5.   8 Justinus, Historiae Philippicae 43, 3: J. Selby Watson (tr.), Justin, Cornelius Nepos and Eutropius (London 1882) p. 287.   9 See P. Mac Cana, 'The theme of king and goddess in Old Irish literature', ÉtC 7 (1955–56) pp 76–114 and 356–413 and ÉtC 8 (1958–59) pp 59–65.   10 See Myles Dillon (trans.), Baile in Scáil 'The Vision of the Fantom', in The cycles of the kings (Oxford 1946) pp 11–14.   11 Stokes (ed.), Echtra mac Echad Muigmedoin 'The Adventure of the Sons of Eochaid Muigmedón', RC 24 (1903) pp 191–207.

the *coincidentia oppositorum* suggested by the Paeonian lady, richly dressed and adorned and acting as a servant, makes her more akin to Niall's mother, the Saxon princess who was concubine and servant to king Eochaid Mugmedón, and whose function was to bring water from the well;[12] or to Eithne, daughter of Catháir Mór, king of the Leinstermen, who followed as a servant the impoverished hospitaller, Buchet, and had been seen milking the cows, cutting rushes, and taking water from the brink of the stream by the future king Cormac who married her;[13] or even better, to the daughter of the rebel prince in Persia who was hidden as a servant to save her life. She offered water from the well to Shâpur and his horse and confirmed the prediction of the oracle, that is his accession to the throne bringing to an end the reign of his father, king Ardashir, the founder of the Sassanid dynasty.[14] Unquenched thirst is a sign of lost sovereignty and death: king Conaire retired from battle to drink and perished of a consuming fever since no drink was left in the house and the rivers and lakes of Ireland had all hidden themselves from Mac Cecht, the chief warrior, who went to find water to fill the royal cup.[15] In that light, the gesture of the Paeonian brothers who sent their sister to fill her jar is without ambiguity.

Like Athena, the warrior goddess and also goddess of spinners and embroiderers, our Paeonian lady is associated with the spindle. Indeed another attribute of Sovereignty is the rope, the net, the knot, the thread … or what produces them. The particular feature of Étaín, another personification of Sovereignty, whom king Eochaid met when she was near a fountain washing her hair,[16] was to be the best at serving drink,[17] but her grand-daughter, and somehow her reincarnation, who became the wife of king Etarscéle and mother of king Conaire, had another attribute – she 'surpassed all women at embroidery. Her eyes saw nothing that her hands could not embroider'.[18] Penelope preserved herself and the land for her husband Odysseus by weaving and unweaving Laertes's shroud. The rope, one of the attributes of Varuna, the Vedic sovereign god (*ŚB*, iii, 2, 4, 18) is also that of Odinn, the Sovereign god of the ancient Scandinavians. When Alexander the Great had the audacity to cut the Gordian knot with his sword, by his bold gesture he acquired the sovereignty of Phrygia (Arrianus, *Anabasis*, ii, 3).

Like Epona, our Paeonian lady is associated with the horse.[19] She holds 'him' by a bridle passed to her arm as if she were married to 'him'. The close relationship of the horse and sovereignty is widespread in the Indo-European world.[20] For example, Varuna is the horse *aśva* (*ŚB*, vii, 5, 2, 18); in the course of the *aśvamedha*, the sacrifice of the horse to ensure Universal Sovereignty, the king is directly united to the Earth. Touching the earth he says: 'You are Manu's mare' and the commentator explains 'that it is under this appearance that Earth carried Manu' (*ŚB*, xiv, 1, 3, 25). In Greece, the horse is specifically linked with Poseidon the god of the sea, progenitor of many mythical genealogies. He pursued Demeter, the mother goddess of the Earth, who took the shape of a mare to escape him; but, assuming the likeness of a horse, he mated with her. When the

---

12 Ibid., § 1.   **13** *Esnada Tige Buchet*, prose version, W. Stokes (ed.), *RC* 25 (1904) pp 18–39; verse version, Mary Hayden (ed.), *ZCP* 8 (1912) pp 261–73.   **14** Levy (trans.), *The epic of the kings: Shah-nama, the national epic of Persia by Ferdowsi* (London 1967) pp 276–7.   **15** Stokes (ed.), *Togail Bruidne Dá Derga* 'The Destruction of Dá Derga's Hostel', *RC* 22 (1901) pp 9–61, 165–215, 282–329, 390–435 at pp 314–22, § 143–56.   **16** *Tochmarc Étaíne*, version Egerton 1782, E. Windisch (ed.), *Irische Texte* I (Leipzig 1880) pp 117–30, § 2. Ch.-J. Guyonvarc'h (trans.), *Celticum* 15 (1966) pp 317–22.   **17** *Tochmarc Étaíne*, version of the Yellow Book of Lecan, O. Bergin and R.I. Best (eds), *Ériu* 12 (1938) pp 137–96, p. 187, § 18; also Ch.-J. Guyonvarc'h (trans.), *Celticum* 15 (1966) pp 283–316.   **18** Ibid. p. 189, § 20.   **19** See H. Hubert, 'Le mythe d'Epona', in *Divinités gauloises* (Mâcon 1925) pp 21–32.   **20** E. Delebecque, *Le Cheval dans l'Iliade; suivi d'un lexique du cheval chez Homère et d'un essai sur le cheval pré-homérique* (Paris 1951) III, 1: 'L'Histoire du cheval indo-européen'; P. Ní Chatháin, 'Traces of the cult of the horse in early Irish sources', *Journal of Indo-European Studies* 19 (1991) pp 123–32.

pretenders to Penelope's hand came to visit her she was always accompanied by two ladies and through the name of one, Hippodamia (*Odyssey*, xviii, 182–3), she is also associated with the horse. On the other hand Helen, as the source of the war between the Greeks and the Trojans, was eventually reconquered by the trickery of the wooden horse.

The attributes with which the Paeonian brothers surrounded their sister are found at a later date associated again with sovereignty. Curtius Rufus in his *History of Alexander* (iv, 9, 24–25) relates an incident before the battle of Gaugamela in 331 when Alexander's army was attacked by a detachment of Persian cavalry. Alexander ordered Ariston, the commander of the Paeonian cavalry, to charge the Persians. Ariston successfully killed the leader of the Persian horsemen and brought his head back to Alexander.[21] And according to Plutarch who finishes the story, Ariston said: 'In my country, O King, such a gift as this is rewarded with a golden beaker. 'Yes' said Alexander with a laugh, 'an empty one; but I will pledge thy health with one which is full of pure wine' (*Life of Alexander*, xxxix, 1–3).[22] And some years later, King Audoleon of Paeonia (*c.*310–284 BC) at the beginning of his reign 'struck silver tetradrachms with the head of Athena on the obverse and a standing horse on the reverse'.[23] Besides, the three attributes associated with the Paeonian lady may be compared to the royal talismans of the Scythians as related by Herodotus (*Hist.*, iv, 5–7) and Curtius Rufus (*History of Alexander*, vii, 8, 16–19). According to Herodotus they fell scorching hot from heaven and the last of three brothers who seized these objects and was not burned became king. They are a plough and a yoke, an axe (for Curtius Rufus, a spear and an arrow) and a cup. The Latin historian adds that the Scythian ambassadors to Alexander said that they used them with their friends and against their enemies:

> To our friends we give the fruit of the earth that brings the work of our oxen, with our friends we use the cup to offer libations to the gods and as to our enemies we attack them from afar with the arrow and from near with the spear; and it is like that we have vanquished the kings of Syria, of the Persians and of the Medes.

According to Dumézil these objects would symbolise the three functions by which the Indo-Europeans tended to represent globally the sacred, mental and social vision of their world.[24] In that light the vessel would associate the Paeonian lady with the priestly function,[25] the spindle with the martial function, while the horse would symbolise the land and all its promises of fecundity.[26] From another point of view, one could say that these attributes overemphasise the

21 According to H. Bardon (ed.), *Quinte Curce, Histoires* (Paris 1961) p. 81 note 2, Ariston would have belonged to the reigning family of Paeonia.   **22** Translated by B. Perrin, *Plutarch's Lives*, vol. 7, Loeb Classical Library (London 1971).   **23** See I.L. Merker, op. cit., pp 45 and 47.   **24** To the first function belongs the administration of the world from the religious and juridical point of view: it is the class of the priest, jurist, poet, magician. To the second function belongs the virile and warlike strength, and to the third fecundity under all its forms. See G. Dumézil, *Les Dieux des Indo-Européens* (Paris 1952) Chap. 1; id. *L'Idéologie tripartie des Indo-Européens* (Bruxelles 1958) chap. 1. See also his *Jupiter, Mars, Quirinus, I* (Paris 1941) pp 155–98 in which he compares the royal talismans of the Scythians to those of the Tuatha Dé Danann, and pp 225–34 their cup and cauldron to the Gundestrup cauldron and the Graal. There is an interesting debate as to the exact provenance of the Gundestrup cauldron. It comes either from Continental Celts, see G.S. Olmsted, *The Gundestrup Cauldron*, Coll. Latomus, vol. 162 (Bruxelles 1979) or from Thracia, see F. Kaul et al., *Thracian tales on the Gundestrup Cauldron* (Amsterdam 1991).   **25** According to Arrianus (*Anabasis of Alexander*, II, 3) King Midas's mother was a priestess whom his father, Gordius, met while she was drawing water at the well when he was looking for the meaning of why an eagle remained sitting on the yoke of his oxen during all the time he was ploughing.   **26** One cannot help thinking of the deep symbolical meaning of the inauguration ritual of the kings of Tír Conaill related by Giraldus

unique and only power that was recognised as belonging to woman – mediation – as she brings men into being and gives them at the same time life and death. And mediation in its most awesome form, that is Sovereignty, is necessary to gain access to power.

Motion is the other important aspect of the scene created by Pigres and Mantyes – their sister is walking while turning the spindle, even her stop at the riverside is action since she lets the horse drink and fills her jar. However this activity is accomplished in silence. She does not speak and one does not know her name: perhaps the Paeonians followed 'the Greek belief that it was disrespectful to mention a woman's name in public',[27] and her brothers may have shared the opinion of Aristotle who, citing Sophocles (*Ajax*, 293), declares: 'Silence is a woman's glory (*kosmos*)' (*Politics*, i, 1260a30). So this silence is positive and 'dynamic' as it allows her brothers to express their ambition. While representing the fecundity of the land she appears potentially in waiting to offer to someone her drink, to mount her horse, to give the flax she spins for a new robe. There is little doubt that the two Paeonian brothers exhibited their sister in order to tempt Darius and offer her as a concubine[28] in exchange for the gift of sovereignty over their own people.[29]

Darius must have understood perfectly what Pigres and Mantyes wanted because he played a scenario (or invented a story) to explain his accession to a throne to which he had no established rights, which is not without similarity to the staged performance imagined by the Paeonian brothers.[30] Herodotus relates that Darius and five other young men who desired the throne decided that 'they would ride out together next morning into the skirts of the city, and he whose steed first neighed after the sun was up should have the kingdom' (*Hist.* iii, 84). Darius asked his groom, Oebares, to find a plan to make his horse neigh first. So when night came, Oebares 'took one of the mares, the chief favourite of the horse which Darius rode, and tethering it in the suburb, brought his master's horse to the place; then, after leading him round and round the mare several times, nearer and nearer at each circuit, he ended by letting them come together' (*Hist.* iii, 85). And when morning came and the six young men met together on horseback, rode about the suburb, and came near the spot where the mare had been tethered the night before, Darius's horse sprang forward and neighed. 'Just as the same time, though the sky was clear and bright, there was a flash of lightning, followed by a thunderclap. It seemed as if the heavens conspired with Darius, and hereby inaugurated him king.' (*Hist.* iii, 86).[31] One already recognises the function of the horse symbolising at the same time the throne and the land. The trickery on the part of Darius to put fate and destiny, as it were, on his side, does not make him different from Pelops, son of Tantalus, king of Lydia, who corrupted the charioteer of his rival, won the chariot race, Hippodamia's hand, and the kingship of Pisa in Elis (Diodorus Siculus iv, 73); or that of Visnu who disguised himself as a woman to obtain the *amrta* (the drink of immortality) from the asuras

Cambrensis (*Topographia Hibernica*, III, 25). The king not only 'marries' the horse, but is also born from the horse as he emerges from the bath he takes in the broth made from the cooked horse, and this same broth and the meat are offered as food to the people: see my article 'Two late inaugurations of Irish kings', *ÉtC* 24 (1987) pp 203–8. **27** M. Brosius, *Women in ancient Persia 559–331 BC* (Oxford 1996) p. 16. **28** Ibid., pp 32–3. Maria Brosius shows that the king's wife was selected from a Persian family, and a woman from a non-Persian background could only be the king's concubine. **29** See M.I. Finley, 'Marriage, Sale and Gift in the Homeric World', *Revue Internationale des Droits de l'Antiquité* 2 (1985) pp 167–94, at p. 177. **30** M. Brosius, op. cit., pp 47–64 tries to elucidate through Darius's different marriages his real role in the revolt against king Cambyses II and the conspiracy against Bardiya, Cambyses's brother which led to his accession to the throne. See also T. Cuyler Young, 'The consolidation of the Empire and its limits of growth under Darius and Xerxes', *The Cambridge Ancient History* 4 (1988) pp 53–111, at pp 53–6. **31** See G. Dumézül, 'Hérodote et l'intronisation de Darius' in *L'oubli de l'homme et l'honneur des dieux* (Paris 1985) pp 246–53.

who had just won it (*Mbh.*, i, 15–18). In the case of Darius's story, the help of the groom and the use of the mare to excite the horse, express the *coincidentia oppositorum* at the source of Sovereignty and the proof is that thunder and the flash in the sky express the agreement of the gods or their co-operation in the election of Darius to the throne. This account shows that it is through the language of symbols that Darius's right to the throne of Persia is justified. But if Darius's story was an affirmation of his access to kingship, the staged performance created by Pigres and Mantyes was a begging for power.

The two Paeonian brothers attracted the attention of Darius to the exceptional spectacle in Asia of a woman exposed to the eyes of men but also to an extraordinary and meaningful scene. Their sister, incarnating the Sovereignty of Paeonia, was to generate the dynamic and awesome forces which elevate one from an inferior to an eminent state. Their scheme does not seem to have brought them the power they were looking for, as Herodotus remains silent about their achievement, but, in a manner they could not have expected, it gave them immortality.

The practical hero

BENJAMIN HUDSON

Heroes and heroism are topics that interest the literary critic very much, and the historian very little. The contrast is stark; a classic study of medieval literature is called simply *The Heroic Age*, while an important work on twelfth-century Irish history is titled *No Hero in the House*.[1] The historian has not always been so wary of the topic, and in the nineteenth century the studies of Thomas Carlyle show how the student of a past century viewed the rôle of the hero. More recently, the idea of the heroic is often associated with the Gaelic culture of Ireland and Britain from the first centuries of the Middle Ages back to the pre-Christian era; in the days before Vikings, much less Normans, had made an appearance. The hero-tales looking to that time are mainly concerned with the martial hero who brings enlightenment to his people and defeats an otherworldly opponent.[2]

Thus it is interesting to glance briefly at the treatment of heroism in Irish and Scottish historical literature during the High Middle Ages, when Gaelic society was undergoing dramatic transformations in the church, economy and statecraft. Several important historical and semi-historical works composed round the eleventh century used a vocabulary and narrative construction that borrowed from the tales and sagas of legendary or early historical heroes. Only a few of these texts can be discussed here, and those only briefly. On this subject, students of Middle Irish literature are indebted to Professor Próinséas Ní Chatháin's important studies on the literary history of early Ireland, especially the Irish reception of foreign works, which have provided important insights into the intellectual tradition.

Throughout western Europe there was a renewed interest in the idea of the heroic that becomes increasingly visible interest in literary and historical writings from the mid-tenth to the early twelfth century. The tenth century has been seen as a transitional period between the Carolingian renaissance and the 'more vigorous minds of the eleventh and twelfth centuries'.[3] Among the Anglo-Saxons contemporary history is told in heroic narratives within poems on the English victory of Brunanburh (937) and the Viking victory at the battle of Maldon (994).[4] In the Anglo-Saxon chronicles the accounts of the Viking/Danish wars of 991–1013 are recorded in fulsome reports with debts to heroic literature, such as the poem Beowulf that was being recopied at this time.[5] In Normandy, the panegyric on the early dukes of Normandy composed by Dudo of St. Quentin is as much a heroic tale as it is historical remembrance.[6] Heroic epics were even

1 H.M. Chadwick, *The heroic age* (Cambridge 1912) and F.X. Martin, *No hero in the house, Diarmait Mac Murchada and the coming of the Normans to Ireland* (Dublin 1975).   **2** T. Ó Cathasaigh, *The heroic biography of Cormac Mac Airt* (Dublin 1977) pp 8–23.   **3** M.L.W. Laistner, *Thought and letters in Western Europe AD 500 to 900* (2nd ed. Ithaca 1976) p. 388.   **4** For Maldon see Katherine O'Brien O'Keefe, 'Heroic values and Christian ethics', in *Cambridge guide to Old English literature*, ed. M. Godden and M. Lapidge (Cambridge 1991) pp 117–23.   **5** *Beowulf with the Finnesburg fragment*, ed. C.L. Wrenn (2nd ed. London 1966) p. 9.   **6** The Latin text is printed in *De Moribus et Actis primorum Normanniae Ducum auctore Dudone Sancti Quintini Decano*, ed. J. Lair (Caen 1865) while a translation and more recent study of the text is by E. Christiansen, *Dudo of St. Quentin, history of the Normans* (Woodbridge 1998) who would date the composition of the text 996–1020, p. xiii.

intruding upon historical events. Sung to the army of William the Conqueror on the night before
the battle of Hastings was the Old French epic called the Song of Roland, which now survives
in a manuscript *c*.1100. The Song of Roland is an odd choice of inspiration for an army about to
go into battle, for its kernel of truth is the description of a defeat inflicted on Charlemagne's army
at the battle of Roncevaux in 778.[7]

The literary culture of Ireland and Scotland shared in this revival. The Gaelic heroic literature
of the seventh and eighth centuries could have provided the inspiration for later historical
enthusiasms. Written versions of several of these fictionalised histories, or historical dramas, were
to be found in the compendium of adventure and heroic tales collected in the eighth century in
a miscellany known as *Cin Dromma Snechta*, which had stories from the Ulster Cycle, adventure
tales and verse.[8] Those who wrote contemporary history in the following decades resisted the urge
to imitate. The ninth-century entries in the Annals of Ulster, for example, are models of restraint.[9]
The passing of the great Uí Néill prince Máel Sechnaill I, arguably the first true high king of
Ireland in the historic period, in 862 is marked by the bare statement that he was king of all
Ireland. When his son Flann *Sinna* ('of the Shannon') died on May 25, 916, the chronological
details are faithfully preserved. We are told that he was 68 years old, that 25 May fell on a Saturday,
and that he had reigned 36 years, 6 months and 5 days, but there is not a word about the
achievements of his reign or his own personal triumphs. At roughly the same time a reworking of
an eighth-century verse history of powerful Irish princes known as *Baile Chuind* ('Conn's Frenzy')
describes the men in picturesque terms, but not in heroic ones.[10] In the last quarter of the tenth
century, the catalogue of kings preserved in the versified biblical history known as *Saltair na Rann*
('Psalter of the Quatrains') gives a list of the great monarchs of Britain and Ireland as well as
several of the continent.[11] The most elaborate tribute is given to the first prince in the list, the
Scots monarch Cináed mac Máel Choluim (Kenneth II, died 995), but the emphasis is on his
kingly rather than heroic stature. To the poet he is merely fair Cináed who ruled Scotland and
part of Ireland, an exaggeration of territory so far as historical verity is concerned.[12] One must be
wary, however, of trying to present too general a reading of the sources of this period, and a look
at the contemporary collection of materials with the modern title *Tripartite Life of St. Patrick*
shows the saint portrayed in distinctly heroic aspect in his dealings both human and divine.[13]

Even as the 'Psalter of the Quatrains' was being composed, there are signs that the heroic was
coming back into scholarly fashion. Popular literature is one guide, as the heroic sagas of the
seventh and eighth centuries, with their larger-than-life characters, were being reworked. While
dating the redactions of these earlier tales must necessarily be general rather than specific, the
eleventh and early twelfth century saw the reworking of such important texts as *Aided
Muirchertaigh meic Erca* ('The Tragic Death of Muirchertach son of Erc'), *Caithréim Cellaig meic
Eogáin Bél* ('The Triumph of Cellach son of Eogan'), *Scéla Mucce meic Dathó* ('The Tale of Mac
Datho's Pig'), and *Togail Bruidne Da Derga* ('The Destruction of Da Derga's Hostel').[14] This

7 G.J. Brault, *The Song of Roland,* 2 vols (University Park, Pa. 1978) i, pp 3–4.   **8** J. Carney, *Studies in Irish literature and history* (Dublin 1955) p. 282.   **9** S. Mac Airt and G. Mac Niocaill (eds), *The Annals of Ulster to AD 1130* (Dublin 1984).   **10** G. Murphy, '*Baile Chuind* and the date of Cín Dromma Snechta', *Ériu* 16 (1952) pp 145–51.   **11** W. Stokes, *Saltair na Rann* (Oxford 1883) p. 34.   **12** Stokes, *Saltair na Rann,* l. 2349–2352: *In amsir Cináeda cáim\ meicc Máel Cholaim for Albain\ for hÉrainn cen, lethrainn lainn\ do Chináed mac Máel Cholaim.*   **13** W. Stokes, *Tripartite Life of Patrick,* 2 vols (London 1887). The dating of the text is less certain than was once thought, see K.H. Jackson, 'Date of the Tripartite Life of St. Patrick', *ZCP* 41 (1986) pp 5–45, especially page 16 where his manuscript stemma suggests that the extant text is a copy of an eleventh-century intermediate recension.   **14** *Aided Muirchertaig meic Erca*, ed. L. Nic

revival was not limited to tales that were Irish in orientation, but extended to those stories where part of the action took place in the Irish community in Britain. *Longes Mac n-Uislenn* ('The Exile of the Sons of Uisliu'), where the heroes take service with the king of Alba, was originally a late Old Irish text that was revised *c.* AD1000.[15] Some of these tales might have had a much wider influence, such as *Scéla Cano meic Gartnáin* ('The Saga of Cano son of Gartnan'), the seventh-century noble of Dál Riata, whose connection with the Tristan legend continues to be debated.[16] The fashion for the heroic stretched across the spectrum of society. In the late eleventh-/early twelfth-century compilation known as *Lebor na hUidre* ('The Book of the Dun Cow') heroic tales mingle indiscriminately with devotional/theological works. The eschatological tract *Dá Brón Flatha Nime* ('The Two Sorrows of the Kingdom of Heaven') is followed by the ancient secular tale *Mesca Ulad* ('The Intoxication of the Ulstermen'), and another eschatological work *Scéla na Esérgi* ('Tidings of the Resurrection') is followed by the *Aided Nath Í* ('Tragic Death of Nath Í').[17] As late as the twelfth century, tales such as *Cath Ruis na Ríg* ('The Battle of Ros na Ríg') were being rewritten.[18] This was not narrowly a native antiquarian movement, for among the heroic tales was *Togail Troí* ('Destruction of Troy') showing both a European view as well as a resurgent concern for the world of classical antiquity.[19] Even the accepted canon of stories necessary for the professional *litterati* was revised during this time. The analysis of the tale-lists in the Book of Leinster shows revision in the late eleventh century, with the addition of some new material, such as *Braflang Scóine* ('The Treachery at Scone'), a tale about the destruction of the Picts by the Scots.[20]

Baile in Scáil *and the prophecy of Berchán*

Among the several historical tracts that use heroic vocabulary and imagery in their narratives, informative examples are two texts that seem to have been written at Armagh at roughly the same time. The first is a pseudo-prophecy known as *Baile in Scáil*, translated variously as the 'Phantom's Frenzy' or the 'Phantom's Prophecy'.[21] This is a list of the 'high kings' of Ireland from pre-history, i.e. before the time of St Patrick, up to the mid-eleventh century; the narrative ends with vaguely eschatological implications about signs preceding the Day of Judgement. The author was Dub-dá-Leithe of Armagh (d. 1064), who is interesting not just because he is one of the few known authors from the eleventh century, but he was also one of the most important men of his day.[22] Dub-dá-Leithe was the *comarba* ('heir') of Patrick from 1049 to 1064, but his scholarship was

Dhonnchadha (Dublin 1964) p. viii; *Caithréim Cellaig*, ed. K. Mulchrone (Dublin 1971) pp ix–x; *Scéla Mucce Meic Dathó*, ed. R. Thurneysen (Dublin 1935) p. ii; *Togail Brudne Da Derga*, ed. E. Knott (Dublin 1936) p. xi; and Dillon, 'Pre-Norman literature', p. 32. **15** V. Hull, *Longes Mac n-Uislenn, The Exile of the Sons of Uisliu* (New York 1949) pp 29–30. **16** *Scéla Cano meic Gartnáin*, ed. D.A. Binchy (Dublin 1963) p. xiv. While Binchy argued that the original story was a composition of the ninth century, arguments have been advanced that it was composed in the eighth century, see B. Hudson, *Kings of Celtic Scotland* (Westport 1994) pp 21–2. **17** R.I. Best and O. Bergin, *Lebor na Huidre, Book of the Dun Cow* (Dublin 1929) pp 47–9, 50–3, 82–8, and 90–4. **18** *Cath Ruis na Ríg*, ed. E. Hogan (Dublin 1897); U. Mac Gearailt, 'Cath Ruis na Ríg and twelfth-century literature and oral tradition', *ZCP* 44 (1991) pp 128–53. **19** Book of Leinster, fol. 217a-244b, for a diplomatic transcript see *The Book of Leinster formerly Lebar na Núachongbála*, ed. R.I. Best et al., 6 vols (Dublin 1954–83) iv, 1063–1117. **20** P. Mac Cana, *The learned tales of medieval Ireland* (Dublin 1980) pp 142–5, and B. Hudson, 'The conquest of the Picts in early Scottish literature' *Scotia* 15 (1990) pp 13–25. **21** A new study is by Dr Kevin Murray, *Baile in Scáil, A Literary and Historical Perspective* (Ph.D. dissertation, University College, Dublin) which will be published by the Irish Text Society in 2001; see also K. Meyer, 'Mitteilungen aus irischen Handschriften', *ZCP* 3 (1899) pp 17–39, and 'Das Ende von Baile in Scáil', *ZCP* 12 (1918) pp 232–38, and R. Thurneysen, 'Baile in Scáil', *ZCP* 20 (1936) pp 213–27. **22** B. Hudson, *Prophecy of Berchán* (Westport 1996) pp 97–98 and 164.

genuine, for he had been the *fer léighinn* or head of the church's schools from 1045 to 1049. He was a dynast of Clann Sinaich, the family that Bernard of Clairvaux would condemn so vituperatively in his *vita* of Malachy.[23] For *Baile in Scáil*, Dub-dá-Leithe was not original in inspiration and his model was the previously mentioned eighth-century list of kings called *Baile Chuind* ('Conn's Frenzy'). Together with *Baile in Scáil*, Dub-dá-Leithe is credited with the production of the manuscript miscellany called the Book of Dub-dá-Leithe, excerpts from which are embedded in the Annals of Ulster. The other contents of Dub-dá-Leithe's book are less certain, although some scholarly opinion would include well-known stories such as the *Scéla Mucce meic Dathó*, *Imram Brain* ('Voyage of Bran son of Febal'), *Tochmarc Emire* ('The Wooing of Emer'), and a legend of St Patrick, Enna son of Loegaire and Michael the Archangel.

The narrative in the *Baile in Scáil* begins with episodes more suited to the heroic adventure than a preface to an historical tract. The semi-legendary king Conn of the Hundred Battles is the first individual introduced, as he goes around the ramparts of Tara to ensure that the people of the fairy mounds or the Fomorians do not attack the Irish unawares. Then he discovers a stone that would be found by a true king, and it would scream the number of times that his descendants would rule after him. Afterwards the king meets a phantom who is the ghost of Lug son of Ethniu, who names the future monarchs and their deeds. The earliest monarchs are legendary, but after moving into the period when historical texts are available, the information in the narrative generally is confirmed by them. Dub-dá-Leithe presents his information in a manner deliberately recalling the heroic. For the ninth-century Uí Néill lord Niall mac Áeda or Niall *Caille* (of the river Callann) (d. 846) there is the cryptic triad: 'Niall in the sea, Niall in the wounding, Niall in the fire' (*Níell hi muir, Níell hi nguin, Níell hi tein*). This is an echo of the threefold death that is associated with heroes such as Muirchertach mac Erca.[24] Niall's grandson Niall mac Áeda or Niall *Glúndub* ('Black-Knee') will 'cleanse the battlefield of Ruadra' (*glanfus rói Rúadra*), and he is the 'high heroic of the Liffey' (*artt láechda Liphi*), where the primary meaning of láechda ('warrior-like') takes the extended meaning of 'heroic'. Animal symbolism is used to describe Máel Sechlainn mac Domnaill, or Máel Sechlainn II (d. 1022), who is the great grouse (*gercc mór*). Not only is *gercc* a synonym for 'champion', but the cry of this bird was believed to be a means of divination.[25] The sixty-second monarch listed in *Baile in Scáil* is the famous hero-deliverer Áed Engach, during whose reign will be born a priest who will make peace.[26] The reign of the last monarch of Tara, Flann Cinuch, will witness the appearance of three suns together for three days, and there is the implication that this is the prelude to the end of time.

Baile in Scáil quickly became a part of the Gaelic literary canon. The contemporary historian Flann Mainistrech refers to it in his verses on the pre-Christian king of Tara named Echu Mugmedón, for whom he notes that the circumstances of Echu's death were written in the *Scálbaile*.[27] In the eleventh century, the canon of tales a professional story-teller was expected to know underwent revision and enlargement, and *Baile in Scáil* replaced the earlier, eighth-century, text that had been a model. All versions of the revised list note that *Fís Chuind* is now *Baile in*

23 St Bernard of Clairvaux, *Liber de Vita et Rebus Gestis S. Malachiæ Hiberniæ Episcopi, PL* 182, col. 1088.   24 B. Ó Cuív, 'The Motif of the threefold death', *Éigse* 15 (1973–4) pp 145–50, especially page 146 for a discussion of Niall.   25 For the association of birds with the supernatural see A.-M. O'Connell, 'L'oiseau surnaturel: approche narrative et figurative', *ZCP* 51 (1999) pp 46–65.   26 For this individual see B. Ó Buachalla, 'Aodh Eangach and the Irish king-hero', in D. Ó Corráin et al. (eds), *Sages, saints and storytellers* (Maynooth 1989) pp 200–32.   27 This stanza from the poem *Ríg Themra dia tesband tnú* is preserved in the Book of Leinster at fol. 132a 47ff (in the edition of Best *et al.*, it is at vol. iii, 508): *Marb iarna rígad don tslóg/ Eocho mínglan Mugmedon/ ro fírad cid cruth aile/ ro*

Scáil, alerting the reader that the older text has been superseded.[28] This is a tribute to Dub-dá-Leithe's scholarship and industry, for his work is a much larger and informative catalogue than its predecessor. At the same time, it is also a reflection of the author's skill as a story teller, and the fantastic opening to his narrative would hold the attention of an audience that had a noticeable taste for history presented with flair and imagination.

Armagh was the most important intellectual centre in the Gaelic cultural world during the eleventh century due largely to the efforts of men such as Dub-dá-Leithe. He might not have been the only historian active at Armagh and another work that seems to have been composed there during his lifetime is the Prophecy of Berchán. There are three *strata* of materials in Berchán, but the main section was composed by one individual in the mid-eleventh century. That person might be a colleague of Dub-dá-Leithe named Dubthach *Albanach* 'the Scotsman.' Little is known of him other than his teaching of the Old Testament in the monastic school and his death there in 1065. The Prophecy of Berchán is entirely in verse and is a survey of the great princes among the Gaels in both Ireland and Britain. Unlike the pre-historic beginning to *Baile in Scáil*, Berchán's narrative begins in the ninth century and continues to the eleventh. The two kingly lists are connected by a section on saints that were venerated in Ireland and Britain: Patrick, Brigit and Columba.

Even though the identity of the princes in the Prophecy of Berchán is obscured by the poet's employment of pseudonyms in place of the monarch's names (with two exceptions), like *Baile in Scáil* the heroic aspect is deliberately cultivated. The ninth-century Uí Néill lord Máel Sechnaill I (d. 862) is the 'luck of Ireland' (*líth nElga*), in which the hero's identification with his people in this instance encompasses the entire island. The prowess in battle of one Scots monarch is noted, 'every face will turn pale before his jewel (i.e. eye)' (*bidh bán gach aighedh fria dhúis*), for King Causantín II (reigned 900–943, d. 952). A later prince, Máel Coluim II (d. 1034) is distinguished as a 'fierce beast over all Scotland,' (*onchú is ar Albain n-uill*), and he will 'leap through battle' (*lém tre chath*). Both these descriptions evoke heroic imagery, as the eye is a prominent feature of the hero and has an association with fire, while the hero is often portrayed as an animal.[29] The heroic association with the animal world is suggested by the identification of Máel Sechlainn I as the trout from the river Liffey (*in brec a Lifi*).[30] His contemporary Fedelmid mac Crimthainn (d. 847), the enigmatic king/bishop of Munster, is the great ram from the plain of Daithi, (*in molt mór á Maig Dathí*)), referring back to the legendary prince Aillil Molt mac Dathí/Nathí who is included in *Baile in Scáil*. Berchán is direct in its reference to Doomsday, with an account of the appearance of the Antichrist and the purification of the great fire.

Heroes for a New Age

Baile in Scáil and the Prophecy of Berchán used heroic vocabulary and imagery derived from the insular tradition. A variation on the idea of hero can be seen in the texts that promoted the interests of the great Munster family of Uí Briain. This was the dynasty of the early eleventh-century high king Brian mac Cennétig who was known more popularly as Brian *bórumha* ('of the cattle tribute'). While his family's literary supporters attempted to promote Brian as the greatest prince of his day, he was a different type of hero. The histories show that unlike his contemporaries, Brian rarely risked a battle

scríbad issin Scálbaile. **28** Mac Cana, *Learned tales*, p. 67. **29** P.L. Henry, '*Furor Heroicus*', *ZCP* 39 (1982) pp 235–6 and 240–2. **30** For the trout see Colum Ó Baoill, 'Gaelic ichthyonymy', *ZCP* 46 (1994) p. 168.

if the odds were too much against him, and would simply lead his army away from the field if the
opposition proved to be more numerous or better prepared than he had anticipated. He held
conquered territory not through the loyalty of adoring followers or former enemies, but through a
series of fortresses, manned not by warriors eager for glory, but by mercenaries fighting for pay.[31]

Of course there has always been a substantial gap between the literary ideal and historical
reality, but this information comes not just from the spare account of the chronicles, but also from
the texts commissioned by his descendants, which were designed to glorify Brian and themselves.
An important work is *Cocad Gáedel re Gallaib* ('War of the Irish against the Vikings').[32] This is based
on an earlier (late tenth century) record of the wars of the Viking period, but it was reworked and
expanded during the reign of Brian's great-grandson Muirchertach (reigned 1086–1119).[33] The material
added to the original text is an account of the heroic career of Brian and the circumstances of his
death during the battle fought beyond the fortress of Dublin at Clontarf on Good Friday in
1014.[34] The opponents were the Vikings of Ireland, the Hebrides and the Orkneys, together with
the Irish of Leinster on one side, and the Irish of Munster and Connacht together with the
southern Uí Néill (who refused to fight at the battle) under the command of Brian. *Cocad Gáedel
re Gallaib* uses a heroic vocabulary in its description of the armies prior to the battle of Clontarf.
The Viking-Leinster army becomes pagan, murderous and unscrupulous; on the other side Brian
and his followers are called simply the champions. But in the place of the expected comparison
of Brian only with the great figures of Irish legend, there are classical or biblical individuals. He
is called Octavian because of his triumphs, Alexander on account of his battles, Solomon for his
wealth, David for his faithfulness and Moses for his personal purity.[35] Implicit in this recital is that
the heroes with whom Brian is compared are famed for good government. Solomon was the great
law giver and figure of wisdom in the Old Testament, Alexander was the ever victorious commander, Augustus brought peace to Rome by ending the civil war and restoring the government's
ability to rule, while Moses delivered his people from captivity.

Such a mix of imagery is not limited to Brian, and almost as fulsome an eulogy is given to his
son Murchad, who led Brian's forces on the day of the battle. He is called the royal champion
(*rígmilid*), and the author exhausts himself in describing Murchad's heroic prowess. He was the
last man of true valour in Ireland, the last who was a match for a hundred men, and the last one
who killed a hundred men in one day.[36] The praise continues with a comparison of Murchad with
the ancient Irish heroes such as Lugh Lagha, Conall Cernach and Lugh Lamha-fóda. Then there
is a sudden shift in orientation and a comparison is made with classical and biblical models.
Murchad is called a match for Hector the son of Priam and the writer claims that the idea of the
champion began with Hector and ended with Murchad and compares championship with human
life. The discussion continues with the comparison of Murchad with Samson, because of his
service to his people, and with Hercules, in a passage in which the Vikings living in Ireland are
represented by serpents and monsters who inhabit the lakes, pools and caverns.[37]

31 B. Hudson, 'Changing economy of the Irish sea province', in *Britain and Ireland, 900–1300*, ed. B. Smith (Cambridge
1999) p. 46.   **32** *Cogadh Gaedhel re Gallaibh, The War of the Gaedhil with the Gaill*, ed. J.H. Todd (London 1867).
33 Hudson, *Prophecy of Berchán*, p. 14.   **34** There are several useful studies of this text, among which are R. Leech,
'*Cogadh Gaedhel re Gallaibh* and the *Annals of Inisfallen*', *North Munster Archaeological Society* 11 (1968) pp 13–21; K.
Hughes, *Early Christian Ireland: introduction to the sources* (Ithaca 1972) pp 288–97; and an important series of papers
by M. Ní Mhaonaigh: 'Bréifne bias in *Cogad Gáedel re Gallaib*', *Ériu* 43 (1992) pp 135–58; '*Cogad Gáedel re Gallaib*: some
dating considerations', *Peritia* 9 (1995) pp 354–77; and '*Cogad Gáedel re Gallaib* and the Annals: a comparison', *Ériu* 47
(1996) pp 101–26.   **35** *Cogach Gaedhel re Gallaib*, p. 204.   **36** Ibid. p. 186.   **37** Ibid. pp 186–8.

A similar mixing of ideals is found in the description of the men of Dál Cais, the dynasty of Brian. They are compared with the sons of Mil for renown, and are called the Franks of Ireland for their valour and the Israelites of Ireland for their dignity. Animal symbolism is also employed as they are compared with the brave lions, the nimble wolfhounds, and they are called the graceful hawks of Europe.[38]

These three examples – Brian, Murchad and Dál Cais – provide some scope for observation and speculation. As the eleventh century passed into the twelfth, the connection with heroism was not exclusively within the Gaelic tradition, but incorporated heroic figures from classical and biblical literature in addition to references to continental Europe. The discussion about heroism in *Cocad Gáedhel re Gallaib* that is connected with Hector and Murchad shows that the author is being deliberate in his choice of vocabulary and presentation of the subject. References to Troy are not surprising, as there was a long-standing interest in the Roman poet Virgil among the Irish and certainly the Irish scholars on the continent were familiar with his *AEneid* by the ninth century. At this time in Britain there were the beginnings of the legend of Brutus and the flight of the survivors from the fall of Troy that would appear in the *Historia Regum Britanniae* by Geoffrey of Monmouth. The appearance of the Trojan hero Hector in an Uí Briain tract suggests that some of their supporters were considering the idea of a connection with that legend. The Irish version of the downfall of Troy, *Togail Trói*, was being composed in the eleventh century, to be joined by a version of the *Thebaid* known as *Togail na Tebe* in the twelfth century.[39]

The appearance of the Franks shows that ideas of heroism were also not entirely antiquarian. So far as eleventh-century Ireland is concerned 'Franks' should be read as 'Normans'. Late in the eleventh century the Uí Briain princes had made diplomatic overtures to the Normans who had recently taken control of England.[40] This contact was maintained into the twelfth century, and transcripts survive of letters to Tairdelbach Ua Briain from Archbishop Lanfranc of Canterbury and from his son Muirchertach to Archbishop Anselm; while Muirchertach's daughter would marry a Norman noble named Arnulf of Montgomery. The reference to the Franks could be an effort to remind the other Irish princes of their association with those successful warriors and their international contacts. The desirability is obvious; the Normans were victorious in battle (such as the conquest of England), modern in policy, favourites of the papacy and international in outlook.

Monarchs were not alone in looking outside Ireland, and the Irish *litterati* were being influenced by their contacts with the intellectual centres of Britain and the continent.[41] In the cathedral schools, scholars had to begin to grapple with the first waves of classical texts that would soon become a flood. The cathedral school at Cologne was among these important centres, and to that town flocked Irish clergy in exile. The chronicler Marianus Scotus first resided at the monastery of St. Martin at Cologne upon his exile from Ireland. Various Uí Briain princes were personally in contact with the intellectual circles at Canterbury, where Archbishop Lanfranc was rebuilding the community and the library, and at Worcester, where the saintly bishop Wulfstan personally supervised the restoration of the cathedral's archives. At these ancient churches the new literary and intellectual fashions were being cultivated in the era of change popularly known as the Gregorian reform movement.

---

38 Ibid. p. 160.   **39** Mac Cana, *Learned tales*, p. 84.   **40** B. Hudson, 'William the Conqueror and Ireland', *IHS* 29 (1994) pp 145–58.   **41** For examples see L. Bieler and B. Bischoff, 'Fragmente zweier frühmittelatlerlicher Schulbücher aus Glendalough', *Celtica* 3 (1956) pp 211–20, and P.P. Ó Néill, 'An Irishman at Chartres in the twelfth century – the evidence of Oxford, Bodleian Library, MS Auct. F. III. 15', *Ériu* 48 (1997) pp 1–35.

Within this international context, it is worth considering that the model for some Irish materials might have come from outside the island. In the example of *Cocad Gáehel re Gallaib* there has been scholarly speculation that some part of its composition imitates the *Life of King Alfred* by Asser, which follows Einhard's *Life of Charlemagne* that took as its model Suetonius' *Lives of the Caesars*.[42] In common with Alfred's biography, Brian's royal lineage is asserted, his wars against the Vikings leads him into the wilderness for guerilla warfare and his eventual triumph inaugurates a period of peace, scholarship and prosperity for Ireland. This was blended into the native heroic tradition, and, unlike Alfred, Brian dies a hero's death with his family's banshee, Aibhinn of Craig Liath, announcing his death on the eve of battle. There might have been other borrowings as well. The report that Brian remained in his tent engaged in prayer during the battle is first mentioned by Marianus Scotus, but he might have taken the image from Bede's account of the death of the saintly king Oswald.[43]

This possibly imitative aspect of *Cocad Gáedel re Gallaib* might have been followed in another Uí Briain production known as *Lebor na Cert* ('The Book of Rights').[44] This is a listing of the stipends that made up the ritual gift-exchange that signified ties of political status in native Irish society. In literature, gift exchange was an important aspect of the recognition of heroic status, and reference need be made only to Beowulf to see its prominence beyond the Celtic world. Not just the quality or quantity of the gift was important, but the very item itself had a real value as an indicator. The text of *Lebor na Cert* was composed probably during the reign of Brian's great-grandson Muirchertach and it pretensions for the supremacy of the dynasty of Dál Cais have been dismissed as wishful thinking on the part of a prince who was never able to have his lordship recognized throughout Ireland. One possible model for *Lebor na Cert* is Domesday Book. While the latter looks to the reign of Edward the Confessor (reigned 1042–1066) as its chronological marker, the former looks to the reign as high king of Brian (1002–1014) for the stipends it lists. *Lebor na Cert*, unlike Domesday Book, anticipates the resumption of that ancient state of affairs should Brian's descendants prove themselves able to succeed to his primacy. Like *Cocad Gáedel re Gallaib*, *Lebor na Cert* tries to make the idea of the heroic more contemporary. There are the expected commodities of livestock (particularly horses), jewelry and articles of clothing, the items well-known from heroic literature. At the same time there are additions to the list. In them practicality has made an appearance, and the new items are considered worthy of a prince. Some are substantial and expensive, such as the ships with beds that are given from the king of Cashel to the king of Dublin or the ships fully rigged that are given to the king of the Deisi.[45] Others are commonplace, and from Connacht come ingots of iron (*cáer íaraind*); while even the title for a lord can reflect this new idea of royalty, and the prince of Meath is described as 'the king of Meath of the market' (*rí Midi inn marcaid*).[46]

Those who wrote chronicles seem not to have been immune to the new interest in the heroic. Reference has been made to the Annals of Ulster in the ninth and tenth century for their sparse eulogies on powerful princes. By the eleventh century that restraint is giving way to more colourful language. The brief and plain account of the battle of Clontarf in the Annals of Ulster finds space to describe the slain Brian as the Augustus of all northern Europe (*Brian mac Cenneitigh ... August*

42 A.J. Goedheer, *Irish and Norse traditions about the Battle of Clontarf* (Haarlem 1938) p. 38. Less convinced was Kathleen Hughes, *Early Christian Ireland*, pp 293–4.   **43** Goedheer, *Irish and Norse traditions*, pp 30–1.   **44** *Lebor na Cert, The Book of Rights*, ed. Myles Dillon (Dublin 1962). A brief discussion is by Hughes, *Early Christian Ireland*, pp 284–7, while an older view is by E. Mac Neill, *Celtic Ireland*, with introduction and new notes by D. Ó Corráin (Dublin 1981) pp 73–95 and 191–2.   **45** Dillon, *Book of Rights*, pp 4 and 38.   **46** Ibid. pp 48 and 144.

iartair tuaisceirt Eorpa uile). In 1034 the Annals of Tigernach describe the Scots king Máel Coluim II as the glory of the whole west of Europe (*ordan iarthar Eorpa uile*), even though his equally powerful father Cináed II was described simply as a king of the Scots. A few individuals might have had a disproportionate amount of influence. An account of a typical cattle raid by the northern Uí Néill prince Áed Ua Neill in 1021, taken from Dub-dá-Leithe's book, reads like an heroic saga. The entry concludes with the statement that Áed carried all before him, although he had only a hundred and twenty warriors (*Crech la* [Flaithbertach] *mac Aedha .H. Neill ... ni raibe acht da .xx. deg oglach*]. Historical writing might have had an influence on the new versions of the old heroic tales. The structure of the tale *Caithréim Cellaig* has been compared with the psuedo-historical sections of eleventh-century composition in the Fragmentary Annals.[47]

The Vikings and the Heroic

New heroes needed new villains. The dynastic and regional rivalries of the earlier sagas were becoming increasingly incomprehensible to an audience of the High Middle Ages. Not entirely surprisingly, a more contemporary nemesis appeared in the form of the Vikings. Despite the fact that by the eleventh-century descendants of the Vikings had settled and lived among the Gaels for several centuries and had converted to Christianity, nevertheless they became the stock enemy. The irony is that there was little literary interest in them during the 'classical' Viking Age of the ninth and tenth century, but as their military threat receded, their literary villainy increased.[48] The Prophecy of Berchán not only uses an heroic vocabulary to describe the powerful princes of Ireland and Scotland, but it also incorporates these new malefactors, the Vikings. They are actually only one of two principal agents of turmoil in this work, the other being the Laigin ('Leinstermen'). One triad sarcastically states 'Welcome thieves, Vikings – what is the third? – and Laigin from the southeast.'[49]

As the saga literature was recopied and edited, the Viking as a figure of evil is incorporated in the new versions. The earlier version of the tale of the conception of Mongan (*Compert Mongáin*) found in the *Lebor na hUidre* claims that Mongan was fathered by Manannán mac Lir, the sea-god, while his mother's husband Fiachna Lurga, lord of Dál nAraide and ruler of Ulaid, was in Britain, fighting for Áedán mac Gabráin of Dál Riata against the English.[50] The later version of the story, found in the Book of Fermoy, has Fiachna going to Lochlann (Scandinavia) in order to avenge himself on the king named Eolgarb Mór, who had failed to honour his commitment to take the red-eared white cow that had restored him to health.[51] Even heroes such as Cú Chulainn contend with the Viking menace. In *Siaburcharpat Con Culaind*, revised in the late tenth or eleventh century, Cú Chulainn goes to Scandinavian in order to impose tribute on the inhabitants.[52] *Cath Ruis na Ríg* gives practically a geography of the twelfth-century western Scandinavian world, and it might have intended as the beginning to a new saga about the hero Conall Cernach.[53] Not all the

47 M. Herbert, 'Caithréim Cellaig': some literary and historical considerations', *ZCP* 49–50 (1999) pp 321–2; she suggests that the composition of the extent text might be as early as 1111 (page 329). 48 P. Mac Cana, 'Influence of the Vikings on Celtic Literature', in *Impact of the Scandinavians on the Celtic-speaking People c.800–1100 AD*, ed. B. Ó Cúiv (Dublin 1975) p. 80. 49 Hudson, *Prophecy of Berchán*, p. 31 (st. 57) for the reign of Ruaidrí Ua Canannáin (d. 950). 50 *Lebor na Huidre*, p. 333; K. Meyer, *Voyage of Bran son of Febal* (London 1895) pp 42–5; Carney, *Studies*, p. 290; and P.L. Henry, *Saoithiúlacht na Sean-Ghaeilge* (Dublin 1978) pp 86–94. 51 Meyer, *Voyage of Bran son of Febal*, pp 54–84. 52 *Lebor na Huidre*, pp 281–282; Mac Cana, 'Influence of the Vikings', p. 81. 53 Mac Gearailt, 'Cath Ruis na Ríg',

references to the Vikings were necessarily unpleasant. The eleventh-century reworking of the seventh- or eighth-century version of *Tochmarc Emire* has embassaries from the *gaill* ('foreigners') bringing gifts of gold and wine.[54]

The usefulness of a universal villain was not lost on the writers of religious texts, and in eschatological literature there is an equally mistrustful view of the Viking settlers. The tract known as the Second Vision of Adomnán, which probably contributed to the panic of 1096, claims that one of the reasons for divine displeasure was that the Irish were behaving as badly as Vikings, except that they did not worship idols.[55] The so-called First Vision of Adomnán (*Fís Adomnán*), composed in the late tenth or early eleventh century, claims that certain occupations were particularly susceptible to damnation, including cloth merchants, artisans, and traders, employments that had become identified with the Viking settlers of Ireland by the eleventh century.[56]

Even as they were becoming the new villains, this new culture could have made its own contribution to the renewed interest in the heroic. While it might seem laughably anachronistic to refer to pre-Norman Ireland as a multi-cultural society, by the eleventh century there were in Ireland two cultures: Gaelic and Norse. The inhabitants of towns such as Dublin, Limerick or Waterford were closely associated with their Gaelic neighbours, but they still maintained ties to their ancestral lands. Norse poets such as Thorgils Grouse-poet (whose *nom de plume* might have owed something to Irish heroic tales) and Gunnlag snake-tongue visited Ireland; the Dublin lords such as Olaf *Cuarán*, the sometimes king of Northumbria, and his son Sitric 'Silken-beard' were their patrons.[57] This continuing cultural association was more than a mere affectation by the powerful lords, there was an equally telling political aspect. Three times in the eleventh century – 1030, 1058 and 1066 – troops from the Scandinavian colonies in Ireland fought outside the island for Danish and Norwegian princes; and for six years – from 1098 to 1103 – Dublin was part of the Norwegian colonial empire. But this culture in Ireland also had an important economic aspect, one recognized by high-kings of the time as they attempted to bring the towns, with their wealth, under their control. The Viking merchants of Dublin had wealth enough to support poets, establish churches (the see of Dublin was established by Sitric, who began the building of Christ Church Cathedral) and the children of their rulers were attractive matrimonial prospects for the Irish aristocracy.

The Gaelo-Scandinavians had a taste for the heroic as can be seen in literature produced for them. The same Olaf who was the patron of Thorgils Grouse-poet was also the patron of the Irish poet Cináed Ua hArtacáin. Cináed wrote for Olaf a poem on the legendary history of the hill of Skreen, near Tara.[58] The heroine of the story is a princess named Achall, who died of grief after her brother Erc was slain in revenge for cutting off Cú Chulainn's head at the battle of Murthemne. The poem goes on to list Achall among the six best women of the world. So a new audience was open to the poets, historians and storytellers of Ireland, who might secure their cooperation with the great Irish princes. By incorporating the Vikings of Dublin into the Irish heroic tradition, even if only through association, then a prince might be able to influence their allegiance. A connection between a living prince and the heroic figures of the past would impress

p. 132.   **54** Mac Cana, 'Influence of the Vikings', p. 81.   **55** W. Stokes, 'Adomnan's Second Vision', *RC* 12 (1891) pp 420–43; B. Hudson, 'Time is short: the eschatology of the early Gaelic Church', in *Last things*, ed. C. Bynum and P. Freedman (Philadelphia 2000) p. 118.   **56** *Lebor na Huidre*, p. 74; Hudson, 'Time is short', p. 112.   **57** B. Hudson, 'The Viking and the Irishman', *Medium Aevum* 60 (1991) p. 262.   **58** E. Gwynn, *The Metrical Dindsenchas*, 5 parts (Dublin, 1903–35) i, 46–53, following the Book of Leinster, fol. 161 a 44–161 b 35, cf. Best et al., *Book of Leinster*, iii, pp 710–12.

not only Vikings, but also the Irish. This consideration of the Scandinavian settlers could be one reason why they are treated so gently in the new stories, and the bad Vikings in the reworked literature usually are from outside Ireland

Changes in Fashion

The interest in the hero on the part of those who would write panegyrics for particular families or individuals as well as those who contributed to the mythological or legendary tales continued into the later twelfth century and beyond; one needs to look no farther than the Book of Leinster and later Irish encyclopedia for evidence. Certainly the stories of the Finn cycle were heroic tales. At the same time, those writing history, or even history in the interests of a particular dynasty, looked for inspiration elsewhere. Changing fashions in composition are apparent by the twelfth century.

Not all approved of this interest in the heroes of an earlier period. The older heroic tales are mercilessly mocked by the satiric piece called *Aislinge Meic Con Glinne* ('The Vision of Mac Con Glinne'). This late-eleventh-/ early twelfth-century tale savagely pillories heroic vocabulary and presentation in its account of the adventures of the gourmand Anér mac Con Glinne, who labours to banish a devil of gluttony that tormented the king Cathal mac Finguine.[59] In a section of the tale that might be a deliberate imitation of Dub-dá-Leithe's *Baile in Scáil*, Mac Con Glinne tells a story about a visitation from a phantom who recites a litany of foodstuffs before sending him off to be cured of his hunger by a wizard.[60] The similarity with the phantom's appearing, identification and recitation of princes in *Baile in Scáil* is striking. A distaste for the fantastic is not limited to history as such, but it extended into the realm of hagiography, as can be seen in the different versions of the *vita* of St Kentigern, the patron of Glasgow and the north British kingdom of Strathclyde (that was annexed to the Scots domain in the early eleventh century). A *vita* of the saint was prepared during the episcopate of Bishop Herbert of Glasgow (1147–1164) and it was subsequently reworked by Jocelin of Furness under instructions from Bishop Jocelin of Glasgow (1174–1199).[61] The earlier *vita* of Kentigern is full of heroic feats, some that verge on the heretical. All this is firmly set aside in the later reworking by Jocelin of Furness; he replaces the archaic fantasy with sensible and rational explanations or, as he explains, seasoning the barbarous narrative with Roman salt.[62]

The work known as *Caithréim Cellacháin Caisil* ('The Triumph of Cellachán of Cashel') demonstrates how tastes in historical writing could alter. This pseudo-historical work was composed in the mid-twelfth century, but it glorifies the career of the tenth-century Munster king Cellachán, who was considered the founder of the powerful Mac Carthy family, in reply to the Uí Briúin tract *Cocad Gáedel re Gallaib*.[63] The Mac Carthy's had risen to power in southern Munster under their king Cormac Mac Carthy (d. 1138) in opposition to the Uí Briúin. As in that earlier work, the protagonist is presented as the tireless foe of the Vikings, but while Cellachán experiences triumph and defeat, there are no screaming banshees, frenzied wildmen or comparisons

---

59 *Aislinge Meic Con Glinne*, ed. K.H. Jackson (Dublin 1990); Henry A. Jeffries, 'The Visions of Mac Conglinne, and their authors', *Studia Hibernica* 29 (1995–7) p. 30.   **60** *Aislinge Meic Con Glinne*, pp 27–39.   **61** Alexander Penrose Forbes, *Lives of S. Ninian and S. Kentigern* (Edinburgh 1874); the fragmentary vita from the time of Bishop Herbert is printed at pages 243–52 while the work of Jocelin of Furness is at pages 159–242.   **62** Ibid., p. 160: *barbarice exarata Romano sale condire.*   **63** *Caithréim Cellacháin Caisil*, ed. Alexander Bugge (Christiania 1905); for a critical study see D. Ó Corráin, 'Caithréim Chellachain Chaisil: history or propaganda', *Ériu* 25 (1974) pp 1–69.

with the heroes of antiquity. Instead Cellachán succeeds through his own ability, the loyalty of his followers and the flaws of his opponents. This work is more in keeping with other European literature of the time, in which piety and moral standing are more important than the paraphernalia of the earlier heroic tales. Like *Cocad Gáedel re Gallaib, Caithréim Cellacháin Caisil* looks to classical texts for inspiration, and its similarity with *Togail Troí* has received comment.[64] This can be compared with writings throughout Europe, such as the afore-mentioned Song of Roland. While Roland is certainly portrayed as a hero, his death is brought about not by supernatural agencies, but through his own sin of pride. *Caithréim Cellacháin Caisil* fits into what Bernard of Clairvaux, the friend of Cormac's spiritual advisor St Malachy, described in another context as the new chivalry.[65] Bowing to contemporary mores had its benefits. Cormac and his son Diarmait Mór were remembered in the necrology of the Schottenkloster at St. Jakob's at Würzburg, (as were the Uí Briúin) and Cormac is portrayed as another Solomon in the *Visio Tnugdali*, whose protagonist claims to have served him.[66]

History and Heroes

Why did hero and heroism interest the Gaels during the period from the late tenth to early twelfth century? This era has been seen as one of political turmoil, during which rivals were employing somewhat pedestrian tactics in their pursuit of power, such as fortress building, establishing alliances and taking control of centres of economic power; all sensible actions, but not heroic ones. Many questions remain about the subject of the heroic and the Gaels, while many texts have not been included in this survey, including the important *Lebar Gabála Érenn* and other synthetic historical works. These few thoughts on the heroic and historical writing must be regarded as tentative, but future scholarly studies of the subject may illuminate many obscure matters. A brief overview of the topic leaves many questions unasked, much less unanswered, but one or two observations can be tentatively made.

A renewed interest in the heroic among those who professed to write history in the eleventh century must have been complementary to the reworking of the tales from three centuries earlier. A pressing reason to 'modernize' the heroic literature of an early period was that the language had evolved from the Old Irish in which the heroic tales had been composed into Middle Irish. More than just the language was different and the eleventh century had changed culturally from the eighth. This was apparent not just in literature, but in other studies such as law, as the vast corpus of legal commentary tried, not always successfully, to interpret archaic legal texts. So not only the language of the old tales had evolved, but the motivations of their characters and the scenarios of the stories seem to have been increasingly unintelligible to an audience of the eleventh century. The Middle Irish words and phrases that mingle with the Old Irish text betray copyists *cum* editors trying to retain the original story while explaining what was no longer sensible.

An impetus for the preservation, through recopying and reworking, of the older heroic tales might have been the physical destruction of the old church libraries. The churches ravaged by the

---

64 *Caithréim Cellacháin*, pp xvi–xvii. **65** St Bernard of Clairvaux wrote his *De Laude Novae Militiae* c.1128 as a constitution for the Knights Templar, in which the basic plan was modelled on the organization of the Cistercians; in *Sancti Bernardi Opera*, vol. 3, ed. Dom J. Leclerq and Dom H.M. Rochais (Rome 1963). **66** D. Ó Riain-Raedel, 'Irish kings and bishops in the memoria of the German Schottenklöster', P. Ní Chatháin and M. Richter

Vikings had also housed the great libraries. They included Bangor, Iona and Kildare; great centres of scholarship, but known now through texts which had been sent away from them. Two great centres of scholarship which, although attacked, continued as important archives, were Clonmacnois and Armagh. At Armagh laboured Dub-dá-Leithe and the Dubthach who might be the author of Berchán, while *Lebor na hUidre* was produced at Clonmacnois. Those churches were protected by two of the powerful dynasties of the Uí Néill confederation: Clann Cholmáin at Clonmacnois and Cenél nEógain at Armagh, where they had a residence. Destruction of materials was not always due to deliberate human attack and fires were a constant danger, such as the one that ravaged Dunkeld in 1027. Dunkeld had been one of the literary centres for the eastern Gaels, and surviving from it are the Scottish Chronicle (which had been sent to St Andrews) and some liturgical works.[67] Even when a fire is known not to have destroyed the library, such as the one at Armagh on 30 May 1020, it still might have inspired concern. The fire at Armagh consumed the great church and several outlying churches in addition to important items such as the preaching chair and the chariot of Patrick. In the same year there were devastating fires at Kildare, Glendalough, Clonard, Clonmacnois and Swords. The fire of 1020 was not the first major conflagration at Armagh: on 27 April 916 lightning had started a fire that destroyed the southern half of the community, including the abbot's house. The narrow miss of the library by the eleventh-century fire at Armagh could have been the impetus for the work of Dub-dá-Leithe, the author of the Phantom's Frenzy, and others who feared for the survival of the old texts.

Besides their scholarly interest, the preservation of these heroic sagas could have had a connection with their political value in glorifying the powerful dynasties or institutions.[68] The tales of Cú Chulainn, for example, record the pre-historical wars between the men of Connacht and the men of Ulster. The Connacht heroes were claimed as ancestors not only by the important families of the province, but also the powerful Uí Néill families. The connection of political power with literature is visible at this time as the lords of Connacht were becoming increasingly powerful in the eleventh century and they would dominate in Ireland during the twelfth. The Ulstermen remained important because of their association with St Patrick and, by extension Armagh, even though their own political importance was declining. By the eleventh century Armagh was recognized as the leading church in Ireland, and through their association with that church's patron the Ulstermen were ensured literary immortality. Looking south, a similar process is visible for the Leinster tales. The preservation of the heroic legends of the Leinstermen is a sign of their increasing political importance during the career of Diarmait mac Máel na mBó and his successors in the middle of the eleventh century, especially after their capture of Dublin in 1052, and the Isle of Man in 1061. Diplomatic purposes are suggested by a story concerning Brandub son of Echdach that appears in the eleventh century.[69] Brandub was the ancestor of Diarmait's kindred of Uí Cheinnselaig, and the story in question is that of Brandub's birth. Not only is the ancestor of Uí Cheinnselaig present, but also present is Áedán son of Gabrán, the ancestor of the Scottish

(eds), *Irland und Europa/Ireland and Europe* (Stuttgart 1984) pp 390–404.   **67** B. Hudson, 'The Scottish chronicle', *SHR* 77 (1998) p. 135.   **68** D. Ó Corráin, 'Historical need and literary narrative', *Proceedings of the Seventh International Congress of Celtic Studies*, ed. D. Ellis Evans, J.G. Griffith and E.M. Jope (Oxford 1986) pp 141–58. **69** R.I. Best, 'The Birth of Brandub son of Eochaid, and of Aedán son of Gabráin', in *Medieval studies in memory of Gertrude Schoepperle Loomis* (Paris 1927) pp 381–90; M.A. O'Brien, 'A Middle Irish Poem on the Birth of Áedán mac Gabráin and Brandub mac Echach', *Ériu* 16 (1952) pp 157–70; Hudson, *Kings of Celtic Scotland*, pp 110–11; M. Herbert, 'Sea-divided Gaels? Constructing relationships between Irish and Scots c.800–1169' in Smith, *Britain and Ireland, 900–1300*, pp 93–4.

monarchs Máel Coluim II, Donnchad I and Máel Coluim III who were the contemporaries of
Diarmait mac Máel na mBó. So heroic tales might also point modern scholars towards otherwise
unknown alliances, or proposed alliances.

In addition to flattering dynastic vanity, the institutions and families that provided the audience
for these earlier sagas might have demanded this literature in order to compensate for political decline,
uncertainty of rule or the need to distract attention from their lack of a suitable antiquity. Dub-dá-
Leithe, for example, was writing during a time of political eclipse (temporary as it would prove to be)
of Armagh's Uí Néill patrons. The ascendancy of Brian of Munster had been the beginning to a period
when the ascendancy of Uí Néill seemed to be no longer assured, and temporarily the fight for
supremacy in Ireland was between Munster, in the person of Brian's son Donnchad, and Leinster,
under the lordship of Diarmait mac Máel na mBó. A similar scenario can be suggested for the
composer for the main section of the Prophecy of Berchán, which was being written at roughly the
same time. The Berchán poet had no particular ties to Uí Néill, so the Irish section is much more a
survey of great lords from various regions: Ossory, Munster, and even the Vikings. The Scottish
section, however, may reflect political uncertainty. The kindred of Cináed mac Alpín (Kenneth I, died
858) of Cenél nGabráin had moved into the lands of the Picts too recently for there to be recourse
to legends of ancient triumphs. Like the Uí Briúin of Munster, they had to legitimise their success
through claims of divine providence and good government. The situation was made more uncertain
by the events of the mid-eleventh century. From the advantage of hindsight, the royal succession
among Cenél nGabráin seems to be a smooth progression. That was not obvious to contemporaries
as there had been a vicious civil war only two generations earlier, and the repercussions from it were
still being felt in the second quarter of the eleventh century. Even the supremacy of Cenél nGabráin
had been eclipsed by their northern rivals of Cenél Loairn. The Berchán poet is sympathetic to Cenél
nGabráin, and the only genuine, and failed, effort at prophecy in the poem is his effort to win for
Máel Coluim III some claim of divine inspiration when he declares that the king would die while
on a pilgrimage to Rome.

Whatever the reason, these historical works that draw some of their inspiration from heroic
literature provide an insight into the intellect of the age. In a time when power was less the
property of the mighty warrior with ties to the fantastic and more an adjunct of fortifications,
alliances and economics, there was a desire to look back to an era that was simply more interesting
or somehow purer. The influence of this brief period on later literature was complex and
enduring.

Tochmarc Étaíne: a literal interpretation

T.M. CHARLES-EDWARDS

The Wooing of Étaín has had a double interest for scholars:[1] at least one part of it was perceived, though not necessarily by the author of the earliest recension, as a *remscél* or prefatory tale to *Togail Bruidne Da Derga*, 'The Destruction of Da Derga's Hostel'.[2] It is also, however, one of the principal surviving stories or groups of stories in what modern scholars have named 'the Mythological Cycle'. My concern is with neither of these two aspects of *Tochmarc Étaíne (TE)*: as my title indicates, what I wish to offer is an interpretation of what is going on in the narrative at a literal level. This is based on the assumption that in the original context of *TE* potential hearers or readers would be accustomed through biblical exegesis to interpreting texts on more than one level. To seek to make sense of the narrative is not to deny that a mythological interpretation may be legitimate, merely to indicate that such an approach is not mine. Within this literal level of interpretation, however, I include elements which are at least half-explicit in the Old-Irish text. This essay began life as a lecture to students who had no specialist knowledge of early Irish literature. It is offered here to Próinséas Ní Chatháin in recognition of, among many other things, her work in extending the teaching of Celtic literature in UCD to those who do not know Old Irish.

In the edition by Bergin and Best, *Tochmarc Étaíne* is divided into three subtales, which we may call *TE* I, II and III. The manuscript tradition of the three subtales is different: we have all three in sequence in a detached portion of *YBL* (Y^1); in *LU* we have the last part of *TE* I (it begins after a lacuna in the MS, and there is no reason to doubt that the MS once had the whole of *TE* I), the whole of *TE* II, and the first part of *TE* III.[3] This is followed by another lacuna in the MS; and thus, again, there is no reason to doubt that it had the full text as in Y^1. Outside this agreement between *LU* and Y^1, matters are very different. *YBL* also contains a quite distinct text of *TE* II at another place in the MS (this I shall call Y^2);[4] there is no suggestion there that it had been accompanied by *TE* I or III. In British Library, Egerton MS 1782 things are rather more complicated:[5] we have a version of *TE* II, with considerable amplification and recasting, nothing corresponding to the first fourteen paragraphs of the Y^1 version of *TE* III and a very different version of the last part, §§ 15–23. Moreover, the Egerton recension declared itself as a text of two stories, the *Serclige Aililla* (here possibly 'Love-Lying' rather than 'Wasting Sickness', *Serglige*) and *Tochmarc Étaíne*, 'The Wooing of Étaín'. The title *Tochmarc Étaíne* is here given only to one part of *TE* III. In Y^1, however, *Tochmarc Étaíne* is a name given to all three subtales; in Y^2 the same title is given to *TE* II. The manuscript tradition thus raises a question: how coherent is this tale

1 *Tochmarc Étaíne*, ed. and trans. O. Bergin and R.I. Best, *Ériu* 12 (1938) pp 137–96.   2 As we shall see, the Late Middle Irish version in British Library MS Egerton 1782, applied the title *Tochmarc Étaíne* solely to a version of the last part of the third tale, *TE* III in the edition by Best and Bergin: *Irische Texte*, ed. E. Windisch (Leipzig 1880) i. p. 130 (§ 30). This made it much easier to see it as a *remscél* to *Togail Bruidne Da Derga*.   3 *Lebor na hUidre*, ed. R.I. Best and O. Bergin (Dublin 1929) pp 323–32.   4 This is given at the bottom of the page in the edition by Bergin and Best.   5 This text is edited, together with the fragments from *LU*, by E. Windisch in *Irische Texte*, i (Leipzig 1880) pp 113–33. See also R. Thurneysen, *Die irische Helden- und Königsage* (Halle 1921) pp 597–8, for an overview of all the material known before the rediscovery of the full text in the missing portion of *YBL*.

composed of three subtales? Their combination as in *Y¹* and *LU* might be a convenient assemblage of texts that indeed had some connection but were not seen as a single literary composition. The worry is made more insistent by the ways in which, in *TE* II, *Y¹* and *LU* agree in variant readings against *Y²*;[6] this raises the possibility that the text as presented in *Y¹* and *LU* did not go back to the archetype of all the manuscripts.

Alongside this question of coherence, two more particular questions may be raised: first, could an Old Irish text evoke a literary motif without committing itself unambiguously to it? There are places in *Tochmarc Étaíne* where it looks as though the familiar motif of the sovereignty goddess is present; but, if so, it is present only as one way in which the reader or audience might take a particular passage, not the only way in which it could be understood. I am certainly not espousing a general principle that sees literary texts as inherently and wholly fluid in meaning. If that were so, a particular instance of fluidity would be utterly unremarkable. Instead, some texts or parts of texts may be relatively unambiguous – that is, ideas or themes are unquestionably part of the workings of the text and are not left to hover on the margins. If that is one's initial stance, the reverse case, where themes or motifs do hover on the margin, becomes much more interesting. The second question concerns the presuppositions shared by the author and his contemporary reader (or audience): can we detect ideas or practices taken for granted in the eighth and ninth centuries, but which can only be deduced by us because they appear to be required in order to make sense of the text?

TE I

With these issues in mind, we may follow the narrative, raising issues of literal interpretation as they arise, so that we can see the problematic passages in context. The beginning of the story is pointedly conventional: 'There was over Ériu a famous king' is, with minor variations, the beginning of several stories. The king in question here bore two names, Dagda 'Good God', and Eochaid Ollathair, Eochaid 'Supreme Father'. The divine nature of the Dagda is introduced as a matter of lineage: his descent was from 'the God Peoples'.[7] In most books this term 'God Peoples' is rendered, as it is by Jeffrey Gantz in his translation, as Túatha Dé Danann, 'The Peoples of the Goddess Danu', and they are compared with the family of Dôn in the Welsh tales, 'The Four Branches of the Mabinogi'.[8] There are, however, grounds for doubting whether this name applied to all the gods, although it was used of the Dagda.[9]

The Dagda, then, is introduced first as possessing divine lineage and then as a miracle-worker among the Túatha Dé, one who controls the weather and the crops. The Dagda was a person of ample sexual appetite, and our story begins as a tale of adultery.[10] To appreciate what is happening we need a little divine-cum-human geography. The home of the Dagda is identified as Uisnech, the centre of Mide, the 'Middle Land' of Ireland.[11] Its role as the symbolic focus of Mide was also

---

6 The significant variations may all turn out to be innovations by *Y²*, in which case they would not pose a problem, but one would need a critical edition to be sure. Examples are: II. 6: the clause 'acht niba isin tsosudh na fírflatha dogentar an col' is omitted by *Y²*; II.9: imlot n-einig, *LU*, im*m*lot n-einig, *Y¹*, lot ar n-enig, *Y²*.   **7** *do Thuathaib De a chenel*, *TE* I.1.   **8** J. Gantz, *Early Irish myths and sagas* (London 1981) p. 39.   **9** J. Carey, 'The Name "Tuatha Dé Danann"', *Éigse* 18 (1981) pp 291–4; *Túatha Dé Danann* occurs at TE I. 15, 18 (in the latter case, the Dagda is included).   **10** If the author or his contemporary readers had read Augustine's *City of God*, Book VII, they would know that this was the kind of thing that pagan gods got up to all the time.   **11** This is a hill in Westmeath, between Mullingar and Athlone, on which there is a series of prehistoric monuments: for a brief account see Lord

picked up by Tírechán, writing about Patrick in the late seventh century, and by the later version of Patrick's life and journeys in the so-called Tripartite Life of the saint.[12] The home of the woman whom the Dagda desired was Brug na Bóinne, the district including Newgrange, the great Neolithic Passage Grave on the lower Boyne known in the Old Irish period as Síd in Broga or Cnoc Síde in Broga, as well as Knowth and other prehistoric monuments. Moreover, the woman after whom the Dagda lusted bore two names, Eithne and Boand. The latter is the name of the River Boyne that flows past Newgrange and is the great river of Mag mBreg, the Plain of Brega.

When the Dagda had slept with Eithne *alias* Boand, the child that was born of the union, Óengus, like his parents, bore two names: as well as Óengus he was 'the Young Son', a name said to have been conferred by his mother when she said, 'Young is the son who was made at the break of day and born between it and evening.'[13] Like any other noble Irish child, Óengus was fostered away from his natal home; in this case, however, there was a special reason – it was imperative that the child of adultery should be well out of the way before the husband of his mother returned. He was fostered at Brí Léith, the 'Hill of a Grey One', namely Ardagh Hill in Co. Longford. Again the geography was precise and unambiguously Irish.

The sites are at least reminiscent of the political geography of Early Christian Ireland. In *Togail Bruidne Da Derga*, the author of the story was quite content to shift his eras: Conaire Már, who was evidently placed close to the time of Christ, was made to march east, past Uisnech Midi towards Tara, across 'the Land of the Uí Néill', namely the midlands from the Irish Sea to the Shannon.[14] This 'Land of the Uí Néill' was divided into three provinces: Brega in the east, Mide in the centre, and Tethbae to the north-west, on the Shannon. The 'Young Son', *in Macc Óc*, had a mother who was the river-goddess of Brega, a father who lived at Uisnech, the centre of Mide, the Middle Land, and a foster-father, Midir, whose home was Brí Léith in Tethbae. There is, then, the possibility that this divine bonding between Brega, Mide and Tethbae may express a more this-worldly relationship among the Southern Uí Néill. The possibility is given rather more weight by comparison with another story in the Mythological Cycle, namely 'The Second Battle of Mag Tuired'. The geography in that tale also is precise and wholly Irish, but instead of the midlands, namely the lands of the Southern Uí Néill, the Second Battle of Mag Tuired runs its course in two second-ranking kingdoms of the north-west, ruled by Cenél Coirpri Dromma Clíab around Sligo Town and the Uí Ailella just to their south.[15] In modern terms it is a tale of Co. Sligo, in early medieval terms of the north-eastern part of the province of the Connachta. In that case, there may be a double level of history behind the mythology: that area was one of the principal fault-lines of early-medieval Irish politics. While, therefore, there is good evidence in the text to think that those deservedly defeated in the tale, the unlovely Fomorians, the enemies of the gods, were, in part, a metaphor for the Vikings of the mid-ninth century, anyone who paid attention to the geography of the text would know that the Vikings were not the only likely target.[16] Behind Fomorian and Viking onslaughts may have lain the older attacks of Cenél Coirpri and their patrons, Cenél Conaill, upon the Connachta.

Killanin and M. Duignan, *The Shell guide to Ireland*, 2nd edn (London 1967) p. 101.   **12** Tírechán, *Collectanea*, c.16, ed. L. Bieler, *The Patrician texts in the Book of Armagh* (Dublin 1979) p. 136; *Bethu Phátraic: The Tripartite Life of Patrick*, ed. K. Mulchrone (Dublin 1939) ll. 867–73.   **13** *TE* I.2.   **14** *Togail Bruidne Da Derga*, ed. E. Knott (Dublin 1936) § 25. For this delimitation of their territory, excluding the Northern Uí Néill, compare Tírechán, *Collectanea*, c.17, ed. L. Bieler, *Patrician texts*, p. 138, whose work is calculated to please Síl nÁeda Sláne at the expense, primarily, of Cenél Conaill; similarly AU 850.3.   **15** *Cath Maige Tuired*, ed. E. Gray, *ITS* 52 (1982) §§ 84–94.   **16** P. Mac Cana, 'The Influence of the Vikings on Celtic Literature', in B. Ó Cuív (ed.), *The impact of the Scandinavian invasions on the Celtic-speaking peoples, c.800–1100 AD* (Dublin 1975) p. 94.

Fig. 1: Kingdom and Genealogy

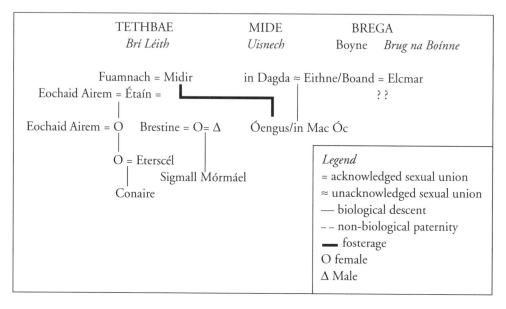

This possibility of contemporary eighth- or ninth-century reference cannot be dismissed or given even a limited acceptance until we look further at some of the implications of the relationships between the gods. Óengus was the son of the wife of Elcmar. Whoever was the physical father, the marriage created a presumption in law that Elcmar was the father, provided that it was first known who was the child's mother (hence the queries in the broken line connecting Elcmar and Óengus in the genealogical table). The rule was that the child begotten on a married woman by someone other than the husband belonged to the husband until that child had been bought from him by the biological father.[17] If, then, it were known that Óengus was the son of Eithne, the wife of Elcmar, and if the Dagda acknowledged parenthood openly, that acknowledgement would render him liable to compensate Elcmar for the insult and he would have to purchase the officially-recognized paternity of his son. The Dagda did no such thing, but the possibility that Elcmar would learn the truth hangs in the air. In the short term, at least, he was kept in the dark by the miraculous powers of the Dagda (expressly asserted at the outset of the text).

The truth began to come out into the open because of an insult. Óengus was put to shame by another fosterling of Midir, Tríath son of Febal (or Gobor), who was of the Fir Bolg. Óengus began the trouble by claiming that Tríath was of servile status, a *mug*. The presupposition was that the Fir Bolg were a subject people while the Túatha Dé were the nobles; the division between noble and commoner was also an ethnic divide.[18] In this case then, the contemporary reference is to social status. We were told at the outset that the divinity of the Dagda and his fellows was a matter of descent. In the playing-field of Brí Léith, however, there was an incongruity: the difference of social status between the Dagda's son, Óengus, and Tríath of the Fir Bolg allowed both to be fosterlings of Midir and to mix on daily terms at Brí Léith; yet, on the other, the social

17 *CIH* 294.13; *CGH* 140 (141 a 15).   18 Cf. the division between the *aithechthúatha*, 'vassal peoples', and the men of Ireland proper: *Audacht Morainn*, ed. and trans. F. Kelly (Dublin 1976) § 1; R. Thurneysen, 'Morands Fürstenspiegel', *ZCP* 11 (1917) pp 56–69; T. Ó Raifeartaigh, *Genealogical Tracts I* (Dublin 1932) pp 107–14, 122–31.

gulf was so great that it amounted to a difference of race, between one people and another. And this incongruity was the point on which tension broke out into conflict, when Óengus declared, 'It causes me pain when the son of a serf attempts to make conversation with me.'

If Óengus had accurately discerned a social inconsistency in Midir's household, the object of his disdain, Tríath, had no difficulty in discerning a social inconsistency in Óengus's own position. Here was one who had the first place among the fosterlings of Midir on account of his descent, among other things, but whose parents were unknown. Tríath's reply implied that Óengus was what the Irish laws called a 'child of darkness' and, as such, should himself be of servile status, if not a serf, a *mug*, then at least an *amus*, a hireling.[19] Moreover, the name of this acute youth of the Fir Bolg meant 'over-king'.[20] His challenge to Óengus revealed the impossibility of the Dagda's abdication of responsibility: the gods could not continue to claim a superiority over the Fir Bolg based on descent if they failed to acknowledge paternity. If nobody knows who has slept with whom, there can hardly be any nobility of blood. The Good God, therefore, was forced to that modest but necessary level of virtue which consisted in admitting publicly what he had done – not forced by his own sense of honour, but by a challenge from the lower classes.[21]

In addition to claiming that Óengus should be acknowledged by the Dagda as his son, Midir asserted that the acknowledged son of the king of Ireland should not be landless. This further demand was necessary to cope with the accusation made by Tríath of the Fir Bolg that Óengus was a hireling, a mere hanger-on in someone else's household, without any sufficient land of his own. The Dagda then revealed a scheme by which Óengus could acquire Brug na Bóinne, namely Elcmar's land. This may seem to be gratuitous beastliness, to use the son whom he had begotten on Elcmar's wife in order to dispossess Elcmar of his land by a piece of legal chicanery. This is perhaps true, but there is more to it than that. If Óengus had been born to Eithne, Elcmar's wife, in the ordinary way – without any miraculous proceedings to prevent Elcmar from knowing what was going on – Óengus would have been officially Elcmar's son, and therefore his heir. The Dagda may have been a malevolent schemer but his plots had some faint legal substance.

There are evidently a number of distinct ideas in the story of the trick by which Óengus came to acquire Brug na Bóinne. First, there was the propriety in the notion that the son of Boand, the Boyne, should have Brug na Bóinne. Yet that notion is only in the background. Also in the background was any direct equation between the political geography of ancient divine Ireland and that of the late-eighth and ninth centuries, when Mide was often the dominant kingdom in Ireland. It seems that the text permits the reader to make this equation without in any way compelling him to do so. What is explicit is the notion that the Dagda, the king of Ireland but also the ruler of Mide, should control lordship over land, even in Brega, with the consequence that, as soon as the Brug was vacant, he would be in a position to give it to whomsoever he wished. In fact, the Brug was not vacant and the Dagda declared himself, rather implausibly, unwilling to annoy Elcmar any further; presumably now that he had acknowledged his son, there was every possibility that Elcmar might find out who was the boy's mother.

The trick by which Óengus obtained possession of Brug na Bóinne involved taking what is sometimes called a formalist view of legal proceedings and a strong view on the inviolability of a contractual promise. As the text says itself: 'He (the Dagda) adjudged everyone's contract according to his undertaking.'[22] For the Dagda, a promise was a promise and was not to be

19 Cf. T.M. Charles-Edwards, *Early Irish and Welsh kinship* (Oxford 1993) pp 61–2, 314. **20** *CIH* 583.7–12. **21** *TE* I.5 (Midir having privately revealed the truth to Óengus in I.4). **22** *TE* I.8.

undone merely because it was unfair; also, the promise was what was said, whatever may have been meant.[23] The promise made by Elcmar, that Óengus should have the Brug for a day and a night, was construed by Óengus one way and by Elcmar another; the Dagda as king of Ireland was the judge and supported his son. The text is, however, sufficiently realistic to allow that the judge needed to reconcile the parties to the dispute as well as judge the mere law of the matter.[24] Elcmar was offered Cleitech, another ancient mound on the southern side of the Brug. From there he would have, so the Dagda says, 'the fruit of the Boyne for your enjoyment.' The cuckold will still have his wife, even though Óengus now has his mother.

In this way, the Dagda sets up the next scene of the tale. Óengus is on his mound, and Elcmar on his; in between them their boys – presumably the fosterlings without whom no Irish king's household would be complete – are in the playing-field. The legal conflict between Óengus and Elcmar and the personal conflict between the cuckold and the son of his wife's adultery have both been transferred to yet another conflict, between the boys attached to both of them, a kind of divine Rangers versus Celtic match. Midir, Óengus's foster-father, again had to come to the rescue and separate the two warring companies of youths. Like some other referees he suffered severe damage in the process; and since he got involved on behalf of Óengus, Óengus owed him reparation. Although Midir's healing was secured through the services of the divine physician, Dían Cécht, and Midir declared himself healed, he would not stay with Óengus unless the latter performed further services for him; these included one crucial item, namely acting as a go-between and negotiator to arrange a marriage between Midir and Étaín, the daughter of Ailill, king of the Ulstermen.[25] Indeed, by this stage the debts of Óengus to Midir made a fairly formidable list. The intended outcome of this first part of the story was thus to get Óengus into such social debt that he had to discharge it by undertaking the severe tasks imposed by Ailill, king of the Ulstermen and father of Midir's intended bride Étaín.

There is another connection between the first part of *TE* I – getting Óengus into the Brug – and the second, namely the first wooing of Étaín. As Ailill, king of the Ulstermen, very reasonably says, 'I will not give her to you, for there is no profit in it. The nobility of your kindred and the extent of your power and that of your father is so great that, if you were to shame my daughter, I would have no redress.'[26] As the treatment of Elcmar of the Brug had demonstrated, this objection was entirely fair. Óengus's response to Ailill's refusal to give Étaín is interesting. To understand it, we need to know that the standard form of marital union in Ireland at the period was one by which the woman's kindred, and usually her father in particular, betrothed her to the man.[27] Subsequently, they were married at a feast. The legal driving-force was principally in the betrothal not in the marriage itself; the latter was simply the fulfilment of the contract made at the

---

23 For the opposition between contractual entitlement on the one hand and fairness on the other, see *CIH* 593.8–22 = *Berrad Airechta*, §§ 28–33, Engl. trans. R. Chapman Stacey, in T.M. Charles-Edwards, M.E. Owen and D.B. Walters (eds), *Lawyers and laymen* (Cardiff 1986) pp 214–15, German trans. R. Thurneysen, *Die Bürgschaft im irischen Recht, Abhandlungen der Preussischen Akademie der Wissenschaften 1928* (Berlin 1928) pp 10–11, and *Di Astud Chor*, ed. N. McLeod, *Early Irish contract law* (Sydney 1996) passim.   **24** That this might be expected of a judge is suggested by the legal tract *Cóic Conara Fugill*, ed. and trans. R. Thurneysen, *Abhandlungen der Preussischen Akademie der Wissenschaften 1925*, Phil.-Hist. Klasse, no. 2 (Berlin 1926) §§ 8–12, pp. 18–20: on the one hand, the 'path to judgement' called *dliged*, 'entitlement', corresponds to the Dagda's initial strategy (a promise is a promise, whether fair or not); on the other hand, the path named *cert*, that which is just, would give grounds for Elcmar to make a rejoinder. The final settlement is meant to satisfy both *dliged* and *cert*.   **25** Another version, alluded to in a poem now within the text, made Étaín the healer of Midir's eye: *TE* I.23.   **26** *TE* I.12.   **27** F. Kelly, *A guide to early Irish law* (Dublin 1988) pp 70–3.

betrothal. In the standard union, part of the negotiations before the betrothal would have consisted in fixing what property each side would bring to the marriage. From an economic of view, a marriage of the most highly esteemed kind created a farm run with property belonging to both husband and wife in collaboration; the dowry remained the property of the wife but in farming terms became part of the one operation.

What Óengus says, therefore, is effectively this: 'Fine, you won't give her, because the rights that a giver of a woman possesses would be of no value to you, since you could do nothing against the power of the Dagda and myself. Instead I shall purchase her.' There is, perhaps, a presupposition bearing on a union by bride-purchase: in such a union the rights of the woman's father and kindred to protect the interests of the woman in such a union against ill-treatment by her husband or her husband's family were either severely reduced or entirely nullified. For the wife's side to contribute property to the marriage gave them an entitlement to protect her. This was the entitlement Ailill proposed to forego, because in reality it would be worthless. If this interpretation is correct, this passage offers important evidence on early Irish marriage.

Ailill, then, is portrayed simply as king of the Ulstermen, with his own kingdom, the particular basis of his power, in Mag nInis, south-east Co. Down, around Downpatrick. This reflects precisely the normal political arrangement in the north-east in the seventh, eighth and ninth centuries.[28] There may have been an implication of the subordinate status of Ulster in an earlier reference to Mag nInis: when Elcmar was sent away to allow time for the union between his wife and the Dagda and for the birth of their son, he was sent to Mag nInis, to Bres mac Elathan; but, in *Cath Maige Tuired*, Bres was a king of Fomorian paternity.[29] Just as with Tríath of the Fir Bolg in the playing-field of Midir, ethnic difference may signify inferiority of rank and power. On the other hand, the tasks that Ailill imposed on Óengus revealed a different Ulster, that of the so-called Ulster Cycle, a period assigned by the synthetic historians to shortly before the reign of Conaire Már, namely about the time of the birth of Christ.[30] In the *Lebor Gabála Érenn*, Book of the Taking of Ireland, one of the things that happened early in the scheme of Irish history was land-clearance, or, more specifically, the clearance of the principal plains or inhabited areas of Ireland.[31] In the versions that survive of the *Lebor Gabála*, which are some three centuries and more later than the Wooing of Étaín, priority in the settlement of Ulster is given to the great rivals of the rulers of Mag nInis, namely the kings of Mag Line, north-west of Belfast, an area which would include Antrim Town and the modern Belfast Aldergrove airport.[32] The Wooing of Étaín, however, flatly contradicts this account. Mag Line, the rival kingdom to Mag nInis, was merely one of the plains cleared by Óengus on behalf of Ailill, king of Mag nInis and Ulster.[33] The other plains named encompassed all the main areas of the legendary Ulster: the list thus placed contemporary reference within an overall context of the remote past.

When the Macc Óc had cleared the plains and had gone on, with the aid of the Dagda, to create the rivers that would drain the province, he naturally thought he had done his bit for Ailill. Ailill, however, who was a good negotiator if ever there was one, remarked cheerily that everything up to then had been done for Étaín's people, namely the Ulstermen, and not for Ailill personally.

---

28 For example, Muirchú, *Vita Patricii*, ed. Bieler, *Patrician texts*, I. 12. 4 (p. 80): '*conuertit cito iter suum ad regiones Ulothorum . . . et rursum peruenit in campum Inis*'. 29 *TE* I.1; *Cath Maige Tuired*, § 21. 30 *TE* I.13–14; cf. *TE* II.1; *The Book of Leinster* [hereafter *LL*], ed. R.I. Best, O.J. Bergin, M.A. O'Brien and A. O'Sullivan, 6 vols (Dublin 1954–83) i. p. 90 (ll. 2885–92). 31 *LL* i. 20 (ll. 624–8) etc. 32 *CGH* 269 (156 a 25–31); cf. F.J. Byrne, *Irish kings and high-kings* (London 1973, repr. Dublin 2001) pp 108–9. 33 *TE* I.13.

For himself he stipulated Étaín's weight in gold and silver – a stipulation which may echo the compensations for an insult against the honour of the highest grade of king.[34] When Óengus finally returned to Brug na Bóinne with Étaín, Midir received his stipulations, the conditions on which he would stay for a year with Óengus.

If the story began with the potential jealousy of Elcmar, it now goes a stage further through the jealousy of a divine woman, Fúamnach. Étaín was not Midir's first wife; and, while the law, even in early Christian Ireland, recognized the legitimacy of a second wife while the first was still alive, it also recognized the legitimacy of the jealousy likely to be felt by the first wife.[35] Midir may have done rather well out of the Dagda's sexual triangle, but he did a great deal less well out of his own. As Óengus warned Midir, Fúamnach was a woman of terrifying ferocity and possessed of all the magical craft of her kindred, namely the Túatha Dé Danann.[36] Étaín, by contrast, is portrayed as a woman of gentleness as well as beauty.

There is, however, more to the contrast, and the conflict, between Étaín and Fúamnach than the difference between a woman of power and self-will and one who was a male ideal of womanhood. Fúamnach was unambiguously of divine descent and kindred. The sorcery of the Túatha Dé Danann was a characteristic that brought them close to the conception of the pagan gods as demons, for the demons were the power behind the sorcerer's wand.[37] Yet the author cannot be thinking of the magical power of the gods as merely demonic, since it was that very power that had cleared the land of Ireland and made it cultivable. The gender difference seems to allow him to handle incompatible views of the gods: the female Fúamnach deploys a magic perceived by the gods themselves as malevolent; the male Midir and Óengus also deploy magical powers but to a good purpose.

Étaín, however, is a somewhat ambiguous character. At the start she seems to be a mere human or perhaps a Fomorian.[38] Her father, Ailill, has no power when confronted by the gods; he is not of their race. In this story, the midlands, the lands of the Southern Uí Néill, may have divine rulers, but Ulster seems to have a lesser being for its king. It is perhaps important, also, that, just as Étaín began as daughter of a king of Ulster, so also, in her second begetting as the daughter of Étar of Inber Cíchmaine, she was also a native of Ulster. Both as the wife of Midir and as the wife of Eochaid Airem, she came from Ulster to be the wife of a ruler in the midlands. This may even be a deliberate point, a metaphorical way of saying that the Uí Néill had no competitors in the northern half of Ireland for lineage and power, in particular not among their old enemies, the Ulstermen. If so, it suggests a period when the Southern Uí Néill, the Uí Néill of the midlands were indeed dominant, and, moreover, a period when the rulers of Mide were the premier kindred among the Uí Néill. Given the language of the story, that points to the period either between 743 and 797 or in the middle years of the ninth century, the reign of Máel Sechnaill I.[39] This is, however, one way in which the text might have been interpreted in the eighth or ninth century; it was not an inescapable corollary.

Yet, if Étaín began as if she were a mere human, she certainly did not stay a mere human. For one thing, she lived, in her various guises, for more than a thousand years; for another, she possessed some clear characteristics of the sovereignty goddess, the divine representative of the land and its fertility, whom a king must marry in order to reign with power and justice. At the

---

34 For gold as part of the honour-price of a *tríath* see *CIH* 583.9.   **35** Kelly, *Guide*, p. 79.   **36** *TE* I.15.
37 Adomnán, *Vita S. Columbae*, ii. 17.   **38** To judge by the allusion to Bres mac Elathan.   **39** Domnall mac Murchada became king of Tara in 743, the first Cland Cholmáin king to do so; his son Donnchad died in 797.

beginning of the second main section of the tale, *TE* II, Eochaid Airem cannot celebrate the Feast of Tara until he has married her. Yet the Feast of Tara was the marriage-feast between the king and the goddess of the land.[40] In this story, the purpose of the Feast of Tara was also to agree the taxes that the king might levy upon his kingdom; but this may be interpreted as the way in which a king enjoyed the fruitfulness of his land, through the renders of his subjects. Again, the goddess of sovereignty is sometimes characterized as the one who pours 'the ales of sovereignty', and of Étaín it is said that 'the serving of drink was her speciality'.[41] Moreover, if Étaín were indeed a sovereignty and fertility goddess, it would help to explain the nature of the tasks imposed by Ailill on Óengus in exchange for her marriage to Midir. What those tasks secured was the fertility of Ulster. Only when that had been obtained from Óengus, the youthful god, the 'Young Son', did Ailill consider that Ulster, if not he himself, had obtained a fair exchange for Étaín. If, then, Étaín began as if she were a human girl sought in marriage by one god on behalf of another, she was subsequently a quasi-divine wife of a human king of Tara. Indeed, there seems to be something emblematic about Eochaid Airem; he is 'Ploughman Eochaid', a title explained within the text, but presumably intended to be contrasted with 'Eochaid the Supreme Father', namely the Dagda.[42] In this tale Eochaid Airem is the human king of Ireland, just as Eochaid 'Supreme Father' had earlier been his divine counterpart.[43]

A possible explanation of this conundrum of the human and divine guises of Étaín is that there may have been different groups among the gods. This is hinted at in the text itself: on the one hand there is the group headed by the Dagda, on the other there is Boand or Eithne, who is much more closely identified with the river than the Dagda is with Uisnech. To explain Étaín's different roles, then, we need a contrast between a dominant family of gods, including the Dagda, Óengus and Midir, and another group, of lesser power and status yet still divine. The lesser group would be the one closely identified with the land, in Boand's case with Brega, in Étaín's with eastern Ulster in the first place, and then perhaps also Ireland as a whole when she married Eochaid Airem. In other words, Étaín as the daughter of Étar, namely in her second incarnation, still remains a woman of Ulster, but the sovereignty of a king of Ireland comes from the subjection of the principal provincial kings. One possible variant of the sovereignty goddess could then be the woman who represented the great provincial kingdoms.

An alternative might be to appeal to the evidence from Antiquity for a Celtic belief in metempsychosis among ordinary humans.[44] But here one must distinguish between the ultimate origin of a motif, exemplified here in the rebirth of Étaín, and its function in a story which has both a Christian author and a Christian audience and readership. The meaning of this motif in the Old Irish tale can hardly be human metempsychosis, whereas there is far more scope for non-natural happenings among the gods. Moreover, we need to ask what is the point of saying that there were 1,012 years between the two incarnations of Étaín. In terms of biblical chronology this would place Étaín's first begetting close to the time of David.[45] In terms of the story, however, it

---

40 D.A. Binchy, 'The Fair of Tailtiu and the Feast of Tara', *Ériu* 18 (1958) pp 134–7.   **41** *TE* III.13. Cf. M. Herbert, 'Goddess and King: the sacred marriage in early Ireland', in L.O. Fradenburg (ed.), *Women and sovereignty* (Edinburgh 1992) p. 269.   **42** It is explained in *TE* III.8 on the grounds that a change in Irish ploughing methods was derived from watching Midir's people at work; on this see F. Kelly, *Early Irish farming* (Dublin 1997) p. 472. **43** Contrast T.F. O'Rahilly, *Early Irish history and mythology* (Dublin 1946) p. 132 n. 2.   **44** Whether the ancient Celts had such a belief is itself problematic: N.K. Chadwick, *The druids* (Cardiff 1966) p. 55.   **45** According to Gilla Cóemáin (*LL* iii. 485–6) Eochu Feidlech was succeeded by Eochu Airem, he being followed by Eterscél, Nuadu Necht and Conaire Már. After Conaire came the period without a king of Tara, contemporary with

places it in a world in which the gods ruled Ireland, where the Dagda, not any mere human such as Eochaid Airem, was high-king. In terms of the broad shape of Irish synthetic history (as opposed to the chronological detail) that places Étaín's first incarnation within the era when the Túatha Dé ruled Ireland and thus before the domination of the progenitors of the Irish, the Milesians. Not that the Túatha Dé were the sole inhabitants – the presence of Tríath of the Fir Bolg and, less certainly, that of Bres mac Elathan, perhaps of the Fomoiri, demonstrates the contrary – but the rulers were of the gods, and Étaín was a king's daughter. The likelihood is, then, that Étaín was more goddess than human.

TE II and III

If we assume that Étaín was indeed a sovereignty goddess, the second and third parts of the tale take on a quite different meaning. The very notion of 'the Wooing of Étaín' becomes a competition for the sovereignty goddess and thus for the kingship. One of her characteristics is that when sex is in question she never says 'no' to a man worthy to be king; the nearest to rejection she comes is a conditional 'no' and even then it is addressed to a god, Midir, that is, to her original husband. Yet she retains female honour, associated with modesty, as when she blushes at the very notion that she might have said to Midir that she would go with him.[46]

There is an astonishing contrast in the second tale. There Ailill Ánguba, the brother of Eochaid Airem, has fallen in love with Étaín at the Feast of Tara, namely the very occasion when his brother's sovereignty could finally be enjoyed to the full, because he was now married to Étaín. Yet Ailill would not say anything to Étaín, apparently because a love for his brother's wife was dishonourable. He would rather die of his love-sickness than acknowledge its source, even to the physician who knew at least what the general nature of his malady must be, though not the object of his love.[47] As soon, however, as Étaín has questioned him, when he is on what everyone takes to be his death-bed, and he has revealed the truth to her, she promptly says:[48]

> A shame you did not tell me sooner, for had I known, you would long since have been well.

Her obligation to Eochaid through the marriage seems to be nothing in comparison with Ailill's obligation to his brother in virtue of kinship.

Although, on the face of things, the story of Étaín and Ailill Ánguba seems to be a gentle tale of harmless passion, in which everything turns out for the best and no one, in the end, misbehaves with anyone, Ailill is not quite the paragon of sexual virtue that he might seem at first reading. It is words, not actions, that arouse his sense of shame. He will not reveal his passion for his brother's wife even to the physician; yet he has no problems, once Étaín has questioned him, over having sex with her. When he has been healed of his wicked passion (by Midir, who caused it in the first place, rather than by sex with Étaín), what he says is odd. Literally it goes as follows:[49]

Conchobor and thus with Christ (cf. The Annals of Tigernach, First Fragment, ed. W. Stokes, *RC* 16 (1895) p. 405). On this scheme the reign of Eochu/Eochaid Airem was less than half a century before Christ. This would place Étaín's first incarnation in the time of King David and thus well after the rule of the Tuatha Dé had come to an end according to the scheme laid out in the *The Annals of Inisfallen*, ed. S. Mac Airt (Dublin 1951) pp 5–6, where the domination of the Tuatha Dea is brief, occurring during the lifetime of Moses.   **46** *TE* III.14.   **47** *TE* II.4.   **48** *TE* II.5.   **49** *TE* II.9.

'Our meeting has turned out well,' said Ailill, 'not only have I now been healed, but you have suffered no injury to your honour thereby.'

The language is somewhat provocative, since *comrac*, 'meeting', is a normal term for making love.[50] Yet, the healing that was to have been obtained by a full sexual encounter has now been secured without it. Not just Ailill but Midir too says that things have turned out fortunately, because Étaín's honour was not injured.[51] Neither of them refers to any possible harm to Ailill's honour or Eochaid's. True, illicit sex has, in Europe at least, been widely considered more damaging to female than to male honour. But one would ordinarily have imagined that it would have been highly damaging at least to Eochaid's honour. And, indeed, Étaín herself proposed that Ailill and she should make love on a hill close to the court, and not in the court itself, on account of her husband. Moreover, the terms in which she makes this condition are interesting. When Ailill says to her, 'And when shall I have from you what is still lacking to cure me?' (namely full sexual union), she replies:[52]

'You shall have it tomorrow,' said she, 'but not in the dwelling of the just ruler shall the sin be committed.'

Although the Bergin and Best translation presents the issue here as one of honour and shame ('but not in the prince's dwelling shall he be put to shame'), that is not what the text itself says.[53] It applies notions of shame and honour only to Ailill and to Étaín.

If one scrutinizes Ailill's original reason for being ashamed, things again look less edifying. A rapid reading might leave one with the impression that the source of the shame is the conflict between Ailill's obligation to his brother and the passion for his brother's wife. Moreover, there is indeed a conflict between virtue and passion; as the text itself, uncharacteristically, comments, 'Desire was stronger than character'.[54] Yet the explanation why Ailill became sick was not lest his brother should endure the shame of being cuckolded but rather lest his own 'honour should be stained' (*naro tubaide fria enech*, LU); and that is odd, since the person in a sexual triangle of husband, wife and lover who is usually least affected by any disgrace is the lover.

If Étaín, however, is a sovereignty goddess, her behaviour is, within the terms of her role, honourable as well as explicable. She is not the Loathly Lady type of sovereignty goddess, as in the story of Niall Noígiallach and his brothers, in which sovereignty appears first as a hag, and only when the union with the incoming king has been consummated does she appear as a beautiful girl.[55] Étaín, throughout her thousand and more years of existence, remains beautiful, even when transformed into a fly. It is the role of the sovereignty goddess to welcome those worthy to be king; and Étaín's declared purpose in expressing willingness to have sexual relations with Ailill was that 'one worthy to be king of Ireland should be saved from the sickness that had befallen him'.[56] What Ailill perhaps feared, and

50 The narrative does not make it explicit whether Étaín and Midir, appearing in the guise of Ailill, made love or not. 51 For Midir, see the end of *TE* II.8. 52 *TE* II.6. Bergin and Best do not render *firfhlaith* by anything more precise than 'prince'. 53 Their translation 'shall he be put to shame' corresponds to *do-géntar an col*, which is, more literally, 'shall the sin be committed' (cf. *TE* II.8: *An fer frisro dalusa ni ar c[h]ul no amleas tiacht ara c[h]ind*, 'The man with whom I have made a tryst, 'tis not for sin or hurt that the tryst has been made with him'). Since Étaín's first incarnation belonged to the period of the *Túatha Dé*, there may be an echo of the notion that the love-making of the gods was sinless, as in *TE* III.10: *combart cen pecadh cen chol*. For her, then, it might have been sinless, even though she refers to it as a sin (for Ailill alone?). 54 *TE* II.3. This is in *Y¹* and in *LU* but not in *Y¹*. 55 Herbert, 'Goddess and king', pp 270–2; Byrne, *Irish kings*, pp 74–5. 56 *TE* II.8: *domnai rig Erenn*; for the *damnae ríg* and *rígdamnae*, see B. Jaski, *Early Irish kingship and succession* (Dublin 2000) pp 236–47, and T.M.

what might have damaged his honour, was a rejection which would thus deny him the status of being 'one worthy to be king of Ireland'.

On the other hand, there is no suggestion that Étaín's willingness to have sexual relations with Ailill entailed an acceptance that he should replace Eochaid as king of Ireland. When Eochaid had returned from his circuit, so we are told, 'Étaín received warm thanks for what she had done until he had come again'.[57] This is somewhat more explicit in the later version in Egerton MS 1782, since it says that Eochaid questioned his brother and that Ailill told him the whole story from beginning to end, and it was then that Eochaid thanked his wife for what she had done.[58] Yet Eochaid would hardly have thanked Étaín if she had been willing to put Ailill in his place as king of Ireland. It seems best to regard Étaín's role as a sovereignty goddess as being something hovering on the margin of the story and as something which the reader or hearer was permitted but not required to invoke. The most that can be said is that the motif may here be linked with the status of 'one worthy to be king of Ireland', *damnae ríg Érenn*, rather than a king of Ireland, *rí Érenn*.

Another oddity in the story of Étaín is her response to the claim made by Midir that she should return to him, as her original, and moreover divine, husband. When she has been told that Midir had paid a bride-price for her, she asks him what is his name. He says that he is Midir of Brí Léith and explains that it was Fúamnach that parted them. But when he then says 'Will you go with me?' she replies simply, 'No, I will not sell the king of Ireland in exchange for a man of whose kindred and lineage I know nothing'.[59] The best she will say is that she will go with him if Eochaid tells her to do so.

I am not sure quite what is going on here. Why is it that Étaín, who was quite willing to sleep with Ailill, is so coy when it comes to returning to her first husband? A possible clue is the way the language of Étaín, and to some extent the others, echoes themes in the first part of the story. Étaín has to be sold rather than given; Midir seeks her with the performance of great tasks, just such tasks as his fosterson, Óengus, performed for the earlier Ailill, the king of Ulster, on Midir's behalf.[60] And when Midir does win her, it is through construing a part as a whole. Just as Óengus won Brug na Bóinne by gaining Elcmar's promise that he might rule there for a day and a night, so Midir won back Étaín by gaining Eochaid's promise that he might put his arms round Étaín and have a kiss from her.[61]

These echoes give a certain coherence to the whole story, but it is not obvious what they signify. What the story does is to suggest connections without specifying them. In order to try and establish quite what narrative coherence may be revealed by these verbal echoes, I propose to look first at the last major section of text, *Tochmarc Étaíne* III, in relation to the first; then we may take a second look at the middle tale, the story of Étaín's dealings with Ailill.

At the outset of the third subtale the position is, as we have seen, that Étaín has refused to 'sell the king of Ireland for a man whose kindred and lineage is not known'. This has echoed passages used in the first subtale, in the first place the occasion when Tríath refused to give way to Óengus, 'to a hireling whose mother or father were not known';[62] but, by contrast, it thereby pointed further, to the exalted lineage of the Dagda, Óengus and Midir. Just as the Dagda was compelled by Tríath's challenge to acknowledge Óengus and so reveal his high lineage, so now Étaín makes the same challenge to Midir. A man 'whose kindred and lineage is not known' is not the equal of Ailill Ánguba, 'worthy to be king of Ireland', let alone of the king of Ireland himself.

Charles-Edwards, *Early Irish and Welsh kinship*, pp 101–10.   **57** *TE* II.9.   **58** *Irische Texte*, ed. Windisch, i. p. 128. **59** *TE* II.8: *Noco ririub rí[g] nErenn ar fer na fedar clainn na cenel dó.*   **60** Cf. *TE* I.12–14 with III.5–8.   **61** *TE* III.9 and 15.   **62** *TE* I.4.

Yet her reply also mentioned 'selling the king of Ireland'; and, of course, she herself had been sold by her father to Midir.[63] By implication she perhaps challenges the validity of what had happened to her: she would be ashamed to do to Eochaid what her father did to her. The challenge is all the stronger because Midir staked his claim on the amplitude of the brideprice he had paid for her: 'I had paid your huge brideprice in the chief plains and streams of Ireland and had left in place of you your weight in gold and silver'.[64] Midir claims to have bought her; she, for her part, will not sell Eochaid. Yet she does not refuse Midir outright; instead she will go to him if Eochaid tells her to do so. The resolution of this challenge is the main subject of the third subtale.

Midir's tactic is to entice Eochaid into some gentle gambling over a game of 'chess', namely 'wood-cunning', *fidchell*. Midir turns up at Tara looking seriously handsome but with a shady pedigree, in more ways than one. Eochaid greets him courteously but evidently expects him to identify himself. After all, Eochaid was king of Ireland and was standing on the rampart of Tara; it was the duty of the inferior and the newcomer to identify himself to a superior and a host, so Eochaid's expectation was inevitable.[65] Midir, however, was notably slow to comply. Eochaid twice has to say he does not know him, and then, a third time, say outright, 'What is your name?' Only then does Midir reply: 'Not well known, Midir of Brí Léith'.[66] The gods of Ireland now pose as shady personages whose clothes are better than their lineages and their lands. Midir declares that he has come to play chess with Eochaid and the king agrees remarking that he is good at chess and will only play for a stake. Also, Eochaid says that the chess-board and pieces are in Étaín's chamber, and that she is asleep; but Midir rapidly says that he himself has brought an equally fine board and pieces, thus fit for the king of Ireland.

They begin by staking equal amounts on the outcome. Within these terms, Eochaid wins twice; Midir pays up with notable promptitude and, when complimented, remarks, with emphasis, 'That which is promised is a debt' – so echoing the Dagda's trapping of Elcmar of the Brug via an incautious promise.[67] But then his foster-father indirectly brings about Eochaid's downfall. This is interesting in itself: fosterage-relationships rescued Óengus and Midir, but they will now trap Eochaid:[68]

> 'You must take great care,' said his foster-father, 'for it is a man of great power who has come to you. Set him difficult tasks, my son.'

As a result, Midir imposed 'these famous great labours: clearing Mide of stones, putting rushes over Tethbae and a wood over Bréifne'. Once this had happened the nature of the matter had changed: it was no longer a stake that either of the two players might win or lose. Eochaid could no more have cleared Mide of stones than fly in the air. From Midir's standpoint it was a new round of tasks imposed before he could win Étaín, only now he had to perform them himself rather than through Óengus.

Eochaid won that round, but cheated on the condition imposed by Midir that no one should watch to see how the tasks were accomplished. (Within the story the cheating had no serious consequence, merely that defects were left in the togher.) When the next game was arranged he was manœuvred into agreeing to play for a stake that would not be specified until it was known

---

63 *TE* I.12.   **64** *TE* II.8. In fact, in our text 'the chief plains and streams' cleared by Óengus on behalf of Midir were not of Ireland but merely of Ulster.   **65** On this custom see T.M. Charles-Edwards, *Early Christian Ireland* (Cambridge 2000) pp 4–5.   **66** *TE* III.2.   **67** Cf. Ingcél Cáech's exploitation of the same debt-relationship: *Togail Bruidne Da Derga*, ed. Knott, ll. 639, 657 etc.   **68** *TE* III.5.

who had won; and that game was the one he lost. Midir could now stipulate that he should be allowed to put his arms round Étaín and have a kiss from her.[69]

All that was a matter between Eochaid and Midir. So far, therefore, Étaín was being treated as a pawn. Things were not quite so simple when Midir arrived to claim his due, just as Étaín was dispensing drink. Midir was greeted and replied that he had come for what had been promised him, adding, in an echo of his earlier remark, 'That which is promised is a debt'.[70] Eochaid replied, rather helplessly, 'I have not thought about that matter until now', to which Midir answered, 'Étaín has promised me herself that she would come to me.' She blushed before the whole company, which evoked from Midir the following plea:[71]

> 'Do not blush, Étaín,' said Midir. 'You have done nothing befitting an evil woman. I have spent a year seeking you with the loveliest gifts and treasures in Ireland, nor have I taken you until I had Eochaid's permission.'

The gifts and treasures in question here were what he gave Eochaid as a result of losing at chess, so that one might reasonably think that he was straining the truth a little. Yet it is true that once Eochaid had imposed the great tasks, he had left behind the moral economy of betting on a game of chess. If Eochaid had lost that game, he could not, as we have noted already, have performed any such tasks himself. In the terms of this tale, massive land-clearance is something only the gods can do (and hence it revealed that his lineage, however shady on the surface, was of the gods). Midir thus had some reason to interpret events as he now did. Yet he was still interpreting it all as bride-purchase.

Étaín's reply shows that she did not accept this interpretation at all:[72]

> 'I have said to you, that until Eochaid shall sell me, I shall not go to you. As for myself, you may take me if Eochaid will sell me.'
> 'But I will not sell you', said Eochaid, 'but let him put his arms about you just as you are in the middle of the house.'

From one point of view, Eochaid and Étaín are at one, but when Eochaid says, speaking to his wife, that Midir is to put his arms around her 'just as you are', one has to remember that Étaín was then serving the drink, a normal action for the woman of the house (as in the opening passage of *Longes mac nUislenn*) but also an action capable of being interpreted as serving 'the ales of sovereignty'.

In this version of the story (as opposed to the significantly different one implied, for example, by one of the Dindshenchas poems, itself quoted in *TE* III.5) this moment is decisive.[73] In the poem Eochaid eventually won back his wife, but in our text he lost her for ever at this point. Moreover, if we take both our text and the others in the same overall narrative continuum, it becomes apparent that the story was not fixed. Our text places this incident, when Midir takes Étaín in spite of Eochaid, in Tara; the Dindshenchas poem places it in Frémainn; according to our text Eochaid sought Étaín from Étar in Ulster; according to *Togail Bruidne Da Derga*, Eochaid Feidlech (not Eochaid Airem) met her at Brí Léith, namely Midir's home, and never had anything

---

69 *TE* III.9. **70** Cf. *TE* III.14 with III.3. **71** *TE* III.14. **72** Ibid. **73** The poem on Ráith Ésa, *Metrical Dindshenchas*, ed. E.J. Gwynn (Dublin 1903–35; repr. 1991) ii. pp 2–9, in which, moreover, the great tasks performed by Midir were part of Eochaid's honour-price for the abduction of Étaín. For yet another version, in which it is Eterscél who digs up Brí Léith and secures the delivery of Ess, daughter of Eochaid Airem and Étaín, see *De Shíl Chonairi Móir*, ed. L. Gwynn, *Ériu* 6 (1912) p. 133.

to do with her father, named Étar but ascribed to the *síd* rather than to Ulster.[74] Some differences are trivial, but whether or not Eochaid ever recovered Étaín from Midir determines the whole shape of the story; and, given the fluidity of the narrative tradition as a whole, the choice made between one development and another would have appeared all the more striking to an informed reader or hearer.[75]

The reason why Eochaid lost Étaín for ever at this point is not evident, but there are enough clues to make a suggestion. While Eochaid holds firm, so does Étaín. Once, however, he allows that Midir has secured the right to embrace Étaín, it appears that she is willing to return to her former husband. One might wonder whether she finally recognizes him when they embrace, but there is no evidence that this is so. In this story she is faithful to Eochaid in the sense that she will not desert him for Midir as long as he remains adamant that she should be his and no one else's. Once he weakens in that resolve and allows them to embrace, she takes that to be tantamount to abandoning her. One might argue that, once another claimant is allowed by a king to embrace sovereignty, that king has effectively forfeited his rights as the husband of the goddess.

A rather different, and perhaps preferable, interpretation stems from the use within the tale of the language of bride-purchase. This is just as explicit when Midir is claiming to have bought Étaín from Eochaid as it was when Óengus, on behalf of Midir, was buying her from her father, Ailill, king of Ulster. The very same verbs, *renaid*, 'sells', and *crenaid*, 'buys', can be applied when a man is buying another man's wife as when he is buying an unmarried girl from her father and kindred.[76] That the person claimed to have sold her was her father in the one case and her husband in the other makes no difference. According to the presuppositions of the text, therefore, a father can sell his daughter to a bridegroom and thereby forfeit rights of protection over her; similarly, a husband may sell his wife to another man, though perhaps only if she were sold to him in the first place. So far the legal presuppositions of the text have a connection with what we know of early Irish law, at least in so far as bride-purchase was one, but only one, recognized form of marital union.[77] Where they add new information is in the effect bride-purchase has on the rights of her natal kin and in revealing that the purchase could be made of the wife of a husband as much as of the daughter of a father. None of this affects the rights of the woman concerned, at least within the terms of our text: Étaín's consent must be obtained by Midir; it is not enough to manœuvre Eochaid into selling his wife.

A further assumption would make the interpretation of the text easier. It looks as though the demand made by Midir when he won the last game of chess may have had a formal significance. It was crucial that the stake won by Midir should not have been specified in advance. Eochaid's reaction when Midir did specify it ('My arms around Étaín and a kiss from her', *TE* III.9) was to fall silent and only then to say that Midir should come in a month's time to receive his due. When the text explains Midir's tactics, it suggests that, when the pledge was specified, it amounted to

---

74 In *Togail Bruidne Da Derga*, this was because their union was of quite a different character, since she gave herself to Eochaid in preference to other suitors, ed. Knott, § 3, very much as Rhiannon gave herself to Pwyll in preference to the suitor preferred by her father: *Pedeir Keinc y Mabinogi*, ed. I. Williams (Cardiff 1930) p. 12. For the lesser status of the union by which a woman gave herself to a man, see *Cáin Lánamna*, ed. and trans. Thurneysen, in D.A. Binchy (ed.), *Studies in early Irish law* (Dublin 1936) § 33, pp 63–8, and T.M. Charles-Edwards, 'Nau Kynywedi Teithiauc', in D. Jenkins and M.E. Owen (ed.), *The Welsh law of women* (Cardiff 1980) pp 30–2. **75** Compare the variants in *TE* itself, I.23, 26; III.21–3. **76** For purchase from the father, *crenaid* is used in *TE* I.12; for the husband selling, *renaid* is used in *TE* III.14–15, 17; the noun *lóg*, *lúag* 'price' is used in *TE* II.8 (*do shárlugaib* for *do shárluagaib* as the variant readings indicate). **77** Thurneysen, 'Heirat', in Binchy (ed.), *Studies in early Irish law*, pp 112–25.

Midir obtaining Étaín from her husband.[78] We can explain Midir's behaviour and his assertions that he has bought Étaín if there is a further presupposition, namely that when a husband sold his wife to another man, the decisive ritual act that sealed the transaction was that the new husband embraced the woman and kissed her.

All this depends, however, on treating the great tasks imposed by Eochaid on Midir as bride-purchase. Here there is a direct clash between the position adopted by Eochaid and that taken by Midir. Eochaid declares to Étaín, 'I will not sell you indeed'; but subsequently Midir says to him, 'You did sell your wife to me.'[79] The reader is encouraged to adopt Midir's standpoint by the resemblance between the great tasks performed by Óengus in *TE* I and those performed by Midir in *TE* III. Yet there are two issues which have to be confused if Midir's position is to be entirely persuasive. On the interpretation advanced above, Eochaid lost Étaín because he lost the last game of chess, and because that game was for an unspecified stake. The great tasks were performed by Midir because he had lost the previous game of chess. There was no intrinsic legal relationship between the one game of chess and the other. Yet Midir's position requires us to take the great tasks he performed after the earlier game, and regard them as bride-purchase, while taking the result of the next game, that Midir might embrace and kiss Étaín, as a formal act sealing the transaction of bride-purchase. There is no reason why the reader should suppose that Midir, who, like the Dagda earlier, is plainly arguing in terms of Old Irish law, must have had a watertight argument. The very gap in his reasoning moves the narrative forward.

Within the text itself, this clash of interpretations between Midir and Eochaid as to whether Étaín has or has not been sold is resolved by a further formal agreement between them, by which Eochaid accepted that, if his wife came to him at the third hour of the next day, he would renounce all claims and actions against Midir.[80] In the event, she did come, but only as one of fifty women all resembling Étaín. Eochaid chose the one who turned out to be his own daughter by Étaín.

The Wooing of Étaín works on several levels. There is the level of ordinary human sympathies, as in the second main section, the love-sickness of Ailill, when Étaín is left behind as Eochaid goes off on circuit to enjoy his new kingship. His new wife is expected to care for Ailill as he sinks closer to death and to see to his mourning when dead. Her sympathy for one worthy to be king of Ireland may perhaps be divine, an attitude proper to a goddess of sovereignty, but it is also human. The echoes of *TE* I contained in *TE* III convey to the reader Midir's view of the situation, a divine view which necessarily remained more or less inaccessible to the human actors within the narrative. In yet another way the narrative works in the sphere of close bargaining and cunning schemes, the sphere of nice calculation, as Midir shepherds the proud king of Ireland towards catastrophic loss or when he gives Eochaid the chance to regain Étaín on condition that he gives sureties that he will never attack Brí Léith again.[81] God though he may be, Midir has to struggle with ordinary human law, not always with complete success, in order to recover his wife. In the person of Étaín, the narrative binds together the world of gods and the world of men, not in terms

---

78 Reading the last sentence of *TE* III.10 together with the first two of III.11.   **79** 'Nid ririubsa immurgu', *TE* III.15; 'Ro renais do mnai frim', *TE* III.17.   **80** The legal nature of the agreement is indicated by the phrases, 'Atumo' = atmu (spoken by Eochaid) and *Naiscis Midir a curu*, *TE* III.17. Cf. *Táin Bó Cúailnge, Recension I*, ed. C. O'Rahilly (Dublin 1976) pp 14–15 (ll. 447–54); *Berrad Airechta*, §§ 51, 57, and, for comment, R. Chapman Stacey, *The road to judgment: from custom to court in medieval Ireland and Wales* (Philadelphia 1994) pp 34–8. The reason why *TE* and *TBC* use the verb atmu (to ad-daim), rather than aicdiu (to ad-guid) as in *Berrad Airechta*, is that atmu is the reply of someone accepting a legal position rather than the act of calling on someone else to appoint a surety. *TE* and *TBC* thus offer helpful supplements to our knowledge about Irish suretyship.   **81** *TE* III.17 (and cf. the beginning of 20).

of some ancient agreement that the gods should have Ireland below ground while men had Ireland above ground, but in the sharper terms of competition for a woman's trust. However clever Midir's pursuit of his former wife, he recovered Étaín because Eochaid deliberately weakened his hold on her and because she was willing to go with him, not because Étaín passively accepted that, yet again, she had been bought.

The learned borrowings claimed for *Táin Bó Fraích*

DEWI WYN EVANS

In a 1956 article entitled 'The Ecclesiastic Background to Irish Saga' (hereafter *EBIS*), James Carney claimed that:

> There is no early Irish saga extant which has not some obvious mark of either learned origin or treatment. But in one particular saga, *Táin Bó Fraích*, written it is thought in the early eighth century, the learned element is so extensive that the saga as a whole can best be considered as a pastiche of various pieces of ecclesiastical writing.[1]

Táin Bó Fraích (TBF) also plays a central role in Carney's *Studies in Irish Literature and History* (hereafter SILH), published in 1955, in which it is argued at much greater length that the early Irish tales extant in manuscripts had had no previous existence in oral tradition, and were rather the written compositions of ecclesiastics, adapted to a great extent from foreign originals.[2]

'This book,' wrote one reviewer, 'is written in a deeply personal style, which becomes infused with a polemical warmth whenever the views expounded in it are not in agreement with those of earlier writers in the same field'.[3] Many years later Carney defended the tone of the work by explaining that, 'When it was written Irish scholarship was dominated by two frustrating, oppressive and powerful orthodoxies, one concerning the nature of early Irish saga, the other concerning the date, career and personality of St Patrick. This book was a perhaps overstrong rebellion against both of these deeply entrenched orthodoxies.'[4]

Where Carney portrays the 'orthodox' position regarding the tales, the descriptions not uncommonly verge on caricature:

> [I] oppose in a general way the common habit exemplified here of denying, or severely limiting, the artistic, individual, and creative achievement of mediaeval authors, especially when they have the misfortune to be anonymous. Modern writers on this subject all too commonly think in terms of 'compilers'. Denial of authorship is made, not always by downright and deliberate statement, but by the use of suggestive impersonal terms. A saga 'comes into being' by some vague process involving the communal will and the creative desire of the 'folk' and has a long life in a wild state to describe which biological terms are

---

1 In A. Furumark et al. (eds), *Artica: Essays presented to Åke Campbell*, Studia ethnographica Upsaliensia 11 (Uppsala 1956) pp 221–7, p. 221.   2 As well as being the focus of the book's opening and longest chapter, TBF also plays an important part in a number of the following analyses, and conclusions drawn about it are used to bolster the arguments made about other tales. It was Carney's opinion that his 'examination of *Táin Bó Fraích* will enable us to make many generalisations with regard to the origin and development of early Irish saga' (*EBIS*, p. 226). See also his remarks in the introduction to E. Knott and G. Murphy, *Early Irish Literature* (London 1966) p. 17.   3 C.R. Ó Cléirigh, *IHS* 11 (1958/9) pp 160–70, p. 161.   4 'Early Irish literature: the state of research', in *Proceedings of the Sixth International Congress of Celtic Studies*, ed. G. Mac Eoin (Galway 1983) pp 113–30, pp 127–8. He adds (p. 128): 'I would hold to most of what I wrote about *Táin Bó Froích*.'

invariably used: hence the saga 'spreads', 'creeps', 'shoots forth' until it is finally 'domesticated', that is, given literary form at a particular time and in a particular place, thus entering on that phase of its existence where literary terms may be substituted for biological.[5]

Underlying (and undermining) Carney's whole approach is his polarization – and thus over-simplification – of possible approaches to the texts, and his antipathy towards the oral tradition which prevents any semblance of an even-handed discussion. His exclusive focus on the literate individual engaged in the deliberate synthesis of written texts, and his general dismissal of the likelihood that any amalgamation of sources occurred over a period of time, and on the oral as well as the written medium, is to my mind a serious failing.[6]

It is not my intention here to review the native / external debate in general, nor even to discuss the possible ecclesiastical contribution to TBF, but merely to consider critically the plausibility of Carney's analysis of the tale, and to bring together some of the objections which others have raised concerning it.

TBF is in Carney's opinion a written tale composed by an ecclesiastic, who based its title on (the written) *Táin Bó Cuailnge*, where he also found some of the characters and the general background.[7] He discerns examples of direct borrowing from six other written sources, five of them in Latin. For convenience I shall summarise the tale's main events.

> Froech son of Idath of the Connachta and Bé Find from the Otherworld hears that Findabair, daughter of Ailill and Medb, loves him due to his great renown. Bearing wondrous gifts given to him by his Otherworld aunt Boand, he travels with a magnificent entourage to Cruachain in the hope of meeting her. They are made welcome. Ailill and Medb play *fidchell*, and then Froech does likewise with one of his people. Medb then plays against Froech, and his harpers provide music while his people prepare dinner. Due to the brightness of the precious stones in Froech's company, Medb continues playing until three days and nights have elapsed unbeknown to her. On hearing that so much time has passed she orders food to be prepared for the warriors, and the feast lasts for three days and three nights. Froech is then asked the purpose of his journey, and he answers that it was to visit them. After a fortnight spent hunting Froech manages to talk with Findabair and asks her to elope with him, but she tells him to ask for her hand, giving him a ring as a token between them.
>
> Suspecting the two are fond of each other, Ailill is favourable to the match, but seeks an unreasonably high bride price which Froech refuses to pay. Fearing a great battle if Froech carry off Findabair by force, Ailill plans that he be killed in what will seem an accident.

---

5 From a review of Carl Selmer's edition of *Navigatio sancti Brendani Abbatis* in *Medium Aevum* 32 (1963) pp 37–44, p. 39. The most relevant pages of *SILH* for Carney's conception of the early tales' background are pp 77–8, 191–92, 276–79, 321–3. Though he rails against the 'nativist' conception of early Irish literature, he admits (*SILH*, p. 280) that 'It is not possible for me to point to any outstanding contemporary work on the subject where faulty assumptions such as those I have referred to are made'.   **6** For a very caustic response to Carney's approach see Howard Meroney's review of *SILH* in *Journal of Celtic Studies* 2 (1958) pp 238–42. It appears that Carney's adoption of his 'anti-nativist' stance was largely 'a result of his reading one particular book – E.R. Curtius's *European literature and the Latin middle ages*' according to Terence McCaughey in 'James Patrick Carney', *Celtica* 23 (1999) pp 188–92, p. 188.   **7** The improbability of this scenario is made clear by Donald E. Meek in his two-part article, '*Táin Bó Fraích* and other "Fráech" texts: a study in thematic relationships' in *CMCS* 7 (1984) pp 1–37, and 8 (1984) pp 65–85. This detailed work is indispensable for a proper consideration of TBF within the broader tradition.

After a morning's hunting, Ailill asks Froech to display his skills as a swimmer in the river, and when he does so Ailill opens Froech's purse and discovers the ring. He throws it into the river and Froech sees a salmon swallowing it. He catches the fish and hides it on the bank. As he is about to get out of the water Ailill asks him to swim to the rowan tree growing on the opposite bank and to bring him a branch, as the berries are so beautiful. Froech does so, and is asked for yet more. As he returns he is attacked by a water monster, and owing to the general fear of arousing Ailill's displeasure, his appeal for his sword goes unheeded until Findabair dives into the water with it. Ailill throws a spear at her which goes through a plait of her hair before being caught by Froech and thrown back so that it pierces Ailill's clothes without, however, injuring him. With the sword Froech beheads the monster.

Ailill and Medb are ashamed of their behaviour towards Froech, and have a curative bath prepared for him, but Ailill vows he will punish Findabair. After being bathed Froech is borne away by women from the Otherworld and returns the following evening fully healed. Ailill and Medb apologize for having maltreated him, they are reconciled and begin to feast. Foreseeing that the ring will be demanded of Findabair, Froech sends a boy to fetch the salmon and give it to her. Later on that evening Ailill orders that his treasures be displayed, and tells Findabair to show the ring. She claims to be unable to find it, and the incensed Ailill threatens to kill her if it isn't produced. She finally relents, and it is brought in to the amazement of Ailill and Medb.

Froech feigns surprise and checks his purse, and Ailill explains that he had found the ring there, recognized it as his own, and, realizing that it had been given away by Findabair, threw it into the river. He then asks for an explanation of how it was retrieved. Froech's answer is that he originally discovered the ring on the ground, and that when he later saw Findabair searching for it, asked her what she would give him if he found it, and was promised her love for a year. He had it in his lodgings at the time, and before he had the chance to meet her again he saw Ailill open his purse and throw it into the river. He saw a salmon swallow it, and he caught the fish and returned the ring. Findabair says she will have no other man but him, and it is agreed that after bringing his cows to the driving of the cattle from Cuailnge, Froech will sleep with Findabair.

Froech sets off for his own lands the following day, and on his arrival is told that his sons, his wife and most of his cattle have been seized and taken to the Alps, while three of his cows are in the lands of the Picts. Accompanied by Conall Cernach, Froech and his men cross the land of the Langobards and reach the Alps. With the aid of two women of Irish descent they attack the dwelling of the raider-king. The fearsome serpent which guards it leaps into Conall Cernach's belt, and the fort is destroyed and looted, and Froech's family freed. The serpent is then released unharmed and having caused no injury. The three cows from the land of the Picts are recaptured on the return journey to Ireland, and Froech then sets out to drive the cattle from Cuailnge.

The first scene in which Carney discerns an obvious borrowing is when Medb and Froech play *fidchell*:

> In TBF the hero's company carries spears adorned with carbuncle. The jewels used to light up the night as if they were sunbeams. The hero and the queen spend three days and three nights playing the board-game called *fidchell*. No food is served and they fail to note that

night has come three times on account of the bright light of the precious stones which illumines the darkness.

   This situation is borrowed in part from a life of St. Brigit, and in part from Isidore of Seville … Just as Froech in this episode visits the household of Medb, so in the religious tale Patrick visits that of Brigit. Patrick, instead of playing *fidchell*, preaches the word of God for three days and three nights, and meanwhile nobody hungers and the sun does not set.

   The author of TBF borrowed this incident, but he could not use the miraculous portion of it, the failure of the sun to set: Christian miracles could not be transferred back to the pagan Irish past. He had, however, to find some equivalent for the miracle, something that would have the same effect, but of which there would be a natural explanation. He found this in the great compendium of the knowledge of that age, the *Etymologiae* of Isidore of Seville. Isidore, in dealing with the precious stone called *carbunculus* associates it etymologically with *carbo*, coal: it is not conquered by night, he tells us, it lights up the darkness so that it causes flames to flicker before the eyes. This passage in the *Etymologiae* gave the author of TBF the mechanism whereby he could allow his characters to sit together for three days and three nights, without noting that night had come.[8]

I find this strained and thoroughly unconvincing. There is hardly any similarity between the present scene and that in Brigit's life other than the passing of a period of three days. In the religious story the day is prolonged due to divine intervention, but here the distinction between day and night is blurred by the brilliance of the precious stones in Froech's company (a detail which dramatically demonstrates his riches and status). Froech is fully aware that what Medb considered a very long day had in fact been three. Carney does not attempt to explain why what he sees as similarities are indeed borrowings, and the premise that such extraordinary and unrealistic events are best explained as 'suppressed miracles', to use his own phrase,[9] strikes me as completely misconceived. As Wolfgang Meid has noted, in *Tochmarc Étaíne* the Dagda's powers keep darkness, thirst and hunger away from Elcmar for a whole nine months, which pass by like a single day.[10]

   Despite Carney's implicit suggestion that it was the carbuncle which caused the change between day and night to pass by unnoticed, the text does not bear this out, but states rather that it was due to the abundance of precious stones. The only reference to carbuncle comes in fact before Froech sets out for Cruachain, when the gifts he received from his otherworld aunt are enumerated. These include:

Coíca scíath n-argdide co n-imlib óir impu, 7 caindel rígthigi i lláim cech áe, 7 coíca semmand findruine ar cech n-áe. Coíca toracht di ór forloiscthi im cech n-áe. Eirmitiuda di charrmocul fóib anís, 7 is di lecaib lógmairib a n-airíarn. No lastais in aidche amal betís ruithni gréni.[11]	Fifty silver shields with rims of gold. And a candle of a king's house (i.e. a spear) in the hand of each of them, each having rivets of white bronze, and fifty bands of burnished gold; the spikes below were of carbuncle and the heads were of precious stones. They used to blaze at night as if they were sunbeams.[12]

---

8 *SILH* pp 82–3. See also p. 34. Carney does not discuss the Latin text at all, and only summarises what he sees as correspondences in a footnote on p. 83. See also *EBIS* pp 222–3. For the Latin life of Brigit see Michael Lapidge and Richard Sharpe, *A bibliography of Celtic-Latin literature 400–1200* (Dublin 1985) item 342, p. 102.   **9** *SILH* p. 82.   **10** *Táin Bó Fraích*, ed. W. Meid (Dublin 1974) [hereafter *TBF2*], p. 32. All quotations from the text are taken from this edition.   **11** *TBF2* pp 1–2 (lines 20–26).   **12** *SILH* pp 1–2. Except for one example noted below I

The references to the unnoticed passing of time are:

Bátar tri láa 7 téora aidche oc imbirt na fidchille la immed na lliac lógmar i tegluch Froích.[13]	They were three days and nights playing chess on account of the wealth of precious stones amongst the company of Froech.[14]
'Atát tri láa 7 téora aidchi and', ol sisi, 'acht nád n-airigmer in n-aidchi la bánṡuilsi inna líac lógmar issin tig.'[15]	'Three days and three nights have gone by,' she said, 'but that we did not notice the night with the bright light of the precious stones in the house.'[16]

Meid has noted examples in *Fled Bricrend* and *Dindsenchas Rennes* of this idea of metals and precious stones making night appear like day, the latter significantly containing no mention of carbuncle. He comes to the conclusion that, 'In view of the fact that the same motif, in a similar setting, occurs also elsewhere in early Irish literature, it is more probable that the author took it from the stream of common tradition of which it was part'.[17]

Though it provides the tale with its title, the final section of TBF where Froech travels to regain his family and cattle, is, as many commentators have observed, a somewhat awkward addendum to the main events. Here Carney sees one obvious borrowing:

> In *Táin Bó Fraích* Conall Cernach and Froech go on an expedition to the region of 'the Alps in the northern territory of the Langobards'. The purpose of the expedition is to recover Froech's wife, sons and cattle, which have been stolen by the king of that territory. During their journey, and on their arrival, they receive warnings that they will have to encounter a dangerous serpent. The serpent guards a fortress or dwelling (*dún*) and has made the lands about inhabitable. Finally when they encounter the serpent there is an anticlimax which at first sight seems inexplicable. The serpent offered no opposition and we are weakly told that it jumped into the belt or girdle (*criss*) of Conall Cernach and neither harmed the other.[18]

This, he affirms, is an adaptation from the Life of Saint Samson of Dol:

> St Samson at the instance of a prince decides to go against a venomous serpent that lives in a cave and makes two territories uninhabitable. A youth accompanies St Samson and they have to cross a river to get at the cave. The serpent is terrified when it sees St Samson and wishes to escape. But the saint takes his *girdle* and places it upon the serpent's neck, drags it after him and throws it over a cliff.

---

quote from Carney's translation of the tale. A list of translations and modernizations is given in J.P. Mallory and R. Ó hUiginn, 'The Ulster cycles: a check list of translations' in *Ulidia: Proceedings of the First International Conference on the Ulster Cycle of Tales*, ed. J.P. Mallory and G. Stockman (Belfast 1994) pp 291–303, p. 300. To these can be added C. Ó Cadhlaigh, 'Táin Bó Fraoigh' in *An Rúraíocht* (Baile Átha Cliath 1956) pp 253–62 and Ciarán Ó Coigligh, 'Táin Bó Fraoích' in *Mangarae: Aistí Litríochta agus Teanga* (Cathair na Mart 1987) pp 112–23. **13** *TBF2* p. 5, lines 119–20. **14** *SILH* p. 5. **15** *TBF2* p. 5, lines 131–32. **16** *SILH* p. 5. **17** *TBF2* p. 33. The word *carrmocul* does, of course, come from Latin, and the rejection of Carney's claim of direct textual borrowing does not imply that its adoption among the dazzling gems cannot be due to an ecclesiastic. Meid, op. cit., adds that the fact that it is included in Isidore 'suggests that it was common knowledge, being at least as old as Herodotus (cp. II 44)'. **18** *EBIS* p. 224. See also *SILH* pp 123–4.

There can be little doubt but that this incident in the life of St Samson is the source of the corresponding incident in TBF.[19]

How the 'inexplicable' episode in the Irish text is made more explicable by reference to the Latin *vita* remains unclear to me, and I can see no reason for positing that we have here any particular similarities, let alone a borrowing. Meid too doubts the relevance of the comparison: 'The resemblance between the two texts is so superficial … that it is not very likely that this particular life has been the direct source of the incident in TBF'.[20]

It is, of course, more than probable that the introduction of the Langobards is an ecclesiastic's contribution, and Donald Meek (and others) have noted the interesting point that Froech's route 'follows one of the main monastic pathways from Ireland to the Continent in the Dark Ages'.[21]

Carney detected the most extensive borrowings by far in the portion of TBF which deals with the wooing of Findabair. The sources he cites are:

(a) The story of Rhydderch's Ring from an early vita of Saint Kentigern, preserved at second hand in Jocelin's twelfth century life of the saint [RhR].

> King Rhydderch gives his wife a ring as a special mark of conjugal love, but she in turn gives it to her lover, a soldier. The king learns of this, and after a day's hunting when the soldier is asleep, obtains the ring and throws it into the River Clyde. He then demands that his wife produce the ring, and when she fails, imprisons her and sentences her to death. God takes pity on her and directs her to send a messenger to Saint Kentigern, who bids the messenger bring him the first fish he catches from the river. The ring is found in the salmon which is caught, the queen is saved, and is thereafter an exemplary wife.

(b) *Aided Fergusa maicc Róig*, The Death of Fergus mac Róig [AF].

> A number of men are swimming in a lake, and Ailill urges Fergus to enter the water. Medb joins him, and entwines herself around him. Ailill becomes intensely jealous and deceives his blind brother Lugaid, who never missed with the spear, into casting at Fergus, who is mortally wounded. Before dying he throws back the spear at the fleeing Ailill, killing a hunting dog in his chariot.

(c) An episode from Book II, chapter 27 of Adomnán's *Vita Columbae* [VC].

> Columba wishes to cross a river where a monster lives. He orders one of his followers to swim to the opposite bank to fetch a boat, but in the middle of the water he is attacked by the monster. Due to the saint's prayers the monster takes flight.

19 *SILH* pp 123–4. For the *vita*, see Lapidge and Sharpe, op. cit., item 951, pp 261–2. The relevant passage is quoted in a footnote in *SILH* pp 123–4. See also p. 58. Another borrowing from the same source is claimed in *SILH* pp 124–5 where Samson gets rid of a different monster by placing a cloak on its neck and exiling it. As this is not even mentioned in the slightly later *EBIS* it will not be considered here.   **20** *TBF2* p. 44. A very different interpretation to Carney's was offered by Anne Ross in her *Pagan Celtic Britain* (London and New York 1967) pp 149–54, where Conall Cernach is identified with the Celtic god Cernunnos. See also Donald Meek, op. cit., pp 68–9.   **21** Op. cit. p. 70. Comparisons with other texts suggest to him that it would be reasonable to suppose that 'the original expedition may have been to the Otherworld, and not to any recognizable country' (p. 71). The three cows of

It is Carney's view that the author of TBF combined elements from these three sources and adapted them to an Irish background and to characters who already had a certain stability in Irish tradition. The framework was borrowed from Rhydderch's Ring, but as Ailill was a weaker character than Medb in existing tradition, it would not permit him to condemn his wife to death, and therefore her place is taken by his daughter Findabair.[22] The disparate elements were combined thus:

- A man receives a ring as a token of love from a woman who has received it from a king [RhR]
- Ailill gets a man to display his skill as a swimmer [AF]
- A ring is thrown to a river and is swallowed by a salmon [RhR]
- A sea monster attacks a man in the middle of the water [VC]
- When the lovers are together in the water, a spear is thrown at them [AF]
- The ring appears and the woman's life is spared [RhR]

Carney sees TBF's dependence on these compositions revealed by a series of unmotivated incidents, which derive from the author's failure to integrate fully his disparate sources. While I personally find it extremely difficult to believe that any work of literature is composed in such a mechanical manner, the claims will be looked at in more detail.

Rhydderch's Ring

> In the story of Rhydderch's Ring we have a closely analogous situation to that which we find in TBF. The king, Rhydderch, gives his wife a ring *in signum conjugalis amoris*. The queen gives the ring to her lover. The king, after a day's hunting rests with the queen's lover by the river Clyde. While the lover sleeps the king secretly takes the ring and throws it into the river. Later in the presence of the court he demands from the queen that she should tell where was the ring he had given her for safekeeping (*ubi anulus suus ad custodiam ei commendatus esset*). The queen fails to produce the ring and is condemned to death. She sends a messenger to St. Kentigern acquainting him with her plight. Kentigern sends the messenger to the river Clyde ... telling him to bring the first fish he should catch. A salmon is caught, the ring is found and the queen is saved ...
>
> The close similarity in detail between TBF and the story of Rhydderch's ring points, not to a vague collateral relationship, but to the direct dependence of the former upon the latter.[23]

A formidable difficulty here is that TBF, whose earliest written form is usually dated to the eighth century, is seen as having a direct dependence on Jocelin's twelfth century text. While Carney would date Jocelin's sources to the seventh century, he offers no evidence to support this.[24]

Froech's which end up in the land of the Picts are quite possibly the remnants of an incompletely suppressed variant tradition. Heinrich Zimmer believed that the continental journey arose due to a misunderstanding of *Alba* (Britain/ Scotland) and *Alpu* (the Alps): 'Keltische Beiträge I' in *Zeitschrift für deutsches Altertum und deutsche Literatur* 32 (1888) pp 196–334, pp 256–63. See also David Dumville, 'Ireland and Britain in *Táin Bó Fraích*' in *ÉtC* 32 (1996) pp 175–87.   **22** Somewhat unfortunately for this argument, it is Ailill, as Carney himself noticed in *SILH* pp 64–5, who is by far the more important character of the two in TBF.   **23** *SILH* pp 37–8.   **24** Carney writes (*SILH* p. 79): 'The text of this episode is of course twelfth century, and was written by Jocelin of Furness. But some general stylistic considerations show that Jocelin has presented his early sources verbatim or nearly so. The fact that

Kenneth Jackson, having made a detailed study of what Jocelin's raw materials are likely to have been, firmly rejects the claims that the story of Rhydderch's Ring, and another episode claimed by Carney to have been borrowed in *Tromdám Guaire*, derive from an early life of the saint:

> The conclusion is, I believe, that nothing remotely like the Life of St Kentigern in the form we see it in Jocelyn existed so early as the seventh century, or probably before the eleventh; that the two motifs in question got into the Kentigern material in the eleventh century, as part of a secondary appendix of a hotch-potch of Kentigern's miracles deriving from popular tales and 'religious folklore' of a predominantly 'Gaelic' background; and that the idea that the whole thing goes back almost to living memory of Kentigern himself is neither proven nor probable.[25]

Though the story of a ring which is swallowed by a fish and later recovered is, in Carney's own words, 'commonly known to folklorists as the "Ring of Polycrates" motif',[26] the possibility that the motif had entered and become part of the oral tradition is regrettably not seriously considered.[27]

Aided Fergusa

Particular similarities here are that Ailill urges Fergus to enter the water, as he does Froech in TBF. In both tales a spear is thrown back, which just misses Ailill. Carney also sees as significant the verbal resemblances in Ailill's words. In AF he says of the swimmers: *nit maithi i n-uisciu* 'they are not good in water', and in TBF he tells Froech, *Adfiadar dam at maith i n-uisciu* 'I am told that you are good in water'.

Carney's opinion that 'There can be no question of incidental resemblance' between these episodes seems reasonable. Though there are certainly many differences between them, there are also undoubted similarities. But while Carney was of the view that TBF borrowed from AF, Thurneysen believed the exact opposite to be the case.[28] One cannot easily refute the claim that we are here dealing with a direct written borrowing (in either direction), but one can hardly demonstrate it either, and the alternative that we have here an episode from the oral tradition used to different purposes in the two tales is at least as attractive a proposition.[29]

Though written in reference to another of Carney's claims, Jackson's words are also relevant in the present context:

> The argument depends on the assumption that if two versions of a story exist, closely similar to one another in their plot, the one must be derived directly from the other. Now, it is well

the present episode can be shown to be a source of TBF is evidence of a seventh century date.' As C.R. Ó Cléirigh noted op. cit. p. 167, 'To quote TBF to prove the antiquity of *Vita Kentegerni*, which has already been postulated as a source of TBF (ch.1) is nothing less than arguing in a circle'. Or in Jackson's words: 'This is the familiar fallacy of assuming what one wishes to prove', 'The sources for the Life of St Kentigern' in N.K. Chadwick et al. (eds), *Studies in the early British Church* (Cambridge 1958) pp 273–357, p. 350 n. **25** Jackson, op. cit. p. 356. **26** *SILH* p. 42. **27** The motif is found in other early texts from Ireland: see T.P. Cross, *Motif-index of early Irish literature* (Indiana 1952) p. 407, and it is quite possible that it was originally introduced into Ireland by an ecclesiastic who had come across it in his reading. On its international distribution see the sources noted by Jackson, op. cit. p. 322. A Welsh parallel is given in T. Jones, 'Gwraig Maelgwn Gwynedd a'r Fodrwy', *BBCS* 18 (1958) pp 55–8. **28** R. Thurneysen, *Die irische Helden- und Königsage bis zum 17. Jahrhundert* (Halle 1921) p. 575. **29** In his review of Thurneysen's *Heldensage* in *ZCP* 14 (1923) pp 299–305, pp 303–4, Wolfgang Schulz, who notes wider parallels to the two scenes, also rejects the suggestion of simple borrowing.

known nowadays that among peoples possessing a rich oral literature, stories – not merely their broad outlines, or single motifs, but complex tales preserving an intricate plot – migrate freely; and that before one can assert that version I is derived directly from version II, rather than both from a more distant third one now lost, it is necessary to produce some very strong and particular reason to think so. In the absence of such reason the only sound assumption is that though admittedly connected, and perhaps closely, the one known version cannot be proved to come straight from the other; that we have no right to claim that it does; and that the hypothesis of the lost common original must, as a matter of method, take precedence.[30]

Vita Columbae

A swimmer is sent to seek something on the opposite bank of a lake in the two tales, and he is attacked by a monster, but saved. Carney sees it as significant that Findabair, despite Froech's dire straits, firstly disrobes before plunging into the water: a lazy adaptation of VC where there is a description of the saint's follower undressing before entering the water.

In Gerard Murphy's view, the argument here 'will hardly convince anyone who is not initially prejudiced in favour of tracing as much as possible in the story to saints' lives'.[31] It is rejected as well by Jacqueline Borsje,[32] and seems implausible to me also. It is difficult to see any close affinity between the episodes, which are completely different in atmosphere and quite dissimilar in incident.

While I cannot agree with Carney's view that the tale can be best explained as the composition of a literary author scouring his Latin reading in order to create an Irish heroic tale, an examination of his objections to TBF as it stands is, I believe, of some value:

> This tale is awkwardly composed. One may ask such questions as: why did the king, who every moment expected the monster to attack Froech, and who presumably had his eyes fixed upon the swimming hero, fail to see Froech catch the salmon and hide it in 'a secret place'? Why does Ailill condemn his daughter to death for the loss of a valuable ring? This is not merely an inexplicably harsh attitude, but also quite inconsistent with his resumption of friendly relations with Froech. Why does Froech indulge in unnecessary heroics, offering to ransom the girl with his most valuable possessions when he knows that [s]he can produce the ring and subsequently does so? Why did Ailill, in the first place, give his daughter a ring 'for safe-keeping' (*dia taiscid*)?[33]

I shall try to reply to each of these questions, taking them in a slightly different order:

1. 'Why did the king, who every moment expected the monster to attack Froech, and who presumably had his eyes fixed upon the swimming hero, fail to see Froech catch the salmon and hide it in "a secret place"?'

30 Op. cit. p. 350. Though 'lost common original' might not be the most apposite wording to describe the more fluid medium of oral tradition, the argument remains valid. Similar objections are expressed by C.R. Ó Cléirigh, op. cit. p. 165, and by Jean Marx in his review of *SILH* in *ÉtC* 7 (1955/6) pp 443–7, p. 446.   **31** In his review of *SILH* in *Éigse* 8 (1956–7) pp 152–64, pp 152–3.   **32** *From chaos to enemy: encounters with monsters in early Irish texts. An investigation related to the process of Christianization and the concept of evil* (Turnhout 1996) p. 144.   **33** *SILH* pp 36–7.

The plausibility of Ailill not seeing Froech catch and hide the salmon is merely a question of how far one is willing to suspend one's disbelief. In a modern realistic narrative the scene would of course be considered highly improbable, but in the context of early Irish narrative (or medieval saints' vitae for that matter) it is far more credible than very many other more fabulous events, and can hardly be cavilled at as being inconceivable within its frame of reference.

2. 'Why does Ailill condemn his daughter to death for the loss of a valuable ring? This is not merely an inexplicably harsh attitude, but also quite inconsistent with his resumption of friendly relations with Froech.'

Carney's explanation is that it is due to the unsuccessful adaptation of Rhydderch's Ring, where the queen's inability to produce the ring was a proof of her infidelity. Here it cannot be accounted for. Jackson too considers it somewhat awkward: 'The father's threat to kill the girl is not explicitly motivated in *TBF*, though it obviously arises from his fury at her suspected fornication'.[34]

A close reading of the tale, however, makes quite clear that the loss of the ring was not the real reason for Ailill's rage, but merely the pretext for gaining revenge on his daughter for defying his wishes by taking the sword to Froech. Ailill was so incensed at her action that he threw a spear at her, and he later predicts how he will punish her for her treachery:

'Issinn aithrech', ol Ailill, 'a ndoringénsam risin fer. Ind ingen immurgu', ol sé, 'atbélat a bbéoilside i mbárach d'adaig, 7 níba cin ṁbreithe in chlaidib mbeithir dí'.[35]

'We regret', said Ailill, 'what we did to the man'. 'But the girl', said he, 'her lips shall expire tomorrow night, and it will not be the crime of bringing the sword that will be brought against her'.[36]

As he wishes now to be reconciled with Froech, Ailill could no longer punish Findabair for saving his life, but he intends instead to use the loss of the ring as an excuse for doing so.[37]

3. 'Why did Ailill, in the first place, give his daughter a ring "for safe-keeping" (*dia taiscid*)?'

The perceived difficulty here is purely of Carney's own making, and due to his hypothesis that TBF is dependent on RhR:

> Most convincing … is the fact that a minor contradiction in Rhydderch's Ring is echoed verbally in TBF. Rhydderch gives his wife the ring *in signum conjugalis amoris*. But when he demands the ring back he is pictured as having merely given it to her primarily 'for safe-keeping' (*ad custodiam ei commendatus*). There is an essential difference between a ring given in *signum amoris* and *ad custodiam commendatus* … It is … of importance to note that the King's phrase ad custodiam is echoed by Findabair's *Dosrat mo athair damsa … dia taiscid* 'My father gave it to me for safe-keeping'.[38]

Even if we follow Carney in disregarding for the present the difficulty of establishing how an eighth-century Irish text can resonate with verbal echoes from the twelfth century Latin one, the arguments are still unconvincing. These are at the two Latin phrases, with the editor's translations appended:

---

34 Jackson, op. cit. p. 352.   **35** *TBF*2 p. 9, l. 222–5.   **36** *SILH* p. 8.   **37** These remarks are obviously not meant to suggest that Ailill had a valid reason for wishing Findabair dead. But there is no inconsistency, as Carney claimed, nor any close connection with RhR.   **38** *SILH* pp 38–9.

Anulum … quei ipse legitimus maritus, in spe- 'A … ring … which her lawful husband had intrust-
ciale signum conjugalis amoris commendaverat. ed to her as a special mark of his conjugal love'.

Ubi anulus suus ad custodiam ei commendatus He demanded where the ring was which he had
esset requisivit.   intrusted to her keeping'.[39]

I can see no contradiction here; even the same verb *commendare* is used in the two examples. There is even less reason for suggesting that there is an inconsistency in TBF where Ailill gives the ring to Findabair to wear, and she in turn gives it to Froech as a sign of commitment between them. Carney's translation of *dia taiscid* as 'for safe-keeping' or 'to take care of it' is also unfortunate and unnecessary, suggesting that Findabair had been entrusted with the ring to safeguard it. This, as her words at greater length show, is groundless:

'Dosrat m'athair damsa', ol sí, 'dia taiscid, 7 'My [father] gave it me to keep, and I shall say I
asbér is cor roda lláus immudu.'[40]   have mislaid it.'[41]

These are hardly the words of someone charged with the ring's protection.[42]

4. 'Why does Froech indulge in unnecessary heroics, offering to ransom the girl with his most valuable possessions when he knows that [s]he can produce the ring and subsequently does so?'
    One might add: Why did Findabair initially claim not to know of the ring's whereabouts and maintain that she is unable to present it to her father?
    The answer is that all the apparent attempts at reasoning with Ailill are in fact part of a successful ploy to goad him into fury. He becomes so enraged that Findabair finally – as if tired of his unreasonable ranting – answers him that it will be brought to him if he so badly wants it, but adding the crucial proviso that if it is, she will no longer be under his power. Overconfident, he agrees to relinquish his authority, and when the ring is brought in, there is no longer any impediment to Findabair and Froech's union. The whole episode is narrated with great skill:

Gaibthir fledugud leu d'adaig. Congair Fráech At night they start to feast. Froech calls a
gilla dia muintir. 'Airg ass', ol sé, 'cosin magin serving-boy of his people. 'Go,' said he, 'to
i ndeochadsa issin uisce. Éicne forácbusa and, where I went into the water. I have left a
donuc do Findabair, 7 irbbad fessin fair, 7 salmon there. Bring it to Findabair, and let her
fonaither int écne lee co mmaith, 7 atá ind see to it, and let her cook the salmon well. And
ordnasc i mmedón ind éicni. Is dóig lim the thumb-ring is inside the salmon. I think it
condessar chuca innocht.'   will be asked of her to-night.'

Gabthus mesca 7 aruspeittet céola 7 airfiti. They became intoxicated, and music and
Asbert Ailill íarum: 'Tucaid mo šéotu damsa minstrelsy are played to them. Then Ailill said:

39 Text and translation are taken from A.P. Forbes, *Historians of Scotland*, vol. 5, as given in *SILH*, 15–24. **40** *TBF*2 p. 6, lines 153–4.   **41** This is the translation given by Mary E. Byrne and Myles Dillon, 'Táin Bó Fraích' in *ÉtC* 2 (1937) pp 1–27, p. 6, except that they give 'mother' rather than 'father'. On reasons why the reading '*m'athair*' is preferable, see W. Meid *TBF*2 p. 34, and his *Die Romanze von Froech und Findabair: Táin Bó Froích* (Innsbruck 1970) p. 166. Carney's translation is 'My father gave it to me to take care of it, and I shall say that I happened to mislay it.' *SILH* p. 6.   **42** See also *TBF*2 p. 11, lines 263–5. *DIL*'s translations of *taiscid* are 'keeping, storing, guarding'. As Jackson, op. cit. p. 353, has pointed out, the giving of a ring to keep (but not to own) is

huili!' ol sé. Dobretha dó íarum co mbátar ara bélaib. 'Amra! Amra!' ol cách. 'Gairid damsa Findabair!' ol sé. Dotháet Findabair cucai, 7 coíca ingen impe. 'A ingen', ol Ailill, 'ind ordnasc doratusa duitsiu inuraid, in mair latt? Tuc dam conda accatar ind óic. Rot biasu íarum. 'Ní fetar', ol sí, 'cid dernad de'. 'Fintasu ém!' ol Ailill. 'Is éicen a cungid nó th'anim do dul as do churp.' 'Nícon fíu', ol ind óic, 'atá mór di maith and chena.' 'Ní fail ní dom šétaibse nád téi dar cend na hingine', ol Fráech, 'dáig ruc in claideb dam do giull dom anmain.' 'Ní fuil lat do šétaib ní nodott ain mani aisce úadi ind ordnaisc', ol Ailill. 'Nicom thása cumang dia tabairt', ol ind ingen. 'An ro chara, dagné dímsa.' 'Tungu día tonges mo thúath, atbélat do béoil meni aisce úait', ol Ailill. 'Is aire condegar chucut, úair is decmaing, ar rofetarsa, co tísat na doíni atbathatar ó thossuch domuin, ní thic assin magin in rolád.' 'Nícon ticfa ri moín nó adlaic thrá', ol ind ingen, 'in sét connegar and. Tíagsa conda tucsa, úair is tricc condegar.' 'Ní regasu', ol Ailill. 'Táet nech úait immurgu dia tabairt.' Foídis ind ingen a inailt dia tabairt. 'Tongusa do día thonges mo thúath, dia faigbither nícon béosa fot chumachtasu ba síre, diandum roib forsa rol mo greis.' 'Nícon gébsa dítsu ón, cid cossin n-echaire théisi, má fogabthar ind ordnasc', ol Ailill.

'Bring me all my treasures', said he. Then they were brought to him, and lay before him. 'Wondrous, wondrous', said all. 'Call Findabair to me', said he. Findabair comes to him with fifty maidens round her. 'Daughter', said Ailill, 'the thumb-ring I gave you last year, have you still got it? Give it to me that the warriors may see it. You shall have it again'. 'I do not know', said she, 'what has happened to it'. 'Find out, then', said Ailill. 'It had better be found or your life will leave your body'. 'It is not worth it', said the warriors. 'There is much wealth here already'. 'There is none of my treasures that shall not go in ransom for the girl', said Froech; 'for she brought the sword to save my life'. 'You have no treasures that can save her, if she does not restore the thumb-ring', said Ailill. 'It is not in my power to give it' said the girl. 'Do with me what you like'. 'I swear by the god by whom my people swear your lips shall perish unless you give it up', said Ailill. 'The reason it is asked of you is because it is impossible, for I know that till the people who have died since the beginning of the world come back, it will not come from where it has been cast'. 'The jewel that is sought will not come for love or money, indeed!' said the girl. 'Let me go fetch it since it is so urgently required'. '*You* shall not go', said Ailill, 'but send someone to bring it'. The girl sent her maid to bring it. 'I swear by the god by whom my people swear, if it be found, I shall not be in your power any longer if I have anyone under whose protection I may put myself'. 'Even if you go to the horse-boy I shall not hold you back if the ring be found', said Ailill.

Dobert íarum ind inailt in méis issa rígthech 7 int éicne fonaithe fuirre, is é fuillechta fo mil. Dogníth lassin ingin co maith, 7 boí ind ordnasc óir forsind éicni anúas. Dosféccai Ailill 7 Medb.[43]

The serving-maid then brought the dish into the palace with the cooked salmon upon it, smeared with honey. It was well done by the girl, and the gold thumb-ring lay upon the salmon. Ailill and Medb stare at it.[44]

---

commonplace in the versions from Ireland, and is found also in oriental versions, which he sees as the possible source of the motif in Celtic. **43** *TBF2* pp 10–2, lines 253–88. **44** *SILH* pp 9–10.

While Carney is at great pains to stress that the early Irish tales are far too sophisticated to be reflections of the oral tradition, his whole approach paradoxically demands that they be unskilful enough for him to discern their foreign sources. Rather than praise TBF he writes of 'careless integration', 'unnatural distortion', 'awkward and unconvincing compound', 'inconsistencies, incoherences, and outright contradictions'. Jackson, too, is dismissive, calling it 'a very broken-down and corrupted tale',[45] and stating that 'the whole story of Fraech hangs together very badly'.[46] Others, however, have been far more appreciative. Miles Dillon writes: 'The story is well told and has some charming passages'.[47] Donald Meek admires 'the stylistic richness of the first part of *TBF*, with its clever use of dialogue and its sophisticated motivation',[48] and Wolfgang Meid too is enthusiastic, describing it as 'der ältesten und schönsten dieser kleineren *tána bó*',[49] and praising the 'elegant erzählten, in seinen Dialogszenen dramatischen ersten Teil'.[50]

I would agree with the favourable commentators, and see the main part of TBF which deals with the wooing of Findabair as displaying a complex and skilful weaving of events rather than being a disjointed account replete with unexplained and unmotivated incidents. Though at first sight a tale of romance and heroic deeds, much of the action derives from the battle of wits between Froech and Findabair on the one hand, and Ailill on the other. Time and time again we can perceive a clear disparity between outward pronouncements and inner intentions, and from the outset, when Froech conceals his true motive for visiting Cruachain, until he fabricates a story to explain how he obtained the ring, he is presented as being prudent, wary and shrewd; qualities which prove essential in his dealings with Ailill.

It is Ailill's malicious designs which ultimately propel much of the plot. When he is refused the bride price which he demands, his attitude towards Froech changes from a sympathetic one into a wish to see him killed. His attempt to cause Froech's death (in which he seeks to hide his own involvement) is thwarted by Findabair's intervention, and from then on she becomes the object of his wrath. When he tries to condemn her to death (concealing his true motive), Froech now comes to Findabair's rescue, and the pair foil Ailill a second time. The ring, given to Froech and then stolen, regained, returned and finally displayed, acquires various functions during the tale. From being originally no more than a tangible sign of the suitors' pledge it is subsequently seen as proof of filial misconduct, then used as the pretext for Ailill's revenge, before eventually becoming the means of facilitating the couple's union.

45 Op. cit. p. 352.   46 Op. cit. p. 355.   47 M.E. Byrne and M. Dillon, *Táin Bó Fraích* (Dublin 1933) p. vii. 48 Op. cit. 85. On p. 28 he writes that it is 'sophisticated in structure, but at times weak in plot'.   49 *Die Romanze* p. 14.   50 Op. cit. p. 16.

Baile in Scáil and *Echtrae Chormaic*

KEVIN MURRAY

A link between *Baile in Scáil* and *Echtrae Chormaic* given in footnotes was noted by Whitley Stokes in his edition of the latter[1] and has more recently been adverted to by Donnchadh Ó Corráin and Kim McCone.[2] The connection between the two texts was made more explicit by John Carey who argues that there is an episode in *Echtrae Chormaic* 'in which close verbal correspondences point to direct derivation from *Baile in Scáil*'.[3] The purpose of this note is to investigate these links further.[4]

The work edited by Whitley Stokes is an amalgamation of three separate texts, as witnessed by its colophon.[5] The opening section (§§1–10) sets the background for an account of what have become known as 'the twelve ordeals' (§11–24) which decide between truth and falsehood. The twelfth of these items which may adjudicate between veracity and lies is Cormac mac Airt's cup, and the story surrounding the obtaining of this in the Otherworld is given in §§25–54.[6] The final section of the edition (§§55–80) knits together the proceeding paragraphs as well as telling a story of its own. §§55–58 seem to be a direct continuation of §§1–10; §§59–78 deal with the third strand of the textual amalgamation, namely the acquiring of Cormac's sword; while from the latter half of §78 to the end, the story is concerned with tying these varying strands together as one text – thus the colophon in §79: *Conidh scél na fír flatha, 7 echtra Cormaic a Tír Tharrngiri 7 Claideb Cormaic an scel sin* (So that is the tale of the Ordeals, and of Cormac's Adventures in the Land of Promise, and of Cormac's Sword). The story contained in §§25–54, *Echtrae Chormaic (i Tír Tairngiri)*, is the text under discussion here.

The thematic parallels between *EC* and *BS* are well known and will only be briefly enumerated here: (1) an unknown figure appears to the king at Tara; (2) this figure induces the king of Tara to journey to the Otherworld; (3) a great mist is used to obscure the real world and reveal the

---

1 Ed. W. Stokes, 'The Irish ordeals, Cormac's adventure in the land of promise, and the decision as to Cormac's sword', *IT* 3.1 (Leipzig 1891) pp 183–229 [esp. §§25–54], at p. 229 (edited from *BB* and *YBL*). The BFer. version is edited by V. Hull, '*Echtra Cormaic maic Airt*: The Adventure of Cormac mac Airt', *PMLA* 64 (1949) pp 871–83. There are several modern Irish versions of the story – for a brief note on some of these, see R.I. Best, *Bibliography of Irish philology and of printed Irish literature to 1912* (Dublin 1913; repr. 1992) p. 108 and Hull, op. cit., pp 873–4. Although Hull has established some of the connections between the different recensions (op. cit., pp 871–5), the relationship between the varying manuscript versions of *EC* has not yet been worked out in detail. For the most comprehensive treatment of *EC* to date, particularly in the context of tales concerning Cormac mac Airt, see T. Ó Cathasaigh, *The heroic biography of Cormac mac Airt* (Dublin 1977) pp 80–5. I have used the following abbreviations: *BS*: *Baile in Scáil*; *EC*: *Echtrae Chormaic*; *EC¹*: *Echtrae Chormaic*, Recension 1 = Stokes' edition; *EC²*: *Echtrae Chormaic*, Recension 2 = Hull's edition; *EC³*: *Echtrae Chormaic*, Recension 3 (also called *Faghail Craoibhe Chormaic Mhic Airt*) = O'Grady's edition (see footnote 11 for details). **2** D. Ó Corráin, 'Irish vernacular law and the Old Testament', *Ireland and Christendom: the Bible and the missions*, ed. P. Ní Chatháin and M. Richter (Stuttgart 1987) pp 284–307, at p. 293n; K. McCone, *Pagan past and Christian present in early Irish literature* (Maynooth 1990) pp 155–8, f 10. **3** J. Carey, 'On the interrelationships of some *Cín Dromma Snechtai* texts', *Ériu* 46 (1995) pp 71–92, at p. 76n. **4** I wish to thank Dr John Carey for his help and advice with this paper. **5** J. Carey ('The testimony of the dead', *Éigse* 26 (1992) pp 1–12, at p. 1) emphasises, however, 'the desirability of considering the work as a whole' because of 'its essential, and very intriguing, thematic unity'. **6** For a convenient summary, see M. Dillon, *Early Irish literature* (Chicago 1948; repr. Dublin 1994) pp 110–12.

Otherworld; (4) in the Otherworld plain a great dwelling is found;[7] (5) the Otherworld figure's remarkable appearance is described; (6) the Otherworld figure is accompanied by a beautiful woman; (7) refreshments are served to the king of Tara; (8) the identity of the Otherworld figure is revealed; (9) the king of Tara returns safely to the mortal world with tokens from the Otherworld.

It may be profitable at this point to compare certain passages in *BS*[8] with their closest corresponding sections in *EC*:

1.   The arrival of the Otherworld figure to the king in Tara.

> *BS* §§1&5 [*ZCP* 20, 218–19]: Laa ro·búi Cond i Temraich iar ndith dona rigaibh at·raracht matin moch for <rig>raith na Temrach ria turcbail greni 7 a tri druid ríam / Co·cualatar trechan an marcaigh ara cend.
>
> *EC*[1] §25 [*IT* 3.1, 193]: Laa n-æin dobai Cormac ua Cuind madan moch i cetamun a ænur for Mur Tea hi Temraig. Conaca in t-æn oclach forosta findliath adochum.
>
> *EC*[2] [*PMLA* 64, 875]: Fechtus do·bi Cormac h-u Cuinn a Liatruim. Co·fhaccaidh aen-oclach furusta finn-líath cugi ar faighthi in duín.
>
> *EC*[3] [*TOS* 3, 212]: Feacht n-ann dá raibh Cormac mac Airt mhic Chuinn cheudchathaigh .i. áirdrigh Eirionn, a Liathdruim, ro chonnairc an t-aon óglach ar fhaithche a dhúin.

2.   Description of the mist which descends upon the plain and which obscures the mortal world to reveal the Otherworld dwelling.

> BS §§5&6 [*ZCP* 20, 219]: A mbatar and iarum co·n-accatar ciaigh móír impu cona·fetatar *cía* do·chotar ar meid in dorcha dus·*fánic* / Do·cotar iarum ass conda·rala assa mag, 7 bile n-orda ann. Tech foa ochtaig findruine and, .x. traigid .xx. a mét.
>
> *EC*[1] §32&37 [*IT* 3.1, 195–6]: Tucad ceo mor for lar in maighi sonnaich doibh. Focerd Cormac a magh mor a ænur. Dun mor ar lar in maighi. Sonnach credhumæ uime / A mbadar and íar trath nona conacadar æn fear chucu isin teach.
>
> *EC*[2] [*PMLA* 64, 876]: Tucadh nél cíach eturra co[n]ach·fídír Cormac cá leth do·chuaidh an t-oclach 7 an righan. Do·rala iar sin Cormac a aenur ar lar mhuíghi moír. Dun m[or] ar lar an mhuighi 7 sondach airgít uime.
>
> *EC*[3] [*TOS* 3, 216]: Agus ro éirigh ceo doilbhthe draoidheachta dho, agus tárla a máigh iongantaigh eugsamhail é.

3.   An account of the king of Tara's entry into the Otherworld dwelling together with a description of the uniqueness of the Otherworld figure therein and of his female companion.

> *BS* §§5&6 [*ZCP* 20, 219–20]: Lotar iarum issa tech co·n-accatar ingen maccthacht i cathair glanidi 7 barr órdhai fora mullach 7 brat co srethaib di or impe … Et co·n-accatar a scál fadeissin isin taig ara ciund inna rígsudiu. Ocus ropu mór a delgnaidhe. Ba dethbir son,

---

7 As pointed out by John Carey ('The location of the Otherworld in Irish tradition', *Éigse* 19 (1982–3) pp 36–43, at p. 41n.), 'an Otherworld hall reached through a "great mist" appears only' in these two Irish texts.   **8** Ed. K. Meyer, *ZCP* 3 (1901) pp 457–66; *ZCP* 12 (1918) pp 232–8; *ZCP* 13 (1921) pp 371–82. Ed. R. Thurneysen, *ZCP* 20 (1935) pp 213–27. It is only the introductory section (§§1–9) of *BS* that concerns us here. *BS* was the subject of my doctoral dissertation presented to the NUI in 1997 – Prof. Ní Chatháin supervised this thesis and, thus, much of the work on which this note is based.

ar ni·frith hi Temraig riam fer a meti nach-a chaime ar aille a delba n[ach a] chrotha 7 ara inganti.

*EC*¹ §36 [*IT* 3.1, 195]: Luidh iarsin isin rightheach. Oen lanamain is[in]tigh forachind. Ba derscai[g]theach dealb in oclaig ar ailli a crotha, ar chaine a dealbha 7 ar ingantus a ecoisce. Ingen immorro macdachta mongbhuidhi, fo barr ordha, fa haillim do mnaib in betha, ina fharradh.

*EC*² [*PMLA* 64, 876]: Taínic Cormac iar sin cum an duín 7 sondach airgít gláin íme 7 ceithre tighi ann 7 en-téach mor etúrra. Lanámhain caem cruthamail ar lar ín tighi.

*EC*³ [*TOS* 3, 220]: agus dhruideas Cormac chum an tighe go n-deachaidh ann, agus ro bheannuigh righ Eirionn. Do fhreagradar lánamha árdhachta ioldathach ro bhá astigh dho.

4. The giving of refreshment / hospitality to the king of Tara.

> *BS* §8 [*ZCP* 20, 220]: 7 ba si do·bert dithait do Chunn .i. damasnæ 7 torcasnæ.
>
> *BS*¹ §52 [*IT* 3.1, 197]: Rodailedh lind 7 biadh doib iarum co mbadar subhaigh soforbailig.
>
> *BS*² [*PMLA* 64, 876]: Do·roighnedh iar sin osáig don righ.
>
> *BS*³ [*TOS* 3, 220]: agus fá mhaith leis aoidheacht na h-oidhche sin d'fhághail.

5. The revelation of the identity of the Otherworld figure.

> *BS* §7 [*ZCP* 20, 220]: '… is he mo slonnud [Lug mac Eth]nen m. Smretha … m. Miled Espaine. Et is dó do·deochad-sa co·n·ecius duit-siu sægal do flatha 7 cacha flatha bias huait hi Temraig co brad'.
>
> *EC*¹ §53 [*IT* 3.1, 198]: "Misi Manandan mac Lir", ar se, "righ Thíri Tarrngiri, 7 is aire doradus alle d'fhechsain Tíri Tarrngire".
>
> *EC*² [*PMLA* 64, 877]: Ro·chan Mananan ceol do Cormac.
>
> *EC*³ [*TOS* 3, 222]: "Más fíor do bhar sgeulaibh," ar Cormac, "is tusa Manánán, agus is í sin do bhean".

As can be seen from the assembled evidence, *EC* and *BS* are not textually similar at these points though there are obvious thematic correspondences, particularly between *BS* and *EC*¹ (which is closer in content to *BS* than are the other recensions of *EC*).⁹ The only textual similarity is between *BS* and *EC*¹ in section no. 3 above, i.e. the scene referred to by John Carey at the start of this article. The introductory portion of *BS* (§§1–9), from which these excerpts are taken, seems amenable on linguistic grounds to a date around AD 900.¹⁰ The language of *EC*¹ is late Middle Irish.

Hull (op. cit., 874–5) compared *EC*¹ (Stokes' edition) with the second recension (his own edition) and came to the following conclusion:

> the second recension is distinguished from the first recension by its omissions. Apparently it omits much. Yet when this omitted material in the second recension is analyzed, one is

---

9 For example, in section 5 (above), the Otherworld figure himself reveals his identity in *BS* and *EC*¹ – in *EC*² and *EC*³ the identity of this figure emerges in a different way. He also gives a reason for enticing the king of Tara to the Otherworld in *BS* and *EC*¹.   **10** See the comment of Gerard Murphy ('On the dates of two sources used in Thurneysen's Heldensage', *Ériu* 16 (1952) pp 145–56, p. 150n.) who gives it as his belief that 'the language of the introductory portion of *Baile in Scáil* … on the whole tends to confirm the belief that its basic framework goes back to the late 9th century'.

led to conclude that these omissions are not vital, that only unimportant details are left out, and that thereby the story itself gains in effectiveness through its conciseness.

The relationship between the three different recensions of *EC* is difficult to establish with any degree of certainty.[11] Dr Carey believes that 'none is based upon either of the others, and that all three go back to a text of the later Middle Irish period'.[12] This interpretation seems to be borne out by the analysis presented here. Though all three recensions have much in common, the differences are too great to posit textual interdependence.[13] Thus, if we just had the testimony of recensions 2 & 3, we would only be able to state that *BS* and *EC* were thematically linked. The parallels in section no. 3 between *EC*¹ and *BS*, however, point towards some minor textual link as well.

This conclusion may help point the way towards solving a dilemma concerning *EC* raised by Hull (op. cit., 875). He asks if

> one may be justified in raising the question whether perhaps the second recension, which as now transmitted was written about the same time as the first recension, does not represent after all the oldest tradition, a tradition which the first recension expanded.

If we believe, however, that *BS* contains the same structural outline utilised by the compiler of *EC* (as seems likely), then the textual correspondence which exists between *BS* and *EC*¹ (and which is not present with recensions 2 & 3) along with the close structural parallels between *BS* and *EC*¹ may indicate that recension 1 is closest to the Middle Irish original. As noted by Hull (op. cit., 874–5) 'the second recension adds nothing new that is of importance' and the third recension has omitted 'the second anecdote without which the tale is incomplete'. These facts may point towards a similar conclusion.

The closest overt link between the two texts is to be found in the final paragraph of Stokes' edition (§80) of the composite text: *Acht adberaid na hecnaidi cach uair notaisbenta taibsi ingnad dona righflathaibh anall – amal adfaid in Scal do Chund, 7 amal tarfas Tír Thairngiri do Cormac –, conidh timtirecht diada ticedh fan samla sin, 7 conach timthirecht deamnach* (The wise declare that whenever any strange apparition was revealed of old to the royal lords, – as the ghost revealed to Conn, and as the Land of Promise was shown to Cormac, – it was a divine ministration that used to come in that wise, and not a demoniacal ministration). It is clear that the story concerning the phantom's appearance to Conn is being explicitly adverted to here. Theoretically, we might argue that this could be either *Baile in Scáil* or *Baile Chuind* [hereafter *BC*] (or more properly the 'lost narrative introduction' to the latter) that is in question here.[14] The evidence points directly towards *BS*, however.[15]

11 The third recension is a Modern Irish version which is extant in numerous manuscripts. There is as yet no critical edition but the story has been printed twice – firstly by S.H. O'Grady, *TOS* 3 (1857) pp 212–29 and again by P. Ó Fithcheallaigh, *Mil na mBeach* (Dublin 1911) pp 7–13 and 82–3.   **12** J. Carey, 'The narrative setting of *Baile Chuinn Chétchathaig*', *ÉtC* 32 (1996) pp 189–201, at p. 197.   **13** It would take more detailed textual analysis, however, to be certain of this conclusion.   **14** This 'lost narrative introduction' is proposed by John Carey (*Ériu* 46, p. 76) and is the subject of further analysis by him in *ÉtC* 32. This position was first intimated by Gerard Murphy (op. cit., p. 152n.) where he notes that 'it is clear that the first hearers of *Baile Chuind* knew of the tradition indicated in the introductory portion of *Baile in Scáil* according to which wedding a goddess, by drinking intoxicating liquor poured by her, marked the inauguration of a reign'. One would not be able to argue for a close link between *BC* (as it has come down to us) and the information presented in §80 of *EC*¹ without positing some form of lost narrative.   **15** The uncertainty of whether a *scál* would necessarily have appeared in the lost

These similarities are sufficiently clear to allow us to say that certain aspects of *EC* (most notably in *EC*[1]) are directly derived from *BS*. However, it is clear from the amount of material in *BS* not drawn upon in *EC* that the compiler of *EC* had a story framework similar enough to *BS* to render borrowing useful but different enough to ensure that the borrowing remained selective.[16] Thus, once more, it may be more profitable to look to the lost narrative section of *BC* as the ultimate basis for the thematic outline of both stories.

narrative introduction to *BC* may also point in the same direction. *BS* also seems to have had greater currency than *BC* in the Middle Irish period, as witnessed, for example, by *LL* 15768 (*ro scríbad issin Scálbaile*) and by the medieval tale lists where *Fís Chuind* is consistently glossed *.i. Baile in Scáil* – see P. Mac Cana, *The learned tales of medieval Ireland* (Dublin 1980). **16** J. Carey, (*ÉtC* 32, p. 198) would argue 'that we cannot explain Cormac's journey as being merely a copy of Conn's: the two are independent realisations of a preexisting story pattern'.

Codes of conduct and honour in *Stair Bibuis*

ERICH POPPE

The late-twelfth-century Anglo-Norman romance *Boeve de Haumtone* is the direct or indirect source for a number of Insular adaptations of the story – these are the various Middle English texts about Beues of Hamtoun, the Middle Welsh *Ystorya Bown de Hamtwn*, the Old Norse *Bevers saga*, and the Early Modern Irish *Stair Bibuis*.[1] The original English version as well as the Welsh and the Norse versions are directly based on an Anglo-Norman source, whereas the Irish version is in all likelihood based on an unknown English source. This Irish version is transmitted incomplete and without a title in a single manuscript, namely Dublin, Trinity College, H.2.7 (= 1298), which has been dated to the second half of the fifteenth century. In addition to *Stair Bibuis*, the manuscript contains the Irish versions of the story of Hercules and of Guy of Warwick, which are also derived from English sources, as well as the native story *Stair Nuadat Find Femin*.[2] Gordon Quin has argued that the scribe of the manuscript, Uilliam Mac an Leagha, was the translator and the author respectively of the four texts which share – beyond the expulsion-and-return formula – a significant number of formal and stylistic features.[3] The same features are also found in five religious texts based on foreign-language sources in another manuscript written by Uilliam Mac an Leagha, namely London, British Library, MS Additional 30512, and Diarmuid Ó Laoghaire has therefore made a case that Mac an Leagha was their translator as well.[4] If Quin's and Ó Laoghaire's arguments are accepted then these texts represent the autographs of their redactor Uilliam Mac an Leagha. He may have produced H.2.7 for a member of the gaelicized Anglo-Irish family of the Butlers, and the manuscript's contents would thus reflect an aspect of the literary tastes of this class.

---

1 For these texts see *Der anglo-normannische Boeve de Haumtone*, ed. A. Stimming (Halle 1899), *The Romance of Sir Beues of Hamtou*n, ed. E. Kölbing, Early English Texts Society, Extra Series, 46, 48, 65 (London 1885–94) (references from this text will be identified by *SBH* plus abbreviation of the manuscript quoted from and line-number), *Ystorya Bown de Hamtwn*, ed. M. Watkin (Cardiff 1958), 'Bevers Saga', in *Fornsögur Suðrlanda*, ed. G. Cederschiöld (Lund 1884) pp ccxvi–ccxli, and 'The Irish Lives of Guy of Warwick and Bevis of Hampton', ed. F.N. Robinson, *ZCP* 6 (1908) pp 9–180, 273–338, 556, at pp 273–320 (references from this text will be identified by *SB* plus page and line). For the date of the Anglo-Norman *Boeve* see J. Weiss, 'The date of the Anglo-Norman *Boeve de Haumtone*', *Medium Ævum* 55 (1986) pp 237–41. For discussions of the Welsh and Irish versions see R. Reck, 'Heiligere Streiter und keuschere Jungfrauen. Religiöse Elemente in der kymrischen Adaption des anglo-normannischen *Boeve de Haumtone*', in *Übersetzung, Adaptation und Akkulturation im insularen Mittelalter*, ed. E. Poppe and L.C.H. Tristram (Münster 1999) pp 289–304, E. Poppe, 'Adaption und Akkulturation. Narrative Techniken in der mittelkymrischen *Ystorya Bown de Hamtwn*', in ibid., pp 305–17, and id., 'The Early Modern Irish Version of Beves of Hamtoun', *CMCS* 23 (1992) pp 77–98. 2 For these texts see *Stair Ercuil ocus a Bás*, ed. E.G. Quin, *ITS* 38 ([London] 1939), Robinson, 'The Irish Lives', pp 24–180, 'Stair Nuadat Find Femin', ed. K. Müller-Lisowski, *ZCP* 13 (1921) pp 195–250. On *Stair Ercuil* see B. Ross, *Bildungsidol – Ritter – Held. Herkules bei William Caxton und Uilliam Mac an Lega* (Heidelberg 1989), on *Stair Nuadat* see E. Poppe, '*Stair Nuadat Find Femin*: Eine irische Romanze?', *ZCP* 49–50 (1997) pp 749–59. 3 See Quin, *Stair Ercuil*, pp xxxviii–xl. 4 See D. Ó Laoghaire, 'Beathaí naomh iasachta i ndeireadh na meánaoise', *Léachtaí Cholm Cille* 15 (1985) pp 79–97, at pp 86–91, and also E. Poppe, 'Favourite expressions, repetition, and variation: observations on *Beatha Mhuire Eigiptacdha* in Add. 30512', in *The Legend of Mary of Egypt in medieval Insular hagiography*, ed. E. Poppe and B. Ross (Dublin 1996) pp 279–99.

Robinson's title 'Beathadh Sir Gui [o Bhar]bhuic'[5] has no decisive support from the manuscript, since it is, according to Max Nettlau, 'written in a later hand'.[6] Quin has suggested the title *Stair Ercuil ocus a Bás* for Mac an Leagha's adaptation of the story about Hercules on the basis of the colophon to the main part of the story (*Conidh i stair Ercuil 7 a bas connicci sin*), and a reference to the writing of Hercules's own history (*sgribhadh a staire budhein*) is also found in the text.[7] On this basis I tentatively suggest the title *Stair Bibuis* for the Irish version of the story of Beues of Hamtoun.

None of the known English versions of *Sir Beues of Hamtoun* was the direct source of the Irish adaptation.[8] Based on a comparison of the English and the Irish texts J.L. Fellows has suggested that the Irish text is 'clearly adapted from a fifteenth-century M[iddle] E[nglish] text, having certain close affinities with both C [Cambridge, University Library, Ff. 2. 38, a late-fifteenth- or early-sixteenth-century manuscript] and M [Manchester, Chetham's Library, MS 8009, *c.*1479/80]'.[9]

The fact that the immediate source of the Irish text is unknown aggravates the methodological problems for the analysis of the translation on the level of contents. Its formal and stylistic integration into the vernacular textual culture is much easier to show, as is the introduction of some concepts which originate in the Irish tradition.[10] With reference to the Irish versions of classical texts W.B. Stanford has emphasized 'the freedom with which the translator adapts or supplements his classical text to suit Irish taste',[11] and this freedom is a characteristic feature of Uilliam Mac an Leagha's adaptations as well. Quin has described *Stair Ercuil* as 'a tale which except for its central theme is thoroughly Irish',[12] and remarks:

> In addition to adopting a peculiarly Irish phraseology and making free use of the commonplaces of the native literature he [the adapter] draws wherever it suits him on other sources and alters proper names at will.[13]

This approach to translation was not exclusively Irish, and seems to be typical for many secular medieval translators.[14] It creates, however, serious methodological problems for the textual analysis of the process of translation. In the case of the texts in H.2.7 we seem to be in the rather unusual position of having at least the autograph of the translator; this implies that the texts have not

---

5 Robinson, 'The Irish Lives', p. 24, the analogous title 'Beathadh Bibuis o Hamtuir', ibid., p. 273, is marked as his conjecture. **6** M. Nettlau, 'On some Irish translations from medieval European literature', *RC* 10 (1889) pp 178–91, p. 187. **7** Quin, *Stair Ercuil*, p. xiv and ll. 2544 and 1830. **8** The same seems to apply to the Irish version of Guy of Warwick: 'the Irish life of Guy makes probable the existence of an English romance which differed in one important feature [i.e., inclusion of material from the *Speculum Gy de Warewyke*], and may have departed in many details, from the known English versions of the story' (Robinson, 'The Irish Lives', p. 16). **9** J.L. Fellows, 'Sir Beves of Hampton: Study and Edition', 5 vols (unpublished Ph.D. dissertation, University of Cambridge 1979) I, p. 51. For an intriguing example where the English A-version seems to be closer to the Irish version than the C- or M-versions, see the discussion below of Bibus' rejection of the pilgrim's offer to read the letter which contains his death-sentence. **10** See Poppe, 'The early modern Irish version', pp 81–96. **11** W.B. Stanford, 'Towards a history of classical influences in Ireland', *PRIA* (1970) p. 36. **12** Quin, *Stair Ercuil*, p. xxvi. **13** Quin, *Stair Ercuil*, pp xxv–xxvi. **14** Compare, for example, H.U. Gumbrecht, 'Literary translations and its social conditioning in the Middle Ages: four Spanish romance texts of the 13th century', *Yale French Studies* 51 (1974) pp 205–22, G. Barnes, 'Arthurian chivalry in Old Norse', *Arthurian Literature* 7 (1987) pp 50–102, and S. Würth, *Der "Antikenroman" in der isländischen Literatur des Mittelalters. Eine Untersuchung zur Übersetzung und Rezeption lateinischer Literatur im Norden* (Basel and Frankfurt 1998). Würth's study contains many useful hints on the general medieval approach to translating (see particularly pp 9–13) as well as a thorough discussion of the characteristics of medieval Icelandic adaptations of classical works, which typologically share many features with their Irish counterparts. For a discussion of a secular approach to the adaptations of legends into medieval German, and its conceptual consequences, see E. Feistner, 'Bausteine zu einer Übersetzungstypologie im Bezugsystem von

undergone further changes in the course of their transmission within the vernacular tradition, as have, for example, the Irish, and the Icelandic, versions of Dares's *De Excidio Troiae Historia*.[15] Their sources, on the other hand, remain unidentified; and in view of the freedom with which Uilliam Mac an Leagha seems to have treated his sources – if, for example, his radical stylistic innovations are a criterion to go by – it is clearly difficult to be certain about the responsibility for differences in relation to content between the known English texts and the Irish version: were they already contained in the unidentified source or were they introduced by Mac an Leagha?

In the following I propose to look at the presentation of concepts of conduct and honour in *Stair Bibuis*. It is striking that the Irish text contains a number of scenes in which the explicit discussion of such codes and of moral standards seems to play a significantly more important role than in their counterparts in the known English texts. One or two such scenes would not suffice to argue that these are the translator's conscious, or subconscious, additions, but their accumulation might. Of course, this is not meant to imply that codes of honour and conduct play no role in the English texts, and many such references to moral standards in the English text are also taken over by the Irish translator. Thus Bonyface comments that *it was neuure churlis dede* (*SBH* M 937) that Beues presented him with a valuable garment, and similarly in the Irish, *adubairt nar duine anuasal tug an brat uasalsin do fein* (*SB* 282.33–4) 'he said that it was no ignoble man who gave this noble garment to him'. Another example is found in the scene in which Beues/Bibus rejects Iosyan/Sisian's wooing on the grounds of their unequal rank and background:

> 'Iosyan, be thou styll! / Me thinkyth, thou spekyst ageynst skyll: / Thou maiste haue one me on-liche, / Bradmond, the kyng, that is so ryche; / In all the world is no man, / Kynge ne duke ne Soudan, / But he wold haue the to quene, / And he had the with eyen sene; / And I am knyght of vncouth ['foreign'] lond, / I haue no more than I in stond!' (*SBH* M 873–82)

'Ní cubaid rit beth agum-sa', are-sé, 'uair ní fuil isin cruinne co comcoitcenn fer nach fuil a saith do mnai innud; 7 a rigan', ar-sé, 'ní fuil inme na ardflaithus agum-sa,' ar-sé, 'acht mina faghar le nert mo loinne é, 7 is uime-sin nach dingmala duit-si misi mur fir', ar Bibus. (*SB* 282.5–10)	'It is not fitting for you to be with me', he said, 'because there is not in the universe anywhere a man for whom you would not be a fitting wife, and, lady,' he said, 'I have neither heritage[16] nor a chief-kingdom,' he said, 'unless I win it by the strength of my valour, and therefore I am not suitable for you as a husband', Bibus said.

But already in this passage the Irish version is slightly more explicit about the differences between Bibus and Sisian in background and rank than the English text.

My first example of a greater emphasis on the codes of conduct and honour in *Stair Bibuis* concerns the confrontation between Bibus and his stepfather and his mother. In the English text Beues pretends to be *a messingere* (*SBH* M 308) when he requests entrance to his stepfather's palace, which was formerly his father's, and the porter sends him away with harsh words:[17]

Rezeptions- und Funktionsgeschichte der mittelalterlichen Heiligenlegende', *Wolfram-Studien* 14 (1996) pp 171–84. **15** See the remarks in L.D. Myrick, *From the De Excidio Troiae Historia to the Togail Troí. Literary-cultural synthesis in a medieval Irish adaptation of Dares' Troy Tale* (Heidelberg 1993) pp 85–91, and Würth, *Der "Antikenroman"*, pp 12–13, for methodological considerations, and pp 46–54 and 148–70, for the different Icelandic versions and the characteristic changes in the course of their transmission. **16** *DIL* gives the following meanings for *indme*: 'wealth, heritage; state, rank, condition'; the same phrase occurs again later in the text (*SB* 286.21, see below on Bibus's argument with God). **17** In the version from the Auchinleck MS (A), Beues does not identify himself, but simply demands *let me in reke!*

'Fye on the rebaude,' said the porter thoo, / 'Horeson, harlot, home thou goo! / There was none, but he was mad, / In message to send suche a lad!' (*SBH* M 309–12)

In the Irish version Bibus correctly identifies himself as *muiccidhi Sir Saber* (*SB* 276.6) 'Sir Saber's swine-herd', but the porter does not realize that this swine-herd is in reality the former earl's son whom his mother had ordered to be killed by his foster-father, Sir Saber. That Bibus does not use the pretence to be a messenger may have to do either with the social status accorded to non-noble messengers in the Irish version – on which see below – or with his sense of honour. Furthermore, in the English text Beues takes the decision to approach his stepfather's palace after a searching monologue in which he refers to his social position as formerly *an Erlis son / And nowe I am but an herde* (*SBH* M 298–99), whereas in the Irish version he is spurred into action by his fellow swine-herd's rebuke *Mor an metachus duit* (*SB* 275.34) 'great [is] your cowardice'.[18] The porter tries to send Bibus away by saying *gur maith in dil esanora e tri iarraidh teacht sa cathraigh* (*SB* 276.6–7) 'that paying him dishonour was proper for asking to enter the castle'. Then, when he has wounded his stepfather, the emperor, and thinks that he has killed him, he tells his foster-father on his return: *Is maith in gnim doronus [...] oir is doigh gur dilus m'athair 7 gur marbus in t-imper* (*SB* 276.34–6) 'The deed I have done is good, because it was to be expected that I avenge my father and kill the emperor'. Here he gives an explicit positive evaluation of his actions justified on the basis of social and moral obligations. In the English text Beues simply tells Sabere what has happened:[19]

'I wyll you tell all to geder: / Bete I haue my stepfader! / With my staff I smote hym on the hede, / That I lefte hym all ffor dede!' (*SBH* M 345–8)

However, the stepfather is not dead, and in the English version his wife, Beues's mother, goes away to accuse Sabere of not having killed Beues (*SBH* M 354–58). In the Irish text, on the other hand, a dialogue between stepfather and mother raises moral issues, in that the stepfather blames his wife for having been untrue to her promise to arrange for Bibus's death, and she gives her word that to the best of her knowledge she has kept it:

Roimderg 7 roaithisigh[20] in t-imper ingin righ Albun 7 adubairt gur gell si bas do tabairt do Bibus, 7 con derrna-si brég ara gelladh. Doraidh in righan: 'Doberim-si mo briathur', ar-si, 'gur sailes co fuair se bas'. (*SB* 277.1–5)	The emperor reproached and reviled the daughter of the king of Scotland [i.e., Bibus's mother] and said that she had promised to put Bibus to death and that she had broken her promise. The lady said: 'I give my word', she said, 'that I thought that he had been killed.'

Social norms, or standards of honour and honesty, appear to be behind Bibus's correct identification as *muiccidhi Sir Saber*, in preference to the English *messingere*, and the Irish gatekeeper refers to his unacceptable behaviour. In the remaining part of the scene, the characters in the English text simply describe and summarize their actions, whereas in the Irish version they

/ *A lite þing ich aue to speke / With þemperur* (*SBH* A 394–6). In the Anglo-Norman version Boeve identifies himself correctly as *fiz de counte* who has been made *bercher*, see Stimming, *Der anglo-normannische Boeve*, l. 263. **18** For a brief discussion of this scene see Poppe, 'The early modern Irish version', p. 84. **19** Similarly in the Anglo-Norman version, see Stimming, *Der anglo-normannische Boeve*, ll. 318–20. **20** For a combination of the same verbs see Quin, *Stair Ercuil*, ll. 1595–96: *ag imdhergadh 7 ag athaisiughudh*.

explore their motives, or explain their actions, in terms of honour, social obligation or expectation, and promise. This tendency is perhaps also reflected in the way Bibus's mother addresses Saber as *A treturaigh, fhallsa* (*SB* 277.6) 'false traitor'; in the English version she calls him *Sabere* without any qualifications (*SBH* M 357).[21] Qualifying epithets are one device used in the Irish text to indicate the narrator's, or the characters', assessment of characters,[22] which is particularly important since other explicit judgements by the narrator are unusual. Examples within the narrative are *an drochben celgach, mailisech* (*SB* 274.17–18) 'the evil, treacherous, and malicious woman' and *an imperi aingidhi, etroccuir* (*SB* 275.12) 'of the ruthless, cruel emperor', which have no parallel in the English text.[23]

In the next scene to be discussed,[24] Bibus's encounter with the Saracens on Christmas Day honour and religion combine: in the Irish version, the Saracens boast *Is iat ar seinnsir-ne docroch hé* (*SB* 278.10–1) 'they, our fore-fathers, crucified him [i.e., Christ]', and Bibus comments that he would like to punish them for this deed: *Is truagh lium-sa [...] gan nert agum a digailt oruibh-si a admail curob iad bur sinsir tug pais dom tigerna* (*SB* 278.12–14) 'I am sorry that I do not have the strength to avenge on you the admission that they, your fore-fathers, inflicted the Passion on my Lord'. This has no parallel in the English version, where Beues gives as his motive for wanting to fight with the Saracens the proof that his God is stronger: *there it shall be right well wiste, / Wheþure were strenger god in hevyn / Or all the mawȝmettes* ['idols'] (*SBH* M 486–8). After the fight Bibus/Beues retreats to his room, and the king wants to summon him to find out what has happened and why he has killed his men. In the English version two knights (*II knyghtes, SBH* M 553) approach Beues and are sent back with angry words:

> 'I will not rise ffro this ground, / To speke with no hethyn hound! / Oncristoned dogges, I rede, you flee, / Your hertes blood ellis wyll I see!' (*SBH* M 565–8)

In the Irish version the king sent messengers (*techta, SB* 278.25) of lower rank, not knights, as is obvious from Bibus's reaction. These are sent away as well, and Bibus comments explicitly on the differences in the treatment accorded to messengers in relation to their social standing:

'Da mad ridiri no lucht gaisgidh dotiucfad leisin techtairecht-sin, ní liccfind eladhach betha beo dibh,[25] 7 ni fiu lium echt anuasal na gillannrach do marbadh.' (*SB* 278.28–31)

'If knights or men of war came with this message, I would not let one of them escape alive, but it is not fitting for me to slay the ignoble or to kill the servants.'

However, Beues/Bibus is finally persuaded by Iosyan/Sisian, the king's daugher, to come to the king, and in the English version the king is moved to tears by Beues's story and his wounds and orders his daughter to look after him (*SBH* M 592–602).[26] In the Irish version the king explicitly forgives Bibus on the grounds of his religious loyalties:

---

21 In the English version she describes Beues in the same context as *That wekyd lad, that ffelown* (*SBH* M 358). No such description occurs in the Irish version. **22** Compare also the systematic use of epithets referring to Mary of Egypt and her spiritual development in Mac an Leagha's Irish version of the legend, see Poppe, 'Favourite expressions', pp 288–9. **23** Compare *SBH* M 146 and 219. **24** This scene has no analogue in the Anglo-Norman version. **25** Compare Quin, *Stair Ercuil*, ll. 813–14: *nar fhagaibh Ercuil eladhach betha beo dib acht Proserpini aonar* 'so that Hercules did not let one soul of them escape alive save Proserpine alone'. **26** This scene is developed even less in the Anglo-Norman version, see Stimming, *Der anglo-normannische Boeve*, ll. 485–90.

'Maithmid duit marbadh na ridiri', ar-se, '7 dobermid cairt do shidha duid, uair tuicmid in tan ata in grad úd agud aran righ nach facais riam curub mó na sin do gradh orum-sa, uair is mé in ri docunncais'. (*SB* 279.3–6)

'We will forgive you slaying the knights', he said, 'and we will give you an assurance of peace, because we understand now that your love for the king, whom you have never seen, is greater than your love for me, for I am the king you have seen.'

The characters' actions are again given greater moral and religious motivation than in the parallel English scene.

In explaining why she does not want to become Bramon's wife Sisian cites, among other things, the honour of her country, that 'this land will be held in contempt without a king being resident in it' (*an tir-so do cur a tarcaisne tre gan rí dobeth a comnaidhe innti*, *SB* 281.6–7).[27] It could perhaps be suggested that in the angry scene between Iosyan/Sisian and Beues/Bibus[28] the Irish version is again more explicit on the code of honour, but it must be stressed that honour is the decisive factor motivating Beues/Bibus's behaviour in both versions. In the Irish version he mentions 'this insult and this reproach without cause' (*in masla 7 in t-imdergadh-sin gan adhbhar*, *SB* 282.18–19) – but in the English version the narrator explains *For Iosyan had him myssaid* (SBH M 908) – and Sisian clearly states that she regrets her words (*is aitrech lem-sa a ndubart re Bibus*, *SB* 282.23 'I regret what I said to Bibus') and has dishonoured Bibus (*ina esonoir*, *SB* 282.25 'for his dishonour'). When Bibus and Sisian afterwards become reconciled and kiss each other, the Irish narrator twice uses the term *pósad* 'act of marrying, betrothal' (*SB* 283.6,8), which gives their kissing a more legal and official meaning than in the English version:

'Forgeve me, Beues, that I myssayd, / I wyll, yf thou be wyll payd, / My fals goddus I wyll forsake / And crystondome for thy love take!' / 'On that comenand,' said Beues than, / 'I wyll the love, Iosyan!' / And he kyssud her to cordment. (*SBH* M 953–9)

Later on in the narrative, Bibus twice describes his relationship with Sisian as proper (*co roibi ingen do righ paganta a cert aigi*, *SB* 289.16, also 289.26–7, 'that he had the daughter of a pagan king properly [as wife]'), and the Pope of India (*papa na hIndia*, *SB* 289.15–16) tells him that it would be appropriate for him to have another wife (*ben ele do beth aigi*, *SB* 289.17) under special circumstances only.[29] All this indicates that the narrator wants to convey the idea that there is nothing improper in the relationship between Sisian and Bibus. Similarly Robinson suggests that '[i]n Guy's interviews with Felice the English [...] suggests that his proposals were improper, whereas the Irish makes no mention of "folye".'[30]

---

27 I have discussed her arguments in greater detail, and with reference to the Irish concept of sovereignty, in Poppe, 'The early modern Irish version', pp 95–6; in the English and Anglo-Norman versions the king's daughter does not participate in the decision.   28 Compare particularly *SBH* M 898–918 and *SB* 282.14–25.   29 Bibus's sojourn with the Pope of India has no analogue in the English version; when he converses with the Patriarch of Jerusalem – who in the Irish version gives him the same advice as the Pope of India – the latter *for-bed him vpon his lif, / þat he neuer toke wif, / Boute þe were clene maide* (*SBH* A 1967–9), without any reference to Iosyan, who is shortly afterwards described as Beues's *lemman* (*SBH* A 1984) 'lover/sweetheart'. In the Anglo-Norman version the *patriarc* gives Boeve a mule, some money, and a blessing, and Boeve afterwards goes away to talk to Josian, see Stimming, *Der anglo-normannische Boeve*, ll. 1356–59, 1364. Only later, when Josian wants to accompany him to England, Boeve tells her that the *patriarc* had ordered him to take a virgin as wife, see Stimming, *Der anglo-normannische Boeve*, ll. 1475–8.
30 Robinson, 'The Irish Lives', pp 14–55.

In the Uriah-letter scene, a number of differences between the known English versions and the Irish adaptation can be noted, which are particularly striking when viewed together. To begin with, king Ermyn has Beues swear that he will not open the letter which contains the order that he should be killed:[31]

> 'But, Beves,' he said, 'thou shalte swere, / Thou wylte be trewe, my letter to bere; / As thou arte trew men and sele, / Vndo not the prynte of my seale!' (*SBH* M 1007–10)

In the Irish version, Ermin put Bibus under obligation by saying that 'it is you whom I consider most faithful of the men of the world' (*is tu is tairisi lium-sa d'feruibh an betha*, *SB* 283.18–19) and orders him not to open the letter (*na scail in litir*, *SB* 283.20), thus perhaps placing greater emphasis on Bibus's sense of honour. Bibus's rejection of the pilgrim's offer to read the letter – 'may I not stay [?] with a lord whom I would suspect to betray me' (*ni ber ag tigerna ara mbiadh amurus agum fell orum*, *SB* 284.7–8)   again plays on the sense of honour and loyalty, but is more difficult to assess. In this instance the closest English analogue appears to be the A-version – *He, þat me tok þis letter an honde, / He ne wolde loue me non oþer, / þan ich were is owene broþer* (*SBH* A 1330–2)[32] – rather than the C- or M-version,[33] so that the relationship between the Irish version and Mac an Leagha's possible source must remain open. We are on perhaps safer ground with Bramon's comment which reflects his sense of rank, when he remarks that Bibus forced him to give homage and tribute 'to a man [i.e., Ermin] who was lower than myself [i.e., Bramon]' (*do duine fa mesa na me fein*, *SB* 285.9). There is nothing on submission in the English A-version, and the C- and M-versions simply have Bradmond state that Beues made him *thrall* without reference to differences in rank between Bradmond and Ermyn (*SBH* M 1233, C 327). In a further addition to the extent English versions Bramon orders that Bibus is supplied with food 'because it is not proper not to honour the servant of a worthy lord' (*Tabur biadh do Bibus [...] uair ni cubaidh oglach tigerna maith gan anoir do denum do*, *SB* 285.10–11), thus at least superficially stressing the values of hospitality and social obligations.[34] But it should be noted that in the Anglo-Norman version Bradmund also offers Boeve food, but here slightly later in the course of events, namely before he has him put into prison.[35] When the king discloses the contents of the letter to Beues/Bibus, the reactions are revealingly different in the English and Irish versions: In the English version Beues insists on his equal rank as knight and demands to fight with the Saracens so that he may *dye in batell right, / As maner is of a doughty knyght* (*SBH* M 1261–2). In the Irish version Bibus first argues with his function as messenger and the protection accorded to messengers and says that 'this is disgraceful, to kill the one who comes with a message' (*Is nar sin [...] i. in nech dothiucfadh le techtairecht do cur cum bais*, *SB* 285.16–17). Only then he demands to fight with the Saracens and again stresses the moral differences between killing a well-equipped

---

31 Similarly in the Anglo-Norman version, see Stimming, *Der anglo-normannische Boeve*, ll. 806–8.   **32** See Kölbing's paraphrase: 'He who commissioned me with this letter loves me so much that he would not send me to a place where my life was in danger' (*SHB*, p. 281). The Anglo-Norman version has *'Oustés,' ce dist Boefs, 'de ceo ne vus dotez / moun seignur ne le freit pur treis cent citez'*, see Stimming, *Der anglo-normannische Boeve*, ll. 860–2. **33** The M-version, to which the C-version is very similar (*SBH* C 155–9), reads: *Nay, as haue I rest or roo, / So couth I my selfe haue do; / Shall it never on-done be, / Tyll the kyng hym selfe it se!* (*SBH* M 1121–4).   **34** In this particular context providing Bibus with food gives Bramon and his retinue the time necessary to consider how to kill Bibus. On the importance of hospitality in another scene see Poppe, 'The early modern Irish version', p. 93.   **35** See Stimming, *Der anglo-normannische Boeve*, ll. 928–32.

warrior in the battle-field and a defenceless messenger in the hall, *is lugha d'adhbur gotha dibh-si misi do marbadh mur sin na mo marbadh ann-so* (*SB* 285.21–2) 'it is less cause for censuring you to kill me like this than to kill me here'.[36]

Even in the hero's dealings with God there may be a difference between the English and the Irish versions, in that the Irish version stresses the importance of mutual obligations. When Beues has suffered in the dungeon of king Bradmond for a long time, he finally implores God for *pite* and *merci* (*SBH* A 1585, 1586).[37] But in the Irish version he argues with God and insists that he has been faithful all the time he lived among the pagans, thus implying that God is obliged to help him now, even if he moderates this implication slightly in the last sentence:

'[...] Doci tú, a tigerna, nar treices do creidem fein fos ge taim coic bliadhna dec a talam na paganach, 7 a thigerna', ar-se, 'is aithnid duid co fuiginn inme 7 ardflaithus mor da treiccinn do creidem-sa; 7 a tigerna nemdha', ar-se, 'foir orum intan is mithi let féin'. (*SB* 286.18–23)

'See, Lord, that I did not abandon faith in you while I was for fifteen years in the land of the pagans, and, Lord', he said, 'you know that I could have obtained a great heritage and chief-kingdom if I had abandoned this faith in you, and, Lord,' he said, 'help me when you consider it timely.'

My final example concerns the confrontation between Beues and Grander's brother and the latter's accusation that Beues stole Grander's horse (*SBH* A 1865–8). In the English version, Beues ignores it and tells the gruesome story of how he killed Grander by breaking open his skull (*made him a kroune brod*, *SBH* A 1870) and thus *made him prest* (*SBH* A 1872).[38] In the Irish version, Bibus explicitly rejects the accusation and denies having stolen Grainnder's horse, but admits at the same time that he killed Grainnder and took his horse by force, thus presumably implying a subtle difference between theft and honorable acquisition through fight: *Ní hé a goid dorinis [...] 7 gideth romarbus inté aga roibhi si, 7 dobenus in t-ech ar ecin de* (*SB* 288.27–9) 'I did not steal it, although I killed him who owned it and took the horse from him by force'.[39]

Politically, Gaelic and gaelicised Ireland in the fifteenth century were characterized by 'local autonomy by both Gaelic and Anglo-Irish lords, and the frequency of warfare between these independent or semi-independent units'.[40] But we know little of the mentality and the attitudes

---

36 Note that a similar argument is advanced in the Irish version of Guy of Warwick and that Beues' final plea occurs nearly verbatim there as well, but Guy's reason is the hospitality that he has had: '*ni fhuil acht fell dibh énridiri na enur dia tugabur biadh do marbadh i nbur tigh, 7 masa duine fíruasal thu, tabur cet dam-sa dul ar m'ech tar dorus na cathrach amach, 7 tabraidh mo cloidhem 7 mo sciath dam, 7 bid ced toraigechta agud orum, 7 is lugha is guth dib mo marbadh mur-sin no marbadh mur-so*' (Robinson, 'The Irish Lives', p. 79) '"it is treachery for you to kill a single knight or a single man to whom you have given food in your house, and if you are a truly noble man, give me permission to go on my horse out of the city and give me my sword and my shield, and you will have my permission to pursue me, and the blame is less for you to kill me like this than to kill me like that."' This scene is clearly derived from the Middle English version, see *The Romance of Guy of Warwick. The first or 14th-century version*, ed. by J. Zupitza, Early English Texts Society, Extra Series, 42, 49, 59 (London 1883–91) p. 364.   **37** The differences between the English versions are minimal here, so that Kölbing gives the text from A. The Anglo-Norman version is again close to the English, see Stimming, *Der anglo-normannische Boeve*, ll. 1040–5.   **38** Similarly in the Anglo-Norman version, see Stimming, *Der anglo-normannische Boeve*, ll. 1305–8. For further parallels in other Middle English texts see Kölbing's note, p. 299.   **39** Note that Beues's joking remark that he made Grander a priest is not taken over by the Irish redactor, as is also neither Gye's wife's disparaging remark that *All day he [i.e., Gye] courith in the churche* (*SBH* M 80) nor the humorous description of Ascaparde's baptism in Cologne (*SBH* M 2309–16), which may indicate a concern with the status of church-matters.   **40** A. Cosgrove,

of the ruling classes. Bardic poetry allows many insights, but analysis of this corpus to date has been mainly confined to the poetic discourse on sovereignty, nationality, and the assessment of the changing political situation.[41] The aristocratic ideal of bardic poetry focuses on military prowess and generosity. In view of the likelihood that H.2.7 was produced for an aristocratic patron it is therefore striking that *Stair Bibuis* reveals rather different concerns.

At least one manuscript written by Uilliam Mac an Leagha appears to be connected with the gaelicised Butler family. This is London, British Library, Additional MS 30512, which may have been written for Edmund mac Richard Butler of Polestown († 1464) who was 'keenly interested in Irish literature' and had a wife from the Gaelic nobility.[42] Robin Flower has suggested more specifically that it may be 'Leabur na carraigi given with Laud Misc. 610 in ransom for Edmond Butler in 1462', but Anne and William O'Sullivan consider this proposal unlikely.[43] Be that as it may, it is clear that the compiler(s) of the manuscript had an interest in a man called Richard Butler, since there are four religious poems in the manuscript associated with that name: (1) a poem on the power of Jesus as exemplified in his dealing with Old and New Testament characters, (2) a poem on the beauty and sweetness of Christ, which Richard is said to have recited on the day of his death, (3) a poem of invocation to God and the angels, and (4) a poem written in sickness and asking help of God.[44] Gearóid Mac Niocaill thinks it most likely that this Richard Butler was Edmund's father.[45] Uilliam Mac an Leagha's version of the legend of Mary of Egypt in

'Ireland beyond the Pale, 1399–1460', in *A new history of Ireland*, vol. 2, *Medieval Ireland 1169–1534*, ed. A. Cosgrove (Oxford 1987) pp 569–90, at p. 583.   **41** See in particular J. Leerssen, *Mere Irish and Fíor-Ghael. Studies in the idea of Irish nationality, its development and literary expression prior to the nineteenth century* (repr. Cork, 1996) pp 151–253, M. O Riordan, *The Gaelic mind and the colapse of the Gaelic world* (Cork 1990), and M. Caball, *Poets and politics. Reaction and continuity in Irish poetry, 1558–1625* (Cork 1998).   **42** J. Carney, *Poems on the Butlers of Ormond, Cahier, and Dunboyne (AD 1400–1650)* (Dublin 1945) p. ix, see ibid., pp viii–xiii for a short history of the Butlers. Carney also notes (ibid., pp xii) that '[i]n view of the extent to which the junior branches of the Butlers, and for a brief period the house of Ormond, patronised Irish bards, the amount of encomiastic verse dealing with them must seem meagre.' He suggests that this is due to a chance survival of the existing texts, reflecting later generations' loss of interest in Irish poetry, and that originally there must have been considerably more poetry (ibid., pp xii–xiii). For further discussion of Edmund mac Richard Butler and Uilliam Mac an Leagha see F. Henry and G. Marsh-Micheli, 'Manuscripts and illuminations, 1169–1603', in *A new history of Ireland*, vol. 2, *Medieval Ireland 1169–1534*, ed. A. Cosgrove (Oxford 1987) pp 781–813, at pp 802–5.   **43** R. Flower, *Catalogue of Irish manuscripts in the British Library [formerly British Museum]*, vol. 2 (Dublin 1992) p. 471; A. and W. O'Sullivan, 'Three Notes on Laud Misc. 610 (Or the Book of Pottlerath)', *Celtica* 9 (1971) pp 135–51, at p. 145. Another Edmund Butler 'became the eighth baron of Dunboyne about 1460 and held this position until his death sometime in 1498–9' (A. O'Sullivan and P. Ó Riain, *Poems on marcher lords from a sixteenth-century Tipperary manuscript*, ITS 53 (London 1987) p. 68).   **44** See Flower, *Catalogue of Irish manuscripts*, pp 496 (no. 90) 497 (no. 94), 498 (no. 98), 499–500 (no. 101). A quatrain in a margin possibly intended as an interpretation of a quatrain on the number of the Tuatha Dé Danann is also ascribed to him, see ibid., p. 504 (no. 114 (h)), but is mostly illegible. Nos 98 and 101 have been edited by Gearóid Mac Niocaill ('Dhá Dhán le Risteard Buitléar', *Éigse* 9.2 (1958) pp 83–8), no. 94 has been edited and translated by Robin Flower (*The Irish tradition* (Oxford 1947) pp 134–5) as an example 'of the practice of Irish verse by the hibernicized English, and as a proof of the penetration of the Franciscan attitude, which so profoundly modified the religious poetry of Europe in the later Middle Ages, into the Irish tradition' (ibid. p. 134).   **45** Flower (*Catalogue of Irish manuscripts*, p. 497) suggests that no. 94 is written in a sixteenth-century hand and also believes (*Irish tradition*, p. 134) that the Richard Butler who is said in the manuscript to have composed this poem on the day he died, lived around 1537, and he attributes to this Butler all poems associated with the name Richard Butler in the manuscript. Mac Niocaill ('Dhá Dhán', p. 84), however, rejects Flower's suggestions about the date of the script of no. 94 and believes that nos 94, 98, 101, and 114 (h) are all written in the same fifteenth-century hand. He also upholds the identification of the poems' author with Richard Butler, the son of James, the third earl of Ormond († 1405), and the father of Edmund, on which my tentative suggestions here are based (the fourth, or White, Earl († 1452) would thus have been Richard's brother and Edmund's uncle). Flower's poem no. 90 is not discussed by Mac Niocaill.

the same manuscript has been interpreted in the light of fifteenth-century reform movements as a 'piece of propaganda for monastic reform and a strict adherence to the monastic rule as well as a call for a greater stress on religious values in secular life'.[46] Flower has classified the contents of Additional MS 30512 as 'miscellaneous theology' and suggested that it

> falls naturally, apart from matter inserted later, into two sharply contrasted parts, which may originally have been independent MSS. The first part (arts. 1–97), in verse and prose, contains, with few exceptions, texts of the pre-twelfth cent. period, the second part (arts. 98–113) divided from the first part by blank leaves and opening with an elaborate initial, contains prose only, in the main of the 14th-15th cent. period, translated from Latin, and in two cases possibly from English, originals.[47]

The invocation to God ascribed to Richard Butler[48] forms the beginning of the second part. If the poem's theme and the contents of the manuscript are indicative of his and his son's tastes it is clear that religious topics were a central concern and that they were interested in native stories as well as in stories derived from foreign-language sources.

The part of Oxford, Bodleian MS Laud Misc. 610 originally written for Edmund mac Richard Butler has a similar thematic pattern and falls 'textually into a religious or hagiological part at the beginning with the glossary [viz. Cormac's Glossary] in the middle cutting the genealogical and historical part into two'.[49] A number of the religious texts are again based on foreign-language sources; the manuscript also contains a text of the Irish version of the *chanson de geste* of Fortibras preceded by an adaptation of the Invention of the Holy Cross.[50] The mixture of the native and the foreign is also repeated in the decoration of the manuscript; Françoise Henry and Geneviève Marsh-Micheli note

> the deliberate acceptance of forms of initials or ornaments current in non-Irish manuscripts of the time, such as fine scrolls or patterns of flowers and the flippant mixing of them with the most traditional Irish patterns. It is not complete integration, [...] it remains juxtaposition. The scribes are obviously well-read and perfectly aware of the methods of decoration of their contemporaries, and perhaps want us to realise that if they are using mostly Irish patterns it is not out of ignorance of other fashions but from deliberate choice.[51]

H.2.7 is the only one of Uilliam Mac an Leagha's manuscripts containing secular texts only, although it has been argued that the English romances of Guy of Warwick and Beues of Hamtoun have a Christian message,[52] and Robinson has stressed the importance of additional religious

---

46 B. Ross, 'Uilliam Mac an Leagha's version of the story of Mary of Egypt', in Poppe and Ross, *The Legend of Mary of Egypt*, pp 259–78, at p. 276. Caoimhín Breatnach's discussion of *Oidheadh Chloinne Lir*, and of its depiction of human suffering and its implied Christian message, within the wider context of religious themes in fifteenth-century Irish literature adds further weight to my argument, see C. Breatnach, 'The Religious Significance of *Oidheadh Chloinne Lir*', *Ériu* 50 (1999) pp 1–40. **47** Flower, *Catalogue of Irish manuscripts*, pp 473–4. **48** This is 'Risderd Botiler' in the manuscript. **49** A. and W. O'Sullivan, 'Three Notes', p. 144. **50** For a catalogue of the contents of the manuscript see M. Dillon, 'Laud Misc. 610', *Celtica* 5 (1960) 64–76, pp 71–6. **51** Henry and Marsh-Micheli, 'Manuscripts and illuminations', p. 803. **52** For a list of his manuscripts with a summary of their contents see Ross, *Bildungsidol*, pp 41–5; for religious elements in the Middle English romances see, for example, D. Mehl, 'Weltliche Epik in England: Von Sir Beues of Hamtoun bis Malorys Morte Arthur', in *Europäisches Spätmittelalter*, ed. W. Erzgräber (Heidelberg 1989) pp 205–20, at p. 208, and S. Crane Dannenbaum, 'Guy of

themes and the insistence on works of piety and charity in Mac an Leagha's adaptation of the story of Guy. My analysis of the fragment of the Irish adaptation of the story of Beues has identified a preoccupation with codes of conduct and honour which is lacking in the extent English versions. The manuscript's association with the Butlers must remain speculative, but Bibus' additional sojourn with the Prior of Rhodes (*SB* 289.20–24) may be connected with the fact that Thomas Bachach Butler, a half-brother to Edmund's uncle, the fourth earl of Ormond, was the prior of the Knights Hospitallers in Ireland in the early part of the fifteenth century.[53] Given the predominantly 'heroic' concerns of bardic poetry and the predominantly Christian concerns of the manuscripts associated with the Butlers, it is tempting – though dangerous – to speculate that the small amount of encomiastic verse dealing with them, noted by Carney,[54] may reflect more than just the vagaries of chance survival.

Uilliam Mac an Leagha produced the texts in H.2.17 for a patron, and he and his patron, as individuals or as members of a particular section of Irish society, would have considered the values transmitted here to be important. Thus the veiled discourse on conduct and honour in *Stair Bibuis* can be seen as an indicator of attitudes and preoccupations of at least some representatives of the Irish intellectual elite at the end of the fifteenth century, and both the focus on religous values and the interest in the adaptation of foreign-language materials could suit the context of the gaelicised Anglo-Norman family of the Butlers.

Warwick and the question of exemplary romance', *Genre* 17 (1984) pp 351–74.   **53** See Poppe, 'The early modern Irish version', pp 97–8.   **54** See Carney, *Poems on the Butlers*, p. xii.   **55** It would be an interesting exercise to analyse all four texts of H.2.7 in terms of their ideological and attitudinal preoccupations; for many useful hints on *Stair Ercuil* see Ross, *Bildungsidol*, who stresses the Irish version's emphasis on Ercuil's heroic and military prowess. I have not found any references to Bibus as a standard of comparison in Irish bardic poetry, which is perhaps not surprising. In Welsh bardic poetry, however, Bown's name is used by poets of the *uchelwyr* between 1450 and 1600, for example by Guto'r Glyn, Tudur Aled, Siôn Ceri, and Siôn Tudur. Keating lists *Bevis of Hamton* among his examples of fictional stories called *fabulae* (*sceoil da ngairthí fabulae*) from countries other than Ireland written in both pagan and Christian times, see Seathrún Céitinn, *Foras Feasa ar Éirinn*, vol. 2, ed. Pádraig Ua Duinnín, *ITS* 8 (London 1908) p. 326.

The poetic self-fashioning of Gofraidh Fionn Ó Dálaigh

ANN DOOLEY

The difficulties of taking a biographical approach to an Irish bardic poet and his work are legion.[1] The corpus is not always easy to establish. Attributions can occur in late manuscripts, the reliability of which it is not always easy to assess; the rate of reliability of these is in inverse proportion to the fame of the poet being claimed as author. This can be particularly confusing in the blurred transmission tradition of southern Ó Dálaigh material.[2] There are some markers that help: in the case of Gofraidh Fionn, one looks for the typical dedicatory quatrain to St Michael, evidence for his family connections with Adare Abbey of similar dedication. But this can be unreliable as the abbey was built and dedicated some years after Gofraidh's death.[3] So the best that can be said is that these quatrains are marks, both of a genuine southern Ó Dálaigh tradition of devotion and of transmission of Gofraidh's poems in a family milieu; the worst that they are a spurious attempt to increase prestige by marking later poetry with a recognizable earlier pattern of attribution to one the greatest of Irish medieval poets.

There is also the general and basic difficulty of constructing a chronology. Bardic poems are notoriously allusive and indirect and refuse to yield their information easily. Many – indeed most – poems to patrons can be dated to a reign if information on the father, grandfather and wife or mother is given. Within this time-frame some conventions can help: for example, an elegy can be pegged to a death date attested from annalistic sources; an inauguration poem – and genuine ones are rare – to succession to a title;[4] one can guess at other occasions; a militaristic incitement to action for a young noble, or individual poems to two siblings, may signal the few years within which succession between rival candidates is being fought out.[5] Poems to women patrons pose a particularly interesting problem. I believe that there are some instances of genuine epithalamia – one in the Magauran Duanaire for example – but one would like to know more about the kinds of significant occasions for which gifts or commissions of poems for women before and after marriage are deemed appropriate.[6]

We still do not know enough about variation in the conditions of patronage at different periods. Does the chief's poet operate under a different set of assumptions about social relations with his patron in the late fourteenth century from those that obtain in the late fifteenth and early

---

1 Brian Ó Cuív has shown the problems of verification in the only poet's 'biography' known to us, the account of Muireadhach Albannach Ó Dálaigh in *AFM*: 'Eachtra Mhuireadhaigh Í Dhálaigh', *Studia Hibernica* I (1961) pp 56–69. James Carney attempted a biographical account of Eochaidh Ó hEodhasa from the internal evidence of his poetry in *The Irish bardic poet* (Dublin 1967). **2** Cf C. McGrath, 'Ó Dálaigh Fionn cct.', *Éigse* 5 (1945) pp 185–95. He did not use the Carew evidence; for this see A. O'Sullivan, 'Tadhg O'Daly and Sir George Carew', *Éigse* 14 (1971–2) pp 27–38. **3** The abbey is a Geraldine foundation. According to McGrath, loc.cit. n. II, 189–90, Margaret wife of Cú Uladh Ó Dálaigh (†1483) caused the Lady chapel to be built. **4** For an example of the uncertain criteria for designating a poem an inauguration ode see Séamus Mac Mathúna, 'An inaugural ode to Hugh O'Connor?', *ZCP* 49–50 (1997) pp 548–75. **5** For examples of this in Gofraidh's own corpus see the poems to Diarmaid and to his brother Domhnall Mág Cárthaigh in L. McKenna S.J. (ed.), *Dioghluim Dána* (Dublin 1938) pp 296–301, 228–35. **6** Cf the poem for Sadhbh, daughter of Cathal Ó Conchobhair and wife of Niall Mág Shamhradháin, *The Book of Magauran*, ed. L. McKenna S.J. (Dublin 1947) pp 130–9, 339–43, 418–20.

sixteenth, the focus of Pádraig A. Breatnach's careful study of the relationship?[7] What exactly is the significance for the biography of the poet of marking some poems with quatrains to local patrons and leaving other poems unmarked as in the case of much of the Gofraidh Fionn corpus? Were such poems 're-edited' by the poet himself, for example? To which patron was Gofraidh an *ollamh* in poetry and when?

All this indeterminacy creates an initial sense of frustration which is further compounded by the nature of bardic poetry itself. In the highly conventional and public poetic forms practised by medieval Irish professional poets, principles of discursive decorum are prized above the idea of a discourse intended to reveal the individual subjective self. So we are perhaps even less likely than those working on this question of subjectivity in other medieval vernaculars to subscribe to the fallacy of mimetic sincerity, that is, to claim to equate the lived experience of the author with the content of the finished poem. In looking at any body of bardic poetry, the effort to distinguish the particular characteristics of an individual poet's voice has to recognize the formal structure of rhetorical play which sustains the semblance of emotion and personal engagement in each unique literary invention, and which gives to a bardic poem its brilliant and Gongoresque façade of impenetrable poetic reserve.

The conventions of bardic poetry are helpful in a number of other ways, however. Firstly, the poem is not entirely other-directed and is by no means intended to be empty of self. Indeed, the projection of self is crucial. The dynamic which animates bardic poetics is the reciprocal relationship between patron and lord; what happens in that relationship constitutes the real matter of the poetry. Thus the poetico-social contract, and the principle of bardic discourse as social engagement, prevents the poet from disengaging himself from the very real play of event and social reality within which the relationship is grounded. Secondly, in a poetic system where the power relations of poet and patron are paramount, the discriminatory wealth and material resources of the patron must be balanced by a display of power transference from the poet, which is necessarily symbolic but also real. The allocutionary act, from composition to public performance, to written record is itself deemed to be a vessel of power. In such a system the convention of a strongly assertive poetic ego is an essential part of the poet's stylized power display. Finally, there is the issue of competition on another level. The poet strives to be heard against a background of other competing poetic voices.[8] Professional competitive anxiety hones the edge of the personal in a particularly complex set of self-measurings and assertions that are always present in poems. Competition forces the patron's hand also; one constantly reads the tension between the lines of the main discourse of praise for the telling moment when the conventionally expected accolade is witheld, or shaded off into less than complete endorsment by a veiled reference to another. These factors put the issue of the poet's individuality squarely back in the discursive agenda and makes it possible for us to assess whether or how an individual poet is pushing the envelope of conventionalized self.

The professional identity of Gofraidh Fionn is initially easiest to establish from his contemporary and subsequent literary reputation. The jealousy of his poetic contemporaries does

7 'The chief's poet', *PRIA* 83 (1986) pp 37–79 See also his comments on Gofraidh's habit, itself marked as unique by other later poets, of referring to pacts made between Gofraidh and patrons to include a quatrain for them in his other poems, 'A covenant between Eochaidh Ó hEodhusa and Aodh Mág Uidhir', *Éigse* 27 (1993) 59–66. **8** The hostility is evident in the poem by Maolmhuire Mág Craith addressed to Gofraidh, *Mairg chaitheas dlús re dhalta, Dioghluim Dána*, pp 352–4.

not prevent them from making generous admission of his literary achievement as the complaint poem from Maolmhuire Mág Craith makes clear:

Ceard Ghofradha as ghlan cridhe	In all sincerity, Gofraidh's art is an ornament to
ag cumhdach ar gceirdei-ne;	our profession; the ornament of his education
maith bláth a oideachta air	sits well on him; it might, perhaps, constitute a
do b'fháth coigealta ar chiontaibh.[9]	reason to keep silent about his transgressions.

He himself ensured that his reputation as a master craftsman and figure of poetic authority in his own right would already be established in his own lifetime, as the recording of his poem on bardic grammer and usage in so proximate a source as the Book of Uí Mhaine attests.[10] The signature quatrain, unusual in itself for the period, is missing from the Book of Uí Mhaine but the scribe of RIA 23 D 14, the text of McKenna's edition and that of the later RIA 24 P 8, 3 who seems to have used a version like M's had no difficulty in accepting it as Gofraidh's work:

Is mé Gofraidh mac meic Thaidhg	I am Gofraidh, grandson of Tadhg, from
a-ndeas ón Mhumhain mhíonaird	smooth lofty Munster in the south; few are
tearc trá ón lios i luighim	they who can answer these questions I send
gá dtá fios a bhfiafruighim.	forth from this fort where I lie.[11]

His conclusions, however, do more than exemplify his command of the craft. This poem is carried forward on a sharply aggressive register and Gofraidh plays the exercise as if it were a contest with an adversary for poetic pre-eminence. At the same time, he seems to be defending the art of Irish bardic verse with a consciousness of perspectives from those intellectual traditions outside the native frame of reference (cf. the references to *soisgéal* (qu. 19), *canóin* (qu. 22) and *feallsamh* (qu.15)). But if innovation is part of Gofraidh's challenge here, his world of competitive learning is also a world that is sustained by the prestige that accrues to his fanciful version of a native title, to *ollamhnaibh na n-airdríogh*. All in all, there is a strong sense that he is also, with this poem, hanging up his shop sign as it were, and serving notice that he will brook no southern rival in the bardic academy business.

Ar na ceasdaibh ad-chluine	If anyone should explore these questions I have
dá n-urmaise énduine	been elucidating, let him do so under my
- an aithnesi ní haisgidh-	direction. Poetry does not come free!
ar mhaithrisi urmaisdir.	

In fhogluimsi an iongnadh libh	Does it not seem odd to you that poets would
da mbeith a haithne ag éigsibh,	have been knowledgeable about poetry, with
is iad lesin ndán druim ar druim,	hands-on experience of the craft, and that they
is gan iad dá rádh romhuinn.	would have never given instruction on it up to now?

---

9 Ibid. qu. 2. The compliment to his *oideacht* is a backhanded one as, on the evidence of this poem, Gofraidh was educated by the Mág Craiths. Translation my own here and elsewhere unless otherwise stated. **10** 'Mad fiafraidheach budh feasach', ed. L. McKenna, 'A Poem by Gofraidh Fionn Ó Dálaigh', in *Féilscríbhinn Torna: essays and studies presented to Professor Tadhg Ua Donnchadha*, ed. S. Pender (Cork 1947) pp 66–76. **11** I translate *luighim* as 'lie' against McKenna's 'dwell', as it may be an allusion to the bardic compositional practice of composing while

Meinic shaoilim ó so suas   From now on I expect that anyone who fails to
- ni hionann do chách coguas -   master it will also blame me for the failure–all
ó nach fuighe uirre eol   are not on the same level of understanding.
duine uime dom áitcheodh.

Tacmhang na héigse uile   Involvement in poetry is perilous for any man;
conntabhairt é ag énduine   few are qualified to speak of the complexities
tearc as ionchomhráidh orra   involved in learning the art. (qq. 50–52, 54)[12]
friothghobhláin na foghloma.

It may well be that this, as well as anxiety about competition for Ó Briain patronage, is what upset
the older Mág Craith poetic establishment so much and occasioned the reproof from Maolmhuire
already cited.

In addition to this professional self-testimonial, I think we can advance, in a major way, our
appreciation of Gofraidh's particularly aggressive type of self-definition if we accept that there are
also sufficient grounds for assigning to him *Damhaidh dúinn cóir a chléirche*, one of the most
important bardic poems from the later fourteenth-century.[13] In this piece, one of the most able
defences of eulogy in the whole of bardic tradition is mounted and a coherent rationale for the
profession of poetry is laid out. At the same time the projection of self in this poem differs from
Gofraidh's teaching poem above in a significant way, in that the entire poem remains rhetorically
anchored in the traditional formulae of request to the patron and counterpointed with hostility
towards another learned adversary. Before looking at the thematic concerns of the poem it may
be well to lay out the reasons why it seems to me likely that the poem is to be attributed to
Gofraidh Fionn. It survives as a single copy, in the Nugent manuscript (National Library of
Ireland, G 992, fol. 38v-40v), and, as its editor Brian Ó Cuív demonstrates, was addressed to
Diarmaid Ó Briain, who died in 1364 after a long and chequered career in which he figured as lord
of Thomond from 1350 on. The editor provided a rich set of contextual references but did not
pronounce on the identity of the poet other than to speculate on the possible literary connections
between this poem and the *Caithréim Thoirdhealdhaigh* in which Diarmaid figured prominently
and which, ironically, was written by a member of the Mag Craith family.[14]

The assembled comparanda that incline me to assign the poem to Gofraidh are the following:

a) Identical metaphor

as bas re buinde roimhear (qu. 24).[15]   as bas re sruth (qu.59).[16]

---

lying down in a confined space.   **12** Presumably, he will be reproached in the future because he has raised the
standard so high that few can reach the level he demands.   **13** Ed. B. Ó Cuív, 'An appeal on behalf of the
profession of poetry', *Éigse* 14 (1971–2) pp 87–106.   **14** Ó Cuív notes of Diarmaid mainly those elements of his
youthful career contained in CT. But if this narrative was written – and Ó Cuív notes the opinion of T.F. O'Rahilly
– *c*.1330, the implication that this might help the dating of the poem is unhelpful. It is more likely to have been
written in the late 1350s after the death of the first earl of Desmond and when both of his sons Muiris (†1358) and
Gearóid (†1398) were coming into adulthood. This is also the period of his other poem to Diarmaid (*Ériu* 16 (1952)
pp 132–9). It is likely that the connection with the O'Briens is a cause of hostility with the family of Mág Craith,
who also look, like Gofraidh, for Ó Briain patronage.   **15** Gofraidh's poem to Diarmaid Ó Briain, 'A toigh bheag
tiaghar a tteagh mór', *Ériu* 16, p. 135.   **16** Noted by Ó Cuív, 'An Appeal', p. 104.

b) Identical set of epithets fixed by rime

tiomna Colmáin ar a cheird
tré diomdha an bhonnbháin
bhéildeirg (qu. 9).[17]

An onóir chédna ar ar gceird
foráil-si, a bhondbháin bhéildeirg (qu. 33).

c) The use of *Saltair Chaisil* to advance an encomiastic argument fixed by rime

Fuair sinn i Saltair Chaisil
go dtiocfa-sa an turais-sin
d'fhéachain fionnphuirt shuairc do shean
ion-Chuirc do chuairt go Caiseal (qu. 10).[18]

Breath Shaltrach caoimhe Caisil
dá dtucca(m s)fan tagraisin
a aomhachdain an áil libh
a ráidh cáomhShaltair Chaisil (qu. 4).

In both cases in c) the Psalter of Cashel is being used to back up a truth assertion claim: in one, the judgement of the Psalter of Cashel stands as a reliable native Irish ecclesiastical source which can refute the claims of a new clericy, and against which all other texts can be dismissed as *leabhar mbriondach*; in the other it is the source of a specific tradition of saintly prophecy, *tarngair na naomh*, which upholds Domhnall's right to the royal site of his ancestors.

d) Similar architectural terms

A chrannghal sa chloch aolta
gar da chéile a ccomhaonta;
dealughadh ga nuaim ni bhfuil
buaidh nealudhan an obuir

Nír snadhmadh dfhiodhbhaidh oile
comhálainn na crannghaile;
an rochloch, ní fhalaigh aol
aghaidh chathrach a comhchaomh

Rogha na cclach is na gcrann
cúirt fhairsing áibhle Cualann;
dairighe dúinte gan dluighe,
sailghe a cúirte cúpluighe (qu. 31–33)

Maith le saoraibh sliochd a lámh
d'adhmoladh ar n-úaim dheaghclár
ar gcur chrandghal gcaol nó chloch
no ar n-amladh bhrugh saor seasbhach (qu. 10).[19]

17 'A Cholmáin mhóir mheic Léinín', *Irish bardic poetry*, ed. O. Bergin and D. Greene (Dublin 1970) p. 71.   18 'In the Psalter of Cashel I have found that you would make a journey to view the beautiful fort of your ancestors; your journey to Cashel would be similar to Corc's' *Beir eolas dúinn a Dhomhnuill* (to Domhnall Óg Mág Cárthaigh), *Dioghluim Dána*, pp 228–35 (qu. 10). 'If we adduce in that dispute the judgement of the fair Psalter of Cashel, are you willing to accept what it actually says' (qu. 4).   19 'Craftsmen like the product of their hands to be praised, when fine boards are joined, after slender wooden joists or stones are placed in position, when [these] noble lasting dwellings are decorated' (qu 10). 'Close is the joining of its timber and its lime-washed stone; there is no gaping where they touch, the work is a triumph of art. From no other forest has timber of such beauty been joined; that great mass of stone, lime covers no citadel its equal. The choicest stone and timber has gone into the spacious court of the Spark of Cualu; the beams of his arched hall are of unspliced oak' (qu. 31–3), ed. E. Knott, '*Filidh Éirionn go haointeach*', *Ériu* 5 (1911) pp 50–69.

The word *crannghal* seems to have a fairly restricted usage. *DIL* cites its use in connection with ships, ploughs and weaponry and suggests a general meaning 'wedge'.[20] The word *cúplach* is, incidentally, another favourite of Gofraidh's, recurring in the phrase *bruidhean chúplach* with reference to the house of Conchobhar Ó Briain in a poem which must be one of Gofraidh's earliest.[21] The relation between *Damhaidh dúinn cóir a chléirche* and the poem on William O'Kelly's feast from which the term *cúplach* is drawn is such that the *topos,* in the former, of envisioning a patron's great culture feast while praising architectural features represents a synopsis of the more extended and *post factum* treatment in the Ó Ceallaigh piece. It thus seems likely that the Ó Briain poem, *Damhaidh dúinn cóir a chléirche,* is somewhat later than 1351, as if Gofraidh is referring almost schematically to a poetic run which he had developed to great effect in the O'Kelly's feast offering. Whatever the case may be, the occurrence of similar architectural terms in both poems brings the larger issue of functional similarities into clear focus.

There is one other term, *cuing,* 'yoke', used in *Damhaidh dúinn cóir a chléirche* on which much of the argument for the status of poetry turns and which also seems to be a favourite term of Gofraidh's, occurring in a number of his poems in related contexts.[22] In *Damhaidh dúinn cóir a chléirche,* the term is first applied to the consequences of the new clerical ordinances: they are not just a *cuing/ ar chách ainfhéle d'fhoghlaim* [an obligation on all to learn to be miserly], resulting in the loss of lords' entertainments; the more serious consequences will be the dangerous yoking together under *aonchuing* of noble families and the sons of slaves.[23] This elicits the rallying cry for a patron who will go to war on behalf of poetry and so break the tyrannous clerical *cuing* (qu. 28) just as heroes and saints, Finnian and Cú Chulainn, did long ago.[24] Only through the free circulation of the learned lore of poets are such examples of honour from the past remembered and made effective for a present generation. The Diarmaids and the Williams will also be made famous and immortal by the poets' invocation of their good example in turn. Thus by his generous action in taking on responsibility for maintaining poets the patron will restore to *cuing* its proper lexical status as the *eneachchuing* (qu. 42) and the *cuing na bhfhileadh* (qu. 43). This yoke, Gofraidh maintains, is the only factor maintaining social solidarity and identity: *faoilidh le gach saorchloind sin/ Gaoidhil fá aonchuing n-einigh* (qu. 43) [That will be pleasing to every noble family – that the Gaoidhil will be under one yoke of generosity/ honour].

This is followed by two quatrains where a suggestion is made to Diarmaid to bring all poets together in one grand *cuairt.* It may be, as I suggest above, that Gofraidh is here thinking again of an occasion such as that provided by Ó Ceallaigh in 1351 for which Gofraidh's poem was

---

20 There is one unascribed poem in the Tinnakill Duanaire – which also has a poem of Gofraidh's – where the bridge of salvation is described as a laying of stones on a crannghal See A. O'Sullivan, 'The Tinnakill Duanaire', *Celtica* 11(1976) pp 214–28; cf. *Dioghluim Dána*, 66–9, qu. 10.   **21** *Dioghluim Dána*, pp 400–2, qu 4. Its first usage in an architectural sense seems to be in an Ó Dálaigh poem from the beginning of the century, celebrating Aodh Ó Conchobhair's new castle at Carn Fraoich (*Dioghluim Dána*, p. 414, qu. 33, where it is specifically recognized as a foreign term; e.g. *sreath cúpladh* with variation between final *ch/dh/gh.* The author is Aonghas mac Taidhg mhic Cearbhaill Bhuidhe Ó Dálaigh and, if the auctorial quatrain is authentic in the poem on metrics discussed above, then Gofraidh may well belong to this family as the son or nephew of this Aongas. The Úa Dálaigh genealogies are suspect even to the later medieval genealogists themselves. In RIA c iv 2, the six sons of Aongas m. Taidg dhoichligh m. Conchonnacht na sgoile are given of which information on three family lines is given. One line does descend from Tadhg m. Taidhg doichligh. In this line is found a Cerbhall Buidhe but the only son listed for him is Cúchonnacht.   **22** See his early poem to Conchobhar Ó Domhnaill [†1342], *A fhir théid i dTír Chonaill, Dioghluim Dána,* pp 200–1, qu. 11) and the poem to St Colmán qu. 7, cited n. 17 above.   **23** I would translate qu. 27cd somewhat differently to Ó Cuív and as follows: 'it was not for you to order the nobility and the lower orders to be joined together under a single yoke.'   **24** Incidentally, the poet's use of a Life of St Finnian in qu. 26 may

intended by him to represent the gratitude of all the learned classes.[25] Certainly the poet is pushing to the fore an opportunistic message of his poetic dominance in this section, balanced by praise of the patron's generosity and a somewhat condescending show of concern for the benefit of all his colleagues:

Cóir don éicsi, a mheic meic Taidhg,	It is only proper, o grandson of Tadhg, that the
do chur im cheand gach énmhaircc	poetic profession should direct every single
d'fhiodhbhaidh bhláith bhionn-	complaint through me to the blooming, mild,
fhoclaigh bhuig,	sweet-worded leader – every one should give to
iomarcaigh cáich dá gcaraid (qu. 46).[26]	others out of their surplus

One may enquire at this point as to what resources, what registers of knowledge, Gofraidh draws upon as he fills out the argument of his poem. Firstly, he shows himself a skilful manipulator of the operations of the poetics of praise, both on a theoretical level in the body of the argument, and, as may be expected, on a practical level, in calling on the expected pattern of traditional patronly response in the conclusion. He goes further, however, in his defense of eulogy and advances into the camp of the enemy clerics themselves by adducing a theological argument. The very subject matter of bardic praise, the human person, was created through the medium of the second person of the Trinity (qu. 9). As such it has been transformed by the Incarnation whereby God has ennobled human nature:

Uasal an t-adhbhar molta;	Noble is the subject-matter of praise; God
táinic Día a ndeilbh shaodhalta,	assumed human form, a worldly covering about
truaill shaodhalta fá a ghnúis ngil;	his bright person; this is the reason why people
cúis dhaonnachda do dháoinibh. (qu. 14)	should be human/generous.

At the very heart of the bardic poetic paradigm we find a Christian validation; it is this privileged human nature, *daonnacht*, that is the source of the other social *daonnacht*, generosity. Here we are, of course, very close to some other major contemporary European formulations of civility, as, for example, the great passage in *Piers Plowman* on Christ's Incarnation and Baptism as the true source of gentilesse in a Christian age.[27] Defiantly shading in to the specifically clerical speech register of the hostile Paris-trained clerics, *an léigheand labhraid cléirigh* (qu. 22), the defense of authentic native poetry, *ar n-ealadha fhírchéilligh*, is also undertaken according to the teaching of the seven books of learning, a traditional phrase here nuanced in the direction of the seven liberal arts schema of the university schools. Gofraidh makes an effort to integrate this with a long-standing Irish argument for the compatibility of native and clerical learning. They are two main

have a sound basis. For Finnian and his reward to a carminator see *Vita S. Finiani* ch. 23, ed. W.W. Heist, *Vitae Sanctorum Hiberniae* (Brussels 1965) pp 96–107.   **25** One may note the phrase in qu. 21, *go seachd leabhraibh an léighinn*, which Ó Cuív suggests refers to the seven liberal arts. There is a similar phrase in the Ó Ceallaigh poem, *na seacht bhfíorghrádha fileadh* (qu. 14), that might suggest a more traditional reading here.   **26** I follow Ó Cuív's alternative translation for *do chur* and translate the fourth line as an independent general axiom which may refer either to the patron's generosity or, more pointedly, to Gofraidh's own overwhelmingly superior gifts which he too must share with other poets.   **27** *And tho that bicome Crysten by conseille of the Baptiste/ Aren frankeleynes, fre men, thorow fullying pat pei toke/ And gentel-men with Iesu, for Iesus was yfolled,/ And vpon Calvarye on crosse ycrouned kynge of Iewes.* (XIX, ll. 32 ff.) The Pauline theme is given a more Irish incarnational frame by Gofraidh, but the underlying social anxieties may be parallel.

streams issuing from a single well: the one is *éicse*, school learning; the other is the art of poetry, *filidheacht* (qu. 23).

Returning this poem to Gofraidh would certainly establish the rationale for the grudging acknowledgement by others of his contemporaries of his dominant role in later fourteenth-century literary politics. But over and above any real or invented occasion of crisis, what can we say about the significance of the poem to the present theme? Behind this poem, as also its companion – if not model – *A theachtaire thig ón Róimh*, one senses an intense desire for social stability in a world which does not necessarily guarantee it.[28] Any attempt to change the rules of cultural discourse by short-circuiting the poet/ patron reciprocal relationship is to threaten society itself. The warning on social chaos, so strenuously argued as a defense of poetry in the earlier poem, resonates in Gofraidh's poem also as we have seen. The claim Irish poets make that theirs and theirs alone is the power to set the fundamental social measure of the individual in their society has long been viewed by scholars as corresponding to a most basic level of insular, indeed, Indo-European poetics. The privileged and privileging aspects of this view of poetry can easily absorb any additional *auctoritas* that the Christian world-view can provide. As Gofraidh by his secular art can take the genealogy of Ó Briain back to Adam, so too, the native poetics of praise have been demonstrated to be of the same nature as the right order of the Christian cosmos itself. But, as with the social order, so too with the literary; newcomers and social change can put that comfortable assumption of stability into question.

The poets claim, then, that the relation of poet and patron ratifies in a fundamental way the very idea of noblesse, of self-identity and social esteem in society in general. But this rhetoric of essential values, while it veils with decorum, must yet negotiate continually the conditions of ego, anxiety and mutability resulting from a mixed and changing social collectivity. Geoffrey's whole career pivots around the ambiguities of his patronage position, located somewhat uneasily between rival Gaelic patrons and the Anglo-Norman Munster magnates. And it sometimes seems as if he wishes to test the limits of his unstable position in various ways. Along with the note of magisterial control, Gofraidh – as with many poets – has a persistent habit of trailing the coat of his argument just this side of outrageousness, issuing challenges, not just to fellow poets but also to patrons, that he cannot expect to go unmarked. One might then describe his typical treatment of his social position and his poetic themes as ironic. There is in his work a persistent sense of meaning as reversible, of shiftings in and out of roles and registers of seriousness, of meaning mediated in playfulness, and with these a sense of the possibilities in such a mode for exploring questions of roles and social identity on his terms. Through his extended use of the exemplum and the allegorical mode, he suggests a world in which literary role-playing is taking on a more self-conscious and competitive value than ever before. In this, one can perhaps speak of Gofraidh's participation in a prevailing mood of fourteenth-century European literature in general.

An example of this sense of playful role-changing provides the basic structure for one of Gofraidh's most important Mág Cárthaigh poems, that to Domhnall Óg which I have already cited.[29] Here, the opening line, *Beir eolas dúinn a Dhomhnaill*, with its play on the meaning of *eolus* involves the reader in the shock of role reversals. The novel position accorded the patron, of bestower of knowledge, is further sharpened by the use of scriptural allegory. Domhnall is the new Moses in whom the poet must believe and who by his wisdom leads his people back to the

28 *Dioghluim Dána*, pp 220–3.   **29** *Dioghluim Dána*, pp 228–35 See my 'Arthur in Ireland: the earliest citation in native Irish literature', *Arthurian Studies* 12 (1993) p. 166.

promised land of Cashel (qq. 19–35). The full allegorical panoply of religious manifest destiny makes of the Eoghanacht *clann Israel* (qu. 35), *pobul Dé* (qu. 28), *deibhléan Dé* (qu. 26), *cuideachta Criosdaoidheadh* (qu. 32). The allegorical mode also forces the reading of the Gall of Munster as the Egyptians. There is every possibility that the earl of Desmond, though notorious as something of a law unto himself, would not have taken kindly to being identified as the Godless Pharaoh.

Irony, then, is a rhetorical device that facilitates both the stratagem of auctorial distancing and the playful intimacy of self-consciously shared courtly assumptions; it is a device for controlling the play of similitude and difference. I should like to take a few other soundings of this theme, bearing in mind that these few strands are just a fraction of a much more complex set of feelings, generated within the mother matrix of bardic poetry, but playing out a quite personal drama of successive involvement and reserve.

In the poem for Uilliam Ó Ceallaigh's Christmas festival of 1351, irony enters in quickly through consideration of the paradox of the festival itself.[30] One man's culture feast becomes other men's famines as Gofraidh registers the massive nature of the poetic invasion of Uí Mhaine by every learned type from every region. This initial irony is then compounded by the fact that the patron could have such power when he himself is totally ignorant of the arts of poetry. But if Uilliam's access to literary fame is not possible through direct professional contribution, Gofraidh is prepared to go further than merely to praise him conventionally for his largesse and hospitality. Gofraidh, in effect, transforms that hospitality through analogy and metaphor into a form of memorable, one might say, monumental literacy. Through Gofraidh's favourite topos of the big house, Uilliam's entertainment is represented as a great literary guest book, a 'Book of Uí Mhaine' *juste avant la lettre*, in which his own castle has pride of place as the great capital letter dominating the writing lines of poets, historians and entertainers. It is the mythical Eamhain rebuilt, it is like a heavenly city glimpsed from afar, a castle of vellum-like clarity of outline above the waters of the Lake of Poetry. It is, in another register of visionary transformation, the tower of Breogan whence Ireland itself was once viewed from the mythical perspective of a primeval European colonising world. It is in this larger view of the *translatio imperii* from Greece to Spain to Ireland, that the Milesian conquest of the earlier groups ultimately created a national group, which in the fourteenth century can now paradoxically be called the *Éireannaigh* (qu. 34). From this perspective, Gofraidh declares, Uilliam himself is not merely Irish but Greek and Spanish as well (qu. 41). Are the originary Europeans, the sons of Míl, considered as *Éireannaigh* because they won Ireland by force of arms? If so then Uilliam, as part of an enhanced national destiny, owes his condition of being *Éireannach* both to descent and to military energy. On the margins of the page of Uí Mhaine are the castle of the Gall, Athlone, and the barony of Clann Riocaird. Hence, in qu. 47, when Gofraidh speaks of this territory of Maonmhagh, the traditional Fenian literary territory of the sons of Morna and the recent domain of the Anglo-Norman Burkes, he can bring a complex node of meaning to his use of the word *osgardha* to describe Uilliam. As Fenian warrior paradigm, as relatively recently dominant in his territory, Uilliam cannot avoid the fact that his very identity as an *Éireannach* has about it – if not the quality of the provisional – the condition of living on swordland, of being constantly reliant on his own warlike spirit and the pronouncement of poets for the right to be called *Éireannach*. The term, then, is not a stable one but one that involves its aspirants in a ceaseless flux of becoming.

---

30 '*Filidh Éirionn go haointeach*'; see n. 19 above.

Éireannach is, of course, one of the key mediating terms of the later fourteenth century as issues of ethnic difference are brought into sharper focus on both the Gaelic and the English side.[31] It is a term that comes into prominence mainly through the writings of Gofraidh himself and the work of his neighbour and contemporary, Gearóid Iarla. It is always very carefully nuanced by Gofraidh and must rank as one of the most important to us as we observe his mediation of cultural identity on a personal as well as a public level. It is for him a concept that always carries with it the shadow of the Other. I would like to conclude this exploration of Gofraidh's mental world by looking at the terms of 'self' and 'other' in some poems from the Mág Cárthaigh/ Fitzgerald drama of patronage.

The first poem, *Fa ngníomraidh measdar meic ríogh*, is a eulogy for Diarmaid Mág Cárthaigh (made lord of Muscraighe in 1353 and died in 1391) and constitutes the most elaborate treatment of one of his favourite topics, namely the evaluation of an individual's personal worth and fame.[32] Gofraidh had already alluded to the theme in the poem for Diarmaid Ó Briain and will go on to provide another version of it in his poem for Maurice Fitzgerald, the third earl of Desmond.[33] In the spirit of the classic medieval formulation of, 'they are gentil who doeth gentil dedes', Gofraidh emphasises the individual's responsibility for the shaping of his own destiny, no matter what the advantages of lineage or personal beauty. The term *Éireannach* occurs in qu. 31:

Gidh uaisle an glan falt-úr fial	However nobler the renowned fair-haired hero
ó Artúr dána gar a ghaol	may be who is closely descended from Arthur,
méin Éireannach ní holc dhún	we, rather, approve of a hero who displays an
fa fholt úr chéimeannach chlaon.	Irish nature beneath fresh wavy flowing hair.

The editor, L. McKenna, was puzzled by this quatrain, finding no-one with the name in the MacCarthy genealogies or any reason why there should be a reference to 'Artúr rí' in a poem of this type and to such a patron.[34] Gofraidh has, in fact, set the terms of his poem in such a way that the reference to King Arthur of courtly romance makes perfectly good sense here. Already in qu. 13, the contrastive models of Gael and Gall have been set out in these same terms of *uaisleacht* comparanda:

Téid a fheidhm do dhearbh gach drong	His bravery, which all have felt, excels his beauty
tar a dheilbh-gá dealbh as fhearr?	– yet whose beauty excels his? all of nobility that
uaisleacht a bhfoil d'fhíonfhuil Ghall	there is in the wine-blood of the Gall cannot
ní thall soin dá ghníomhaibh geall.	match his deeds.

The poet has also established as his essential rhetorical figure the analogy between Diarmaid and his earlier Mág Carthaigh namesake, Diarmaid († 1185), who is here represented as the aggressive enemy of the intrusive Anglo-Norman barons during the first phase of their invasion of Ireland.[35] Indeed, for the purposes of this poem, the exemplary value of this figure from a heroic Munster

31 For earlier usage of the term see T.F. O'Rahilly, *Early Irish history and mythology* (Dublin 1946) pp 75–84. See the excellent discussion of this term in Joep Leerssen, *Mere Irish and Fíor-ghael* (Amsterdam 1986) pp 190–3. See also F.X. Martin, 'Medieval Ireland: introduction' in *Medieval Ireland 1169–1534*, ed. Art Cosgrove, *A new history of Ireland*, vol. 2 (Oxford 1987) pp li–lii.   32 *Dioghluim Dána*, pp 296–301.   33 *Irish bardic poetry*, pp 73–80.   34 I have pointed out the significance of the reference to Arthur in my 'Arthur in Ireland' (see above n. 29) pp 166–9. I accept here the editor's emendation of ms. *da ngaire* in line *b* of the quatrain.   35 This too is coat-trailing of a kind. The earlier historical Diarmaid was not, in fact, a very aggressive chaser of the newly-arrived Anglo-Normans.

past can be seen to reside primarily in his resistance to, and his difference from the foreigners (qq. 24–5). The whole effect of the poem, then, resides in the carefully articulated contrast between the values of the native Gaelic mythos of conquest and the British Arthurian mythos of conquest that the rivals of the present Diarmaid for paramountcy in Munster, the Anglo-Norman earls of Desmond, may be assumed to exemplify. In a famous passage from another poem addressed to Maurice's brother Gerald, Gofraidh sets up, only to collapse into broadly ironic double-speak, the facts of the presence of two cultural communities in Ireland:

Dá chineadh dá gcumthar dán
i gcrích Éireann na n-uarán
na Gaoidhil-se ag boing re bladh
is Goill bhraoin-inse Breatan.

I ndán na nGall gealltar linn
Gaoidhil d'ionnarba a hÉrinn
Goill do shraoineadh tar sál sair
i ndán na nGaoidheal gealltair.[36]

There are two peoples for whom poems are composed in cool-streamed Eire: the Gaoidhil known to fame and the Goill of Britain, isle of brimming beauty.

In poems to the Gall we pledge the expulsion of the Gael from Ireland; in those to the Gael we promise to hurl the Gall east across the sea.

Éireannach, then, is a carefully nuanced term; it can smooth over ethnic difference on the one hand and on the other, may be taken back and appropriated as a badge of exclusive Gaelic identity.

All of this implies a sharpening in the later fourteenth century of a sense of a wider culture field within which various groups position themselves strategically with varying degrees of identification of self and other. There is some further evidence from Gofraidh's work that he is well capable of projecting Irish cultural identities on a European scale of value. His poem to Maurice, the second earl of Desmond, *Mór ar bhfearg riot a rí Saxan*, suggests as much.[37] Here the young Maurice is about to attend the English king's court and to take part, as one of Edward III's retinue in the English campaign in France. As part of that expedition he can look forward to some new cultural experiences:

Lé a oide, lé hairdrígh Saxan,
siobhal díoghainn,
téid isan bFraingc n-ealaigh n-áloinn
bhfleadaigh bhfíonduinn

Sgéla na Fraingce, fios Saxan,
suairc an comhrádh,
do-gébhthor 'gan ghasda ghealmhór,
bhlasda bonnbhán (qq. 12–13).

With his mentor, the great king of England, he is going – a mighty expedition! – to France, land of the beautiful swans, of feasts and of dark red wine.

The bright tall hero, gracious and white-footed, will discover the romances of France, the learning of England–delightful the dalliance.[38]

In this poem Gofraidh executes a kind of reverse poetic seduction, as it were, of the young Anglo-Norman aristocrat, by countering the mentorship of Edward III with his mentorship. Whatever the career and cultural attractions of the English view of Europe, Gofraidh as mentor can show a more coherent and satisfying – because more dazzling – literary tour-de-force, in equalling Maurice with the great Lugh of Irish mythological tradition (qq. 20–47), or even, in view of his family origins, with Manannán of Irish and British significance (qu. 50). In fact, Gofraidh

---

36 'A Ghearóid, déana mo dháil', *Dioghluim Dána*, pp 201–6, qu. 45–6. Note here the manner in which Gofraidh uses a neutral and Arthurian term, Britain, rather than Saxon to refer to the Anglo-Normans.   **37** *Irish bardic poetry*, pp 73–80.   **38** At this time the tales of France, i.e. French romances, were dominant among the aristocratic

suggests, his family fame gives the young heir more than an English-French prestige. It comprises an older trans-national status that could well be counted as superior to, because more ancient than this. It is moreover an occasion for Gofraidh to solicit the favour of the young man's father, the

Do líonadh a los a athar
as úr méine,
an dá oilén arda úaine,
Alba is Éire (qu. 53).

The fame of his father's ardent character has filled the two lofty green islands, Albion and Ireland.

first earl:

The visit of Maurice to England has, in fact, quite a rich historical and cultural background of its own. It was in 1356 that the English campaign in France resulted in the successful siege and battle of Poitiers in which Jean le Bon, king of France, was captured. In the winter of that year an extraordinary round of courtly tournaments and entertainments took place in England in which the royal French party took part. Through Edward's wife, Philippa of Hainault and her Flemish entourage (which included Froissard), the English court had already become noted for its musical brilliance for the first time since Henry II. Guillaume de Machaut had already introduced into this court his particular line of ironic misogynist courtliness through such works as the *Jugement dou Roy de Navarre* (1349) and his *Querelle des Dames*. It was during this winter of festivities that, in all likelihood, the idea of the neo-Arthurian order of the Garter was first conceived.[39] It seems to me that Gofraidh may well have been aware of the rather special cultural context of Maurice's venture from the way he sets out for him the agenda of the journey. That it was a journey that ended in the young man's death makes the freshness and lightness of this little 'Mirror for Earls' Sons' all the more poignant.

But perhaps the most poignant of all Gofraidh's ego-plays occurs in one of his latest poems to Maurice's half-brother Gerald, the fourth earl, *Iongaibh thú orm, a Iarla*.[40] Here the challenge is to write a poem which will chide the earl for his followers' disregard for the poet's property in such a way as not to alienate him. Here, neither the social self, projected as professional poet, nor the more 'sincere' self offered in friendship, nor even the presence of the physical self are a match for the willed 'unknowing' brought on by the rancour of a broken relationship. The 'I' of both poet and patron are annihilated in the quarrel. The pain is evident and made even more poignant by the difference in age between Gearóid Iarla and Gofraidh. I justify the extended quotation by the

Fear aithne na n-uile cheard
dom thréagadh truagh an díbhearg;
gá dú acht ni aithnighe inn
gidh tú as aithnighe i nÉirinn.

The man who knows all men of art is now casting me out–this is a grievous wrong. Though you know more people than any man in Ireland, yet you will not recognize me.

Feabhas th'aithne, a fhir Theamhra,
córaide dhamh doimheanma
th'anáir faoi o nach fuighinn;
fagháil gnaoi do ghnáthuighinn.

It is a great thing to be recognized by you, this is why I am the more downcast; I who am always seeking recognition can win none from you.

---

public in England. Irish students frequented Oxford, however, as their main centre of University schooling; hence the appropriateness of Gofraidh's division.   **39** For an account of court life in England at this period see Nigel Wilkins, 'Music and poetry at court: England and France in the late Middle Ages' in V.J. Scattergood (ed.), *English court culture in the later middle ages* (London 1983) pp 190–7; See also James I. Wimsatt, *Chaucer and his French contemporaries: natural music in the fourteenth century* (Toronto 1996) pp 43–82.   **40** *Dioghlum Dána*, pp 338–43.

Dar leat nocha rabha riamh
id bhrugh, a bharr na bhfinnchiabh,
is ná faca sibh sinne,
a fhir dhathta Dhuibhlinne.

It is as if I was never in your castle, o fair-haired prince, and that you had never seen me, o colourful grandee of Dublin.

Da dteagmhainn duid ar druim róid
seocham do ghéabhtha, a Ghearóid,
gan mé na thú rinn do rádh
agus rinn chlú ar mo chomhrádh.

If I were to meet you on the high road, you would go straight past me, Gearóid; and never say neither 'me' nor 'thee', though my witty talk is most famous.

Beag má do-bheirim aithne
ort gidh adhbhar machtnuighthe
mar do-chuaidh th'aigneadh tar ais
uainn ar gcaidreamh bhar gcádhais.

I can barely recognize you, though what is truly extraordinary is how much your feelings have changed towards me when once I enjoyed so much honour from you.

Ní chongbha th'aghaidh mhóir mhoill
feadh a haithinte oruinn;
deacair dhamh aithne uirre
gan char aighthe oruinn-ne.

You do not turn your great stately face long enough towards me for me to recognize it. It is hard for me to recognize it if you keep your head turned away from me.

Dar leat ni tu-sa a-tá ann
gér dhlúith da chéile ar gcumann,
nó no ní mei-si mé féin
gidh bé dan treise a thoibhéim.

It is as if it were not really you that was there, even though once we were once so close; or else that I am not really I! I do not know who is more insulted by it.

Baramhail aithne agam
a-tá, a chraobh fhial fhabhradhdonn
ar do ghlár 's ar ghné th'aighthe
gidh lán mé dod mhearaithne. (qq. 38–45)

O noble dark-browed hero, there still comes to me the echo of having known you, made up of the sound of your voice and the shape of your face, and this even among your weird way of knowing.

sheer emotionality of the passage, a value not normally associated with bardic poetry:

What I have been trying to assemble in this paper, is a kind of plea; that, in assessing the formal and essentialist patterns of bardic poetry, we nevertheless remain sensitive to the ways in which individual poets make the most apparently public and rigid of literary conventions and genres bend to the personal by inscribing into its forms disparate elements of personal contrariety. We can never hope to discover in these Irish poets that desired pure entity posited as the teleologically desired object, 'the socially undetermined subject' that person for whose advent the new historicists, and the medieval and renaissance literary critics eagerly scrutinise and debate the signs.[41] We can, however, more modestly describe Gofraidh's corpus as representing sustained and insistent acts of self-speaking, self-fashioning by one whose social ideology all but precluded self-consciousness.

41 For a discussion of these issues as they pertain to other European vernacular poetry see M. Zink, *La subjectivité littéraire autour du siècle de saint Louis* (Paris 1985). For the relevance of the idea of self-construction in medieval English literature see Lee Patterson, *Chaucer and the subject of history* (Wisconsin 1991) pp 3–41.

A monstrance for an absent poem:
the reciting of *Amra Coluim Cille* in the sixteenth-century Life of Colum Cille

JAN ERIK REKDAL

The final part of the Columban hagiographical tradition is made up by the sixteenth-century Life (1532) – *Betha Coluim Chille* – written in Irish in Tír Conaill under the auspices of the chieftain-to-be Maghnus Ó Domhnaill. In this Life a lot of attention and space is given to the Old Irish praise-poem *Amra Choluimb Chille*,[1] or to the Middle Irish glossed and prefaced recension of that poem[2] and more to this later preface than to the poem itself. This encomiastic poem as it stands stems from the time of Colum Cille's death in 597 or the years just after that and represents the oldest extant portrayal of the saint to which the material of the preface adds later features. In the following I want to look at the implications of this attention for the shape of the Life, why it was given, and finally to what extent this makes it differ from earlier Columban Lives.

The only edition of the Life is based on a copy in the Bodleian manuscript, Rawlinson B 514 and all references are to this edition.[3] In the depiction of Colum Cille's life in Iona (from § 202) in the Life proper (§§ 51/52 – 376) there is a break or an interlude (§§ 315–50). The interlude consists narratively of his return to Ireland and gives the story of Colum Cille's attendance and mediating at the convention of Druim Cett. The story is based on material from the preface to the *Amra* as it surfaced in writing at the very beginning of the eleventh century. What will be concentrated on here is the part of it which gives the context of the *Amra*: who wrote it, where, when and why – with special attention to the reward of that poem: 'heaven to everyone who recites it'. We shall see that the insertion of this story into the depiction of Colum Cille's life in Iona or into the Life as a whole, is not done for lack of composing skill, but for the importance given to it at the time.

This Life is reputed to be characterised by lack of composing skill. If discrimination of available material on the subject is the ideal this text may always come short in comparison with the other Lives of the saint.[4] Many scholars of Columban hagiography will of course find the Life disturbing in its unorthodoxy of including secular and popular material which consciously was for the most part kept out of the previous ones. But in so doing this Life only does what the previous ones were on the verge of doing – and as one shall see, to a modest extent did. The carpet

---

1 M. Herbert, *Iona, Kells and Derry* (Oxford 1988, repr. Dublin 1996) p. 10, see references cited there. 2 M. Herbert, 'The Preface to the *Amra Coluim Cille*' in D. Ó Corráin et al. (eds), *Sages, saints and storytellers: celtic studies in honour of James Carney* (Maynooth 1989) pp 67–75. 3 A. O'Kelleher and G. Schoepperle, *Betha Colaim Chille* (University of Illinois 1918, repr. Dublin 1994). 4 The disapproval has been expressed clearly by some, more discretely by others. Gertrud Brüning, 'Adamnans Vita Columbae und ihre Ableitungen' *ZCP* 11 (1917) pp 213–304 at p. 284, formulated it harshly: 'das sonderbare Machwerk' an option which has stuck to it. Although Maghnus Ó Domhnaill has been praised as a chieftain, the work has never been given a sincere estimation (with the exception of P. Ó Fiannachta, 'Betha Choluimb Chille. Ár naomhsheanchas' *Léachtaí Cholm Cille* 15 (1985) pp 11–33. For an attempt of an appraisal, see J.E. Rekdal, 'From profile to face: an analysis of the portrayal of Colum Cille in his sixteenth-century Life by Maghnus Ó Domhnaill', unp. thesis., univ. of Oslo, 1995.

of Latin hagiography has been bulging with Irish praise-poems, secular or not, since the very Adomnán wrote his *Vita Columbae c.700* and probably earlier. With the Early Modern Irish Life that carpet seems to be so worn that what lies underneath has become transparent.

The context of the composition of the present Life is given in its preface (§§ 1–20). Of its *causa scribendi* we are there informed that it is to honour God, to hold up Colum Cille's name and to benefit (*tarb*) the soul and body of the hagiographer and of the readers and listeners of the Life. (§ 20). The benefit provided by the Life lies in what the Life tells us about how to attain heaven. Heaven is attained, it says, through the commemoration of Colum Cille. And how do we commemorate the holy man? By memorising the *Amra* as heaven is attained by everyone who recites it. How do we memorise the Amra? By reciting it daily and in full. This is illustratively demonstrated by two episodes (§§ 337 & 434). – The Irish verb used in the Life for memorise is the etymologically closely related *mebraigh* (the most frequent spelling of it in the text).[5]

The first episode (§ 337) is given within the Life proper and within the interlude attached to an episode where the reward for the *Amra* is settled. The other much longer episode (§ 435) given outside the Life proper makes up the last of the three final paragraphs of the entire narrative, all of which relate of miracles worked posthumously by Colum Cille. Structurally the second episode echoes the first by also being attached. They both read like anecdotes from a popular and possibly oral tradition.[6]

The shorter, first episode (§ 337) is about an Armagh water-clerk who because of sinfulness can not memorise the last half of the *Amra*. So he fasts at the tomb of Colum Cille to obtain this part and obtains it. But while memorising the latter half he forgets the former. This is explained by the fact that his life did not merit salvation from God nor had he prayed to Colum Cille to remember the two together.

The longer, second anecdote is about a certain Mac Taidg mic Toirrdelbaigh ua Briain.[7] In spite of the sureties of the chiefs of Leth Mogha and Turcall, king of the Gaill (the Norse) and Úeinne,[8] archbishop of Ireland, he is seized and imprisoned by the king of Munster. After a long time in prison without any hope of help, he plans to enter into an alliance with the devil to be freed. But when the devil comes to make a pact with him, Colum Cille intervenes because mac Taidg has 'memorised the book called the *Amra*' (*do mebraigh se an leabhar darub ainm Amhra Coluim Cille*). When the devil sees that he cannot have Mac Taidg's soul, he avenges this on his body and by breathing on him makes him a leper. Colum Cille consents to this because of Mac Taidg's bad faith, which made him want to make a pact with the devil and not with God. He is to spend his life as the leader of the lepers of Mochuda's Lismore, but Colum Cille promises that his soul shall obtain heaven.

In both instances it is a matter of having memorised the whole poem. I take 'the book called Amra' as to mean the entire poem. We do not dare to think what would have happened to Mac

---

5 We should notice that at the time of the composition memorizing seems to imply reciting. See the stanza in Mág Uidhir's *duanaire* where it says (in D. Greene's translation, *Duanaire Mhéig Uidhir* (Dublin 1972) p. 24): 'The highking of Fermanagh has taken the advice of Cormac of the battles; he has it from books and he memorized it when it was recited.' (*Comhairle Chormaic na ccath/do ghabh airdrí Fher Manach/ atá sí ó leabhraiph leis/ do mheabhraigh hí ar aithriss*).   **6** See C. Gallagher and S. Greenblatt, *Practicing new historicism* (Univ. of Chicago Press 2000) pp 47–51 about anecdotes outside the literary offering access to the everyday, 'the place where things are actually done.'   **7** He may be indentified as the Domnall mac Taidg who in 1107 was taken captive in Dublin by his uncle Muirchetrach Ua Briain, king of Munster; see S. Duffy, 'Irishmen and Islesmen in the kingdoms of Dublin and Man, 1052–1171', *Ériu* 43 (1992) pp 108–16 at pp 114–15.   **8** This could be a misreading by the scribe or the editors of Gréine (Gregor) who was bishop of Dublin, but in time his predecessor Samuel Ua hAingliu (1095–1121) would fit better.

Taidg if he had memorised only a half of it. Also in both episodes there is a matter of having
grasped its sense – that it is not sufficient to memorise if you do not believe in it and live
according to it. This is clearly pointed out in the preface of the *Amra*,[9] but even more so in the
Life by Baithin. He objects that a man who has done evil will attain heaven if only he memorises
the praise. Colum Cille denies this by saying that a damned person will not be able to memorise
it properly (§ 336).

Quite in accordance with its program of modernisation, the Modern Irish[10] Life describes the
way one is to memorise it as *con a ceill agus gon a tuicsin* (with its sense and its understanding/of
it). Understanding has in this Life ousted the 'sound' (*fogur*) which is the word used in the
prefatory matter of the *Amra* as we find it in the Bodleian MS.[11] Considering the extremely
difficult language employed in this Old Irish poem, one may wonder how an understanding of it
could be achieved. I would suggest that an understanding was believed to be achievable by means
of the present Life, the task of which, it claims in the preface (§§ 10 & 11), was to make all extant
testimonies concerning the saint accessible to everybody both in substance and form through its
collection and modern rendering – either by reading or listening.

The hagiographer explicitly mentioned in the text is Maghnus Ó Domhnaill. In spite of what
the text claims we cannot be sure of what part Maghnus actually played in the composition of the
Life and to what extent he engaged himself in that process. But we know from the text itself that
he wanted it to be read as if he had composed it. From poems signed by him we know further that
Maghnus had committed half a dozen of poems and obviously was a chieftain (the Ó Domhnaill
from 1537–55) with some literary pretensions.[12] So about the hagiographer presented to us we
know that he was a chieftain-to-be and an amateur poet.[13] And like every chieftain he was utterly
aware of the danger of satire and the importance of praise-poems for the renown of himself and
his chieftaincy.[14] This may to a large extent explain why the Life is permeated by poetry as the
whole text is interspersed with quatrains (248 is the number of quoted quatrains).

The Life could be described as a narrative based on a poem (the *Amra*) which itself is not
quoted only the story about it. The way the Life holds up the first extant poem portraying the
saint makes it resemble an empty monstrance. The story about the poem would then be the vessel
part of the monstrance. This story is not only about the importance of praise-poems and of their
producers, the professional poets and of properly reward for such poems. It is also a story about
the danger of vainglory as a result of being praised. To avoid that praise-poems should be recited
posthumously. This is what the poet in question here, Dallán the high-poet of Ireland, does with
the *Amra*. As all this is demonstrated through Colum Cille's own experience the story implicitly
also depicts him. But the portrayal of the saint given by the poem itself is not quoted. Thus the
Life reads as if the absent portrayal of that poem is filled up with the portrayal of the present Life

9 W. Stokes (ed.), 'The Bodleian *Amra Choluimb Chille*', RC 20 (1899) pp 30–55, 132–83, 248–89, 400–37 at pp
134–5.   10 As opposed to above where Early Modern follows the traditional definition of historical periods I call
it here Modern Irish because that is what this text is linguistically speaking. Its falling between two stools may
explain why it is not treated in *Stair na Gaeilge* under Early Modern nor Modern Irish. This extensive prose-text
seems to demand a reconsideration of the linguistic definition of these two periods.   11 Stokes, 'Bodleian *Amra
Choluimb Chille*', pp 134–5.   12 T. O'Rahilly, *Dánta Grádha* (Cork Univ. Press 1926) pp 70–4.   13 The professional
bard Tadhg Mór Ó Cobhthaigh seems to have been his tutor in poetry, see P.A. Breatnach, 'In Praise of Maghnas
Ó Domhnaill', *Celtica* 16 (1984) p. 64.   14 A treaty made in 1539 between Maghnus and Ó Conchobhair of Sligo
shows clearly the power of satire where Ó Conchobhair is threatened by excommunication by representatives of
the church and by being satirised by representatives of the poets. (M. Carney, 'Agreement between Ó Domhnaill
and Tadhg Ó Conchobhair concerning Sligo Castle (23 June 1539)' *Irish Historical Studies* 3 (1943) pp 282–96.

and consequently demonstrates the parallel between the *Amra* and the Life. Maghnus does in the Life what Dallán once did in his *Amra*: commemorates the saint. The Life is constructed around the story about an old poem portraying the subject of the narrative. As the poem itself is left out we are presented with a double framed empty picture in which we ultimately may discern the hagiographer – a chieftain and a descendant of the saint and an amateur poet portraying the saint, his ancestor.

When the Life was written there was still a prevalent tradition that every nobleman should have his *duanaire* – a poem book consisting of a collection of eulogies and elegies composed for different members of his family.[15] There are reasons to suggest that the manuscript Rawlinson 514 may represent a copy of Maghnus's own *duanaire*, or poem book. This manuscript contains in addition to the Life (60 leaves) 18 leaves of poems related to the Ó Domhnaill family (or to the entire Cenél Conaill of which the Ó Domhnaill branch did not become prominent until the tenth century[16]).[17]

This latter part of Rawlinson B 514 contains 49 poems which makes out more than thousand stanzas as each poem consists of several stanzas, 66 of which are ascribed to Colum Cille.[18] Included is also the prose-piece giving the *buannacht bhuna* – the basic billeting rights[19] of the Ó Domhnaill over the other chiefs of the province of Ulster in peace-time – an important item in a list of virtues.

The numerous quatrains interspersed throughout the narrative of the Life consist mostly of poems praising Colum Cille or poems attributed to him as poet.[20] Although many of the poems are recited by Colum Cille and not addressed to him, it is nevertheless possible to see all these poems as Colum Cille's *duanaire* embedded in the Life. Colum Cille the poet is the most conspicuous feature of the portrayal the Life sets out to give. This becomes particularly evident through the space and attention given to the episode of the synod at Druim Cett for which Colum Cille returns from Iona to talk the poets' case for not being thrown out of the country. Colum Cille's argument (§ 332) is that praise lasts, men and wealth perish. He refers to God who commissioned David to write him 150 praise-poems. The importance of the exchange of praise and reward is underlined by the example of God bestowing on David a rich earthly life as well as one in heaven. This is echoed by the price given for the *Amra*. Colum Cille goes as far as saying that there has nowhere been written that no man was made holy without generosity and largesse (*gan fheli, gan einech*).

In this perspective the Life could be regarded as Maghnus' poem to Colum Cille and it thus becomes the first of the poems contained by Rawlinson B 514. The preface informs us about this Life poem, that Maghnus recited it or 'composed it out of his mouth' (§ 11: *do decht as a bel fein hí*).[21] The

15 B. Ó Cuív, *The Irish bardic Duanaire or 'Poem-Book'* (Dublin 1973).   **16** F.J. Byrne, *Irish kings and high-kings* (London 1973, repr. Dublin 2001) p. 258.   **17** While some poems are on the remote history of the Ó Domhnaill family, twenty-six of the poems are composed for members of the same family from the thirteenth to the sixteenth century. B. Ó Cuív (*The Irish bardic Duanaire*, p. 34) regards this collection of poems as en edited duanaire made specially for Maghnus as he is the latest chief addressed.   **18** E.C. Quiggin, *Prolegomena to the study of the later Irish bards 1200–1500* (London 1913).   **19** K. Simms, *From kings to warlords* (Woodbridge 1987) pp 139, 171, 172.   **20** Very few of the poems, however, in Laud 615 believed to have been a scrapbook put together for the writing of the Life, very few seems to be quoted or referred to. Some may have been overlooked as this judgment is based only on a comparison of the list of poems given as Appendix III in M. Herbert and A. O'Sullivan, 'The provenance of Laud Misc. 615' *Celtica* 10 (1973) pp 174–92, with the list of first lines of quatrains given by O'Kelleher and Schoepperle. Indeed, the former is indexed according to the first line of the first stanza of the entire poem (which contains more than one quatrain or stanza). So some of the quatrains given in the Life may be the equivalent to a stanza other than the first one in the Laud-list. I have not had the opportunity to compare each stanza in the Life with the stanzas of more than one thousand in Laud 615.   **21** 'It' refers to all the material on Colum Cille Maghnus had collected. This it is that he 'composes'. I agree with Paul Walsh, *Irish men of learning* (Dublin 1947) pp 170–1, that this does not reflect the true situation of how the work was composed.

verb *decht* which in the preface is used about the poets (*filid*) (§ 8), about Adomnán (§ 8) and about Maghnus himself (§ 11), draws a parallel between the three and places Maghnus composition between that of the poets and of the exemplary hagiographer. In the Life a relation between the verb *decht* and *mebraigh* is established by the fact that this is the verb most frequently used about Adomnán when his *Vita Columbae* is explicitly quoted which it is throughout: 'as A. memorises in his Life … '(§ 353,406, etc.). This brings us back to the anecdotes which tell how the praise-poem is to be memorised. Thus Mac Taidg does what Adomnán does but with a different text, although commemorating the same holy man. Of course, implicitly we are led to understand that this is also what the present hagiographer does.

This may explain why in this Life the compositional structure resembles in many ways the prefaced *Amra* of the early eleventh century. Formally they both consist of a narrative body equipped with a preface. The prefaces share common features giving the *locus, tempus, persona* and *causa scribendi*. In the *Amra*-preface they are: Druim Cett, the time of king Áed mac Ainmuirech, Dallán Forgaill and 'to attain heaven for himself et *aliis per se*.'[22] In Maghnus Life they are: 'Port na Tri Namat', 1532, Maghnus Ó Domhnaill mac Aedha and to honour God, to hold up Colum Cille' name and to benefit (*tarb*) the soul and body of the hagiographer and of the readers and listeners of the Life, etc.[23] Similar prefaces are not found in the Columban Lives preceding the sixteenth-century one.[24]

I read this preface as information added to Maghnus' Life-poem similar to that of the prefatory material added to the *Amra* conveying information about how the poems can provide salvation for their readers, listeners and reciters. Maghnus composed his Life-poem to make the *Amra* comprehensible in order to recite it not only in sound but also with understanding as required.

His other concern was to make it complete. As a poem from the *Amra*-preface puts it:

> Colum's *Amra* every day
> whoever recites it *in full*[25]
> will have the bright heaven
> that God gave to Dallán.[26]

Turned to Colum Cille Maghnus himself puts it like this in his preface (§ 20): '… that I may finish completely this work I wish to do for you …' (… indus go crichnuiginn go foirfe an saethar-so dob ail lim do dhenam duid fen …). There are several incidents throughout the Life of concern for completeness. Everything available should be included in the Life although all available pieces put together would still not make a complete picture, as completeness is not achievable. (§ 431: 'Till now I have written all I found of the Life, but one should not think that all is here. It would be boasting to consider it achievable to witness it unless it were witnessed by the angels of God, considering the length of his life, and the amount of his grace and the multitude of his miracles revealed every day.') This paragraph reads as an introduction to the three miracles post-mortem concluding the entire Life. It tells us that only a few of the posthumous miracles will be related, 'though it would not be possible for anybody at all to finish them because of their number and amount.' (§ 432) This resembles the discourse of a court-poet referring to his

---

22 Stokes, 'Bodleian *Amra Choluimb Chille*', pp 36–9.   **23** In the twenty paragraphs making up the preface in Maghnus Life *persona* is given in § 10, *locus* and *tempus* in § 13 and *causa* in § 20.   **24** Adomnán does not mention himself by name until in the opening of the Life immediately preceding the story about the reciting.   **25** The emphasis is by me.

patron's virtues. Both these paragraphs make use of the first person – the latter plural and the former singular – referring to the hagiographer. The poetry had to be included to render a portrayal as complete as possible the way Maghnus, a secular hagiographer if at all, saw it.

That was not the case for this Life's predecessors. In the homiletic Life written in Irish almost four hundred years earlier there is no mention of the *Amra* or the story of its context. As mentioned by Herbert,[27] for a homily addressing a monastic audience the depicting of the saint involved in worldly affairs like the convention of Druim Cett pleading the cause of the poets would not seem appropriate. But from the poems from the prefatory matter of the *Amra* which are nevertheless included in the homily, we understand that the hagiographer was familiar with the Middle Irish glossed recension of that text.[28]

On the other hand, in later (fifteenth-century) versions of this Life as they occur in The Mac Sweeney Book and in the Scottish MS Adv. 72.1.40, the story of the context of the *Amra* surfaces.[29] However not even here do we find any anecdote giving an example of the effect of the reciting of the old elegy.

Four hundred and fifty years further back in time there is the Life written in Latin by Adomnán, himself an abbot in Iona – a Life which was to become the example of Columban Lives and still is among Columban scholars. This Life does refer to the miraculous power of reciting praise-poems in Irish in commemoration of the saint, but neither the poems nor the poets are named. The story is, nevertheless, given a prominent place at the opening of the Life proper (*VC* I, 1). The anecdote[30] relates of bloodstained robbers being delivered from their enemies who had surrounded their house at night and set it on fire. Those among them who were not delivered, according to the story, perished. Adomnán tells us that similar miracles are reported in such a number both in Ireland and Irish speaking parts of Britain that they should be given credence to. Adomnán underlines that all these miracles are caused in the same way: the reciting of songs in commemoration of Columba.

Of course we do not know if any of these praise-poems (*carmina*) referred to contains the *Amra*, but as Adomnán refers to more than one poem, it is most likely that the *Amra* was thought of as one of them.[31] Speculation about this is futile, but in our context the importance is the fact that the reciting of praise-poems in Irish in commemoration of Columba is referred to as something that works miracles, in a Latin Life not addressing an Irish-speaking audience and populace.

So while the former Lives on Colum Cille have their hagiographic carpets bulging with praise-poems in Irish, secular or not, the present one lets the tradition concerning the *Amra* make up its pattern.

We have seen how a full inclusion of the prefatory material of the *Amra* is innovated by the sixteenth-century Life by Maghnus Ó Domhnaill presented to us as its hagiographer. The inclusion is related to the context of the Life and caused by the hagiographer's concern for completeness and attention to praise-poems (and satire). For a secular hagiographer – traditionally a contradiction in terms – the poems may have been regarded as the only unchanged parts – and thus closer to the original picture – of a pattern hardly discernible in the constant flow of hagiographic prose.

---

26 Stokes, 'Bodleian *Amra Choluimb Chille*', pp 134–5; *The Irish Liber Hymnorum* I, p. 166. 27 Herbert, *Iona, Kells and Derry*, p. 202. 28 Ibid. p. 201. 29 Ibid. pp 215–16. 30 Adomnán refers himself to this story as an aside, so it reads as something that is only attached to the Life as such. I see it as an anecdote from a popular tradition not a part of the hagiographic canon as it stood then. See R. Sharpe, *Adomnán of Iona. Life of St Columba* (London 1995) pp 59–60. 31 R. Sharpe, 'Maghnus Ó Domhnaill's source for Adomnán's *Vita S. Columbae* and other vitae', *Celtica* 21 (1990) pp 604–7 and id., *Adomnán of Iona. Life of St Columba*, n. 46.

The Old-Irish glosses of the *prima manus* in Würzburg, m.p.th.f.12: text and context reconsidered

PÁDRAIG P. Ó NÉILL

Würzburg M.P.Th.F.12 is a copy of the Pauline Epistles well known for its Old-Irish glosses. These are traditionally dated 'about the middle of the eighth century',[1] making them the earliest of the three collections that together form the basis of our knowledge of classical Old Irish.[2] But the Würzburg manuscript (Wb) also contains a stratum of Old-Irish glosses entered by an earlier scribe, the linguistic archaisms of which have ensured for it a special prominence in Early Irish studies. Thus, when cited in grammars and dictionaries, these glosses are individually identified as *a prima manu*, an acknowledgement both of their importance and the fact that their scribe was the first glossator of that manuscript.[3]

The Glosses in their Manuscript Context

Given the special status of these glosses it is worth examining them in their immediate, physical, context.[4] The fact that they are linguistically of the late seventh/early eighth century, that is, more than half a century earlier than the date of their appearance in Wb, suggests that they were copied. This conclusion is supported by occasional errors consonant with copying from an exemplar; for example, the probable omission of abbreviation marks (gll. 10, 41 and 54) and the presence of certain defective spellings (gll. 66 and 71).[5] That their linguistic forms consistently harmonize both with the proposed date of *c.*700[6] and with each other would suggest that they are a homogenous group of glosses drawn from a common exemplar of that date.

And since these glosses were copied by the same scribe who wrote the main Latin text, one might surmise that the two were present together in the one exemplar and were copied

---

1 R. Thurneysen, *A grammar of Old Irish*, trans. by D.A. Binchy and O. Bergin (Dublin 1946) p. 4. The manuscript itself is generally dated to the second half of the eight century. See B. Bischoff and J. Hofmann, *Libri Sancti Kyliani: die Würzburger Schreibschule und die Dombibliothek im VIII. und IX. Jahrhundert*, Quellen und Forschungen zur Geschichte des Bistums und Hochstifts Würzburg (Würzburg 1952) p. 98, who dated it 'nach der Mitte des 8. Jh.'; and E.A. Lowe, *CLA* IX, no. 1403, who dated it 'saec. VIII ex.'.   2 The standard edition of the Würzburg glosses is W. Stokes and J. Strachan, *Thesaurus Palaeohibernicus. A collection of Old-Irish Glosses, scholia, prose and verse*, 2 vols (Cambridge 1901–3; repr. with supplement (Dublin 1975) I, pp 499–712 (Hereafter referred to as *Thes. Pal.*).   3 Despite the reservations expressed in *Thes. Pal.* I, pp xxiv–v, it is now generally accepted that the *prima manus* also copied the main text; see, for example, the palaeographical evidence below and n. 8. Likewise, it is clear that the glosses of the *prima manus* were entered into the manuscript before those of the main glossator, not only from instances where the latter had to redirect his gloss around a previously existing gloss by the *prima manus*, but also from cases where the main glossator linked his gloss to an adjacent one of the *prima manus* by means of *uel*. For example, at fol. 29a20, TESTOR (I Tim. 5:21) has directly above it the gloss 'adiuro' (*prima manus*) and to the left of the latter the gloss '.i. guidimm uel' (main glossator).   4 I have used the facsimile of L. Ch. Stern, *Epistolae Beati Pauli glosatae* ... (Halle 1910).   5 Here, and throughout, the numbering of the glosses is that of the text given in the Appendix.   6 On which see R. Thurneysen, 'Das Alter der Würzburger Glossen', *ZCP* 3 (1901) pp 47–54, and K.H. Schmidt, 'Die Würzburger Glossen', *ZCP* 39 (1982) pp 54–77, at 64–8.

simultaneously. In support of this hypothesis is evidence physical and palaeographical. First, the glosses are written in the same dark-brown ink that was used for the Latin text – in contrast with the lighter brown ink of the main body of glosses. Second, many of them were written in a script whose formal ductus (with a marked tendency to separate letters), occasional large letters (e.g., gll. 1, 34, 36, and 39), and consistent use of semi-uncial *d* (with a very short vertical shaft slanting to the left)[7] recall the formal minuscule of the main text. This evidence suggests that the same scribe copied text and gloss at the same time and probably with the same pen.[8] Significantly, when correcting an omission in the main text at fol. 11b23 by adding *in macelluo* on the margin, he also supplied above the latter an Old-Irish gloss (in very large letters), presumably because both were present together in his exemplar.[9]

In writing the Old-Irish glosses, he observed a consistent and often distinctive set of conventions. The most striking of these, no less telling for being negative, is the absence of any indication of vowel length. He used neither the older system of doubling the vowel (except in gl. 55), nor the more common one of adding an acute accent, the normal diacritic employed by Old-Irish scribes to indicate a long vowel.[10] Conversely, he sometimes supplied slanted (acute) strokes above an Old-Irish word to identify it as vernacular (gll. 2–4, 23, 26–7, 56, 60). But in doing so he took care to locate the strokes above consonants, as if aware that placing them above vowels might cause them to be confused with acute accents.[11] This hypothesis, if correct, would imply that he was aware of the function of accent marks, but perhaps did not wish to use them because they were not present in his exemplar.

Frequently he marked the completion of a gloss with a mid point dot, a practice also well attested in the seventh-century glosses to the Usserianus Primus Gospels (Uss. I).[12] He sometimes used a suprascript dot (occasionally two dots, as in gll. 2, 40, 43) to link a gloss on the margins with its lemma in the main text. Although such linking is commonplace, the symbols or *signes de renvoi* employed for this purpose by other Old-Irish scribes are more elaborate, normally consisting of curves with one or more points, or of various arrangements of dots.[13] A close parallel to this simple system of the *prima manus* glosses is found in Uss. I where two words in the main text are linked to each other by a single dot.[14] Another feature shared by the glosses of these two manuscripts is the writing of only the first three/four letters of a word, rounded off with an arbitrary suspension stroke above. This technique is very common in Uss I.[15] In Wb the suspension stroke occurs in gll. 1, 60, 63, and was probably originally present in gll. 10 and 54, and perhaps gll. 5 and 51.[16]

---

7 This *d* is the most distinctive feature of the *prima manus* glosses, especially so since Old-Irish glossators normally use the *d* derived from uncial script. Admittedly, the main Wb glossator sometimes used a semi-uncial d, but his form has either an elongated or a looped shaft. Other features of the *prima manus* are an open-headed *p*, and a preference for triangular *a*.   **8** By contrast, the main glossator used a pen and employed a ductus eminently suited to glossing in a small script.   **9** See gl. 17 below.   **10** On which see now K. McCone, *Towards a relative chronology of ancient and medieval Celtic sound change*, Maynooth Studies in Celtic linguistics 1 (Maynooth 1996) p. 28. See also n. 33 below.   **11** Although well aware of the function of these strokes (which they called 'apices'), the editors of *Thes. Pal.* were careless about reproducing them, often placing them over vowels. See gll. 2, 3, 4, 26, 27, 56 below.   **12** See P. Ó Néill, 'The earliest dry-point glosses in Codex Usserianus Primus', in T. Barnard et al. (eds), *A miracle of learning: studies in manuscripts and Irish learning. Essays in honour of William O'Sullivan* (1998) pp 1–28, at p. 5. The one exception is gl. 12 which he ended with a colon.   **13** Cf. for example, the systems used in the Milan Commentary on the Psalms; R.I. Best, *The commentary on the Psalms with glosses in Old-Irish preserved in the Ambrosian Library*, p. 29. The only exception in Wb is gl. 13 which is accompanied by a slanting virgule with single dot underneath, but has no complement in the main text.   **14** See Ó Néill, 'The earliest dry-point glosses', p. 23 (gl. 132).   **15** Ibid. p. 5.   **16** See relevant commentary on these glosses.

Also noteworthy is the relative infrequency of the symbol *.i.* (*id est*) to introduce a gloss; only 12 of the 84 glosses have it.[17] This tendency is in marked contrast to that of the main Wb glossator who almost always uses it, and to the other two major collections of Old-Irish glosses, where *.i.* heavily predominates. Again, the parallel with Uss. I comes to mind, since the latter does not employ *.i.* at all.

But the most distinctive feature of the *prima manus* glosses is the degree to which they are subordinated to the main text. Of course such subordination is normal in Irish manuscripts, being usually expressed by employing a smaller and lower grade of minuscule script. But the *prima manus* made the dependent relationship more obvious: in marked contrast to the main Wb gloss, which is sprawled all over the page, filling every available space, his glosses tend to be brief in content and discreet in location. Thus, most of them consist of a single word or a phrase. And almost half of them (37) are located on the margins (normally the margin to the left of the relevant text).[18] Admittedly, for some of these, the marginal location could be explained by the physical accident of proximity to their lemmata; yet the fact that the glossator chose this position over the conventional location above the lemma, suggests a deliberate practice of marginalizing them. Moreover, in at least seventeen of these occurrences there can be little doubt about his conscious preference for the marginal space, since it put him to the trouble of using a system of dots to connect gloss and lemma.[19] He also followed, not infrequently, the same practice with his (more numerous) Latin glosses,[20] leading one to conclude that he wished to keep the main text as clean as possible. In this respect he resembles the seventh-century glossator of Uss. I, who achieved the same effect by writing his glosses in dry-point.

Thus, the techniques of glossing employed by the *prima manus* share some remarkable similarities with those of Uss. I: in use of symbols, the mid-point dot to mark the end of a gloss, the single dot as a *signe de renvoi*, and suprascript strokes to highlight a gloss; in content, the predilection for succinct glosses; in abbreviations, the use of the arbitrary suspension stroke; and most importantly, in presentation, the effort to prevent the glosses from visually interfering with the main text. Even if in some respects the usages of Uss. I seem to be older, notably, in the total absence of *.i.* and in the use of horizontal rather than slanting strokes for highlighting glosses,[21] the similarities are significant. Together they suggest that the *prima manus* glosses have preserved scribal usages consonant with the late-seventh/early-eighth century date suggested by the linguistic evidence.

The nature of the Glosses

The glosses of the *prima manus* have been described as 'explanations of single words'.[22] For the most part this characterization is true. Not only do most of the glosses provide a literal translation of the Latin lemma, they even copy the case of nouns and adjectives, the tense and person of verbs. The main exception to the latter is a small group of glosses that render verbs with verbal

---

17 Gll. 1, 21, 29, 51–2, 54, 57, 67–8, 73–4, 78.   18 For example, gll. 1–4, 11–13, 19–20.   19 Gll. 2–4, 13, 20, 22–3, 28, 35, 38–40, 43–4, 51, 53, and 63. For what it is worth, one gets the impression that he became less rigorous about this practice as he went along.   20 Among the Latin glosses of the *prima manus* are two uncharacteristically lengthy comments. Significantly, both were relegated to the outer margins: one was entered on the bottom margin (fol. 5v, col. d) well below the main text and distant from its lemma; the other on the upper left margin (fol. 24v, col c) adjacent to the Argumentum and the decorated initial *P* that preceded the epistle proper.   21 See Ó Néill, 'The earliest dry-point glosses', p. 5 and note 42.   22 *Thes. Pal.*, p. xxiii.

nouns or nouns; thus, *fomnas* (CADAT; gl. 15), *folog* (SUBPORTATE; gl. 31), *het* (AEMULOR; gl. 32), *tobe* (EXCIDANT; gl. 33). A few other glosses might be loosely described as grammatical in function if not in content. For example, the glossing of MAGNUM (a word which would not normally present a lexical challenge) by *macdath* (gl. 34) was presumably intended to highlight a substantival use of the adjective. The glossing of GRATIA by *robe* (gl. 46) was meant to indicate that a prayer was implied; that of QUOMODO by *cair* (gl. 52), that the lemma was not a conjunction but an interrogative adverb.[23]

A few of the glosses offer more than lexical or grammatical explanation, notably *diltuth* (gl.1), *dindiboiprib* (gl.12), *praidches* (gl. 19), *manam* (gl. 38), *demon* (gl. 49), *is fech* (gl. 51), *sabati* (gl. 53), *kal* (gl. 54),[24] but their slant is decidedly literal, and probably influenced by Pelagius' commentary on the Pauline Epistles.[25] Overall, the predominantly lexical nature of these glosses, their elementary character, and their tendency to literal interpretation, suggest that they were intended for an audience of beginners.

Whether the distribution of the glosses throughout the Pauline Epistles can reveal much about their purpose, or even their source, is doubtful. The Old-Irish glosses begin almost at the end of Romans and effectively end with I Thessalonians.[26] All of the epistles within this group are glossed except for Colossians. Most striking is the attention given to I and II Corinthians which together received almost half of the glosses (40). It would be tempting to think that these epistles attracted the original glossator's attention because of their discussion of practical moral and doctrinal issues. But this thought fades quickly when one considers the literal and mundane character of many of the lemmata chosen by him, for example, in gll. 35–40. The absence of glosses on I and II Timothy, Titus, and Philemon is understandable, given their 'minor' status. But the lack of glosses (both Old-Irish and Latin) on Hebrews may be more significant, hinting perhaps that the exemplar did not have this epistle, or as with Pelagius, did not gloss it.

Yet the most striking feature of the *prima manus* is the contrast it affords with the main glossator. Whereas the former is austere and discreet, the latter is exuberant and prolific.[27] One produced a plain text of the Pauline Epistles with some light, explanatory, glossing; the other almost overpowered that text, transforming it into a scholarly, didactic, commentary.[28] This radical change, apparently occurring after a relatively short period,[29] raises the possibility that the manuscript's function and purpose was then re-assessed, perhaps even that it changed owners.

The text of the prima manus *glosses in* Thesaurus Palaeohibernicus

The standard edition of the Wb glosses, that of *Thesaurus Palaeohibernicus*, vol. 1, pp 499–712, is a re-working of an earlier edition by Stokes,[30] the faults of which had already been remorselessly

23 See also gl. 29. 24 See relevant commentary below. 25 At least one of the Latin glosses of the *prima manus* drew on Pelagius. A long introductory comment on I Thessalonians, fol. 24v, col. c, '*Thessolonicenses primo non solum ipsi in omnibus perfecti erunt sed etiam …prouocat et inuitat*' corresponds to Pelagius, p. 417, lines 1–3. Also noteworthy here is the use of the older abbreviation for *sed*, consisting of *s* followed by a mid-point dot, rather than the later form, *s* with a contraction mark above. 26 The Latin glosses of the *prima manus* begin earlier in Romans and apparently end with I Tim. 27 He supplied about 3,000 Old-Irish glosses, not counting an even larger number in Latin. 28 Judging by the interpretative contents of the Old-Irish glosses and such pedagogical tools as the presence of construe-marks. On the latter in Wb, see M. Korhammer, 'Mittelalterliche Konstruktionshilfen und altenglische Wortstellung', *Scriptorium* 34 (1980) pp 15–55. 29 I rely here on Bischoff's assessment of the main glossator's hand as 'nicht viel jünger als der Text' (Bischoff-Hofmann, *Libri Sancti Kyliani*, p. 98). 30 W. Stokes,

pointed out by H. Zimmer.[31] Despite these criticisms, as well as corrections by Stern[32] (most of which were later recorded in a Supplement to *Thes. Pal.*), the text of the glosses remains significantly flawed by inaccuracies and omissions. Most noticeable among the latter is the failure (even taking into account the corrections made in the Supplement) to record at least four glosses (gll. 26, 49, 51, 84) as *a prima manu.* To make matters worse, *Thes. Pal.* provided a separate list of the *prima manus* glosses in the Introduction to vol. 1 (p. xxiv), one which incorporated some of the errors of the edition while adding new ones. Thus, two of its glosses, *indarbe* (Wb 10d6) and *iarmoysi* (Wb 33b10) are not *a prima manu*; and a third, *car* (Wb 18a2a; gl. 41), although *a prima manu*, could more plausibly be read as Latin *car<ne>.* Furthermore, the list omitted six other Old-Irish glosses, five of which (gll. 10, 15, 49, 51, 56) are certainly, and the remaining one (gl. 54) probably, by the *prima manus.*

Thes. Pal. also failed to acknowledge and distinguish the various symbols accompanying these glosses. For example, it occasionally omitted the *.i.* symbol before a gloss (e.g., gll. 67 and 73) and, conversely, supplied it without manuscript authority (e.g., gll. 58 and 80). It misrepresented the slanted strokes that occasionally occur above glosses, serving to mark them as vernacular words. First, it printed them over vowels, when in fact the scribe had placed them over consonants, arguably so that they would not be confused with marks of length. For example, *tuercomlassat* (gl. 2) has slanting strokes over *t, m, l,* and *s* (2°), whereas *Thes. Pal.* prints them over *u, o, a* and *a.*[33] Secondly, it misread some of these strokes as marks of length; for example, *ni* (gl. 27), which has a slanting stroke over *n,* is printed as ní; *tete* (gl. 56), with slanting strokes over each *t,* is printed as *téte.*

Thes. Pal. sometimes linked an Old-Irish gloss to the wrong Latin lemma (e.g., gll. 11, 13). This, despite the fact that the *prima manus* was generally careful to link gloss and lemma either by physical proximity or by the use of dots (one or two) that served as *signes de renvoi.* Some of these errors in *Thes. Pal.* may be the result of a desire to separate the glosses of the *prima manus* from those of the main glossator in the edition, even if that meant assigning them different lemmata. Also unreliable is the text of the Pauline Epistles in *Thes. Pal.*, which occasionally deviates from the manuscript in spelling (by normalizing) and sometimes even in readings.[34] The present paper attempts to correct these errors by providing a new collation of the Old-Irish glosses of the *prima manus*, one that also takes into account their manuscript context.

Appendix: a new Collation of the Old-Irish Glosses

In presenting the glosses, the following format is used: first, location in the manuscript, by folio, column (a and b [recto]; c and d [verso]), and line number (as provided in Stern's facsimile); next the relevant scriptural lemma, printed as it appears in the manuscript; then the Old-Irish gloss, parenthetically identified by the numbering assigned to it in *Thes. Pal.*, beginning with 'Wb'. Finally, a brief commentary provides a translation of the gloss, a note on its location, and corrections of errors in *Thes. Pal.*'s transcription.

The Old Irish glosses at Würzburg and Carlsruhe, Part 1 (Cambridge and London 1887).   **31** Especially in 'Zu den Würzburger Glossen', *ZCP* 6 (1908) pp 454–530, and 7 (1909) pp 271–87.   **32** L. Ch. Stern, 'Bermerkungen zu dem Würzburger Glossencodex', *ZCP* 6 (1908) pp 531–45. Stern was at the time preparing a facsimile of the manuscript (see note 2), so his readings are especially valuable.   **33** I give this example because it was recently cited from *Thes. Pal.* by K. McCone, *Towards a relative chronology*, p. 28, who (understandably) drew the wrong conclusions from its inaccurate evidence.   **34** See also the commentary on gl. 28 below.

The following abbreviations and short titles are used:

P. Ní Chatháin, 'Notes' 'Notes on the Würzburg Glosses', in P. Ní Chatháin and M. Richter, *Irland und die Christenheit* (Stuttgart 1987) pp 190–9.

DIA (*Contributions to a*) *Dictionary of the Irish Language.*

Pedersen, *VGK* H. Pedersen, *Vergleichende Grammatik der keltischen Sprachen*, 2 vols (Göttingen 1909; rpr. 1976).

Pelagius *Pelagius's Expositions of Thirteen Epistles of St Paul*, ed. A. Souter, 2 vols (Cambridge 1922–6; rpr. Wiesbaden, 1967), vol. II (text).

Stern, 'Bemerkungen' L. Ch. Stern, 'Bermerkungen zu dem Würzburger Glossencodex', *ZCP* 6 (1908) pp 531–45.

Thes. Pal. W. Stokes and J. Strachan, *Thesaurus Palaeohibernicus. A Collection of Old-Irish Glosses, Scholia, Prose and Verse*, 2 vols (Cambridge 1901–3; rpr. Dublin 1975).

Thes. Pal. Supplement A Supplement to *Thesaurus Palaeohibernicus*, in *Thes. Pal.* II (1975 edn.) pp 423–506.

Thurneysen, 'Das Alter' R. Thurneysen, 'Das Alter der Würzburger Glossen', *ZCP* 3 (1901) pp 47–54.

Thurneysen, *Grammar* R. Thurneysen, *A Grammar of Old Irish*, trans. by D.A. Binchy and O. Bergin (Dublin 1946).

1. fol. 6c2 [Rm 14:10] NE PONATIS OFFENDICULUM FRATRI UEL SCANDALUM: *.i. diltuth* ut man<ducetis> quod non uult (Wb 6c2), 'that is, a scandal that you should eat what he does not wish to eat'. Left margin above –DALUM; the *.i.* is scarcely visible. *Thes. Pal.* omitted *.i.* and expanded *man~* to *manducet*. But Paul is explaining how the liberal dietary practices of those Christians whom he is addressing (plural) may be a source of scandal to a fellow-Christian (singular); cf. v. 15, 'noli cibo tuo illum perdere'.

2. fol. 7a14 [Rm 15:26] PROBAUERUNT ENIM MACEDONIA ET ACHAIA CONLATIONEM ALIQUAM FACERE IN PAUPERES SANCTORUM: *tuercomlassat* (Wb 7a5a), 'they have gathered'. Left margin, adjacent to SANCTIS of the previous verse; slanting strokes above *t*, *m*, *l*, *s* (2°); linked to PROBAUERUNT by two dots. The gloss serves to explain not the meaning but the object of PROBAUERUNT; cf. Pelagius, 119, 19–20, 'Probauerunt hoc sibi utile fore, si collationem aliquam sumptuum facerent [in] sanctis'. On the incorrect numbering and treatment of this gloss in *Thes. Pal.*, see gl. 3 below, and p. 234 above.

3. fol. 7a15 [see gl. 2] CONLATIONEM: *comtinol* (Wb 7a6a), 'a contribution'. Left margin, adjacent to ACHAIA; slanting strokes above *m*, *t*, and *n*; linked to CONLATIONEM by a single dot. *Thes. Pal.* both incorrectly united gll. 2 and 3 and linked them to FACERE, as noted by Stern, 'Bemerkungen' p. 536, and corrected in *Thes. Pal.*, Supplement, p. 468 (with renumbering from Wb 7a7 to 7a5a and 7a6a, respectively). These two glosses have separate lemmata (indicated by double and single dot, respectively) and are on separate lines; and the first ends with a punctum, the usual mark of a completed gloss.

4. fol. 7b17 [Rm 16:10] SALUTATE APPELLEN PROBUM IN X̅P̅O: *pr(o)umthe* (Wb 7b17a), 'tested, proven'. Right margin, adjacent to SALUTATE, linked to PROBUM by a single dot; slanting strokes above *p*, *m*, and possibly *e*; read as *prumthe*. Omitted from *Thes. Pal.*, but supplied in Addenda and Corrigenda, p. 725, and Supplement, p. 468, though without slanting strokes.

5. fol. 7c16 [Rm 16:25] QUI POTENS EST UOS CONFIRMARE IUXTA EUANGELIUM MEUM ET PREDICATIONEM IHU: *isech* (Wb 7c11). Above PREDICATIONEM. Stern, 'Bemerkungen' p. 536, emends to *.i. sech* (also adopted in *Thes. Pal.*, Supplement, p. 469), and treats it as 'a rare occurrence of the absolute use of the conjunction *sech*', with the meaning 'besonders angeführt'. In support he notes Wb 22b22, 'Christi et Dei', the latter glossed *.i. sech*; cf. also Tur 93a3. Alternatively, one might read *i sech<im>*, 'in following, imitating'; cf. Wb 26d17, *imsechim agníme*: SECUNDUM OPERATIONEM EIUS; and Pelagius's comment on this verse, 126, 1–2, 'Ut sic uiuatis quo modo ego Christi exemplo et auctoritati pra[e]dicaui'.

6. fol. 8d3 [I Cor 3:15] DETRIMENTUM PATIETUR: *dernum* (Wb 8d3), 'trouble, anxiety'. Left margin, adjacent to DETRIMENTUM. For the proposed etymology of this otherwise unattested word, see DIA, s.v. *dernum*. Stern, 'Bemerkungen' p. 536, queried if *dernum* might be a scribal error for *damnum*.

7. fol. 8d8 [I Cor 3:18] STULTUS FIAT: *baid* (Wb 8d8), 'foolish'. Above STULTUS. Cf. gl. 20.

8. fol. 8d10 [I Cor 3:19] COMPREHENDAM SAPIENTES IN ASTUTIA EORUM: *ifoili* (Wb 8d13), 'in craftiness'. Above ASTUTIA.

9. fol. 9b18 [I Cor 5:8] NON IN FERMENTO MALITIAE ET NEQUITIAE: *esbetu* (Wb 9b15), 'worthlessness, emptiness'. Above NEQUITIAE; dot over *esbetu*.

10. fol. 9b27 [I Cor 5:11] CUM HUIUSMODI NEC CIBUM QUIDEM SUMERE: *isam* (Wb 9b22). Above HUIUS-; the *s* is scarcely visible. *Thes. Pal.* expanded to *isamlaid*, 'it is so', an interpretation that does not fit the nominal character of HUIUSMODI. Perhaps read *i sam<ail>*, 'in that likeness' or emend to *.i. sam<la>*, 'that is, of that type'.

11. fol. 9c3 [I Cor 6:5] HABENS NEGOTIUM ADUERSUS ALTERUM IUDICARI: *fugell* (Wb 9c5), 'a case for judgement'. Right margin, above ADUER-, presumably glossing NEGOTIUM, not ALTERUM as given in *Thes. Pal.*

12. fol. 9d20 [I Cor 7:5] NOLITE FRUDARE INUICEM NISI FORTE EX CONSENSU: *dindiboiprib* (Wb 9d19), 'of the two activities' [*sc.* the mutual sharing of sexual intercourse]. Left, inter-columnar, margin, adjacent to NOLITE. *Thes. Pal.* (and Thurneysen, 'Das Alter' 50, n.1) proposed emending to *dindib-oiprid* ('das ihr euch betruegt'). But Pedersen's linguistic argument, *VGK* II, 469, that *oiprib* is dat. pl. of *opar* (a euphemism for sexual activity) is supported by the exegetical comment of Pelagius, 161, 3–4, 'de duobus incontinentibus dicit'.

13. fol. 10c26 [I Cor 9:1] NON SUM LIBER NON SUM APOSTOLUS NONNE IHM XPM DOMINUM UIDI: *cani* (Wb 10c15), 'is it not?'. Thes Pal. confused this occurrence of *cani* with an earlier one on the same page by the main glossator (Wb 10c7); and also attached it to the wrong lemma: although located on the left margin above *sum* (1º), its accompanying *signe de renvoi* indicates for *cani* a different location, almost certainly above *nonne*, though the latter shows no sign of a complementary sign. On this use of *cani* to render *nonne*, see Thurneysen, Grammar, §465.

14. fol. 11a5 [I Cor 9:24] HII QUI IN STADIO CURRUNT: *i routh* (Wb 11a3), 'in a race'. Above STADIO.

15. fol. 11b2 [I Cor 10:12] ITAQUE QUI SE EXISTEMAT STARE UIDEAT NE CADAT: *fomnas* (Wb 11b1a), 'beware' (?). Above CADAT. *Thes. Pal.* identified UIDEAT as the lemma, and emended to *fomnar*, 'let him beware'; see also Supplement, p. 472. Stern, 'Bemerkungen' p. 537, retained *fomnas*, treating it as a noun, 'das Achtgeben'. But see also DIA, s.v. *fo-moinethar*, 286, 12–15, for examples of *fomnais* apparently used with the force of an imperative.

16. fol. 11b5 [I Cor 10:13] FACIET CUM TEMPTATIONE ETIAM PROUENTUM: *torbe* (Wb 11b3), 'an advantage, increase'. Above PROUENTUM.

17. fol. 11b23 [I Cor 10:25] OMNE QUOD UENIT IN MACELLUO MANDUCATE: *i cundrattig* (Wb 11b19), 'in a marketplace'. Above MACELLUO, the latter located on the right margin after UENIT as an addendum. *Thes. Pal.* read *icundrathtig*, but according to Stern there is no *h* visible after the first *t*, a reading subsequently accepted in Supplement, p. 472. P. Ní Catháin, 'Notes' pp 194–5, points to a close parallel in an early eighth-century Northumbrian copy of the Pauline Epistles (Cambridge, Trinity College, MS B.10.5, fol 4r21), which glosses MACELLO with Old English *.i. ceopstoue* ('that is, a marketplace').

18. fol. 12c19 [I Cor 14:1] MAGIS AUTEM UT PROPHETETIS: *forcanit* (Wb 12c18), 'you may prophesy'. Above PROPHETETIS. There is a dot above MAGIS, but no complement is visible.

19. fol. 12c24 [I Cor 14:4] QUI AUTEM PROPHETAT AECCLESIAM DEI AEDIFICAT: *praidchas* (Wb 12c27), 'who preaches'. Above PROPHETAT, on right margin.

20. fol. 12d28 [I Cor 14:23] INTRENT AUTEM IDIOTAE AUT INFIDILES: *in baid* (Wb 12d35), 'the unlearned, foolish'. Right margin, adjacent to AUT, though presumably intended for IDIOTAE (cf. gl. 7). *Thes. Pal.* incorrectly supplied *aut* before the gloss; corrected in Supplement, p. 474.

21. fol. 13d25 [I Cor 15:54] ABSOR<B>TA EST MORS IN UICTORIA: *.i. roslogeth* (Wb 13d24), 'that is, it has been swallowed up'. Above ABSORTA.

22. fol. 14a20 [I Cor 16:12] UENIET AUTEM CUM EI UACUUM FUERIT: *dilmain* (Wb 14a24), 'free'. Left margin, linked to UACUUM by a single dot.

23. fol. 14b18 [II Cor 2:4] UT POSSIMUS ET IPSI CONSULARI EOS QUI IN OMNI PRESURA SUNT: *on<dair>cur* (Wb 14b12), 'from the oppression'. Right margin, adjacent to SUNT; stroke above *o*. Since the margin is shaved (on this type of damage to the manuscript, see Stern, 'Bemerkungen' pp 532–3), the loss of a few letters after *on* on one line and before *cur* on the next line is very likely; cf. also *aircur* (gl. 73 below) glossing PRESSURA.

24. fol. 14b31 [II Cor 1:8] ITA UT TEDERET NOS ETIAM UIUERE: *toncomra* (Wb 14b23), 'so that it tires us'. Right margin, adjacent to TEDERET. *Thes. Pal.* incorrectly supplied *.i.* before the gloss.

25. fol. 15b24 [II Cor 4:8] PATIMUR SED NON ANGUSTIAMUR: *nitam toirsech* (Wb 15b21), 'we are not distressed'. Left margin, adjacent to NON ANGUSTIAMUR.

26. fol. 15b24 [II Cor 4:8] APORIAMUR: *frisbrudemor* (Wb 15b22), 'we are rejected'. Above APORIAMUR. *Thes. Pal.* failed to identify the gloss as *a prima manu*, misread the slanting strokes above *r* and *m* as marks of length above *u* and *e*, and incorrectly supplied *.i.*

27. fol. 15b24 [II Cor 4:8] SED NON DESTITUIMUR: *ni dergemor<ni>* (Wb 15b23), 'we are not abandoned'. Right margin, adjacent to DESTITUIMUR. *Thes. Pal.* incorrectly printed the gloss as *.i. ní dergemarni eter*, and misread the first of two slanting strokes (above first *n* and *g*) as a mark of length over the first *i*. Supplement, p. 477, corrected *dergemarni eter* to *dergemor*, in partial accord with Stern's reading, *ni dergemorni* (the *-ni* of which I could not verify), p. 538. But see K.H. Schmidt, 'Die Würzburger Glossen', *ZCP* 39 (1982), pp 54–77, note 35, who reads 'ní-dergemarni'.

28. fol. 15c26 [II Cor 5:8] AMBULAMUS ET NON PER SPICIEM AUDEMUS AUTEM ... : *laimirsni* (Wb 15c20), 'we dare'. Left margin, adjacent to -BULAMUS, but linked to AUDEMUS by dots. *Thes. Pal.* suggested emending to *laim<imm>ir-sni* (scribal haplography ?); and indicated a loss of letters before the gloss by supplying two dots, no doubt thinking of preverbal *ro-* (cf. gl. 36). In fact, there is no indication in the manuscript of missing letters; and the absence of *ro-* may have another explanation; see Thurneysen, *Grammar*, §543. Several lines of the main text missing after AUTEM were supplied by the second (main) glossator.

29. fol. 15d8 [II Cor 5:13] SIUE SOBRII SUMUS UOBIS: *.i. dubsi* (Wb 15d8), '[it is] for you'. Above UOBIS. *Thes. Pal.* incorrectly supplied a mark of length over *u*. The gloss is not lexical but rhetorical, to mark the contrast with parallel 'Deo' of the previous line: 'if we were out of our mind – it was for God; or if we are sane – it is for you'.

30. fol. 17b5 [II Cor 10:10] ET SERMO CONTEMPTIBILIS: *deroil* (Wb 17b4), 'contemptible, insignificant'. Above CONTEMPTIBILIS.

31. fol. 17b25 [II Cor 11:1] SED SUPORTATE ME: *folog* (Wb 17b23), 'tolerating'. Above SUPORTATE.

32. fol. 17b25 [II Cor 11:2] AEMULOR ENIM UOS DEI AEMULATIONE: *het* (Wb 17b25), 'jealousy'. Above AEMULOR. Perhaps a shorthand for *is het limm*, 'I am jealous'.

33. fol. 17b29 [II Cor 11:3] ET EXCIDANT A SIMPLICITATE: *tobe* (Wb 17b30), 'a cutting-off'. Above EXCIDANT. As noted in *Thes. Pal.*, the glossator misread *excidant* (with short *i*) as *excidant* (with long *i*). *Thes. Pal.* incorrectly supplied *.i.*

34. fol. 17c15 [II Cor 11:15] NON EST ERGO MAGNUM SI MINISTRI EIUS TRANSFIGURENTUR: *macdath* (Wb 17c9), 'a great wonder'. Above MAGNUM.

35. fol. 17c22 [II Cor 11:17] IN HAC SUBSTANTIA GLORIAE: *maidem* (Wb 17c14), 'boasting, glorying'. Left margin, adjacent to -NTIA.

36. fo. 17c29 [II Cor 11:21] IN QUO QUIS AUDET IN INSIPIENTIA DICO AUDEO ET EGO: *rulaimur* (Wb 17c21), 'I dare'. Right margin, adjacent to AUDEO. *Thes. Pal.* gave the lemma as EGO.

37. fol. 17d1 [II Cor 11:24] QUINQUIES QUADRAGENAS UNA MINUS ACCIPI: *cetarcoti* (Wb 17d1), 'forty [lashes]'. Above QUADREGENAS.

38. fol. 17d8 [II Cor 11:27] IN LABORE ET ERUMPNA: *manam* (Wb 17c4a), 'my life' (*mo + anan*). Intercolumnar margin, adjacent to LABORE. *Thes. Pal.* (and Supplement, p. 479) identified it as a gloss on II Cor 11:10, but did not give a specific lemma, while Stern, 'Bemerkungen' p. 539, linked it to II Cor 11:9; both looking to the main text of the c-column, to the left of the gloss. But given its closer proximity to LABORE, and the glossator's normal practice of locating his glosses on the margin to the left of the lemma, it seems better to take *m'anam* as a gloss on II Cor 11: 23–7 of the upper d-column, where Paul describes the numerous physical threats to his life. If this is so, then the gloss should be renumbered Wb 17d7a.

39. fol. 17d16 [II Cor 11:32] DAMASCI PREPOSSITUS GENTIS ARATHAE REGIS: *rectire* (Wb 17d13), 'governor'. Left margin, adjacent to -MASCI, linked to PREPOSSITUS (and DAMASCI and GENTIS) by a single dot. *Thes. Pal.* incorrectly supplied *.i.* and linked the gloss to REGIS (the latter error corrected in Supplement, p. 479).

40. fol. 17d18 [II Cor 11:33] ET PER FENISTRAM IN SPORTAM DIMISUS SUM: *aincis* (Wb 17d15), 'a rush basket'. Left margin, adjacent to (CONPRE)HENDERET, the last word of the previous verse; linked to SPORTAM by two dots.

41. fol. 18a3 [II Cor 12:10] CUM ENIM INFIRMOR TUNC POTENS SUM: *car* (Wb 18a2a). Above INFIRMOR. *Thes. Pal.* read OIr *car*, 'brittle', a rare word apparently attested only in glossaries; but Stern, 'Bemerkungen' p. 539, more plausibly argued for Latin *car<ne>*.

42. fol. 18a6 [II Cor 12:11] AB HIS QUI SUNT SUPRAMODUM APOSTOLI: *in mar* (Wb 18a5), 'greatly'. Above SUPRAMODUM.

43. fol. 18a10 [II Cor 12:13] DONATE MIHI HANC INIURIAM: *dilgid* (Wb 18a11), 'forgive'. Left margin, adjacent to UOS of the previous verse; linked to DONATE by two dots. *Thes. Pal.* incorrectly supplied *donate* before *dilgid*; corrected in Supplement, p. 479.

44 fol. 18a26 [II Cor 12:20] AEMOLATIONES ANIMOSITATES DESENSIONES: *menmnihi* (Wb 18a21), 'high-spirited attitudes'. Right margin, adjacent to DESEN-, but linked to ANIMOSITATES by a

single dot. *Thes. Pal.* incorrectly identified the lemma as DESENSIONES; corrected in Supplement, p. 479. See Stern, 'Bemerkungen' p. 539, who suggested that it is an etymologizing gloss.

45. fol. 18a35 [II Cor 13:2] PREDIXI ET PREDICO UT PRESENS ET NUNC ABSENS: *cenathe* (Wb 18a25), 'absent'. Above NUNC AB-. *Thes. Pal.* incorrectly supplied *.i* .

46. fol. 18c5 [Gal 1:3] gratia uobis: *robe* (Wb 18c4), 'may there be'. Above GRATIA.

47. fol. 18c12 [Gal 1:7] EUANGELIUM QUOD NON EST ALIUD: *nadni* (Wb 18c7), 'which is nothing'. Above EST ALIUD.

48. fol. 19b3 [Gal 3:1] O INSENSATI GALATIAE: *dasachtaich* (Wb 19b3), 'insane'. Above INSENSATI GAL-.

49. fol. 19b3 [Gal 3:1] QUIS UOS FASCENAUIT: *demon*, 'the Devil'. Above QUIS. Although not recorded by previous editors as an Old-Irish word, I take it as a borrowing from Latin *d(a)emon*, to denote Satan. The gloss is not likely to be (eccclesiastical) Latin, which eschews the use of the singular form with this meaning. By contrast, both this form and meaning are well attested in Old Irish (cf. Wb 21b2). If so, the gloss should be numbered Wb 19b4a.

50. fol. 19b3 [see gl. 49] FASCENAUIT: *adobragart* (Wb 19b5), 'he [the Devil] has seduced you'. Above FASCENAUIT. Although this meaning for the verb *ad-gair* is otherwise unattested, see W. Stokes, *Revue Celtique* 4 (1879–80), pp 324–48, at 340–1, who compared *adobragart* to Old Breton *aruuoart* (=*ar-guo-garth*), glossing UOS FASCINAUIT in Paris, BNF, ms. lat. 12021 (ninth or early tenth century).

51. fol. 19d2 [Gal 4:2] SED SUB CURATORIBUS EST ET ACTORIBUS USQUE AD PREFINITUM TEMPUS A PATRAE: *.i. is fech* (Wb 19d4), 'that is, it is an obligation' or 'that is, he is under obligation' (?). Left margin, close to (CURATO)-RIBUS. *Thes. Pal.* linked this gloss to PATRAE, though more likely it is a comment on the whole verse; and failed to identify it as *a prima manu*. Strachan, Addenda and Corrigenda, p. 726, suggested emending to *is sech* 'and further', but rescinded this reading in Supplement, p. 480. Stern, *Epistolae Beati Pauli glosati* (see n. 3), p. xiii, n. 4, suggested either (1) *is fech*, 'it is an obligation' or (2) *is fech*, 'he is under obligation', the latter adopted by *Thes. Pal.*, Supplement, p. 480, 'he is a debtor'.

52. fol. 19d16 [Gal 4:9] QUOMODO CONUERTIMINI: *.i. coir* (Wb 19d10), 'that is, why?'. Above QUOMODO. *Coir* here could be read as an interrogative particle, 'why?' or simply as a marker of a following question (see DIA, s.v. 2 *cair*). In either case, the glossator may have wanted to highlight that QUOMODO was an adverb and not a conjunction (as in gl. 78, where it is glossed *ci crud*).

53. fol. 19d18 [Gal 4:10] QUIBUS DE NOUO UULTIS SERUIRE DIES OBSERBATIS ET MENSES: *sabati* (Wb 19d13). 'sabbaths'. Left margin, adjacent to *(uul)-tis*, the beginning of the line; no visual link to a lemma in the the main text, though presumably intended for DIES; cf. gl. 54.

54. fol. 19d18 [see gl. 53] ET MENSES: *.i. kal* (Wb 19d14), 'that is, the beginnings of months'. Above MENSES; *Thes. Pal.* incorrectly supplied an abbreviation mark after *kal*. Although not identified as *a prima manu* by previous editors, its broad-headed *a* and bold *.i.* mark it as such. Moreover, the gloss fits well into a tripartite set of glosses on this verse, the other two of which are *a prima manu*; thus: DIES: *sabati*; MENSES: *.i. kal*; ANNOS: *.i. iubili-* (leg. *Iubil<ae>i* or *iubili<os>* ?). However, in place of OIr *kal<anda>* one could also read Lat. *kal<endas>*. Cf. Pelagius, 325, 10, 'non enim calendas colimus'; and Pseudo-Primasius (Cassiodorus's revision of Pelagius), 'non enim calendas colimus … Et annos. Forte … dicit … de … quinquagesimo, id est jubilaeo' (*PL* 68, 595C).

55. fol. 20a15 [Gal 4:26] QUAE SURSUM EST: *soos* (Wb 20a8), 'above'. Above SURSUM.

56. fol. 20b28 [Gal 5:19] QUAE SUNT FORNICATIO INMUNDITIA LUXORIA: *tete* (Wb 20b17), 'luxury, comfort'. Right margin, adjacent to LUXORIA (which has a dot above it). *Thes. Pal.* failed to identify it as *a prima manu* and incorrectly read a mark of length over first *e*, which is actually one of two slanting strokes over the two *t*s of *tete*.

57. fol. 20b29 [Gal 5:20] IDOLORUM SERUITUS UENEFICIA: *.i. aipthi* (Wb 20b20), 'spells'. Above UENEFICIA.

58. fol. 20c12 [Gal 6:2] ALTER ALTERIUS HONERA PORTATE: *fulget* (Wb 20c5), 'sustain!'. Above PORTATE, which also has a dot over it. *Thes. Pal.* incorrectly supplied *.i.*

59. fol. 20c14 [Gal 6:3] NAM SI QUIS ESISTIMAT SE ALIQUID ESSE: *besni* (Wb 20c7), 'that he be something'. Left margin, adjacent to -QUID ESSE. *Thes. Pal.* incorrectly supplied *.i.*

60. fol. 20d6 [Gal 6:17] EGO ENIM STIGMATA IH̄U IN CORPORE MEO PORTO: *inda errend .i.* turmenta flagil- (Wb 20d5), 'the marks, that is, the pains of the lashings'. Left margin, adjacent to STIGMATA. *Thes. Pal.* (following Thurneysen, 'Das Alter' pp 53–4) printed two slanting strokes, above *a* and initial *e*, respectively. Actually, the first of these is located above the first *d*, while the second is a dot linking the gloss to its lemma, STIGMATA. *Thes. Pal.*'s translation, 'the stigmata', misleadingly conveys the impression of Paul carrying the marks of Christ's passion. As indicated by the Latin gloss that follows, the glossator was thinking of the physical punishments endured by Paul; cf. gl.37

61. fol. 21a10 [Eph 1:13] IN QUO ET RECENTES SIGNATI ESTIS SPU PROMISIONIS SANCTO: *siglithi* (Wb 21a4), 'sealed'. Left margin, adjacent to SIGNATI which has a *signe de renvoi*.

62. fol. 21c22 [Eph 3:4] PROUT POTESTIS LEGENTES INTELLEGERE: *amail* (Wb 21c10), 'as'. Although *amail* properly belongs with PROUT, its location above POTESTIS was perhaps intended to warn the reader that the latter is a verb, not a noun.

63. fol. 21d14 [Eph 3:17] IN CARITATE RADICATI ET FUNDATI: *clan-* (Wb 21d6), 'planted'. Left margin, adjacent to IN. *Thes. Pal.* (and Stern, 'Bemerkungen' p. 540) omits the abbreviation stroke above *n*, and expands to *clan<tai>* for *clandtai*. Since there is no defining dot over either Latin verb, the gloss may be intended for both.

64. fol. 22a4 [Eph 4:9] QUOD AUTEM ASCENDIT QUID EST NISI QUIA ET DISCENDIT PRIMUM: *cith* (Wb 22a5), 'even'. Above ET.

65. fol. 22a6 [Eph 4:10] IPSE EST ET QUI ASCENDIT SUPER OMNES CAELOS: *cith isse* (Wb 22a7), 'even he himself'. Above QUI and ASCENDIT, respectively. *Thes. Pal.* conjoins the two words; corrected in Supplement, p. 481. On *isse*, see *DIA*, s.v. 2 *os*.

66. fol. 22b22 [Eph 5:4] AUT TURPITUDO: *dronei* (Wb 22b16), 'vile practices'. Above TURPITUDO. Thurneysen, 'Das Alter' p. 50, agrees with Zimmer that the gloss derives from *droch-gné*, and would attribute the loss of the guttural to scribal negligence or incompetence. Perhaps the guttural was represented by *h* in the exemplar and the latter was then confused with *n*. But see also *Lexique Etymologique de l'Irlandais Ancien de J. Vendryes*, ed. Y.-P. Lambert (Paris, 1996), D-201, s.v.

67. fol. 22b23 [Eph 5:4] AUT SCURILITAS: *.i. enchache* (Wb 22b18), 'that is, scurrility'. Above SCURILITAS. *Thes. Pal.* omitted *.i.*

68. fol. 22c26 [Eph 5:28] ITA UIRI DEBENT DELEGERE UXORES SUAS UT CORPORA SUA: *.i. amail ata* (Wb 22c14), 'that is, as they are' [*sc.* in love with their own bodies]). Above CORPORA SUA.

69. fol. 22d19 [Eph 6:11] INDUITE UOS ARMATURA DEI: *aithirgabu* (Wb 22d10), 'arms, weapons'. Left margin, adjacent to ARMATURA (misread by Stern, 'Bemerkungen' p. 512, as ARMATURAM).

70. fol. 22d35 [Eph 6:18] ET IN IPSO UIGILANTES IN OMNI INSTANTIA: *ingreschi* (Wb 22d23), 'in perseverance'. Left margin, adjacent to INSTANTIA.

71. fol. 23b2 [Phil 1:10] UT PROBETIS POTIORA: *dersciddu* (Wb 23b8), 'better things'. Above POTIORA. The spelling is problematic; perhaps read *derscigdu* as suggested by Pedersen, *VGK*, II, p. 618. See also Thurneysen, 'Das Alter' p. 50, and *Thes. Pal.*, Supplement, p. 482.

72. fol. 23b8 [Phil 1:13] in OMNI PRAETORIO: *rigteg* (Wb 23b8), 'a royal residence'. Left margin, adjacent to -TORIO.

73. fol. 23b16 [Phil 1:17] EXISTIMANTES PRESURAM SE SUSCITARE: *.i. aircur* (Wb 23b19), 'that is, affliction'. Above PRESURAM. *Thes. Pal.* omitted *.i.*. Cf. gl. 23.

74. fol. 23b17 [Phil 1:18] DUM OMNI MODO CHRISTUS...ADNUNTIATUR: *.i. saichi crud* (Wb 23b22), 'that is, in whatever way'. Left margin and above DUM OMNI. *Thes. Pal.* omitted *.i.*

75. fol. 23c1 [Phil 1:27] QUIA STATIS IN UNO SPIRITU: *ol* (Wb 23c1), 'since'. Left margin, above QUIA. Cf. gl. 83.

76. fol. 23d30 [Phil 3:2] UIDETE CONCISSIONEM: *adcumbe carnis* (Wb 23d22), 'a cutting of the flesh'. Above – CISSIONEM. *Thes. Pal.* translates 'recutting *carnis*'.

77. fol. 23d31 [Phil 3:3] NOS ENIM SUMUS CIRCUMCISSIO: *coirttobe* (Wb 23d24), 'circumcision'. Left margin, above -CISSIO.

78. fol. 24a11 [Phil 3:11] SI QUOMODO OCCURRAM AD RESURRECTIONEM: *.i. ci crud* (Wb 24a9), 'that is, in what manner'. Above QUOMODO (which also has a dot above it). *Thes. Pal.* omitted *.i.*

79. fol. 24a17 [Phil 3:14] AD DESTINATUM PERSEQUOR BRADIUM SUPERNAE UOCATIONIS: *boid* (Wb 24a16), 'victory'. Above BRADIUM. On the latter spelling (for BRABIUM), see P. Ní Chatháin, 'Notes', p. 194.

80. fol. 24b9 [Phil 4:8] QUAECUMQUE AMABILIA: *eslabre* (Wb 24b8), 'generosity'. Above AMABILIA. *Thes. Pal.* incorrectly supplied *.i.*

81. fol. 24c7 [Argumentum to I Th] PER THITHICUM DIACONEM ET HONESSIMUM ACOLITUM: *caindleoir* (Wb 24b32), 'a candle-bearer, an acolyte'. Right margin, adjacent to ACOLI-. The *n* of *caindleoir* was added above the word.

82. fol. 24c23 [I Th 1:6] ET UOS ... EXCIPIENTES UERBUM IN TRIBULATIONE MULTA: *fresdel* (Wb 24c11), 'receiving'. Above EXCIPIENTES.

83. fol. 25b27 [I Th 4:14] QUIA NOS QUI UIUIMUS: *ol* (Wb 25b15), 'for, since'. Above QUIA. Cf. gl. 75.

84. fol. 27d21 [Argumentum to I Tim] INCIPIT ARGUMENTUM AEPIS<TOLAE> AD TIMOTHEUM: *haecosc* (Wb 27d17), 'indication of what follows, summary'. Above ARGUMENTUM. *Thes. Pal.* did not identify this gloss as a *prima manu*, though in Addenda and Corrigenda, p. 727, it cited Zimmer's opinion that it is in the hand of the main text.

Index of Old-Irish words

Words are identified by the number of the gloss in which they occur; forms marked with an asterisk are doubtful for one reason or another.

A fragment of a Latin grammar

PATRICIA KELLY

The question of the native or external provenance of aspects of early medieval Irish learned tradition has fuelled a lively debate in recent years. In particular the areas of law and historico-literary narrative have come in for much renewed scrutiny of their putative origins. As regards the field of language study, there was never any room for doubt about the substantial foreign input, ample testimony to the study of the works of the Latin grammarians in the monastic schools being supplied by a rich textual heritage, in both Hiberno-Latin and Early Irish. Indeed the very earliest records of the Irish language, lapidary inscriptions, some of which may be as old as the fifth century, also testify to this knowledge: the Ogham alphabet in which these documents are inscribed was devised by someone familiar with the grammarians' analysis of the letters of the Latin alphabet into vowels and consonants.[1]

Two further substantial bodies of text bear witness to the long tradition of language study in medieval Ireland. *Auraicept na nÉces* 'the scholars' primer', comprises an Old-Irish nucleus, amplified by extensive Middle Irish commentary.[2] Its claim to being considered a separate strand in the linguistic tradition is two-fold. First, the main focus of its interest is Irish rather than Latin. Secondly, while it uses terminology based on Latin grammar, this is in many cases flanked by terms attributed to native Gaelic learning. This hybrid quality of *Auraicept na nÉces* has been characterized as follows: 'Although the native element in the *Auraicept* is quite marked, the work was clearly composed by someone who had studied the Latin grammarians.'[3] The remaining major strand in medieval Irish linguistics is the 'Bardic Grammatical Tracts', which provide an analytical tool for the assessment of correct practice in the writing of Classical Irish poetry from the thirteenth to the seventeenth century. For Bergin, this shows the 'native Irish grammarian' *par excellence*, in that this material reflects 'a complete break' with the earlier *Auraicept* tradition.[4]

Recent work has shown that there may be more continuity between the above strands of linguistic tradition than was at first apparent.[5] The present article examines a Latin grammatical fragment which illustrates both the continuity and the heterogeneity of medieval Irish grammatical learning.

The fourteenth-century National Library of Ireland manuscript G 2–3 is the earliest known source for the didactic material from the Bardic schools: it contains an eclectic collection of texts of linguistic interest, including two whose primary orientation is towards Latin.[6] One is an Early Irish poem on the gender and declension of Latin nouns. David Greene noted that the poem is based, probably directly, on books v–vii of Priscian's *Institutiones Grammaticae*. Assigning a

---

1 D. McManus, *A guide to Ogam* (Maynooth 1991) pp 27–30. 2 G. Calder, *Auraicept na nÉces. The scholars' primer* (Edinburgh 1917). The Old-Irish core has been re-edited in A. Ahlqvist, *The Early Irish linguist* (Helsinki 1983). 3 B. Ó Cuív, 'Linguistic terminology in the mediaeval Irish bardic tracts', *Transactions of the Philogical Society* 1965 (1966) pp 141–64, at p. 159. 4 O.J. Bergin, 'The native Irish grammarian', *Proceedings of the British Academy* 24 (1939) pp 205–35, at p. 7. 5 Cuív, Ahlqvist. 6 B. Ó Cuív, *The linguistic training of the mediaeval Irish poet* (Dublin 1973) p. 5. For the manuscript, see N. Ní Shéaghdha, *Catalogue of Irish manuscripts in the National Library of Ireland*, Fasciculus 1 (Dublin 1967) pp 12–28.

possible eleventh-century date to the poem, he concluded that 'it constitutes a proof … that the scientific study of Latin grammar continued into what we call the Middle Irish period'.[7]

Further, and more immediate, testimony to the survival of interest in the Latin grammarians in Ireland is supplied by a fragment of the 'Irish' version of Priscian's grammar on a vellum scrap retrieved from the binding of the thirteenth-century Trinity College Dublin manuscript C.1.8 (No. 229).[8] It is in an Irish hand which has been dated to the eleventh century, and was probably written in Ireland.[9] At least one Hiberno-Latin grammar was also still being studied in Ireland at this period: an eleventh or twelfth-century date has been suggested on palaeographical grounds for fol. 16 of the British Library composite manuscript Egerton 3323, which is written in an Irish hand and contains a fragment of the *Ars grammatica* of Clemens Scottus.[10]

Some basic elements of the work of the Latin grammarians remained in circulation even longer still in Ireland. This is reflected in the second of the two Latin-oriented texts in manuscript G 2–3 noted by Ó Cuív (note 6 above). It is a short tract in Later Middle or Early Modern Irish which classifies the letters of the alphabet into vowels and consonants, semi-vowels, mutes and liquids, according to the doctrine of classical grammar. It is one of two similar tracts which have been published by Meyer in 1918,[11] and Ahlqvist (from G2–3) in 1987.[12] Another remains unpublished. One copy of it has been noticed, namely that in the Trinity College Dublin manuscript H.3.18 (now No. 1337), p. 414f.[13] This is the verso of a single leaf which is bound into the surrounding folios by means of a strip which obscures the initial and final letters of each line on recto and verso respectively. Fortunately this deficiency can be remedied for much of the text by a copy in the Royal Irish Academy Stowe vellum of fifteenth or sixteenth-century date[14] C i 2 (No. 1234, fol. 39 r a1–39 v b24). This copy is itself, however, also defective, as it ends imperfect owing to a chasm in the manuscript.

All three tracts have at their core the elementary classification of the letters of the alphabet. They also share the question and answer format of exposition, which itself is also derived ultimately from the Latin grammarians.[15] Yet they differ too much in expression and partly also in content for a common archetype to be posited. The third text in particular has 'a good deal

7 D. Greene, 'A Middle Irish poem on Latin nouns', *Celtica* 2 (1954) pp 278–96, at p. 278.   8 T.K. Abbott, *Catalogue of the manuscripts in the library of Trinity College, Dublin* (Dublin 1900) p. 32. The fragment is noted in M. Esposito, 'Classical manuscripts in Irish libraries: Part I', *Hermathena* 19 (1922) pp 123–40, at p. 136. For a full description of the fragment and its contents, the 'Irish' Priscian, see R. Hofman, *The Sankt Gall Priscian commentary*. Part 1. Volume 1 (Münster 1996) p. 39.   9 L. Bieler and B. Bischoff, 'Fragmente zweier frühmittelalterlicher Schulbücher aus Glendalough', *Celtica* 3 (1956) pp 211–20, at p. 220 note 1. This fragment was evidently unknown to Margaret Gibson, 'Milestones in the story of Priscian, *c.*800–*c.*1200', *Viator* 23 (1992) pp 17–33, who writes (at p. 26): 'It should be remembered that the insular evidence is entirely lost. Not a word, not a scrap of parchment concerning the text or the exposition of Priscian survives in Ireland today, nor in a manuscript which can be associated with any medieval library in Ireland. All the surviving evidence is Continental.'   10 Bieler and Bischoff, 'Fragmente', pp 211–16. Arguments for a more precise dating, to 1106, and for Glendalough as *locus scribendi*, are presented op. cit. p. 212. On the wider context of these two fragments see also D. Ó Cróinín, 'Na mainistreacha agus an léann', in M. Mac Conmara (ed.), *An léann eaglasta 1000–1200* (Baile Átha Cliath 1982) pp 19–30.   11 K. Meyer, 'Mitteilungen aus irischen Handschriften: Vom Buchstaben', *ZCP* 12 (1918) pp 294f. (from the Book of Lecan).   12 A. Ahlqvist, 'An Irish text on the letters of the alphabet', in A.M. Simon-Vandenbergen (ed.), *Studies in honour of René Derolez* (Ghent 1987) pp 3–16. I am grateful to Professor Ahlqvist for providing me with a copy of this paper.   13 Ahlqvist, *Early Irish linguist*, pp 16f. See also idem, 'Gramadóirí Gaeilge agus Laidine', *Léachtaí Cholm Cille* 16 (Maigh Nuad 1986) pp 54–70, at p. 64. T.K. Abbott and E.J. Gwynn, *Catalogue of the Irish manuscripts in the library of Trinity College, Dublin* (Dublin 1921) p. 149, merely states that this page contains 'various short notes'.   14 K. Mulchrone, *Catalogue of Irish manuscripts in the Royal Irish Academy*, Fasciculus 26 (Dublin 1942) pp 3414–18, at p. 3414. The text in question is noticed as a 'linguistic item' in B. Ó Cuív, 'Irish words for "alphabet"', *Ériu* 31 (1980) pp 100–10, at p. 108.   15 T. Charles-Edwards, '*The Corpus Iuris Hibernici*' (review article), *Studia Hibernica* 20 (1980) pp 141–62, at p. 147.

of supplementary material'.[16] It opens with a statement of the number of letters in the alphabet, and proceeds to the familiar division of letters into vowels and consonants. The section on the vowels is of considerable interest, especially in that it incorporates some lines in Latin, interspersed with Irish. These lines occur immediately after the listing of the five vowels, and before the definition of a vowel. The Latin falls into four short sections, each followed by Irish material introduced by the abbreviation .i. which signals explanatory glossing. In the TCD manuscript, the Latin portions are distinguished from the Irish by being written in the large script normally reserved for canonical text which is to be glossed. Thus, recourse can be had to the accompanying Irish text to retrieve the meaning of the latin, which is unfortunately corrupt.[17]

The Latin passage is also found independently of the tract on the alphabet, and without the explanations in Irish, on a small trapezoid-shaped piece of vellum inserted into the composite Trinity College Dublin manuscript H.4.22 (now No. 1363) after p. 158.[18] There it follows some eleven lines largely in Irish, consisting of material which occurs in the Yellow Book of Lecan recension of *Auraicept na nÉces*. This Irish material falls into two parts. Lines 1–7, which deal with the accent in Latin *circumdamus,* correspond to *Auraicept* 4103–35.[19] Thurneysen points out that this is an interpolation between the third and fourth 'books' of the *Auraicept*.[20] Nevertheless it is written in large 'text' script, and partly accompanied by an Irish explanatory text.[21] The second part comprises lines 8–11, and is concerned with the concept expressed by OIr *nihelas* 'nullity (of phonetic value)',[22] as instanced by *u* when it follows *q, g* or *s*. This passage corresponds to *Auraicept* 2836–43.[23] It incorporates a Latin quotation (*s in principio uel ut sillabam sonat = Auraicept* 2840–1) attributed to Ogricus, which Thurneysen recognized as the name of the grammarian Agroecius.[24] The Latin passage under consideration here begins on line 11, and occupies the final six lines. These are of decreasing length, as the vellum scrap here tapers away to a point. The vellum is so buckled, and the right-hand edge of the narrow piece is so worn that some letters are indecipherable by me.

The defective state of two of the manuscripts, and the corrupt transmission of the Latin, make it hazardous to attempt an edition. A full transcription of all three versions is here offered in the hope that it may enable a Latin specialist to restore the text to a greater degree than is achieved in this article. The abbreviations C, H1 and H2 stand for the manuscripts C i 2, H.3.18 and H.4.22 respectively. I have supplied minimal punctuation, capitalization and word-division, mainly of the Irish. The division into four sections corresponds to the four units of Latin plus Irish explanation. The Irish text is that of manuscript C, which supplies letters missing in H1, and which differs only inessentially from it.

Angled brackets indicate both the letters in H1 which have been obscured by the binding, and those in H2 which are illegible to me. Round brackets are placed around tentative readings, square brackets around editorial emendations to the Irish text.

16 Ahlqvist, 'An Irish text', p. 6. Another noteworthy feature is its attestation of the hitherto unknown Early Irish *liccit* 'liquid', borrowed from Latin, discussed in P. Kelly, 'Variation in Early Irish linguistic terminology' in A. Ahlqvist and V. Čapková (eds), *Dán do oide: essays in memory of Conn R. Ó Cléirigh* (Dublin 1997) pp 243–6. 17 Ahlqvist, *Early Irish linguist,* p. 16. 18 Abbott and Gwynn, *Catalogue,* pp 199–216, at p. 209. The occurrence of the Latin passage in question on this fragment is noted in Ahlqvist, *Early Irish linguist,* p. 16. 19 Calder, *Auraicept* pp 228f. 20 R. Thurneysen, 'Auraicept na n-Éces, *ZCP* 17 (1927) pp 277–303, at p. 285 note 2. 21 Calder, *Auraicept,* pp 228f. 22 On this term see R. Hofman, 'Isidore in the St Gall glosses', in P. Ní Chatháin and M. Richter (eds), *Ireland and Europe in the early middle ages: learning and literature* (Stuttgart 1996) pp 173–86, at p. 179. 23 Calder, *Auraicept,* pp 188f. 24 Thurneysen, 'Auraicept na n-Éces', p. 278. Thurneysen locates the original in *GL* vii 118.7. The Agroecius passage is quoted more literally by Donatus ortigraphus, a Hiberno-Latin grammarian of the ninth century: J. Chittenden (ed.), *Donatus ortigraphus, Ars grammatica, CCCM* 40 D (Turnhout 1982) p. 35.759–66.

C   Ca mét nguthi*dhe* ata ann? Ni *hansa*. a .v. .i. a e i o u

§ 1

C   Ce*s*tio fit talis cura sit primo uocalis ipsa gradu primo retenet sub pectoris imo
H1   Cestio fitalis cura sit primo uocalis ipso < >rimo retinet sub pectaris imo
H2   Ce*s*ñio fitailis cúr .á. sit primo u< > ipsa gradu prima retinet supectoris primo.

C   .i. Cad do-beir cu*r*ob i .a. is c*ét* guth*idhe* an*n*? Ni *hansa*: ar son gu*r*ob isin ucht
     fog*r*aidhis.

§ 2

C   .E. que secunda dat*ur* quia gutiris imo sonat*ur*
H1   E qe secunda dat*ur* quia gutaris imo
H2   <   > dator que gutiris imo sonator

C   .i. a ci*n*d na sgornaighe do gab*ur* .e.

§ 3

C   Hi. streipit extermo sonat o inter dentibus e(u)ia
H1   strepit extrema so< >ter dentibas iena
H2   I <   >mat sonat .o int*er* dentes e < >

C   .i. l*eth* atuas do*n* sgornaigh do gabur .í. ET e*t*ir na fiacl*a* fog*r*aidhis .o

§ 4

C   .u. sub p*r*ima dat*ur* quia labis hora sonat*ur*
H1   U. qe sub pror< >qe labis ore sonatur
H2   .u. que supr(em)< > labis

C   .i. as í .v. is deghi*n*aidh dibh oí[r] is e*t*ir na meillibh fog*r*aidhas.

NOTES
§ 1 H1 *fitalis*: a second *t* has been added above the line in a fainter ink.
§ 3 H1 *dentibas*: a correction to be inserted after *t* has been entered below the line, possibly
     to be read as *es*.
§ 4 *deghinaidh*: H1 *degincha* ‖ *ói[r]*: C *oí*, H1 *ór*.

While the Latin has suffered in transmission, enough of the original can be pieced together from the three manuscripts for the gist of its contents to be retrieved with the help of the Irish, which is clearly a rough translation, and which is fully intelligible:

'How many vowels are there? Not difficult: five, that is, *a e i o u*.
Why is it that *a* is the first vowel? Not difficult: because it is in the breast that it sounds.
e is said at the back of the throat.
In the upper part of the throat *i* is said, and *o* sounds between the teeth.
u is the last of them because it is between the lips[25] that it sounds.'

25 Literally 'protuberances'. *DIL* lists only *mell*, with meanings (a) ball, sphere, round mass, (b) round protuberance, swelling, used of various body parts. A doublet *meill* is noted by T.F. O'Rahilly, 'Notes, mainly

This is evidently an attempt to explain the order of the vowels in the alphabet on the basis of their perceived points of articulation, beginning with the innermost organs and proceeding up the throat and gullet towards teeth and lips. What is clearly fundamentally the same doctrine is found in somewhat different form in the commentary on Donatus, *Ars Maior* I 2[26] by Sedulius Scottus:

SVNT AVTEM NVMERO QVINQVE: A E I O V. Quaeritur, quare hunc ordinem uocales habeant. Ideo quia a in pectore, e in gutture, i inter fauces, o inter dentes, u paene extra labia sonat. Quod non ita intelligendum est, quasi singulae uocales in his omnibus locis non sonent. Sonant etenim, sed magis tamen in pectore quam in aliis locis sonat; quod et de ceteris uocalibus in suis locis similiter est intelligendum.[27]	[The vowels] are five in number: a e i o u. It is asked why the vowels have this order. For the reason that *a* sounds in the breast, *e* in the throat, *i* in the pharynx, *o* between the teeth, *u* almost outside the lips. Which is not to be understood as if to mean that the individual vowels do not sound in all these places. They do, indeed, but [*a*] however sounds more in the breast than in other places; which is also to be similarly understood of the other vowels in their own places.

In essence the content is the same as in our text, in that both purport to show the phonetic basis to the order of vowels. This material is also positioned in both texts in the same place, after the statement of the number of vowels and their identity. There are nevertheless interesting divergences in expression. The opening question is formulated quite differently, and in our text may perhaps be restored as follows: *Cestio: [cur] fit talis cur[a] a sit prima uocalis?*[28] In the answer, whereas Sedulius compresses the detail into one concise sentence, our text offers a somewhat expanded version. Each of the vowels receives a separate clause, and Sedulius's single verb *sonat* is supplemented by the more colourful *retinnit* (sic leg. § 1) for the letter *a*, and *strepit* in the case of *i*. A comparison of two other phrases again shows how our text is slightly more prolix. For *in pectore* 'in the breast' and *in gutture* 'in the throat', our version has *sub pectoris imo* and *sub gutturis imo* 'at the bottom of the breast' etc. The entry for the letter *i* in §3 shows the greatest difference. In place of *inter fauces* 'in the pharynx' our text presumably had something like *in gutturis extremo* 'at the end of the throat' corresponding to the Irish. In the case of *o*, the element following *inter dentes* (sic leg. with H2) remains unclear to me. The phrase introducing the letter *u* in § 4 is presumably of the same structure as *e que secunda datur* in § 2, and to be restored *u quae suprema datur*. The 'phonetic' detail is again worded differently from Sedulius. The reading *ore* (H1) may perhaps be taken as 'from the mouth', corresponding to *extra labia* in Sedulius: it may not have been understood by the glossator, as it does not have a counterpart in the Irish version. The final two sentences in Sedulius (*Quod non ita ... est intelligendum*), which seem to be specifying primary as opposed to secondary points of articulation, may be the clue to the puzzling *ipso gradu primo* in § 1 of our text.

This work of Sedulius Scottus is closely related to two other ninth-century commentaries on Donatus, those of Murethach[29] and Anonymus of Lorsch,[30] in that all three have a common

etymological', *Ériu* 13 (1942) pp 144–219, at p. 194. Under *meill*, P.S. Dinneen, *Foclóir Gaedhilge agus Béarla. An Irish-English dictionary* (Dublin 1927) p. 734, gives the related meanings 'a mouth, a cheek, a deformity of mouth, a protruding lip'.   **26** *GL* iv 367.11–12 = L. Holtz (ed.), *Donat et la tradition de l'enseignement grammatical* (Paris 1981) p. 603.8–9.   **27** B. Löfstedt (ed.), *Sedulius Scottus in Donati Artem maiorem, CCCM* 40 B (Turnhout 1977) p. 8.1–8.
28 This suggestion I owe to Professor G.L. Huxley. Thanks are also due to the editors of this volume for assistance with the Latin.   **29** L. Holtz (ed.), *Murethach in Donati Artem maiorem, CCCM* 40 (Turnhout 1977).   **30** B. Löfstedt (ed.),

source in a Hiberno-Latin commentary on the *Ars Maior* written in Ireland in the early ninth century.[31] Neither Murethach nor Lorsch, however, deals with the question of the order of the vowels at this point. Nor does Löfstedt's *apparatus fontium* in his edition of Sedulius' commentary furnish any parallels for this section in other Latin grammars. Only the *Ars Brugensis*, which is largely a collection of excerpts from Sedulius and Murethach,[32] is shown by Löfstedt's *apparatus criticus* to contain this passage.[33]

Holtz observed that Sedulius can be contrasted with Murethach and Anonymus of Lorsch through the extent to which he amplifies the source commentary, resulting in a text which is at least twice as long as theirs.[34] Two other passages which distinguish Sedulius' text deal with matters analogous to the analysis of the vowel sounds. His commentary on the opening sentence of the *Ars Maior*, which begins with a section *De voce* (*Vox est aer ictus sensibilis auditu, quantum in ipso est*),[35] incorporates a quotation from Fulgentius Mythographus on the ten organs of speech, which concludes: *His igitur decem instrumentis omnis uox articulata formatur*).[36] His discussion of lengthening and shortening in vowels (*Latinae vocales omnes et produci et corripi possunt*)[37] relates this feature to the primary point of articulation, stating that the long variants are produced further back in the throat (*Nam quando producuntur, maxime in gutture sonant, quando uero corripiuntur, magis in faucibus resonant*),[38] a suggestion which approaches an understanding of the physical dimension of allophonic variation.

It would appear therefore that an interest in the phonetic aspect of speech sounds was not as lacking in this early period of language study as has been thought.[39] Another pointer towards such an interest is a short text in a ninth-century Berne manuscript which lists the letters of the alphabet and adds a brief description of where and how each one is produced in the mouth.[40] The details for the vowel sounds are however somewhat different from those of the Sedulius commentary. A further text in the same manuscript[41] also lists the letters of the alphabet in order, adding miscellaneous details, but not of a 'phonetic' nature. The section on the letter *a* asks: *Quare prima ex litteris est a?*, but the answer given is that it is because Adam was the first man.

As regards the source of the doctrine on the pronunciation of the vowels, its presence in the work of Sedulius Scottus, and the existence of the version preserved in the late Irish tract on the letters of the alphabet, do not of course amount to a proof of Irish origin. Grammatical works of non-Irish origin are frequently quoted in the Middle-Irish commentaries on the *Auraicept*.[42] Some, of course, may have entered the *Auraicept* tradition via a Hiberno-Latin intermediary.[43] Nevertheless, a striking confirmation of an Irish concern with the physiological basis to speech sounds is found in an early vernacular text. This is the *Bretha Nemed Déidenach*, a 'poetico-legal' tract.[44] In addition to much detail about the legal rights and duties of poets, it contains, as the

---

Ars Laureshamensis, CCCM 40 A (Turnhout 1977). **31** L. Holtz, 'Sur trois commentaires irlandais de *l'Art Majeur* de Donat au IXe siècle', *Revue d'Histoire des Textes* 2 (1972) pp 45–72. See also Löfstedt, *Ars Laureshamensis*, p. xiii, for a modification of Holtz's stemma. **32** Löfstedt, *Sedulius*, p. ix. **33** Note that the *Ars Brugensis* is closer to the Irish in featuring *inter* for Sedulius's *extra* (*labia*). **34** Holtz, 'Sur trois commentaires', p. 59. **35** *GL* iv 367.5 = Holtz, *Donat*, p. 603.2. **36** Löfstedt, *Sedulius*, p. 4.65–74. **37** *GL* iv 367.20 = Holtz, *Donat*, p. 604.8. **38** Löfstedt, *Sedulius*, p. 11.7–9. **39** V. Law, *Grammar and grammarians in the early middle ages* (London and New York 1997) p. 262. **40** *GL* viii 307f. **41** *GL* viii 302.4, noted in Ahlqvist, *Early Irish linguist*, p. 16 note 44. **42** Cf. E. Poppe, 'The Latin quotations in *Auraicept na nÉces*: microtexts and their transmission', in P. Ní Chatháin and M. Richter (eds), *Ireland and Europe in the early middle ages: texts and transmission* (Dublin, forthcoming). **43** Such a text may have been the channel for the 'quotation' from Agroecius mentioned above (see note 24). **44** E.J. Gwynn, 'An Old-Irish tract on the privileges and responsibilities of poets', *Ériu* 13 (1942) pp 1–60, 220–36 = *CIH* iii 1111–1138. For a brief description of this text see F. Kelly, *A guide to early Irish law* (Dublin 1988) pp 268f.

editor puts it, some lines on 'the physiology of the voice, conducted by the method of question and answer'.[45] In what follows I have changed the presentation of the material from that in the manuscript, in which the questions are first grouped together in block, followed by a block of answers, to a more conventional arrangement of the 'question-and-answer' units:[46]

Caide i nduine aitreibh an ghotha? .i. i bfulachtaibh taoibh 7 tromchridhe i reibh urbruinne.
Cisne conair do cing i nduine? .i. tre tromchridhe i reibh urbhruinne.
Cis lir a uidhe? .i. an céduidhe go ling mbruinne, an tanaisde go hubhall mbraghad an tres uide go beola, an cethramhadh o bheola amach ... [47]

Where is the dwelling of voice in man? In the cavities of side and liver [and] in the spaces of the breast.
What paths does it take in man? Through the liver, in the spaces of the breast.
How many are its routes? The first to the cavity of the breast, the second to the apple of the throat, the third to the lips, the fourth from the lips outwards.

After the response to the last question, the following variant on the above appears:

Itté cúig tairismhe an gotha, 7 na hanáile .i. i ttaobh, i ndruim, i mbruinne, i mbráighid, i mbeola. Itte a ceithre huide .i. a fulacht go druim, a druim go bruinne, a bruinne go braighe, a bráighe go beóla.

These are the five fixed points (?) of the voice and the breath: in the side, in the back, in the breast, in the throat, in the lips. These are their four routes: from the cavity [of the side] to the back, from the back to the breast, from the breast to the throat, from the throat to the lips.

The section of Gwynn's text which contains the above also appears independently of the *Bretha Nemed* context in a second manuscript,[48] the first half of which consists largely of a version of the *Auraicept*,[49] followed by another legal text on the qualifications and privileges of the poets.[50] It occurs after two Middle Irish poems: one is based on the commentary on the material relating to poets in the legal tract *Uraicecht Becc*;[51] the second derives from the *Trefhocal* tract on metrical faults often found in association with the *Auraicept*.[52] These two contexts, *Auraicept* and law, also constitute the manuscript environment for our Latin passage on the order of the vowels, and also for one copy of the Irish tract on the alphabet in which it is embedded. We have seen above that the fragment H2 is appended to two passages which appear in the Middle Irish commentary to the *Auraicept*. Version H1 features a similar juxtaposition: it is followed[53] by 'etymologies' of the words *gutta* 'vowel' and *consain* 'consonant' similar to those found in the *Auraicept* commentary (ll 358–76; 2735–61),[54] and the remainder of the page consists of a few lines of legal matter, some of which is in the same hand as our text.[55] Indeed the greater part of this section of the composite

45 Gwynn, op. cit., p. 5. **46** This solution is adopted from the edition of an adjacent passage from this section of Gwynn's text: J. Carey, 'Vernacular Irish learning: three notes: 2. *compóit mérda*', *Éigse* 24 (1990) pp 39–41. **47** *CIH* iii 1127.4–23, Gwynn, 'Privileges', p. 36.5–28. The reply to the following query *Cis lir a ʃuidhe?* 'How many are its seats?', seems to be a conflation of the answers to the first and last of the above questions. **48** *CIH* vi 2342.16–2343.21. **49** Ahlqvist, *Early Irish linguist*, pp 22f. **50** L. Breathnach, *Uraicecht na Ríar* (Dublin 1987) pp 19, 63. **51** Ibid. pp 19, 171–75. **52** Ahlqvist, *Early Irish linguist*, p. 29. **53** H.3.18, p. 414.29–35. **54** The correspondence is noted in Ahlqvist, *Early Irish linguist*, p. 16.

manuscript H.3.18 is devoted to legal material.[56] This nexus of language and law is particulary evident in the texts of the 'poetico-legal' school or schools,[57] and it supplies the broader context which can encompass both the Latin passage in question here and the vernacular piece on the 'paths' etc. of the voice.

One remaining noteworthy feature of the Irish context for our Latin piece shows a further link with the *Auraicept*, in which both canonical text and commentary pay particular attention to Ogham.[58] Our tract on the letters of the alphabet does not make any explicit reference to Ogham, and its use in the passage on the order of the vowels would seem to be precluded by the discrepancy between the Ogham and Latin systems in this regard. Nonetheless, version H1 flies in the face of the Latin explanation and its Irish gloss by listing the vowels in the Ogham order, viz *a o u e i*.[59] The retention of the Ogham sequence here may be compared with its use as an active ordering principle in two alphabetical lists in Early Modern Irish texts.[60] Among the many strands in the variegated weave of language study in medieval Ireland, a number of which are represented in our text, the cultivation of the Oghamic tradition throughout the centuries has been one of the most enduring, and it has been an abiding interest in the scholarship of Próinséas Ní Chatháin.

55 *CIH* iii 947.22–27.   **56** *CIH* iii 809.4–951.z.   **57** Ahlqvist, *Early Irish linguist*, pp 11–14.   **58** Op. cit. p. 10. See also McManus, *Guide to ogam*, (note 11 above) pp 137f., 148.   **59** This is also the order of the vowels in the tract edited by Meyer, p. 294.21.   **60** Ó Cuív, 'Irish words for "alphabet"', pp 102f, 108; idem, *The linguistic training*, p. 3; idem, 'Miscellanea 1. A fragment of bardic linguistic tradition', *Éigse* 11 (1964–6) pp 287f.

Thanks are due to the officers of the Royal Irish Academy and the Board of Trinity College Dublin for permission to publish extracts from manuscripts in their care.

Virgilius Grammaticus and the earliest Hiberno-Latin literature

DAMIAN BRACKEN

The curious grammarian Virgilius Grammaticus has been difficult to place in an historical milieu.[1] For some he was Septimanian, for others a Jew and for more he was an Irishman. Professor Michael Herren examined the possible influence of Old Irish on Virgilius's Latin[2] and Professor Dáibhí Ó Cróinín has shown that the earliest quotations from his works appear in Irish sources.[3] In a series of articles and a recent monograph, Dr Vivien Law has shown that Virgilius was more than a strange grammarian.[4] His works can be placed in the tradition of wisdom literature for they show a preoccupation with wisdom, its attainment and how this is incompatible with the pursuit of worldly wealth. Law examined two florilegia and found the same themes in a number of shared passages. Some of these passages are attributed to Virgilius in the florilegia. Law concluded that the content, style, attribution and the position within sections of these fragments in the florilegia made it likely that they were derived from lost portions of Virgilius's *Epitomae*. There are other overlapping passages from the florilegia which also concern wisdom and have some affinity with Virgilius. These passages may not necessarily have been written by Virgilius himself for some are before his floruit of *c.*AD650, but their content allows us to call them 'Virgilian material'. This Virgilian material, in turn, is found in one of the earliest examples of Hiberno-Latin literature: the biblical commentary by Scottus Anonymus written, it seems, in the 640s. This commentary is, therefore, the earliest source to quote Virgilian material and this can help to establish a milieu for Virgilius and his 'circle'.[5]

To begin, something needs to be said about the main texts considered here. Scottus Anonymus's commentary on the Catholic Epistles is the earliest commentary in the Western tradition on this part of the Bible to survive.[6] The figures named in the commentary show that its author shared his scholarly milieu with some writers active in Ireland around the middle of the

1 I have used two editions of Virgilius's works: G. Polara and L. Caruso, *Virgilio Marone Grammatico: Epitomi ed Epistole* (Naples 1979) and D. Tardi, *Les Epitomae de Virgile de Toulouse* (Paris 1928). References to the *Epistolae* (*Epist.*) and the *Epitomae* (*Epit.*) are by chapter and section numbers of Polara and Carnso. I am very grateful to Professor Donnchadh Ó Curráin for reading this article and his suggestion for its improvement. 2 M. Herren, 'The pseudonymous tradition in Hiberno-Latin: an introduction', in J.J. O'Meara and B. Naumann (eds), *Latin script and letters: AD 400–900. Festschrift presented to Ludwig Bieler on the occasion of his 70th birthday* (Leiden 1976) pp 121–31; id. 'Some new light on the life of Virgilius Maro Grammaticus', *PRIA* 79 (1979) pp 27–71; id. 'Virgil the Grammarian: a Spanish Jew in Ireland?', *Peritia* 9 (1995) pp 51–71. 3 D. Ó Cróinín, 'A seventh-century Irish computus from the circle of Cummianus', *PRIA* 82 (1982) pp 405–30 and 'The date, provenance, and earliest use of the works of Virgilius Maro Grammaticus', in G. Bernt, F. Rädle and G. Silagi (eds), *Tradition und Wertung. Festschrift für Franz Brunhölzl zum 65 Geburtstag* (Sigmaringen 1989) pp 13–22. His nationality is considered by M. Richter, *Ireland and her neighbours in the seventh century* (Dublin 1999) p. 167. 4 V. Law, 'Fragments from the lost portions of the *Epitomae* of Virgilius Maro Grammaticus', *CMCS* 21 (1991) pp 113–25; ead. *Wisdom, authority and grammar in the seventh century: decoding Virgilius Maro Grammaticus* (Cambridge 1995). 5 Herren, 'Some new light', 51, is sceptical about Virgilius's circle as is Alexandru Cizek, 'Virgile le grammairien: un auteur hiberno-aquitain?', in J.-M. Picard (ed.), *Aquitaine and Ireland in the middle ages* (Dublin 1995) p. 136. 6 Ed. R.E. McNally, *Scriptores Minores Hiberniae* i, *CCSL* 108B (Turnhout 1973) pp 3–50.

seventh century.[7] The eighth-century *Florilegium Frisingense*[8] [*Flor. Fris.*] and the ninth-century *Collectaneum* of Sedulius Scottus[9] are the two florilegia from which Law recovered lost portions of Virgilius's *Epitomae*. The *Collectaneum* compiled by Sedulius is a vast florilegium made up of 'excerpts from classical, biblical, patristic, late antique and medieval Latin sources'.[10] *Flor. Fris.* is drawn from biblical, patristic and Insular Latin sources. Ps-Bede's *Collectanea* is another text of significance for the present argument. It is a short work of around nine-thousand words and very different in scale and character to Sedulius's *Collectaneum*. To avoid confusion, Ps-Bede's *Collectanea* will be referred to for the future as 'Ps-Bede' and Sedulius's *Collectaneum* in the abbreviated form *Coll.* The manuscript of Ps-Bede's work is lost. It survives because it was printed among Bede's works in a sixteenth-century edition.[11] Many of the sources from which Ps-Bede compiled his information have associations with Insular literature. It is accessible in an excellent, new edition.[12] The editors conclude that it was compiled in southern Germania in the eighth century. However, it contains examples of the earliest Hiberno-Latin literature. The entry numbered 207 in the new edition is presented as prose. No source or analogues are given. It reads:

Cauete, filioli [mei]   Beware, little sons,
feminarum species   the beauties of women
per quas mors ingreditur   through which death enters
[et] non parva pernicies.   and no little danger.

This is recognisable as poetry with seven syllables per line, a characteristic of early Hiberno-Latin poetry, significantly it comes from Columbanus's *De mundi transitu.*[13] Dr David Howlett says this may have been written by Columbanus as early as 590 before he left Bangor for the Continent.[14] The presence of Hiberno-Latin literature that predates Virgilius in Ps-Bede makes it less surprising that the compiler(s) had access to the works of Virgilius himself. Virgilius's etymology of *philosophia* is found in Ps-Bede.[15]

Ps-Bede has a lengthier example of Virgilian material that is related to sections in *Flor. Fris.*, *Coll.* and other texts. I propose to show how this piece concerning the Virgilian motif of wisdom and its attainment has influenced Scottus Anonymus's commentary. On the basis of present knowledge, it seems that Scottus was writing slightly earlier than Virgilius. If Virgilius is to be

7 On these scholars, see P. Grosjean, 'Sur quelques exégètes irlandais du VIIe siècle', *Sacris Erudiri* 7 (1955) pp 67–98; A. Breen, 'Some seventh-century Hiberno-Latin texts and their relationships', *Peritia* 3 (1984) pp 204–14. See also the comments of M.M. Gorman, 'A critique of Bischoff's theory of Irish exegesis: the Commentary on Genesis in Munich Clm 6302 (Wendekpunkte 2)', *Journal of Medieval Latin* 7 (1997) pp 178–233: 192, n 29 and the reply of M. Herren, 'Irish biblical commentaries before 800', in J. Hamesse (ed.), *Roma, magistra mundi. Itineraria culturae medievalis. Mélanges offerts au Père L.E. Boyle à l'occasion de son 75e anniversaire* (Louvain-la-Neuve 1998) pp 391–407: 403–5.   8 Ed. A. Lehner, *Florilegia, CCSL* 108D (Turnhout 1987) pp 3–39.   9 Ed. D. Simpson, *Sedulii Scotti Collectaneum Miscellaneum, CCCM* 76 (Turnhout 1988).   10 *CCCM* 67, ix.   11 M. Lapidge and R. Sharpe, *A bibliography of Celtic-Latin literature 400–1200* (Dublin 1985) no. 1257 with reference to J. Herwagen, *Opera Bedae venerabilis* (Basel 1563). This is the edition repr. in *PL* 94.   12 M. Bayless and M. Lapidge, *Collectanea Pseudo-Bedae, SLH* 14 (Dublin 1998).   13 Lapidge and Sharpe, no. 819. Ed. G.S.M. Walker, *Sancti Columbani opera, SLH* 2 (Dublin 1970) p. 182: 'Caveto, filiole, feminarum species, per quas mors ingreditur, non parva pernicies'; *AL* 51 (Leipzig 1886–1922) p. 352 give 'mox' for 'mors'. Unless stated otherwise, all translations are my own.   14 D.R. Howlett, 'The earliest Irish writers at home and abroad', *Peritia* 8 (1994) pp 1–17: 1–2. D. Schaller shows this poem to be the work of Columbanus in '"De mundi transitu": a rhythmical poem by Columbanus?', in M. Lapidge (ed.), *Columbanus: studies in the Latin writings* (Woodbridge 1997) pp 240–54.   15 Polara and Caruso, p. 26; Tardi, p. 51 = Ps-Bede, §144.

located in seventh-century Ireland, this suggests that the sapiential motif in his works is part of an already established tradition there. It also makes Scottus Anonymus the first writer to use what has been called 'Virgilian material'.[16]

Remigius of Auxerre, in his glosses on Martianus Capella, also wrote on the incompatibility of wealth and wisdom. The theme is illustrated with an account of the philosopher Crates's dramatic renunciation of his inheritance.

Contempserant enim divitias amore philosophiae quia cupiditas multum obest studiis, unde et nonnulli amore philosophiae diuitiis abrenuntiabant sicut legitur fecisse Crates philosophus qui magnum pondus auri quod uendito patrimonio adquisierat in mare proiecit dicens: 'Ite pessum malae cupiditates, ego vos demergam ne a uobis ipse demergar'.[18]	They disdained wealth for the love of philosophy because greed greatly hinders studies. Therefore some renounced riches for the love of philosophy, as one reads of the philosopher Crates. Having amassed a great load of gold by selling his inheritance, he threw it into the sea, saying: 'Go to your ruin … '

At the same point in his commentary on Martianus Cappella, the commentator identified as Dúnchad of Reims looks at the damaging effects of material wealth on the pursuit of wisdom. He tells us that the son of Fabricius, in similar fashion, threw his gold into a river to pursue wisdom more freely.[19] Although this theme is by no means exclusive to Virgilius, it is found with characteristically greater frequency in his writings or in work attributed to him. Indeed, he begins *Epit.* I, I ('Concerning wisdom') on this subject.

Toto proficit in polo nostrae connumeratio litteraturae, quia non pecuniarum contractus, sed sapientiae quaestus ratiocinamur.	The examination of our writings profits the whole world because we reckon with the pursuit of wisdom, not with commercial gain.

The Goballus Story

One of the more arresting treatments of this theme is found in both Ps-Bede and *Coll.* V.I.[20] This is the story of the great bird Goballus. It gives birth to an 'exceedingly beautiful and noisy chick' but goes in search of a precious stone in the ocean 'that is sometimes visible and at other times is covered by the sands'. During the unsuccessful search for the stone, a sea-monster devours the chick and Goballus, returning to find the nest empty, cries out seven times, sheds huge tears and

---

16 Not all sections common to both *Coll.* and *Flor. Fris.* are concerned with wisdom. *Coll.* XIII.xx.13 ('Quatuor uirtutibus homo sanatur: patientia, timore, spe, amore …') = *Flor. Fris.* §428. It is also found in the *Apgitir Chrábaid,* ed. and trans. V. Hull, 'Apgitir chrábaid: the Alphabet of Piety', *Celtica* 8 (1968) pp 44–89 (as Simpson notes) and in the Reference Bible (Paris, BN lat. 11561, fol. 102r). Ps-Bede and the other florilegia contain clusters of quotations from the wisdom books of the Old Testament: Ps-Bede, §30 (Ecl. 7:6) = *Flor. Fris.* §404; Ps-Bede, §32 (Prv. 16:32) = *Flor. Fris.* §§331 and 399. 18 C.E. Lutz, *Dunchad: Glossae in Martianum* (Lancaster PN 1944) p. xxiii. 19 Ibid. p. xxiii: 'Fabricii filius ob sapientiam exquirendum omnibus facultatibus abrenuntians magnam partem auri in fluuium quedam, ut sapientiae liberius uacasset, proiecit'. 20 The parallel is noticed in P. Kitson, 'Lapidary traditions in Anglo-Saxon: part I, the background; the Old English Lapidary', *Anglo-Saxon England* 7 (1978) pp 9–60: p. 23; *CCCM* 67, p. 19; Law, 'Fragments', p. 124 and *Wisdom, authority and grammar,* p. 45; *SLH*

'plunges itself into the deep and dies'.[21] At this point, *Coll.* launches into a moral explanation of the story. A somewhat garbled version is found in Ps-Bede. The moral presents the Virgilian motif of the incompatibility of wealth and wisdom as the key to interpreting the story. Indeed, Ps-Bede attributes the moralising piece to a figure mentioned by Virgilius. The longest account of the moral is found in *Coll.*, but Ps-Bede had some version of this before him. The extended moral has received little attention and there are compelling reasons for associating it with Virgilius or his circle. The style of the story itself, however, is so different from Virgilius's that Law says 'it represents an independent recasting of this characteristically Virgilian motif into folktale form, whether by a member of his circle or by a later reader'.[22] The eastern associations of tales of great birds make it more likely that if there was adaptation it was the other way around – from folktale to moral.[23] Professor Martin McNamara shows how one such tale is found in the Insular glosses on the Psalms in Vatican, MS Pal. lat. 86 written perhaps in the late seventh century.[24] This brings such exotic tales closer to the time of Virgilius. However, the moral itself can be shown to be a borrowing from some wisdom text that was attached at some time to the Goballus story.

The basis for Law's recovery of the lost fragments by Virgilius was that they are found in both *Coll.* and *Flor. Fris.* In both, the fragments are independent borrowings and therefore go back to a common source that she says was probably a lost section of Virgilius's *Epitomae*. It is significant, therefore, that part of the moralising piece that follows the story is found in both *Coll.* and *Flor. Fris.* This is the longest, continuous text on a Virgilian theme common to both *Coll.* and *Flor. Fris.* so far discovered. Parts of the moral also overlap with Ps-Bede and, taking account of the variations among the three witnesses, it is possible to attempt a reconstruction of the moralising section. The following is from *Coll.* and Ps-Bede, but is not found in *Flor. Fris.* The Virgilian tenor of the piece is clear.

Et tu, homo, Goballus es, habens naturam decoram nimis quae generat sapientiam uenustam. Lapis autem in mari amor diuitiarum est, quae seducit hominem et, relicta sapientia, uolat ad diuitias congregandas. Cetus autem magnus stultitia est quae aufert sapientiam simul cum divitiis. Stultitia nascitur et homo perdit sapientiam, perdit diuitias et infelici rapitur morte.[25]

And you, man, with such a beautiful nature which begets pleasing wisdom, are Goballus. Now the stone in the sea is the love of riches which seduces man. Once wisdom has been abandoned, he flies to accumulate riches. The great monster is stupidity which carries away wisdom as well as the riches. Stupidity grows, the man loses both wisdom and riches, and an unhappy death carries him off.

At this point, Ps-Bede attributes the rest of the moralising section to a Gelflidius. This brings the moral very close to Virgilius for Gelflidius has been identified as the Gelbidius named by him in the *Epitomae*.[26] What follows is found in *Coll.* and Ps-Bede with minor but significant variations. Text peculiar to *Coll.* is given in round brackets, text peculiar to Ps-Bede in square brackets.

14, p. 139.   **21** Latin text in *SLH* 14, p. 128.   **22** Law, 'Fragments', p. 124.   **23** A discussion of the eastern origins of these tales is found in P. Kitson, 'The jewels and the bird *Hiruath* of the "Ever-new tongue"', *Ériu* 35 (1984) pp 113–36 and M. McNamara, 'The bird *Hiruath* of the "Ever-new tongue" and *Hirodius* of Gloss on Ps. 103:17 in Vatican Codex Pal. Lat. 68', *Ériu* 39 (1988) pp 87–94.   **24** Ed. M. McNamara, *Glossa in Psalmos: the Hiberno-Latin gloss on the Psalms of Codex Palatinus Latinus 68*, Studi e Testi 310 (Vatican 1986) p. 213.   **25** *CCCM* 67, p. 20; *SLH* 14, p. 128. The bird is named Goballa in *Coll.*   **26** Polara and Caruso, p. 56; Tardi, p. 71. On these names mentioned by Virgilius, see G. Calder, *Auraicept na n-Éces: the Scholar's Primer* (Edinburgh 1917, repr. Dublin 1995)

[Unde Gelflidius ait]: Melior [est] sapientia auro, et consilium pretiosius argento, et (prudentia prelatior) [praeclarius] omni lapide pretioso et disciplina praeeminentior omni uestitu gemmato. [Sapientia, quae de fontis aurei liquidissima uena prorumpit, gemmis omnibus, uariisque margaritarum generibus, et cunctis pretiosior inuenitur gazis, quae suos sectatores ad aulam coelistis paradisi deducit. Melius est una hora vivere cum sapientibus, quam vinum bibere cum insipientibus].[27]

[Of this Gelflidius says], 'Wisdom is better than gold, counsel is more valuable than silver, (prudence is preferable to) [is brighter than] all precious stones and learning excels all jewelled clothes. [Wisdom, which flows in the purest stream from a golden fount, is found more valuable than all gems, than pearls of different kinds and every treasure, for wisdom leads its followers to the heavenly court of paradise. It is better to live one hour with the wise than to drink wine with the foolish'].

Here Ps-Bede reports Gelbidius/Gelflidius teaching on the triad of wisdom, counsel and learning. The evidence found in *Coll.* and supported by a range of texts discussed below indicates that behind the *praeclarius* of Ps-Bede lies a fourth quality, *prudentia*. The base text of the piece found in Ps-Bede therefore refers to a tetrad of wisdom, counsel, prudence and learning. The contrasting of riches with the attributes that lead to wisdom is a typically Virgilian concern. The final statement that it is better to spend an hour with the wise than to drink with the foolish has also the Virgilian flavour of forsaking the mundane in the search for wisdom. Ps-Bede finishes his moral on the story of Goballus at this point, but in *Coll.* the tetrad is developed further by 'a certain philosopher' for the tetrad of wisdom, counsel, prudence and learning is said to increase the intellectual stature of the one who cultivates them and, significantly, this is also found in *Flor. Fris.* §§448–50—a section with Virgilian borrowings. Text peculiar to *Coll.* appears in square brackets and text found in *Flor. Fris.* alone in round brackets.

[Denique quidam sophus hoc probleuma inferens aiebat:] Quatuor flumina uidi uno ex fonte manantia, lignum quoque humillimum omnium lignorum inter ea situm. Cumque ab his indesinenter fluminibus circumdaretur atque irrigaretur, factum est super omnia ligna in altum ita ut summo cacumine sidera pertingeret. Haec sunt autem quatuor flumina: sapientia, consilium, prudentia, et disciplina; [quae quatuor ex eadem natura omnium bonorum fonte procedunt]. Lignum [autem] humile homo est pauper et ignobilis nudus[que] quem haec quatuor (flumina) irrigant (uirtutum bona): sapientia illuminat, consilium stabilitat, prudentia astutum facit, disciplina informat actus.[28]

[Therefore a certain philosopher referring to this puzzle said], 'I saw four streams flowing from one fount and also a tree – the smallest of all the trees – placed among them. When it was incessantly watered and surrounded by these streams it grew in height above all the trees so that it could reach the stars in the highest summit. These are the four streams: wisdom, counsel, prudence and learning. [These four flow from the same nature, which is the fount of all good things]. Now, the small tree which these four (good rivers of the virtues) water is the poor, undistinguished, naked man: wisdom enlightens, counsel supports, prudence makes wary and learning directs the impulses'.

p. xli and Herren, 'Some new light', p. 35. Calder says that Zimmer believed these names were Celtic in origin. On the identification of Gelflidius with Gelbidius, see P. Kitson, 'Lapidary traditions in Anglo-Saxon: part I', 23; Law, *Wisdom, authority and grammar*, 46. **27** *CCCM* 67, 20; *SLH* 14, 128. **28** *CCCM* 67, 20. The text in the *Florilegium Frisingense* is edited in *CCSL* 108D, 37 and divided into three entries. The next entry continues the theme: 'In tantum hic omnes supercrescit, ut etiam regibus proceribus ac diuitibus merito praeponatur'.

This gives us compelling reasons for believing that the Goballus story or, more precisely, its moral explanation, has some connection with Virgilius. The tetrad and its elaboration are found in both *Flor. Fris.* and *Coll.*, the two sources from which Law recovered lost fragments of Virgil's works. Secondly, the tetrad occurs in the context of a discussion of the nature of wisdom and its incompatibility with worldly wealth, a theme that preoccupied Virgilius. This is not to suggest the tetrad is by Virgilius himself because it is to be found in sources that predate him, but that Virgilius and these sources come from a similar milieu.

This is supported by the *Prebiarum* [sic] *de multorium* [sic] *exemplaribus*,[29] a work that shares the same historical context as Ps-Bede and *Flor. Fris. Flor. Fris.* was compiled by Peregrinus at the episcopal scriptorium of bishop Arbeo of Freising (764–84). The manuscript containing the *Prebiarum* was also written in Arbeo's scriptorium. This area of southern Bavaria was influenced by Insular culture at this time. According to some, this was where Columbanian monasticism lasted longest.[30] Robert E. McNally, the editor of the *Prebiarum*, believed that it originated in a circle of Irish or Irish-influenced scholars in this region in the eighth century. He wrote that Salzburg and its monastery of Saint Peter was its focus. St Virgilius of Salzburg, who left Ireland for the Continent *c*.742, was abbot of St Peter's.[31] The association of Salzburg with the see of Freising and its bishop Arbeo is interesting. Arbeo was a friend of Virgilius of Salzburg[32] and Virgilius's successor, Arno, appointed by Charlemagne, was educated and ordained in Freising.[33] The *Prebiarum*'s sources are varied and include Insular Latin and patristic material. It, too, shows a concern with theories of wisdom and of Creation; it opens with a consideration of the nature of wisdom and ends with a series of questions taken from a dialogue on Genesis attributed to Augustine and Orosius.[34] It brings together the disparate elements of the works considered here. The opening sections are quoted here as they appear in the edition:

<1> Quod sunt sapiencia generis? Id III, deuitare mala, facere bona, sperare premia … <3> Ubi est locus proprius in homine de quo uenit sapientia? Id, ex natura. <4> Ubi sunt quae commituntur sapientiam? Id, consilium, disciplina, prudentia. Ex uno fonte fleunt, id ex natura. <5> Ubi est opus uniuscuiusque ex his tribus in homine? Sapientia inluminat. Consilium stabiliat. Prudentia astutum fecit. Disciplina firmat actum.[35]

What are the types of wisdom? Answer, three: to avoid evils, do good things, to hope for rewards … Where is the proper place whence wisdom comes to man? Answer, from nature. Where are the things that are combined to give wisdom? Answer, counsel, learning and prudence. They flow from a single fount, that is, from nature. Where is the work of each of these three in man? Wisdom enlightens, counsel supports, prudence made wary and learning directs the impulse.

29 *CCSL* 108B, pp 161–71.   **30** F. Clark, *The Pseudo-Gregorian Dialogues*, Studies in the History of Christian Thought 37–38 (Leiden 1987) i, p. 291.   **31** Virgilius administered the diocese of Salzburg from his monastery of St Peter, see J.F. Kenney, *The sources for the early history of Ireland: ecclesiastical*, Records of Civilization: Sources and Studies XI (New York 1929, repr. with corrections by L. Bieler (Dublin 1979)) p. 523; H. Wolfram, 'Virgil of St Peter's at Salzburg', in P. Ní Chatháin and M. Richter (eds), *Irland und die Christenheit: Bibelstudien und Mission* (Stuttgart 1987) 415–20: 416'.   **32** See NcNally's; introductory remarks to the *Prebiarum* in *CCSL* 108B, pp 158–9; M.J. Enright, *Iona, Tara and Soissons: the origin of the royal anointing ritual*, Arbeiten zur Frühmittelalterforschung 17 (Berlin 1985) pp 97–8, n 112; M. Garrison 'The *Collectanea* and medieval florilegia', *SLH* 14, pp 63–7.   **33** R.E. Reynolds, 'Canon law collections in early ninth-century Salzburg', in S. Kuttner and K. Pennington (eds), *Proceedings of the Fifth International Congress on Medieval Canon Law*, Monumenta Iuris Canonici (Series C: Subsidia) 6 (Vatican 1980) p. 17.   **34** The *quaestiones* at the end of the work are not directly from Augustine as McNally says, but from Ps-Augustine's *Dialogus quaestionum lxv* (*PL* 40, col. 733–52); see Bracken, 'Immortality and capital punishment: patristic concepts in Irish law', *Peritia* 9 (1995) pp 167–86: p. 184.   **35** *CCSL* 108B, p. 161.

The *Prebiarum* gives the tetrad found in *Coll.* and *Flor. Fris.* Like *Coll.*, it names the actions of each of the qualities that lead to wisdom and says that wisdom originates in nature. The substance of the moral and the texts in which it is found suggests a connection with Virgilius Grammaticus. *Coll.*, *Flor. Fris.*, Ps-Bede and the *Prebiarum* show that the tetrad of wisdom, counsel, learning and prudence and its elaboration are taken from a source that was joined at some time to the Goballus legend where it became the basis for the moral explanation.

The commentary on the Catholic Epistles by Scottus Anonymus is a key text in the identification of a group of ecclesiastical scholars active in Ireland in the seventh century. This commentary is important because its date (before 650) and provenance (southern Ireland) can be established with more than the usual degree of certainty for early Hiberno-Latin works.[36] It would seem that Scottus Anonymus was writing at about the same time as Virgilius Grammaticus. Scottus also shows a certain concern with wisdom, its nature and origin. In his comment on Jm 1.6, 'If any of you lacks wisdom, let him ask God …', he quotes 2 Ch 1.10, 'Give me wisdom and knowledge', and gives a series of apophthegms on wisdom. Like the *Prebiarum*, the comment begins by defining the three types of wisdom:

Prima sapientia hominis est deuitare mala, facere bona, sperare proemia.	The first part of man's wisdom is to avoid evils, do good things and to hope for rewards.

This is also found in *Flor. Fris.* §423 and twice in the *Prebiarum* (§§1 & 29). Scottus Anonymus names the three categories of worldly and sacred wisdom before describing the origin of wisdom. Like *Coll.* and the *Prebiarum* it is said to begin in good nature and like them Scottus uses the verb *procedere*. He then presents the Virgilian tetrad of wisdom, counsel, prudence and learning as found in Ps-Bede, the *Prebiarum* and also, most importantly, in both *Flor. Fris.* and *Coll.*

Sapientia ex natura bona procedit. Sapientia inluminat, consilium stabiluit *(sic)*, prudentia astutum facit, disciplina firmat actus.[37]	Wisdom comes from good nature. Wisdom enlightens, counsel supports, prudence makes wary and learning directs impulses.

The grammatical work of Virgilius is very different from the exegetical work of Scottus Anonymus. It is significant that the tetrad of wisdom, counsel, prudence and discipline is found in the commentary by Scottus Anonymus and in texts associated with Virgilius since it strengthens the ties between the enigmatic Virgilius and this group of Irish Latin scholars. Furthermore, the bearer of the strange name Gelbidius/Gelflidius to whom Ps-Bede attributes the piece containing the tetrad – or a garbled version of it – would seem to have been a real writer and not a figment of Virgilius's fertile imagination. It is possible that the circle of friends and associates mentioned by Virgilius has some basis in fact. Scottus Anonymus may also be considered the earliest Insular writer to use what has been termed Virgilian material.

Of all the analogues, the *Prebiarum* comes closest to Scottus Anonymus. It is the clearest witness to the text on which Scottus drew. This was probably a wisdom text, although there are hints that suggest a connection with another type of literature in which Virgilius himself shows a considerable interest. Interpretations of the opening of Genesis and the story of the Creation also preoccupied Virgilius.[38] He claims to have written a commentary on 'the creation of the world'

---

36 See Grosjean, 'Sur quelques exégètes irlandais' and Breen, 'Some seventh-century Hiberno-Latin texts', passim.
37 *CCSL* 108B, p. 7. McNally's punctuation has been changed and some needless emendation omitted.   **38** For

directed, it is interesting to note, 'against the pagans'.[39] He says in *Epit.* 4:13 that everyone who is wise should know and examine how man is composed of two elements: a body made from the mire (*ex limo*) and a soul (*affla* "breath") from on high. This is based on exegesis of Gn 2:7, 'God formed the man of the slime (*de limo*) of the earth, and breathed into his face the breath of life'.[40] A quotation he takes from a figure he names as Origen the African concerns the nature of the immortality enjoyed by prelapsarian man: '... if the condition of man were to remain as it was at the start, it would have no infirmity, but would be esteemed somehow immutable and eternal'.[41] The moral attached to the Goballus story itself contains paradisical imagery and the allegorising of the four streams flowing from the same spring recalls the exegesis on the four rivers of paradise in Gn 2.10–14.

Ps-Bede also shows an interest in the interpretation of Genesis. Indeed, the Goballus story occurs immediately after what appear to be selections from a commentary on Genesis. Comparing them to a Genesis commentary that shares a connection with Ps-Bede's south German provenance can show this. This commentary is found in Paris, BN lat. 10616 and was compiled in the scriptorium of Bishop Egino/Heginus of Verona. He died at Reichenau in 802.[42] It is arranged as a *discipulus-magister* dialogue. A comparison with Ps-Bede indicates that the compiler(s) of the *Collectanea* had access information like that in the Genesis commentary of BN lat. 10161. §§58–59 of Ps–Bede read:

Quid est malum? Corruptio boni. Quid est mors? Absentia uitae. | What is evil? The corruption of good. What is death? The absence of life.[43]

Ps-Bede gives the Augustinian definition of evil as an abstract value having no existence in a positive sense.[44] The same line is taken in the definition of death. A close parallel is found in BN lat. 10616:

Quid est igitur malum nisi corruptio boni? Quid est mors nisi absentia uite?

examples other than those mentioned here, see Law, *Wisdom, authority and grammar*, pp 38–40. **39** He quotes the opening in *Epist.* 7:4: 'Multa sunt huius rei exempla iuxta illud quod et ego hesterno feceram anno, cum librum de mundi creatione commentatorium aduersus paganos ediderim, cuius principium est: "absque deo nullus est solo, qui omnia creat"', Polara and Caruso, p. 322. **40** 'Illud quoque omni sapienti sciendum atque scrutandum est quomodo et qualiter sese plastus homo habeat, qui primum plastum ex limo, dein afflam ex superioribus et haec ineffabiliter coniuncta habet, dissimili natura in semetipso perfruens ... affla, quae est anima ...' Polara and Caruso, p. 36; Tardi, p. 59. **41** '... hominis ... status si in coepto permaneat, nihil instabilitatis habebit, sed inmotabilis quodammodo et aeternus aestimabitaur [sic]', Polara and Caruso, 236. Augustine maintains that man would have received immortality as part of his nature and not merely as the gift of his Creator had he not sinned in *De genesi ad litteram* VI.22–25, *PL* 34, col. 353–4. Virgilius's contemporary, the Irish Augustine, in *De mirabilibus sacrae scripturae*, *PL* 35, col. 2153, says the same. The idea is also found in Ps-Isidore's *Liber de ordine creaturarum*, ed. M.C. Díaz y Díaz, *Liber de ordine creaturarum: un anónimo irlandés del siglo VII*, Monografías de la Universidad de Santiago de Compostela 10 (Santiago de Compostela 1972) pp 160, 164–6. **42** On the manuscript and commentary, see E.A. Lowe, *CLA* 5, 601; J.E. Cross, *Cambridge Pembroke College MS 25: a Carolingian sermonary used by Anglo-Saxon preachers*, King's College London Medieval Studies 1 (Exeter 1987) p. 77; B. Bischoff, 'Turning-points in the history of Latin exegesis in the early Irish Church: AD 650–800', in M. McNamara (ed.), *Biblical studies: the medieval Irish contribution*, Proceedings of the Irish Biblical Association 1 (Dublin 1976) pp 103–4: no. 3; J.F. Kelly, 'A catalogue of early medieval Hiberno-Latin biblical commentaries: I', *Traditio* 44 (1988) pp 555–6: no. 20; T. O'Loughlin, *Teachers and code-breakers: the Latin Genesis tradition, 430–800* (Steenbrugge 1998) pp 150–4. I am very grateful to Dr Helmut Flachenecker for providing information on this figure. **43** Ed. and trans. *SLH* 14, pp 126–7. **44** On Augustine's definition of evil as an abstract value, see C. Journet, *The meaning of evil* (London 1963) pp 31–49.

The next entries (§§60–61) in Ps-Bede are also significantly close to BN lat. 10616.[45] Although there is no reference in this part of Ps-Bede to the rivers of paradise, §§110–11 name the four paradisical rivers and the waters of this world:

Quot sunt flumina paradisi? Quatuor: Phison, Geon, Tigris, Euphrates; lac, mel, uinum et oleum. Aquae mundi quod sunt? Duae: sal et aqua.

How many are the rivers of paradise? Four: Phison, Geon, Tigris, Euphrates; milk, honey, wine and oil. How many are the waters of the world? Two: salt and (fresh-)water.[46]

Parallels are found in the Genesis commentaries of BN lat. 10616, fol. 27v and the Reference Bible, BN lat. 11561, fol. 12v which name seven *liquora*. Although the Goballus story follows a series of entries relating to exegesis on Genesis, Ps-Bede does not relate the four sapiential virtues to the four rivers. He writes, however, that wisdom 'springs forth from the most pure vein of the golden fountain'. When compared to BN lat. 10616, Ps-Bede's wording and the description of the four rivers in the other sources provide further evidence to link the moralising section attached to the Goballus legend to interpretations of Genesis.

    Coll. says that the four rivers of wisdom, counsel, prudence and learning flow from a single fount which is defined as nature (this is not found in the parallel section of *Flor. Fris.*). *Prebiarum* §3 states that wisdom comes from a single fount which it too calls nature. In his edition of *Prebiarum*, McNally says that the source is Pelagius's commentary on Paul's First Letter to the Corinthians.[47] In his comment on 1 Co 1.19, 'I will destroy the wisdom of the wise', Pelagius cites Si 1.1, 'Indeed it is written "All wisdom comes from the Lord"'. His high estimation of man's natural goodness independent of grace led him further to refine this statement on the origin of wisdom: … *id est, de bona natura ducit exordium* 'that is, it [wisdom] takes its origin from good nature'.[48] Pelagius presents the same ideas as the texts considered here, but his formulation is very different. The commentary in BN lat. 10616 gives the usual topoi when considering the four rivers of paradise. It compares them to the four evangelists and to the four theological virtues of prudence, fortitude, temperance and justice. However, the description of the origin of the virtues comes very close to the account of the origin of wisdom and the sapiential virtues in the *Prebiarum* and *Coll.* The Paris commentary reads:

Sicut enim ab uno fonte quattuor ueniunt flumina, sic ab uno fonte bone nature cetere procedunt uirtutes (BN lat. 10616, fol. 90r).

Just as the four rivers come from a single fount, so the other virtues flow from the one fount of good nature.

Coll. allegorises the four rivers in the moral on the Goballus legend and compares them to wisdom, counsel, prudence and learning. It describes the origin of the four rivers and their sapiential qualities as follows,

> … quae quatuor ex eadem natura omnium bonorum fonte procedunt.

45 §60, 'Est enim uita carnis anima, uita animae Dominus', is widely attested, as the editors say, but no text has this exact wording. The closest analogue they give is from Bede who has *carnis*; the other analogues give *corporis*. However, the parallel in BN lat. 10616, fol. 93r is close and it also gives *carnis*: '"Mortalis eris ab ista die in qua manducabis, siue morieris ipsa die morte animae". Uita enim carnis anima, uita animae deus est'. §61, 'Despicit Deus, si quis exsultet in malis alterius, nam posuit Deus ordinem ut terra seruiret corpori, corpus animae, anima menti, mens Deo' = BN lat. 10616, fol. 90v.   **46** Ed. and trans, *SLH* 14, pp 134–5. See J. O'Reilly, 'The Hiberno-Latin tradition of evangelists and the Gospels of Mael Brigte', *Peritia* 9 (1995) pp 290–309.   **47** *CCSL* 108B, p. 161.   **48** *PLS* 1, col. 1184; *PL* 26, col. 749.

The Genesis commentary and *Coll.* link wisdom with good nature flowing from a single fount and both use the verb *procedere*. Law holds that the works of Virgilius Grammaticus are a reaction against the trammelling of scholarly thought within narrow, clerical lines. If so, it would not be going too far to suggest that the tetrad of wisdom, counsel, prudence and learning looks like a "humanistic" counterpart to the four theological virtues. *Flor. Fris.* refers to the 'four good rivers of the virtues'. Furthermore, if this tetrad is connected with exegesis on Genesis, it would be in keeping with the cosmogonical interests of Virgilius.

Scottus Anonymus, Virgilius and Ps-Jerome

There are other parts in his commentary where Scottus Anonymus shows some association with Virgilius. Ps-Bede begins with a definition of the woman breast-feeding her children as wisdom[49] which comes from Virgilius's *Epist.* XV.[50] It is also found in *Coll.* II.1. Among the figures mentioned by Scottus Anonymus is Laithcenn mac Báith. He is the author of the *Egloga de Moralibus in Iob*, an abridgement of Gregory's *Moralia*. He is associated with the midlands monastery of Cluain Ferta Molua and the annals record his death in 661. He is numbered among the circle of Latin scholars active in the southern part of Ireland in the seventh century and Scottus mentions him twice, first as 'Lodcen', in the second reference his name appears as the abbreviated 'Lath'.[51] In the comment on *lac rationabile* of 1 P 2.2, Scottus Anonymus associates the breast-feeding woman with wisdom:

Lodocenses dicit: 'Lac rationabile', id est in uberibus matris que rationabili\<s est\> quia adheret pectori, loco rationabili. Unde dicitur. Larga ubera sapientiae conspicite.

So says Lodocenses: *Lac rationabile*, that is in the breasts of the mother which is rational because it clings to the chest, the place of reasoning. Hence it is said, 'Regard the bountiful breasts of wisdom'.

It is significant that Scottus Anonymus should include a definition given by Virgilius and repeated by Ps-Bede. The attribution of this piece is also important. Could 'Lodocenses' be a garbled reference to Laithcenn or 'Lodcen', as Scottus Anonymus referred to him earlier, or to 'a follower – or followers – of Laithcenn'? If it is the work of Laithcenn, it would seem to indicate a certain currency of ideas among Laithcenn, Virgilius and Scottus Anonymus.

Law discovered that some apophthegms attributed to a Jerome in *Coll.* VIII.i.6 are like Virgilius's writing in style and content. She says that although they may be the work of some medieval Ps-Jerome, they may possibly be by Virgilius himself.[52] It is also possible that this Jerome was another of Virgilius's circle. *Flor. Fris.* §§78–97 bears the general heading *Hieronymus: De lectionis adsiduitate*. §§96–97 are repeated in §§440–41 at the very end of the florilegium in the section containing the moral on the Goballus story. (§96 = *Coll.* II.5; §97 is attributed to Virgilius). In all, eleven sentences in this section are attributed to Jerome, including one *item* that applies to him. Albert Lehner, the editor, found sources for seven in the genuine works of Jerome. Another is from Ps-Clement's *Recognitiones*. The entries for which no sources are named by the

49 *PL* 94, col. 539: 'Dic mihi, quaeso, quae est illa mulier quae innumeris filiis ubera porrigit, quae quantum sueta fuerit, tantum inundat. Mulier ista est sapientia'.   **50** On this, see Richter's chapter, 'Ubera sapientia sapientiae', in *Ireland and her neighbours*.   **51** *CCSL* 108B, pp 15 and 49.   **52** Law, 'Fragments', p. 123.

compiler of *Flor. Fris.* have mostly to do with wisdom. §86, *Uelocitas audiendi docibilem hominem facit*, is one such entry without attribution, although it is preceded and followed by entries attributed to Jerome and it has some association with his commentary on Ecclesiastes.[53] Scottus Anonymus's comment on Jm 1.19–20, 'Let every man be quick to hear, slow to speak, slow to anger', is significant for two reasons. Firstly, it provides yet another example of material known to both the compiler of *Flor. Fris.* and to Scottus Anonymus. Secondly, it shows how §86 is definitely to be associated with the enigmatic 'Jerome' for, although there is no direct reference 'Jerome' in *Flor. Fris.*, Scottus Anonymus, in the following extract, names him as the source.

… *ut Hieronimus dixit: Velocitas audiendi facit hominem docibilem. Tarditas adloquendi hominem mansuetum facit. Pithagorici per quinquennium silent. Ita et nos prius discamus et postea doceamus.*	… as Jerome said: Quickness of listening makes a man instructable, slowness of speaking makes a man gentle. The Pithagorians keep silent for five years. So should we first learn and then teach.

Again, this piece pertains to wisdom. It occurs, in part, in *Flor. Fris.* in the midst of sentences attributed to Jerome and in Scottus Anonymus where Jerome is named as the source. This Jerome may therefore have been a member of Virgilius's circle or he may have been influenced by the ideas on wisdom that also affected Virgilius. From this we can infer that Scottus Anonymus may in part have known the work of the 'Jerome' associated with Virgilius.

Another seventh-century commentary on the Catholic Epistles is attributed to a Ps-Hilary. Dr Aidan Breen has tentatively suggested that this Ps-Hilary could be an Irish writer.[54] He proposes a floruit of 670–90. Ps-Hilary repeats Ps-Jerome's aphorism without naming him as the source.[55] He names the three types of wisdom[56] as found in Scottus Anonymus and *Flor. Fris.* §423. Breen says that Ps-Hilary used material known to Virgilius.[57] It seems that Scottus Anonymus also used works associated with Virgilius. He is therefore the earliest Irish writer to attest to Virgilian material. The nature of this material indicates that it derives from sapiential literature, a type of writing that appealed to Virgilius. If Scottus Anonymus is contemporary with or slightly earlier than Virgilius, then Gelbidius and Ps-Jerome must have been writing before him and certainly before Virgilius. The conclusion is that Virgilius was following an established tradition of wisdom literature practised by these writers and this helps to establish an historical context for him.

---

53 Scottus Anonymus and Ps-Hilary repeat in abbreviated form Jerome's advice on how to follow the Pithagorians who maintain silence while learning before presuming to teach, *CCSL* 72, p. 276.   **54** Breen, 'Some seventh-century Hiberno-Latin texts', p. 213.   **55** *CCSL* 108B, p. 61.   **56** *CCSL* 108B, p. 58.   **57** Breen, 'Some seventh-century Hiberno-Latin texts', p. 214, where the reference is to knowledge of 'Virgilian material or of its common source'.

The biblical text of Sankt Gallen Stiftsbibliothek codex 51: with special reference to the fourth gospel

MARTIN McNAMARA

My first serious involvement with the text of the Latin Bible in Ireland was at the request of Professor Proinséas Ní Chatháin for the 1984 third international colloquium on Ireland and Europe in the Middle Ages, on the theme "Ireland and Christendom. The Bible and the Missions".[1] I am happy to be able to make this contribution on one small aspect of the ongoing work on this subject to this volume of essays in her honour.

The text of the Latin Gospels presents a rich field of study, both with regard to the Old Latin text (the *Vetus Latina*) and that of the Vulgate. For the period before AD 900 , there are about four hundred and fifty manuscript texts of the Latin Gospels, representing the *Vetus Latina*, the Vulgate and mixed texts of both of these. For the period between AD 600 and 1200 we have about thirty Gospel texts from Ireland, or connected with Ireland – while a significant number in itself, small when considered against what must be the vast number circulating during that period in the Western Church.

Overall studies of the Latin Gospel tradition are, of course, as welcome as they are necessary. Examination of the Latin Gospel transmission in particular countries, or cultural areas, is also legitimate, since by such studies of particular areas the larger picture is better understood.

The present study has to do with the Irish transmission of the Gospel text, in particular as witnessed to in one manuscript, Sankt Gallen, Stiftsbibliothek Codex 51. Before we turn to a detailed study of this text it seems indicated that we set our enquiry in the context of the history of research of the 'Irish' or 'Celtic' Gospel text. This, in turn, will of necessity bring us into consideration of the need for developing a methodology in this branch of study.

Brief history of research on Irish/Celtic gospel texts

Serious interest in Latin texts of the Gospels from Ireland can be said to have begun with the publication of J.O. Westwood's *Palaeographia Sacra* in 1843–5.[2] In this work Westwood examines in more or less detail great codices that will later be brought together under the rather generic term 'Celtic' or 'Irish' Gospel texts – for instance the Gospels of Saint Chad (Lichfield Gospels), the Mac Durnan Gospels, the Irish Domnach Airgid, the Book of Kells, Leabhar Dimma, the Würzburg Gospels, the Book of Armagh, the Stowe Saint John. He has a section specifically on Irish manuscripts, in which he treats of the Gospels of Máel Brigte and the Gospels of Saint Mulling. Westwood considers further Irish and Celtic texts in his other work *Facsimiles of*

---

1 Published with other papers of the colloquium, as indicated in the next note. 2 J.O. Westwood, *Palaeographia sacra pictoria* (London 1843–5) reprinted under a new title: *The art of illuminated manuscripts. Illustrated sacred writings* (London 1988). For more on this early stage of study on the manuscripts and the Irish Biblical text, see M. McNamara, 'The text of the Latin Bible in the Early Irish Church: some data and desiderata', in *Ireland and Christendom. The Bible and the missions*, ed. P. Ní Chatháin and M. Richter (Stuttgart 1987) pp 7–55.

Miniatures and Ornaments in Anglo-Saxon and Irish Manuscripts, published some time later.[3] Interest in Irish and related manuscripts carrying Latin Gospel texts continued, and was soon to turn from the manuscripts to the form of the Latin biblical text in these same works, as was the case in an essay by Brooke Foss Westcott on the Vulgate published in 1863.[4] Work on the Irish and British Biblical text was continued by A.W. Hadden[5] and Henry Julian White, in conjunction with John Wordsworth.[6] This in due time led to the critical edition of the Vulgate Gospels under the editorship of J. Wordsworth and H.J. White.[7] By this time the view had emerged that there is to be found a special form of Mixed Text (of Vulgate and Old Latin) of the group of the Celtic/Irish manuscripts given the sigla DELQR (respectively the Book of Armagh, BL Egerton 609, the Lichfield Gospels, the Book of Kells, the Rushworth or Mac Regol Gospels). Two of those, we may note, are not Irish: Lichfield was written very probably on the Welsh-English borders, while Egerton 609 was written in a scriptorium in Tours. Wordsworth and White regularly use twenty-nine manuscripts for the critical edition of the Gospels. They found it impossible to establish a *stemma codicum* for the manuscripts they used for this critical edition of the Gospels, which for this reason they divide into two, or rather three, classes. The first class they considered to be represented by older codices (13 in number) that are free of additions; the second class is the Celtic/Irish DELQR, to which can be added the Gallic family and a Spanish family. While this work on the critical edition of the Latin Vulgate was in progress, Samuel Berger – through his book on the history of the Vulgate in the Early Middle Ages – was promoting the view that the European Mixed Text of the Gospels was due to the influence of Irish manuscripts, brought to Europe by Irish missionaries.[8] Particularly from 1963 onwards a strong reaction to a number of these positions came from Bonifatius Fischer, who has devoted a life's study to the history of the Latin Gospel texts.[9] His researches made him acutely aware of the complexity of the situation – with some 450 manuscripts for the period before AD 900 alone! In 1986 Fischer announced his plan to take a new approach to the question, in the form of a exhaustive collation of all the manuscripts for four test pericopes from each of the four Gospels – sixteen pericopes in all. In yearly volumes between 1988 and 1991 he produced the results of his work in four volumes, one for each of the four gospels, with an announced plan for a fifth volume on the use of the material he had assembled in these volumes.[10] The renowned author died in 1997 before he could complete this final work. In the introduction to each of these volumes Fischer notes that the critical edition of the Gospels in the concise edition (*Handausgabe*) of the Stuttgart Vulgate rests

3 J.O. Westwood, *Facsimiles of miniatures and ornaments in Anglo-Saxon and Irish manuscripts* (London 1868). **4** B.F. Westcott, 'Vulgate (Latin Version of the Bible)', in Smith's *Dictionary of the Bible* (London 1863) vol. 3, pp 1688–1718. See also McNamara, 'The text of the Latin Bible', pp 17–18. **5** A.W. Hadden in A. W. Haddan and W. Stubbs (eds), *Councils and Ecclesiastical documents relating to Great Britain and Ireland*, vol. I (Oxford 1869), excursus on 'Latin versions of the Holy Scriptures in use in the Scoto-Brittanic Churches', pp 170–97. **6** H.J. White (with J. Wordsworth), 'The Latin versions', vol. 2: chapter III, ed. F.G.A. Scrivener's, *A plain introduction to the criticism of the New Testament for the use of Biblical students* (London 1894) pp 41–90; id. 'Vulgata' in Hasting's *A Dictionary of the Bible*, vol. 4 (Edinburgh 1902) pp 873–90. See further McNamara, 'The text of the Latin Bible', pp 19–21. **7** J. Wordsworth, and H.J. White, *Nouum Testamentum Domini Nostri Iesu Christi secundum editionem Sancti Hieronymi* (Oxford 1889–1898): critical edition of the Vulgate Gospels. **8** S. Berger, *Histoire de la Vulgate pendant les premiers siècles du Moyen Age* (Paris 1893, repr. New York 1961). **9** B. Fischer, 'Bibelausgaben des frühen Mittelalters', in *La Bibbia nell'alto medievo*, Settimane 10 (Spoleto 1963) pp 519–600. (= *Lateinische Bibelhandschriften im frühen Mittelalter* [Aus der Geschichte der lateinischen Bibel 11] (Freiburg 1985) pp 35–100). **10** B. Fischer, *Die lateinischen Evangelien bis zum 10. Jahrhundert. I. Varianten zu Matthäus; II. Varianten zu Markus; III. Varianten zu Lukas; IV. Varianten zu Johannes* [Aus der Geschichte der lateinischen Bibel 13, 15, 17, 18] (Freiburg im Breisgau 1988, 1989, 1990, 1991). The title of the fifth volume, with the key to his collected material, was to be *Untersuchung und Auswertung des vorgelegten Materials aus den lateinischen Evangelien* (planned, but not carried out; B. Fischer died 19 April 1997).

on sure foundations. And with this, Fischer remarks, the certainty ends. The sea of manuscripts outside of this is still uncharted waters. 'The researcher must venture forth unprejudiced, without map, into this unknown territory, and must himself outline his own plans, which may serve as a landmark, possibly even as a co-ordinate system, for future researchers.'[11]

It is unfortunate that Fischer was unable to complete his work, however, he presents evidence that must be taken into consideration in any collation of the Irish Gospel texts. This leads us on the question of methodology in this branch of study.

Reflections and Methodology

Much work remains to be done in the study of the transmission of the Latin text of the Gospels in Ireland, and through Irish sources. This can only be properly done after each of the known manuscripts has been fully examined and collated. While the group DELQR (possibly with the addition of Ep^{mg} = the Echternach Gospels marginalia), the so-called Celtic/Irish group of texts, has served and will continue to serve, a useful purpose. It seems to have originated by an accident of history rather than from a careful examination of all the evidence. Four of the manuscripts (DLQR) are among those made known by Westwood and later scholars. One of the manuscripts (E = BL Egerton 609) was written in Tours, another (L) is Welsh rather than Irish. We will have a truer picture only after the full Irish evidence has been examined.

In 1990 Patrick McGurk published a full collation of the text of Q.[12] Some years later the present writer published a full collation of the text of Matthew in Cod. Amb. I.61 sup. of the Ambrosian Library, Milan.[13] This manuscript contains the four gospels in the usual order. It came to Milan from the monastery of Bobbio. It is in Irish minuscule script of the seventh or eighth century (opinion is divided regarding the exact date). From the palaeographical point of view the manuscript could have been written in Ireland or Italy. Its textual affiliations remained to be determined. It is classed by Fischer with Italian manuscripts (and given the siglum Ji). One of the intentions of the collation was to see if specific text affiliations could be identified, especially whether chiefly 'Celtic/Irish' or 'Italian'. The collation was made first against the critical apparatus of the Wordworth-White critical edition of the Gospels (from some 29 manuscripts). Computer analysis of the results showed a rather high number of agreements with the individual witnesses LREDQ Ep (in that order), and also a number of agreements with multiple witnesses of the Irish/Celtic family (DE 119 times; DEL 12; DELQ 5; DELQR 4: DE Ep 63; EL 40; ELQ 4; LQ 66; LQR 49; LR 78; DLR 10; DL 31; EL 25; QR 32). However, when the collation was controlled against Fischer's full collation for his four trial pericopes of Matthew, evidence for a special textual relationship with the Celtic/Irish text was less clear. The conclusion which seems to emerge from this full collation of these passages is that the variants (from the Vulgate text) of Amb I. 61 sup. are well attested both in the Italian (Fischer's J) and Irish (Fischer's H) group of texts, at times somewhat more strongly in one than in the other. Further and more refined analysis of the evidence may yield some more satisfactory conclusion.

Seeing that the results from the collation of Matthew in this manuscript yielded no clear conclusion, the collation of the remaining three Gospels was not pursued. My attention then turned to another of the neglected Irish Gospel texts, namely Sankt Gallen, Stiftsbibliothek codex 51.

11 Fischer, *Die lateinische Evangelien*, pp 7–8.   12 P. McGurk, 'The Gospel Text', in *The Book of Kells. MS 58 Trinity College Library Dublin. Commentary*, ed. by Peter Cox, Fine Arts facsimile publications of Switzerland (Luzern 1990) pp 37–152.   13 M. McNamara, 'Non-Vulgate readings of Codex Amb. I.61 sup. I. The Gospel of Matthew',

Introduction to Codex Sankt Gallen Stiftsbibl. 51

Codex no. 51 of the Stiftsbibliothek of St. Gallen contains the four Gospels in the usual order, in Latin. It has subdivisions marked off by larger initials, probably intended for liturgical reading.[14] The text in the normal hand of the manuscript scribe ends on page 265, at the second last verse of John's Gospel, John 21.24, with the reading: *et scimus quia testimonium uerum est* (instead of *quia uerum est testimonium eius*). Page 264 has 25 lines of text, while on page 265 there are only thirteen full lines in the normal hand of the manuscript. Why the original scribe ended here, with an erroneous ending for verse 24 and omitting the last verse of John (John 21:25) we cannot say. The final verse (John 21.25) is omitted by the first hand in the Greek Codex Sinaiticus (a*; added by a later hand), but we can hardly assume that it was missing in the Latin exemplar of St. Gallen Codex 51. A later hand completed the Latin text in two further lines (repeating the true reading *testimonium eius* of v. 24). On the reverse of p. 265 there is a miniature of the crucifixion scene, and facing this another miniature of Christ in glory (probably in a judgement scene).[15]

The existence of these Gospels has been noted for a long time. However, more attention has been devoted to the illumination of the work than to an examination of the biblical text it carries, although this has not been forgotten. The Gospels feature in Gregory's *Textkritik*.[16] Samuel Berger examined them for his study of the Vulgate in the early Middle Ages.[17] He says they have the mixed Irish type of text, and is particularly mixed in the first chapters of Matthew. He notes some rare or unique readings: Mat 1:25: *filium suum unigenitum* (= Q, g2); 2:4: *et congregatis omnibus pontificis et scribis populi*; 2:6: *domus Iuda ... rex*; 2:7: *exquessiuit*; 3:3: *Hoc enim quod dictum est*; 3:7: *ab ira uentura*; 4:18: *Transens autem secus mare Galileae*, 10:31: *timere eos, multo magis passeribus;* 16:6: *Adtendtite uobis et;* Mark 1:42: *Inspiciens autem uultu iecit eum* (cf. Q); John 13:10: *non indiget ut lauet nisi pedes lauare* (doublet); 21:25 is omitted (= a*); end of v. 24: *quod testimonium uerum est.*

W.M. Lindsay[18] has examined the manuscript's script: an Irish half-uncial or large minuscule. Lindsay remarks that at the conclusion (p. 265: that is the concluding verse) the scribe relapses into what we may suppose his everyday hand. This is the continental type of minuscule. For Lindsay this indicated that the manuscript was very likely written on the continent, but by an Irish scribe as there was no trace of the use of continental script in Ireland at so early a date. He expressed the opinion that certain ligatures and abbreviations, although few in number, seemed to confirm this impression of continental origin.

E.H. Zimmermann[19] took quite a different stance, finding Lindsay's arguments unconvincing. He regarded the postscript, which Lindsay regarded as contemporary with the main text, as much later (from the tenth century), and argues for Irish origin for the manuscript, assigning it a date of *c.*750–60. K. Löffler[20] later took up the question of the place of origin and date of the manuscript. He noted the predominant opinion regarding it to be of Irish origin and of a mid-

Sacris Erudiri 33 (1992–3) pp 183–257.   **14** On this manuscript see Kenney, *Sources*, p. 649; J. Duft, in J. Duft and P. Meyer, *The Irish miniatures in the abbey library of St Gall* (Olten, Berne and Lausanne 1954) pp 69–71.   **15** On these miniatures see M. McNamara, 'Bible text and illumination in St Gallen Stiftsbibliothek Codex 51: with special reference to Longinus in the crucifixion scene', in *Proceedings of the Fourth International Insular Art Conference Cardiff* 1998 (forthcoming).   **16** C.R. Gregory, *Textkritik des Neuen Testamentes*, 3 vols (Leipzig 1900–9) vol. 1, p. 708, no. 1923.   **17** S. Berger, *Histoire de la Vulgate*, pp 56 and 416.   **18** W.M. Lindsay, 'Irish cursive script', *ZCP* 9 (1913) pp 301–8, at 304; similarly idem, in *Notae Latinae. An account of abbreviations in Latin MSS. of the early minuscule period* (*c.750–850*) (Cambridge 1915) p. 483.   **19** E.H. Zimmermann, *Vorkarolingische Miniaturen* (Berlin 1916) pp 99–102, at 240–2.   **20** K. Löffler, 'Die Sankt Galler Schreibschule in der 2. Hälfte des 8. Jahrhunderts', *Palaeographia Latina*, ed. by W.M. Lindsay, part 6 (Oxford 1929) pp 5–66, at 13–15.

eighth-century date. He returns to the end lines in Carolingian minuscule, and defends Continental origin (possibly St Gallen itself) and a mid- or late-ninth-century date for the manuscript. The most authoritative examination of the manuscript has been made by Johannes Duft, former librarian of the Stiftsbibliothek. Duft remarks that the time of origin can only be decided on palaeographical and art-historical grounds. He thinks that it was written about, or probably later than, 750. In his view the manuscript was probably written in Ireland; at all events it is the work of an Irish scribe and of at least two book-illuminators.[21]

The biblical text, to my knowledge, has thus far been generally neglected. The first serious analysis is that of the 16 passages (4 from each Gospel) examined by Bonifatius Fischer in his four volumes on the Latin Gospels before 900.[22] B. Fischer has given the siglum Hs (Hibernia, Sankt Gallen) to the biblical text of Codex 51. In the first of the four sections collated from Matthew, viz. Matt 2:19–4:17: Fischer says that Hs is as far removed from the Vulgate text as is Vetus Latina manuscript Xd (that is the Latin side of Codex Bezae) and scarcely less that Xk, that is the Bobiensis, with the African text of the Vetus Latina.[23]

In a work published in 1990 the present writer carried out a partial collation of chapters from all four Gospels of this manuscript. This partial collation indicates that in this codex we are in the presence of some curious phenomena, ranging from readings otherwise unattested in the early chapters of Matthew to an extraordinary correspondence with the Irish texts D and R (the Book of Armagh and the Mac Regol Gospels) throughout John.

In the article refered to above,[24] I have also given attention to the last two lines of the biblical text which have been used, by Lindsay and Löffler in particular, for assigning a date later than the eighth century to the work. Analysis indicates that the biblical text of the ending of John is disturbed and that the much-discussed ending in the last two lines has a contraction and abbreviation system different from the main text. This, in my view, seems to indicate that the ending in Carolingian minuscule is not by the main scribe, and thus provides no basis for a late (ninth century) date for the main biblical text.

Collation of John: Introduction and Methodology used

It is agreed that this St Gall manuscript is by an Irish hand. Indications are that it was written in Ireland rather than on the Continent, more probably in the middle or in the latter part of the eighth century. We may now turn our attention once more to the biblical text it carries. The textual tradition it represents will be determined only after a complete collation. There are indications that for Matthew's Gospel, apart from sections of chapters 2, 3 and 4 this is of the Irish/Celtic type of DELQR. At Mat 27:49 it has an interpolated passage (*Alius autem accepta lancea pupungit latus eius et exit aqua et sanguis*) found almost exclusively in Irish Gospel texts.

There are valid arguments why the complete collation of the biblical text of St Gallen Codex 51 could profitably begin with the Fourth Gospel. As already noted, an initial, but partial, collation of John's Gospel made in 1990 showed that it has a close correspondence with the texts of the Irish Gospels in the Book of Armagh (D) and in the Mac Regol (Rushworth) Gospels (R). The full collation I have made of the manuscript shows that the agreement between St. Gallen 51

---

21 See n. 14 above.   **22** See n. 10 above.   **23** Fischer, *Die lateinischen Evangelien* I. *Varianten zu Matthäus*, p. 6.
24 See note 15 above.

and D runs right through the Gospel of John, from beginning to end. The same holds for the relationship of Codex 51 to R.[25] However, use of the full collation of Fischer for the four test pericopes of John brought an awareness that many of the variants of Codex 51 were shared by other manuscripts beyond D and R.

The Irish affiliations of the St. Gallen text appears especially in a special interpolation in the Crucifixion scene in John. We have also already examined the interpolation at the crucifixion scene of Matt 27.49. We have another and extremely significant interpolation (from Matt 27:51 or Mark 15:38) at John 19:30, again at the account of the death of Christ, added after the words 'He handed over the spirit':

> 19:30 (*tradidit spiritum*). *Cum ergo expirasset uelum templi scisum est* a *summo usque deorsum.*
> (*Iudei ergo* ...).

This addition is all the more significant in that it is known otherwise in Latin only in Irish Gospel texts: in the Vulgate texts DREp[mg] BL Harley 1023 Harley 1802 (Gospels of Mael Brigte, AD 1138: Fischer Hz), Cadmug Gospels (Fulda, Fischer Hf); in VL only r (Fischer Xr; Usserianus Primus; Irish). It is also found in some late (12th and 14th century) Greek minuscule texts, but also in the earlier Syriac (Syr[her]) and Syro-Palestinian translations.[26]

The full collation of John's Gospel will in the first instance have to be done against the variants in the critical edition of the Vulgate text edited by Wordsworth and White. The limitations of this edition (made from 29 Gospel manuscripts) must be borne in mind, and for this reason the results must be controlled against the full collation (from some 450 manuscripts for the period before AD 900) carried out by B. Fischer for the four pericopes of the Fourth Gospel John 2:18–3:31; 7:28–8:16; 12:17–13:6; 20:1–21:4).

Another point worth bearing in mind in the collation of St Gallen Codex 51, and of John's Gospel in particular, is the analysis of the text of the Book of Armagh so meticulously carried out by J. Gwynn. In this analysis he notes all the deviation of the text of D from the Vulgate. In examining Gwynn's analysis I was struck by the manner in which these deviations of D corresponded in good part with the text of Codex 51, thus apparently confirming the special textual affinity of the two biblical texts. Here, again, however, it is necessary to compare the results of Gwynn's analysis with the fuller evidence made available by Fischer for the four pericopes in question.

In my view, Fischer's fuller range of texts only confirms the 'Irish' nature of the variants of D and St Gallen Codex 51 in question. However, Fischer's full evidence also indicates that a proof of a peculiar overall relationship of St. Gallen Codex 51 with D and R cannot be confidently asserted without a much fuller collation against all the Irish known Gospel texts.

---

25 We may note that the text of D (the Book of Armagh) has been published by John Gwynn, *Liber Ardmachanus. The Book of Armagh* (Dublin 1913) p. clxvii. The text of R (Mac Regol or Rushworth Gospels) hade been published much earlier by the Surtees Society: J. Stevenson, J.G. Waring, et al., *The Lindisfarne and Rushworth Gospels*, 4 vols (Durham 1854, 1861, 1864, 1865).   **26** See the apparatus to John 19:30 in A. Merk, *Novum Testamentum graece et latine*, 6th edn (Rome 1948) and in C. Tischendorf, *Novum Testamentum Graece*. Editio octava critica maior, 2 vols (Leipzig 1872.); earlier in J.J. Griesbach, *Novum Testamentum Graece*. 2 vols (London 1818) vol. I, p. 512. With regard to these interpolated passages in the crucifixion scenes in the Gospel of Matthew and John we may legitimately ask whether they have been preserved by textual transmission alone, or whether their presence is due to prominence of the crucifixion scene in Irish devotion.

The Irish contribution to Anglo-Latin hermeneutic prose

JANE STEVENSON

Insular Latin prose – both Anglo-Saxon and Irish – often seems to represent a battleground between two opposing stylistic impulses: one towards a plain style, which may be seen as classicising, or as Augustinian *sermo humilis*,[1] the other towards exuberant ornamentation of one kind or another.[2] At the head of the latter tradition stands the massively influential figure of the sixth-century Briton Gildas, whose highly ornate prose may be linked stylistically with the discourse of Gaulish contemporaries such as Sidonius Apollinaris.[3] In the context of the British Isles, however, ornamented styles in literature are a parallel case to styles of ornament such as interlace in Insular art. A number of schools can be readily distinguished, with a certain amount of interconnection between them, while the establishment of appropriate taxonomies materially helps to bring the development of cultures over time into focus.

The mutual influence of Celtic and Germanic tradition of ornament (culminating in the 'Celto-Saxon' style of the great Insular gospel books offers a model for thinking about Irish and Anglo-Saxon literary style: or more precisely, Latin style. Anglo-Latin underwent some distinctive stylistic developments in the tenth century. Various writers, notably Michael Lapidge, have detached the Anglo-Latin style of the tenth century from the irrelevant and confusing adjective 'hisperic', which implicitly links it with the Latinity of seventh-century Ireland, and substituted the word 'hermeneutic' (which has problems of its own; though I shall continue to use in this paper).[4] But extracting tenth-century Anglo-Latin from the shadow of the *Hisperica Famina* is not the end of what can be said on the subject. I want in this paper to address the question of Irish influence on late Anglo-Latin more precisely: there is one, but it is more narrowly focused and less radical in its effects than the use of the term 'hisperic' would have implied.

The main sources for tenth-century hermeneutic writing are not far to seek. The writers draw on the Anglo-Latin stylistic tradition of copious, often rather poetic vocabulary and chiastic construction which came to its first florescence in late seventh and early eighth-century writers such as Aldhelm and Boniface. They also draw on recent and contemporary continental writers, for Frankia also displayed a considerable enthusiasm for obscure diction and exotic vocabulary in the ninth and tenth centuries. Leaders of the monastic reform movement which is so important

---

1 F. Auerbach, *Literary language and its public in late antiquity and the middle ages*, trans. Ralph Mannheim (Princeton, New Jersey 1965) pp 25–66. 2 The development of ornamented prose styles in early medieval Ireland and Anglo–Saxon England can be exemplified by the prose styles of two of the earliest Insular writers, the Irish Columbanus, and the Anglo-Saxon Aldhelm: see C. Mohrmann, 'On the earliest continental Irish Latin', *Vigiliae Christianae* 16 (1962) pp 216–53 and M. Winterbottom, 'Aldhelm's prose style and its origins', *Anglo-Saxon England* 6 (1977) pp 39–76. 3 Neil Wright, 'Gildas's Prose Style and its Origins', in *Gildas: new approaches*, ed. M. Lapidge and D.N. Dumville (Woodbridge 1984) pp 107–28. See also N.K. Chadwick, *Poetry and letters in early Christian Gaul* (London 1955). 4 M. Lapidge, 'The hermeneutic style in tenth-century Anglo-Latin literature', *Anglo-Saxon England* 4 (1975) pp 67–112. M. Lapidge: 'The present state of Anglo-Latin Studies', in *Insular Latin studies: papers on Latin texts and manuscripts of the British Isles: 550–1066*, ed. M.W. Herren (Toronto 1981) pp 45–82. As a term of art in the study of Insular Latin, it has a meaning widely divergent from the principal dictionary definition of 'hermeneutic', which is 'the science of the methods of exegesis'. 5 *Occupatio*, ed. Antony Swoboda (Leipzig

268

to the history of this time, though they otherwise led lives austere in all respects, allowed an otherwise sternly repressed exuberance to burst forth in prose compositions such as the *Occupatio* of Odo of Cluny, and the third book of Abbo's *Bella Parisiacae Urbis*.[5] The great Benedictine reformers of England crossed to the Continent to learn about the new developments in monasticism at first hand; and with it, they also learned about new developments in Latin literature.[6] Secular English Latinists such as Æthelweard were also influenced by these new stylistic developments.[7] I am not, in this paper, attempting to reverse or even greatly to modify, the picture as I have just sketched it. The point I wish to make is essentially that the flight of Irish Latinists to the continent in the time of Charlemagne and his successors resulted in the appearance, in Continental milieux, of quantities of Hiberno-Latin literature. The *Hisperica Famina* were copied, probably at Fleury, in the ninth century, and their vocabulary and diction influence the writings of Continental writers such as Odo of Cluny and Lios Monocus. So when the English reformers imported new Continental literature into their new centres of learning, some of it was flavoured with Hiberno-Latin.

The wealth of the Carolingian court and the increasing threat from Vikings at home combined to draw many Irish clerics to the Continent, to live by their wits, scholarship or literary talents, in the hope of attracting the benevolence of the Emperor or some other wealthy and powerful protector.[8] A number of such Irish scholars in exile, including Sedulius Scottus and 'Hibernicus exul', drew attention to themselves by writing Latin poetry.[9] There were also other Irishmen who, faithful to the literary and exegetical traditions of their own land, achieved a less desirable publicity and were accused of pedantry, verbosity, overweening arrogance, and triviality. While one literary trend visible in the Carolingian world is towards straightforward, no-nonsense exposition, another, more potentially welcoming for the highly selfconscious productions of the faminators, was a fashion for poetry and prose which could only be understood by a tiny band of *cognoscenti*. This was not practised exclusively by Irishmen, but by Continentals as well, such as Hincmar of Laon,[10] accused by his uncle, Hincmar of Reims, of writing with deliberate obscurity.[11] One cannot but reflect that Hincmar of Reims' description of his nephew's style admirably fits the *Hisperica Famina*, and might also be relevant to the reception of *Rubisca*, and the works of Virgilius Maro Grammaticus. An Irishman trying to live by his wits in a Carolingian world which was beginning to feel that it already had a superfluity of learned Irishmen, and hoping to distinguish himself from the mass by his talents in a scholarly milieu where abstruse writing was admired, would find in his native *Hisperica Famina* an instrument well suited to his needs. Michael Lapidge, in discussing the genuine Greek scholarship

1900).The third book of Abbo's *Bella Parisiacae Urbis* (*MGH, PL* 4, 1, pp 72–122, at pp 116–21) was heavily used in Anglo-Saxon England, on which see Lapidge, 'The hermeneutic style', pp 71–2 and 75–6, and P. Lendinara, 'The third book of the *Bella Parisiacae Urbis* by Abbo of Saint-Germain-des-Prés and its Old English gloss', *Anglo-Saxon England* 15 (1986) pp 73–90.   **6** David Dumville has suggested that the revival of English learning of which the rise of consciously stylish Latin prose writing in late Anglo-Saxon England is a part, predates the monastic reform: it is, rather, a symptom of England's recovery from the Viking wars ('The English element in tenth century Breton book production', in *Britains and Anglo-Saxon in the early middle ages* (Aldershot 1993) XIV, pp 1–14, p. 9. This does not invalidate the basic point that the English revival is associable with renewed links with the continent, even if its epicentre should perhaps be shifted from the reforming monasteries to, perhaps, the court.   **7** *The Chronicle of Æthelweard*, ed. A. Campbell (London and Edinburgh 1962) pp xlv–lv.   **8** See, for example Sedulius's poems to Hartgar of Liège, in James Carney, *Medieval Irish lyrics, and the Irish bardic poet*, new ed. in one vol. (Dublin 1985) pp 46–55 (nos. xix–xxi). The complete poems are in *MGH, PL* 2, ed. Ludwig Traube (Berlin 1896) pp 151–237.   **9** Sedulius also distinguished himself as a grammarian and a student of Greek (see M. Lapidge and R. Sharpe, *A Bibliography of Celtic-Latin literature, 400–1200* (Dublin 1985) pp 177–80, nos. 672–86).   **10** M. Lapidge, 'The hermeneutic style', pp 70–1.   **11** Hincmar of Reims, *PL* 136, col. 290–494, col. 448. The lack of sympathy between Hincmar of Reims and the macaronic school was mutual, as John Scotus's biting epigram on him bears witness (*Iohannis Scotti Eriugenae Carmina*, ed. M.W. Herren, *SLH* 12 (Dublin 1993) App 9 a,b,c, pp 126–7).

of John Scotus Eriugena, and considering the simultaneous cultivation of real Greek and hisperic literature in tenth-century Fleury, poses the question: 'néanmoins, n'est-il pas probable qu'un goût pour la poésie érigénienne ait pû entraîner un goût pour les poèmes hispériques?'[12]

The euphuistic tendencies noted in Hincmar of Laon did not quickly wither. The hermeneutic tradition of writing continued to develop in Frankia during the tenth century, associable with a variety of individuals and centres, not least with Fleury.[13] The monks of Fleury seem also to have had an interest in the *Hisperica Famina*, since Hisperic manuscripts appear to have been copied there. They also had a copy of 'Altus Prosator' by the eleventh century (which they may not have associated with Ireland, since it was travelling with Julianus Pomerius's *De vita contemplatiua*.)[14] The poetry of the ninth-century Breton Lios Monocus, whom Grosjean regarded as an important link in the transmission of the *Famina*, is also associable with Fleury.[15] Oda, archbishop of Canterbury from 942 to 958, took the monastic habit at Fleury.[16] Furthermore, Fleury was a major resource for the tenth-century English monastic reformers. Apart from Oda of Canterbury, Oswald of Worcester, his nephew, Osgar (from Abingdon), Germanus (from Winchester) and Abbo (who taught for two years at Ramsey) were all students at Fleury and teachers in England.[17] The reflorescence of English culture after the Viking age may not be a direct consequence of the monastic reforms, but it was certainly encouraged by them: the many connections between the reformers and Fleury offers a channel for hisperic influence on Anglo-Latin diction.

Another, equally important chain of connexions can be drawn between Hiberno-Latin, Brittany and the Continent, which again, was drawn on by tenth-century English writers. The possible role of the Breton Lios Monocus, who makes use of hisperic words in his *Libellulus Sacerdotalis*, has already been mentioned. The B- and C-texts of the *Hisperica Famina* have Breton glosses.[18] The St Omer manuscript which includes the second text of 'Adelphus, adelpha' is also glossed in Breton.[19] There is a single Breton gloss (*aincrum*) on the hisperic-influenced poem *Rubisca* (l. 64) in the Cambridge manuscript.[20] Early Breton writers such as Wrmonoc and Paul Aurelian used Gildas as a stylistic model: the only writers outside the British Isles so to do. And, as we have already observed, the Breton writer Lios Monocus made use of Hisperic vocabulary. The Harley Glossary (discussed below) appears to have passed through Brittany, as did many other works, as David Dumville has pointed out:

12 'L'influence', p. 448.   13 Jean Vezin has discovered the presence of an English scribe called Leofnoth in two tenth-century manuscripts from Fleury, who writes in the manner of a Fleury scribe though his script retains some traces of Insular origin: 'Leofnoth, un scribe anglais à Saint-Benoît-sur-Loire', *Codices Manuscripti* 3 (1977) pp 109–20. Similarly an Æthelgar went to Fleury after the death of Dunstan in 988 (Amoin, *Miraculi S. Benedicti*, ed. A. Vidier, *L'historiographie à Saint-Benoît-sur-Loire* (Paris 1965) p. 228. How many such Englishmen were there in late tenth century Fleury? See also for additional evidence of connections between England and Fleury *The Winchcombe Sacramentary* (Orléans, *bibliothèque municipale* 127 [105], ed. Anselme Davril (London 1995). 14 Orléans, Bibliothèque municipale 169 (146) (Fleury provenance, s. xi) ff. 300–8, printed by C. Cuissard, 'La prose de Saint Columba', *RC* 5 (1882–3) 205–12.   15 *MGH, PL* 5.1, ed. Paul von Winterfeld (Berlin 1894) pp 276–95. P. Grosjean, 'Confusa Caligo', p. 40. See also Lapidge, 'L'influence', p. 448.   16 Frank Stenton, *Anglo-Saxon England*, 3rd edn (Oxford 1971) pp 447–8.   17 John Godfrey, *The Church in Anglo-Saxon England* (Cambridge 1962) pp 298–306. Lapidge, 'L'influence', p. 448. The third book of Abbo's *Bella Parisiacae Urbis* (*MGH, PL* 4.1, 72–122, pp 116–21) was heavily used in Anglo-Saxon England, on which see Lapidge, 'The hermeneutic style', pp 71–2 and 75–6, and Patrizia Lendinara, 'The third book'.   18 M. Lapidge, 'A seventh-century insular Latin debate poem on divorce', *CMCS* 10 (1985) pp 1–23, p. 8.   19 St Omer, Bibliothèque municipale MS no. 666, from St Bertin, s. x, ff. 43a–b. The text is glossed in Old Breton as well as Latin.   20 *The Hisperica Famina II: related poems*, ed. M.W. Herren (Toronto 1987) p. 20.

The transmission of Amalarius's *liber officialis* to England seems to conform to what is now a recognizable pattern ... a Breton manuscript came to England *c.*AD 900 and gave rise to a local progeny. This was part of the process of the revival of English learning and ecclesiastical life after the destruction caused by the viking-wars (the reception of this text in England seems to have had nothing to do, at least initially, with the Benedictine reforms in the later tenth century).

As I shall hope to show, this Breton influence on Anglo-Latin may have disseminated from the court rather than from the principal monasteries. Besides all this, we have contact between the kingdoms of the Welsh, Ireland, and Britain. The family of Sulien in eleventh-century Llanbadarn, as Lapidge showed, were familiar with the *Hisperica Famina* and otherwise culturally linked to Ireland,[21] while other evidence, such as the *Liber Commonei* in 'St Dunstan's Classbook', the Nennian material, and so on, serves to link Wales and England. Thus, we have a variety of evidence to suggest that Hiberno-Latin texts wandered far from their point of origin, and a whole range of possible avenues of reception into England.

One specific work which shows clear traces of travel from Ireland to the continent and thence to England (or conceivably, from Ireland to England and thence to the continent) is the *Lorica* of Laidcenn. The early transmission of the *Lorica*, though it was certainly written in Ireland in the mid-seventh century, is mainly through English books.[22] The only Irish copy is very late; the fourteenth-century Leabhar Breac.[23] But there are two continental copies of the ninth and tenth centuries, Cologne, Dombibliothek 106 (formerly Darmstadt 2106), s. ix, ff. 60–62,[24] and Verona, Biblioteca capitolare LXVII (64), s. x, ff 32–32v (incomplete).[25] The earliest, Cologne, Dombibliothek 106, contains beside the *Lorica* exegesis and poems by Alcuin, the hymn 'Sancte sator, suffragator' (which may also be by Alcuin),[26] and two hymns by Bede, all of which suggests that this manuscript originated in an Anglo-Saxon (rather than an Irish) centre on the Continent.[27] This provides some indication, further substantiated by the Echternach manuscript of the B- and C-texts of the *Famina*, that Hisperic texts were of interest both to Celtic and Anglo-Saxon readers in the eighth and ninth centuries, and that the vagaries of literary fashion on the Continent ensured that they were read and copied (bristling with glosses) in Carolingian Francia, and transmitted on to tenth-century England as an element of the literary revival of Æthelstan's age.

The tendency to the elaboration of Latin vocabulary in men such as Hincmar of Laon has already been noticed. An important element of this style, the use of Greek, is associated particularly with Irish scholars of the late ninth and tenth century. The most distinguished of these is John Scotus Eriugena, but his fellow-countrymen Sedulius and Martin of Laon were also

21 M. Lapidge, 'The Welsh-Latin poetry of Sulien's family', *Studia Celtica* 8/9 (1973–4) pp 68–106.   **22** 'The Book of Nunnaminster', London, British Library Harley 2965 (*c.*800), 'The Book of Cerne', Cambridge, University Library Ll.i.10 (s. ix), glossed in Mercian in a tenth-century hand, and the medico-magical text 'Lacnunga', London, British Library Harley 585, ff. 130 193 (*c.*1000).   **23** L. Gougaud, 'Le témoignage des manuscrits sur l'oeuvre littéraire du moine Lathcen', *RC* 30 (1909) pp 37–46, at pp 43–4.   **24** *Ecclesiae metropolitanae Coloniensis codices manuscripti*, ed. P. Jaffé and W. Wattenbach (Berlin 1874) pp 43–4.   **25** A. Riefferschied, 'Bibliotheca patrum Latinorum Italica I', *SBB* 49 (1865) pp 4–112, p. 10.   **26** Blume, 'Hymnodia hiberno-celtica', pp 299–300. The apparently Anglo-Saxon character of this hymn has been discussed by Lapidge, 'The school of Theodore and Hadrian', *Anglo-Saxon England* 15 (1986) pp 45–72, p. 47, who emphasises its *trochaic* rhythm, found in demonstrably Anglo-Latin octosyllables, and not in demonstrably Hiberno-Latin octosyllabic poems, which have an iambic rhythmic pattern. I know of only one possible exception to this, the two-line verse in Virgilius Maro Grammaticus, *epitome* IV, 2: '*Phoebus surgit, caelum scandit / polo claret, cunctis paret*' (*Epitomi ed epistole*, ed. Polara, p. 18).   **27** Jaffé and Wattenbach, *Ecclesiae metropolitanae Coloniensis codices*, pp 43–4.

notable Greek scholars by the standards of the time. Eriugena set a fashion for the writing of Latin verse in hexameter and other metres which was heavily sprinkled with Greek words.[28] This was eagerly taken up by the school of Laon, and a substantial body of macaronic Greek-Latin poetry survives from this centre.[29]

Thus, cultural and stylistic developments on the continent, and the various levels of interaction between the Anglo-Saxons, the Bretons, and continental scholars and reformers, create a context in which it is reasonable to expect that some Hiberno-Latin texts would appear in England.

Charters

The first group of Anglo-Latin texts I want to examine is charters: particularly useful, because they are dated and localisable. The Anglo-Latin charter tradition in general is remarkably conservative. There is a great deal of continuity as well as variation in the proems and anathemas on which the composers, particularly those working under Æthelstan, lavished their hermeneutic skills. The earliest charter to contain demonstrably Hiberno-Latin vocabulary is Sawyer 206 (Birch no. 488/9), a charter addressed by King Burhred of Mercia to bishop Alhwine of Worcester, in 855.[30] It begins, '*Regnante in perpetuum agio et alto prosatori nostro uniuersitatus creatore in seculorum secula amen*'. This is quite obviously drawing on the first stanza of the early Hiberno-Latin hymn, 'Altus Prosator':[31]

> *Altus prosator* uetustus dierum et ingenitus
> erat absque origine primordii et crepidine,
> est et erit *in secula seculorum* infinita

This charter therefore demonstrates that 'Altus Prosator' was in Southern England by the mid-ninth century. However, the poem is not used again in charters for another century, when a cluster of half-quotations, words and concepts show that the poem was greatly admired in the royal writing-office of Æthelstan, which developed an elaborate and highly distinctive style of its own. It seems as if 'Altus Prosator' (particularly its first stanza) became a source-text for royal scribes under both Æthelstan and Eadwi, probably quite independently of its use by the compiler of the charter of Burhred. One of the clearest instances is Sawyer 629,[32] written in AD 956.

> Altus positor omnium ex nichilo rerum ante omnes tempus angelos condidit et informem materiam quam Adam prothoplastus in Eden primo formatus apparuit.

---

28 Lapidge, 'L'influence', p. 441. See *MGH, PL* 3, pp 518–56, especially pp 537–48.   **29** *MGH, PL* 3, pp 685–701. A non-Irish follower of this fashion was Rather of Verona, who comments on his own work, '*graecizando uanus, cum non sit saltem Latinus*', in *Qualitatis Coniectura Cuiusdam*, ed. Migne, *PL* 136 col. 521–50, col. 524.   **30** Simon Keynes assures me that there is no reason to doubt its authenticity.   **31** Clemens Blume's edition of 'Altus Prosator' in 'Hymnodia Hiberno-celtica', *Analecta Hymnica Medii Aevi* 51 (1908) pp 257–365, pp 271–83 is based primarily on the relatively early continental manuscripts. The English manuscript, London, British Library Cotton Galba A.xiv (Winchester provenance, s. xi in – xi 1) ff. 7–19, is printed by B. Muir, *A pre-conquest English prayerbook* (London 1988) pp 32–9. See for a full description of the poem, Jane Stevenson, 'Altus Prosator', *Celtica* 23 (1999) pp 326–68.   **32** *Cartularium Saxonicum*, ed. Walter de Gray Birch, 3 vols and index (London 1885–9), III, p. 90,

This draws on three stanzas of the poem: the opening (quoted above), the second, which stresses that the angels were created before anything else, and the fifth stanza, which describes the creation of Adam, using the word *protoplastus* to describe him.

In the reign of King Æthelstan, Simon Keynes has drawn attention to the existence of a scribe and composer of charters whom he calls 'Ælthelstan A'. This person was a user of 'Altus Prosator'. Charters attributed to Æthelstan A include a number of words from this poem; *prosator* itself, *poliandria*, used in 'Altus' to mean 'cemetery' (Birch no. 703, T2), and notably, *iduma* (Birch no. 669, M3), a rare word of indisputably Hiberno-Latin provenance.[33] More conclusively, Æthelstan A twice seems to paraphrase the first line of stanza S, '*stantes erimus pauidi ante tribunal domini*', in Birch 676 and 701:[34]

> (701) quam horribile erit *standum ante tribunal* et conspectum aeterni iudicis, quando totius mundi machina uorax flamma in fauillam redigendo consumat.

Less conclusively, the phrase *mundi machina* (first used by Lucretius), which appears here, is also found in 'Altus Prosator', stanza E1. The phrase '*lubricus ille et tortuosus serpens*' in Birch 663 (AD 928) is probably based on '*qui fuit serpens lubricus*' in AP D2.[35] Another Æthelstan A charter, of 930, also clearly draws on the poem for the phrase 'tuba perstrepente archangeli bustis sponte dehiscentibus': compare T1–2:

> *Tuba* primi *archangeli strepente* admirabili
> Erumpent munitissima claustra ac poliandria.

The same charter also includes the phrase '*edacibus innumerabilium tormentorum flammis*', from N3, '*ardens flammis edacibus*'. This accumulated weight of evidence appears to suggest that 'Altus Prosator' was known in court circles from the mid-ninth century,[36] and taken up with enthusiasm in the tenth, as the style considered appropriate to charter-prologues was increasingly elaborated.

The fact that he clearly admired 'Altus Prosator' is far from exhausting the interest of 'Æthelstan A' for the reception-history of Hiberno-Latin. Birch 663 makes it clear that this writer also knew the poem *Rubisca*, which may have been written on the Continent, or even in England, but which is clearly dependent on Hisperic texts, notably the *Lorica*.[37] He uses the word *giboniferum*, 'fiery', which is only attested in *Rubisca* (l. 50), and also *forceps*, which in *Rubisca* means 'beak' (l. 33), with the meaning 'pen-nib', an obvious transference. The odd word *tanaliter*, used in Æthelstan's charter of 28 May, 934, Birch no. 702, derives from the third line of 'Adelphus, adelpha', a poem which is found side by side with *Rubisca* in a later English manuscript, Gg. 5. 35, and which appears to have travelled together with it.[38]

no. 921).   **33** Aidan Breen, 'Iduma (*idouma*)', *Celtica* 21 (1990) pp 40–50.   **34** Birch II, pp 400 2 (no. 701), AD 930 (for 934?).   **35** Birch II, pp 340–2.   **36** Mercia was close to Wessex, and intermittently subordinate to it, in the ninth century. Burgred of Mercia, the issuer of the ninth-century charter quoted here, was son-in-law to Æthelwulf of Wessex (F.M. Stenton, *Anglo-Saxon England*, 3rd ed. (Oxford 1971) pp 244–5).   **37** Cambridge University Library Gg 5 35, from St Augustine's Canterbury, s. xi med., fol. 419v – 420r, and Paris, Sainte-Geneviève 2410, English, probably also from Canterbury, s. x–xi, part iii (s. xi 2) fol. 118–21. On the provenance of the Sainte-Geneviève MS, see *Anglo-Latin Litanies of the Saints*, ed. M. Lapidge (London 1991) p. 14. Most recently edited in *The Hisperica Famina II: Related Poems*, ed. M.W. Herren (Toronto 1987). See also for further discussion of its origins J. Stevenson, 'Rubisca, Hiberno-Latin, and the hermeneutic tradition', *Nottingham Medieval Studies* 36 (1992) pp 1–27.   **38** The Cambridge MS glosses *tanaliter* with *equaliter*, the St Omer MS with *mortaliter*.

The probable context for the knowledge of both *Rubisca* and 'Adelphus, adelpha' (though not, so far as can be demonstrated, of 'Altus Prosator') in Æthelstan's writing-office is the presence at court of the distinguished scholar Israel the Grammarian. Michael Lapidge has demonstrated the mutual relatedness of a series of manuscripts associable with Israel, some of which are also associable with tenth-century England.

1. Leningrad, Public Library F.v.vi.3, ff. 39–44, a quire of six leaves dating to *c*.1000,[39] which includes two poems by Israel, one of which is his *De arte metrica*, two medical poems,[40] and a series of glosses on 'Adelphus, adelpha'.
2. The Harley Glossary, BL Harley 3376, discussed below, also written in England *c*.1000, which shares a gloss (on *crunicula*) with the Leningrad manuscript, and as we shall see, also includes glosses from *Rubisca* and 'Adelphus, adelpha'.
3. Paris, Bibliothèque Sainte-Geneviève 2410, ff. 118–21, which was written at St Augustine's Canterbury and which includes a text of *Rubisca*, Israel's *De arte metrica* and a Greek litany.
4. Cambridge, University Library Gg.5.35, which includes *Rubisca*, 'Adelphus, adelpha' and the two medical poems also found in the Leningrad MS.
5. Vatican city, Biblioteca apostolica vaticana reg. lat. 421, ff. 5–15, which includes Israel's *De arte metrica* and the aforementioned Greek litany also found in Ste-Geneviève 2410.

The Greek litany which appears in the Paris and Vatican manuscripts mentioned above has an additional importance, in that it helps to link this 'Israel dossier' with the court of king Æthelstan. Its other early appearance is in BL Cotton Galba A xviii, 'Æthelstan's Psalter',[41] written in Northern France in the late ninth century, where it appears in a collection of material added to the main manuscript in the second quarter of the tenth century.[42] Israel's own presence at the court of Æthelstan is established by the well-known note on the 'Gospel Dice' (*alea euangelii*) copied into a twelfth-century Irish gospel book, Oxford, Corpus Christi College 122, written *c*.1140 at Bangor:[43]

Incipit alea euangelii quam Dubinsi episcopus Bennchorensis detulit a rege Anglorum id est a domu Adalstani regis Anglorum depicta a quodam Francone et a Romano sapiente id est Israel.	Here begins the Gospel Dice which Dub Innse, bishop of Bangor, brought from the English king, that is from the household of Æthelstan, king of England, drawn by a certain Franco (or by a Frank) and by a Roman scholar, i.e. Israel.

Thus, the overlap of material between the various manuscripts brought together by Michael Lapidge suggests that Israel the Grammarian arrived at the court of King Æthelstan bringing with him a collection of interesting texts, some of them of Greek origin, which included two heavily

---

39 Lapidge, 'Israel the Grammarian', pp 102–3, and see also E. Jeauneau, 'Pour le dossier d'Israel Scot', *ADHLMA* 52 (1985) 7–71.   **40** These poems are printed by Lapidge in 'The hermeneutic style'.   **41** London, BL Cotton Galba A. xviii, the so-called 'Athelstan Psalter', fol. 178–200. The main part of this MS is a late-ninth-century illuminated psalter written in north-east France, with additions in Anglo-Saxon scripts of the tenth century at the beginning and end of the book. The additions in the last three quires, our fol. 178–200, are written in Phase II Anglo-Saxon Square minuscule. See D.N. Dumville, 'English square minuscule script: the background and earliest phases', *Anglo-Saxon England* 16 (1987) pp 147–79, p. 176. Æthelstan's ownership of this manuscript is probable but cannot be established beyond doubt (Lapidge, 'Israel the Grammarian', p. 112).   **42** Lapidge (ed.), *Anglo-Saxon litanies of the saints*, no. xvii, pp 172–3.   **43** Lapidge, 'Israel the Grammarian', p. 99.

Greek-influenced poems, *Rubisca* and 'Adelphus, adelpha', which became part of the repertory of writers associated with the court. Israel the Grammarian was with Æthelstan probably in the 930s, when 'Æthelstan A' , familiar with 'Altus Prosator', *Rubisca* and 'Adelphus, adelpha', was at work there.[44]

The presence of these Hiberno-Latin texts at Æthelstan's court and their use in his writing-office must be seen in the context of his outlook more generally. Æthelstan's circle was cosmopolitan: he maintained extensive contacts both with Ireland and with Brittany,[45] as well as with France and Germany.[46] We also have two books which show that Æthelstan's court had connections with Ireland itself. The first of these is the Mac Durnan Gospels.[47] The book is provenanced as follows:

Maielbrithus Mac Durnani	Maelbrigte Mac Durnan proclaims this text, by
Istum textum per triquadrum	God's will, throughout the world,
Deo digne dogmatizat	
[Ast] Athelstanus Anglosaexna	while Æthelstan, king and ruler of the Anglo-
Rex et rector Doruuernensi	Saxons, gives it for ever to the city of Canterbury.
Metropoli dat per aeuum.	

This is an octosyllabic, alliterative poem, if we allow synezesis of Dor(u)uernensi (four syllables), and set *ast* outside the structure as a connective. It implies that this Gospel-book was given by Maelbrigte, coarb of St Patrick, and 'head of the piety of all Ireland' to Æthelstan, since the book is palaeographically too early to have been written or commisioned by him. Note that the word *triquadrum* for 'world' is found in the charters of 'Æthelstan A'. This would seem to give us a useful connection between the king's household, where a dedication describing the books's history and marking its transfer from the royal library to that of Canterbury is likely to have been written, and the production of Æthelstan's charters. It also seems to show a connection between Ireland and English court, rather than ecclesiastical, circles. The description of the game called *alea euangelii* (already mentioned in connection with Israel the Grammarian) in the Corpus Gospels provides a further witness for direct connections between Irish bishops and the English king, since it reveals that Dubinsi bishop of Bangor (who died in 953, and was thus a younger contemporary of Maelbrigte, who died in 927) had visited Æthelstan. Dubinsi, as Armitage Robinson suggested, may have been visiting the court along with his older contemporary, Maelbrigte. In any case, the snippet gives us a fascinating glimpse into the exchange of books and concepts between the English king in his cultivated court, and senior Irish clerics.

The Mac Durnan Gospels is not the only book which Æthelstan is known to have presented to Canterbury: a gift of two Frankish gospel-books is also attested.[48] Since the royal writing-office and Canterbury are the two centres where we can be surest that *Rubisca* was known, his generosity

---

44 Ibid.   **45** Lapidge and Sharpe, *A bibliography*, p. 229 (no. 830).   **46** J. Armitage Robinson, *The times of St Dunstan* (Oxford 1923) pp 51–80.   **47** See Lapidge and Sharpe, *A Bibliography*, p. 137 (no. 528), and M. McNamara, 'The Echternach and MacDurnan Gospels: some common readings and their significance', *Peritia* 6–7 (1987–8) pp 217–22, pp 217–18.   **48** Now London, Lambeth Palace 1370 (Armagh, s. ix ex), London, British Library Cotton Tiberius A ii (s. ix), and Royal I A xviii (s. x in) (the last belonged to St Augustine's, not Christ Church). See discussion in J. Armitage Robinson, *The times of St Dunstan* (Oxford 1923) pp 51–61.

towards Canterbury may have included other less prestigious texts, such as the kind of scholarly collection brought in by Israel the Grammarian.

To sum up: the influence of Hiberno-Latin on writing emanating from the royal court in the tenth century can be subdivided into three stages. The first is of texts used in England in the seventh century, which influenced such writers as Aldhelm and the Canterbury glossators, and which can fairly be described as naturalised by the tenth century. There was perhaps a second point of entry during or shortly after the Viking age, which made the *Lorica* available to the compilers of the late eighth or early ninth-century Books of Cerne and Nunnaminster and brought 'Altus Prosator' to the royal writing-office by 855. This second introduction may be a witness for the revival of English culture before the monastic reforms, as Dumville has suggested.[49] The third point of entry is the introduction of a dossier of Grecizing texts into Æthelstan's court by Israel the Grammarian, which included works heavily influenced by Hiberno-Latin.

The Harley and Cotton Glossaries

Another important set of evidence for Irish influence on Anglo-Latin is from tenth-century glossaries, in particular, the so-called Harley glossary,[50] which has already been mentioned as related in some way to the 'Israel dossier'. The glossary tradition parallels the development of Anglo-Latin style in its use of Hiberno-Latin. There is a first stage of Irish input into the Anglo-Latin glossarial tradition from as early as the seventh century, as is witnessed by the appearance of a number of Irish words in the Epinal-Erfurt glossaries.[51] The earliest of these is the Epinal glossary, recently argued by Julian Brown to have been copied in Mercia at the end of the seventh century.[52] The first Erfurt glossary is a slightly shorter version of Epinal: the two derive from a common exemplar. Both are glossed in Latin with occasional glosses in Old English. The source of the common ancestor of these glossaries appears to be Canterbury.[53]

---

49 'The English Element', p. 9. **50** Other Latin-Latin glossaries from late Anglo-Saxon England include Antwerp, Plantin-Moretus Museum 47, London, BL Additional 32246, Oxford, Bodleian Library MS Digby 163, Cambridge, *CCC MS* 356, pt. 3, London, BL MSS Royal 7.D.II and Harley 3826. Antwerp, Plantin-Moretus Museum 47, London, BL Additional 32246, Oxford, Bodleian Library MS Digby 163, Cambridge, *CCC MS* 356, pt. 3, London, BL MSS Royal 7.D.II and Harley 3826. **51** J.D. Pheifer, *Old English glosses in the Epinal-Erfurt glossary* (Oxford 1974) p. 82. There is a full facsimile edition, with discussion, in *The Epinal, Erfurt, Werden and Corpus glossaries*, ed. B. Bischoff et al., EEMF 22 (Copenhagen 1988). Both Erfurt glossaries are printed in full in Goetz (ed.), *Corpus Glossariorum Latinorum*, V, pp 337–401 and 259–337. There is an earlier facsimile edition of Epinal by H. Sweet (ed.), *The Epinal glossary* (London 1883), and editions of the Corpus glossary by J.H. Hessels (ed.), *An eighth-century Latin-Anglo-Saxon glossary preseved in the library of Corpus Christi College, Cambridge* (Cambridge 1890) and W.M. Lindsay (ed.), *The Corpus glossary* (Cambridge 1921). The principal sources for this group of glossaries were set out by K.W. Gruber, *Die Hauptquellen des Corpus- Epinaler und Erfurter Glossares* (Erlangen 1904). The most important source by far is Jerome (p. 62–95), but others, in order of importance, are the Vulgate (pp 19–50), canons, councils and decretals (pp 54–59), the *regula S. Benedicti* (pp 60–1), and the *uita S. Eugeniae* (pp 61–2). **52** T.J. Brown, 'The Irish element in the Insular system of scripts to circa AD 850', *Die Iren und Europa im früheren Mittelalter*, ed. H. Löwe, 2 vols (Stuttgart 1982) I, pp 101–19, at p. 109, n. 12. **53** H. Bradley, 'Remarks on the Corpus Glossary', *Classical Quarterly* 13 (1919) 89–108, pp 101–2 suggested that the archetype might have derived from Aldhelm's school at Malmesbury: Aldhelm, however, received part of his education in the school of Theodore and Hadrian and maintained contact with Hadrian, so the accuracy of the Aldhelmian glosses is just as explicable if the archetype was created at Canterbury. M. Lapidge, 'The school of Theodore and Hadrian', *Anglo-Saxon England* 15 (1986) pp 45–72, p. 58, discusses the relationship of the various witnesses to the Canterbury *glossae collectae* and the reasons for connecting them with the school of Theodore and Hadrian. **54** The fragments of the Harley Glossary are discussed by Jessica Cooke, 'The Harley manuscript 3376: a study in Anglo-Saxon

The renewed glossarial activity of the tenth century shows, as do the royal charters, a second stage of input from Hiberno-Latin texts. This is particularly clear in the case of the Harley glossary, London, British Library Harley 3376, which is fragmentary – the main section goes only up to letter F, and there are two separate fragments of I.[54] It is arranged in AB-order, and was once very large. The lemmas and glosses of this collection come from a wide variety of sources, and include quite a large number of Greek words. The existing edition, by Robert Oliphant, makes only sporadic attempts to track the sources.[55] His occasional comments to the effect that he 'does not understand the lemma' seem to carry the corollary that lemmas not so indicated, and not otherwise explained, are quite straightforward and obvious. But many of them strike me as thoroughly problematic; and a number, though they have no place in what Virgilius Maro Grammaticus called *lingua Latina ussitata*, are manifestly Hiberno-Latin.[56]

Its Hiberno-Latin contents, which are various, and indicated both by some exceedingly rare words, and by others which are collocated so as to show that they are derived from a particular Hiberno-Latin source. Many of the glosses in Harley 3376 are in Old English, and it is unquestionably an English compilation (Jessica Cooke suggests it was compiled and kept at Worcester Cathedral until at least the mid-thirteenth century),[57] but it includes two glosses, apparently Celtic, but not Irish, C1847, *guohioc*, and C2227, *petellerion*, which may be Breton or, in the latter case, Cornish; reinforcing the case for seeing it as connected in some way with Israel the Grammarian.[58]

The Hiberno-Latin sources for Harley 3376 include the *Lorica* attributed to Laidcenn, 'Altus Prosator', a seventh-century poem misattributed to St Columba,[59] 'Adelphus, adelpha' and *Rubisca*, which I believe to have been written in the late ninth or tenth century, by an Irishman working on the Continent.[60] We also find traces of the colloquy known as *De Raris Fabulis*, possibly Welsh in origin, Gildas's *De Excidio Britanniae*, and the *Epitomi* of Virgilius Maro Grammaticus. Each of this group of Celtic Latin texts contains several words which are unusual or even unique. I will identify the most important of these, before listing them together in the order of the glossary.

The *Lorica* words which appear in the Harley glossary include *bathma*: 'femora, þeoh', and *catacrinas*: glossed '*hypban*'. This last is significant, since *cata* is the Greek κατα, 'with', and thus should not be part of the lemma at all. Other words which are significant are *carsum*,[61] and *foribus*, lemmatized in the same case in which they are found in the *Lorica* (usually the case with the Hiberno-Latin lemmas). The spellings and glosses of the Harley *Lorica* batch align it with the *Lorica* texts of Cerne and Harley 585, though it is not identical, so the source-text for the Harley Glossary's version is almost certainly part of Herren's 'delta' tradition, which consists mainly of English MSS.

The use of *Rubisca* is proved by the lemma bifaxo ales (B212), glossed '*binos oculos habes*', among others. This lemma is a metrical adonic verse from this curious poem, and the gloss is

glossography', Cambridge Ph.D. 1994. The I fragments are now Lawrence, University of Kansas Kenneth Spencer Research Library Pryce MS P 2 A;1 and Oxford, Bodleian Library Lat. misc. a.3, fol. 49. **55** *The Harley Latin Old English Glossary, edited from BM MS Harley 3376*, ed. Robert T. Oliphant (The Hague 1966). On the Harley Glossary, see N.R. Ker, *Catalogue of manuscripts containing Anglo-Saxon* (Oxford 1957) no. 240, and T.A.M. Bishop. 'The Corpus Martianus Capella', *Transactions of the Cambridge Bibliographical Society* 4 (1964–8) pp 257–75, at p. 258. **56** J.D. Pheifer's promised edition will doubtless clarify the position very substantially: see for the present M.W. Herren in the Gneuss Festschrift, and Jessica Cooke, 'The Harley Manuscript'. **57** Cooke, 'The Harley manuscript', p. 28. **58** K.H. Jackson, *Language and history in early Britain* (Edinburgh 1953, repr. Dublin 2000) p. 67, and Lapidge, 'Israel the Grammarian', p. 103. **59** See my article 'Altus Prosator'. **60** See n. 37 above. **61** Herren thinks from Heb. *kares* with Lat. –*um*; the spelling *charassum* reflecting an original *karesum. So spelt in some *Lorica* MSS, and in the Harley glossary.

nearly identical to one found with the poem itself in the Cambridge manuscript, Gg. 5. 35. It is of course slightly incorrect, in the same way as *catacrinas*: the gloss should refer only to *bifaxo*. *Cisfores* (C949): '*ante fores*', is another clear *Rubisca* lemma, and so are *fidiamus* (which is not otherwise attested anywhere at all, as far as I know), and *becca*, 'beak', mistakenly glossed with '*cauda*' in both MSS, and also here in the Glossary. We also find *edenis*, which *Rubisca*, and no other text that I know of, uses for *auribus*. The text of *Rubisca* used in the Harley Glossary is very close to that of the two surviving MSS, and was possibly copied from the same exemplar – which was apparently Breton, since a Breton gloss crept into the Cambridge text of line 64.

The use of 'Adelphus, adelpha' (which accompanies *Rubisca* in the Cambridge MS) in the Harley Glossary is proved by three words; *bethuen, biblion*, and *bolen. Bolen* is glossed 'consilium', as it is in both MSS of 'Adelphus, adelpha'.

With 'Altus Prosator', the absolutely unambiguous examples are the phrase *ceruleus turbinibus* (C702), taken directly from the poem, and the word *flammaticus*, which appears nowhere else at all.[62] I might emphasize that the list I give is not intended to cover all the possible borrowings from these Hiberno-Latin works. Many words – *cenodoxia, constipatio, edax*, and so on – are found both in the glossary and in this group of poems, but they are not so conspicuously unusual that they had to come from these sources, and can therefore bear no burden of proof.

Another highly distinctive Hiberno-Latin writer, Virgilius Maro Grammaticus, was read in seventh- and eighth-century England both North and South of the Humber.[63] His highly distinctive Latinity is not generally an influence on the Anglo-Latin glossorial tradition, but the Harley Glossary includes two words for 'fire', *cociabin* and *calax* (both glossed *ignis*), which can derive from no other source. In Virgilius's remarkable list of twelve kinds of Latinity, *ignis* is used as an example: 'in ussitata enim Latinitate *ignis* primo habetur, qui sua omnia ignit natura, II *quoquihabin* … IIII *calax calacis*, ex calore'.[64] I know of nothing else which confirms that Virgilius was read in tenth-century England. The word *caraxare* appears three times in the Harley Glossary (C386–8): it was used by Virgilius, but also by many other Insular Latin writers.[65]

Harley 3376 does not show the same kind of dependence on Gildas, except that the word *ciulas*, glossed '*ceol*' (an unusual instance of a word being glossed by itself), is almost certainly taken from *De Excidio*. Gildas was lemmatized by Anglo-Latin glossators as early as the Leiden glossary, and is also a source for Aldhelm's vocabulary, but the word *ciula* does not appear eleswhere in the Anglo-Latin glossarial tradition. Apart from the word *ciulas*, nothing in this glossary is diagnostic of a re-lemmatization of *De Excidio*, except perhaps *flebo, flebilis* (F465). Another possible one-word derivation from a Celtic source is C550: Catus. doctus. ingeniosus. sacer, which may perhaps come from St Patrick's *Confessio*, in which he refers to the British bishops as *domini cati rhetorici*.

De Raris Fabulis is practically a glossary in itself; a many-layered text which has accumulated words down the centuries like a snowball.[66] It borrows from the Anglo-Latin glossarial tradition,

---

62 This was first pointed out by O.B. Schlutter, 'Lexical and glossographic notes, I', *Modern Language Notes* 15 (1900) pp 206–11, p. 210.   **63** Vivien Law, *The Insular Latin grammarians* (Woodbridge 1982) pp 42–52, at pp 48–50, demonstrates that Virgilius was read by Boniface, Bede, and probably by Aldhelm, and his works were transmitted to the continent, perhaps from England, in the ninth century.   **64** Virgilius Maro Grammaticus, *Epitomi ed Epistole*, ed. and trans. G. Polara and L. Caruso (Naples 1979) p. 6.   **65** The word has been very fully discussed by M.W. Herren, 'Insular Latin c(h)araxare (craxare) and its derivatives', *Peritia* 1 (1982) pp 273–80. **66** W.H. Stevenson (ed.), *Early scholastic colloquies* (Oxford 1929) pp 1–11 (no. 1). For commentary, see M. Lapidge, 'Latin learning in dark age Wales: some prolegomena', *Proceedings of the Seventh International Congress of Celtic Studies*, ed. D. Ellis Evans, John G. Griffith and E.M. Jope (Oxford 1985) pp 91–107 at pp 94–7, and references in Lapidge and Sharpe, *A bibliography*, p. 31 (no. 85).

but it also feeds into it. *De Raris Fabulis* also overlaps with the Harley Glossary, of which the most significant words are *crouitorium* (C2128), very rare indeed, *colestrum* and *caelia*, which in both cases share a rather unusual spelling, and *fordalium* (which does, however, appear in other glossaries, and more than once in 3376 itself). The meaning *bella* attached to *fabula* in the Harley Glossary (F43) is explicable in terms of *De Raris Fabulis*: the interlocutor in the latter text asks the visitor for 'news', and is promptly told of a list of battles. *Cipus* (C1059), an onion or leek of some kind, is another word which may derive from *De Raris Fabulis*: it does not appear in the *Dictionary of Medieval Latin from British Sources*, suggesting that it was not used in Anglo-Latin. Considering that the Harley Glossary runs from A–F only, and that *De Raris Fabulis* is not very long, a surprising number of its more peculiar words also appear in the Glossary. It may simplify matters to present my findings on Hiberno-Latin in the Harley Glossary in tabular form:

Hiberno-Latin in Harley 3376

AA = 'Adelphus, adelpha'
AP = 'Altus Prosator'
DRF = *De Raris Fabulis*
HF = *Hisperica Famina*
L = *Lorica*
R = *Rubisca*
Reference is by line-number, except for AP, where reference is by opening letter of stanza, and line within it; and DRF, which I cite by section.

Sigla:
With respect to AA, I note glosses from C (CUL Gg.5.35, the 'Cambridge Songs' MS) and S (St Omer, 666)
With respect to L, I note glosses from C (CUL Ll.1. 10 ('the Book of Cerne')), and H (BL Harley 585 ('Lacnunga')).
With respect to R, I note glosses from G (CUL Gg. 5.35, the 'Cambridge Songs' MS) and P (Paris, Bib. S. Geneviève 2410).

B85	Bariona. filius columbe: used by Adomnán and Columbanus
B104	Bathma .i. femora. þeoh. L36 [gl. þeoh CH]
B114	Becca . cauda R63 [gl. cauda GP]
B153	Bethuen .i. domus idoli AA34
B171	Biblion graece .i. liber bibliotheca AA11 [gl libro C canone S]
B212	Bifaxo ales . binos oculos habes R6 [gl. binos oculos habens GP]
B327	Bolen consilium AA8 (glossed consilium CS)
B331	Bolla . ornamenta cinguli . forthgegyrdu DRF bullo § 11
B402	Bucina. tuba. dicta qua uocina AP
B528	Brumalia. uernalia. rosina AP
C133	Calax. ignis. Virgilius, *Epitomi* 1.4
C147	Caladum . ceruix R34 [gl. collum P]

C306   Capitula . origo . vel heafod boster . angin

C374   Carsum . uentrem R49 [gl. uentrem G]

C386   Caraxari . scribi Adomnán, among others

C415   Caribdis . uerticosum mare . gurgis . baratrum AP K5

C502   Catacrinas . hypban L60 [gl. hypban]

C550   Catus. doctus. ingeniosus. sacer. uel *bolla. *Confessio*, domini cati?

C676   Cerula. uel celina. i.e. nigra. obscura. unda. uel *laguflod vel nox AP

C684   Ceruisa. siue a cerere .i. fruge uocata est DRF § 3

C686   Ceruical .i. capitale bolster . uel wongere DRF § 17

C749   Celeum . ceruise . ealu DRF § 3, celea [gl. ceruisia], HF A302

C702   Ceruleis turbinibus . lægflodum †odenum AP I3

C797   Cenodoxia .i. uana gloria AP

C840   Cephal. gr*aece* caput L33

C949   Cisfores . ante fores R27 [gl. ante G]

C1037   Ciula . ceol *De Excidio* § 23.3

C1059   Cipus . croplec DRF § 5

C1076   Clangor. tubarum.uel uox tubae. *dyne. *geþun. *cyrm AP

C1303   Compagines .i. coniunctiones . iuncture . *gefeg AP T4

C1286   Compes . uinculum pedis DRF § 11

C1610   Colestrum . beost DRF § 5, colestrum

C1729   Cociabin . ignis Virgilius, *Epitomi* I.4

C1780   Condensa. .i. spissa. secreta. *þicce. vel overþeaht AP

C1921   Conclauia . cubicula DRF § 4, conclauium

C1985   Conas . oculos L33 [gl. ond eagan CH]

C2013   Crasum . dorsum L35 [gl. breost C, hryncg H]

C2128   Crouitorium . gaerstun DRF § 2

C2167   Cubile . burcot DRF § 17, cubile

C2189   Culina . coquina DRF § 9

D404   Dealibus .i. deificis . godlicum AP M1

D811   Dodrans .i. malina . egur AP I2

E34   Edenis .i. auribus R38 [gl. auribus]

F33   Fabrefactum . ornate compositum . uel ornatum .uel gesmithodum L83

F43   Fabula .i. bella . spel uel unnyt spræc DRF § 24

F111   Fatimine . loquele AP B6

F319   Fibula . siue dicta quod ligat . cnæp . sigl . spennels. chorda DRF § 11

F351   Fidibus .i. chorde cithare . strengum R66

F352   Fidiamus . amicus R 72 mufidiame P, mufidiane C

F400   Flammaticus . ligen AP N6

F465   Flebo . bilis . wependlic *De Excidio*

F567   Foribus .i. ianuis L82 [gl. durum CH]

F601   Fordalium . gesoden wyrtmete DRF § 5 fordalium

Though it is the longest and most important, the Harley glossary is not the only late Anglo-Latin glossary to lemmatize Celtic-Latin. Another such glossary, London, British Library Cotton

Cleopatra A III, has more than fifty words from Gildas, as Jenkinson first pointed out.[67] This manu-script contains both a vocabulary arranged by subjects (possibly suggested by Isidore's *Etymologiae*) and a long glossary, assembled from batches taken from glossed manuscripts, and put into A-order.[68] Aldhelm is a readily identifiable source for many of the words in this glossary. Like the Harley Glossary, it seems to point to a renewal of interest in exotic vocabulary, but achieves this principally by re-exploring texts already available in England rather than drawing on new works coming in from abroad. Gildas aside, there are few manifestly Celtic-Latin lemmata. One which is of some interest is *bariona*, glossed, in Old English, as 'culfran sunu': 'son of the dove'. The popularity of Columba/ Columbanus/ Colmán in Ireland ensured that *bar iona* was a well-known Hebraism: it is translated as *filius columbae* by Columbanus and by Adomnán. No diagnostic vocabulary appears in the Cotton glossary which could be used to link it with one or the other. *Bariona* also appears in the Harley Glossary (B85), where Oliphant suggests that it derives directly from Jerome's commentaries.

However, one additional Celtic-Latin text which may have been used by the compilers of the Cotton glossary is *De Raris Fabulis*. *Spatula,* with the meaning 'bed' rather than 'shoulder' is a lexical oddity, which is found in three places; *De Raris Fabulis*, the subject-glossary of Cotton Cleopatra A III, and the eighth-century Felix's *Life of St Guthlac*. It may be that Felix was ultimately the source for both, in which case, its appearance here should perhaps be connected with the interaction between Celtic-Latin and Anglo-Latin writers in the eighth century. Another interesting Cotton Cleopatra gloss is on *alleluia: alle* is glossed 'pater', *lu* 'filius', and *ia* 'spiritus sanctus',[69] transforming the alleluia into a triple invocation of the Trinity: an example of the kind of philological free invention often thought particularly characteristic of Hiberno-Latin. Its earliest appearance, however, is in the seventh-century Whitby *Life* of Gregory the Great.[70] The word *alle*, glossed 'pater', also appears in, 'Adelphus, adelpha', which is preserved in a Canterbury MS, Gg. 5. 35, together with *Rubisca*.[71] The fact that the Cotton glossary gives the full, triple etymology and 'Adelphus, adelpha' only the first element, suggests that it is the Northumbrian text on which the Cotton glossator is drawing. But the transmission of this word does appear to be further evidence of the way that Celtic, Anglo-Saxon and Frankish literary traditions cross-fertilise.[72] Whereas the Harley glossary opens a window on the use of Celtic-Latin texts in England, the Cotton glossary seems, rather, to point towards the reciprocal use of Anglo-Latin texts by Celtic scholars.

Conclusions

In addition to the charters and glossaries which have been under discussion here, several manuscripts from Anglo-Saxon England of the tenth century or later contain Celtic-Latin items. They include Cotton Galba A XIV, which contains a text of 'Altus Prosator', as well as another probably Irish hymn attributed to Columba in the Irish *Liber Hymnorum*, 'Adiutor Laborantium',

67 Jenkinson, *Hisperica Famina*, p. xxi; *Anglo-Saxon and Old English glossaries, by Thomas Wright, Esq., M.A., F.S.A., Hon. M.R.S.L.*, ed. Richard Paul Wülcker, 2 vols, 2nd edn (London 1884) cols 338–473.   **68** Wright-Wülcker, I, cols 338–473.   **69** Ibid. col. 411.37   **70** *The earliest Life of Gregory the Great by an anonymous monk of Whitby*, ed. B. Colgrave (Lawrence, Kansas 1968) p. 97.   **71** The gloss to the first stanza of 'Adelphus, adelpha' found in one of the texts of the 'Israel dossier', Leningrad Public Library F.v.vi.3, glosses *philus* but not *alle,* thus supporting the St Omer manuscript, which omits alle, adding it only as a correction, suggesting that the text originally read 'pilus hius tegater'. The Cotton glossary, if it is drawing on the poem at all, is therefore presumably drawing on the Canterbury redaction. **72** 'Adelphus, adelpha' seems to have been written on the Continent in the tenth century, by a writer of unknown race whose resources included substantial knowledge of Greek and some acquaintance with Hisperic texts.

found in no other manuscript.[73] Then there is Harley 585, the medical manuscript known as 'Lacnunga', which contains one of the three Anglo-Saxon copies of the *Lorica* (the others are the late eighth- or early ninth-century Books of Cerne and Nunnaminster).[74] The mid-eleventh-century manuscript Cambridge Gg.5.35, as has already been mentioned, contains *Rubisca* and 'Adelphus Adelpha', it was probably written at Canterbury. Paris, Ste Geneviève 2410, an English manuscript of the end of the tenth century, also contains a text of *Rubisca*.

The use of *Rubisca* even later in Anglo-Saxon England is also shown by two sets of verses attached to the corpus of material which goes under the name of Nennius, in Corpus Christi College, Cambridge 139, f. 168v, a manuscript written at Durham, which make use of an exotic vocabulary mainly based on *Rubisca*. The poem is introduced as being by Nennius, and addressed to 'Samuel', son of the poet's magister, Beulan. David Dumville has dated this recension of the *Historia Brittonum* to the mid-eleventh century, and was the first to point out the resemblance between these two poems, 'Adiutor benignus' and 'Fornifer qui digitis scripsit', and *Rubisca*.[75] Also in the eleventh century, the marginalia of Cambridge, Corpus Christi College 41 contain another Hiberno-Latin text not otherwise attested in later Anglo-Saxon England, the last three and the first stanzas of 'Audite Omnes', a sixth- or seventh-century hymn on St Patrick, here used as a charm.

It should be evident from this list of Hiberno-Latin texts visibly preserved in English manuscripts that there is a rather close correlation between these actual survivals of Irish or Irish-influenced texts in English manuscripts and the texts drawn on by royal scribes and the glossators. 'Audite Omnes', which almost certainly dates from a period of Irish culture when it was prose rather than verse which was adorned with lexical bizarrerie, is quite plain and unadorned in its diction. There is nothing in it to interest a hermeneutic writer, and it has left no apparent trace in the glossaries. But *Lorica*, *Rubisca*, 'Altus Prosator' and 'Adelphus, Adelpha' are all better witnessed in England than they are in Ireland. Knowledge of the *Lorica* may go back to Aldhelm, who seems to quote a line from it, and *Lorica* words form part of the Canterbury glossarial tradition. *Rubisca* survives only in English MSS, 'Adelphus, Adelpha' in an English and a Breton one. And 'Altus Prosator' is not witnessed in Ireland before the compilation of the Irish *Liber Hymnorum* in the eleventh century, though it has a long Continental history going back to the ninth.

What is the context for this literary activity? The monastic reform movement took tenth-century English church leaders over to the continent, and that they brought back with them new literary styles as well as new developments in monasticism. The fact that Fleury has a considerable claim to be the main centre for the copying of Hisperic writing, the importance of Abbo of Fleury to the history of English education, and the connection of Fleury with various leading lights of the reform movement has generally meant that commentators have linked the use of Hiberno-Latin texts with the monastic movement. However, the main focus of this investigation has been on texts collected at, and disseminated from, the court of King Æthelstan. This seems to strengthen the case for regarding the royal court, rather than the reform monasteries, as a principal centre for cultural development and stylistic innovation.

73 Muir, A pre-conquest English prayer-book, pp 32–41.   **74** See n. 22 above.   **75** D.N. Dumville, 'Nennius and the *Historia Brittonum*', *Studia Celtica* 10–11 (1975–6) pp 78–95, pp 83–4. He notes (p. 83, n. 2) 'the fact that the unusual words (except *ben* and *fornifer*) in these two sets of verses can be paralleled in *Rubisca* is striking: we have no reason to assume borrowing, but we are naturally led to seek some connection. A common glossary-source would be the obvious deduction, but only *fonis*, *obtalmus* and *ros* may be discovered in the glossaries'. It may also be noticed that 'Adiutor Benignus', like *Rubisca*, makes use of tmesis. Alistair Campbell discusses tmesis in 'Some linguistic features of early Anglo-Latin verse and its use of classical models', *Transactions of the Philological Society* (1953) 1–20, p. 20. The poems are also discussed by V.H. Friedel, 'Les vers de pseudo-Nennius', *ZCP* 3 (1901) pp 112–22 and 515.

The first Jew in England: 'The game of the Evangel' and a Hiberno-Latin contribution to Anglo-Jewish history

DAVID J. WASSERSTEIN

More than twenty years ago, when I was about to move to a post in University College, Dublin, my late teacher Chaim Rabin, in Jerusalem, told me to look out for an old friend and former pupil of his when I got there. I noted the name and, when I arrived, asked around and looked in the 'phone book for Frances O'Kane. In vain. I could not find her. There seemed to be no such person. It was not until some months had past, and I had met Próinséas Ní Chatháin several times, that she happened to mention that she had studied Hebrew long years before with – perhaps I knew him? – Chaim Rabin. The intricate and sometimes arcane mysteries of Irish identity, linguistic, onomastic and other, took years to make themselves understood to me. It is a pleasure to contribute to a volume in honour both of Próinséas and of Frances, and I hope that this little note, bringing together as it does three loves, English, Irish and Jewish, will remind her happily both of a former colleague and of our common teacher.

The earliest documentary evidence for the presence of Jews in England – indeed in the British Isles – dates from some little time after the Norman Conquest of 1066. Cecil Roth suggests that there may have been Jewish captives or slaves in Britain in the first and second centuries, and notes that Jerome, in the fourth century, thought that there were.[1] There had been Jews in the Norman possessions of William the Conqueror, and some may even have come across with him.[2] For the period before the Conquest, however, although there have been guesses, like those of Roth, in the past, there has until now not been any evidence which points conclusively to the presence of Jews in Britain before 1066. It is occasionally suggested that some Jewish traders, in slaves and other commodities, may have visited the country at various stages under the Anglo-Saxon kings.[3] But such suggestions, like others relating to Jewish captives or slaves in earlier periods, rely more on impressions of what may have been than on any hard evidence.

Given what we know of the presence of Jews in north-western Europe in later centuries, after the turn of the millennium, it may seem somewhat strange that testimony to Jews in the first millennium should be so scarce, not to say non-existent. But such is the situation: we know almost nothing of Jewish populations in north-western Europe at any time before the end of the first millennium. Occasional suggestions that there will have been Jews here and there thanks to Jewish activity as merchants all over the Roman empire, and as a result of the destruction of the year 70, which led to the scattering of Jews as slaves everywhere, seem to derive more than anything else from wishful thinking, and the desire to push back the date for a Jewish presence in different places as far as possible. A couple of references in the *Codex Theodosianus* show that there

---

[1] Cecil Roth, *A history of the Jews in England*, second ed. (Oxford 1949) pp 1–2. See also ibid., additional note I (a) p. 269, on other, apocryphal pieces of early material on Jews in England. [2] See Norman Golb, *The Jews in medieval Normandy, a social and intellectual history* (Cambridge 1998), who perhaps overstates his case somewhat. [3] Roth, *Jews in England*, pp 2–3.

were Jews in Cologne in the first half of the fourth century, when Constantine imposed the obligation to undertake curial duties upon them, but Cologne was a major city in the empire of the period, and if we are to find Jews anywhere at all, it is surely here and at this time. And whatever else these references show us, they tell us nothing as to numbers.[4] The only inscriptions associated with Jews that have been found in Germany (none has been found in the British Isles datable to before the Norman Conquest) from the first millennium have recently been rejected as Jewish by the latest editor of such material.[5]

It is therefore of more than merely antiquarian interest to be able to point to material which is capable of changing this impression, and of showing that there were Jews, or that there was a Jewish presence, in north-western Europe, before the start of the second millennium. My aim here is to present a piece of evidence – the only one, so far as I know – which seems to demonstrate and to document the presence of at least one Jew in England as early as the first half of the tenth century, that is to say, well over a century before the arrival of the Normans.

Corpus Christi College, Oxford, possesses a manuscript of the Gospels copied, apparently, in Bangor, Co. Down, in about 1150, and possibly even earlier, during the eleventh century.[6] The manuscript came to the college as a gift from Henry Parry, in 1619, presumably from his estate, since he had died three years earlier. Parry (1561–1616) was connected with Corpus from the age of 15, when he became a scholar there, graduating B.A. and M.A., as well as, later on, B.D. and D.D. (this last on 14 February 1595–6), and also becoming a fellow in 1586. He served as chaplain to Queen Elizabeth, and was with her at her death, when, 'speechless, she signified by signs her adhesion to the faith she had caused to be professed'. Under James I, still enjoying royal favour, he became successively dean of Chester (in 1605), bishop of Gloucester (in 1607) and finally, to the grief of the people of Gloucester, to whom he had been very generous, bishop of Worcester (in 1610). According to his epitaph (in the cathedral of Worcester) he was a man *multiplici eruditione, trium linguarum cognitione*, as well as a man of generosity to the poor and to the University of Oxford, where he contributed to the building of the arts schools.[7] His knowledge of the three languages (*trium linguarum cognitio*), which must be a reference to Latin, Greek and Hebrew, is of interest in the present context, for Parry's college, Corpus, was a centre of the little Hebrew learning that existed in Tudor England. Erasmus refers as early as 1519 to its 'trilingual library' – though it does not seem actually to have possessed anything Hebraic (other than a copy

---

4 Cod. Theod. 16:8, 3–4, dated 321 and 330. See also discussion in Amnon Linder (ed.), *The Jews in Roman imperial legislation* (Detroit and Jerusalem 1987) no. 7, pp 120–24 (of AD 321), and no. 9, pp 132–38 (of AD 330) (= Hebrew edition (Jerusalem 1983), no. 7, pp 87–89 (of AD 321), and no. 9, pp 96–100 (of AD 330)). See however especially n. 12 to no. 9 (pp 137–8 in the English edition, p. 99 in the Hebrew), where Linder argues against seeing a reference to Cologne in this edict. If he is right, then our material for Cologne is reduced to no. 7 alone, and, as pointed out above, whatever else this text may tell us about Jews, it does not testify to large numbers of them. Its isolation in our sources may hint that there were not many there, or anywhere.   5 See J.-B. Frey, *Corpus Inscriptionum Iudaicarum, Recueil des Inscriptions juives qui vont du IIIe siècle avant Jésus-Christ au VIIe siècle de notre ère* (Città del Vaticano 1936–52, repr. with an introduction by B. Lifshitz, New York 1975) I, pp 485–6, nos 673–4: both are inscriptions not on buildings and the like but on amulets, in other words, movable objects. One was found in Regensburg, the other in Badenweiler; one is on a small sheet of gold, the other on a small sheet of silver. The amulets were clearly made for wearing. The most recent discussion of them is D. Noy, *Jewish Inscriptions of Western Europe*, I, *Italy (excluding the City of Rome), Spain and Gaul* (Cambridge 1993) Appendix 2, pp 303, no. 227 (= Frey, *CIJ*, no. 673) and 304, no. 228 (= Frey, *CIJ*, no. 674). For Noy they are "not considered Jewish". His arguments against them seem conclusive. The result is that we have virtually no hard evidence for the first millennium.
6 H.O. Coxe, *Catalogus Codicum MSS. qui in collegiis aulisque oxoniensibus hodie adservantur*, II (Oxford 1852) p. 43, no. CXXII. The dating to the eleventh century is from Coxe; for the later dating, see Armitage Robinson, below, note 12.   7 For all these details, see *Dictionary of national biography* (Oxford 1917) vol. XV, p. 375.

of Reuchlin's *De Rudimentis Hebraicis*, published in Pforzheim in 1506) until 1537, when its president, John Claymond, presented it with seven Hebrew manuscripts. But even in 1527, John Fisher could speak of the college as 'well endowed with teachers in Hebrew, Greek and Latin and in whatever ministers to the true study of Theology'.[8] Later in the same century, another President of Corpus, John Rainolds (president from 1598 to 1607, therefore a contemporary of our Parry), wrote of Hebrew being indispensable to the study of the Bible, and urged a correspondent to persevere in his study of the language. That Rainolds practised what he preached we can confirm from the survival of what appear to be his notes on Hebrew grammar.[9]

The Corpus manuscript contains a large number of glosses and other marginalia which contribute greatly to our knowledge of Old Irish. One of these scribal additions is a description of a board game, based in some fashion on the Four Gospels and on the so-called Eusebian Canons, tables drawn up by Eusebius with the help of which a reader could find passages in different Gospels parallel or similar to the passage which he was reading in one of them. The Canons are to this day often printed, as they were also in the past often written in manuscripts, at the start (occasionally also at the end) of editions of the Gospels in Latin or in Greek.[10] In the present case we have such a situation, for the canons come at the start of the manuscript, occupying fol. 1–5a.

On fol. 5b of the manuscript we have a schematic representation of the canons in tabular form, followed by a picture of the board on which the game was to be played. This has as a superscription the following text in three lines:

Incipit alea euangelii quam dubinsi episcopus bennchorensis detulit * a rege anglorum id est a domu adalstani regis anglorum * depicta a quodam francone et a romano sapiente id est israelita

Here begins the game of the evangel which Dubinse, bishop of Bangor, brought back from the king of the Angles, that is from the house of Athelstan king of the English, drawn by some Frank and by a learned Roman, that is an Israelite.

The word *israelita* is written in the form *isrl*,[11] Gilbert, who published this page of the manuscript in his fine collection of facsimiles of important Irish manuscripts,[12] regarded this as an abbreviation for *israelita*, and there seems indeed to be nothing else which might be offered as an alternative interpretation. In addition, as will be seen, there is a useful piece of material confirmatory of Gilbert's view in what follows.

The next two pages in the manuscript, fol. 6a and 6b, after the illustration of the board on which the game was to be played, contain a long description and explanation of the game associated with the canons. This begins as follows:

8 See Gareth Lloyd Jones, *The discovery of Hebrew in Tudor England: a third language* (Manchester 1983) pp 94–5, with references to sources. **9** Ibid. pp 159–61. **10** Cf. *Oxford dictionary of the Christian Church*, ed. F.L. Cross and E.A. Livingstone, 3rd edn (Oxford 1997) pp 573–74, with useful bibliography. **11** In Coxe's catalogue, the last word is printed in the form *irril.* **12** The picture of the board, and the text introducing it, are reproduced in J.T. Gilbert, *Facsimiles of the national manuscripts of Ireland* (Dublin 1874–84) II, plate 46, with a facing transcription into modern printing. For a transcription of the long description and explanation following the picture, see J. Armitage Robinson, *The times of Saint Dunstan* (Oxford 1923) pp 174–7.

Iudeus Romanus et Franconus peritissimi .IIII. evangeliorum ut per ordinem canonum .X. multiplicationem .IIII. evangelistarum intellexerunt quadrangulam paribus figuram quatuor lateribus .X. et .VIII. tramites in longitudine et in latitudine habentem consignaverunt.	A Roman Jew and a Frank, very skilled in the four Gospels, as (?) they understood through the order of the 10 canons the multiplication of the 4 evangelists, drew a figure with four equal sides having ten plus eight lines (boxes? squares?) on each side.[13]

It is clear from this that the Roman Jew and the Frank must be the same men as the isr[ae]l[ita] and the Frank whom we met just a few lines before, and this incidentally confirms for us Gilbert's reading and interpretation of *isrl*.[14]

The English king Athelstan held power between the years 924 and 939 (he was actually crowned only in 925). Dubinse seems to be identified by Armitage Robinson, on the basis of an entry in the *Annals of the Four Masters*, as follows (s. a. 951, for 953): 'Duibhinnsi, a sage and bishop of the family of Beannchair, died'.[15] We cannot know what brought him to the court of Athelstan. In consequence of our lack of knowledge, on this aspect of this story as on so many others, we cannot fix the date of this episode with any certainty more closely than to somewhere in the fifteen years of Athelstan's reign. But what is of special interest about this story of the game and its history, going beyond the game itself, is that, as Armitage Robinson says, 'somebody knew about it in K. Athelstan's marvellous court, whence Dubinsi 'the sage and bishop' fetched it away to Ireland in those far-off spacious days'.[16]

Since our only other references in pre-Conquest literature mentioning Jews are in contexts which demonstrably go back to older and foreign sources, in law codes and in other works like commentary on holy scripture,[17] it is impossible to know whether the use of the term *israelita*, meaning 'Jew', as a substitute for Judeus, here is as curious as it might appear to be. Certainly in later periods words connected with *Iudeus* seem to provide the normal terms for things connected with Jews and Judaism, and the term *Israel* seems to be confined, adjectivally, to the word *lapis*, and to refer to engraved gems, cameos, and the like. It is not clear whether the word *israelita* is found, whether adjectivally or nominally, with the meaning 'Jew' (outside biblical contexts) other than here.[18]

However all this may be, the sentences which we have here are difficult enough in other ways too. Why should *israelita*, whatever interpretation we give to its background and its use here in relation to a Jew, be employed here as a suitable synonym (for it is as this that it occurs here) also for *romano sapiente*, 'a wise Roman', 'a Roman sage'? How can we explain the statement that an Irish bishop obtained detailed information about a game wholly dependent on a deep knowledge of the Christian Gospels from a Jew, albeit a learned one? What might such a Jew have been doing in England, and what, further, at the court of the king of the English? And how might he have come there?

None of these questions is susceptible of a simple or an easy answer. Nevertheless, a number of comments seem worth making on these short pieces of text, more particularly in view of their apparently indubitable authenticity and also because of their potential importance as showing a Jewish presence in England at such an early date.

---

13 The Latin is crabbed; I cannot be sure that this translation is fully correct. **14** Coxe, in transcribing the beginning of the description of the game, adds a comma after Judeus, which seems to make the Romanus a separate person from the Jew. As has been seen, however, the context seems to argue against such an interpretation. **15** Armitage Robinson, p. 70, referring to the *Annals of the Four Masters*, ed. O'Donovan, 1856, ii, 69, and saying also that the *Annals of Ulster* are quoted there in a note. **16** Ibid., p. 71. **17** Cf. note. 1 above. **18** See R.E. Latham, *Revised medieval Latin word-list from British and Irish sources* (London, Oxford 1965) ss.vv. *Israel* (p. 261), and *Judaismus*

A learned Jew from Rome is far from an impossibility at this time. Rome, unlike northern Europe, had a Jewish community whose existence is fairly well documented from Antiquity. And it is precisely around the tenth century that we witness among the Jews of Rome the beginnings of a revival of learning, with the existence in the city of a *yeshivah*, a religious academy, and the activity of men like R. (= Rabbi) Jacob, the 'Gaon' of Rome, the poet Solomon ben Judah, 'the Babylonian', and R. Kalonymus ben Moses and his son R. Meshullam;[19] and above all R. Nathan ben Jehiel (1035-*c*1110), whose *Arukh* is one of the most remarkable and widely learned books to emerge from this obscure period of Jewish history.[20] Solomon ben Judah, R. Kalonymus and his son R. Meshullam have another, special, claim on our attention here, for they are of the tenth century, they are active in Rome, or elsewhere in Italy, and in addition to this they all seem to have moved from there northwards, to Germany, settling in different cities, places like Mainz and elsewhere in the Rhineland. The journey from there to England is far easier, and much shorter, than that from Rome, but a Jew of their sort, visiting England in the tenth century, might easily have been seen, and then described, as Roman. These men may well represent the sort of background from which our visitor to Athelstan's court came. We may perhaps compare them with another such wandering Jew, the still greater Abraham Ibn Ezra (1089–1164). He certainly came in his wandering to England, remaining there, in London, for at least a year, in 1158.[21] If a Jew in England in the first half of the tenth century was to be described as learned, then probably Rome was the obvious place for him to have come from, whether directly or indirectly.

We cannot say what such a Jew might have been doing in England. However, the fact that he was at the court of the king, and not simply visiting the country or someone else in it, does perhaps offer a hint. Could he have been on a mission similar to the one that lies behind our first real reference to Jews and Ireland: seeking a home for Jews in an inhospitable world? We hear about this in the *Annals of Inisfallen*, under the year 1079, a century and a half after the time of our visitor to Athelstan: 'Five Jews came over sea with gifts to Tairdelbach and they were sent back again over sea'.[22] Unfortunately, we are not told anything about the purpose of this trip to England. How the man came to England is also not clear. Slightly later, he might have come via Flanders.[23] And earlier, too, such relations need not surprise.[24] The continent was, of course, not cut off from England in this period. What does surprise, in fact, is the absence of links, or of evidence for links, between continental Jews and the British Isles at any time before the Norman arrival. And as a result of this, our reference in this text is of interest and value not just because of its content but, even more so, because of its rarity, indeed its uniqueness.

What is more mysterious than all of these questions is the link between this Jew and the 'game of the evangel'. If we had only the first reference to the Jew, in the form *isrl*, then Coxe's reading,

(p. 263); C. Du Cange, *Glossarium Mediae et Infimae Latinitatis* (Graz 1954) (repr. of edition of 1883–7) IV, 429, s.v. *Israel*, where only the nominal use is listed. No other meaning of *Israel* is given in either of these dictionaries. See also Du Cange, pp 433–7, for *Judaeus* and words related to it; J.F. Niermeyer, *Mediae Latinitatis Lexicon Minus* (Leiden 1976) p. 561, ss.vv. *judaismus, judaizare, judearia* (It is telling that there is no entry at all for *Israel* in this work).   **19** For all of these see Cecil Roth, *The history of the Jews in Italy* (Philadelphia 1946, repr. Farnborough 1969) index, under their names; and also the *Encyclopaedia Judaica* (Jerusalem 1970) under their names, and, more generally, the entry 'Rome', vol. 14, especially col. 245.   **20** On Nathan ben Jehiel and his *Arukh* see *Encyclopaedia Judaica* (Jerusalem 1970) vol. 12, cols 859–60; *Jewish encyclopedia*, New York, Funk and Wagnalls, 1905, vol. IX, pp 180–3 (both with useful bibliographies).   **21** See the entry on him in *Encyclopaedia Judaica*, vol. 8, cols 1163–70. **22** Quoted in Louis Hyman, *The Jews of Ireland from earliest times to the year 1910* (Shannon 1972) p. 3, with reference to the *Annals of Inisfallen*, ed. Séan Mac Airt (Dublin 1951) p. 235.   **23** Cf. P. Grierson, 'The relations between England and Flanders before the Norman Conquest', *Transactions of the Royal Historical Society*, 4th series 23 (1941) pp 71–112.   **24** W. Levison, *England and the continent in the eighth century* (Oxford 1946).

irril, might have been acceptable, despite its obscurity; in that case we should not see any reference to a Jew in the word. However, the occurrence of the expression Judeus in the following passage both confirms the correctness and the interpretation of the reading *isrl*, and strengthens its significance. It does nothing, however, to explain its obscurity. Here perhaps we should see some relevance in the Roman aspect of the Jew's background. May it be possible that not only his background in the learning of the Roman Jewish community of his day accounted for his description as a Roman *sapiens*? Could it be also that coming from Rome, rather than from anywhere else, that the special character of Rome as a Christian centre, had actually given him access of a special sort to knowledge of the type necessary to make him an expert on this very Christian game? Alternatively, could it be that he possessed mathematical skills and understanding of a type well suited to analysing and explaining the rules and functioning of the game? Certainly some small degree of mathematical knowledge is necessary for this game, and a learned Roman Jew might well have possessed that, given the importance among Jews of mathematical knowledge for calendrical calculations connected with the dates of festivals. If these cannot be more than speculations, they do, nevertheless, offer the sort of considerations which we need to look at if we are to place this curious text in its truest perspective.

At the end of his description and discussion of this game, Armitage Robinson says 'We may wonder whether after all this *alea Evangelii* is not rather a puzzle than a game'.[25] As we can see from the references to a Jew, the puzzles do not end with the game itself. Nonetheless, this brief text in this Hiberno-Latin manuscript does appear to offer us our earliest solid piece of testimony to a Jewish presence, if for all that a thin and tantalising one, in the British Isles before the end of the first millennium and the coming of the Normans.[26]

25 Robinson, p. 180.   **26** I should like to record my thanks to Dáibhí Ó Cróinín, who first discussed this passage with me twenty years ago, to Michael Richter for encouraging me to write about it for Próinséas Ní Chatháin, to Hannah Cotton for reminding me of the material in the Codex Theodosianus and its relevance for Cologne, and to James Howard-Johnston and Sarah Newton (Librarian-in-Charge, Corpus Christi College, Oxford) for answering my queries about the manuscript with friendliness and alacrity.

On the linguistic background of the personal pronouns of Old Irish

KARL HORST SCHMIDT

Thurneysen distinguishes for Old Irish (OIr.) between 1. 'fully stressed forms of the personal pronouns' and 2. 'proclitic or enclitic' elements.[1] This differentiation coincides in principle with the Indo-European (IE) reconstruction model:

> 1. 'Die Nominative der Personalpronomina wurden von uridg. Zeit her in der Regel nur dann gebraucht, wenn auf ihnen ein Nachdruck war'.   2. 'Die Formen der obliquen Kasus waren seit uridg. Zeit in weitem Umfang enklitisch'.[2]

The two classes of stressed vs. enclitic personal pronouns are confirmed by the later discovered IE languages Hittite (Hitt.) and Tocharian (Toch.).[3]

1.1 In OIr. the fully stressed or absolute forms of personal pronouns occur in the nominative case:

sg.	1		*mé*;	emphatic *messe, meisse, mese*
	2		*tú*;	emphatic *tussu, tusu*
	3	masc.	*(h)é*;	emphatic *(h)é-som*
		fem.	*sí*[1];	emphatic *sis(s)i* (late)
		neut.	*(h)ed*;	no emphatic form
pl.	1		*sní*;	emphatic *snisni*
	2		*sí*;	emphatic *sissi*
	3		*(h)é*;	emphatic *hé-ssom*

(Thurneysen, *GOI*, § 405)

In OIr. the IE personal pronouns underwent a number of changes, as e.g.

a) levelling of suppletivism in the 1sg., probably a Proto-Celtic transformation, by which the nominative sg. takes over the stem of the oblique cases: Vedic (Ved.) *ahám : mām* (*mā*), Old Bulgarian (OBulg.) *azъ: mene* (*mę*), Greek ἐγώ: ἐμέ(με), Old Lat. *ego : mēd*, Gothic (Goth.) *ik : mik*, Hitt. *uk : ammuk* vs. OIr. *mé : *mé*.[4] This process has a typological parallel in late Hittite.[5]

1 R. Thurneysen, *A grammar of Old Irish*, trans. by D.A. Binchy and O. Bergin (Dublin 1946, repr. 1975) p. 251, § 401.   2 Brugmann, *Grundriss der vergleich. Grammatik der idg. Sprachen* II 2/1 u. 2nd ed. (Strassburg 1911) pp 391–2.   3 J. Friedrich, *Hethitisches Elementarbuch* I 2nd ed.(Heidelberg 1960) pp 62–6; W. Krause/W. Thomas, *Tocharisches Elementarbuch* I (Heidelberg 1960) pp 162–5.   4 Cf. O. Szemerényi, *Einführung in die vergleichende Sprachwissenschaft* 4th ed. (Darmstadt 1990) p. 225.   5 Cf. Friedrich, *Hethitisches Elementarbuch*, p. 62: 'Die Sprache des Neuen Reiches aber gebraucht die Akkusative (wie die romanischen Sprachen) auch als Nominative, so daß *uk* und u̯ēš fast verdrängt sind.'

b) modelling of the genitive sg. of the 1st person on the 2nd: 'Proclitic *mo* lenites like *do*, whereas in Welsh nasalization persists after *fy* (< *my*), which seems to point to an apocopated genitive *men*; cp. O.Slav. *mene*, Avest. *mana*' (*GOI*, p. 281).

c) levelling of suppletivism in the 3sg., *so *sa *tod > *so-, attested in Gaulish[6] and Celtiberian (Botorrita),[7] in Slavic and Baltic, however, with an expansion of *to-: Lith. *tàs*, *tà* : *taī* (*taī* neut. 'so'), OBulg. *tъ*, *ta*, *to*.

Celtic examples of *to- are preserved in OIr.: *tó* 'yes' < *tod* 'that' and the infixed pronouns of class B: *t^n* [*d^n*] < *tom*, *t^l* [*d^l*] < *to* < *tod*, *ta^g* [*da^g*] < *tons*, *tās*.[8] The Irish evidence of *to-* may be taken as an example of the preservation of an archaism both outside the paradigm (cf. *tó* 'yes') and possibly petrified in a secondary function.[9]

The 3rd person *(h)é sí (h)ed* corresponds to Goth. *is si ita*, Lat. *is id*, Ved. *id-am*, Lith. *jìs*, fem. *jì* (*GOI*, § 450; Szemerényi 1990 [footnote 4], pp 218 f.). The problem of the IE paradigms of *so *sā *tod and *is *ī *id[10] in Celtic needs to be scrutinized.

1.2 The absolute forms of the personal pronouns are used a) as predicative nominatives after the copula, b) as subjects in nominal clauses without a verb:

  a) *is mé, is messe* 'it is I', *ní mé* 'it is not I'; *is snisni* 'it is we';
  b) *apstil i tossug, sissi íarum* 'Apostles first, ye afterwards'; *ce hé* 'who is he?'[11]

As pointed out by Thurneysen, *GOI*, § 407, 'the predicative nominative pronoun normally agrees with the subject in gender; e.g. *Críst didiu is sí in chathir* 'Christ, then, the city is he' Wb. 21^{c}5 (*cathir* fem.), i.e. 'he is the city'.' This agreement corresponds to an IE nominal clause of the type *omnia praeclara* (*in chathir*) *rara* (*is sí*). In addition to that, the grammatical analysis of *is sí*, i.e. copula plus predicative nominative pronoun, is identical with that of OIr. *at* 'you are', etc. consisting of the proclitic 2sg. of the copula with suffixed personal pronoun: *esi-tu > *ei-tu > *ētu (W. *wyt*) > *ě-t (with reduced vowel) > *at* (with *ě* > *a* in proclitic position).[12]

1.3 In connection with the predicative nominative pronoun in the sg. and 1 and 2pl. the copula is in the 3sg., but the 3pl. form of the pronoun always agrees with the copula in the plural: *is snisni* 'it is we', *is sissi in tempul sin* 'ye are that temple' (lit. 'that temple is ye') vs. *it é* 'it is they', *ce-btar é* 'though it was they'. This differentiation between the 3pl. and 'all the other persons' (*GOI*, § 540) has a parallel in the passive construction:

6 P.–Y. Lambert, *La langue gauloise* (Paris 1995) p. 66.   7 F. Villar, *The Celtiberian language*, ZCP 49–50 (1997) pp 898–949: 918 f.   8 Thurneysen, *GOI* pp 259f., 286; K.H. Schmidt, 'Zum Personalpronomen und der Kategorie 'Person' im Kartvelischen und Indogermanischen', HS 107 (1994) pp 179–93: 182 f. In contrast to Thurneysen, C. Watkins, 'Preliminaries to a historical and comparative analysis of the syntax of the Old Irish verb', *Celtica* 6 (Dublin 1963) pp 1–49: 26–8 gives a different explanation of the element -*d*- tracing it back to the enclitic particle *de (Greek δέ).   9 Cf. J. Kuryłowicz, *The inflectional categories of Indo-European* (Heidelberg 1964) p. 11. In addition to that, the preservation of OIr. *tó* 'yes' is comparable to that of Lith. *taī* neut. 'so', since the neuter has been generally lost in the pronominal paradigm of Lithuanian.   10 Szemerényi, *Einführung in die vergleichende Sprachwissenschaft*, pp 216–20; Lewis/Pedersen, *CCCG* 3rd ed. (Göttingen 1974) pp 193–207.   11 Thurneysen, *GOI* p. 254.   12 Thurneysen, *GOI* pp 483 f.; Lewis/Pedersen, *CCCG*, p. 322; Brugmann, *Grundriss* II 3/2, pp 593 f.; R. Trautmann, *Die altpreußischen Sprachdenkmäler* (Göttingen 1970) pp 273 f.: OPruss.: *astits* 'ist, sei' < *asti-tas (*tas = Lith. *tàs* 'this'), *billāts* 'sprach' < *billatas beside *billa: Bhe Deiws Rikijs billa* 'Und Gott der Herr sprach' (Trautmann, l.c., p. 63: 18).

1sg.	*no-m.charthar* 'I am loved' : pl.	*no-n.carthar*
2sg.	*no-t.charthar*	*no-b.carthar*
3sg.	*carthair, .carthar*	*cart(a)ir, .cartar*[13]

The central position of the 3sg. is in accordance with the features by which it is characterized; it is a) unmarked, 'non-personal' and b) 'of high text frequency':

a) 'la '3ᵉ personne' n'est pas une 'personne'; c'est même la forme verbale qui a pour fonction d'exprimer la *non-personne*. A cette définition répondent: l'absence de tout pronom de la 3ᵉ personne, fait fondamental, qu'il suffit de rappeler, et la situation très particulière de la 3ᵉ personne dans le verbe de la plupart des langues'.[14]

b) 'to posit, tentatively at least, a hierarchy in which the third person was the least marked, and the second person the most marked, with the first person intermediate. This is in general supported by the frequency data which are available'.[15]

2 As concerns the proclitic or enclitic elements, four different classes must be distinguished:

1. emphasizing particles (*notae augentes*),
2. infixed pronouns (*pronomina infixa*),
3. suffixed pronouns after verbs,
4. suffixed pronouns after prepositions (conjugated prepositions).

2.1 Emphasizing particles 'can be combined with all classes of pronouns described in the present section[16] as well as with verbs' (*GOI*, p. 252):

sg.	1		*se, sa*	*baitsim-se* 'I baptise', *tíagu-ssa* 'I go'
	2		*siu, so*	*for.regae-siu* 'thou wilt help', *do-mointer-so* 'thou thinkest', but also *as.bir-so* 'thou sayest' beside *as-bir- siu*
	3	masc.	*som, (sem)*	*ad.cobra-som* 'he desires'
		fem.	*si*	*dénad-si* 'let her do'
		neut.	*som, (sem)*	*as.beir-sem* 'he says'
pl.	1		*(s)ni, (nai)*	*laimir-sni* 'we dare', *guidmi-ni* 'we pray'
	2		*si*	*berid-si* 'ye say'
	3		*som, (sem)*	*ráncatar-som* 'they have reached'[17]

13 Thurneysen, *GOI* § 540; cf. also Lewis/Pedersen, *CCCG* p. 309. As to the central position of the 3sg. cf. also Trautmann, *Die altpreußischen Sprachdenkmäler*, p. 273; T. Burrow, 'The Sanskrit precative', in *Asiatica. FS F. Weller* (Leipzig 1954) pp 35 42: p. 36; C. Watkins, *Indo-European origins of the Celtic verb. 1. The sigmatic aorist* (Dublin 1962) pp 90–6; K.H. Schmidt, 'Miscellanea Svanica', *Annual of Ibero-Caucasian linguistics* 9 (Tbilisi 1982) pp 62–73: 65–7. **14** E. Benveniste, 'Structure des relations de personne dans le verbe', *BSL* 43, fasc. 1 (1946) = *Problèmes de linguistique générale* (Paris 1966) pp 225–36: p. 228. As to the term 'non-personal' cf. Watkins, *Indo-European origins*, p. 91: 'It [the 3sg.] is characterized uniquely by being non-personal; the correlation of subjectivity is unspecified, since this is contingent upon the presence of personalness'. **15** J.H. Greenberg, 'Language universals', in T.A. Sebeok (ed.), *Current trends in linguistics III* (The Hague/Paris 1966) pp 61–112: 85. **16** Cf. e.g. 1.1, the emphatic forms of the fully stressed pronouns. **17** The vocalic alternation, e.g. '1sg. After palatal consonants and front vowels (*-e, -i*) *se* (very rarely *sea*), otherwise *sa*' (*GOI*, p. 252) reflects a kind of vowel harmony, as we know it among others from Turkish.

Emphasizing particles also occupy a position after the noun (*GOI*, p. 253), a) as they 'cannot come immediately after the copula, which is itself proclitic and hence incapable of supporting an enclitic': *am cimbid-se* 'I am a captive', *is día-som* 'he is God'; b) 'in sentences which have no verb': *fáelid-sem* 'he (is) joyous', *maic-ni dosom* 'we (are) sons of his'.

There are different explanations of the etymological origin of emphasizing particles[18] the most convincing of which seems to be their tracing back to the demonstrative stem **so-*.[19]

From a typological point of view the emphasizing particles overlap functionally with the postponed article of Classical Armenian:

> a) *-s* 'hic', *-d* 'iste', *-n* 'ille' referring to the first (*-s*), second (*-d*), third (*-n*) person;
> b) the third person (*-n*) exhibits especially high text frequency, followed by the first person, the second person being least attested;[20]
> c) the Armenian article may be attached to a verb, especially in a relative clause:

> Lk 16.2 *zinčᶜ*? *ē ays zor lsems zkⁱēn* τί τοῦτο ἀκούω περὶ σοῦ; (*lsem* ἀκούω plus article *-s* 1sg.) (Klein, l.c., p. 53);
> Mt 8.13 *orpēs hawatacᶜerd elicᶜi kᶜez* ὡς ἐπίστευσας γενηθήτω σοι (*hawatacᶜer* ἐπίστευσας plus article *-d* 2sg.) (Klein, l.c., p. 96).

d) 'the use of the local adverbs *anti* [illinc], *and* [illic], and *andr* [illuc] in articular value following, respectively, an ablative, a locative, and an accusative' (Klein l.c. p. 23):

> Lk 3.2 *elew ban $\overline{AY}$ i veray Youhannów ... yanapati and* ἐγένετο ῥῆμα θεοῦ ἐπὶ Ἰωάννην ... ἐν τῇ ἐρήμῳ (*y-anapati and* ἐν τῇ ἐρήμῳ) (Klein, l.c., p. 23).
> Mt 4.21 *Ew matowcᶜeal anti yaraj* καὶ προβὰς ἐκεῖθεν (and coming forward from there [anti]) (Klein, l.c., p. 25).

In principle, the use of local adverbs may be compared with the OIr. adverbs of place following a noun with the article: 'Present place and time are expressed by the enclitic particles *so* and *sa* ..., after palatal auslaut usually *se*, *seo*, and *sea*; e.g. in *lebor-so* or *-sa* 'this book', *ind libuir-se* or *-seo* or *-sea* 'of this book', etc.' (*GOI*, p. 300).

'Its counterpart is enclitic *-sin* (likewise with unlenited *s-*), which is never really deictic but always refers anaphorically to something already mentioned; e.g. *a cetharde-sin* 'those four above-mentioned things'" (*GOI*, p. 300).

Cf. also *in salm-so sís* 'the Psalm following here below', *in fer tall* 'the man there, yonder man', *in rí túas* 'the king above', etc. (*GOI*, p. 300).

2.2 The infixed pronouns are governed by the following rules (*GOI*, pp 255–7):

> a) They are always unstressed.
> b) They are attached to the first element of the finite verb form (conjunct particle, first preposition, verbal particle *no*).

---

18 Cf. e.g. *LEIA, RS* p. S-3, H. Pedersen, *VGKS* 2 (1913) pp 137f., Thurneysen, *GOI*, p. 282, Lewis/Pedersen, *CCCG*, pp 221 f. **19** Cf. Pokorny, *IEW* p. 978 f., *LEIA, RS* p. S-155 and see 1.1c. **20** Cf. J.S. Klein, *On personal deixis in Classical Armenian. A study of syntax and semantics of the* n-, s-, *and* d-*demonstratives in manuscripts E and M of Old Armenian Gospels* (Dettelbach 1996) p. 4.

c) With active or deponent forms of transitive verbs they express the direct object; e.g. *ro-m.gab* 'he has taken me', *ní-s.n-ágathar* 'he does not fear them'. With the verb 'to be' … they express the indirect (dative) object, which otherwise is generally expressed by means of the prep. *do*; e.g. *ro-t.bia* 'erit tibi', 'thou shalt have'.

d) With passive forms … the pronouns of the 1st and 2nd persons regularly indicate the subject; e.g. *ro-b.hícad* 'ye have been saved'.

e) The forms of the infixed pronouns fall into three classes (*GOI* p. 257):

Class A is used after all particles and most prepositions which originally ended in a vowel (*GOI* p. 257)

Class B is used after prepositions ending in a consonant; the pronouns of this class are characterized throughout by an initial *d*, which is always unlenited and hence often written (*GOI* p. 257);

Class C has syntactic rather than phonological significance (*GOI* p. 257).

If we take the classes B and C as later innovations,[21] we come to the conclusion 'that there was originally only a simple set of enclitic pronouns (A), used in both relative and non-relative sentences'.[22] The connection between Tmesis, Wackernagel's Law of 1892 and the infixed pronouns of class A had already been observed by the turn of the 20th century. The comparisons with Old Latin (Gaidoz and Sommer), Greek (d'Arbois de Jubainville), and Vedic Sanskrit (Windisch) were supplemented half a century later by Hittite parallels provided by Dillon.[23]

Old Irish *du-s-gní* MI 29a,3 'he carries it (fem.) out';
Old Latin *ob vos sacro; sub vos placo* Fest. 190,309;
Greek πρό μ' ἔπεμψε ἄναξ ἀνδρῶν 'Αγαμέμνων A 442;
Vedic *sam mā tapanti* RV 1,105,8 'they torment me';
Hittite *n(u)-an pešta* 'he gave him'.

In addition to that we find Gaulish evidence as well:

to-med-ec-lai Obalda natina 'ponit or posuit me Obalda filia (or *filiola*)' (Voltino), **to-so-ko[n]de[de]* 'posuit eos' (Vercelli).[24]

2.3 The suffixed pronouns after verbs are in a complementary distribution with the infixed pronouns. 'The most numerous class consists of pronouns of the third person attached as a direct object to the 3sg., absolute flexion, of an active verb in the indicative. To the verbal ending is added *-i* for the 3sg. masc. neut., *-us* for the fem. sg. and the plural of all genders … *beirthi* 'bears it, applies it' from *berith berid … mórthus* 'magnifies her' from *móraid … selgus* 'he cut them down' from *selaig … firiánichthi* 'justifies him' from the deponent *firiánigidir*' (*GOI*, p. 270).

21 cf. Watkins, op. cit. above footnote 8, pp 26–8. **22** Ibid. pp 26 f. **23** Cf. K.H. Schmidt, 'The Celtic languages in their European context', in *Proceedings of the Seventh International Congress of Celtic Studies* held at Oxford, 1983 (Oxford 1986) pp 199–221: p. 200; H. Gaidoz, 'Des pronoms infixes', *RC* 6 (1883) pp 86–91; F. Sommer, 'Das Pronomen Personale Infixum im Altirischen', *ZCP* 1 (1897) pp 177–231; H. d'Arbois de Jubainville, 'L'infixation du substantif et du pronom entre le préfixe et le verbe en grec archaïque et en vieil irlandais', MSL 10 (1898) pp 283–7; E. Windisch, 'Pronomen infixum im Altirischen und im *Rgveda*', *IF* 14 (1903) pp 420–6; M. Dillon, 'On the syntax of the Irish verb', *TPS* 1955 (London 1956) pp 104–16. **24** Cf. Thurneysen, *ZCP* 14 (1923) pp 8–10, writing *posiit* instead of *posuit*; J. Koch, 'The sentence in Gaulish', *PHCC* 3 (1983) pp 169–215: p. 187; cf. also *tioinuoru* (Banassac), interpreted by Lambert, *ÉtC* 30 (1994) pp 216–19 as *tio–(s)in–uōru* and the criticism of J.J. Rubio Orecilla, *Veleia* 15 (1998) p. 235 f.

In connection with the verb 'to be' the suffixed pronouns express the indirect (dative) object, comparable to the infixed pronouns.[25] 'Pronouns of all persons are often used in a dative sense after *táith, the 3sg. absolute form of the present indicative of the substantive verb, which occurs only in this combination' (*GOI*, p. 430): 2sg. *táthut* 'est tibi, thou hast', 3sg. masc. *táth(a)i*, fem. *táthus*, 1pl. *táthunn*, 2 *táthuib*, *bíthi* 'he possesses', lit. 'there is wont to be to him' (consuet. pres.).[26] The preservation of suffixed pronouns of the 1st and 2nd persons after uncompounded transitive verbs must be regarded as an archaism confined to poetic language. The limited number of suffixed pronouns in Early Irish confirms 'the gradual decline of the suffixed *vis-a-vis* the infixed pronouns'.[27] This development is in great contrast to Tocharian, a language that evidently lost the inherited infixed pronouns, preserving just two classes of personal pronouns: 1. Independent personal pronouns, 2. suffixed personal pronouns.[28]

2.4 The *conjugated prepositions* govern personal pronouns in the accusative, dative, or both accusative and dative (*GOI*, pp 272–6). 'The pronouns of the first and second persons are reduced to -*m*, -*t*, -*n*, -*b* (= β)' (*GOI*, p. 272). The conjugated prepositions 'resulted from old formations in British and Goidelic, whereby the preposition was closely joined to the personal pronoun which it governed. In Welsh the preposition is very similar to that of the verb, and has been influenced in its later development by verbal forms'.[29] As the early attested IE languages show, prepositions develop from IE case-syntax: case > case + postposition > preposition + case:

> 'Im sanskrit kann man oft 10 bis 20 seiten lesen, ohne irgend einer präposition mit einem von ihr regierten casus zu begegnen' (Grassmann, *KZ* 23, 1877, 560). 'Das Hethitische hat Postpositionen, nicht Präpositionen … Das Hethitische kann die syntaktischen Verhältnisse, die wir durch Präpositionen bezeichnen, oft durch Kasusformen allein (ohne Postpositionen) zum Ausdruck bringen'.[30]

The postpositions/prepositions originated from adverbs 'primarily used to modify the meaning of verbs' (cf. 2.2 Tmesis). These words 'came to be connected independently with the cases governed by the verbs they modified'.[31] The origin of the prepositions leads to the conclusion that the conjugated prepositions resulted from a late innovation of Celtic, possibly limited to British and Goidelic where it has been developed by language contact.[32]

---

25 Cf. also 'infixed pronouns' after the copula (*GOI* § 427): *iss-um écen* 'it is necessary for me', *iss-id n-aithrech* 'he repents'. There occur occasionally two innovations of this construction: a) the pronoun expresses an accusative relationship: *bes-id fiu* 'which shall be worth it' (*bes* pres. subj. rel.); b) the pronoun is suffixed to the prepositions *do* or *la: is écen dam* 'it is necessary for me', *nipa aidrech lib* 'ye will not regret'.   **26** The Celtic languages have no means of expressing the notion 'to have' synthetically by a single verb, a feature which must be classified as archaic in accordance with the principles of diachronic typology (cf. K.H. Schmidt, *Celtic: a western Indo-European language?* (Innsbruck 1996) pp 16–8). In this context the use of 'to be' in combination with a noun or personal pronoun in the dative case is more archaic than the periphrastic constructions with prepositions of the type *tá ag* (denoting temporary possession) and *is le* (denoting permanent possession). Similarly, periphrastic constructions of physical or mental state of the type *iss-id n-aithrech* [cf. above, n. 25] are more archaic than the type *nipa aidrech lib* 'ye will not regret' (consisting of 'to be' and preposition). Cf. A. Ó Corráin, 'Spatial perception and the development of grammatical structures in Irish', in F. Josephson, *Celts and Vikings. Proceedings of the Fourth Symposium of Societas Celtologica Nordica* (Göteborg 1997) pp 89–101 and K.H. Schmidt, *IF* 103 (1998) pp 301–2.   **27** L. Breatnach, 'The suffixed pronouns in Early Irish', *Celtica* 12 (1977) pp 75–107: 75.   **28** Krause/Thomas, *Tocharisches Elementarbuch*, pp 162–3.   **29** D.S. Evans, *A grammar of Middle Welsh* (Dublin 1964) p. 58.   **30** Friedrich, *Hethitisches Elementarbuch*, p. 129.   **31** A.A. Macdonell, *A Vedic grammar for students* (London 1916, repr. 1966) p. 207; cf. also Brugmann, *Grundriss II*, 2 Mu.2 p. 761 who calls the connection of a postposition/preposition with a noun 'syntaktische Gliederungsverschiebung'.   **32** Cf., however, Classical Armenian *cʿ-is* 'to me', 'mili', *cʿ-na* 'to him', 'ei', *z-na* 'him', *y-awr* 'on the day' (the prepositions *cʿ*, *z-*, *y /i-* merge into a group with the following word.

The making of myth: Old Irish *Airgatlám*, Welsh *Llaw ereint*, Caledonian Ἀργεντοκόξος

STEFAN ZIMMER

Elsewhere, I have demonstrated that mythological details may have possibly originated in misunderstandings concerning traditional epithets of gods and heroes.[1] In this contribution, intended to congratulate another good friend and esteemed scholar, I'll present a similar case, that of Old Irish *Airgatlám*, Welsh *Llaw ereint*, and Caledonian Ἀργεντοκόξος, together with an attempt of elucidating the background of these formations, so strange at first sight. What is meant by 'silver-hand' or 'silver-foot'? Are there parallel cases outside Celtic literature?

§1. The epithet 'silver-handed' is doubly attested in Celtic. First, it is found in Old Irish form with Nuadu *Airgatlám* 'Nuadu with the silver hand (or arm?)', the king of the Tuatha Dé Danann. He is reported in *Cath Maige Tuired* to have lost his right arm in battle against the Fir Bolg. Dian Cécht (the great doctor and grandfather of Lug Lámada) provided him with an artificial replacement 'with the motion of every hand', we are told.[2] Unfortunately, Nuadu's W equivalent, Lludd *Llaw ereint* (the father of Creiddylad[3] in *Culhwch ac Olwen*), is not much more than a name for us, all possible mythological lore, apart from an indirect reference to his grievous imprisonment, being lost in W. The identical names and epithets allow us to understand both figures as a form of a Celtic deity attested in inscriptions from Britain as *Nodons*, and identified with the Roman Mars. W *Ll-* in place of expected *N-* is due to alliteration with the epithet, as already seen by J. Rhŷs.[4] Though a Nodons sanctuary has been excavated in *Lydney* (on the Severn, Gloucs., built *c*.AD 364), no hint of a silver arm of the god could be found there. It is curious to note that both name forms, *Lludd* and *Nudd* occur in W literature[5] without any allusion to their original identity.[6] The former identity of the two names must have been forgotten after the end of Roman rule in Britain, and the pertaining turmoil.

§2. Speaking of artificial silver hands, one has also to remind the Caledonian warrior Ἀργεντοκόξος – mentioned by Dio Chrysostomus (76,16,5; *c*.AD100). His name has –ε– for genuine Celtic -α- through influence from Greek (less likely from Latin, as Holder thought).[7] OIr

---

1 S. Zimmer, 'On the prehistory of OIr *lámada*, W *llawir*', in D. Ó hAodha (ed.), *Féilscríbhinn Ghearóid Mhic Eoin* (forthcoming). **2** W. Stokes (ed.), 'The second battle of Moytura,' *RC* 12 (1891) pp 52–130, 306–8 ch. 11: *go tarad Dien-cecht an liaigh laim airgid foair co luth cecai láma, ocus Creidhne in cerd ag cungnam fris* 'So D.C. the leech put on him a hand of silver with the motion of every hand, and C. the brazier was helping him'. Similarly in ch. 33: *go luth cecha lamha indhe* 'with the motion of every hand therein'. E.A. Gray (ed.), *Cath Maige Tuired, The second battle of Mag Tuired, ITS* 52 (Kildare 1982) p. 25, gave a slightly freer translation: '… hand that moved as well as any other hand'. **3** The name is attested in OW form as *Creurdilad merch Lut* in the Black Book of Carmathen, p. 97.13. **4** H. Wagner, 'Zur Etymologie von keltisch Nodons, irisch Nuadu, kymrisch Nudd/Ludd', *ZCP* 41 (1986) pp 180–8. **5** For references, see P.C. Bartrum, *A Welsh classical dictionary, people in history and legend up to about AD 1000* (Aberystwyth 1993) pp 416–8, 509–10 (cf. also p. 507). **6** Sir J. Rhŷs, *Lectures on the origin and growth of religion as illustrated by Celtic heathendom*, 3rd edn (London 1899) p. 127. **7** A. Holder, *Alt-Celtischer Sprachschatz I–III* (Leipzig 1896–1910); cf. also Leo Weisgerber, *Die Sprache der Festlandkelten* (Frankfurt 1931) p. 186.

cos is both 'foot'[8] and 'leg' according to DIL, but only one attestation for the latter meaning is given, and even this is doubtful: *fuil chuise* in the Law text *Bretha Crólige* ('judgements of blood-lying') ch. 63, where it is understood as either 'une blessure sur la jambe'(*LEIA*) or 'a wound on a foot'.[9] *Cos* is presumably one of the replacements for the inherited root noun **ped-/pod-* which became too short after the loss of *p-* and fell out of use. Its former existence in Celtic is, of course, proven by the old loc. pl. **pēd-su* > OIr W *is* 'lower' > 'under'. The other Celtic word for 'foot' is OIr *traig*, gen. *traiged*; W *troed*, pl. *traed*, an old nom. agentis 'runner'.[10]

§3. It is difficult to think of a warrior 'with a silver foot or leg'. It is therefore appropriate to look for a different explanation. In discussing two possibilities I should like to remark that they are similar with respect to the underlying semantics, and that none of them has ever been applied to Celtic before.

The first is based on a suggestion by Françoise Bader on Gr compounds with ἀργυρο-.[11] She observed that Apollo ἀργυρότοξος could, for several obvious reasons, not have had a bow made from silver. According to the system discovered by W. Caland, no adjective in *-ro-* is to be expected as first member (FM) of a compound. What would be expected is **ἀργί-τοξος* with **argi-* as in Hitt *harki-*, TochA *ārki-* 'white'; this **argi-* is well attested in Greek, e.g. in ἀργι-βρέντας (Pi., epithet of Poseidon) and ἀργι-κέραυνος (Hom. etc., of Zeus), both 'with brilliant lightning'; ἀργι-λοφος 'white-crested', etc.[12] But **ἀργί-τοξος*, with its creticus structure [long-short-long-X], does not fit into the dactylic metre. This led, F. Bader supposed, to its substitution by ἀργυρό-τοξος [long-short-short, long-X]. This assumption is supported, she claims, by the artificial case endings of Ilias A 49 ἀργυρέοιο βιοῖο (hapax) and ἀργυρέῳ τόξῳ (Pi. O. 9,32). If her theory is to be accepted, the structure of other Greek compounds may also be better understood, e.g. ἀργυρό-πεζα (epithet of Thetis, etc.) instead of ἀργί-πους, which itself is never found in the nominative: in this case, it is consistently replaced by ἀργυρό-πεζα (for **ἀργί-πεζα), just as ποδάς ὠκύς is used where ποδώκης cannot fit into the metre. For the meaning of ἀργυρό-πεζα 'silver-footed', F. Bader considers also 'with feet white (from foam)', comparable to ἀργυρο-δίνης 'of silver eddying', an epithet of rivers.

There are several criticisms to be raised: First, the possibility that Apollo's bow might have had silver applications; second, 'silver' is often found as FM of a compound as a means of describing colour, and not always necessarily of indicating the matter something is made of. Furthermore, such colour indications tend to be rather vague, especially in poetical texts. (One might recall the many W cpds. in *eur-*).[13] More important is the fact, that 'silver' is not the basic meaning of ἀργυρός. The suffix **-ro-* is typical for adjectives, and the etymological connection to the root **h₂erǵ–* as found in Skt *rj-rá-* beside *árjuna-* < **arǵu-no-* is clear enough to postulate a basic meaning 'brilliant, shining'. On top of that, the comparison of Greek and Sanskrit terms and their usage allows us to identify a further step in the development of the semantics. The meaning 'swift' is as old as 'shining', both going back to qualities of natural light. Many such lights, forest fires, lightning or star showers are both 'brilliant' and 'swift'.

8 OIr *coss* gl. *pes* Wb 12a20 reflects standard usage.   **9** D.A. Binchy, 'Bretha Crólige', *Ériu* 12 (1938) pp 1–77.
10 According to K.H. Jackson, *Language and history in early Britain* (Edinburgh 1953, repr. Dublin 2000) p. 455, W *troed* is from **troget-s,* but all other forms from **traget-,* which would point to independent parallel innovation in Goidelic and Brittonic.   **11** F. Bader, 'Vocabulaire et idéologie tripartie des Indo-Européens: La racine **swer-* 'veiller sur' en grec', *Bulletin de la Société de Linguistique* 66 (1966) pp 139–211: 206–7.   **12** See P. Chantraine, *Dictionnaire éytmologique de la langue grecque* (Paris 968) s.v. ἀργός.   **13** For their formation and interpretation, see S. Zimmer, *Studies in Welsh word-formation* (Dublin 2000) pp 136–8.

But these are purely semantic objections which hardly affect the formal side of Bader's theory. Her idea that an exceptional form of the adjective might have arisen out of metrical constraints is sensible, and might be applied, with due caution, to non-Greek cases should occasion arise.

§4. In the light of these possibilities, one might ask whether W *ereint* in the epithet *llaw ereint* is not simply a feminine adjective, going back to CC **arg-ant-ī* < IE **h₂r̥ǵ -n̥t-ih₂* 'brightly shining', the regular athematic feminine present participle of the root **h₂erǵ-*. The corresponding neuter is found e.g. in Av *ərəzata-*, L *argentum*, Co *argant* 'silver', etc., < IE **h₂r̥ǵ-n̥t-ó-* 'the silvery shining (metal)'; Skt *rajatá-* 'shining like silver, brilliant white' has a slightly modified structure; Mayrhofer considers an irregular vr̥ddhi.[14] The W epithet *llaw ereint* is then not a reversed BV compound, but a syntagm of substantive + adjective **pl̥m-eh₂ *h₂r̥ǵ-n̥t-ih₂* 'the hand (is) brilliant'[15] paraphrasing, as it were, OIr *airgatlám*, just as *Dolgorukyj* is identical with *Dolgaja Ruka* in the ORu chronicle. Incidentally, there is an Irish parallel with 'silver eye' to be found in the Genealogies, viz. *Derc nArgit* (CGH), which supports such an interpretation.[16]

The idea of the silver artificial limbs may be a Celtic, or more probably a Goidelic pre-Christian innovation after the original meaning (which, however, may still be reflected in Caledonian Ἀργεντοκόξος) had become opaque. Such a development could have been supported by other maimed gods in IE mythology, especially the ON *Týr* who, however, did not get an artificial arm. The IE origin of the Celtic epithets seems clear thanks to the obvious parallels found in Homeric diction. Having 'bright' or 'swift' hands, arms or feet is a typical epithet for gods and warriors.

§5. This allows a solution to the old unanswered question why there is no trace to be found of any parallel to the myth about Nuadu Airgatlam in any other Celtic, or even in any other old Indo-European literature. When the old meaning of IE **h₂erǵ-*, CC **arg-*, viz. 'to move or shine brilliantly', was lost – perhaps because **arganto-* 'silver', later also 'money' became so prominent – inherited compounds or collocations describing heroes or gods as 'characterised by swift/brilliant hands/feet' etc. became opaque. Consequently, the poetical diction was no longer understood in the old meaning and had to be filled with renewed, transparent semantics.[17] If Nodons now seemed to be rather 'silver-handed', the poets were obliged to explain for what reasons. And they found a perfect solution which was, fortunately enough, handed down until confined to parchment, and preserved to the present day. There is, unfortunately, nothing comparable transmitted on the Welsh side, and nothing at all recorded from the Caledonians. So, we'll never exactly know when and where the story of Dian Cechts masterwork was invented, but the first centuries AD in Ireland seem to be a reasonable guess. Our honouree herself deserves to be given the very epithet. We all, full of admiration for her humane and scholarly excellence, wish her many happy returns, and many more occasions to demonstrate her 'brilliant hand'.

---

14 M. Mayrhofer, *Etymologisches Wörterbuch des Altindoarischen* (Heidelberg 1986) II, p. 426, with references.   **15** Less likely, so it seems, would be the assumption of genetival construction with two genitives, one a *genitivus qualitatis*, the other a *genitivus materiae*, **pl̥m-eh₂-s *h₂r̥ǵ-n̥t-ieh₂-s*, 'of a silvery hand', but Uhlich's idea to take the second word to be an old genitive **h₂r̥ǵ-n̥t-ī* cf. L *argentum*, is a perfect alternative: Jürgen Uhlich, *Die Morphologie der komponierten Personennamen des Altirischen* (Witterschlick/Bonn 1993) p. 4.   **16** The older meaning would have been 'brilliant eye', or rather 'with brilliant eyes', CC **derkon *arganton*, replacing an IE cpd. **derko-h₂r̥ǵ-n̥t-ó-*. Cf., with a partly different explanation, Uhlich, *Die Morphologie*, p. 4. Other personal names with 'silver': OIr: *Argatmár* m. Sírláim (CGH), Eanna *Airgthioch* at a place called *Airgedros* (Keating I, 27, 2019), W. Kadellin *Tal Aryant* (C&O 289, Hettwn *Tal Aryant* (C&O 344).   **17** The desire to 'explain', and thereby to 'understand' words and names of no longer transparent structure is one of the main incentives of human intellectual activity. This is most prominent in the interest for names so popular all over the world. In Ireland, whole literary genres came into being through such 'explications', viz. Dinnshenchas – cf. E. Gwynn, *The Metrical Dindshenchas* (Dublin 1903–35, repr. 1991), pp 91–2 – and Banschenchas. Old Irish saga literature makes free use of the device – cf. A. Dooley & H. Roe, *Tales of the Elders of Ireland (Acallam na Senórach),* (Oxford 1999), p. ix. For the historical and intellectual background, see the two articles in R. Welch (ed.), *The Oxford Companion to Irish Literature* (Oxford 1996), p. 31, and pp 149–50.

Zu irisch *grád* 'Liebe'

WOLFGANG MEID

In meinem Vortrag über 'Freundschaft' und 'Liebe' in keltischen Sprachen, gehalten am 17. März 1998 (St Patrick's Day) in Konstanz und abdruckt in den Akten jener Tagung, bin ich über die mit irisch *grád* verbundenen Probleme – Lautung, Form und Etymologie – etwas zu leicht hinweggegangen, da das Eingehen auf Details dem Vortrag nicht bekömmlich gewesen wäre und letzten Endes auch nicht allzuviel erbracht hätte. Diese Probleme, die so bedeutend nicht sind und auch nicht zu voller Zufriedenheit gelöst werden können (ein Rest von Zweifel wird immer bleiben), sollen hier jedoch zumindest erörtert werden.

Das Wort, das im Neuirischen zum geläufigen Ausdruck für 'Liebe' geworden ist (*grádh, grá*), taucht erst im Mittelirischen in der Überlieferung auf, tritt zunächst neben das ältere Wort *serc*, um dann später an seine Stelle zu treten. Noch in dem in seiner kompilatorischen Form unverkennbar mittelirischen Text *Serglige Con Chulaind* ist *serc* häufiger als *grád*, das nur zweimal vorkommt, beide Male aber in stark emotional getönten Äußerungen, so wenn Emer, Cú Chulainns Gattin, diesem zur Schande anrechnet, wegen der Liebe zu einer Frau (*ban-grád*) in Liebeskummer dahinzusiechen: '*Is mebul duit*', *or sí*, '*laige fri bangrád, úair dogénad galar duit sírligi*' (ed. Dillon, 389 f.), oder wenn Fand, die Geliebte, als sie von Cú Chulainn scheiden muß, von Gefühlen überwältigt wird, eben weil das Übermaß an Liebe (*ro-grád*), das sie Cú Chulainn gegeben hatte, sie aufwühlt: *ro búadir in rograd hí dorat do Choin Chulaind* (729 f.). An den anderen Stellen findet sich noch das ältere Wort *serc*, dem das Wort für die Liebeskrankheit, *serg*, ja so lautähnlich ist, daß es Assoziationen wecken kann. Dieses Nebeneinander der lautähnlichen, zum Überfluß noch gleich geschriebenen Wörter findet sich bekanntlich ja auch in dem älteren Text *Aislinge Oengusso*. Es ist interessant, daß an der oben zitierten Stelle, in der *ban-grád* erscheint, die Krankheit *galar* genannt ist.

Serc ist ein Wort mit erotischem Flair, wenngleich dies von der Etymologie her nicht vorgegeben ist (die Verwandten im Griechischen, στέργω, στοργή, drücken eher pietätische Liebe aus). *Grád* kann, wie die obigen Beispiele zeigen, auch die erotische Komponente haben (vgl. etwa noch *tuc grád … dó* 'verliebte sich in ihn'), die zugrunde liegende Bedeutung ist aber eher eine emotional-affektische, denn *grád* kann auch Nächstenliebe (*cardoit a caritate .i. grad*, Corm. Y 282), Liebe zu Gott (zusammen mit *serc: cen serc cen grád Dé accu*, FA 27), die Liebe eines Volkes zu seinem Herrscher (*do thuatha oc do grád*) oder ein Vertrauensverhältnis (*fer gráda, oés gráda*) bezeichnen, ähnlich wie dies 'lieb' in altgermanischen Sprachen kann. Die generelle Bedeutung 'Liebe', die dieses Wort angenommen hat, ist also aus einer breiter angelegten Gefühlsbasis erwachsen.

Die Frage stellt sich dann, woher das Wort kommt und was es ursprünglich bedeutet hat. Der Verdacht liegt nahe, daß es kein einheimisches Wort ist, sondern ein Lehnwort, wobei praktisch nur das Lateinische in Frage kommt. Das Mißliche an der Situation ist, daß es bereits ein im Altirischen gut bezeugtes Lehnwort *grád* gibt, daß aus lateinisch *gradus* stammt und dessen geläufige Bedeutungen – 'Stufe, Rang, Grad' usw. – fortführt. Obwohl man sich Wendungen wie *gradus amicitiae, gradus amoris* vorstellen könnte, gibt es doch keinerlei Anzeichen, daß sich *grád* 'Liebe' daraus abgezweigt hätte.

Auch sind *grád* 'Grad' und *grád* 'Liebe' nur isoliert betrachtet homophon, sie unterscheiden sich in Stammbildung und Flexion. *grád* 'Grad' flektiert als neutraler *o*-Stamm, *grád* 'Liebe' als *u*-Stamm (Genitiv *gráda*). Dies ist einigermaßen merkwürdig, denn *u*-Flexion wäre eher für *grád* aus lateinisch *gradus* (*u*-Stamm!) angemessen als für *grád* 'Liebe', für das von H. Pedersen und (ihm folgend) J. Pokorny Herkunft aus lateinisch *grā̆tum* angenommen wird (substantiviertes Neutrum von *grā̆tus* 'lieb, angenehm'). Es hätte also paradoxerweise *grád* 'Grad' (obwohl aus lateinischem *u*-Stamm) im Irischen die Stammbildung (und das Genus) von *grā̆tum*, während *grád* 'Liebe' (aus lateinischem *o*-Stamm) die von *gradus* (*u*-Stamm) hätte.

Dies sieht nach gegenseitiger Beeinflussung der beiden Wörter aus, die sich auch im Lautlichen zeigt. Wir unterstellen dabei, daß *grád* 'Liebe' tatsächlich aus lateinisch *grā̆tum* stammt, aus einem Wort, das in fast alle romanischen Sprachen eingegangen ist: italienisch *grato* (archaisch), *grado*,[1] französisch *gré*.[2] J. Pokorny nimmt an, daß irisch *grád* aus Wendungen wie *gratum facere alicui* erwachsen wäre.[3] Lateinisch *grā̆tus* 'angenehm, gefällig, beliebt' ist dem Ursprung nach ein Wort der Lobpreisung, das in besonderem Maße dem dichterischen und religiösen Sprachgebrauch angehörte (lateinisch *grā̆tus* = altindisch *gūrtá-*, litauisch *gìrtas* 'gepriesen'); die indogermanische Wurzel ist im Keltischen durch 'Barde' vertreten.[4]

Nun aber zum Lautlichen. Aus *gradus* 'Grad' sollte man irisch **grad (gradh)* mit kurzem *a* erwarten (vgl. kymrisch *gradd*). Aus *grā̆tum* 'Belieben' sollte man irisch **gráth*, mit stimmloser Spirans im Auslaut (wie regulär bei Einsilblern), erwarten. Auch aus dieser Gegenüberstellung ist zu ersehen, daß sich die beiden Wörter aneinander angenähert haben. *grád* 'Grad' hat den langen Vokal von *grád* 'Liebe', dieses wiederum hat die auslautende stimmhafte Spirans von *grád* 'Grad', wo sie regulär ist.

H. Pedersen hat diese analogische Beeinflussung erkannt, denn er weist an zwei Stellen seiner Vergleichenden keltischen Grammatik darauf hin: I 133 (§ 85.3) läßt er *grád* 'Liebe' (: lat. *grā̆tus* 'lieb') unter Hinweis auf *grád* 'Grad' 'volksetymologisch beeinflußt' sein,[5] und I 193 (§ 121.4) führt er als Beispiel für gelegentliche Dehnung eines lateinischen *a* 'unter analogischem Einfluß' *grád* 'Grad' als beeinflußt von *grád* 'Liebe' an.

Da Pedersen die beiden Fälle lautlicher Beeinflussung an verschiedenen Stellen behandelt, ist nicht klar, ob ihm bewußt geworden ist, daß beide *grád* sich dann gegenseitig beeinflußt haben müßten. Wenn dies aber der Fall gewesen sein sollte, ergibt sich ein interessantes chronologisches Problem aus dem Umstand, daß *grád* 'Grad' ja älter (und häufiger) bezeugt ist als *grád* 'Liebe'. Wenn das später bezeugte Wort das früher bezeugte beeinflußt haben soll (denn die Länge von *grád* 'Grad' ist schon altirisch bezeugt), dann muß auch *grád* 'Liebe' schon in altirischer Zeit existiert haben. Dies ist an sich nicht unplausibel; man hat dann anzunehmen, daß das Wort von der Überlieferung, die zu jener Zeit wenig Raum für Mitteilung subjektiver Empfindungen ließ, nicht begünstigt worden ist.

---

1 Redewendungen: *di buon grado* 'volontieri', *a suo grado* 'a suo piacimento', *a suo mal grado* 'mal volontieri', *avere in grado* 'ritenere caro' etc. **2** *à mon gré, malgré moi* usw. **3** Es wäre sinnvoll, der Verwendung von *gratum* im mittellateinischen, und besonders im hibernolateinischen, Schrifttum nachzugehen. **4** J. Pokorny, *Indo-germanisches etymologisches Wörterbuch*, p. 478 f.; E. Campanile, *Studi e saggi linguistici* 20 (1980) p. 184. **5** Das andere Beispiel, das Pedersen an der Stelle zitiert und wo ebenfalls *th* zu erwarten wäre, ist *táid* 'Dieb' (< **tātis*, vgl. altslavisch *tatĭ*); in diesem Fall nimmt Pedersen Einfluß der Nomina agentis auf *-id* an.

The four names of St Patrick

GEARÓID MAC EOIN

In a series of texts going back to the seventh century there is to be found a tradition that St Patrick had four names. Making allowance for variations in language (Latin or Irish) and in spelling we find that the texts are in essential agreement about the names in question. But the nature and extent of the extra information supplied allows us to arrange the texts in three groups which may be summarised here in advance of a more detailed discussion below:

A. Texts which give a simple translation or etymology of the name.
B. Texts which state the occasions on which Patrick received the various names.
C. Texts which give the same information as group B but which identify the name-givers, Patrick's parents, Miliuc, Germanus, and Pope Celestine.

Texts of Group A – Tírechán and Derivatives

Text 1

Tírechán's collection of material on the Life of St Patrick, assembled in the second half of the seventh century and preserved in the Book of Armagh (c.AD 807, henceforth LArm), informs us on the authority of a book in the possession of Ultán of Ard mBreccán near Navan, Co. Meath, who is described as bishop of Dál Conchobair and who died in AD 657 (AU), that Patrick had four names:

Inueni quattuor nomina in libro scripta Patricio apud Ultanum episcopum Conchuburnensium: sanctus Magonus, qui est clarus; Succetus qui est …, Patricius …, Cothirthiacus, quia seruiuit quattuor domibus magorum; et empsit illum unus ex eis, cui nomen erat Miliuc maccu Boin magus, et seruiuit illi septem annis omni seruitute ac duplici labore

I have found four names for Patrick written in a book in the hands of Ultán, bishop of Connor [recte Dál Conchubair]: the saint (was named) Magonus, that is: famous; Succetus, that is …, Patricius …; Cothirthiacus, because he served four houses of druids; and one of them, by name Miliuc moccu Bóin, a druid, bought him, and he served him for seven years in all submission and in works of all kinds.[1]

Text 2

The Brussels manuscript of Muirchú's Life of St Patrick may have been written in the *Schottenkloster* of Würzburg in the eleventh century. The script points to an Italian origin for the

1 L. Bieler (ed. and trans.), *The Patrician texts in the Book of Armagh, SLH* 10 (Dublin 1979) pp 124.16–21. Here and in the following, in order to reproduce accurately the text of the manuscripts, I have removed material inserted by Bieler in text and translation and collated the text with the facsimile of the manuscript published by the Irish

manuscript as a whole, but not necessarily for the Muirchú text.[2] The Prologue to the *Life* is a very confused passage, consisting of the introduction to a *Life* of St Basil into which three sentences relating to Patrick have been inserted. Two of these are taken from a text of Tírechán's *Life*, though not, it would seem, directly from LArm[3], while the third is a text of the Group B type, which will be given in its proper place below (Text 3). The sentence quoted from Tírechán relating to Patrick's names is as follows:

Inueni quattuor nomina in libro scripta Patricii abud Uldanum episcopum Concubrensum: Sanctus Magonus, qui est clarus; Sucsetus ipse est ..., Patricius ..., ... quia seruiuit quattuor domibus magorum; et emit illum ab illis unus, cui nomen erat Miluch Mocuboín magus, et seruiuit illi septem annis.	I have found four names of Patrick in a book in the possession of Ultán, bishop of Dál Conchubair: Holy Magonus, that is 'famous'; Sucsetus himself is ..., Patricius ..., ... because he served four households of druids; and one of them bought him, whose name was Milúch moccu Bóin, the druid, and he (Patrick) served him for seven years.[4]

Texts 1 and 2 are badly transmitted and show common lacunae. It should be noted that of the four names mentioned in the Book of Armagh the Brussels manuscript gives only three, *Cothirthiacus* being the missing one, though the survival of the pseudo-etymology shows that a name capable of bearing this explanation must once have existed in the text. There is no certainty that the presence of *Cothirthiacus* in the text of LArm was due to Tírechán in the seventh century and not to Ferdomnach, scribe of LArm in the ninth, or to some intervening scribe – perhaps to fill a gap such as we find in the Brussels manuscript. In LArm and in the Brussels manuscript only two of the three names are explained. These explanations differ from those found in later documents in that they are lexical or etymological, while in most later documents they are more historical, stating the occasions on which Patrick received each of his names. However in the glosses to Fiacc's hymn in the Trinity College, Dublin MS. E. 42 of the eleventh-century *Liber Hymnorum* we also find etymological glosses: '*Succat*: Bretnas sein 7 *deus belli* a Laten (That is British, and the Latin of it is *deus belli*)', while the corresponding gloss in the Franciscan manuscript of the same text is: 'Bretnas sen, *deus belli uel fortis belli* a Laten, uaire *su* isin Bretnais is *fortis* uel is *deus*, *cat* is *bellum* (That is British, the Latin of it is *deus belli* or *fortis belli*, because *su* in British is *fortis* or *deus*, *cat* is *bellum*)'.[5]

Texts of group B: the Occasions of Patrick's naming

Text 3
Following on the Tírechán quotation in Muirchú's *Life* of Patrick, cited above as Text 2, the text of the Brussels manuscript continues:

Manuscripts Commission with an Introduction by Edward Gwynn (Dublin 1937), and with the edition of the Brussels manuscript in J. Gwynn, *Liber Ardmachanus, The Book of Armagh edited with introduction and appendices* (Dublin 1913) p. 443. The symbol ... indicates that some material is missing from the manuscript text. **2** Bieler, *Patrician texts*, pp 3–4. **3** J.B. Bury, 'The tradition of Muirchu's text,' *Hermathena* 28 (1902) pp 172–207. Bieler, *Patrician texts*, p. 194, §6, believed that LArm is the 'ultimate source' of the passage in the Brussels manuscript. **4** Bieler, ibid. pp 62–3, B 299ra, 6. Again I have adapted Bieler's translation to represent more closely the defective text of the manuscript. **5** W. Stokes and J. Strachan (eds), *Thesaurus Palaeohibernicus* (Cambridge 1901–3, repr. Dublin 1975) II, p. 308, gl. 5.

Patricius [C]alforni filius quattuor nomina
habuit: Sochet quando natus est, Contice
quando seruiuit, Mauonius quando legit,
Patricius quando ordinatus est.

Patrick son of [C]alforni[us] had four names:
Sochet when he was born, Contice when he
was a slave, Mauonius when he studied,
Patricius when he was consecrated.[6]

Text 4

In the *corpus* of genealogies of the Irish saints we find the same tradition repeated in Irish but with
Cotraige instead of *Contice*.

Succait tra ainm baitse Patraic. Cotraige
immurgu a ainm a ndoire; inand on 7 fer
nofhognad do cethrar i n-oenfhecht. Mogonius
a ainm oca fhoglaimm. Patricius a ainm la
Romanchu. Ut dixit:
Succait a ainm baiste iar mbuaid,
Cotraige a ndoire dimbuain,
Patricius i lLetha luind,
Magonius 'ca fhogluimm.[7]

Succait, then, was Patrick's baptismal name.
Cotraige, however, was his name in servitude –
that is to say a man who used to serve four at
once. Mogonius was his name when he was
studying. Patricius was his name among the
Romans. Ut dixit:
Succait his baptismal name after victory,
Cotraige in temporary servitude,
Patricius in violent Letha [i.e. Rome],
Magonius at his studies.

The date of this entry is not easy to determine. The *Recensio major* to which it forms an addition
was compiled from earlier materials probably in the eleventh century[8] and the entry is later than
that.

Text 5

In the two eleventh-century manuscripts (F and T) of the *Liber Hymnorum* there is preserved a
copy of the poem on the life of Patrick which begins *Génair Pátraic i Nemthur* and is usually
known as 'Fiacc's Hymn'. This has been dated *c*.AD 800 but Professor Pádraig Ó Riain argues that
it 'could hardly have been composed earlier than the middle of the ninth century'.[9] In the text of
this poem two of Patrick's four names are included:

> St. 2a. Succat a ainm i tubrad (Succat (was) his name in which he was carried off).
> St. 3cd. batar ili Cothraige / cetharthrebe dia fognad (many were there whom Cothraige of
> the four households used to serve).[10]

On the name *Cothraige* we find the following among the eleventh-century glosses on the hymn:
.i. rolenastar int ainm as Cothraige 'the name Cothraige adhered to him' (emending to *ra*-) and *.i.
cetharaige arinni dogníth* (recte *fognith*) *tribubus .iiii.* 'four masters, because he used to serve four

---

6 Bieler, *Patrician texts*, p. 62, B 299ra(7), 63. 7 P. Ó Riain, *Corpus Genealogiarum Sanctorum Hiberniae* (Dublin
1985) p. 2. The prose section of this entry is found again but with the omission of the sentence *inand ... oenfhecht*
in the *Recensio minor*, p. 78. 8 P. Ó Riain, *Corpus*, xviii. 9 P. Ó Riain, 'When and why *Cothraige* was first
equated with *Patricius*', *ZCP* 49–50 (1997) pp 698–711: 707–9. 10 Stokes/Strachan, *Thesaurus* II, pp 308–9. The
syntax of the first line quoted, as interpreted by Stokes and Strachan, is faulty. It is likely that an *n*-stroke has been
lost over the *a* before *ainm* so that it should be taken as the neuter article rather than as a possessive particle.
Translate: 'Succat was the name in which he was brought [here]'.

houses' (L. *tribus* used in the sense of OIr. *treb*) T , while F has *.i. cethair aige .i. agens .iiii. domibus seruitium* 'four masters, i.e. serving four houses'. *Cethair áige* is, of course, a fanciful etymology of *Cothraige* which is explained as though it contained the numeral 4 and the plural of *áige* 'post, prop, pillar, chief'.[11] This pseudo-etymology is clearly based on some form of Cothraige and provides the basis for the 'four-master' story as told in several texts which do not give the etymology.

Texts of group C: the Name-Givers are Identified

Text 6

This group is found principally in the Tripartite Life of Patrick and in the related *Vita Secunda* and *Vita Quarta*. The expanded story of Patrick's captivity and naming is told in the Tripartite Life in a passage which may be of tenth-century date. However, for much of this passage it so happens that the Egerton manuscript is lacking, so that we have to depend for the text on the Rawlinson manuscript and on the Homily on Patrick from the *Leabhar Breac*, which derives from the Tripartite Life:

Lotar for muir iarom .uii. maicc Fechtmaidi 7 Patraic 7 a di fíer léu i mbraitt. Is ed dolotar timchell nHerenn fáthuaid co ngabsat isin túaiscert, 7 ró rensat Patraic fri Miliuc mac Búain (.i. fri ríg Dál Araidi), 7 ro rensat a di fieir hi Conaille Muirtheimne, 7 ni 'mafítir dóib. Cethrar uero ro cennaigseom; oín dib-side Miliuc. Is dó sein arroétside in n-ainm as Cothraige iarsindí foruigénai do cethartreib.

Ro técht dano ceithir anmand [*here Egerton breaks off*] fair .i. Sucait a ainm o thuistidib, Cothraigi dia mbai ic fognam do cethrur, Magonius a Germano, Patricius id est pater ciuium, a papa Celestino. O'tconnairc imorro Miliuc gurbo mog hiressach, ro cendaig on triur aili co fognad dó a oenur, 7 foruigénair-som .uii. mbliadnai fo bés na nEbraidi. Occus iss ed ro herbath dó, ingaire mucc, 7 ba comrorcu dontí ron ortaig samlaith uair ba córu a bith combad aegairi cairech .i. na mac mbethath. Is ed dorala dó iar tain co rúndai .i. comba haegairi na hEcailsi.[12]

The seven sons of Fechtmaid then put to sea taking with them as booty Patrick and his two sisters. The way that they went was in a northerly direction around Ireland until they landed in the north. They sold Patrick to Miliuc mac Búain (i.e. to the king of Dál nAraide), and they sold his two sisters in Conaille Muirthemne, and they did not know about one another. Four men bought him, one of whom was Miliuc. From that he received the name Cothraige, since he served four houses.

He received then four names: Sucait was his name from his parents, Cothraige when he was serving four, Magonius from St Germanus, Patricius, that is the father of the people, from Pope Celestine. When Miliuc saw that he was a faithful slave he purchased him from the other three so that he would serve himself alone, and he served him for seven years in the manner of the Hebrews. And what was entrusted to him was the tending of pigs, and it was a mistake on the part of the person who arranged it thus, for it would have been more suitable for him to be a tender of sheep, that is of the elect (lit. sons of life). That is what happened to him at a later date in a mystical fashion, that he was the shepherd of the Church.

11 Stokes/Strachan, *Thesaurus* II, p. 309, gl. 4.   12 K. Mulchrone (ed.), *Bethu Phátraic: The Tripartite Life of Patrick* (Dublin 1939) pp 196–212. A similar text occurs as a gloss on the name *Cothraige* in Fiacc's hymn, Stokes/Strachan, *Thesaurus* II, p. 309, gl.1.

The homily on St Patrick in the *Leabhar Breac*[13] tells the same story, the only noteworthy difference being that Patrick's four masters are said to have been four brothers, as in the *Vita Quarta*.

Among the differences which the *Vita Tripartita* (VT) shows over against Tírechán's version of the story we find that Miliuc is now not a druid but king of Dál nAraide,[14] that Patrick is sold to four masters at once but is later bought by Miliuc from the other three in order that he might serve himself alone, that the four names are no longer explained by their lexical significance but by the occasions on which Patrick had received them, including the identification of three of those who named him: his parents, his period of slavery, his teacher Germanus, and Pope Celestine who, according to VT but not Muirchú or Tírechán, ordained Patrick and his companions and gave him the name *Patricius: Celestinus, abb Rómae, is é ró erleg gráda fair-seom … 7 is and dano doratad fair-seom int ainm is Patricius (.i. ainm cumachtai le Rómanchu) .i. fer fuaslaicthea gial[l].*[15] Furthermore *Cothirthiacus*, the form found in Tírechán, is in the VT replaced by *Cothraige*, as found, in a wide variety of spellings, in other texts.

The related texts of the *Vita Secunda* and *Vita Quarta* of Patrick tell the same story with the difference that in the *Vita Secunda* the four masters are *divites*, 'wealthy men', while in the *Vita Quarta* they are four brothers. In these texts Patrick's names show the following variations: in V2 *Succet* and *Quadriga* or *Quotirche* and in V4 *Suggeth* and *Quadriga*. On these forms see further note 67 below. Furthermore in V2 and V4 the giving of the name *Patricius* is expressly connected with his elevation to episcopal dignity (*episcopalem gradum praesumendo* V2, *episcopalem gradum assumendo* V4). Compare the less specific *ordinatus est* in the version of the story from Muirchú in Text 3 above.

Text 7

The Franciscan manuscript of the *Liber Hymnorum* adds a further marginal note to Fiacc's hymn:

Succat mac Calpuirnd (there follows a 13-generation pedigree of Patrick). Multa Patricius habuit nomina ad similitudinem Romanorum nobilium .i. Succet cetus suum nomen baitse a parentibus suis. Codrige a ainm inna doere i nErind. Magonius, .i. magis agens quam caeteri monachi, a ainm ica foglaim ic German. Patricius a ainm fo gradaib, 7 is Celestinus comarba Petair dorat fair.	Sucat son of Calpurn (pedigree omitted). Patrick had many names after the manner of the Roman nobles i.e. first, Sucat his baptismal name from his parents. Cothraige his name in his captivity in Ireland. Magonius i.e. accomplishing more than the other monks, his name when studying with Germanus. Patricius his name when he was ordained, and it was Celestinus, successor of Peter, that conferred it on him.[16]

Text 8

The preface to the hymn of Secundinus, *Audite omnes*, in the Franciscan manuscript of the *Liber Hymnorum* and in the *Leabhar Breac* also contain the tradition of the four names of Patrick:

> Franciscan MS: Sucat dano ainm Patraic apud parentes eius. Cothraige nomen eius apud Miliuc. Magonius apud Germanum. Patricius nomen eius a papa Celestino.

13 W. Stokes, *The Tripartite Life of Patrick with other documents relating to that Saint*, 2 vols, *RS* (London 1887) II, pp 438. 20–440.12. **14** As in Muirchú, Bieler, *Patrician texts*, p. 80.4 and 12ff., though in the earlier part of the narrative he was referred to simply as *homo*, p. 78.19, which is how Patrick also describes him in the *Confessio* (cap. 17). **15** Mulchrone, *Bethu Phátraic*, pp 302–8. **16** Stokes/Strachan, *Thesaurus* II, p. 308. The Latin phrases omitted from the translation in the edition are here translated.

Leabhar Breac: Batar dino .iiii. nomina for Patraic .i. Succat a ainm ica thustidib, Cothrige a ainm dia mbuí oc fognam do chethrur, Magonius a ainm o German. Patricius a ainm a papa Celestino.[17]

The passages quoted in the foregoing allow us to see the growth of the story of Patrick's four names from the seventh century, when they were recorded by Tírechán with pseudo-etymological explanations in a passage which has survived only in two faulty copies, to the eleventh when the story was supplemented by the identification of those who gave Patrick his names.

Patrick's four names

Magonus

The first of Patrick's four names was *Magonus* in Tírechán and in the Tírechán quotation in the Brussels manuscript of Muirchú and *Magonius* in Fiacc's Hymn, the *Vita Tripartita* and the *Corpus Genealogiarum Sanctorum*. The second occurrence in Muirchú (Text 3) has the interesting form *Mauonius* with the British change of intervocalic /g/ > /γ/ > /w/. Tírechán interprets the name as the equivalent of L. *clarus*.

Etymologically Stokes compares Gaulish *Magonius* and Welsh *Maun*, Greek Μαχάων and Sanskrit *maghávan* 'generous' and renders the name as 'gross, mächtig'.[18]

One might also consider that *Magonus* has the appearance of a British or Gaulish divine name, with the suffix *-on*, as in Welsh *Mabon* (Gaulish MAPONOS), *Rhiannon*, *Teyrnon*, British and Gaulish EPONA. The root may be that identified by Stokes and found in W. *magu* 'nourish', Irish *magda* / *mogda* 'great, vast', *do-formaig* 'increases', *mag-* prefix 'with intensive or amplicative force' (*DIL*, s.v.). The meaning of the name would be, then, something like 'the great one'. The semantic transition from 'great' to *clarus* 'illustrious', the meaning given for Magonus in Tírechán, is insignificant. Note also L. MOGOVNO, MOVNO etc. as divine name in Roman inscriptions in Gaul and Britain.[19] There is a MAGUNO (gen.) in an Ogam inscription in Co. Waterford, translated by Rhys and Macalister as 'boy'.[20] According to Jackson[21] British /γ/ < /g/ between back vowels survived until the eighth century, so that the further change /γ/ > /w/ is too late to be of use in dating *Magonus*. In the *Historia Brittonum* (AD 829/30) the name appears as *Maun*, which 'would descend regularly from a British *Magunos* "servant-lad."'[22] Bury takes it as the Roman cognomen *Magonus* for which he cites CIL, v, 4609, viii, 9515.[23] This is echoed by Bieler who applies the full name, Magonus Sucatus Patricius, to Patrick.[24] In any event, the name appears to be British with a Latin termination.

Succetus

In Tírechán Patrick's second name is given as *Succetus* and in the Tírechán quotation in the Brussels manuscript of Muirchú as *Sucsetus*, where *cs* represents the pronunciation of Latin *-cc-*

---

17 Stokes, *Tripartite Life*, II, pp 384, 390. **18** W. Stokes, *Wortschatz der keltischen Spracheinheit* (Göttingen 1894, repr. 1979) p. 198. **19** K. Jackson, *Language and history in early Britain* (Edinburgh 1953, repr. Dublin 1994) p. 444. **20** Macalister, *Corpus Inscriptionum*, pp 268–9. **21** Jackson, *Language and History*, pp 445, 470.6, 697. **22** D. Dumville et al. (eds), *St Patrick, AD 493–1993* (Woodbridge 1993, repr. 1996) p. 90, n. 8. The relevant texts are cited on pp 223, 227, and 230. **23** J.B. Bury, *Life of St Patrick and his place in History* (London 1905) p. 292, n. 1. **24** L. Bieler, *Libri Epistolarum Sancti Patricii Episcopi, introductions, text, and commentary* (Dublin 1952, repr. 1993) p. 5.

before *e* in the eleventh century or later. The Irish forms are *Succat* in Fiacc's Hymn, *Sucait* in the *Vita Tripartita*, and *Succet* in the marginal note to Fiacc's Hymn, in the *Vita Secunda*, and in the *Vita Tertia*. In the *Vita Quarta* it is always *Suggeth*.[25] In a separate occurrence in the Brussels manuscript of Muirchú's *Life*, not found the Book of Armagh, the name is spelt *Sochet*.[26] This spelling occurs also in the *Life* by Probus.[27] It is notable that in these Latin lives of Patrick, apart from Tírechán and Muirchú, though they show Latin forms of many Irish names, the Latin form *Suc(c)etus* does not occur.

Stokes, followed by Bury, Jackson, Guyonvarc'h and others,[28] has analysed *Sucat* (his preferred form though actually unattested) as containing the prefix *su-* as found in Welsh *hy-*, Irish *su-/so-* 'good, excellent' and the noun **katu-*, W. *cad* 'battle', Ir. *cath*. He thereby treats the name as identical with W. *hygad* 'warlike', which suits the translation *deus belli uel fortis belli* given in the glosses to 'Fiacc's Hymn'. However, Stokes's interpretation presupposes a Latin form **Sucatus*, which does not occur, and since Tírechán's *Succetus* is supported by a majority of Irish forms which show *-e-* in the second syllable, we ought surely to take it as the starting-point for investigation. I suggest that *Suc(c)etus* can be more plausibly explained as a Latinised form of a British **su* − + *ced* 'gift, boon, favour, *fig.* of a generous person'. *Suc(c)etus* would then be the equivalent of W. *hyged* 'bountiful, generous, helpful, benign', attested since the 12th or 13th century, to which *Geiriadur Prifysgol Cymru* compares the Old Breton personal name *Hocet*.[29] There is no doubt but that 'generous' is a more suitable epithet for a British Christian, as Patrick was, than 'warlike'. Again this is clearly a British name.

Cothraige

Like the two foregoing names, instances of *Cothraige*, with a few exceptions to be mentioned in the following, are confined to versions of the story of Patrick's four names. This is testimony to the almost total replacement of *Cothraige* by *Pátraic* before our records in the Irish language began.

The usual modern explanation of the origin of *Cothraige* is that it is a borrowing of the Latin name *Patricius* at a period before the sound /p/ had developed in Irish so that in borrowed words it was replaced by the labiovelar /kᵘ/ which later lost its labial element and became /k/, written *c-*. The change of *-a-* to *-o-* is due to the labial element of the labiovelar. Since *Cothraige* also shows lenition of interior consonants and a reduced final syllable it must have been borrowed early enough to participate in these changes. St Patrick was thought to be reliably dated to the first half of the fifth century so that the borrowing was considered to provide a *terminus a quo* for these developments, which totally transformed the Irish language from its primitive, patently Indo-European, form and gave it in essence the distinctive appearance which it retains to this day. Through exemplifying these phonological changes in what was regarded as a datable context the name *Cothraige* became a linguistic milestone. But this neat dating has worried many scholars because it meant that a large number of phonological developments had to be packed into a relatively short period, between the coming of Patrick, traditionally dated to AD 432, and the first attestation of the new form of the language shortly before AD 600.[30] The interval during which these phonological changes may have occurred has to be further shortened if we accept the

25 Bieler, *Four Latin Lives of St Patrick* (Dublin 1971) pp 62.16, 67.17.   **26** Bieler, *Patrician texts*, p. 66.19.   **27** Bieler, *Four Latin Lives*, p. 192, 1.   **28** Stokes, *Tripartite Life*, pp 413n., 616; id., *Wortschatz der keltischen Einheit* (Göttingen 1894, repr. 1979) p. 304; Bury, 'Tradition of Muirchú's Text', pp 186 ff.; id., *Life of St Patrick*, p. 291; Jackson, *Language and history*, p. 518; C.J. Guyonvarc'h in *Ogam* 19 (1967) pp 490, 492; *Geiriadur Prifysgol Cymru* 31 (1981) s.v. *hygad*.   **29** *Geiriadur Prifysgol Cymru* 31 (1981) s.v. *hyged*.   **30** D. McManus, 'A chronology of the

opinion of the majority of historians nowadays, that Patrick, on the evidence of his own writings, lived not in the first but in the second half of the fifth century.[31] John Koch, however, expanding on a theory first set forth by Mario Esposito over forty years ago, has sought to date the period of Patrick's missionary activity to the years 390–430, thereby aiming to extend the interval between Patrick and the completion of the phonological developments to which I have referred.[32]

Some years ago, in an effort to detach historical phonology from the name, Dr Anthony Harvey discussed *Cothraige* with its variant spellings and *Cothirthiacus*, the form in which it appears in Text 1 above from Tírechán.[33] Developing a very speculative argument of James Carney's[34] he emphasised the early attestation of *Cothirthiacus* and suggested that the two are 'entirely separate words', neither of which is borrowed from *Patricius*.[35] He saw in *Cothraige* a tribal or place-name, while *Cothirthiacus* may be 'in origin a real additional name for St Patrick'[36] and the source of the 'four-house' etymology. Dr Harvey's suggestions have found support from Professor Pádraig Ó Riain who has dealt with the tribal name *Cothraige /Cathraige* and sought to identify the motivation for the identification of *Cothraige* with Patrick.[37] Professor Patrick Sims-Williams is non-committally sympathetic towards Harvey's suggestion but John T. Koch, though he has words of praise for Harvey's article, continues to regard *Cothraige* as the borrowed form of *Patricius* and categorises *Cothirthiacus* as 'a book form with a very limited claim to be a close reflection of speech'.[38] On the face of it the separation of the name *Cothraige* from the historical phonology of the Irish language would be an attractive contribution to the solution of the dating problems above referred to, a view with which I think the two authors just cited would agree. However I have reservations about the validity of the arguments proposed.

Before going any further, it must be granted that there certainly existed in early medieval Ireland several widely-dispersed placenames or tribal names which were variously spelled *Catraige*, *Cathraige/-i, Cothrugi, Cothrugu* (dat.).[39] With this variety of orthographic forms it is possible that we are dealing with more than one name, according as one accepts the vowel of the first syllable to have been *-a-* or *-o-* and the following *-t-* to have been lenited or unlenited. *Cat-* 'cat', *Cath-* 'battle', and *Coth-* 'food' are possible readings of the first element of the compound. The second element is the common neuter suffix *-r(a)ige* 'kingdom, people', frequently found in Irish tribal names and also in Gaulish *-riges* – a tribal name *Caturiges* actually occurs in Gaulish.[40] This is a common type of Irish (and Gaulish) gentilic name-formation[41] and there is no difficulty in recognising two of the names quoted by Dr Harvey as of this type, *Catrige* (altered from *Cotrige*) LArm 18ra17–18 in the *Additamenta* to Tírechán and *Cothrugu* LArm 18vb6 from below, in the so-called *Notulae*.[42] In both cases the context shows these to be placenames, not personal names.

Latin loan-words in Early Irish', *Ériu* 34 (1983) pp 21–69, esp. 26. A. Harvey, 'The Significance of *Cothraige*', *Ériu* 36 (1985) pp 1–9, esp. 2. **31** See 'The Floruit of St Patrick-Common and less Common Ground' in Dumville et al., *St Patrick*, pp 13–18. **32** J.T. Koch, '*Cothairche, Esposito's theory, and neo-Celtic lenition,' in A. Bammesberger and. A. Wollmann, *Britain 400–600: language and history* (Heidelberg 1990) pp 179–202. **33** Harvey, 'Significance', pp 5–7. **34** J. Carney, *Studies in Irish literature and history* (Dublin 1955, repr. 1979) pp 362–3. **35** Harvey, 'Significance', p. 7. **36** Ibid. p. 6. **37** See above n. 9. **38** P. Sims Williams, 'Dating the transition to neo-Brittonic: phonology and history, 400–600', in Bammesberger/Wollmann, *Britain 400–600*, pp 217–61. **39** E. Hogan, *Onomasticon Goedelicum* (Dublin 1910, repr. 1993) pp 171, 298. Note also Ogam MAQQI CATTINI in Macalister, *Corpus Inscriptionum*, p. 149.153 from the extreme west of Corca Dhuibhne, Co. Kerry, and Hui Caitin, a Laigin family, in *CGH*, p. 38, n. 0. In Scotland we find *Caitt* (pl.) 'Caithness' and *Inis Chatt* (gen. pl.) 'Shetland Islands'. **40** K.H. Schmidt, 'Die Komposition in Gallischen Personennamen', *ZCP* 26 (1957) pp 33–301: 260–1, 168. **41** J. Mac Neill, 'Early Irish population-groups, their nomenclature, classification, and chronology', *PRIA* 29 (1911) pp 59–114: 67–9, 81. id., *Ériu* 3 (1907) p. 46. **42** Bieler, *Patrician texts*, pp 174.23, 180.18. The text of the *Notulae* entry is given in full in Stokes, *Tripartite Life*, pp 348–51, where the two key

It is more difficult to agree that the two instances of *Petra Coithrigi* which he discusses contain the same gentilic name or placename or that they are unconnected with St Patrick.[43] The first of these relates to the baptism of the sons of Nad Fraích: *et baptitzauit filios Nioth Fruich i tír Mumae super Petram (hi) Coithrigi hi Caissiul*,[44] where the first *hi* 'in' is clearly a scribal mistake, anticipating the following *hi*, each of them preceding a name beginning with *c*. Were *Coithrigi* governed by the preposition *hi* it would show a dat. sing. ending, *-(i)u*, for in the OIr texts in LArm *io*-stems consistently show *-u* in the dat. sing. Cf. Bieler, *Patrician Texts, i nduiniu* 174.8, *di suidiu* 174.26, *i suidiu* 174.27, *ier /iar suidiu* 174.30, 31, 176.24, 31. Note particularly *i Cothrugu* 180.18. The only grammatical case which corresponds to the spelling *Coithrigi* and suits the syntax is the genitive singular, so that *super Petram Coithrigi* must mean 'on the rock of Coithrige'. Here the connection with Patrick is clear: Tírechán's sentence telling of the baptism of the king of Munster and his brothers in Cashel follows closely on the story of the foundation of a church called *Domus Martyrum* at Druimm Urchaille (mod. Dunmurraghil, near Donadea in north County Kildare). There the episode concludes: *et est hic petra Patricii in via.*[45] The parallelism between these two sentences, the identity of their onomastic aim, and their proximity in the text demand that *Coithrige* be equated with *Patricius*, as did the author of the *Vita Tripartita* who used an alternative form of the placename, *Lecc Pátraic* 'Patrick's Rock', in the passage where the baptism of the sons of Nad Fraích is narrated.[46] In the corresponding passage in the Homily on Patrick in the *Leabhar Breac*, a text which is closely related to the *Vita Tripartita,* we find *for Leicc Cathraigi fora n-ordnaigter na rig i cCaissel.*[47] In the *Vita Tertia* the name is *Lecc Coithirgi* in both recensions of the text, so that the reading is to be posited for the archetype which was written in Ireland between *c.* AD 800 and *c.*1100.[48] These readings corroborate both the emendation of *hi Coithrigi* in LArm and the interpretation of *Petra Coithrigi* as 'Patrick's Rock'.

The second instance of the name discussed by Dr Harvey is *Petra Coithrigi* in Uisnech. The context is that Patrick was on a missionary journey through the north midlands, founding churches as he went. He came to Uisnech and halted at Petra Coithrigi where some of his foreign companions were killed by the son of Fiachu mac Néill in whose territory Uisnech lay: *In hUisniuch Midi mansit iuxta Petram Coithrigi sed occissi sunt circa se alii perigrini a filio Fechach filii Néll.*[49] It should be noted that Bieler's punctuation in this sentence is incorrect. He assigns in *hUisniuch Midi* to the previous sentence which refers to St Brigid receiving the veil from Mac Caille *in campo Teloch*. In fact In *hUisnech Midi* is the opening phrase of the sentence quoted above, as is evident from the fact that Uisnech is not in Mag Teloch, which is east of Loch Ainninn (Lough Ennell), but in Mag Assail to the west of the lake. Stokes punctuated the passage correctly in his transcription of the text.[50]

This mention of *Petra Coithrigi* in these cases is not an integral part of the narrative, which has already stated the location of the murder of Patrick's 'foreigners' as *In Uisniuch Midi* and the site of the baptism of *filii Nioth Fruich* as Cashel. It is rather part of a series of placenames inserted in Tírechán's text to substantiate Patrick's connection with the ecclesiastical foundations involved and consequently their inclusion in the *paruchia* of Armagh. Note the stridency of Tírechán's claim in passages like that on Caill Boidmail (Boidmal's wood) where Patrick's charioteer,

---

manuscripts also preserve the form *Cothrugu*.   **43** Harvey, 'Significance', p. 7–8.   **44** Bieler, *Patrician texts*, p. 162.32–3 = LArm. 15vb10.   **45** Ibid. p. 162.25–7.   **46** Mulchrone, *Bethu Phátraic*, line 2290.   **47** Stokes, *Tripartite Life*, II, p. 470.7.   **48** Bieler, *Four Latin Lives*, p. 159, 25–7. Dating discussed on pp 25–6.   **49** Bieler, *Patrician texts*, 136.16 = LArm. 11ra20. On the punctuation see Bieler's note on p. 220.   **50** Stokes, *Tripartite Life*, II, p. 310.24.

Boidmal, was buried, and the wood was given to Patrick: *et immolatum erat Patricio* (138.3), or his claim on the independent church founded by Mathona at Tamnach, Co. Sligo, which, it is said, later became part of Patrick's *familia* but was being claimed by Clonmacnois: *sed quaerit familia Clono, qui per vim tenent locos Patricii multos post mortalitates nouissimas* (142.6–7) or Tírechán's claim on the burial place of Loegaire's two daughters whom Patrick had converted to Christianity: *et immolata est* ferta *Deo et Patricio cum sanctarum ossibus et heredibus eius in saecula et aeclessiam terrenam fecit in eo loco* (144.27–9).

A less assertive way of claiming authority over a church or other foundation was to allude to a placename containing Patrick's name, implying that Patrick and Armagh had a claim on the place: Thus the monastery on Inse Maccu Chor, the islands off the coast of north County Dublin where Patrick began his mission, is claimed for his *familia* by the mention of *insola orientali[s] ... Insola Patricii* (126.7–8) which is still called St Patrick's Island. Twice Tírechán mentions an *ecclesia magna* belonging to Patrick, one in the modern County Meath (132.10) and the other in County Mayo (134.25–6) on each occasion proclaiming a close connection between Patrick and the ruling family of the district. In Dunseverick, Co. Antrim, there is said to have been a rock called *Petra Patricii*, that on which Patrick sat, but Tírechán's motive in alluding to it is to strengthen Patrick's and Armagh's claim to authority over the church in Airther Maige (Armoy) over which he appointed one of his fosterlings, Olcán (160.31).[51] Similarly Tírechán's reference to *Collunt Patricii* (162.18), Slieve Gallion, Co. Derry, is elucidated by the enumeration in VT 1972–5 of the seven churches named *Domnach* in Uí Thuirtri (all churches so named were claimed as part of Patrick's *familia*[52]). Thereafter Patrick travelled southwards and entered the territory of the Laigin by the traditional route over the river Rye on the border of Counties Kildare and Dublin. He came thus into the land of Uí Dúnlainge, the dynasty which held the kingship of North Leinster. According to Tírechán he founded a church there, called Domus Martyrum, at Druim Urchaille (Dunmurraghill) in the valley beside the highway where there is a rock named *Petra Patricii*. This allusion represents a claim to contact with the ruling family of North Leinster (expanded in VT 2167–70) and to authority over a church within the territory usually seen as belonging to the *familia* of Kildare. It should be remembered that standing stones and immovable rocks, with or without ogam inscriptions, were accepted as evidence of ownership in early Irish law.[53]

The practice of including such placenames in the narrative claiming or reinforcing a tradition of Patrick's connection with the places in question is to be found also in Muirchú, and in the *Vita Tripartita*.[54] The two *Petrae Coithrigi* have the same onomastic or polemic function as the two *Petrae Patricii*, establishing Patrick's connection with the rulers of two important sites, Uisnech and Caisel, just as his connections with the king of Tara and with the daughters of the king of Cruachain had already been established.[55] It confirms, incidentally, that Tírechán could use *Cothraige* as an alternative name for Patrick just as he used *Succetus* in the story of the conversion of the children of Miliuc.[56]

Regarding *Cothirthiacus* it is to be noted that the form is nowhere attested but in the text of Tírechán in LArm. The extract from a text of Tírechán in the Brussels manuscript of Muirchú's *Life* (Text 2 above) has a lacuna at this point and thus contains neither this name nor anything

51 For Olcán and Airther Maige see Mulchrone, *Bethu Phátraic*, ll 1869–79; 1885–8; 1916–36.   **52** Bieler, *Patrician texts*, p. 188.6–9.   **53** F. Kelly, *A guide to early Irish law* (Dublin 1988) p. 204 and references there given.   **54** See G. Mac Eoin, 'The dating of Middle Irish texts,' *Proc. of the British Academy* 68 (1982) pp 109–37, esp. 127–32.   **55** Bieler, *Patrician texts*, pp 132.23–30, 142.8–144.29.   **56** Ibid, p. 162.5, 8, 12 = LArm. 15va10, 15, 21.

corresponding, though the survival of the etymological explanation indicates that some form of *Cothraige* must have been present in the text at an earlier stage. The poor state of the text of this passage in both LArm and Brussels indicates that it was already defective in their archetype. It is therefore impossible to say with certainty that the form *Cothirthiacus* entered the text any earlier than LArm, *c.* AD 800, a possibility allowed for by Dr Harvey.[57] The fact that the rest of the Brussels text of Muirchú is independent of LArm may indicate that this passage also derives from a source other than LArm or its descendants.[58]

It is clear that *Cothirthiacus* is the Latinisation of an Irish name achieved by the addition of the ending *-acus*, presumably to provide it with a Latin appearance like the other three names of Patrick, just as *Coirpre* is latinised *Coirpriticus* in Tírechán 132.3ff.[59] The element to which the suffix was added was *Cothirthi*,[60] a variant of **Cothirchi*. This form may be due to the simple misreading of *c* as *t* or to the substitution of a dental fricative for the palatal fricative, an alternation well documented in later Irish.[61] It is impossible to say whether this change was made by Ultán, Tírechán, Ferdomnach, scribe of the Book of Armagh, or by some other writer.

In the stories of Patrick's names documented here there are two separate traditions, each based on the number '4': First, Patrick is said to have had four names because he was named on four separate occasions by four different people. Secondly, he acquired the name *Cothraige* because he served four different masters before being bought over by one of them. The simplest form of the first tradition included etymological explanations of the names, including *Cothraige*, so that the tradition of Patrick's serving four masters must have existed before the text explaining Patrick's four names was compiled. The latter text was contained in Ultán's book in the middle of the seventh century, so that the explanation of *Cothraige* based on the story of the four masters must be older than that. But the form *Cothraige* is phonetically so different from both L. *quattuor* and OIr *cethair* that it is unlikely to have given rise to an etymology based on the number '4'. On the other hand the postulated earlier form of the name, **Quathriche* < **Quatrikias* is so much closer to L. *quattuor* and even to early Irish **quethores, *quethris*, the pre-forms of nom. masc. *cethair* and acc. masc. *cethri* '4', that it is much more likely to have been the basis for the etymology. Since the change of **qᵘ* to /k/ (written *c-*) before back vowels took place, it is thought, in the first half of the sixth century,[62] the story of Patrick's four masters must go back to that period also. In any event this story clearly belongs to Patrick's hagiography rather than to his biography, for he himself states that he served only one master for the full period of his enslavement: *intermisi hominem cum quo fueram sex annis* (*Confessio* §17).

Patricius/Pátraic

In the texts quoted above, whether in Latin or in Irish, Patrick's fourth name is always given in its Latin form, *Patricius*, never in the form, *Pátraic*, which became normal in Irish right down to the present day. This may, of course, be because the context in which Patrick received this name was seen as a purely Latin one, his alleged ordination by Pope Celestine. It may also be that the tradition of the four names goes back to a time before the form *Pátraic* had emerged. The earliest attestations of *Pátraic* seem to be the twenty examples of the name in the Irish sentences of the

57 Harvey, 'Significance', p. 5.   **58** Bieler, *Patrician texts*, pp 20–30.   **59** In this connection note the distaste for names in their Irish form expressed by the redactor of the *Additamenta* in the Book of Armagh, Bieler, *Patrician texts*, p. 178, 12–17.   **60** Koch, '*Cothairche*', p. 185 notes the attestation of this form (with *-e*) in the *Vita Secunda*. **61** *DIL*, T, col. 1, 9–13. Note other Irish names in LArm with the ending *-acus*: *Cethiacus* Tír 6.2, *Camulacus* ibid., *Muirethachus* Tír 6.3, 45.2, and finally *Hiberionacum* in *Liber Angeli*, §13, presumably taken over from *Confessio* 23 and *Epistola* 16, which may have been the model for the formation of the other names.   **62** Jackson, *Language and history*, p. 139; McManus, 'Latin loan-words', pp 21–69: 45.

Additamenta to Tírechán in LArm between fol.17r33 and 18va32.[63] The language of these sentences has been dated to the 'early eighth century'.[64] The name occurs also in the *roscad* attributed to Dubthach maccu Lugair in the pseudohistorical prologue to the *Senchas Már* which has been dated by D.A. Binchy on linguistic grounds to the eighth century and by Kim McCone to the early years of that century.[65] The *terminus ad quem*, then, for the existence of the form *Pátraic* is *c.* AD 700. The *terminus a quo* is the time of the borrowing from British Latin of a considerable number of loan-words showing certain phonological features, also seen in *Pátraic*. These features are, briefly, the emergence of the sound /p/ which did not previously exist in the language, the voicing of the two intervocalic consonants, *t* and *c*, (it should be noted that the orthographic *t* and *c* denote voiced consonants), and the loss of the final syllable, the sole relic of which is the palatalisation of the final consonant of *Pátraic*. Kenneth Jackson dated the 'Pádraig group of borrowings' to the sixth century, while Damian McManus regards the borrowing of *Patricius* in the form *Pátraic* as later than AD 550.[66] This means that the borrowing of Patrick's name in its 'British' form, *Pátraic*, took place well after Patrick's time, possibly as late as the seventh century, and that the 'Irish' form of the borrowing, *Cothraige*, would have been the form of Patrick's name in the Irish language until then. Although *Pátraic* eventually prevailed, *Cothraige* was remembered as part of the 'four names' story right down to the seventeenth century. Examples of *Cothraige* used independently of this story are rare. There are three examples in the *Vita Tripartita*: VT 221 (from TCD MS H. 3. 18), in the prose narrative of Miliuc's vision of Patrick, where *Cothraige* occurs at the beginning of the extract and is immediately replaced by *Pátraic*,[67] VT 2389 where it occurs in an isolated stanza, and VT 2501 which is the opening line of a poem about the *Cáin Pátraic* 'Patrick's Law', promulgated in AD 737 (AU) but here regarded as having been enacted by Cothraige himself. However, the Law is called *Cáin Pátraic* in the poem (2517), which relates that it was first contravened by Dungalach mac Faelgusa úa Nad Froích, who is probably to be identified with Donngal mac Faelgusa m. Nad Fraích of the genealogies.[68] Since these show Donngal to have been great-grandson of Colcu († 678 AU) son of Faílbe Flann († 637 AU) he must have lived in the mid- to late eighth century, so that the poem cannot be earlier than that date.[69] Neither can it be much later as the name *Dungalach* occurs in the *Notulae* of LArm[70] in a context which guarantees the identity of the reference. Since Dúngalach is not mentioned in the prose of the *Vita Tripartita* but only in the poem the date of its composition must have been early enough to allow for the compiler of the *Notulae* to include it in his index and for Ferdomnach to transcribe it in the first half of the ninth century. Thus it would appear that *Cothraige* could be used as a poetic name for Patrick at least until the ninth century.

P.S. By the way, if the fifth-century Irish form of Patrick's name was not *Cothraige*, what was it?

63 Bieler, *Patrician texts*, pp 172.24–178.9.   **64** Stokes/Strachan, *Thesaurus* II, p. xv.   **65** Diplomatic text in Binchy, *Corpus Iuris Hibernici* II, 340–1. Discussion: D.A. Binchy, 'The pseudo-historical prologue to the *Senchas Már*', *Studia Celtica* 10–11 (1975/6) pp 15–28. Partial translation and commentary: D. Ó Corráin et al. (eds), 'The Laws of the Irish', *Peritia* 3 (1984) pp 382–438: 387–91. Edition, translation and discussion: K. McCone, 'Dubthach maccu Lugair and a matter of Life and Death in the pseudo-historical Prologue to the *Senchas Már*', *Peritia* 5 (1986) pp 1–135.   **66** Jackson, *Language and history*, p. 143, McManus, 'Latin loan-words', p. 59.   **67** Bury, 'Tradition of Muirchu's Text', pp 200–2 held that the spellings *Quadriga, Quotirche* in this same episode of Miliuc's vision in *Vita secunda* and *Vita quarta*, represent 'a q-form of the name, older than Cothraige.' It is much more likely that the redactor of the episode in the common ancestor of these two recensions introduced the spelling *Quadriga* to fit his etymology *quia equorum quatuor domibus seruiebat*.   **68** *CGH*, pp 216–8 (R 150b20, 24, 25, 26, 34, 37 also footnote i on p. 217, where he is given as an ancestor of Cathal mac Finguine), 362 (LL320b10).   **69** L. Bieler, *Patrician texts*, p. 50.   **70** L. Bieler, *Patrician texts*, p. 182.21.

Plebs et *populus* dans les pays celtiques

PIERRE-YVES LAMBERT

Comme ancien élève de Proinséas Ní Chatháin, je suis heureux de lui offrir ce témoignage de reconnaissance et d'amitié.

Comme on sait, les Irlandais du Haut Moyen Age ont été des latinistes féconds, avides d'assimiler la culture latine et désireux de la transmettre aussi complètement que possible à leurs élèves. Cependant, ils n'ont jamais été romanisés comme c'était le cas des Bretons de Grande-Bretagne, et si leur entrée dans la latinité a été extrêmement productive, elle n'en était pas moins tardive, et un peu 'orientée' par l'ardeur des néophytes. Cela transparaît dans certains traits de l'hiberno-latin: ainsi lorsque le latin avait plusieurs synonymes, les Irlandais choisissent d'employer le plus expressif, le plus marqué. Ils n'ont pas craint de fabriquer des néologismes, ce qui a produit le latin dit 'hispérique'. Mais la plupart du temps, l'hiberno-latin se caractérise par le choix des mots: il retient ceux qui sont les plus savants, les plus recherchés – certainement en réaction contre l'usage courant dans la Romania, où la langue latine s'était quelque peu 'abâtardie'. Les Irlandais se risquent à employer des termes littéraires au lieu des termes usuels: c'est ce que l'on pourrait appeler la tentation du 'purisme'.

Comme les Irlandais sont évangélisés par des Bretons, on devrait s'attendre à trouver la même forme de latin chez les uns et les autres. Effectivement, la majorité des emprunts irlandais au latin présente des traits phonétiques qui dénoncent une prononciation brittonique du latin – c'est l'exemple bien connu de *Pātrīcius*, prononcé Pa: dri :gius en Grande Bretagne (avec la lénition brittonique) et donnant l'irl. *Pádraig* /Pa:drig'/. Rares sont les emprunts latins qui échappent à cette règle.

D'autre part, nous voyons les mêmes auteurs latins recopiés et glosés de part et d'autre de la Mer d'Irlande (Commentaire de Philargyrius à Virgile; Priscien, Orose, Isidore, Bède); et les gloses sont souvent identiques. C'est donc la même culture latine qui était travaillée par les Irlandais, les Gallois et sans doute aussi les Bretons armoricains.[1] Aussi pourrait-on se demander si l'étiquette 'hiberno-latin' est adéquate: on a proposé parfois de lui substituer celle de 'latin celtique'. C'est notamment le cadre proposé pour un programme de banque de données patronné par la Royal Irish Academy.

Or, après avoir moi-même relevé un certain nombre de correspondances qui semblaient confirmer l'existence d'un 'latin celtique',[2] je dois reconnaître aujourd'hui qu'il existe aussi des différences marquées, dans le choix des mots, l'ordre des mots, et d'autres problèmes de style. Je

---

1 C'est le thème d'une mienne étude: 'Relations culturelles entre Irlandais et Bretons dans le Haut Moyen-Age: le témoignage des gloses', *Irlande et Bretagne, Vingt siècles d'histoire*, Actes du colloque de Rennes (29–31 mars 1993), ed. C. Laurent, H. Davis (Rennes 1994) pp 96–106.   2 C'est ce que j'ai pu montrer pour des termes grammaticaux (cf. '"*Fraudatiuus*" : une dénomination ancienne du "datiuus incommodi" dans le monde celtique', *Revue de Philologie* 57 (1983) pp 39–45; 'Le nom du génitif en vieil-irlandais', *ÉtC* 25 (1988) pp 213–20), et aussi, parfois, pour d'autres lexèmes rencontrés dans les gloses ('Celtic Latin *uigilare* "to wait for"', *Ériu* 36 (1985) pp 187–90). Une comparaison systématique des gloses brittoniques et irlandaises sur les mêmes mots latins révèlerait certainement les mêmes significations, les mêmes interprétations du vocabulaire latin.   3 Sur les emprunts latins en irlandais,

voudrais attirer l'attention ici sur une différence de vocabulaire qui pourrait presque constituer un test de provenance: là où les Bretons (les Brittoniques: Gallois, Corniques, Bretons armoricains) emploient le mot *plebs*, les Irlandais ont préféré le mot *populus*.

Les emprunts au latin

Les emprunts au latin[3] en sont la première preuve. Pour désigner la 'paroisse', les langues brittoniques emploient uniformément un emprunt au lat. *plebs (plēbem)*:

> vbret. *pluiu*, devenu *ploe*, *ploue* (*Plou*, *Plu-* etc. dans les noms de lieux);
> gall. *plwyf*;
> corn. *plui* (Vocabularium Cornicum).

Mais les Irlandais ont préféré utiliser l'emprunt au lat. *populus*. Cet emploi de l'irlandais *pobal* apparaît encore dans un certain nombre d'expressions, comme *teach an phobail* 'église paroissiale' (m.-à-m. 'maison du peuple'). On peut dire en irlandais moderne: *dúirt an sagart le muintir a phobail ...* 'le prêtre a dit aux habitants de son *pobal* ...'.[4] Le latin *parochia* s'est trouvé employé dans un autre sens.[5] Beaucoup plus tard, l'emprunt au fr. *paroisse* (sous une forme dialectale *paroche*) a donné *paróiste*,[6] par ex. dans *sagart paróiste* 'prêtre de paroisse, curé de paroisse'.

Nous allons tenter d'expliquer cette divergence entre le brittonique et l'irlandais.

D'autres divergences apparaissent dans les emprunts latins. Par exemple pour le nom du prêtre, l'irlandais a fait choix de l'emprunt à *sacerdos* (*sagart*, d'ailleurs d'origine brittonique), tandis que le gallois a créé un nom de métier à partir du nom de la messe (*offeren > offeiriad*) et que le breton a retenu une épithète descriptive, *baelec* remontant à **bagl-og*, signifiant celui qui a un bâton, une crosse (en gall. moy. *baglawc* est employé en particulier pour désigner le prêtre auquel un évêque confie sa crosse; c'est une sorte de vicaire général; cf. aussi v.irl. *bachlach*, dont les sens sont très nombreux).

Seul le cornique semble avoir couramment utilisé l'emprunt au latin *presbyter* – sous sa forme la plus courante en latin tardif, **premiter* ou *promiter*: c'est le cornique *prounder* gl. *sacerdos*. Dans ce cas, il semble que le cornique reflète l'usage le plus courant dans la Romania des premiers siècles (IIe-Ve s.). L'emprunt à *presbyter* est connu dans les autres langues celtiques, mais il n'y est attesté qu'à l'état de survivances:[7] mot de glossaire en gallois, mot archaïque et de glossaire en irlandais, simple nom propre en bret. moy.

Presbyter devait être le mot préféré pour désigner le prêtre responsable, le curé: c'est d'ailleurs la traduction de *presbiter* dans le *Vocabularium Cornicum*, '*hebrenchiat plui*, conducteur de paroisse'

depuis la thèse latine de J. Vendryes, voir D. McManus, 'A chronology of the Latin loan-words in Early Irish', *Ériu* 34 (1983) pp 21–71: 46–7; idem, 'On final syllables in the Latin loan-words in Early Irish', *Ériu* 35 (1984) pp 137–62; Sur les emprunts latins en brittonique: cf. J. Loth, *Les mots latins dans les langues brittoniques* (Rennes 1892) paru dans les *Annales de Bretagne* 6 (1890–1) et 7 (1891–2); H. Lewis, *Yr Elfen Ladin yn yr Iaith Gymraeg* (Cardiff 1943); K. Jackson, *Language and History in Early Britain* (Edinburgh 1953, repr. Dublin 2000).   **4** C'est une phrase que je cite d'après un roman récent: P. Standún, *An t-Ainmhí* (Indreabhán 1992) p. 115: '... *stopfadh sé anseo is ansiúd ... le caint a chur ar mhuintir a phobail*.   **5** Comme on sait, *parochia* est réservé à la désignation de la juridiction de l'évêque, en Irlande – avec extension aux abbés de monastère, cf. *paruchia Columbae*; cf. Colmán Etchingham, 'The implications of *paruchia*', *Ériu* 44 (1993) pp 139–62. Aussi l'emprunt irl. à *parochia*, *fairche*, désigne aujourd'hui le diocèse; cela correspondait à l'un des sens du mots dans le latin ecclésiastique.   **6** Cf. Henry Risk, 'French loanwords in Irish', *ÉtC* 12, 2 (1970–1) pp 584–655; 14, 1 (1974) pp 67–98. Plus particulièrement 14, 1 (1974)

(Voc. 106). Il est possible que dans l'usage latin des pays celtiques, il ait été évincé par *sacerdos* à partir d'une certaine date. *Sacerdos* (qui peut désigner l'ensemble prêtre + évêque) était moins précis, mais devait passer pour le meilleur latin que **premter*. [L'emploi de *persona* au sens de 'curé' est tardif: en irlandais comme en breton, il paraît provenir du français ancien *person, persun*].

Un autre cas intéressant est le nom du sacrement de confirmation: v.irl. *cosmit* ne trouve un correspondant que dans le bret. *kouzoumenn*, tous deux en relation avec un latin tardif *consummāre*, exprimant l'achèvement de la formation chrétienne (la confirmation est le sacrement destiné à marquer l'entrée dans un ensemble d'adultes) ainsi chez Jérôme et plusieurs pères de Gaele.

La Differentia d'Isidore

S'il n'y avait que les emprunts, on pourrait encore hésiter. Après tout, c'est peut-être une réaction de purisme qui a fait préférer *populus*, comme le montre une *Differentia* d'Isidore (*Differentiae* I, 445: *Inter plebem et populum*) qui insiste sur la distinction sociale de *plebs, pars (populi) humilis et abiecta*.[8]

> I. 330 (445) *Inter plebem et populum. Plebs a populo eo distat, quod populus est generalis universitas ciuium cum senioribus, plebs autem pars humilis et abiecta.*

Ce qui est en effet le sens de *plebs* en latin classique. Le latin classique, rappelle Isidore ibid., avait aussi des nuances de sens différentes pour le singulier et le pluriel de *populus*. On retrouve la même idée dans les *Étymologies* d'Isidore, IX.4.5–6.

L'emploi courant de plebs

Nous devons cependant remarquer qu'Isidore, en dehors de ses traités de grammaire, peut refléter l'usage courant du mot *plebs* dans la Romania, cf. un extrait du *De Officiis*, II, 5 c.12, cité dans la compilation des *Canones Hibernenses*:[9]

> *Isidorus.* Huic [episcopo] cum consecratur datur baculus ut ejus indicio subditam plebem vel regat vel corrigat vel infirmitates infirmorum sustineat… (ici, *plebs* = l'ensemble soumis à la juridiction de l'évêque).

Et Isidore lui-même ne fait que se conformer à l'usage courant: cf. encore un *Synodus Romana* cité *ibid.* V.2 (pp 23–4):

> *Synodus Romana.* Lector cum ordinatur, facit episcopus verbum de eo ad plebem, indicans ejus fidem ac vitam et ingenium. Post haec spectante plebe tradet ei et codicem, de quo lecturus est … (= *Statt. eccl. ant.* c.8 (96); ici, *plebs* = l'assemblée présente à l'office).

---

p. 70, 85.   **7** Cf. bret. moy. *Runiter / Runuiter / Rumiter*, dans la Vie de Sainte Nonne (*RC* 8 (1887) pp 230–301, 406–91) N 74 (p. 244), N 86 (p. 246), ce qui continue certainement le *Criumther* de la Vie de Saint David par Rhigyfarch; v.gall. *premter*, cité dans le glossaire de Cormac, Corm.219, et *prifder?*, dans le Livre de Taliesin, *BT* 23.12; v.irl. *cruimther*, d'emploi sporadique.   **8** Cf. C.C. Codoner, *Isidoro de Sevilla Differencias, Libro I* (Paris 1992).
9 H. Wasserschleben, *Die irische Kanonensammlung* (Leipzig 1885) I.6, p. 5.

Car il est sûr que l'emploi de *plebs* pour désigner une communauté paroissiale – généralement rurale – était habituel dans l'Europe occidentale du haut Moyen Age.[10] C'est pourquoi l'on trouve des paroisses rurales de Toscane et d'Ombrie portant le nom de *Pieve*. Les pays brittoniques (Armorique, Cornouailles, Pays-de-Galles) ne sont pas du tout isolés de ce point-de-vue. Nous ne pouvons traiter ici de l'entité juridique 'pieve' en Italie centrale et septentrionale, ni du 'plou' breton. Des études remarquables[11] ont été écrites sur ces questions. Le système de la *pieve* s'étend jusqu'en Latium, en Sardaigne et dans une bonne partie de l'Italie du Nord (surtout au sud du Pô, en Vénétie et en Engadine). Pour nos besoins, il suffira de renvoyer à l'étude de Paul Aebischer,[12] qui s'attache à déterminer l'extension géographique, et l'évolution sémantique de l'ital. *pieve*: d'abord communauté paroissiale, puis division territoriale (district de l'administration religieuse).

On emploie parfois le terme de '*pieve* publique' (en relation avec la communauté laïque sous-entendue) pour rappeler l'origine laïque de cette division. Un faux débat a opposé quelque temps les partisans d'un *plou* laïc et ceux d'un *plou* religieux. C'est un faux problème, comme on peut s'en rendre compte en lisant, par exemple, une étude de Luce Piétri, Yves Duval et Charles Piétri[13] de 1992.

On peut d'ailleurs retrouver cet emploi de *plebs* non seulement chez les écrivains bretons comme Patrice et Gildas, ou leurs descendants (comme Rhigyfarch, ou 'Nennius') mais aussi dans la première traduction de la Bible (Vetus Latina):

> et in Osee dicit, uocabo non plebem meam plebem meam et non misericordiam consecutam misericordiam consecutam et erit in loco ubi dictum est: Non plebs mea uos, ita uocabuntur filii Dei uiui (cité par Patrice, *Confessio* § 40).

Comparer le texte de la Vulgate, Osée I, 9, 8, 10:

> Et dixit ei: Voca nomen eius non populus meus, quia uos non populus meus ... et ablactauit eam, quae erat absque misericordia.... Et erit in loco ubi dicetur eis: Non populus meus uos, dicetur eis Filii Dei uiuentis.[14]

Plebs *dans les écrits patriciens, et en hiberno-latin*

Patrice lui-même utilise le mot habituel, *gentes*, ou *populi*, pour les nations encore païennes, mais sitôt qu'elles sont évangélisées – même de fraîche date, il préfère le mot *plebs*, qui semble être doté d'une certaine charge affective:

> quia ualde debitor sum Deo, qui mihi tantam gratiam donauit ut *populi* multi per me in Deum renascerentur et postmodum consummarentur et ut clerici ubique illis ordinarentur ad *plebem* nuper uenientem ad credulitatem (*Confessio* § 38).

---

10 Sur le sens ancien de bret. *ploe* 'paroisse', cf. A. de Courson, *Cartulaire de Redon* (Paris 1863) Introd.; Imbart de la Tour, *Les paroisses rurales du IVe au XIe s.* (Paris 1900) p. 115 s.; H. Sée, 'Étude sur les classes rurales en Bretagne au Moyen-Age', *AnBret* 11 (1896) pp 28–31; R. Largillière, *Les saints et l'organisation chrétienne primitive dans l'Armorique bretonne* (1925, rééd. Crozon 1995) chapitres IX et X (exploitation des toponymes en Plou-). **11** Voir G. Forchielli, *La pieve rurale. Ricerche sulla storia della costituzione della chiesa in Italia e particolarmente nel Veronese* (Roma 1951); C. Violante, 'Pieve e parrochie nell'Italia centro-settentrionale durante i secoli XI e XII', in *Le istituzioni ecclesiastiche*, *MCSM* 8, pp 644–97. Pour la Bretagne, voir les ouvrages d'Henri Sée, et de René Largilliere, cités n. 10. **12** P. Aebischer, 'La diffusion de plebs 'paroisse' dans l'espace et dans le temps', *Revue de Linguistique Romane* 28 (1964) pp 143–65. **13** L. Pietri, Y. Duval, C. Pietri, 'Peuple chrétien et *plebs*: le rôle des laïcs dans les élections ecclésiastiques en Occident', in *Actes de la table ronde autour de l'œuvre de A. Chastagnol* (Rome 1992) pp 373–95. **14** On pourrait multiplier les exemples où s. Jérôme a remplacé *plebs* par *populus*, dans sa traduction de la Bible.

Cependant *populus* (sg.) est aussi possible, lorsqu'il s'agit du peuple en train de se convertir:

> ut ubique essent clerici qui baptizarent et exhortarent populum indigentem et desiderantem (*Confessio* § 40).

On le comprend bien, nous n'essayons pas de prouver que les Irlandais ignorent le mot *plebs* ou les Brittoniques le mot *populus*. Il est clair que l'irlandais *pobal* est un emprunt qui est lui aussi arrivé par l'intermédiaire brittonique. Les latinistes bretons et irlandais connaissaient bien les deux mots: mais il y a dans le choix du mot *plebs* en brittonique, et du mot *populus* en irlandais, l'indication d'un usage qui a évolué: la communauté paroissiale s'appelait *plebs* à l'époque de Patrice, mais elle était couramment désignée sous le nom de *populus* quelques siècles plus tard en Irlande.

Ainsi, l'emploi de *plebs* au sens de communauté dans les textes hiberno-latins est rare et archaïque: on l'a relevé en particulier dans le *Synodus Episcoporum*, ou Premier synode de saint Patrice, un texte qui accorde une grande importance à l'autorité des évêques et qui semble décrire le premier état de l'église irlandaise. La date de ce texte est contestée: d'après Richard Sharpe,[15] les datations hésitent entre le Ve et le VIIe s. Pour moi, il est symptomatique que des textes se rapportant à un état 'brittonique' de l'Église irlandaise emploient précisément le mot *plebs*, le mot que les Bretons préféraient pour désigner la communauté laïque, dans l'Église, ou l'unité paroissiale.

Le paysage irlandais, libre de toute agglomération urbaine, était parfaitement adapté au concept de 'plebs' comme communauté chrétienne rurale: on peut estimer que c'est bien ainsi que les premières communautés paroissiales se sont appelées, en Irlande.

L'un des derniers textes (apparemment) où *plebs* aurait encore un sens religieux semble être la *Vita Columbae* d'Adomnán: encore faut-il relever que le sens de 'l'ensemble des laïcs d'une paroisse' n'est conservé que dans deux dérivés, un diminutif *plebicula* (éd. Anderson, 26a) et un dérivé en -*ius*, *plebeus* 'laïc'; au simple, *plebs* désigne la population d'un territoire d'étendue très variable, qu'elle soit christianisée au non. C'est à peu près la situation que l'on trouve dans les premiers écrits hagiographiques consacrés à Saint Patrice: Muirchú et Tírechán emploient *plebs* ou *populus* de façon indifférenciée. On notera le sens fortement local de *plebs* chez Tírechán: *quacumque plebe aut quacumque regione (essent)* (§ 26); et surtout: *usque dum ad nostram plebem peruenerimus* (§ 14).[16]

Les différents sens de gall. plwyf, moy.-bret. ploe

Notons seulement que *plwyf* est usuel en moyen gallois pour désigner la communauté paroissiale – ainsi, dans les poèmes de Dafydd ap Gwilym, les paroissiens réunis à l'église pour l'office du dimanche (*Merched Llanbadarn*: dans l'église de Llanbadarn, le poète se retourne pour regarder l'assistance – *plwyf* – à travers les plumes de son chapeau, *GDG* 130.23–24; dans la messe des buissons, *Offeren y Llwyn*, il imagine un office célébré par la Nature, c'est un oiseau qui 'lit l'évangile aux paroissiens', *darllain i'r plwyf… efengyl GDG* 323.23–24); ou les habitués de l'église de Ty Dewi, réunis pour écouter un sermon de Gildas (*Buchedd Ddewi*, 3.18). Cet emploi de *plwyf* au sens de 'paroisse' est bien attesté jusqu'à nos jours.

15 R. Sharpe, 'Some problems concerning the organization of the Church in early medieval Ireland', *Peritia* 3 (1984) pp 230–70 (p. 234, 236 et n.4, référence à *plebs* passim et p. 243 n.2).   **16** Parmi les vies de saint Patrice, la *Vita Tertia* comporte plusieurs exemples de *plebs* au sens de *populus* (Ludwig Bieler, *Four Latin Lives of St Patrick* (Dublin 1971) pp 135 § 29, 150 § 45, 186–7 § 91) mais ses attaches bretonnes sont bien connues et se révèlent en particulier par l'irruption de quelques passages en brittonique ancien: voir D. Dumville, 'St Patrick in Cornwall? The origin and transmission of *Vita Tertia S. Patricii*', a Celtic florilegium, *Studies in memory of Brendan O Hehir*, ed. K.A. Klar,

Néanmoins, on peut rencontrer *plwyf* dans un sens plus large, 'l'humanité, les habitants de la terre': ainsi dans *Arymes Dydd Brawt*, 'La Prophétie du Jour du Jugement', *HGC* VIII.7:

> *Ny ganet yn dyd plwyw neb kystal a Duw* 'Il n'est jamais né, dans la population du jour, quelqu'un d'aussi bon que Dieu'

(incertitude sur la construction de *dyd*: nous comprenons *dydd* 'jour', en composition lâche avec *plwyf*, le sens est incertain: la population qui ne dure qu'un jour?). En tout cas, *plwyf* rimant avec *Duw*, ce dernier doit être prononcé avec l'ancienne diphtongue: *plwyw / Dwyw* est certainement une réminiscence de l'expression religieuse *plebs Dei*.

Le même élargissement de sens existait pour moy.bret. *ploe*: tout d'abord, *ploe* avait pris le sens de territoire géographique (occupé par la *plebs*), d'où le sens plus général de 'campagne' (opposé à la ville); de plus, *ploeou*, au pluriel, est l'équivalent de *poblou*. Le dérivé *ploeis* (avec le suffixe issu des noms d'habitants en *-enses* > *-is*), se rencontre soit avec le premier sens: habitants des campagnes, soit avec le deuxième sens: habitants du même pays, ou même habitants du monde (l'équivalent de *bed-is*).[17]

Traces d'un emprunt irlandais à lat. plebs *?*

D'après ce qui a été dit, *plebs* a dû exister en hiberno-latin dans les premiers siècles – avant d'être évincé au profit de *populus* au VIIe ou au VIIIe s. Il ne faudrait donc pas s'étonner de rencontrer un écho du lat. *plebs* dans les textes irlandais archaïques. Il se présente un cas qui mérite la discussion.[18] Dans l'Hymne à sainte Brigide, ou Hymne de Broccán,

> amra sámud sanct-Brigte
> amra plea conhúala
> Wondrous was St Brigit's congregation:
> wondrous was Plea to which it went[19]

Le commentaire ancien semble identifier *plea* comme le nom d'un lieu:

> *Amra Plea .i. Bl[asantia] .i. cathir sen fil do Brigit in Italia; nó Plea cathir fil do Brigit for Muir Icht* "Placentia, a convent which Brigit has in Italy. Or Plea, a convent which Brigit has on the sea of Wight …'.[20] Même commentaire, Fél. 64.29.

Vendryes, *RC* 42 (1925) p. 403, y voyait un emprunt au bas-latin *plagia*, *plaia* 'endroit ouvert'.

Plea pourrait être abrégé de *pleab, archaïque pour *plíab 'plebs'. Curieusement, dans les deux localisations proposées (Plaisance en Italie, et rivage de la Manche, ce qui est imprécis: sud de l'Angleterre, Cornwall, ou Normandie, Bretagne ?) Brigide pouvait rencontrer le système de la *plebs* – paroisse.

E.E. Sweetser, C. Thomas (Andover Mass. 1997) pp 1–7 et quelques références dans mon étude citée plus haut note 1.   **17** Pour moy-bret. *ploe* et son dérivé *ploeis*, on trouvera toutes les références chez Émile Ernault, *Dictionnaire étymologique du breton moyen*, Supplément à *Le Mystère de Sainte-Barbe* (Paris 1888) pp 354–5. Notes complémentaires par le même, *Glossaire Moyen-breton* (Paris 1895) pp 498–9.   **18** La variante *pleo* pour *breo*, dans Fél. Epil. 258b (*La Petar, breo prímdae*) ne paraît pas pouvoir être expliquée par *plebs*: on attend ici une apposition à Petar.   **19** Stokes, *Thesaurus Palaeohibernicus*, II p. 328.7 = Hymn, V.13.   **20** Ibid. p. 328.32.

Le témoignage des gloses

Le témoignage des gloses est une sorte de sanction pour l'usage *courant* des mots latins. Le glossateur qui utilise le latin cherche à simplifier la lecture, il utilise donc les mots latins les plus accessibles. Or les manuscrits latins d'origine brittonique présentent fréquemment la glose 'nomen plebis' sur les noms de peuples, tandis que les manuscrits d'origine irlandaise présentent 'nomen gentis', 'nomen populi' etc.

C'est particulièrement remarquable dans les manuscrits d'Orose:

Des manuscrits avec gloses bretonnes, Vatican Reg. lat. 1974 et sa copie, Vatican Reg. lat. 691, présentent uniquement la glose nomen gentis:

> III, 13.8 triballi[.i. gentes
> III, 23,11 Seres[s. gens
> III, 23.25 argiraspidas[proprium nomen gentis…
> III, 23,36 auiaenatas[s. gentes
> IV, 11,2 Euboicorum[.i. gens
> IV, 13.15 Insubrium[nomen gentis

Mais d'autres manuscrits avec gloses brittoniques présentent la glose *nomen plebis*, ainsi, Venise, Marcianus Zanetti 349:

> f° 12r, II, 4.7 ou II, 19.3 Vehientibus[plebs in Italia

Berne 160, avec une seule glose brittonique:

> f°18, Birocis (= Boeotiis)[.i. nomen plebis
> f°21v, Triballa[nomen plebis

Vatican lat. 296, avec une trentaine de gloses brittoniques:

> f° 33b2 ple(bs) est une glose répétée, sur les noms de peuples.

Un corpus de *glossae collectae* à Orose, présente un cas très intéressant. Il s'agit d'un texte latin avec quelques mots irlandais anciens,[21] le Vatican Reg. Lat. 1650. Apparemment, son témoignage contredit les observations précédentes:

> I, 2.9 *Ausitar* nomen plebis… uel *Superiores* nomen plebis….
> I, 2.14 *Serecus* de plebe Seres.
> I, 2.25 *Chymericum*, id(est) de plebe Cimeriorum
> I, 2,74 *Vacei Celtibri Oretani* id est gentes Ispaniae Vlteriores (ceci, à proximité des citations de mots irlandais, en I, 2.81)

21 Voir édition de la première partie par O. Szerwiniack, 'Un commentaire hiberno-latin des deux premiers livres d'Orose, *Histoires contre les Païens*', *ALMA* 51 (1992–3) pp 5–137. La fin du texte m'a été soumise par O. Szerwiniack comme travail de recherche (thèse E.P.H.E., 2000).

dans la partie encore inédite:

> I, 5.1 *Tacitus* id est de nomine gentis
> I, 8.10 *Diupolitana* id est de nomine genti[s]
> (ici, première vague de gloses sur le début du livre II: aucun exemple de *plebs*)
> II, 8.8 *Platensibus* nomen plebis
> II, 12.7 *Aequi Vlciscique* de plebes Latinorum
> II, 12.8 *Aequis* id est nomen plebis
> II, 14.4 *Regini* plebs Siciliae qui a Rigus ciuitate
> II, 14.4 *Veterani* ples Sicilie
> II, 15.1 *detentus* id est a sua plebe
> II, 18.7 *Locri* ples Italiae

Le début du livre II d'Orose est traité deux fois, comme si le compilateur avait utilisé deux séries de gloses distinctes; la première série ne présente pas *plebs*, la seconde le présente 6 fois; on trouve *gens* à la place de *plebs* à proximité des mots irlandais (I,2, 74 ci-dessus): il est donc raisonnable de conclure que le corpus est formé au moins de deux sources distinctes, l'une utilisant le mot *plebs*, l'autre préférant le mot *gens* et véhiculant quelques mots irlandais. La première est vraisemblablement d'origine brittonique, et la seconde certainement d'origine irlandaise.

Conclusion

De plus amples dépouillements (à travers les canons, les règlements ecclésiastiques, les vies des saints) pourront conduire à une analyse plus fine. Comme on l'a vu, quelques sources archaïques irlandaises (comme le *Synodus Episcoporum*) utilisent encore le mot *plebs* au sens de communauté paroissiale: il serait utile de préciser jusqu'à quelle date.

A présent, il apparaît que l'emploi de *plebs* pour désigner une communauté paroissiale était habituel dans l'Europe occidentale des Ve-VIIe s. Mais cet usage n'a plus cours dans l'Irlande cultivée du VIIIe s., où l'on a élaboré un latin épuré. D'autre part, les glossateurs brittoniques employaient le mot *plebs* non seulement pour désigner leur communauté paroissiale, mais aussi toute sorte de peuplement, distinct par le nom, la langue ou les coutumes. Cet emploi, d'abord attesté chez les Irlandais (Adomnán, Tírechán), semble avoir été petit à petit abandonné sous l'influence de puristes tels qu'Isidore. Cependant les premières communautés irlandaises (fondées par des brittoniques) se désignaient sous le nom de *plebes*, on peut se demander si cet usage n'a pas été modifié de façon soudaine – peut-être au moment de la réforme culturelle et liturgique introduite par les *Romani* au cours du VIIe s.

The hymn of saint Columba in praise of saint Ciaran:
an English translation

PETER DAVIDSON

Born of the soaring apostolic company
(glass of Jerusalem exalted ineffably)
raised on thrones as sunlight lustrous,
came Ciaran, priest and messenger glorious;

Borne to the sky by angel infantry
fulfilling thus his folded family,
Christ's herald, shining apostle of grace
Sent to Ireland in these last, sad days.

Latin text

Hymnus Sancti Columbae in laudem S. Ciarani

Alto et ineffabile apostolorum coeti
celestis Hierusolimae sublimioris speculi
sedente tribunalibus solis modo micantibus
Quiaranus sanctus sacerdos insignis nuntius

Inaltatus est manibus angelorum celestibus
Consummatis felicibus sanctitatum generibus
quem tu Christe apostolum mundo misisti hominem
gloriosum in omnibus nouissimus temporibus

Contributors

DAMIAN BRACKEN, Lecturer, Department of History, University College Cork

EDEL BHREATHNACH, Post-Doctoral Fellow, National University of Ireland, Galway

FRANCIS JOHN BYRNE, Emeritus Professor of Early Irish History, University College Dublin

THOMAS CHARLES-EDWARDS, Jesus Professor of Celtic, University of Oxford

PETER DAVIDSON, Regius Professor of English, University of Aberdeen

ANN DOOLEY, Professor of Celtic Studies Program, University of Toronto

DORIS EDEL, Professor emerita of Celtic languages and civilisation, University of Utrecht

MICHAEL ENRIGHT, Professor, Department of History, East Carolina University

DEWI WYN EVANS, Lecturer, Department of Welsh, University College Dublin

MARIE THERESE FLANAGAN, Lecturer, School of Modern History, The Queen's University of Belfast

STEFANIE HAMANN, Mauerkircherstrasse 100, Munich

ANN HAMLIN, Former Director of the Built Heritage, The Department for the Environment of Northern Ireland

MÁIRE HERBERT, Associate Professor, Department of Early and Medieval Irish, University College Cork

BENJAMIN HUDSON, Professor, Department of History, State University of Pennsylvannia

PATRICIA KELLY, Lecturer, Department of Early and Medieval Irish, University College Dublin

D.P. KIRBY, Emeritus Professor of History, University of Wales, Aberystwyth

PIERRE-YVES LAMBERT, Professor of Celtic Philology, École pratique des Hautes Études, Paris

PROINSIAS MAC CANA, Emeritus Professor, School of Celtic Studies, Dublin Institute for Advanced Studies

GEARÓID MAC EOIN, Emeritus Professor of Old Irish, Scoil na Gaeilge, National University of Ireland, Galway

MARTIN MCNAMARA, Emeritus Professor, Milltown Institute of Theology and Philosophy, Dublin

WOLFGANG MEID, Emeritus Professor, Institut für Sprachwissenschaft, Universität Innsbruck

HERMANN MOISL, Senior Lecturer, Department of English Studies, University of Newcastle upon Tyne

KEVIN MURRAY, Lecturer, Department of Early and Medieval Irish, University College Cork

PÁDRAIG Ó NEILL, Professor, Department of English, University of Chapel Hill, North Carolina

JEAN-MICHEL PICARD, Lecturer, Department of French, University College Dublin

YOLANDE DE PONTFARCY, Lecturer, Department of French, University College Dublin

ERICH POPPE, Professor of Celtic and General Linguistics, University of Marburg

HILARY RICHARDSON, former Lecturer, Department of Archaeology, University College Dublin

MICHAEL RICHTER, Professor of Medieval History, University of Konstanz

JAN ERIK REKDAL, Lecturer, Department of Linguistics, University of Oslo

KARL HORST SCHMIDT, Emeritus Professor Sprachwissenschaftliches Institut, University of Bonn

JANE STEVENSON, Reader, Department of English, University of Aberdeen

DAVID J. WASSERSTEIN, Professor of Islamic History, Tel Aviv University

STEFAN ZIMMER, Professor, Sprachwissenschaftliches Institut, University of Bonn

Index